ALTERNATIVE TRAVEL DIRECTORY

1998

The Complete Guide To
Work, Study, & Travel Overseas

GENERAL EDITOR
Clayton A. Hubbs

CONTRIBUTING EDITORS
Susan Griffith, Cynthia Harriman,
Deborah McLaren, William Nolting,
Susan Sygall, Kathy Widing, Arline K. Wills

Transitions Abroad Publishing, Inc.
Amherst, MA

Contributing editors:
Kathy Widing (Chapter 1), Arline K. Wills (Chapter 3),
Cynthia Harriman (Chapter 5), Susan Sygall (Chapter 6),
Deborah McLaren (Chapter 8), Susan Griffith (Chapter 17),
William Nolting (Chapters 10, 16)

Copyright © 1998 by Transitions Abroad Publishing, Inc.
All Rights Reserved
Published by Transitions Abroad Publishing, Inc.
P.O. Box 1300, Amherst, MA 01004-1300

Manufactured in the United States of America

ISBN 1-886732-05-1
Fourth Edition

Cover and book design by David Cline
Cover photo by Peter Keegan
Typesetting and editorial assistance by Janis Sokol

CONTENTS

S T U D Y

W O R K

Preface to the Fourth Edition

The *Alternative Travel Directory*, published each January since 1993, is a one-volume compilation of essential practical information on the overseas alternatives to mass tourism—independent travel, ecologically and culturally responsible travel, work, living, and study abroad. All information in this 1998 edition was updated immediately before press time.

The steady growth in the number and variety of listings in each volume of the *Alternative Travel Directory* indicates a burgeoning interest in avoiding the international tourist trails. The readers of *Transitions Abroad* magazine, from which this information was compiled, recognize the enormous rewards that come from seeing the world from our hosts' perspective—whether as independent travelers, students, volunteers, or simply as paying guests in private homes.

But personal enrichment is only one reason our readers travel. More and more of them are going abroad to live and to work—either as "working travelers," who pay for their journeys with short-term jobs, or to find more permanent positions in the new global economy. The work of our contributing editors over the past year reflect this growing interest in living and working abroad:

Work Abroad Editor Susan Griffith has just published much expanded new editions of her classic *Work Your Way Around the World* and *Teaching English Abroad*.   Education Abroad Editor, Bill Nolting, the International Opportunities Advisor at the University of Michigan, put together the first comprehensive bibliography of resources on work abroad.

Together, these two authorities on overseas jobs helped us compile the first edition of *Work Abroad: The Complete Guide to Finding a Job Overseas*. Thanks to Susan and Bill, this new volume from *Transitions Abroad* is the most complete and up-to-date reference of its kind for the international job seeker.

On the study abroad front, Education Abroad Editor Bill Hoffa has edited another monumental edition of *NAFSA's Guide to Education Abroad for Advisers and Administrators*. Also for NAFSA: Association of International

Educators, Bill has written a guide to international education for parents and is preparing a similar guide for students (see his introduction to Study Abroad, page 111).

Bringing together in one volume much of her work which has appeared in *Transitions Abroad* over the years, Responsible Travel Editor Deborah McLaren published *Rethinking Tourism and Ecotravel: The Paving of Paradise and What You Can Do to Stop It,* a comprehensive groundbreaking overview of the history and global development of tourism and its consequences.

Congratulations to all our editors for their important accomplishments over the past year and sincere thanks to all reader-contributors who have shared their first-hand experience and information in the pages of *Transitions Abroad.*

Meanwhile, here in Amherst we've been busy putting the information we've gathered over the past 20 years into easily retrievable forms. Our Database Manager, Andrew Gerard, now has all our up-to-date alternative travel resources and programs available on the World Wide Web. Just click on "Where do you want to go?" or "What do you want to do?" at www.transabroad.com.

Finally, thanks to the advertisers and subscribers who help us continue to gather and publish information on the individual alternatives to mass tourism. If you find this information valuable, and you are not already a subscriber to *Transitions Abroad,* we hope you'll become one and spread the word about us to your travel-minded friends.

Medical Insurance and Assistance for Americans traveling or studying overseas.

MedHelp Worldwide provides $500,000 medical coverage for Americans **living or studying** overseas for up to one year.

HealthCare Global provides $100,000 medical coverage for Americans **traveling or studying** overseas for up to six months.

Both MedHelp Worldwide and HealthCare Global provide coverage for hospitalization expenses, doctor's office visits, prescription medicines, etc. and medical evacuation to a better hospital or back to a hospital near your home in the U.S.A.

The policies also include the services of an international network of assistance centers, staffed 24 hours a day with highly experienced multi-lingual travel advisors to assist you with finding medical care and solving other problems a traveler might encounter.

(800) 237-6615 or (540) 687-3166

107 West Federal Street, Post Office Box 480
Middleburg, Virginia 20118-0480 USA
Fax: (540) 687-3172   E-mail: Wallach_R@mediasoft.net

INTRODUCTION

In 1977 I launched *Transitions Abroad*, a magazine of practical information for independent travelers who go abroad to live, work, study, or travel for reasons other than those connected with mass tourism. The title "Transitions" was meant to suggest the changes that occur when travelers leave home behind and truly immerse themselves in a new environment.

Many of the first writers for *Transitions Abroad* were students, just back from a semester or year of travel and study abroad. Writing in the first issue, Gary Langer, then a student at the Univ. of New Hampshire, described staying at a Jerusalem guesthouse of an old Armenian called Mr. A. Those who sought out Mr. A were travelers, not tourists:

"Travelers and tourists, the distinction is simple: Tourists are those who bring their homes with them wherever they go, and apply them to whatever they see. They are closed to experience outside of the superficial. Travelers left home at home, bringing only themselves and a desire to see and hear and feel and take in and grow and learn. Tourists do not go to Mr. A's. They would not appreciate him, nor he them. And the main reason travelers go to Mr. A's is for Mr. A."

Taken out of context, Langer's contrast between travelers and tourists may sound a bit exaggerated and smug (after all, we are all in one sense tourists when we travel to another country). But the distinction has long been made between those who seem to travel more to confirm what they already know than to gain new understanding of themselves and of others. One thinks of Mark Twain's 1860s satirical novel on American travelers who brought so much cultural baggage with them that they were only "In-a-Sense" Abroad.

The stereotypical tourist—whether of Twain's time or ours—doesn't so much abandon his own familiar environment for the sake of engaging with a new one as have himself transported to a foreign place, taking with him as much of his familiar environment as possible. He views the unfamiliar people, places, and culture through the windows or walls of the familiar and pretends that he is still at home. If he must speak to the natives he does so loudly, thereby giving them every opportunity to understand him.

The modern traveler, on the other hand, is increasingly interested in experiencing new people, places, and cultures on their own terms and precisely because they are unfamiliar. The transition is not simply a passage from one place to another; it is a change in perspective and perception.

Interest in alternative travel, or travel for enrichment, grew rapidly in the 1970s and 1980s, in part a result of international air travel becoming affordable to a much larger group of people. In 1989 *Travel & Leisure* magazine commissioned Louis Harris Associates, Inc. to survey thousands of traveling Americans to find out why they traveled. To their surprise, the interviewers found that three travelers out of four took their last trip to improve their minds, to gain new perspectives, and to meet new people. Asked to name their dream vacation, only 10 percent named a place in the U.S. The conclusion of the pollsters was that international travel for personal growth was increasing more rapidly than any other form of nonbusiness travel.

In 1991 Arthur Frommer wrote: "After 30 years of writing standard guidebooks, I began to see that most of the vacation journeys undertaken by Americans were trivial and bland. . . . Travel in all price ranges is scarcely worth the effort unless it is associated with people, with learning and ideas. To have meaning at all, travel must involve an encounter with new and different outlooks and beliefs. . . . At its best, travel should challenge our preconceptions and most cherished views, cause us to rethink our assumptions, shake us a bit, make us broader-minded and more understanding."

"Not to have met the people of other cultures in a nontouristic setting," Frommer concludes in *The New World of Travel*, "is not to have lived in this century."

Detailing the ways and the means to meet people of other cultures in a nontouristic setting has been the major purpose of *Transitions Abroad* since its beginning 20 years ago. In each issue of the magazine we select and publish the most important sources of information on alternative travel along with a selection of programs and other opportunities for the curious and independent-minded.

We revise and update this information continuously. At the end of each year we bring it all together in one volume: the *Alternative Travel Directory*. The three sections—Independent Travel, Study Abroad, and Working Abroad—contain our selection of the major alternatives to mass tourism.

Alternative Travel. The experience of travel involves a continuum or a progression from the familiar to the new. On the one extreme are the unadventurous packaged tourists or mass tourists described above who spend a good portion of their trip in a literal bubble being whisked along on a guided tour, usually in an air-conditioned bus. They make virtually no decisions on their own and are taken, on a fixed schedule, from one attraction (often man-made for their benefit) to another. They observe and photograph but rarely actively experience their surroundings.

On the other extreme are those relatively few travelers who avoid the tourist scene altogether and strike out on their own. They are on no fixed schedule or itinerary and settle where they like for as long as they like, finding casual work when necessary to cover their modest expenses or to pay for moving on.

Between these two extremes are those of us in that growing group of travelers who like to go on our own, often to pursue a particular interest, but only after enough planning and preparation to insure that our limited time and money will be well spent. We don't want to be bound to a group or have our experience spoiled by hordes of tourists; on the other hand, we want to be comfortable and feel sufficiently secure to accomplish our goals.

Independent Travel Abroad. The travel resources and programs in the first nine chapters are grouped under the heading of independent or "life-seeing travel." The latter term comes from the concept of the Scandinavian School for Life (adult continuing education schools to enrich the mind, sometimes but not always to teach a vocational skill) which we described in the first issue of *Transitions Abroad* in 1977. Axel Dessau, director of the Danish Tourist Office, is credited with applying the concept to tourism. Visitors to Denmark are able to engage in activities that match their particular interests—for example, educators may visit schools and stay in the homes of teachers.

The fact that similar home and hospitality exchanges are proliferating throughout the world–as more of us travel from one foreign host's home to another rather than to tourist hotels–is just one indication of the increasing desire on the part of international travelers for an authentic engagement with the local people. For more and more travelers, including the readers of *Transitions Abroad*, life-seeing has replaced sightseeing.

Chapter 1 is a country-by-country guide to the best guidebooks and background reading to consult as you begin to make your overseas travel plans.

Chapters 2 through 7 cover the best travel information resources and selected programs for seniors, for families traveling with children, and for persons with disabilities.

Chapters 8 and 9 cover the major resources and programs exemplifying culturally and environmentally responsible travel, the fastest growing of all forms of alternative travel. How precisely one defines responsible travel and how one travels responsibly is a central topic of each issue of *Transitions Abroad* .

Study Abroad. In Chapter 10 we list the most useful resources for learning opportunities abroad.

Whereas all travel is at least potentially educational, the programs for people of all ages described in chapters 12 through 15 are structured learning experiences. Those organized for undergraduates carry academic credit. Older adults are welcome to take part in most academic programs for no credit, usually at a reduced price.

Working Abroad. There is perhaps no greater learning opportunity and no more rewarding form of travel than getting to know your hosts by working alongside them—whether as an unpaid volunteer or a well-paid professional. The resources, organizations, and programs described in this section make you aware of all that's available.

Chapter 16 is the most detailed and comprehensive existing review of information on jobs abroad.

Chapter 17 covers employers and organizations offering short-term jobs abroad.

The final three chapters, 18 through 20, outline the opportunities for volunteering, interning, and teaching abroad.

Whatever your age, whatever your reason for travel, we think you'll find the overseas travel alternative you're looking for here. If not, let us know and we'll try to include it in the next issue of *Transitions Abroad* and next year's edition of the *Alternative Travel Directory*. Our address is Transitions Abroad, P.O. Box 1300, Amherst, MA 01004-1300; trabroad@aol.com; www.transabroad.com.

Clay Hubbs
Amherst, MA
December 1997

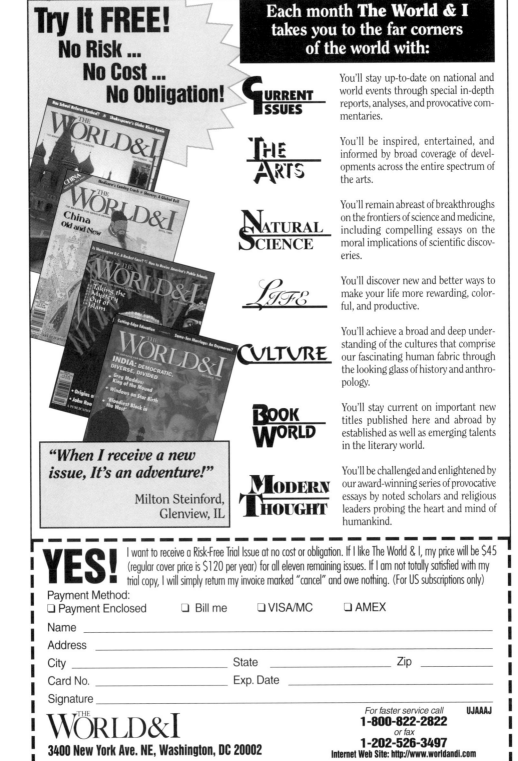

INDEPENDENT TRAVEL

A new aspect of citizen diplomacy involves people from various countries using their vacation time to share their skills, knowledge, and professional contacts to support individuals and local groups in areas that are undergoing rapid social, economic, and political changes.

—DIANNE BRAUSE, PAGE 17

Citizen Diplomacy

Engaged Travel in the Post Cold War Era

By Dianne Brause

Citizen diplomacy is the act of consciously choosing to travel with the objective of connecting with host country citizens, the culture, and the environment in a way that fosters peace, understanding, and a saner, safer world. In the 1970s, citizen diplomats were the first people to discover-- when we sneaked away from the Intourist tours--that the Soviet people had no desire at all to bomb us and were terrified that we might want to bomb them.

Suddenly it made lots of sense to visit the Soviet Union and meet as many people as possible to let them know that since we *all* wanted peace maybe we could join together to make a difference. Eventually the Soviet Union broke apart, the Berlin Wall crumbled, and the Cold War began to melt away.

Meanwhile, in Central America the U.S. Government continued to protect the status quo against would-be revolutionary forces despite the apparent desires of the local people. North Americans in increasing numbers began to travel to Nicaragua and our other southern neighbors to express solidarity with the wishes of the people. They picked coffee, built water systems, lived and worked with the locals, and on some occasions served as human shields for individuals and groups whose lives had been threatened. The problems in these countries remain, but the governments and the majority of citizens have finally agreed that peace is the first goal, and progress is being made year by year in this direction.

While many early citizen diplomats were making a statement about their opposition to their own country's politics, many others chose to go into areas of ongoing war or civil strife, in order to act as a neutral force for understanding and peace. In Northern Ireland, South Africa, and the Middle East seemingly endless efforts to bring together people who have seen each other as mortal enemies for years or generations have led to shifts towards an ethic of peace.

In recent years nations have moved away from lining up along prearranged political lines. The United Nations is now expected to launch peacekeeping missions rather than to automatically take sides on who has the right to kill whom.

While citizen diplomats alone cannot be credited for this turn of events, without the individual efforts of many ordinary citizens the human race might now be off the list of endangered species and on the cosmic list of those now extinct.

As we near the end of the 20th century several major themes are important to citizen diplomacy. One is putting pressure on national governments that continue to act in ways that do not support the needs of the people or the planet--such as in China or Burma where the record on human rights is abysmal--or in Korea--where child prostitution is rampant.

Within the U.S., citizens are pressing hard to have our government ease the ban on travel and the embargo of goods to Cuba. Citizen diplomats are currently traveling to Cuba in spite of the ban and emphasizing the ludicracy of the ban on trade in a post cold war period.

Participants in past conflicts are finding ways to heal wounds as they interact through joint work projects in Vietnam, Bosnia, and Jordan. Nelson Mandela has set an incredible example by conducting war trials in which the criminals receive amnesty simply for the act of confessing the truth. Former Viet Cong soldiers and survivors are removing land mines and planting trees in their place with their former American enemies along the DMZ.

Finally, a new aspect of citizen diplomacy involves people from various countries using their vacation time to share their skills, knowledge, and professional contacts to support individuals and local groups in areas that are undergoing rapid social, economic, and political changes. In the former Soviet republics and throughout Eastern Europe, Westerners are flocking to help their former enemies to learn to set up small businesses, organize democratic elections, design environmental quality standards, create women-run cooperatives, and learn English, the new international language. Throughout the globe people everywhere are beginning to understand that we all share the same planet and the same resources and that sooner or later whatever is done in one corner of the world is going to affect all the other areas as well.

If you are healthy and wealthy enough to travel to another country, chances are that you can also offer something of benefit to your fellow citizens. And chances are that they will have equally beneficial offerings to give back.

*The authentic **American** certificates...*

WORLDWIDE TEACHERS PROFESSIONAL CERTIFICATES:

C.T.E.F.L. (Certificate in Teaching English as a Foreign Language)

The Boston TEFL Certificate Method® is a three-week immersion course (150 hours) offered monthly.

Part-time courses are also available. Emphasis is on practice rather than theory.

* Limited enrollment
* Second career persons are welcome
* No second language is necessary
* Global placement guidance
* Supervised teacher training on-site
* Features a special module on "Teaching Young Learners" (no extra cost)

Tuition: $2,300 includes all texts and materials. Accommodation assistance available.

Cert.T.B.E. (Certificate in Teaching Business English)

Sponsored by The American English Language Foundation

This intensive , one-week, 50 hour course is specially designed for qualified EFL/ESL teachers and offered monthly. This training course is targeted toward developing practical skills and teaching American Business English. The course is specifically designed to expand the repertoire of classroom activities and techniques and to help build a substantial file of immediately usable American Business English material. Participants will liaison with the Better Business Bureau of Boston, Boston Chamber of Commerce, Harvard Business School, Boston University School of Management, and MIT in addition to several other universities and international corporations. **Tuition: $1,400** includes all materials and site visits. If one chooses to take this course upon completion of The Boston TEFL Course®, the tuition will be reduced by 50% ($700). Alumni of The Boston TEFL Course® will also enjoy this 50% tuition reduction. RSA/Cambridge TEFL Certificate graduates will receive a 20% tuition reduction.

Distance Learning Certificates

Internationally approved programs invite you to become part of the technology revolution. A practical teaching component is required. This is the only Distance Learning TEFL course in North America or South America authorized by the Accreditation Council for TESOL Distance Education Courses.

Tuition: $2300, covers all materials and 24 hour access to faculty. Call for special brochure.

Course Director: Thomas A. Kane, Ph.D. Appointed Visiting Scholar at Harvard University, is Director of the Boston TEFL Certificate Course®. Dr.Kane is author of the recent best-seller, *Teach American English Around the World*. The International Employment Gazette recognizes him as the American authority on "teaching English abroad." Inc. Magazine, April 1997, featured him in an article about the turbulent TEFL Industry.

•All courses at Worldwide Teachers Development Institute are eligible for Professional Development Points for recertification by the Massachusetts Department of Education.
We welcome on-site visits by any prospective students, educators, or language industry professionals.

Worldwide Teachers Development Institute

266 Beacon Street, Boston, MA. 02116
Toll free: 1-800-875-5564
Admissions office: (617)262-5722
Fax: (617) 262-0308
Email: BostonTEFL@aol.com
Web Site:http://www.to-get.com/BostonTEFL

CHAPTER 1

TRAVEL RESOURCES

Whether you intend to go abroad for a week or a month, every trip requires planning. The more you learn about your destination, the better equipped you are to embark on your adventure.

Each year, as more and more travel titles are released, we at Transitions Abroad select the best books for independent travelers. In order to help you make informed choices, we've gone even further, using an asterisk to indicate the "best of the best," for both individual books and series guides. These titles offer the most detailed and reliable practical and cultural coverage to enhance your planning and ultimately your travel experience.

Round out your research at your local library or bookstore by picking up literary works from or about the countries you'll visit. Two references worth seeking out are Maggy Simony's Traveller's Reading Guide (Facts on File) and Anderson's Travel Companion by Sarah Anderson (Scolar Press), both guides to travel fiction and non-fiction.

Guidebook Series

*Access Guides (Harper Collins). Well-organized guides with informative walking routes. Titles on London, Paris, Rome, Venice, Milan, Florence, Mexico, Caribbean, Budget Europe, Montreal, and Quebec City, French Wine Country.

Around the World Program (McDonald and Woodward). A new series sponsored by the American Geographical Society provides substantive introductions by authorities to single countries. Titles include: Japan, Switzerland, Fiji, Australia, Malta, and Brazil.

Baedeker's Guides (Macmillan). The oldest sightseeing series covering major cities, regions, and countries. Many European titles plus Japan, Mexico, Caribbean, Israel, Turkey, Bangkok, Hong Kong, Singapore, Tokyo, Jerusalem, Australia, Brazil, Tuscany. New this year: Barcelona, Crete, Nepal, South Africa.

*Berkeley Guides (Fodor's Travel Publications/Random House). Budget guides, with offbeat and adventurous travel ideas. Written by Berkeley students. Titles include: Eastern Europe, Mexico, France, Central America, Europe, Italy, Paris.

Berlitz Travel Guides (Berlitz Publishing). These insightful and literate guides provide the independent traveler with good background as well as practical information on the destination. Titles cover: Australia, Mexico, Ireland, France, Canada, Turkey, Spain, Portugal. Also from Berlitz is the Discover series, with lots of good background and pre-trip information. Titles include: France, Italy, Prague, Israel, Singapore, Portugal, Tuscany. Plus the classic series the Berlitz Pocket Guide. Titles for over 100 destinations including Budapest, Cuba, Edinburgh, Madeira, Tunisia.

Best Places to Stay Guide (Houghton Mifflin). Excellent selection of quality lodging. Available for U.S., Mexico, and the Caribbean.

*Blue Guides (W. W. Norton and Co.). Incredibly detailed British series covering history, culture, walks, driving tours, etc. Titles include Egypt, Istanbul, Jerusalem, Morocco, Denmark, Barcelona, Tuscany, Amsterdam, Albania, Southwest France, Sweden, Tunisia, Jordan, Budapest. New this year: Thailand, Rhodes & Dodecanese, Vienna, Madrid.

Bradt Guides (Globe Pequot Press). Reliable guides originating in the U.K. covering unusual and less traveled destinations for the adventurous traveler. Titles include: Albania, Burma, Estonia, Lebanon, Senegal, Zanzibar, Africa by Road, Eritrea, Malawi, Madagascar Wildlife, Venezuela, Hiking in Romania. New this year: Antarctica, Mozambique, Greece by Rail, Backpacking in Mexico.

*Cadogan Guides (Globe Pequot Press). Excellent, all-purpose guidebooks at moderate prices. Titles include detailed regional guides to the Caribbean, India, Turkey, Morocco, Amsterdam, Southern Spain, Mexico, Paris, Sicily, Cyprus, Malta, Germany, Southwest France, Brussels, London, Southwest Ireland, Andalucia, Henry Kelly's West of Ireland, London Markets, The Algarve, Crete, Northern Spain, Central Asia, Tuscany, Provence. New this year: China: The Silk Route, Loire, Belize, Lombardy and Italian Lakes, Antarctica and The Falklands.

*Culture Shock! Series (Graphic Arts). Guides to customs and etiquette of various cultures. Titles include: Thailand, China, Pakistan, France, Britain, Israel, India, South Africa, Burma, Canada, Philippines, Australia, Korea, Nepal, A Globe-Trotter's Guide, Ireland, Morocco, Switzerland, Syria, Vietnam, Successful Living Abroad: Wife's Guide, Turkey, Germany, Denmark. New this year: Bolivia, United Arab Emirates, Czech Republic, Living and Working Abroad.

Customs and Etiquette in... (Talman Company). Pocket guides to customs, manners, and culture of individual countries. Available for: Arabia and the Gulf States, China, Germany, Russia, Greece, Hungary, Japan, England, India, Israel, Thailand, Singapore. New this year: Holland, Italy, Ireland, Vietnam.

Day Trips Series by Earl Steinbecker (Hastings House). Oriented to public transportation. Titles: Day Trips in France, Germany, Holland/Belgium/Luxembourg, Italy, Israel. Daytrips from London. New this year: Ireland, Spain/Portugal.

Exploring Rural Europe Series (Passport Books). Driving tours of 1 day to 1 week acquaint the traveler with the history, character, and cuisine of the region. Titles for Austria, France, England, Germany, Ireland, Greece, Portugal, Spain.

Eyewitness Guides (Dorling Kindersley Publishing). Well designed with lots of color and illustrations, many in 3-D. Good for art and architecture. Titles include: London, Paris, Rome, Prague, Vienna, France, Provence, Venice, Italy, Loire Valley, Seville, and Andalucia. New this year: Greece, Greek Islands.

Fielding's Guides (Fielding Worldwide). Good general guidebooks for all budget levels. Titles: Europe, Italy, France, Caribbean, Portugal, Amazon, Southeast Asia, Vietnam. Borneo, Thailand. Also a series of Fielding's pocket-size guides called **Fielding's Agenda**. Titles include: London, Paris, Rome. New this year: Asia's Top Dive Sites, Diving Indonesia, Surfing Indonesia, Sydney Agenda.

Fodor's Guides (Fodor's Travel Publications/Random House). **The Fodor's Gold Guides and Pocket Guides**: The largest all-purpose series with approx. 100 titles covering countries, cities and regions all over the world. **Fodor's Exploring Guides**: Well-organized guides with good maps, color photos, detailed information on sights, and lots of interesting facts. Titles include: Paris, Germany, Spain, Rome, Thailand, Australia, Caribbean, Florence, Mexico, Prague, Turkey, China, Egypt, Israel. New this year: Greek Islands, Costa Rica, South Africa. **Fodor's Affordable Guides** for the cost-conscious traveler, include: France, Germany, Great Britain, Italy, Caribbean. **Fodor's Citypacks**, pocket-sized guides with fold-out maps, include: Amsterdam, Berlin, Florence, Hong Kong, Montreal, Paris, Prague, Venice.

***Footprints Handbooks** (NTC Publishing). The original book in the series is the old reliable **South American Handbook**. Now the series has changed its name to **Footprints Handbooks**. Other titles following the same format include: Caribbean Islands, Mexico/Central America, India, North Africa, East Africa, Egypt, Sri Lanka. New this year: South Africa, Indonesia, Burma, Andalucia, Namibia, Tunisia/Libya.

Frommer's Guides (Macmillan). Solid, all-purpose favorite of many travelers. Frommer's comprehensive series covers all price ranges from deluxe to inexpensive. The **Dollar-a-Day** series is more budget-oriented. City guides available for many major cities. **Walking Tour Series** includes: Paris, London, Berlin, England's Favorite Cities, Venice, Tokyo, Spain's Favorite Cities. **Food Lover's Companion Series** includes: France, Italy. **Frommer's Irreverent Guides** include: Amsterdam, London, Paris, Virgin Islands. **Frommer's Driving Tours** (Macmillan) present interesting regional driving routes with lots of tips and sightseeing information. Titles include: Britain, France, Ireland, Mexico, Scotland, Austria, Australia, Scandinavia, Switzerland. New this year: Western Europe.

***Insight Guides** (APA Publications). In-depth background, historical, cultural discussion with good destination information. Over 150 guides to most international destinations. **Insight Pocket Guides** include a fold-out map and cover over 100 locales including Alsace, Corsica, Maldives, Sabah, Sikkim. New this year: Algarve, Brussels, Nepal. **Insight Compact Guides**, have expanded beyond Europe to include Bahamas, Bali, and Beijing. New this year: Cotswolds, Devon, Italian Riviera, Italian Lakes, York, Yorkshire Dales.

Karen Brown's Country Inns and Itineraries Series (Globe Pequot). Offers some great choices throughout Western Europe. Primary selections, organized as part of an itinerary, can be quite expensive but there are usually moderate and sometimes low-cost alternatives as well. Titles include: Austria, France, England, Germany, Ireland, Italy, Spain, Switzerland.

Knopf Guides (Knopf). Heavy focus on art and architecture with lots of photos, drawings, and plans. Titles include: Amsterdam, Istanbul, London, Vienna, Egypt, Provence, Ireland. New this year: Louvre, Bali, Loire Valley.

*****Let's Go Guides** (St. Martin's Press). Still the best all-purpose budget guides around. Thoroughly updated annually. Titles available: Europe, Britain/Ireland, France, Greece, Israel/Egypt, Italy, Mexico, Spain/Portugal/Morocco, Germany/Austria/Switzerland, London, Paris, Eastern Europe, Southeast Asia, Central America. New this year: India/Nepal, Ecuador and Galapagos Islands.

*Lonely Planet Guides (Lonely Planet Publications). **On a Shoestring Guides**: Ultra-low-budget guides of considerable reputation. Titles: **Africa on a Shoestring** and similar titles on Eastern Europe, Northeast Asia, South America, Southeast Asia, West Asia, Central America, Western Europe, Mediterranean Europe, Scandinavian and Baltic Europe, and Middle East. **Travel Survival Kits:** Excellent guides for the adventurous traveler. All-purpose, all price ranges with plenty of low-cost choices. Wide range of titles throughout Africa, Asia, Europe, Oceania, South America. New this year: Africa: The South, Bermuda, Malawi/Mozambique/Zambia, Portugal, Spain. **City Guides** new this year: Amsterdam, Jerusalem. **Walking/Trekking Guides** titles include: Australia, New Zealand, Nepal, Patagonia, Switzerland, Turkey. New this year: **Walking in Britain**. New line of travel literature, "**Journeys**," with titles on Australia, Japan, New Guinea, Syria, Jordan, Africa.

*****Michelin Green Guides** (Michelin Guides & Maps). The best sightseeing guides with good maps and historical notes. English lan-

guage titles cover countries and cities of Western Europe and regions of France plus Mexico and Canada. New this year: Scandinavia, Wales, Michelin Red Guides are comprehensive symbol-oriented guides to restaurants and hotels throughout Western Europe.

Maverick Guides (Pelican Publishing). General guidebooks covering accommodations, sights, background, etc. Titles include: Australia, New Zealand, Thailand, Bali and Java, Prague, Berlin. New this year: Great Barrier Reef.

*****Moon Travel Handbooks** (Moon Publications). These guides provide thorough cultural, historical, and political coverage, as well as exhaustive practical information aimed at getting travelers the best value for money. Titles include: Bali, Nepal, Indonesia, Southeast Asia, South Pacific, Tahiti, New Zealand, Fiji, Egypt, South Korea, Micronesia, Pakistan, Belize, Jamaica, Outback Australia, Thailand, Moscow/St. Petersburg, Tibet, Virgin Islands, Costa Rica, Honduras, Dominican Republic, Cuba, Japan, Mexico (plus individual regional guides), Vietnam/Cambodia/Laos. New this year: Australia, Alberta and Northwest Territories, Singapore.

Nelles Guides (Seven Hills Books). Cover culture and history plus basics on lodgings, sights, and getting around. Good maps. Titles available: Cyprus, Morocco, Paris, Spain (North and South), Turkey, India (North and South), Provence, China, Cambodia/Laos, Bali, Philippines, Moscow/St. Petersburg, Corsica, Israel, Portugal, South Africa. New this year: Scotland.

*****New Key Series.** Good all around general guidebooks with strong emphasis on ecotourism and the environment. Titles include: Costa Rica, Cancun and Yucatan, Belize, Ecuador, Guatemala. New this year: Baja.

Passport Regional Guides (Passport Books). This series divides countries into several areas and provides detailed information. Countries regionalized: China, France, Italy, Indonesia, India, Great Britain, Malaysia, Russia.

*Rick Steves' Series (John Muir). Offers annually updated budget travel insights by *Transitions Abroad* contributing editor on the cities and regions of Europe. Also tips on transport, lodging, and dining. Titles include: Europe, Italy, Scandinavia, France, Great Britain, Baltics and Russia.

*Rough Guides (Penguin). For independent budget travelers. Rough Guides are written with a political awareness and a social and cultural sensitivity that makes them unique. Titles include many European destinations plus Mexico, Kenya, Morocco, Peru, Yugoslavia, Czech Republic, Poland, Nepal, Holland/Belgium/Luxembourg, Prague, Barce- lona, Egypt, Thailand, Tunisia, England, Corsica, Pyrenees, Tuscany/Umbria, Sicily, London, India, Moscow, Romania, Germany, Canada, Costa Rica, First-Time Europe, Goa, West Africa. New this year: China, Sweden, Norway, New Zealand, Jamaica, South Africa.

Sierra Club Adventure Guides (Sierra Club Books). Fine guides to every adventure under the sun. Titles available: Adventuring in.... Australia, Belize, Caribbean, Central America, East Africa, the Pacific, North Africa, Trekking in Nepal, West Tibet and Bhutan. New this year: Adventuring in Indonesia.

Travelers' Tales (O'Reilly and Assoc.). Not regular guidebooks with sights and lodgings, but a collection of travelers' tales from experienced travelers. Titles include: Mexico, France, Paris, Thailand, Gutsy Women, India, A Woman's World, Brazil, Hong Kong, Spain. New this year: Food, Nepal, Italy.

Travellers' History Series (Interlink). Concise background on cities and countries.

Easy reference. Titles include: England, Scotland, France, Paris, Spain, China, Japan, India, Turkey. New this year: North Africa.

Treasures and Pleasures of. . . (Impact Publications). New series designed for people who want to appreciate local cultures by shopping from artists and craftspeople: Caribbean, Hong Kong, Thailand, Indonesia, Singapore and Malaysia, China, Italy, Paris, and the French Riviera.

Walking Easy (Gateway). Titles for recreational walkers of all ages include: Austrian Alps, Italian Alps, Swiss Alps, French Alps.

Planning Guides

1997 International Travel Health Guide by Stuart R. Rose ($17.95 plus $3 shipping from Travel Medicine, Inc., 351 Pleasant St., Suite 312, Northampton, MA 01060; 800-872-8633). Updated annually in spring; recommended by U.S. State Department.

*A Journey of One's Own: Uncommon Advice for the Independent Woman Traveler by Thalia Zepatos (The Eighth Mountain Press). 2nd ed. Detailed advice on practical matters for women traveling abroad alone.

Adventure Holidays 1996: Your Complete Guide to Thousands of Active Vacations Worldwide (Vacation Work). Bicycling, windsurfing, canoeing, and more.

Adventures in Good Company: The Complete Guide to Women's Tours and Outdoor Trips by Thalia Zepatos (The Eighth Mountain Press). Profiles more than 100 companies worldwide that offer trips for women.

AIDS and International Travel (Council Travel with Stanford Univ. and San Francisco AIDS Foundation). Free from Council. Sound advice to international travelers.

Air Courier Bargains: How to Travel Worldwide for Next to Nothing by Kelly Monaghan (6th ed. $17.50 postpaid from The Intrepid Traveler, P.O. Box 438, New York, NY 10034). Complete guide to courier travel in U.S. and around the world.

The Archaeology Handbook: A Field Manual and Resource Guide by Bill McMillon (John Wiley & Sons). Comprehensive how-to and where-to guide for volunteers.

Big Book of Adventure Travel, by James Simmons (John Muir Publications). A source book of worldwide guided adventure tours.

Budget Lodging Guide. (B&J Publications, P.O. Box 5486, Fullerton, CA 92635; 800-525-6633). Lists more than 600 institutions worldwide with bed and breakfast, including 41 in London.

Bugs, Bites and Bowels by Dr. J. Howarth (Globe Pequot). A Cadogan series guide on healthy travel covering prevention, diagnosis, and cure.

Consolidators: Air Travel's Bargain Basement: A 73-page list of U.S. and Canadian companies that buy blocks of seats from the airlines at discounts and pass savings on to the consumer. $8.95 postpaid from The Intrepid Traveler, P.O. Box 438, New York, NY 10034.

Cooking Schools. Directory of culinary vacations and short cooking classes for the non-professional cook. $13 postpaid from Athabasca Univ., Educational Travel, Box 10,000, Athabasca, AB TO6 2RO Canada.

Do's and Taboos Around the World: A Guide to International Behavior by Roger Axtell (John Wiley & Sons). Advice for the business and pleasure traveler on what to do and not to do in other cultures. Titles include: **Gestures: Do's and Taboos of Body Language Around the World, Do's and Taboos of Using English Around the World.**

Earth Fact Book: Facts & Maps (Interarts). Interesting maps and information.

Ford's Freighter Travel Guide (Ford's Travel Guides). Very informative. Updated semi-annually.

Hostelling International (Hostelling International—International Youth Hostel Federation). Lists nearly 5,000 hostels in over 70 countries for all ages. Two annual volumes: Europe and Africa/Americas/Asia/Pacific.

Institute of International Education (IIE), IIE Books, P.O. Box 371, Annapolis Junction, MD 20701-0371; (800) 445-0443, fax (301) 953-2838; iiebooks@iie.org, www.iie.org. Publisher of authoritative directories for study or teaching abroad and financial aid, and distributor of Central Bureau (U.K.) publications on working abroad. Add $2 each shipping for books under $25; $4 each for books over $25, or 10% for orders over $100.

International Travel and Health 1997 (World Health Organization). Vaccination requirements and health advice.

Language Schools. Directory of hundreds of language learning vacations around the world. $13 postpaid from Athabasca Univ., Educational Travel, Box 10,000, Athabasca, AB TO6 2RO Canada.

Passport to World Band Radio (International Broadcasting Services). Hour-by-hour, country-by-country listings for world band radio programming.

Peterson's Learning Adventures Around the World 1998 Peter S. Greenberg, ed.

(Peterson's). 2nd ed. December 1997. Comprehensive guide to 2,500 learning vacations in 110 countries around the globe—handling the U.S.

*Pocket Doctor by Dr. S. Bezruchka (Mountaineers). A compact health guide for the traveler.

Shaw Guides. Published in more than 20 print editions since 1988, Shaw Guides' educational travel guides are now available exclusively on the internet: www.shawguides.com. Contains descriptions of more than 2,000 cooking schools, photo workshops, writers' conferences, art and craft workshops, learning and language vacations, and golf schools and camps worldwide. Searchable by keyword, name, state, country, region, month, and specialty. Site also lists organizations and publications relating to each subject.

Specialty Travel Index. Biannual directory/magazine of special interest and adventure travel listing over 600 tour operators worldwide including addresses, phone, and fax numbers. $10 per year for two issues from Specialty Travel Index, 305 San Anselmo Ave., San Anselmo, CA 94960; (415) 459-4900, fax (415) 459-4974; www.spectrav.com.

Staying Healthy in Asia, Africa, and Latin America by Dirk Schroeder (Moon Publications). Deals with illness prevention, health supplies, suggestions on eating and drinking.

Tips for the Savvy Traveler by Deborah Burns and Sarah May Clarkson (Storey Publishing). Hundreds of valuable tips from planning to coming home.

Transformative Adventures, Vacations and

Retreats by John Benson (New Millennium). Worldwide organizations offering programs for personal change—meditation retreats, health spas, etc.

Travel and Learn by Evelyn Kaye (Blue Panda). Describes more than 2,000 vacations in arts, archaeology, language, music, nature, and wildlife.

Travel by Cargo Ship (Cadogon).

Vacation Home Exchange and Hospitality Guide by John Kimbrough (Kimco Communications). Guide to opportunities for vacation home exchanges all over the world. Information on associations/agencies that will put you in touch with contacts. Call (503) 524-0956.

Volunteer Vacations by Bill McMillon (Chicago Review Press). 5th ed. More than 500 opportunities worldwide.

Work your Way Around the World by Susan Griffith (Peterson's Guides). 7th ed. Excellent first-hand information, by country, on short-term jobs by Transitions Abroad contributing editor.

Work, Study, Travel Abroad: The Whole World Handbook (St. Martin's Press). Excellent but dated resource for students and learning travelers of all ages from Council.

World's Most Dangerous Places by Robert Young Pelton and Coskun Aral (Fielding Worldwide). First-hand experiences, advice on avoiding scams, regions to be aware of, protecting yourself, etc. Some areas covered: Gulf States, Golden Triangle, Cuba, Eastern Turkey.

Africa/Middle East

Series: Baedeker, Bradt, Berlitz, *Blue Guides, *Cadogan, Citywalks, *Culture Shock!, Customs and Etiquette, Fielding, Fodor, *Footprints, Frommer, Knopf, Insight, *Let's Go, *Lonely Planet, *Michelin, *Moon Handbooks, Nelles, *Rough Guides, Sierra Club, Traveller's History.

Distributors: Rafiki Books (45 Rawson Ave., Camden, ME 04843; 207-236-4244, fax 207-236-6253): Over 200 titles on Africa.

Africa's Top Wildlife Countries by Mark W. Nolting (Global Travel Publishers). Excellent reference by an authority on African wildlife.

Africa: Literary Companion by Oona Strathern (Passport Books). Compilation of literature, background, and cultural information.

African Customs and Manners by E. Devine and N. Braganti (St. Martin's Press). Dos and taboos on the African continent.

Backpacker's Africa by Hilary Bradt (Bradt Publishing). Best hikes in 17 countries. 3rd ed.

The Bazak Guide to Israel and Jordan 1996-1997 by Avraham and Ruth Levi (Sterling). Detailed practical guide, includes map.

Bicycling in Africa by David Mozer (International Bicycle Fund, 4887 Columbia Dr. S., Apt. T-7, Seattle, WA 98109-1919). How to do it, with supplements on 17 separate countries.

Cycling in Kenya by Kathleen Bennett (Bicycle Books). Biking and hiking safaris.

Guide to Lebanon by Lynda Keen (Bradt Publishing).

Guide to South Africa by Briggs (Bradt). Detailed guide to the new South Africa.

Israel: Traveler's Literary Companion edited by M. Gluzman and N. Seidman (Whereabouts Press). Literature, cultural and background information.

Israel on Your Own by Harriet Greenberg (Passport Books). 2nd ed. All-purpose guide to independent travel.

Kenya: A Visitor's Guide by Arnold Curtis (Bradt Publishing). Good orientation by long time resident.

Lebanon: A Travel Guide by Reid, Leigh and Kennedy (Pelican Publishing). General guide.

Namibia: Independent Traveler's Guide by Scott and Lucinda Bradshaw (Hippocrene). A must for anyone making their way across the country's vast expanse.

Saudi Arabia Companion Guide by Gene Linsdey (Hippocrene). Good general guide to the area.

The Safari Companion: A Guide to Watching African Mammals by Richard Estes (Chelsea Green Publishing). Good reference.

Spectrum Guides (Interlink Publishing). Beautifully photographed, good cultural and background information. Available for: Kenya, Seychelles, Zimbabwe, African Wildlife Safaris, Uganda.

Albania

Series: Blue Guides, Bradt.

Asia

Series: Baedeker, *Blue Guides, *Cadogan, *Culture Shock!, Customs and Etiquette, Fielding, Fodor, *Footprints, Frommer, *Insight Guides, *Let's Go, *Lonely Planet, *Moon Handbooks, Passport Regional Guides, Sierra Club, *Rough Guides, Traveller' Tales, Travellers' History, Treasures and Pleasures of....

All Asia Guide (Charles E. Tuttle Co.). 17th edition. Comprehensive guide to the continent.

Asia Overland by Mark Elliott and Will Klass (Trailblazer). Routes and planning for overland options across Asia.

*Asia Through the Back Door by Rick Steves and Bob Effertz (John Muir Publications). Inexpensive ways to experience the region.

Southeast Asia: Literary Companion, by Alistair Dingwell (Passport Books). Compilation of literature, background, and cultural information.

Staying Healthy in Asia, Africa, and Latin America by Dirk Schroeder (Moon). Excellent, compact.

Teaching English in Southeast Asia by Jerry O'Sullivan (Passport Books). Practical information on finding a job, teaching and living in Cambodia, Hong Kong, Indonesia, Malaysia, Singapore, Thailand, Laos, Philippines, and Vietnam.

The Traveler's Guide to Asian Customs and Manners by Elizabeth Devine and Nancy Braganti (St. Martin's Press).

Australia

Series: Baedeker, Berlitz, *Culture Shock!, Driving Tours, Fielding, Fodor, Frommer, *Insight Guides, *Lonely Planet, Maverick, *Moon, Nelles, *Rough Guides, Sierra Club, Treasures and Pleasures of... (Lonely Planet also covers each state: Victoria, N.S.W. and A.C.T., Queensland, Northern Territory, South Australia, Western Australia, Tasmania and the Outback, Great Barrier Reef, and Sydney and Melbourne.)

Australia and New Zealand by Rail (Bradt Publishing).

The Australian Bed and Breakfast Book by J. and J. Thomas (Pelican). Stay in private homes with friendly hosts.

Bicycle Touring Australia by Leigh Hemmings (Mountaineers). Cycling tours of the most popular and accessible areas.

Bushwalking in Australia by John and Monica Chapman (Lonely Planet Publications).

Stepping Lightly on Australia by Shirley LaPlanche (Globe Pequot). Traveler's guide to ecotourism in this land of diverse flora and fauna.

Austria

Series: Baedeker, *Berkeley, Berlitz, *Blue Guides, Citywalks, Driving Tours, Exploring Rural Europe, Eyewitness, Fodor, Frommer, Insight Guides, Karen Brown, Knopf, *Let's Go, *Lonely Planet, *Michelin, Off the Beaten Track, *Rick Steves.

Walking Easy in the Austrian Alps (Gateway Books). Hiking guide for active adults.

Baltic Countries

Series: *Bradt, *Lonely Planet, *Rick Steves.

Benelux

Series: Baedeker, Berlitz, *Blue Guides, *Cadogan, Customs and Etiquette, Daytrips, Eyewitness, Fodor, Frommer, *Insight Guides, Knopf, *Michelin, *Rick Steves, *Rough Guides.

Backroads of Holland by Helen Colijn (Bicycle Books). Scenic excursions by bicycle, car, train, or boat.

On the Rails Around France, Belgium,

Netherlands, and Luxembourg by Roger Thomas (Passport Books). Routes, maps, transport information.

Bulgaria

Series: *Rough Guides.

Essential Bulgaria, by David Ash (Passport Books). Pocket size guide.

Bulgaria: A Travel Guide by Philip Ward (Pelican). Comprehensive.

Canada

Series: *Access, Baedeker, Berlitz, *Culture Shock!, Fodor, Frommer, *Insight Guides, *Let's Go, *Lonely Planet, *Michelin, *Moon, Off the Beaten Track, Nelles, *Rough Guides, Sierra Club.

Canada Campground Directory (Woodall/ Globe Pequot). New: **Atlantic Canada Bed & Breakfast** (Seven Hills).

Canada Compass Guide (Random House). History, background, maps, and resource information. Nicely illustrated.

Canadian Bed & Breakfast Guide by Gerda Pantel (Chicago Review Press). 1,500 choices including chalets, farmhouses, and city homes.

Cycling Canada by John M. Smith (Bicycle Books).

Guide to Eastern Canada and Guide to Western Canada by Frederick Pratson (Globe Pequot). Both guides provide thorough information on all aspects of travel in Canada.

Maritime Provinces Off the Beaten Path by Trudy Fong (Globe Pequot).

Nova Scotia and The Maritimes by Bike by Walter Sienko (Mountaineers).

Series of Canadian Guides (Formac Publishing/Seven Hills). Titles available for Nova Scotia, New Brunswick, Prince Edward Island, Manitoba, Halifax. New this year: Ottawa, Toronto.

Toronto Ultimate Guide, and Vancouver Ultimate Guide (Chronicle). Comprehensive guides covering all aspects of travel to these 2 Canadian cities.

Trans-Canada Rail Guide by Bryn Thomas (Trailblazer).

Vancouver Best Places by K. Wilson (Sasquatch Books). 2nd ed.

Caribbean/West Indies

Series: *Access, Baedeker, Berlitz, *Cadogan, Fielding, Fodor, *Footprints, Frommer, *Insight Guides, *Lonely Planet, *Moon, Nelles, *Rough Guides, Sierra Club, Treasures and Pleasures of...

Adventure Guide to ... Barbados, Bermuda, Dominican Republic, Jamaica, Puerto Rico Trinidad/Tobago, and the Virgin Islands (Hunter Publications). Practical guides for the adventurous traveler.

Best Dives in the Caribbean by J. and J. Huber (Hunter Publications). Covers 24 islands.

Caribbean Afoot! by M. Timothy O'Keefe (Menasha Ridge Press). A walking and hiking guide to 29 Caribbean islands.

Caribbean Walking & Hiking Guide by Leonard M. Adkins (Hunter Publications). Pocket size guide offering easy strolls to longer hikes.

Caribbean Literary Companion by James Ferguson (Passport Books). Compilation of literature, background and cultural information.

Diving Bermuda by Jesse Cancelmo and Mike Strohofer (Aqua Quest Publications). Diving sites, information on marine life, shipwrecks, and travel in Bermuda.

Diving Off the Beaten Track by Bob Burgess (Aqua Quest Publications). Diving in various Caribbean destinations.

Guide to Cuba by Stephen Fallon (Bradt Publishing).

Outdoor Traveller's Guide to the Caribbean by Kay Showker (Stewart, Tabori and Chang). Enticing guide covers the Caribbean's natural history and outdoor activities.

Reader's Companion to Cuba edited by Alan Ryan (Harcourt Brace). Selection of travel writing about the island.

Rum and Reggae by J. Runge (Villard). An insider's guide to the Caribbean.

Undiscovered Islands of the Caribbean by Burl Willes (John Muir Publications). Undiscovered is a relative term, but good ideas abound.

Central America

Series: *Berkeley, Bradt, *Culture Shock!, Fodor, *Footprints, Frommer, *Insight Guides, *Let's Go, *Lonely Planet, *Moon, *New Key, *Rough Guides, Sierra Club.

Adventure Guide to Belize by Harry S. Pariser (Hunter Publications). Practical guide for the adventurous traveler.

Belize: A Natural Destination by S. Wotkyns (John Muir). Focus on nature travel.

Choose Costa Rica by John Howells (Gateway Books). Wintering and retirement in Costa Rica (includes Guatemala).

Costa Rica Traveler's Literary Companion by B. Ras (Whereabouts Press). Compilation of literature, background and cultural information.

Costa Rica's National Parks and Preserves by Joseph Franke (Mountaineers). Guide to these beautiful natural areas.

Costa Rica: A Natural Destination by Ree Strange Sheck (John Muir). Focus on nature travel.

The Costa Rica Traveler by Ellen Searby (Windham Bay Press). Good background notes. All price ranges.

Diving Belize by Ned Middleton (Aqua Quest Publications). Diving sites, information on marine life and travel in Belize.

*Guatemala Guide, Belize Guide, Costa Rica Guide by Paul Glassman and Travel Line Press (Open Road). Comprehensive guides for these 3 countries.

Guatemala: A Natural Destination by R. Mahler (John Muir). Focus on nature travel.

Honduras and Bay Islands Guide by J. Panet (Open Road). Good all-around guide.

Latin America by Bike by W. Siekno (Mountaineers). From Mexico through Central America to the tip of Argentina.

On Your Own in El Salvador by Jeff Brauer. New. Comprehensive.

South and Central America: Literary Companion by Jason Wilson (Passport Books). Compilation of literature, background and cultural information.

Traveller's Survival Kit: Central America by Emily Hatchwell and Simon Calder (Vacation Work). Extensive practical information and town-by-town guide to the 7 countries of this region.

China/Hong Kong

Series: Baedeker, Berlitz, *Blue Guides, *Culture Shock!, Customs and Etiquette, Fodor, Frommer, *Insight, *Lonely Planet, Maverick, *Moon Handbooks, Nelles, *Rough Guides, Travelers' Tales, Treasures and Pleasures of...

Biking Beijing by Diana B. Kingsbury (China Books). Tours through Beijing to popular tourist destinations.

China by Bike: Taiwan, Hong Kong, China's East Coast by R. Grigsby (Mountaineers).

China Bound by Anne F. Thurston (National Academy Press). Prepares long- and short-term visitors for everyday life in China.

China Regional Guides (Passport Books). Includes Fujian, Xian, Beijing, Yunnan.

Essential Chinese for Travelers by Fran Zhilong (China Books). Basic phrasebook, and cassette, includes sections on hotels, transportation, money, food, and business. Rev. 1996.

Trekking in Russia and Central Asia: A Traveler's Guide by Frith Maier (Mountaineers).

Czech Republic and Slovak Republic

Series: Baedeker, Berlitz, *Berkeley, *Blue Guides, Citywalks, *Culture Shock!, Customs & Etiquette, Eyewitness, Fodor, Frommer, *In-sight Guides, Knopf, *Let's Go, *Lonely Planet, Nelles, Off the Beaten Track, *Rough Guides.

The Czech Republic by Astrid Holtslag (Hippocrene). For the budget-conscious.

Prague Traveler's Literary Companion by P. Wilson (Whereabouts Press). Compilation of literature, background, and cultural information.

Visitor's Guide to Czech/Slovak Republics by Andrew Beattie (Hunter Publishing). Comprehensive (except dining and accommodations), with good regional information and driving itineraries.

Europe

Series: *Access, Baedeker, *Berkeley, Berlitz, *Blue Guides, Bradt, *Cadogan, Fielding, Fodor, Frommer, *Insight Guides, *Let's Go, *Lonely Planet, *Michelin, Nelles, *Rick Steves, *Rough Guides.

Best European Travel Tips by John Whitman (Harper Collins): 2,001 tips for saving money, time, and trouble in Europe.

Biking Through Europe by Dennis and Tina Jaffe (Williamson Publishing). Excellent, well-researched.

Cambridge Guide to the Museums of Europe (Cambridge Univ. Press). Over 2,000 entries, includes art collections and cathedral treasures.

Camp Europe by Train by Lenore Baken (Ariel Publications). Touring and camping information using public transport.

Central & Eastern Europe: Literary Companion by James Naughton (Passport Books). Compilation of literature, background, and cultural information.

Eastern Europe by Rail by Rob Dodson (Globe Pequot). Practical guide.

*****Eurail Guide—How to Travel Europe and All the World by Train** by Kathryn Turpin and Marvin Saltzman (Eurail Guide Annual). Covers train travel throughout the world.

Euroad: Complete Guide to Motoring in Europe by Bert Lief (VLE Ltd.). Maps include driving times and distances in miles; documents required.

*****Europe 101: History and Art for the Traveler** by Rick Steves and Gene Openshaw (John Muir Publications). Wonderful.

Europe by Bike: 18 Tours Geared for Discovery by Karen and Terry Whitehill (Mountaineers). 2nd ed. First-rate.

Europe by Eurail by G. and L. Ferguson (Globe Pequot). How to tour Europe by train.

Europe by Van and Motorhome Shore and Campbell (Shore/Campbell Publications). The how-to of van travel throughout Europe.

Europe for Free: Hundreds of Free Things to Do in Europe by Brian Butler (Mustang Publishing).

Europe the European Way by James F. Gollattscheck (Gateway Books). Living (or extended stays) in the world's great cities for $2,000 per month for 2.

*****Europe Through the Back Door** by Rick Steves (John Muir Publications). The best "how-to" and preparation book for Europe with lots of useful hints and information.

*****Europe Through the Back Door Travel Newsletter** Rick Steves, ed. Quarterly. Free from Europe Through the Back Door, Inc., 120 4th Ave. N., Edmonds, WA 98020. Our favorite travel newsletter.

Exploring Europe by Boat by B.R. Rogers and S. Rogers (Globe Pequot). Practical guide to water travel in Europe.

Exploring Europe by RV by Dennis and Tina Jaffe (Globe Pequot). Practical guide to RV travel in Europe.

Festival Europe! by Margaret Johnson (Mustang Publishing). Fairs and celebrations throughout Europe.

First-Time Europe: Everything You Need to Know Before You Go by Louis CasaBianca (Rough Guides). Complete trip-planning resource for low-budget independent travelers.

*****Mona Winks: A Guide to Enjoying Europe's Top Museums** by Rick Steves and Gene Openshaw (John Muir Publications).

Moto Europa by Eric Bredesen (Seren Publishing). P.O. Box 1212, Dubuque, IA 52004; (800) 387-6728. In-depth details on renting, driving, buying, and selling a car.

On the Rails Europe edited by Melissa Shales (Passport Books). Routes, maps, transport information.

*****Rick Steve's Europe Through the Back Door Phrase Books** (John Muir). French, Italian, German, Spanish/Portuguese, and French/Italian/German (3 in 1).

Ski Europe by Charles Leocha (World Leisure). Rev. 1997.

Teaching English in Eastern and Central Europe by Robert Lynes (Passport Books). Practical information on finding a job, teaching and living in Czech Republic, Slovakia, Poland, Hungary, Romania, and Bulgaria.

Thomas Cook European Timetable. $27.95 plus $4.50 shipping from Forsyth Travel Library, Inc., 1750 E. 131 St., P.O. Box 480800, Kansas City, MO 64146; (816) 942-9050, (800) 367-7984; www.forsyth.com. Rail schedules for over 50,000 trains on every European and British main line.

Travel Guide to Jewish Europe by Ben Frank (Pelican). Jewish historical sites, Holocaust memorials, neighborhoods, restaurants, etc.

Traveler's Guide to European Camping by Mike and Teri Church (Rolling Homes Press). Explore Europe economically at your own pace using an RV or tent. Lots of campground listings.

Traveling Europe's Trains by Jay Brunhouse (Pelican). Detailed itineraries.

Understanding Europeans by Stuart Miller (John Muir Publications). Insights into European behavior, historical and cultural heritage.

Walking Europe from Top to Bottom by Susan Margolis and Ginger Harmon (Sierra Club Books). Follows the Grande Randonnée Cinque on a 107-day journey. (You can do smaller portions.)

Walks (VLE Ltd.). Street by street walking maps through 13 principal European cities.

France

Series: *Access, Baedeker, *Berkeley, Berlitz, *Blue Guides, *Cadogan, Citywalks, *Culture Shock!, Customs and Etiquette, Driving Tours, Daytrips, Exploring Rural Europe, Eyewitness, Fielding, Fodor, Frommer, *Insight Guides, Karen Brown, Knopf, *Let's Go, *Lonely Planet, *Michelin, Nelles, Off the Beaten Track, Passport Regional Handbooks, *Rick Steves, *Rough Guides.

Bed and Breakfasts of Character and Charm in France (Rivages Guides).

Camping and Caravaning France (Michelin Publications). Campgrounds, town plans, location information, plus facilities.

Cheap Sleeps in Paris and **Cheap Eats in Paris** by Sandra A. Gustafson (Chronicle). Guides to inexpensive lodgings, restaurants, bistros, and brasseries.

France by Bike: 14 Tours Geared for Discovery by Karen and Terry Whitehall (Mountaineers).

France: Literary Companion, by John Edmondson (Passport Books). Compilation of literature, background and cultural information.

Gites Guide (Hunter Publications). Details over 1,200 rental houses/cottages throughout France (includes booking information).

French Country Welcome 1997 (Gites de France). Available in U.S. from Ulysses Books and Maps, 3 Roosevelt Terr. #13, Plattsburgh, NY 12901 or 4176 Saint-Denis, Montreal, PQ H2W 2M5, Canada (Mailing address only. For telephone orders call 514-843-9882.) Information on 3,200 B and Bs throughout France.

Hotels and Country Inns of Charm and Character in France (Rivages Guides).

Literary Cafés of Paris by Noel Riley Fitch (Starrhill Press). Sit in famous Parisian cafes and read about the writers who made them famous.

On the Rails Around France, Belgium, Netherlands and Luxembourg by Roger Thomas (Passport Books). Routes, maps, transport information.

Paris for Free (Or Extremely Cheap) by Mark Beffart (Mustang Publishing).

Paris Inside Out by Anglophone S.A. (below). An insider's guide for resident students and discriminating visitors on living in the French capital.

Paris-Anglophone by David Applefield (Anglophone S.S., 32, rue Edouard); (011-33-1-48-59-6-58). Print and online directory of essential contacts for English speakers in Paris.

The Unknown South of France: A History Buff's Guide by Henry and Margaret Reuss (Harvard Common Press). A guide to the history and culture of the south of France.

Through the French Canals by Philip Bristow (Talman). Exploring the waterways of France.

Undiscovered Museums of Paris by Eloise Danto (Surrey Books). Guide to little-known, hard-to-find (and major) museums and galleries.

Walking Easy in the French Alps (Gateway Books). Hiking guide.

Wild France (Sierra Club). Travel and nature guide to wilderness areas of France.

Germany

Series: Baedeker, *Berkeley, Berlitz, *Blue Guides, *Cadogan, Citywalks, Customs and Etiquette, Daytrips, Driving Tours, Exploring Rural Europe, Fodor, Frommer, Insight Guides, Karen Brown, *Let's Go, *Michelin, Off the Beaten Track, *Rick Steves, *Rough Guides, Traveller's History.

Germany by Bike: 20 Tours Geared for Discovery by Nadine Slavinski (Mountaineers).

Traveler's Guide to Jewish Germany by Hirsch and Lopez (Pelican). Sites, synagogues, memorials, and exhibitions.

Greece

Series: Baedeker, Berlitz, *Blue Guides, *Cadogan, Customs and Etiquette, Exploring Rural Europe, Fodor, Frommer, *Insight Guides, Knopf, *Let's Go, *Lonely Planet, *Michelin, Nelles, Off the Beaten Track, *Rough Guides, Traveller's History.

Greece: A Traveler's Literary Companion edited by Artemis Leontis (Whereabouts Press).

Greek Island Hopping by Richard F. Poffley (Passport Books). Valuable advice on ferries, island itinerary planning.

Trekking in Greece by Marc Dubin (Lonely Planet). Hiking guide.

Hungary

Series: Baedeker, Berlitz, *Blue Guides, Customs and Etiquette, Fodor, Frommer, *Insight Guides, *Lonely Planet, Nelles, *Rough Guides.

Budapest: A Critical Guide by András Török (Zephyr Press, 13 Robinson St., Somerville, MA 02145). Detailed inside information.

People to People Czech-Slovakia, Hungary, Bulgaria by Jim Haynes (Zephyr Press, 13 Robinson St., Somerville, MA 02145). Latest in a series of books on Eastern Europe for travelers who want to experience life as the locals live it. Lists over 1,000 locals to contact.

Indian Subcontinent/ Himalayas

Series: Berlitz, *Cadogan, *Culture Shock!, Customs and Etiquette, Fodor, *Footprints, Frommer, *Insight, *Let's Go, *Lonely Planet, *Moon Handbooks, Nelles, Passport Regional Guides, *Rough Guides, Travelers' Tales.

ALTERNATIVE TRAVEL DIRECTORY

Bhutan: Himalayan Kingdom by Booz (Passport Books). Focuses on background, history, etc. (not the practical).

India by Stanley Wolpert (Univ. of California Press). A concise and comprehensive guide to Indian history and culture by an authority.

India by Rail, also Sri Lanka by Rail, both by Royston Ellis (Bradt).

India, Nepal & Sri Lanka: The Traveler's Guide by Peter Meyer and Barbara Rausch (Riverdale Co.). Popular German budget-oriented guide.

India: Literary Companion by Simon Weightman (Passport Books). Compilation of literature, background and cultural information.

Northern India: Rajasthan, Agra, Delhi by Philip Ward (Pelican). First-person account by well-informed writer.

Passport Regional India Guides (Passport Books). All-purpose guides with planned itineraries and good orientation. Titles include: Museums of India, Bhutan and Bombay/Goa, Delhi, Agrand Pakistan, Jaipur, The Hill Stations of India, The Kathmandu Valley.

Silk Route by Rail by Dominic Streatfield-James (Trailblazer).

Tibet: Roof of the World (Passport Books). 3rd ed. Good overall coverage, focuses more on background, history, etc., than on practical travel information.

Trekking in Indian Himalayas by G. Weare (Lonely Planet).

Trekking in the Annapurna Region by Bryn Thomas (Trailblazer).

*Trekking in Nepal by Stephen Bezruchka (Mountaineers, 6th ed.). Detailed guide.

Trekking in the Everest Region by Jamie McGuinness (Trailblazer).

Trekking in Tibet: A Traveler's Guide by Gary McCue (Mountaineers).

Indonesia/Malaysia/ Singapore

Series: Berlitz, Bradt, *Culture Shock!, Customs and Etiquette, Fielding, *Footprints, *Insight Guides, Knopf, *Lonely Planet, Maverick, *Moon Handbooks, Nelles, Passport Regional Guides, *Rough Guides, Treasures and Pleasures of...

Passport Regional Indonesia Guides (NTC Publishing). Excellent coverage of the islands of the Indonesian Archipelago. Titles include Bali, Java, Spice Islands, Sumatra, Underwater Indonesia, and more.

Thailand, Malaysia, Singapore by Rail by Brian McPhee (Bradt).

Ireland

Series: Baedeker, *Berkeley, Berlitz, *Blue Guides, *Cadogan, Customs and Etiquette, *Culture Shock!, Day Trips, Driving Tours, Exploring Rural Europe, Eyewitness, Fodor, Frommer, *Insight Guides, Karen Brown, Knopf, *Let's Go, *Lonely Planet, *Michelin, Nelles, Off the Beaten Track, *Rick Steves, *Rough Guides, Traveller's History.

Bed and Breakfast Ireland by Elsie Dillard and Susan Causin (Chronicle). Guide to over 300 of Ireland's best B and Bs.

Ireland by Bike: 21 Tours Geared for Discovery by Robyn Krause (Mountaineers).

Ireland: Complete Guide and Road Atlas (Globe Pequot). Comprehensive guide, organized by regions. Color road maps and street maps.

Joyce's Dublin: A Walking Guide to Ulysses by Jack McCarthy (Irish Books & Media). Fascinating.

See Ireland by Train by Fergus Mulligan (Irish Books & Media). Compact, helpful.

Wild Ireland (Sierra Club). Travel and nature guide to wilderness areas.

Italy

Series: *Access, Baedeker, Berkeley, Berlitz, *Blue Guides, *Cadogan, Citywalks, Customs and Etiquette, Daytrips, Driving Tours, Exploring Rural, Eyewitness, Fielding, Fodor, Frommer, *Insight Guides, Karen Brown, Knopf, *Let's Go, *Lonely Planet, *Michelin, Nelles, Off the Beaten Track, Passport Regional Guides, *Rick Steves, *Rough Guides, Traveller's History.

Cento Citta: A Guide to the "Hundred Cities and Towns" of Italy by Paul Hofmann (Henry Holt). Beyond the major tourist cities.

Cheap Sleeps in Italy and Cheap Eats in Italy by Sandra A. Gustafson (Chronicle). Guide to inexpensive, charming lodgings and restaurants.

Hotels and Country Inns of Character and Charm in Italy (Rivages Guides).

Northern Italy: A Taste of Trattoria by Christina Baglivi (Mustang). Eat with the locals.

Teaching English in Italy by Martin Penner (Passport Books). Practical information on finding a job, teaching, and living in Italy.

Touring Club of Italy Guides (Monacelli Press). Established series of Italian guidebooks recently translated into English. Excellent maps. Titles for: Italy, Rome, Venice, Florence.

Undiscovered Museums of Florence by Eloise Danto (Surrey Books). Guide to little-known, hard-to-find (and major) museums and galleries.

Walking Easy in the Italian Alps (Gateway Books). Hiking guide.

Wild Italy (Sierra Club). Travel and nature guide to wilderness areas.

Japan

Series: Baedeker, Berlitz, *Cadogan, *Culture Shock!, Customs and Etiquette, Fodor, Frommer, *Insight Guides, *Lonely Planet, *Moon Handbooks, Traveller's History.

Cycling Japan by B. Harrell (Kodansha).

Hiking in Japan by Paul Hunt (Kodansha). Mountain trails, maps, great geological notes.

Japan-Think, Ameri-Think by Robert J. Collins (Penguin). An irreverent guide to understanding the cultural differences.

Japan: A Literary Companion by Harry Guest (Passport Books). Compilation of literature, background and culture.

Ski Japan! by T.R. Reid (Kodansha).

Teaching English in Japan by Jerry O'Sullivan (Passport Books). Practical information on finding a job, teaching, and living in Japan.

Korea

Series: *Culture Shock!, Fodor, *Insight Guides, *Lonely Planet, *Moon Handbooks.

Malta

Series: Berlitz, *Blue Guides, *Cadogan, *Insight Guides.

Mexico

Series: *Access, Baedeker, *Berkeley, Berlitz, Birnbaum, Bradt, *Cadogan, Daytrips, Driving Tours, Fielding, Fodor, Footprints, Frommer, *Insight Guides, Knopf, *Let's Go, *Lonely Planet, *Michelin, *Moon Handbooks, Nelles, *New Key, *Rough Guides, Travelers' Tales.

Adventure Guide to Baja California by Wilbur Morrison (Hunter Publications). Practical.

Baja by Kayak: The Ultimate Sea Kayaking Guide to Baja by Lindsay Loperenza (White Cloud).

The Best Mexican and Central American Travel Tips by John Whitman (Harper Collins).

Bicycling Mexico by E. Weisbroth and E. Ellman (Hunter Publications).

Choose Mexico by J. Howells and D. Merwin (Gateway Books). Guide for those interested in retiring or residing in Mexico.

Diving Cozumel by Steve Rosenberg (Aqua Quest Publications). Diving sites, information on marine life, archaeological sites, and travel.

Mexico by Rail by G. Poole (Hunter Publications).

Mexico: A Hiker's Guide to Mexico's Natural History by Jim Conrad (Mountaineers). Steers hikers through Mexico's natural landscape while illuminating its natural history.

***The People's Guide to Mexico** by Carl Franz (John Muir Publications). A wonderful read—full of wisdom, too.

***The People's Guide to RV Camping in Mexico** by Carl Franz (John Muir Publications). Extensive camping information and advice.

The Yucatan: A Guide to the Land of Maya Mysteries by Antoinette May (Wide World Publishing). Now includes Tikal, Belize, Copan. A respected guide focusing on cultural considerations.

Myanmar (Burma)

Series: Bradt, *Culture Shock!, Fielding, *Footprints, *Insight Guides, *Lonely Planet, *Moon Handbooks. (*Transitions Abroad* urges you not to visit Burma.)

New Guinea

Series: *Lonely Planet, Passport Regional Guides.

Bushwalking in Papua New Guinea by Riall Nolan (Lonely Planet Publications).

New Zealand

Series: Berlitz, Fielding, Fodor, Frommer, *Insight Guides, *Lonely Planet, Maverick, *Moon, Nelles, Sierra Club.

The New Zealand Bed and Breakfast Book by J. and J. Thomas (Pelican). Lists over 300 private homes and hotels.

New Zealand by Bike by Bruce Ringer (Mountaineers, 2nd edition). Bike tours through scenic countryside.

Pacific

Series: *Lonely Planet, *Moon Handbooks, Sierra Club. Lonely Planet and Moon Handbooks have many titles that focus on this area by island groups and individual islands. Titles include: South Pacific Handbook (Moon Handbooks), Micronesia (Lonely Planet), Fiji (both companies), Vanuatu (Lonely Planet), Samoa (Lonely Planet).

Adventuring in the Pacific (Sierra Club). For the adventurous traveler.

Philippines

Series: *Culture Shock!, *Insight Guides, *Lonely Planet, *Moon Handbooks, Nelles.

Poland

Series: Bradt, Customs and Etiquette, *Insight Guides, *Lonely Planet, Off the Beaten Track, *Rough Guides.

Hiking Guide to Poland and Ukraine by Tim Burford (Bradt).

People to People Poland by Jim Haynes (Zephyr Press, 13 Robinson St., Somerville, MA 02145). One of a series of books on Central Europe for travelers who want to experience life as the locals live it. Lists over 1,000 locals to contact.

Polish Cities (Pelican). A guide to Warsaw, Krakow, and Gdansk.

Portugal

Series: Baedeker, Berlitz, *Blue Guides, *Cadogan, Citywalks, Daytrips, Exploring Rural Europe, Fielding, Fodor, Frommer, *Insight Guides, *Let's Go, *Michelin, Off the Beaten Track, *Rick Steves, *Rough Guides.

Romania

Series: Bradt, *Lonely Planet, *Rough Guides.

People to People Romania by Jim Haynes (Zephyr Press, 13 Robinson St., Somerville, MA 02145). One of a series of books on Central Europe for travelers who want to experience life as locals live it. Lists over 1,000 locals to contact.

Romania Travel Guide by L. Brinkle (Hippocrene). Good background.

Russia and the NIS

Series: Baedeker, Berlitz, *Blue Guides, *Cadogan, Customs and Etiquette, Fodor, Frommer, *Insight Guides, Knopf, *Lonely Planet, *Moon, Nelles, *Rick Steves, *Rough Guides, Traveller's History. Distributors: Russian Information Services, 89 Main St., Montpelier, VT 05602; (800) 639-4301. Free **Access Russia** and **Central Europe** catalog.

Explorer's Guide to Moscow by Robert Greenall (Zephyr Press).

Georgian Republic by Roger Rosen (Passport Books). First comprehensive guide in English.

Russian Life Magazine (Russia Information Services). A monthly color magazine on Russian travel, culture, history, business, and life. One-year subscription $29 (U.S.), $53 (foreign). Contact publisher for free trial subscription: (802) 223-4955, fax

(802) 223-6105; 73244.3372@compuserve.com.

Russia Survival Guide by Paul Richardson (Russian Information Services). Comprehensive guide with practical information.

Russia: People to People by Jim Haynes (Zephyr Press). One of a series of books on Central Europe for travelers who want to experience life as locals live it. Lists over 1,000 locals to contact.

Trans-Siberian Handbook by Bryn Thomas (Trailblazer). Solid information.

Trans-Siberian Rail Guide by Robert Strauss (Hunter Publishing). Excellent.

Trekking in Russia and Central Asia: A Traveler's Guide by Frith Maier (Mountaineers).

Where in Moscow by Paul Richardson (Russian Information Services). Practical information, maps, and information on the city.

Where in St. Petersburg by Scott McDonald (Russian Information Services). Practical information, maps, and information on the city.

Scandinavia

Series: Baedeker, Berlitz, *Blue Guides, *Culture Shock!, Driving Tours, Fodor, Frommer, *Insight Guides, *Lonely Planet, Nelles, Off the Beaten Track, *Rick Steves, *Rough Guides.

Visitor's Guides (Hunter Publishing). Touring guides with suggested routes and information on sights, places of interest, town tours, background: Denmark, Norway, Finland, Sweden, and Iceland.

Slovenia

Series: *Lonely Planet.

South America

Series: Berlitz, Bradt, *Cadogan, Fielding, Fodor, *Footprints, Frommer, *Insight Guides, *Let's Go, *Lonely Planet, *Rough Guides, Travelers' Tales.

Backpacking and Trekking in Peru and Bolivia by Hilary Bradt (Bradt).

Best Places to Stay in South America by Alex Newton (Hunter).

Latin America by Bike by W. Sienko (Mountaineers). From Mexico through Central America all the way to the tip of Argentina.

South America's National Parks by William Leitch (Mountaineers). A long-needed introduction to South America's great ecological treasures.

South and Central America: Literary Companion by Jason Wilson (Passport Books). Compilation of literature, background and cultural information.

Traveler's Guide to El Dorado and the Inca Empire by Lynn Meisch (Viking Penguin). A superb practical guide.

Traveler's Guide to Latin America Customs & Manners by N. Braganti and E. Devine (St. Martin's Press). An important aid in understanding Latin American culture.

Trekking in Bolivia/Bolivia Climbing Guide both by Yossi Brain (Mountaineers).

Spain

Series: *Access, Baedeker, Berlitz, *Blue Guides, *Cadogan, Citywalks, *Culture Shock!, Daytrips, Driving Tours, Exploring Rural Europe, Eyewitness, Fielding, Fodor, *Footprints, Frommer, *Insight Guides, Karen Brown, *Let's Go, *Michelin, Nelles,

Off the Beaten Track, *Rick Steves, *Rough Guides, Traveller's History, Travelers' Tales.

Trekking in Spain by Marc Dubin (Lonely Planet Publications). Gives both day hikes and overnight treks.

Wild Spain (Sierra Club). Travel and nature guide to the wilderness areas of Spain.

Switzerland

Series: Baedeker, Berlitz, *Blue Guides, Bradt, *Culture Shock!, Driving Tours, Fodor, Frommer, *Insight Guides, Karen Brown, *Let's Go, *Lonely Planet, *Michelin, Off the Beaten Track, *Rick Steves.

Switzerland by Rail by Anthony Lambert (Bradt Publishing).

Switzerland: The Smart Traveler's Guide to Zurich, Basel and Geneva by Paul Hofmann (Henry Holt).

Walking Easy in the Swiss Alps by C. and C. Lipton (Gateway Books). Hiking guide for active adults.

Walking Switzerland the Swiss Way by Marcia and Philip Lieberman (Mountaineers). Great ideas.

Taiwan

Series: *Culture Shock!, *Insight Guides, *Lonely Planet.

Thailand

Series: Berlitz, *Cadogan, *Culure Shock!, Fielding, Fodor, *Footprints, Frommer, *Insight Guides, *Let's Go, *Lonely Planet, Knopf, Maverick, *Moon Handbooks,

Nelles, *Rough Guides, Travelers' Tales, Treasures and Pleasures of...

Chiang Mai: Thailand's Northern Rose (Passport Books). Good planning information.

Diving in Thailand by Collin Piprell (Hippocrene). Best diving sites with information on preparation, facilities, etc.

Thailand, Malaysia, Singapore by Rail by Brian McPhee (Bradt).

Turkey

Series: Baedeker, Berlitz, *Blue Guides, *Cadogan, *Culture Shock!, Fodor, Frommer, *Insight Guides, Knopf, *Let's Go, *Lonely Planet, Nelles, *Rough Guides, Traveller's History.

Strolling Through Istanbul by Hillary Sumner Boyd and John Freely (Columbia Univ. Press). A classic that focuses on the city's antiquities.

Trekking in Turkey by Marc Dubin (Lonely Planet Publications). Trekking information for this country of varied terrain.

Ukraine

Hiking Guide to Poland and Ukraine by Tim Burford (Bradt).

Language and Travel Guide to Ukraine by L. Hodges (Hippocrene).

United Kingdom

Series: *Access, Baedeker, *Berkeley, Berlitz, *Blue Guides, *Cadogan, Citywalks, Customs and Etiquette, Daytrips, Driving Tours, Exploring Rural Europe, Eyewitness, Fielding, Fodor, Frommer, *Insight Guides,

Karen Brown, Knopf, *Let's Go, *Lonely Planet, *Michelin, Nelles, Off the Beaten Track, Passport Regional Guides, *Rick Steves, *Rough Guides, Traveller's History, Treasures and Pleasures of...

Best Bed and Breakfasts: England, Scotland, Wales 1996-97 by Sigourney Wells (Globe Pequot). Alphabetical by county.

The Best of Britain's Countryside—Heart of England and Wales by Bill and Gwen North (Mountaineers). Two-week drive and walk itinerary for northern England and Scotland, southern England, heart of England and Wales.

Brit-Think, Ameri-Think by Jane Walmsley (Penguin). An irreverent guide to understanding the cultural differences.

Cheap Eats in London and Cheap Sleeps in London (Chronicle Books). 100 inexpensive places to eat and sleep.

CTC Route Guide to Cycling in Britain and Ireland by Christa Gausden and Nicholas Crane (Haynes Publishing). First rate. Not available in U.S.

Cycle Tours in the U.K. (Ordnance Survey). Sixteen different guides, each describing around 24 different one-day trips in the U.K.

Cycling Great Britain by Tim Hughes (Bicycle Books).

England by Bike: 18 Tours Geared for Discovery by Les Woodland (Mountaineers).

English and Scottish Tourist Board Publications. Selection includes titles on Hotels, B and Bs, Self-Catering, Staying on a Farm, Activity Breaks (Distributed by Seven Hills).

Hotels and Restaurants of Great Britain by British Hospitality Association (Globe Pequot).

Literary Villages of London by Luree Miller (Starrhill Press). The author has mapped her favorite walks past the London homes and haunts of celebrated writers.

London for Free by Brian Butler (Mustang Publishing).

National Trust Handbook (Trafalgar Square). Lists National Trust properties including homes, gardens, castles, lighthouses.

On the Rails Around Britain and Ireland edited by Neil Wenborn (Passport Books). Routes, maps, transport information.

Passport Guide to Ethnic London by Ian McAuley (Passport Books). A guide to history, food, culture—neighborhood by neighborhood.

Scotland Bed and Breakfast (British Tourist Authority). Over 2,000 B and Bs listed.

Undiscovered Museums of London by Eloise Danto (Surrey Books). Guide to little-known, hard-to-find (and major) museums and galleries.

Wild Britain (Sierra Club). Travel and nature guide to wilderness areas of Britain.

Vietnam/Laos/Cambodia

Series: Bradt, *Culture Shock!, Customs and Etiquette, Fielding, *Footprints, *Insight Guides, *Lonely Planet, Maverick, *Moon, Nelles, *Rough Guides.

Guide to Vietnam by John R. Jones (Bradt). Every province and area of interest is described in detail, along with fascinating ethnic and cultural information.

Vietnam: Traveler's Literary Companion edited by J. Balaban and N. Qui Duc

(Whereabouts Press). Compilation of literature, cultural and background information.

Worldwide Destinations

Jewish Travel Guide by Stephen Massil (ISBS). Provides listings of Jewish organizations throughout the world.

More Women Travel (Penguin). From Rough Guide series.

Travel Books Worldwide: The Travel Book Review. $36 per year (10 issues), Canada $48, rest of the world $72 or £42 per year from: Travel Keys Books/Travel Books Worldwide, P.O. Box 162266, Sacramento, CA 95816-2266. A 12-page newsletter devoted to new travel books.

Travel Smarts: Getting the Most for Your Travel Dollar by H. Teison and N. Dunnan (Globe Pequot). Some useful tips and advice.

Traveler's Handbook: Essential Guide for Every Traveler (WEXAS/Globe Peqout). Good resource.

U.S. State Department Travel Advisories. Available through Inter-L or by calling (202) 647-5225, these periodic advisories alert U.S. travelers to health and safety risks worldwide.

Wild Planet! 1,001 Extraordinary Events for the Inspired Traveler by Tom Clynes (Visible Ink). Thorough compendium of festivals, cultural events, and holidays spanning the globe.

The World Awaits: Comprehensive Guide to Extended Backpack Travel by Paul Otteson (John Muir Publications). Practical book preparing travelers with details for life on the road.

World Music from the Rough Guides Series (Penguin). References and information on music spanning the globe.

Web Sites

Eco-Source: The Ecotourism Specialists; ecosource@podi.com, www.podi.com/eco-source. Managed by working professionals, Eco-Source is a dynamic global resource for the ecotourism industry that includes: employment opportunities, educational content, professional consulting, development assistance, "list and link" library, project development, networking, armchair travel, and more.

Journeywoman Online is a magazine for women who love to travel. It's free and on the internet. Visit this award-winning site at www.journeywoman.com and get the real female scoop on travel. They post hundreds of travel tips, stories, and money-saving opportunities all from a woman's point of view. Sign on for a free e-mail newsletter and it's delivered to you in minutes.

Passport to Web Radio (International Broadcasting Services, www.passport.com). Explains how to hear hundreds of local AM/FM stations audible worldwide over the internet.

CHAPTER 2

SPECIAL INTEREST VACATIONS

The following listing of specialty travel vacations was supplied by the organizers. Contact the program directors to confirm costs, dates, and other details.

Africa

Borton Overseas. Borton Overseas specializes in unique adventures to Africa and Scandinavia. We own our own land transportation company and award-winning lodge in Tanzania. We offer programs to Kenya, Tanzania, Uganda, Zimbabwe, Botswana, Namibia, Ghana, Egypt, Morocco, and South Africa.

Dates: Scheduled and custom departures. Contact: Borton Overseas, 1621 E. 79th St., Bloomington, MN 55425; (612) 883-0704 or (800) 843-0602; travel@borton.com, www.borton.com/overseas.html.

Americas

Trek America. Small group adventure camping tours. USA, Canada, Alaska, Mexico, Guate-mala, and Belize. We do the driving and supply all the camping equipment. National and state parks, big cities and small towns, famous places and hidden wonders. Tours from 7 days to 9 weeks from 14 cities. Hike, bike, horseback ride, raft and more.

Dates: Year round. Cost: $40-$120 per day (avg. $60 per day). Contact: Jeff Hall, Trek America, P.O. Box 189, Rockaway, NJ 07866; (800) 221-0596, fax (973) 983-8551; trekamnj@ix.netcom.com.Australia

Trek Australia/New Zealand. Fourteen-31 days exploring Australia and New Zealand with a small (13 max.) international group, utilizing Hostelling-International accommodations. Explore the Great Barrier Reef, the bush and outback, and stunning parks. Detailed dossier available upon request.

Dates: Monthly departures year round. Cost:

From $1,289, includes transportation, accommodations, sightseeing, entrances to parks, adventure excursions. Contact: Roadrunner Worldwide, 6762A Centinela Ave., Culver City, CA 90230-6304; (800) 873-5872, fax (310) 390-1446; amadlax@attmail.com.

Austria

Internationale Hochschulkurse. German courses at the University for beginners and advanced students, perfectionist courses (6 levels). Lectures on German and Austrian literature, music, linguistics, introduction to Austria. Special courses: translation into German, commercial correspondence, business German, medical terminology, communication, phonetics, Vienna waltz, choir singing. Language laboratory. Excursions.

Dates: Jul 6-Aug 2, Aug 3-30, Aug 31-Sep 20. Cost: Course fee (4 weeks): approx. ATS4,300; accommodations: approx. ATS 6,000. Contact: Magister Sigrun Anmann-Trojer, Wiener Internationale Hochsch ulkurse, Universität, Dr. Karl Lueger-Ring 1, A1010 Wien, Austria; (011) 43-1-405-12-54 or 405-47-37, fax 405-12-5410.

Bali, Indonesia

Ann Barros' Yoga in Bali. Package includes: Roundtrip airfare, deluxe accommodations, daily Iyengar yoga classes, language and cultural orientation, gourmet meals and more. The perfect vacation to walk into and enjoy. All details addressed by a very thoughtful and competent tour leader who is also an excellent yoga instructor. Nineteenth tour.

Dates: Feb 6-21 and Jul 18-Aug 1, 1998. Cost: $2,900. Includes airfare, accommodations, breakfasts, excursions. Contact: Ann Barros, 341 26th Ave., Santa Cruz, CA 95062; Tel./fax (408) 475-8738.

Belize

CHAA Creek Caribbean Cookery. Our week-long culinary course combines half days of cooking classes with food-related touring to Mayan sites, local markets, and native kitchens. Special emphasis on tropical ingredients, the foods of Belize, and decadent desserts. Enjoy staying at a jungle lodge on the Macal River while learning how to create gourmet meals.

Dates: Jun 1-Dec 15, alternate weeks. Cost: $1,500 per person, based on double occupancy. Contact: Bill Altman, CHAA Creek, P.O. Box 53, San Ignacio, Cayo, Belize, Central America; (011) 501-92-2037, fax 92-2501; chaa_creek@btl.net.

Brazil

Amazon Jungle Tour. Focus is on the Anavilhanas Islands and the Rio Negro river. Includes a flood forest survival course on biodiversity, medicinal plants and evolutionary adapation—an intimate experience with the jungle. A hands-on way to share experiences with the Amazon people.

Dates: Weekly departures, minimum 2 persons. Cost: $1,250 except for airfare from Miami all inclusive. Contact: Brazilian Views, Inc., 201 E. 66th St., New York, NY 10021-6480; (212) 472-9539.

Canada

Archaeological Digs in Canada. Join scientists from the world-renowned Royal Tyrrell Museum at a field research site in fossil-rich Alberta. You'll prospect for and collect fossils, study the rocks for clues about ancient environments, and learn how the fossils formed. The fossils you find and the information you gather will be used in published scientific studies. On-site training and tools provided. Ages 18 and over.

Dates: Jun 8-Aug 31 (1997). Cost: CAN$800 per week. Includes meals and accommodations. Discounts for booking multiple weeks. Contact: Becky Kowalchuk, Royal Tyrrell Museum, P.O. Box 7500, Drumheller, AB T0J 0Y0, Canada; (403) 823-7707, fax (403) 823-7131; rtmp@dns.magtech.ab.ca, http://tyrrell.magtech.ab.ca.

Hostelling Treks. Two weeks exploring Canada's Rocky Mountains and Alaska's wilderness traveling with a small group from many different countries, staying in Hostelling International-approved accommodations. Hike a glacier, view spectacular wildlife, raft wild rivers. Detailed trek dossier available upon request.

Dates: Weekly departures, May-Oct. Cost: From $859. Contact: Roadrunner Worldwide, 6762A Centinela Ave., Culver City, CA 90230-6304; (800) 873-5872, fax (310) 390-1446; amadlax@attmail.com.

Northern Lights Alpine Recreation. Mountaineering and hiking trips to earnest participants with a sincere interest in meaningful wilderness experiences. Scheduled and customized guided trips. Introductory to experienced. British Columbia Rockies and Purcell Mountain Ranges.

Dates: Year round. Cost: $80 per day, 8-day trips $535-$610. Guiding only. Participants responsible for transportation, equipment, and food. Contact: Kirk or Katie Mauthaer, Box 399, Invermere, BC, V0A 1K0 Canada; (250) 342-6042.

Wilderness Lodging. Purcell Lodge is Canada's finest remote mountain lodge. It sets a new environmental standard in sustainable tourism development. A few miles beyond the crowds of Banff and Lake Louise lies true solitude. A spectacular helicopter flight leaves the familiar far behind. Inside, the comfort of a fine country manor. Outside, your own natural paradise. Peaceful walks in alpine meadows, guided ski tours in stunning surroundings.

Dates: Late Jun-early Sep, Dec-Apr. Cost: All-inclusive American plan $85-$140 per night. Contact: Russ Younger, Manager, Purcell Lodge, Places Less Travelled Ltd., P.O. Box 1829, Golden, BC, Canada V0A 1H0; (250) 344-2639, fax (250) 344-5520; places@rockies.net, www.purcell.com.

Working Landscape Micro-Tours. Explore sustainable alternatives in community development. Small groups; 3-5-day tours. Visit local artisans and community leaders and walk Cape Breton's highlands and wild beaches. Accommodations, meals, local transportation, guides, facilitation, entertainment provided.

Dates: Jun 19-22, 24-29; Sep 11-14, 16-21 (1997). Cost: CAN$1,241 (3 days/nights); CAN$1,973 (5 days/nights). Contact: Ruth M. Schneider, Working Landscape Micro-Tours, R.R. 4, Baddeck, NS B0E 1B0, Canada; (902) 929-2063, fax (902) 929-2348; rschneid@sparc.uccb.ns.ca.

Caribbean

Sonrise Beach Retreat. Jamaica's best ecotourism project: affordable cottages on idyllic private white sand cove, unspoiled wilderness, great swimming, snorkeling, hiking, camping, birding, eco-adventure tours, empty beaches, waterfalls, ruins, rivers, mountains, popular weekend family beach party. Experience the best of Jamaica's natural, cultural, and spiritual life. Special interest low group rate.

Dates: Year round. Cost: From $280 up with accommodations and meals for 1 week. Contact: Robert or Kim Chase, Sonrise Beach Retreat, Robins Bay, St. Mary, Jamaica, WI; Tel./fax (876) 999-7169; www.sonrise-retreat.com.

Tall Ship Adventures. Sail on the historic tall ship Sir Francis Drake. Share the most relaxing vacation afloat with only 30 sailmates. Seven-night cruises in the British Virgin Islands in winter and spring and other exotic Caribbean ports of call in summer and fall.

Dates: Year round. Cost: $995-$1,395 cruise fare only. Contact: Tall Ship Adventures, Inc., 1389 S. Havana St., Aurora, CO 80012; (800) 662-0090 or (303) 755-7983, fax (303) 755-9007; info@tallshipadventures.com, www.tallshipadventures.com.

Costa Rica

Costa Rican Language Academy. Costa Rican-owned and- operated language school offers first-rate Spanish instruction in a warm and friendly environment. Teachers with university degrees. Small groups or private classes. Included free in the programs are airport transportation, coffee and natural refreshments, excursions, and Latin dance, Costa Rican cooking, music, and conversation classes to provide students with complete cultural immersion.

Dates: Year round (start anytime). Cost: $135 per week or $220 per week for program with homestay. All other activities and services included at no additional cost. Contact: Costa Rican Language Academy, P.O. Box 336-2070, San José, Costa Rica; (011) 506-221-1624 or 233-8914 or 233-8938, fax 233-8670. In the U.S.: (800) 854-6057; crlang@sol.racsa.co.cr., www.crlang.co.cr/index.html.

Instituto de Lenguaje "Pura Vida". Only minutes from the capital in the fresh mountain air of Heredia. Intense total immersion methods of teaching. Morning classes and daily cultural activities all conducted in Spanish, maximum 5 students per class. Teachers hold university degrees. Latin music and dance lessons, tours, trips, parties. Learn Spanish fast.

Dates: Classes for all levels start every Monday year round. Cost: Language only, 20 hours per week $230; total immersion, 35 hours per week with homestay $370; children's classes with homestay $370 per week, daycare available. Contact: Instituto de Lenguaje "Pura Vida," P.O. Box 730, Garden Grove, CA 92842; (714) 534-0125, fax (714) 534-1201; BS7324@aol.com, www.arweb.com/puravida.

Language School on Wheels. See the country and learn Spanish. Travel to Costa Rica's beaches, volcanoes, and rainforests aboard comfortable converted coaches. Study Spanish enroute or on the beach from local teachers. Call for trip dates or have us custom design a tour to fit your group. Immerse yourself in the country.

Dates: Feb 1 and Mar 15 (1997). Cost: $449 (land), $101 (food). Contact: Green Tortoise Adventure Travel, 494 Broadway, San Francisco, CA 94133; (800) 867-8647, fax (415) 956-4900; www.greentortoise.com.

Learn Spanish While Volunteering. Assist with the training of Costa Rican public school teachers in our latest language learning techniques, using classroom computers, K-8 school targeted by Costa Rican government as a model ESL/technology school. Enjoy learning Spanish in the morning, volunteer work in the afternoon/evening. Spanish classes are 2-5 students plus group learning activities; conversations with middle-class homestay families (1 student per family). Homestays and volunteer project are within walking distance of school in small town (14,000 population) near the capital, San Jose.

Dates: Year round, all levels. Classes begin every Monday, volunteer program is continuous. Cost: $295 per week for 25 hours of Spanish classes. Includes tuition, all meals (7 days a week), homestay, laundry, all materials, Costa Rican dance and cooking classes, and airport transportation. $25 one-time registration for Spanish classes; $100 additional one-time registration fee for volunteer program. Contact:

Susan Shores, Registrar, Latin American Language Center, 7485 Rush River Dr., Suite 710-123, Sacramento, CA 95831; (916) 447-0938, fax (916) 428-9542; lalc@madre.com.

Europe

Arts and Culture in Europe. Accent offers 2 arts and culture programs this summer for adults: The Art, Music and Gardens of London and Paris—a Tale of Two Cities; and Art, Music and Culture in Florence. Both programs offer a wide variety of activities including: cultural visits, lectures, performances, and excursions outside these extraordinary cities.

Dates: Art, Music and Gardens of London and Paris: Jun 5-Jun 22; Art, Music and Culture in Florence: Jun 27-Jul 26 (1997). Cost: Art, Music and Gardens of London and Paris: $3,200. Includes accommodations, transfer from London to Paris via the Eurostar and all lectures, visits, performances, and excursions. Art, Music and Culture in Florence: $2,800. Includes accommodations, lectures, visits, performances, and excursions. Contact: Accent, 425 Market St., 2nd Fl., San Francisco, CA 94105; (800) 869-9291, fax (415) 904-7759; sfaccent@aol.com.

En Route Travel Experiences. Affordable, engaging, off-the-beaten-path group tours with a wide variety of topics from aromatherapy and hiking to sailing and environmental studies and historic architecture and gardens. Destinations in 1997 include France's château region, Iceland, Copenhagen, Oslo, Stockholm, Norway's Jotunheimen Mountains, the Baltic Sea, Jewish Poland, Wales, Prague, Czech Republic, Italy, England, Provence, and Budapest. Call for free catalog.

Dates: Trip season is Apr-Nov; program length varies, from 7-19 days. Cost: Start at $1,000. Contact: Scandinavian Seminar/En Route, 24 Dickinson St., Amherst, MA 01002; (800) 316-9833 or (413) 253-9736, fax (413) 253-5282; www.enroute.org.

European Hostelling Trek. Eleven-24 days from London, includes all accommodations, transportation in your own minicoach, sightseeing in all major cities, breakfast daily and plenty of time to explore on your own: Amsterdam, Rhône Valley, Prague, Budapest, the Alps, Italy, France, Ireland, and Wales. Detailed trek dossier on request.

Dates: Monthly departures year round. Cost: From $999. Contact: Roadrunner Worldwide, 6762A Centinela Ave., Culver City, CA 90230-6304; (800) 873-5872, fax (310) 390-1446; amadlax@attmail.com.

European Snowboard Tour. Chamonix, France is the crown jewel of alpine sports. Experience European culture, art, architecture, and more while snowboarding with other young people (ages 18 to 38) in the legendary French and Italian Alps. Participate in your favorite outdoor sport for 1 week, in another country, in a friendly international resort atmosphere. Make lifelong friends, take your boarding global.

Dates: Mar 21-29 (1997). Cost: From $1,050. Contact: Julio Buelna, Global Travel Etc., P.O. Box 86226, San Diego, CA 92138; (800) 290-4276, fax (619) 299-5293; goglobal@adnc.com.

Motorcycle Tours and Rentals. In their 10th anniversary year as an incoming motorcycle tour and rental operator in Germany, Bosenberg Motorcycle Excursions offers scheduled, group and custom tours, individual and group rentals, and individual and group travel incentives for a great ride in the heart of Europe.

Dates: Apr-Oct 1998. Cost: Tours start at $2,475 and rentals at $99 per day. Contact: Bosenberg Motorcycle Excursions, Mainzer Str. 54, 55545 Bad Krueznach, Germany; (011) 49-671-67312, fax 67153;

47

bosenberg@compuserve.com, www. bosen-berg.com

Wine and Walking Weekends. Tutored by wine expert Jon Hurley, enjoy delicious food, stay in English country houses, and take lovely, gentle walks in the Wye Valley.

Dates: Year round. Cost: £165-£195 includes accommodations, 2 breakfasts, 2 dinners, 2 tastings, guided walks, all wines. Contact: Jon Hurley's Country House Wine and Walking Weekend, Upper Orchard, Hoarwithy, Herefordshire HR2 6QR, U.K.

France

Artists' Salon of 20th Century Paris. You will explore the world of the writers and artists who lived and worked in Paris in the early 20th century. Highlights include visits to museums, sites of artists' salons, and more. The course is open to anyone with an interest in art, literature, and the nature of creativity.

Dates: Jun 10-24 (1997). Cost: $1,860. Includes airfare, hotel, breakfast, program costs, and tuition. Contact: Jody A. Dudderar, Rockland Community College, 145 College Rd., Suffern, NY 10901; (914) 574-4205, fax (914) 574-4423; jduddderar@sunyrockland.edu.

Cooking with Friends in France. Housed in Julia Child's Provence kitchen. This week-long cultural immersion includes classes in English by Kathie Alex and French chefs. Includes a market tour, restaurant visits. Afternoons free to explore the French Riviera.

Dates: May-Jul; Sep-Nov. Other dates based on availability. Cost: $1,850. Accommodations (double occupancy), most meals, classes. Contact: Jackson & Co., 29 Commonwealth Ave., Boston, MA 02116; voice mail (617) 350-3837, fax (617) 247-6149.

Domaine D'Esperance Cooking. Six times a year, 1-week seminars are held in the spacious kitchen. Enrollment maximum is 9. Each morning is devoted to theoretical instruction, in the afternoon you gain practical experience, preparing the evening meal under the supervision of the chef. The D'Esperance is located in Gascony.

Dates: Oct, Dec, Jan, May, Jun. Cost: FF8,500 per week (10 percent discount for 2 enrollments). Includes full board, lessons. Contact: Claire de Montesquiou, Domaine D'Esperance, 40240 Mauvezin, D'Armagnac, France; (011) 33-5-58-44-68-33, fax 44-85-93.

FPI Piano Festival. The French Piano Institute presents a 2-week piano festival in Paris each July for advanced performers, teachers, and music lovers. Total immersion in French piano repertory is offered by internationally acclaimed guest artists who appear in concert and conduct daily master classes on style and interpretation.

Dates: Jul 3-20, 1998. Cost: $1,024 up, includes tuition, lodging. Contact: Gail Delente, French Piano Institute, 9908 Old Spring Rd., Kensington, MD 20895-3235; (301) 929-8433, fax (301) 929-0254; gdelente@msn.com, www.mmsw.com/fpi.

French and Cookery in a Château. Live and study in 18th century château. Adult courses in French language and Provençal cookery. Relaxed family atmosphere and good food. Château has 13 acres of park and pool. Single/en suite and shared rooms. Close to Burgundy, Beaujolais, Auvergne, and cities of Lyons and Roanne. One- to 12-week courses.

Dates: Every Sunday Apr-Nov. Cost: From $999 full board and classes in Château. Contact: Michael Giammarella, P.O. Box 640713, Oakland Gardens, NY 11364-0713; (800) 484-1234 ext 0096 or

Ecole des Trois Ponts, Chateau de Matel, 42300 Roanne; (011) 33-477-70-80-01, fax 477-71-53-00: info@3ponts.edu,www.3ponts.edu.

French in France. Among the ways to learn French, total immersion is the most enjoyable and the most effective. We have been doing it for 20 years in a small historical city located in Normandy (west of Paris, close to the seaside). We welcome people at any age and any level in from 1- to 10-week programs, intensive or vacation type, from mid-March to mid-November.

Dates: Spring: Mar 23-May 29; summer: Jun 15-Aug 28; fall: Sep 7-Nov 13, 1998. Cost: From $525 per week (tuition, room and board, and excursions). Contact: Dr. Almeras, Chairman, French American Study Center, 12, 14, Blvd. Carnot, B.P. 176, 14104 Lisieux Cedex, France (011) 33-2-31-31-22-01, fax 31-22-21.

Homestay in France. Live with a French family to share their everyday life from 1 week to 1 month. Best way to learn French language, culture, life. Families are located in the south of France: Aix en Provence, Avignon, Nice, Toulon.

Dates: Year round. Cost: One week full board $240. Contact: E.C.I., 62 ave. doPattre de Tossigny, 13090 Aix en Provence, France; (011) 33-4-42-21-07-68, fax 21-42-93; eci@aixpacw.net.

Horizons in Provence. Live and study in a hilltop medieval village and absorb Provence. A week combining workshops with field trips structured to introduce you to the diversity and beauty of Provence—from village markets to wineries to medieval villages and cities such as Avignon. Classes include Painting, Photography/Polaroid Transfers, and Fabric Printing and Design.

Dates: Sep 12-19 (1997). Cost: $1,425 (tu-ition, room and board, field trips). Contact: Horizons, Jane Sinauer, Director, 108 N. Main St.-1st, Sunderland, MA 01375; (413) 665-0300, fax (413) 665-4141.

Le Marmiton - Cooking in Provence. Visit Avignon and Provence and learn, hands-on, about French and Provencal cuisine with the city's best chefs. Up to 12 participants share the large sycamore table and marble counters of our 19th-century period kitchen with its wood fired cast iron stove.

Dates: Each month one 5-day program except in Jul and Aug. Cost: From FF600 for 1 session to FF9,370 for a 5-day, 6-night stay in a deluxe double room with a cooking class every day. Contact: Martin Stein, Hotel de la Mirande, 4, place de La Mirande, F-84000 Avignon, France; (011) 33-490-859393, fax 826685.

Painting and Photography. Atelier Le Bez, located in the beautiful Parc National of Haute Langedoc, brings together small groups to pursue painting and photography and to immerse themselves in French culture and language. The courses are suitable for all levels and include field trips, demonstrations, and language sessions. Year-round retreats available.

Dates: Jun-Oct week-long courses. Cost: FF2,700 tuition, room, and board. Contact: Mabel Odessey, Atelier Le Bez, Brassac 81260, France; Tel./fax (011) 33-5-63-74-56-22.

REMPART. REMPART aims to preserve the French cultural heritage through the restoration of threatened buildings and monuments. It consists of a grouping of more than 140 autonomous associations organizing workcamps that provide a wide variety of work projects involving the restoration of medieval towns, castles, churches, ancient walls, wind/watermills, and industrial sites. Work includes masonry, excavations, woodwork, stone cutting, interior decorating, and clearance work. Opportunities for sports, exploring the region, and taking part in local festivities. Minimum age is 13. Previous experience is not necessary. Some knowledge of French required.

Dates: Workcamps last from 2 to 3 weeks. Most of them are open during Easter holidays and from Jul to Sep. A few camps are open througout the year. Cost: FF220 for insurance, FF40-FF50 per day for food and accommodations. Volunteers help with camp duties, pay their own fares and should bring a sleeping bag. Contact: REMPART, Foreign Secretary: Sabine Guilbert, Union des Associations pour la réhabilitation et l'Entretien des Monuments et du Patrimoine Artistique, 1 rue des Guillemites, 75004 Paris, France; (011) 33-1-42-71-96-55, fax 71-73-00.

Germany

German as a Foreign Language. We offer the following educational programs: various levels of German year round; intensive, crash, and long-term courses, individual tuition; special feature: German and Theater; special programs: business German for professionals, German for teachers, German in a teacher's home, German for special purposes. Academic year for high school students, international study year, internship, guest studentship, homestays for groups, courses for firms and other institutions (banking, insurance, doctors, lawyers, etc.), residential language camps for juniors, examination preparation. Various types of accommodations. Full range of activities.

Dates: Year round. Contact: GLS Sprachenzentrum, Barbara Jaeschke, Managing Director, Kolonnenstrasse 26, 10829 Berlin, Germany; (011) 49-30-787-41-52; fax 41-92; gls.berlin@t-online.de.

Ghana

ABA Tours. The focus of our tours is the art and culture of Ghana. Visit museums, galleries, outdoor markets, and crafts centers. Interact with Africans in their villages and workplaces. Take lessons from the Ghanaian craftspeople or observe how they work.

Dates: Jan-Apr-Aug every year. Cost: $1,700. Includes transportation in Ghana, accommodations, tips, some meals, lessons for 2 weeks. Contact: Ellie Schimelman, ABA Tours, 45 Auburn St., Brookline, MA 02146; Tel./fax (617) 277-0482; abatours@ultranet.com.

Greece

An Archaeological Tour of Greece. Obtain first-hand knowledge of the art and architecture of ancient Greece through on-site archaeological visits and museum tours. This is the only course of its kind in which students are invited to have one of their lectures inside the Parthenon. Other highlights include visits to Sparta, Corinth, Mycenae, the Olympia Grounds, Delphi, Thermopylae, and Mystra, the world's best-preserved medieval city. The trip ends with 4 days on the island of Mykonos and a visit to the "birthplace" of Apollo.

Dates: Jun 7-Jun 29, 1998. Cost: $2,800 (3 credits) includes roundtrip airfare, double occupancy rooms, breakfast daily, bus, ship, and airport transfers. Contact: Dora Riomayor, Director of International Studies, School of Visual Arts, 209 E. 23rd St., New York, NY 10010-3994; (212) 592-2543, fax (212) 592-2545.

Iceland

Iceland 1998. Thoroughgoing backpacking and mixed lighter walking and motorized tours in Iceland, mainly with indoor sleeping-bag accommodations.

Dates: Mid-May to early Sep. Cost: Typically $640 (backpacking) to $1,600 (motorized) for 12 days. ex-Reykjavík, totally inclusive. Contact: Dick Phillips, Whitehall House, Nenthead, Alston, Cumbria CA9 3PS, England; Tel./fax (011) 44-1434-381440.

India (Asia/Southeast Asia)

Kolam Tours. Personalized tour programs for groups and individuals which are people oriented, culturally sensitive, ecologically aware, and politically conscious.

Dates: Individually customized tours from Aug to Mar. Cost: From $75 per person per day for group tours for accommodations (3-star), most meals, all surface travel (road and rail), tours with guides. No hidden costs. Contact: Ranjith Henry, Kolam, Responsible Tours and Soft Travel, B22 Bay View Apts., Kalakshetra Colony, Besant Nagar, Chennai/Madras 600 090 India; (011) 91-44-4913404/4919872, fax 4900939/4915261; http://ourworld.compuserve.com/homepages/kolam.

Ireland

Irish Language and Culture. Irish language programs at all learning levels for adults are offered by Oideas Gael, which also offers cultural activities, learning programs in hillwalking, dances of Ireland, painting, tapestry weaving, Raku-Celtic pottery, and archaeology.

Dates: Apr-Sep, 1998 (weekly). Cost: $150 plus accommodations (from $90 per week). Contact: Liam O'Cuinneagain, Director, Oideas Gael, Gleann Cholm Cille, County Donegal, Ireland; (011) 353-73-30248; oidsgael@iol.ie.

Issues in Public Safety in Ireland. Explore historic and current public safety issues in Ireland. Field study will take place at Dublin Castle, the courts, Probation, Aftercare and Correction Services, and Garda Police College. Tours of historic Dublin will enhance your understanding of Ireland's history and the relationship to the challenges in public safety today.

Dates: Jul 7-21 (1997). Cost: $1,660. Includes airfare, housing, program costs, and tuition. Contact: Jody A. Dudderar, Rockland Community College, 145 College Rd., Suffern, NY 10901; (914) 574-4205, fax (914) 574-4423; jdudderar@sunyrockland.edu.

Joe Mooney Summer School of Traditional Music, Song, and Dance. Workshops in flute, tin whistle, concertina, banjo, button accordion, villeann pipes, fiddle, harp, piano, accordion, bodhrán, traditional singing and set dancing. Lectures, recitals, and concerts. Céilitre. Sessions. Detailed brochure available.

Dates: Jul 18-Jul 25, 1998. Cost: £30 covers workshops and lectures. Contact: Nancy Woods, Joe Mooney Summer School, Drumshanbo, Co. Leitrin, Ireland; (011) 353-78-41213.

Walking and Trekking Holidays. Countryside Tours, set up in 1990, is the specialist in providing leisurely guided and more challenging self-guided hiking tours. A varied program includes all the major areas of interest such as Kerry, Connemara, Wicklow Mountains, and Ulster. Good food, comfortable accommodations in Irish guesthouses.

Dates: Please ask for brochure. Cost: IR£420 for guided tours, from IR£205 for self-guided tours. Contact: Nick Becker, Countryside Tours Ltd., Glencar House, Glencar, County Kerry, Ireland; (011) 353-66-60211, fax 66-60217; country@iol.ie.

Israel

Tel Dor Excavation Project. The Tel Dor Excavation Project is devoted to investigating one of the largest coastal cities in ancient Israel. Volunteers will be engaged in all facets of field archaeology, and in some of the preliminary work of artifact analysis.

Dates: Jul 1-Aug 12, 1998. Cost: $27 per day and $65 participation fee per week. Contact: Dr. I. Sharon, Tel Dor Excavation Project, Institute of Archaeology, Hebrew Univ., Jerusalem, Israel.

The Israel Archaeological Society. The Israel Archaeological Society's Expedition 1998, invites the participation of students, seniors, and families at archaeological digs in Israel and Jordan; work hard, but sleep in comfortable hotels. We will also visit archaeological and historical sites in Israel, Jordan, Syria, and Egypt with a cruise on the Nile. From 1-7 weeks. University students may earn from 4-6 credits from Hebrew Univ.

Dates: Jun 13-Aug 1, 1998. Cost: $1,095-$4,995 land only plus roundtrip airfare. Contact: Arthur D. Greenberg, Israel Archaeological Society, 467 Levering Ave., Los Angeles, CA 90024; (800) 477-2358, fax (310) 476-6259.

Italy

Art Workshop Int'l., Assisi. Live and work in a 12th-century hilltown surrounded by the Umbrian landscape. Instructional courses: painting, drawing, artmaking, all media, art history, creative writing, fiction, poetry. Independent program for professional painters/writers. Two- to 6-week sessions. Visiting artists. New York painters/instructors.

Dates: Jun 23-Aug 3, 1998. Cost: $2,470-$5,670 for tuition, room and board, 4-star hotel, studio space, lectures. Contact: Bea Kreloff, 463 W. St., 1028H, New York, NY 10014; Tel./fax (800) 835-7454; www. vacation-inc.artworkshop.html.

Biking and Walking Tours. Specializing in Italy for over 10 years, Ciclismo Classico distills the "Best of Italy," offering more unique Italian destinations than any other active vacation company.

Educational, active tours for all abilities in Umbria, Tuscany, Piedmont, the Dolomites, Puglia, Sicily, the Amalfi Coast, Cinque Terre, Sardegna, Abruzzo, Campania, Corsica, and Elba, and Ireland, too. Charming accommodations, expert bilingual guides, cooking demonstrations, wine tastings, support vehicle, detailed route instructions, visits to local festivals, countryside picnics—an unforgettable cultural indulgence.

Dates: Apr-Nov (70 departures). Call for specific dates. Cost: $1,500-$3,000. Contact: Lauren Hefferon, Director, Ciclismo Classico, 13 Marathon St., Arlington, MA 02174; (800) 866-7314 or (781) 646-3377.

Italiaidea. Italiaidea is a center for comprehensive Italian instruction. We offer every level and format of Italian study from intensive short-term "survival Italian courses" to advanced semester-long courses meeting once or twice a week. We offer on-site lectures and visits to historic sites in Italian, conversation, and flexible scheduling. For over 10 years we have been offering college credit courses at numerous U.S. college and university programs in Italy; we now offer both academic assistance and travel/study assistance to our client institutions. Homestays are offered as well as accommodations in shared apartments.

Dates: Year round. Cost: Sixty-hour group course LIT750,000; 25-hour one-on-one program LIT1,170,000; 15 hour-specific purposes or culture LIT1,150,000 (taxes not included). Contact: Carolina Ciampaglia, Co-Director, Piazza della Cancelleria 5, 00186 Roma, Italy; (011) 39-6-68307620, fax 6-6892997; italiadea@ nexus.it, www.italiadea.com.

Italian Renaissance. Based in Florence and Rome, explore the achievements of writers, painters, sculptors, and architects of the Italian Renaissance. Highlights include visits to the David, the Duomo, Giotto's Bell Tower, the Vatican Museums, the Sistine Chapel, and St. Peter's Basilica. Experience Italian Renaissance literature, art, and architecture where it was created.

Dates: May 28-Jun 11 (1997). Cost: $1,995. Includes airfare, hotel, breakfast, program costs, and tuition. Contact: Jody A. Dudderar, Rockland Community College, 145 College Rd., Suffern, NY 10901; (914) 574-4205, fax (914) 574-4423; jdudderar@sunyrockland.edu.

Tuscany: Art and Art History. Workshops in an Italian villa, set in the midst of the glorious Tuscan landscape surrounded by vineyards and olive groves. Classes include Painting, Glass Beads, Metals/Jewelry-Making, Photography, Ceramics, Book Arts, Mosaics—combined with field trips to medieval hilltop villages plus Florence and Siena with an art historian.

Dates: May 7-24, Sep 20-27 (1997). Cost: $1,325 (tuition, room and board, field trips). Contact: Horizons, Jane Sinauer, Director, 108 N. Main St.-1st, Sunderland, MA 01375; (413) 665-0300, fax (413) 665-4141.

Malta

Fortress Malta. An exhilarating program for enthusiasts of military history. Malta's rich legacy extends far beyond the time of the knights. Visits include bastions, batteries, medieval ramparts, 20th-century war rooms, lectures and presentations by local experts. Other highlights are the Maritime Museum, Palace Armoury, Aviation Museum, Ft. St. Elmo, WWII Museum. Escorted.

Dates: Jun 14-22; Sep 13-21; Nov 15-23 (1997). Cost: Land cost: $1,387, 8 nights hotel accommodations, all meals, all features. Contact: The OTS Foundation, P.O. Box 17166, Sarasota, FL 34276; (941) 918-9215, fax (941) 918-0265; otsf@aol.com.

Vanishing Ancients. This interactive adventure in archaeology and anthropology on a sunny Mediterranean island visits megalithic temples and explores the mysterious people who built the oldest stone monuments still existing in the world (from 3,800 BCE). Lectures, expert presentations, site visits and behind-the-scenes looks contribute to a comprehensive experience. Conducted in English.

Dates: Apr 12-20; May 24-Jun 1; Oct 11-19 (1997). Cost: Land cost: $1,487, 8 nights hotel accommodations, all meals, all features. Contact: The OTS Foundation, P.O. Box 17166, Sarasota, FL 34276; (941) 918-9215, fax (941) 918-0265; otsf@aol.com.

Mexico

Art and Archaeology in Oaxaca. Live and study in the historic Oaxaca Valley of Mexico, considered the folk art capital of Mexico and set in the midst of an archaeologist's dream. A week combining art and field trips including the ancient Monte Alban ruins plus craft villages. Classes include Ceramics, Hats and Masks, Metals/Jewelry, Baskets and Paper, Painting, Wood Sculpture and Mesoamerican Archaeology.

Dates: Mar 8-15; Sep 17-25 (1997); Jan 5-12, 1998. Cost: $995 (tuition, room, board, field trips). Contact: Horizons, Jane Sinauer, Director, 108 N. Main St.-1st, Sunderland, MA 01375; (413) 665-0300, fax (413) 665-4141.

Flavors of Mexico. Week-long cooking vacations to various regions in Mexico featuring Diana Kennedy, Mexican cooking authority; also includes meals and demonstrations in homes of local cooks, visits to food markets, tours of historical and archaeological sites.

Dates: Year round. Cost: Approx. $2,500.

Includes classes, meals, accommodations, and in-country transportation. Contact: Marilyn Tavsend, Culinary Adventures, Inc., 6023 Reid Dr., NW, Gig Harbor, WA 98335; (253) 851-7676, fax (253) 851-9532; cul-adv-inc@ibm.net.

Intensive Spanish in Cuernavaca. Cuauhnahuac, founded in 1972, offers a variety of intensive and flexible programs geared to individual needs. Six hours of classes daily with no more than 4 students to a class. Housing with Mexican families who really care about you. Cultural conferences, excursions, and special classes for professionals. College credit available.

Dates: Year round. New classes begin every Monday. Cost: $70 registration fee; $650 4 weeks tuition; housing $18 per night. Contact: Marcia Snell, 519 Park Dr., Kenilworth, IL 60043; (800) 245-9335, fax (847) 256-9475; lankysam@aol.com.

Jewelry in San Miguel de Allende. Explore your creativity and practice your Spanish through silver jewelry classes in San Miguel de Allende, Mexico. Innovative, bilingual 5-day workshop in lost wax casting. All skill levels. No experience required. Individual instruction, small groups. All tools provided. Day trips to historical/archaeological sites available.

Dates: Year round. Contact us for a brochure and latest schedule. Cost: $475 for 5-day courses (includes registration, tuition, supplies, and housing). Contact: Raúl Ybarra, 1900 Fox Dr., Box 84-400T, McAllen, TX 78504; (011) 52-415-27358, fax 415-26153, Attn: R. Ybarra.

Language and Culture in Guanajuato. We work with innovative teaching techniques, tailoring instruction to each student's needs. Spanish, Mexican History, Politics, Culture-Cuisine, Folk Dancing and Latin American Literature.

Dates: Year round. New classes begin every Monday. Cost: $925. Includes 4 weeks of classes and homestay with 3 meals daily. Con-tact: Director Jorge Barroso, Instituto Falcon, A.C., Guanajuato, Gto. 36000 Mexico; Tel./fax (011) 52-473-2-36-94, infalcon@redes.int.com.mx, www.infonet.com.mx/falcon.

Yoga Vacation in Mexico. Enjoy a tropical yoga vacation in Islas Miyeres, a tiny island just off Mexico's Turquoise Coast: an ideal place for a truly relaxing yoga vacation, offering sun-washed days on white coral and sand beaches, meditation and Hatha Yoga classes, and delicious vegetarian meals.

Dates: Nov (1997) and Winter 1998. Cost: $695, includes program, double room accommodations, and 3 vegetarian meals daily. Contact: Ashram Reservation Center, Rt. 1, Box 1720, Buckingham, VA 23921; (804) 969-3121, fax (804) 969-1303.

Namibia

Photographic Safaris. Byseewah is a 15,000-hectare game farm near Etosha National Park in Namibia. Accommodations in thatched rondawals, with solar lighting. Swimming pool, game drives, and photographic opportunities of places and people, birds, and wild game including elephant and rhino. Tented camp also available.

Dates and cost: on request. Each safari tailor-made. Contact: Byseewah Safaris, Box 495, Outjo, Namibia; fax (011) 264-651-30-4294; satellite tel: (011) 8716 86490286, satellite fax: 90287.

Papua New Guinea

Trans Niugini Tours. Nature and culture programs are operated in three areas: the Highlands, the Sepik Area, and a marine environment on the North Coast. Each area has its own distinct culture and environment, with comfortable wilderness lodges located in each.

Dates: Weekly departures during 1998 7. Cost: $889-$3,570 per person (land cost). Contact: Bob Bates, Trans Niugini Tours, P.O.

Box 371, Mt. Hagen, Papua New Guinea; (800) 521-7242 or (011) 675-542-1438, fax 675-542-2470; travel@pngtours.com, www. pngtours.com.

Peru

Peruvian Amazon Rainforest Expedition. Unique 1-week Amazon adventure on thatched-roof expedition boat. Piranha fishing, hiking, canoeing, camping, and more. For the adventurous traveler only.

Dates: Weekly during Jul and Aug, 1998. Cost: For 2 or more people $600 each per week. Contact: Orlando Hoyos, 8 Eden St., Chelsea, MA 02150; (617) 889-0740.

Russia and the NIS

Off the Beaten Path. Unique, flexible, and affordable travel opportunities for individuals and small groups. MIR is a 12-year veteran specialty tour operator with representation in Moscow, St. Petersburg, Kiev, Irkutsk, Ulan Ude and Tashkent. Homestays, Trans-Siberian rail journeys, Central Asian explorations, Mongolian adventures, European brewery adventures. Customized independent and group travel.

Dates: Year round; scheduled departures for tours. Cost: Homestays from $40 a night; full packaged tours from $1,175. Contact: MIR Corporation, 85 S. Washington St., Suite 210, Seattle, WA 98104; (800) 424-7289 or (206) 624-7289, fax (206) 624-7360; mir@igc.apc. org, www.mircorp.com.

Scotland

Highland Walks and Tours - Also Audio. Guided walking and Bespoke Tours in Highland and islands: ecology, history, coastal, glens. Jean Stewart's 10th year of showing folks around her favorite Highland haunts— and ensuring their comfort.

Dates: Easter to end Oct. Cost: From £525 full board, guide. Contact: Jean Stewart, Island Horizons, Kirkton, Lochcarron, IV54 8UF, Scotland; (011) 44-1520-722232, fax 722238; jeannie@dial.pipex.com, www. glen.co.uk/rc/horizons.

South Africa

Cheetah Trail Hostelling Safari. Three-week hostelling trek, roundtrip to Johannesburg, includes entrances to game parks, national parks, museums, caves, ostrich and crocodile ranches. Travel with a small group (12 maximum) of people from all over the world. Detailed trek dossier on request.

Dates: Monthly departures year round. Cost: $1,199. Contact: Roadrunner Worldwide, 6762A Centinela Ave., Culver City, CA 90230-6304; (800) 873-5872, fax (310) 390-1446; amadlax@attmail.com.

South America

Incan/Mayan Trail Hostelling Treks. Three 2-week treks exploring Mexico, Peru, or Argentina/Chile with a small, international group, utilizing youth hostels and camping. Explore native ruins, lush jungles, unspoiled beaches, and amazing mountains. Detailed dossier available upon request.

Dates: Monthly departures year round. Cost: From $839, includes transport, accommodations, entrances to parks and archaeological sites, adventure excursions, and some meals. Contact: Roadrunner Worldwide, 6762A Centinela Ave., Culver City, CA 90230-6304; (800) 873-5872, fax (310) 390-1446; amadlax@attmail.com.

Spain

La Coruña Summer Program. Intensive language program providing participants with the opportunity to study Spanish language, civilization, and culture in one of the most beautiful regions in Spain. Cultural immersion is further achieved through homestays with Spanish families. Cultural excursions include Madrid and nearby Santiago de Compostela, site of the famous pilgrimage of Saint James.

Dates: Approx. Jul 1-31. Cost: Approx. $1,700 (tuition and room and board). Contact: Darci Wahl, Study Abroad Advisor, Central Washington Univ., Office of International Studies and Programs, 400 E. 8th Ave., Ellensburg, WA 98926-7408; (509) 963-3623, fax (509) 963-1558; wahld@cwu.edu.

Painting in Barcelona. A celebrated Spanish faculty made up of Tom Carr and Carme Miquel will conduct a 3-week advanced painting workshop at the spacious studio of Escola d'Arts Plastiques i Disseny "Llotja." Included are 3 museum tours to the Antonio Tapies Foundation, the Miro Foundation, and the Picasso Museum. Three credits.

Dates: Jul 3-Jul 25, 1998. Cost: $2,850. Includes airfare, double occupancy rooms, continental breakfast daily, and 3 tours. Contact: Dora Riomayor, Director of International Studies, School of Visual Arts, 209 E. 23rd St., New York, NY 10010-3994; (212) 592-2543.

Summer in Madrid. Students study Spanish language and/or culture: Spanish 2 (Beginning Spanish 2); Spanish 3 (intermediate Spanish 1); Spanish 9 (civilization of Spain); Spanish 4 (intermediate Spanish 2).

Dates: Jun 28-Jul 25, 1998. Contact: Nancy Nieman, Santa Monica College, 1900 Pico Blvd., Santa Monica, CA 90405; (310) 452-9270, fax (310) 581-8618; nnieman@smc.edu.

Sweden

Uppsala Univ. International Summer Session. Sweden's oldest academic summer program focuses on learning the Swedish language. All levels from beginners to advanced. Additional courses in Swedish history, social institutions, arts in Sweden, Swedish film. Excursions every Friday. Extensive evening program includes both lectures and entertainment. Single rooms in dormitories or apartments. Open to both students and adults. Credit possible.

Dates: Jun 21-Aug 14; Jun 21-Jul 17; Jul 19-Aug 14, Jul 5-Aug 14, 1998. Cost: SEK21,400 (approx. $2,740) for the 8-week session, SEK11,700 (approx. $1,500) for the 4-week session. Includes room, some meals, all classes, evening and excursion program. Contact: Dr. Nelleke Dorrestÿn, Uppsala Univ. Int. Summer Session, Box 513, 751 20 Uppsala, Sweden; (011) 31-71-541-4955, fax 71-541-7705; nduiss@worldaccess.nl, www.uuiss.uu.se.

United Kingdom

Crash Courses. Individual tuition in Russian, French, Welsh, and English.

Dates: Any time. Cost: £300 includes tuition, room and board. Contact: Daphne Percival, Bodyfuddam, Transfynydd, Gwynedd, Wales LL41 4UW; (011) 44-1766-540-553; daf@meirionnyddlanguages.force9.co.uk.

Discover Cornwall. Week-long guided mini bus tours (Spring and Autumn). Walking. Mineral collecting, houses, gardens, archaeology, natural history, heritage. Discover unspoiled Cornwall. Cliffs and coves. Wild flowers and birds. Moorland ancient remains. Mining history and much more. Full board included. Small groups. Individuals welcome.

Dates: Mar, Apr, May, Jun, Sep, Oct. Cost: £200 includes accommodations. Some courses extra for entrance fees. Contact: Sheila Harper, Chichester Interest Holidays, 14 Bay View Terr., Newquay, Cornwall TR7 2LR, U.K.; (011) 44-1637-874-216.

Edinburgh Univ. Summer Courses. Scotland past and present: Art, Architecture, History, Literature, Archaeology, Presentation skill, Ethnology, Gaelic, Music, Drama, Creative Writing, Film, Ecology, the Edinburgh Festival. Courses last 1-4 weeks each. Instruction by University professors: highest academic standards. Integral field trips; theatre/concert/cinema tickets provided. Social program. Choice of accommodations.

Dates: Jun-Sep. Contact: Elaine Mowat, Univ. of Edinburgh, Centre for Continuing Education, 11 Buccleuch Pl., Edinburgh EH8 9LW, U.K.; (011) 44-131-650-4400, fax 131-667-6097; CCE@ed.ac.uk, www.ed.ac.uk/~cce/summer.

Green-Wood-Working. Instruction and holiday courses in ancient woodland crafts. Live the life of a last century woodlands craftsman and learn to operate a pole-lathe, or weave wattle fencing; traditional rake making, chair making, candlestick and goblets using 200-year-old technology.

Dates: Courses open to groups of 3-6 people, program on request. Cost: Tuition £30 per day (8 days to make a chair). Contact: Richard King, Old Hall, E. Bergholt, Colchester, Essex CO7 6TG, U.K.; (011) 44-206-298294.

International Summer School. Laban Centre London is the largest institution for professional contemporary dance training in Europe. The Centre has an eminent faculty with an unrivaled range of expertise. The international summer school offers you the chance to study with leading dance artists. Classes for beginners to professional level.

Dates: Jul 20-Jul 31, 1998. Cost: £175-£350 tuition. Contact: Peter Curtis, Laban Centre London, Laurie Grove, London SE14 6NH, U.K.; (011) 44-181-692-4070, fax 694-8749; info@laban.co.uk.

RSPB Voluntary Wardening Scheme. The Voluntary Wardening Scheme operates throughout England, Scotland, and Wales, providing an opportunity for those people interested in ornithology and conservation to gain practical experience of the day to day running of a royal society for the protection of birds reserve. Volunteers not only carry out practical conservation work but work in visitor centers and help with education work.

Dates: Year round. Cost: Free (does not include food and transportation). Contact: Voluntary Wardening Scheme Administrator (TA), Youth and Volunteers Department, RSPB, The Lodge, Sandy, Bedfordshire SG19 2DL, U.K.; (011) 44-1767-692365. For information pack enclose 2x International Reply Coupons.

Segedunum Roman Fort Wallsend. Excavations in and around fort site for large new museum, with reconstructed bath house and field study center. All types of excavation work, including planning and surveying. Write for application pack.

Dates: Ongoing to Dec 1998. Cost: No fees. Pay own board and lodging. Contact: Elizabeth Elliott, Tyne and Wear Museums, Baring St., South Shields, U.K.; (011) 44-191-454-4093, fax 427-6862.

Study in London. Fall, spring, or academic year study abroad program offering regular university courses in liberal arts, business or performing arts at Middlesex Univ. University housing, on-site orientation program, 12-15 undergraduate credits per semester. Qualifications: Sophomore or above in good academic standing.

Dates: Fall: mid-Sep-late Dec; spring: early Feb-early Jun. Cost: Approx. $6,400 per semester. Includes tuition, fees, room and board, and insurance. (Non-New York state residents add $750 per semester.) Contact: Office of International Education, SUNY New Paltz, HAB 33, New Paltz, NY 12561; (914) 257-3125, fax (914) 257-3129; international@newpaltz.edu, www.newpaltz.edu/oie.

Teach English as a Foreign Language. Courses in central London leading to the

Cambridge/RSA Certificate (CELTA), regarded internationally as the ideal qualification in TEFL. International House has 40 years experience in training teachers and can offer jobs to those recently qualified in its 110 schools in 27 countries.

Dates: Four-week (110 hours) intensive courses begin Jan 5, Feb 2, Mar 2, Apr 14, May 11, Jun 8, Jul 6, Aug 3, Sep 1, Sep 28, Oct 26, Nov 23, 1998. Cost: £944 includes Cambridge/RSA registration. Contact: Teacher Training Development, International House, 106 Piccadilly, London W1V 9FL, England; (011) 44-171-491-2598, fax 171-499-0174; teacher@dial.pipex.com.

Two to 8-Day Painting-Drawing-Craft Courses. In beautiful Broads National Park. Resident tutor: Angela Dammery. Watercolor, oil, acrylic. "Old Master" techniques, textiles, printmaking. Unique watercolor cruises aboard a Thames barge, canal boat, Norfolk sailing wherry. Eight days in Venice—pastel/oil. Custom designed courses for art club/college groups.

Dates: Mar-Nov. Cost: From £70-£500. Includes tuition and lunch to full board. Contact: Angela Dammery. NDD. ATC Course Director, Broadland Arts Centre, The Old School, Dilham, North Walsham, Norfolk, U.K.; (011) 44-1702-75361 or 1692-53486.

Univ. of Cambridge International Summer Schools. Largest and longest-established program of summer schools in the U.K. Intensive study in Cambridge as part of an international community. Term I (6 weeks) and Term II (2 weeks) of the International Summer School offer over 60 different courses. Three-week specialist programs: Art history, Medieval Studies, History, English Literature, and Shakespeare. Wide range of classes on all programs. U.S. and other overseas institutions grant credit for study at the Univ. of Cambridge Summer School. Guidelines available.

Dates: Jul 5-Aug 15, 1998. Cost: Tuition from £460-£625 (2 to 4 weeks), accommodations from £240-£925 (2 to 4 weeks). Six-week period of study also possible by combining 2 summer schools. Contact: Sarah Ormrod, Director, International Division, Univ. of Cambridge Board of Continuing Education, Madingley Hall, Madingley, Cambridge CB3 8AQ, England; (011) 44-1954-210636, fax 210677; rdi1000@cam.ac.uk, www.cam.ac.uk.

Visual Arts and Crafts Courses. Week and weekend courses in painting and drawing, blacksmithing, calligraphy, gardening and garden design, glass engraving, photography, pottery, sculpture, silversmithing, soft furnishing, textiles, and woodcarving and woodworking. Courses for different levels of ability, from complete beginners to master classes, run parallel to 7 full-time Diploma courses.

Dates: Year round. Cost: Short course (residential) weekends £150; 5 days £359; 7 days £483. Contact: Heather Way, Public Relations Coordinator, West Dean College, West Dean, Chichester, West Sussex, PO18 OQZ U.K.; (011) 44-1243-811301, fax 811343; westdean@pavilion.co.uk, www.pavilion.co.uk.

Walking Holidays in Britain. Deluxe, relaxed walking tours for all abilities. Both inn-to-inn and centered, using top quality, character country hotels informed local guides take you through idyllic villages and countryside. Tours are vehicle supported and your bags transported between hotels discover the Cotswolds, York Dales, Devon, Dorset, Lake District, Scotland, etc.

Dates: May-October. Cost: $1,290 land only, 6 nights dinner and breakfast. Contact: Andrew D. Bull, Greenscape (UK), Milkaway Ln., Croyde, Devon EX33 1NG, U.K.; (011) 44-1271-890677; walkbrit@greenscape.co.uk, www.greenscape.co.uk.

Worldwide

American-Int'l Homestays. Stay in English-speaking foreign homes in over 30 countries.

Explore foreign cultures responsibly. Learn foreign languages. Perfect for families or seniors. Learn how other people live by living with them in their homes.

Dates: Year round. Cost: From $59 per night. Contact: Joe Kinczel, American-Int'l Homestays, P.O. Box 1754, Nederland, CO 80466; (303) 642-3088 or (800) 876-2048, fax (303) 642-3365; ash@igc.apc.org.

Amizade Volunteer Vacations. Programs offering mix of community service and recreation that provide volunteers with the opportunity to experience firsthand the culture they are working in—Brazilian Amazon, Peruvian Amazon, Bolivian Andes, or Greater Yellowstone region. Volunteers do not need any special skills, just a willingness to serve.

Dates: Year round. Cost: Varies. $1,500-$2,600 for Latin America; $150-$600 for Yellowstone. Contact: Amizade, 1334 Dartmouth Ln., Deerfield, IL 60015; (847) 945-9402, fax (847) 945-5676; amizade@worldnet.att.net, http://amizade.org.

Archaeological Fieldwork Opportunities. The AFOB is an international guide to excavations and field schools with openings for volunteers, students, and staff. Designed to introduce both student and amateur archaeologists to the experience of actual excavation, it is available every year on January 1. Over 250 opportunities listed. Price: $16. Call (800) 228-0810.

Dates: Year round (mainly summer). Cost: Varies. Contact: Susanna Burns, Archaeological Institute of America, 656 Beacon St., Boston, MA 02215-2010; Tel./fax (617) 353-9361; aia@bu.edu, http://csa.brynmawr.edu/aia.html.

Archaeology. The Archaeological Institute of America publishes the Archaeological Fieldwork Opportunities Bulletin (AFOB), a comprehensive guide to excavations, field schools, and special programs with openings for volunteers, students, and staff throughout the world. The cost is $10 for AIA members, $12 for nonmembers plus $4 shipping and han-

dling for the first copy and 50¢ for each additional copy. All orders must be prepaid and be made in U.S. dollars or by an international money order to: Kendall/Hunt Publishing Company, Order Dept., 4050 Westmark Dr., Dubuque, IA 52002. Visa and Mastercard accepted. Call (800) 228-0810, (319) 589-1000.

Dates: Available every January 1. Contact: Archaeological Institute of America, 656 Beacon St., Boston, MA 02215-2010; (617) 353-9361, fax (617) 353-6550; aia@bu.edu, http://csa.brynmawr.edu/aia.html.

Coral Cay Conservation Expeditions. Volunteers needed to join major expeditions to help survey and protect coral reefs and tropical forests in the Caribbean, Asia-Pacific, Philippines, Indonesia, Red Sea. No previous experience required. Full accredited training provided (including scuba certification if required). Thousands of CCC volunteers have already helped establish 8 new marine reserves and wildlife sanctuaries worldwide.

Dates: Expeditions depart monthly throughout the year. Cost: From $995 (2 weeks) to $4,415 (12 weeks) excluding flights. Contact: Coral Cay Conservation Ltd., 154 Clapham Park Rd., London SW4 7DE, U.K.; (305) 757-2955 (U.K. office 011-44-171-498-6248, fax 498-8447); ccc@coralcay.demon.co.uk, www.coralcay.org.

Customized Special Interest Trips. Information—customized tours—travel planning: eco and special interest outdoor adventures—hiking, canoeing, biking, snorkeling, natural history, birding, etc. Clothing optional recreation. Cultural exchanges. World peace. Health. Permaculture. Rainforests. Also budget travel.

Dates: Year round. Cost: $55-$255 per person per day inclusive. Contact: Peter Bentley, Sense Adventures, P.O. Box 1466, Murwillumbah, NSW 2484, Australia; (011) 61-414-854-255.

Earthwatch. Unique opportunities to work with leading scientists on 1- to 3-week field research projects worldwide. Earthwatch sponsors 160 expeditions in over 30 U.S. states and in 60 countries. Project disciplines include archaeology, wildlife management, ecology, ornithology and marine mammalogy. No special skills needed—all training is done in the field.

Dates: Year round. Cost: Tax deductible contributions ranging from $695-$2,800 support the research and cover food and lodging expenses. Airfare not included. Contact: Earthwatch, 680 Mt. Auburn St., P.O. Box 9104MA, Watertown, MA 02272; (800) 776-0188, (617) 926-8200; info@earthwatch.org, www.earthwatch.org.

Educational Adventures. Educational Travel off the beaten path in Asia and South America. Customized for individuals and small groups. "Classrooms without Walls" offer cultural, craft/art, religion, holy site, traditional healing and folk medicine, and natural history/environmental travel study programs, and "Trekking with a Mission" in the world's special and untouristed places.

Dates: Year round. Cost: Vary. See free catalog. Contact: Myths and Mountains, Inc., 976 Tee Court, Incline Village, NV 89451; (800) 670-MYTH (6984), (702) 834-4454; edutrav @sierra.net,www.mythsandmountains.com.

Green Volunteers. The World Guide to Voluntary Work in Nature Conservation lists more than 100 projects and organizations worldwide where you can volunteer from 1 week to 1 year. Projects on marine mammals, primates, sea turtles, African wildlife, birds, and on conservation work in general are listed. Some of the projects do not require a financial contribution from the volunteers.

Dates: Year round. Cost: $16 plus $5 postage. Contact: Green Volunteers: in the U.S.: 1 Greenleaf Woods Dr., #302A, Portsmouth, NH 03810; (800) 525-9379. In Europe: P.O. Box 23, Sandy, Bedfordshire SG19 2XE, U.K.; Tel./ fax (011) 44-767-262481; info@greenvol. com, www.greenvol.com.

Offshore Sailing School. Learn to sail, bareboat cruising preparation, live aboard cruising. Courses meet the needs of varying sailing abilities from beginners to advanced. Offshore has awarded diplomas to over 78,000 successful sailors over 30 years.

Dates: Year round. Cost: Start at $895 including course and accommodations. Contact: Steve and Doris Colgate's Offshore Sailing School, 16731 McGregor Blvd., Ft. Myers, FL 33908; (800) 221-4326, fax (941) 454-1191; offshore@packet.net, www.offshor-sailing. com.

Outer Edge Expeditions. Outer Edge provides small adventurous expeditions from Australia to Zimbabwe. We are devoted to making exciting wilderness areas accessible to the active traveler. Active trips to the Amazon, Africa, Argentina, Australia, Botswana, Borneo, Canada, Chile, Indonesia, Irian Jaya, Mongolia, Namibia, New Zealand, Patagonia, Peru, and Zimbabwe.

Dates: Year round. Cost: Start at $940. All trips include meals, guides, accommodations. Contact: Brian Obrecht, Outer Edge Expeditions, 45500 Pontiac Trail, Walled Lake, MI 48390-4036; (800) 322-5235, (810) 624-5140, fax (810) 624-6744; oedgeexp@ aol.com, www.adventure~travel.com/combo/ oee/oee-idx.htm.

Penn Summer Abroad. Academic programs granting Univ. of Pennsylvania credits. Courses focusing on language, culture, economics, theater, anthropology, Jewish studies, cinema, art history, traditional folk medicine, performing arts, and religion. Several programs offer homestays, some offer internships.

Dates: Mid-May-late Aug (2-8 weeks). Cost: Tuition: $1,420 per course. Living costs vary. Contact: Elizabeth Sachs, Penn Summer Abroad, College of General Studies, Univ. of Pennsylvania, 3440 Market St., Suite 100, Philadelphia, PA 19104-3335; (215) 898-5738, fax (215) 573-2053.

Roadrunner Hostelling Treks. Roadrunner combines hostelling and adventure travel for the young and young at heart, a balance between traveling independently and the advantages of small group touring. Destinations include Europe, Australia/New Zealand, South America, and the Middle East.

Dates: Year round. Cost: Starting from $60 per day. Contact: Roadrunner, 1050 Hancock St., Quincy, MA 02169.

Student Hosteling Program, Inc. The Student Hosteling Program offers bicycle touring trips for teenagers through the countrysides and cultural centers of the U.S., Canada, and Europe. Trips range in length from 1-9 weeks and cost between $650 and $5,000. Small coed trips of 8-12 bicyclists and 2 leaders grouped in very compatible grade groupings. Easy, moderate, and challenging trips are offered. Our 28th year; accredited by the American Camping Association. Free brochure and free video.

Dates: Jun 25-Sep 1, 1998. Cost: $750-$5,000. Contact: Ted Lefkowitz, Student Hosteling Program, 1 Ashfield Rd., Conway, MA 01341; (800) 343-6132, fax (413) 369-4257; shpbike@aol.com.

The Culinary Travel Company. Cooking vacations to wonderful destinations. Small groups. One-on-one cooking classes. Visit wineries, olive oil factories, fresh food markets, historical and gastronomic landmarks, first-class hotels.

Dates: Year round. Cost: Starts at $2,350 per person (dbl. occup.) Includes meals and ground transportation. Contact: Dan Strebel, The Culinary Travel Company, 210 W. Pickwick, Arlington Heights, IL 60005; (888) 777-0760.

Women in the Wilderness. From the Arctic to the Amazon: Cultural, archaeological, wildlife tours, for women of any age. Current/recent destinations include the Peruvian Amazon, Macchu Picchu and the Andes, Greece, Finnish Lapland, Honduras, Virgin Islands. We work with indigenous guides.

Cost: One week-16 days is from $900-$3,500. Contact: Judith Niemi, Women in the Wilderness, 566 Ottawa Ave., St. Paul, MN 55107-2550; (612) 227-2284, fax (612) 227-4028.

World Affairs Council Tours. Council trips offer all the sightseeing and cultural highlights of quality touring plus access to political leaders, journalists, and other local experts who give behind the scenes views and briefings. Enjoy an insider's view of Egypt, China, Albania, Sweden, Provence, Borneo, Baltics, Oman, and other destinations. Includes substantive trip materials.

Contact: Joan Russell, Travel Director, World Affairs Council of Philadelphia, 1314 Chestnut St., Philadelphia, PA 19107; (215) 731-1100 or (800) 942-5004, fax (215) 731-1111; wac@libertynet.org.

Zimbabwe

Art in Africa. A forum for the in-depth study of African culture and art, including Shona and Ndebele sculpture, fiber, iron and beadwork. Highlights include visits to museums, market, wildlife parks, a traditional village, and trips to Victoria Falls and the Great Zimbabwe.

Dates: Jun 2-17 (1997). Cost: $2,800. Includes airfare, hotel, program costs, and tuition. Contact: Jody A. Dudderar, Rockland Community College, 145 College Rd., Suffern, NY 10901; (914) 574-4205, fax (914)574-4423; jdudderar@sunyrockland.edu.

CHAPTER 3

SENIOR TRAVEL RESOURCES

The dynamics of travel have changed in the last several years–for seniors as well as for the general population. Older travelers once wanted a comfortable tour of castles and churches in familiar territory; foreign travel meant a tour of the Continent. Today they are heading for exotic destinations like Sulawesi and Zimbabwe.

Now that they have the time and the energy, seniors also want more interesting and intellectually challenging traveling experiences. They want to get out and meet people in the countries they visit–people with ideas and experiences to enrich their own lives. They like to combine travel with homestays, volunteer work, teaching, and language study.

The travel industry is aware of this growing demand for travel for enrichment, and more and more tour operators are gearing their offerings in this direction. Instead of three countries in 10 days, operators offer longer stays in one area, opportunities to meet families, lectures, and hands-on programs.

The following resources will not only help seniors get ready to go but will help assure a safe and pleasant journey.

Planning Guides

Adventures Abroad: Exploring the Travel/ Retirement Option by Allene Symons and Jane Parker (Gateway Books). Introduction to vacation and retirement living in 17 countries with first-hand experiences of people living abroad. Information on housing, medical, cost of living, laws, finances, etc.

American Society of Travel Agents. Call their Consumer Affairs department at (703) 706-0387 if you need their help to mediate a travel dispute.

Auto Europe Wallet Card. Toll-free telephone access codes to reach AT&T, MCI, and Sprint in 20 countries; (800) 223-5555.

Dept. of State Publications. Travel Tips for Older Americans, Tips for Americans Residing Abroad, Your Trip Abroad, and A Safe Trip Abroad are $1.25 each from Superintendent of Documents, U.S. Government Printing Office, Washington, DC 20402; (202) 647-1488, fax on demand (202) 647-3000; http://travel.state.gov.

Get Up and Go: A Guide for the Mature Traveler by Gene and Adele Malott, 1989. $10.95 from Gateway Books, 2023 Clemons Rd., Oakland, CA; (800) 669-0773.

Hostelling International (International Youth Hostel Federation). Hostels throughout the world. Senior membership $15. Two hostel directories: Europe and Africa/Americas/Asia/Pacific.

Mature Outlook, a travel magazine available by subscription. Send request for information to: 6601 North Clark St., Chicago, IL 60660; (800) 336-6330.

The Mature Traveler's Book of Deals by Gene and Adele Malott, 1997. $7.95 plus $1.95 s/h from Gem Publishing Group, P.O. Box 50400, Reno, NV 89513-0400; (800) 460-6676. Itemized deals for experienced travelers in U.S. and abroad. (Free with subscriptions to their monthly newsletter, *The Mature Traveler.*)

The Seasoned Traveler by Marcia Schnedler. Country Roads, 1992, $10.95.

Secrets Every Smart Traveler Should Know by Wendy Perrin (Fodor's), 1997. Specific ways to smooth the traveler's path by the former "Ombudsman" of *Condé Nast Traveler.*

Taken by Surprise: Travel after 50 ($5.95) and **Taken by Surprise: Travel after 60,** both by Esther Mock ($6.95). R & E Publishers, 1991.

Unbelievably Good Deals and Great Adventures That You Absolutely Can't Get Unless You're Over 50 by Joan R. Heilman. Contemporary Books, 8th ed., 1996, $9.95.

A World of Options edited by Christa Bucks (Mobility International USA, 3rd ed., 1997). $25 (members), $30 (non-members), $40 (organizations) plus $5 s/h from MIUSA, P.O. Box 10767, Eugene, OR 97440; (541) 343-1284, fax (541) 343-6812. A comprehensive guide to international exchange, study, and volunteer opportunities for people with disabilities with more than 1,000 resources on exchanges, rights, travel, and financial aid. Includes personal experience stories.

Health and Safety

1997 International Travel Health Guide by Stuart R. Rose ($17.95 plus $3 shipping from Travel Medicine, Inc., 351 Pleasant St., Suite 312, Northampton, MA 01060; 800-872-8633). Updated annually in spring; recommended by U.S. State Department.

American Lung Association. For advice on traveling with oxygen call (800) 586-4872.

Citizens' Emergency Center, U.S. Dept. of State, 2201 C St., NW, Washington, DC 20520; (202) 647-5225. Handles emergency matters involving U.S. citizens abroad.

Doctor's Guide to Protecting Your Health Before, During and After International Travel by Dr. W. Robert Lange. 1997. Addresses travelers' health issues with particular emphasis on seniors; includes a special section on retiring or relocating abroad, as well as tips and precautions for travelers with chronic health problems, disabilities and handicaps. $9.95 plus $2 s/h from Pilot Books, 127 Sterling Ave., P.O. Box 2102, Greenport, NY 11944; (800) 79PILOT.

Health Information for International Travel, Supt. of Documents, U.S. Government Printing Office, PO Box 371954, Pittsburgh, PA 15250-7950; (202) 512-1800, fax (202) 512-2250. Stock # 017-023-00197-3. $20 (prepaid, Visa/MC accepted). Discusses health precautions and immunizations for travelers to foreign countries.

International Assn. for Medical Assistance to Travelers, 417 Center St., Lewiston, NY 14092; (716) 754-4883. Provides a directory of English-speaking doctors in 500 cities in 116 countries. Also information on health risks and immunizations worldwide.

International SOS. Emergency medical evacuation coverage; (800) 523-8930.

A Senior's Guide to Healthy Travel by Donald L. Sullivan. 1994. $14.95 plus $3.50 shipping from Career Press, Inc., 3 Tice Rd., P.O. Box 687, Franklin Lakes, NJ 07417.

Travel Assistance International, (800) 821-2828. The largest global support system for travelers. Provides emergency medical payments, transportation, referrals, monitoring, and interpretation services. Also insurance for medical, trip cancellation, baggage, accidental dismemberment, evacuations, repatriations, return of mortal remains, and death.

Senior Tour Organizers

Accessible Kiwi Tours New Zealand, Ltd. Adventure or leisure tours for all, including disabled or elderly. Group or individual tours New Zealand-wide. Accessible Kiwi Tours New Zealand, Ltd., P.O. Box 550, Opotiki, New Zealand; (011) 64-7-315-7867, fax 315-5056; kiwitours@wave.co.nz.

Elderhostel, 75 Federal St., Boston, MA 02110; (617) 426-8056. Educational adventures for older adults. Sponsors over 2,000 nonprofit, short-term programs in 70 countries. Must be 55 or over; younger companions are allowed.

Eldertreks, 597 Markham St., Toronto, Ontario, Canada M6G 2L7; (800) 741-7956, fax (416) 588-9839; passages@inforamp.net. Exotic adventures for the young at heart over 50 crowd.

Familyhostel, 6 Garrison Ave., Durham, NH 03824; (800) 733-9753; www.learn.unh.edu. Ten-day learning and travel programs in foreign countries for families (parents, grandparents, school-age children).

France Photogenique has a 12-day tour of Brittany for amateur photographers at all levels. $2,600 plus air includes all accommodations, most meals, TGV fare from Paris to Brittany, all ground transportation in a minibus, all entry fees, and photographic instruction. France Photogenique, 3920 W. 231st Pl., Torrance, CA 90505; (310) 378-2821, fax (310) 375-6356.

Gadabout Tours, 700 E. Tahquitz, Palm Springs, CA 92262; (800) 952-5068.

Golden Age Travelers, Pier 27, The Embarcadero, San Francisco, CA 94111; (800) 258-8880, fax (415) 776-0753.

Grand Circle Travel, 347 Congress St., Boston, MA 02210; (800) 248-3737. More than 200 programs worldwide. Free booklet: "101 Tips for Mature Travelers."

Insight International Tours, 745 Atlantic Ave., Boston, MA 02116; (617) 482-2000.

Interhostel, 6 Garrison Ave., Durham, NH 03824; (800) 733-9753. Over 50 educational travel programs per year worldwide for mature travelers age 50 and up.

National Senior Sports Association, (800) 282-6772. Golf vacations.

Photo Explorer Tours has three programs: a 15-day tour to Tibet and two 16-day tours to China, all led by English-speaking photographer-guides. Tours include programs in the Guilin area and in Longsheng with custom arrangements, all transportation in China, hotels, meals, and fees. Prices are $3,595 for Tibet and $2,995 for China, plus air. Photo Explorer Tours, 2506 Country Village, Ann Arbor, MI 48103; (800) 315-4462, fax (313) 996-1481.

Safari Travel offers a tour of the wine country of South Africa plus an optional week to Victoria Falls, Zimbabwe, and Chobe Game Lodge in Botswana. Non-smokers only. Safari Travel, P.O. Box 5901, Maryville, TN 37802; (888) 445-8340, fax (423) 981-1706.

Saga Holidays, "Road Scholar" Educational Travel Programs, 222 Berkeley St., Boston, MA 02116; (617) 262-2262 or (800) 621-2151.

Seventy Plus Ski Club, (518) 399-5458.

Smithsonian Study Tours, 1100 Jefferson Dr., SW, Washington, DC 20520; (202) 357-4700. Study tours and seminars providing a combination of study, discovery, adventure, and vacation.

Sterling Tours offers an 11-day Performing Arts tour featuring theater and music in London and the Edinburgh festival. $2,353 plus airfare. Sterling Tours, 2707 Congress St., Suite 2-G, San Diego, CA 92110; (800) 727-4359, fax (619) 299-5728.

Travelearn, Ten-day to 3-week programs for adults in 17 countries on 6 continents.

On-site lectures and field experiences by local resource specialists. Travelearn, P.O. Box 315M, Lakeville, PA 18438; (800) 235-9114.

Single Travelers

Handbook for Women Travelers by Maggie and Gemma Ross. Piatkus Books, 5 Windmill St., London W1P 1HF, England; (011) 44-631-0710.

Mesa Travel Singles Registry, P.O. Box 2235, Costa Mesa, CA 92628; (714) 546-8181.

Society of Single Travelers, Travelcare, 3000 Ocean Park Blvd., Suite 1004, Santa Monica, CA 90405; (310) 450-8510.

Travel Companion Exchange, P.O. Box 833, Amityville, NY 11701; (800) 392-1256 (US only), (516) 454-0880, fax (515) 454-0170. $48 yearly, $6 sample newsletter. Widely recommended listings and newsletter for travelers seeking companions. The only major nationwide service of this nature.

Transportation

How to Select a Package Tour. U. S. Tour Operators Assn., 342 Madison Ave., Suite 1522, New York, NY 10173; (212) 599-6599. Free.

Ocean and Cruise News. Ratings, classifications, and features of ships. World Ocean and Cruise Liner Society, P.O. Box 92, Stanford, CT 06904. $28 for a year's subscription (12 issues).

Tips on Renting a Car. Council of Better Business Bureau, 4200 Wilson Blvd., Arlington, VA 22209; (703) 276-0100. $2 with long SAE. Guide to getting the most service for your money from car rental companies. Ask for their other "Tips On" publications.

TravLtips Association. Unusual cruises: freighters, yachts, expeditions. Membership includes magazine and free reference book. $15 a year. P.O. Box 580218-C9S, Flushing, NY 11358; (800) 872-8584.

Volunteering and Other Options

Archaeology Abroad, 31-34 Gordon Sq., London WC1H OPY, England. Three annual bulletins list worldwide archaeological digs with details of staffing needs and costs.

Earthwatch Expeditions, 680 Mt. Auburn St., Watertown, MA 02172; (617) 926-8200. Be a paying volunteer on scientific expeditions worldwide.

Golden Opportunities: A Volunteer Guide for Americans over 50 by Andrew Carroll. Peterson's Guides, 1994, $14.95.

National Senior Sports Association, (800) 282-6772. Golf vacations.

Over the Hill Gang, 3310 Cedar Heights Dr., Colorado Springs, CO 80904; (719) 685-4656. Skiing, hiking, and biking for those over 50.

Smart Vacations: The Traveler's Guide to Learning. 1993. 320 pp. $14.95 plus s/h from Council-Pubs Dept., 205 E. 42nd St., New York, NY 10017-5706; (888) COUNCIL. Adult traveler's guide to learning abroad includes, in addition to study tours, opportunities for voluntary service, field research and archaeological digs, environmental and professional projects, fine arts, and more.

Smithsonian Study Tours, 1100 Jefferson Dr., SW, Washington, DC 20520; (202) 357-4700. Study tours and seminars providing a combination of study, discovery, adventure, and vacation.

Volunteer Vacations by Bill McMillon. Chicago Review Press, 6th ed., 1997, $16.95. Includes 2,000 opportunities worldwide plus personal stories.

CHAPTER 4

Senior Travel Programs

The following listing of senior travel programs was supplied by the organizers. Contact the program directors to confirm costs, dates, and other details. If you do not see the program you want in the country of your choice, look in the "Worldwide" listings at the end of the section for programs located in several different regions.

Australia

Special Interest and Study Tours. Personalized programs for individuals and groups of all ages. We combine education, recreation, accommodations (homestay available), and transportation. Based in tropical Cairns with coverage throughout Australia. Subject areas include: aboriginal dreamtime and culture, Great Barrier Reef, rainforest and savannah. Diving, environmental interpretation, flora and fauna, bird watching, tropical islands and wilderness, adventure safaris and farmstay.

Dates: Year round. Start any date. Cost: Prices and customized itineraries on application. Contact: Murray Simpson, Study Venture International, P.O. Box 229A, Stratford Qld., 4870 Australia; (011) 61-70-411622, fax 552044; svi@ozemail.com.au; www.ozemail. au/~svi.

Costa Rica

Learn Spanish While Volunteering. Assist with the training of Costa Rican public school teachers in our latest language learning techniques, using classroom computers, K-8 school targeted by Costa Rican government as a model ESL/technology school. Enjoy learning Spanish in the morning, volunteer work in the afternoon/evening. Spanish classes are 2-5 students plus group learning activities; conversations with middle-class homestay families (1 student per family). Homestays and volunteer project are within walking distance of school in small town (14,000 population) near the capital, San Jose.

Dates: Year round, all levels. Classes begin every Monday, volunteer program is continuous. Cost: $295 per week for 25 hours of Spanish classes. Includes tuition, all meals (7 days a week), homestay, laundry, all materials, Costa Rican dance and cooking classes, and airport transportation. $25 one-time registration for Spanish classes; $100 additional one-time registration fee for volunteer program. Contact: Susan Shores, Registrar, Latin American Language Center, 7485 Rush River Dr., Suite 710-123, Sacramento, CA 95831; (916) 447-0938, fax (916) 428-9542; lalc@madre.com.

Ecuador

Academia Latinoamericana (Quito). Ecuador's number-one private Spanish language institute in former diplomat's mansion with swimming pool, hot tub, sauna, sport facilities. Instruction by university-trained teachers, all one-on-one. Customized study programs tailored to the individual. Select host family accommodations. Excursions to haciendas, Indian markets, etc. College credit and internships available.

Dates: Year round. Cost: One-week tuition, lodging, meals $294. Contact: Suzanne Bell, Admissions Director, U.S., 640 East 3990 South, Suite E, Salt Lake City, UT 84107; (801) 268-4608, fax (801) 265-9156; latinoa1@spanish.com.ec, http://ecnct.cc/academia/learnspa. htm.

Europe

Untours. Fully equipped private apartments in areas off the beaten path. Live among the locals and set your own itinerary with the help of our resource books and on-site staff. Destinations: Paris, Prague, Budapest, Vienna, and smaller towns in Provence, Tuscany, Ticino, Bernese Oberland, Central Switzerland, Austria, Rhineland Germany, and Holland.

Dates: Every 2 weeks. First term starts Mar 26, last term starts Oct 22. Cost: $1,411-$2,323 (2 weeks, includes airfare from east coast gateway). Contact: Idyll

Untours, P.O. Box 405, Media, PA 19063; (610) 565-5242, fax (610) 565-5142; untours@netreach.net, www.netreach.net/~untours.

France

French and Cookery in a Château. Live and study in 18th-century château. Adult courses in French language and Provençal cookery. Relaxed family atmosphere and good food. Château has 13 acres of park and pool. Single/en suite and shared rooms. Close to Burgundy, Beaujolais, Auvergne, and cities of Lyons and Roanne. One- to 12-week courses.

Dates: Every Sunday Apr-Nov. Cost: From $999 full board and classes in Château. Contact: Michael Giammarella, P.O. Box 640713, Oakland Gardens, NY 11364-0713; (800) 484-1234 ext 0096 or Ecole des Trois Ponts, Château de Matel, 42300 Roanne; (011) 33-477-70-80-01, fax 477-71-53-00; info@3ponts.edu, www.3ponts.edu.

French in France. Among the ways to learn French, total immersion is the most enjoyable and the most effective. We have been doing it for 20 years in a small historical city located in Normandy (west of Paris, close to the seaside). We welcome people at any age and any level in from 1- to 10-week programs, intensive or vacation type, from mid-March to mid-November.

Dates: Spring: Mar 23-May 29; summer: Jun 15-Aug 28; fall: Sep 7-Nov 13, 1998. Cost: From $525 per week (tuition, room and board, and excursions). Contact: Dr. Almeras, Chairman, French American Study Center, 12, 14, Blvd. Carnot, B.P. 176, 14104 Lisieux Cedex, France (011) 33-2-31-31-22-01, fax 31-22-21.

French Language Immersion. International institute on Mediterranean coast. Short- and long-term French courses. Modern air-conditioned premises in large park. Restaurant with terrace. Top-quality homestay, hotels, apartments. Minimum age 17, maximum unlimited. Students, business people, employees, airline staffs, retired people. Charming medieval town linking Provence to Riviera, lively marina, unspoiled beaches.

Dates: Year round. Cost: From FF1,500 per week (tuition). Contact: Institut ELFCA, 66 ave. du Toulon, 83400 Hyeres, France; (011) 44-4-94-65-03-31, fax 65-81-22; elfaca@ compuserve.com, www.worldwide.edu/ france/elfca.

Friendly French Immersion/Riviera Vacation. French Riviera specialist: B and B in villa/ apartment. Discover the charming provencal heritage through 9 educational and cultural tours: architecture, arts, crafts, gastronomy. Mini-cruises from St. Tropez to Menton. Seasonal programs include Nice/Menton/ Mandelieu Carnival (Feb), authentic provencal folkfairs (May-Sep). Two flexible and congenial language programs. Colorful 28-page brochure.

Dates: Year-round and seasonal programs. Cost: (1) Two weeks, homestay, half-board accommodations, 40 hours of visits plus 10 optional hours of informal French discussion, transfer to and from the airport: single $1,710, double $3,350. (2) Seasonal programs: Nice carnival in Feb, Cannes Film Festival in May, Wine Fair in Sep: single $1,990, double $3,780. (3) B and B from U.S. $45-$55 single, $60-$85 double. Accommodations in apartment/villa downtown. Contact: Friendly French Immersion, c/o Michael Grynberg (Marketing and Sales Manager), 4810 Queen Mary, Suite 16, Montreal, PQ H3W 1W3, Canada; (800) 334-0266 or (514) 344-4605, fax (514) 344-6222; ffi@generation.net, www.generation.net/~ffi. In Europe: FFI, c/o Gisele Ninio-Grynberg (President), Val d'Azur, 60 Vallon Barla Bat. C, 06200 Nice, France; Tel./fax (011) 33-93 21-67-26.

Immersion Course in French. Intensive 2- to 4-week course for professional adults in picturesque Villefranche overlooking the French Riviera's most beautiful bay, 8 1/2 hours a day with 2 meals. Audio-visual classes, language lab, practice sessions, discussion-lunch. Evening film showings with discussions, evening outings with teachers, excursions to cultural and scenic landmarks. Accommodations provided in comfortable private apartments.

Dates: Courses start May 5, Jun 2, Jun 30, Aug 4, Sep 1, etc. (year round). Cost: May-Nov (1997): FF16,700 for 4 weeks. Accommodations from FF2,300 to FF5,800 for 4 weeks, depending on type of lodging (individual room, family, studio apartment, etc.) Contact: Elisabeth Martin, Institut de Francais, 23 ave. Général Leclerc, 06230 Villefranche/Mer TR7, France.

India

Project India. A unique 3-week service program open to people of all ages and backgrounds run by a highly qualified staff of educators, social workers, and cultural advisors. Positions include health care, education, social development, arts/recreation, and more. No skills or experience is required. Volunteers pay a fee which covers all expenses.

Dates: Three-week programs run year round. Longer term placements can be arranged. Cost: $1,650 covers all India-based expenses. International airfare, insurance, and visa not included. Program fee is tax deductible. Contact: Steven C. Rosenthal, Cross-Cultural Solutions, P.O. Box 625, Ophir, CO 81426; (970) 728-5551 or (800) 380-4777, fax (970) 728-4577; CCSmailbox@aol.com, http://emol.org/emol/projectindia.

Latin America

Language Travel Programs. For all ages and all Spanish levels. Spanish classes, excursions, cultural activities. One-week to 6 months. Various settings: beaches, mountains, small towns, large cities, etc. Countries: Mexico, Costa Rica, Guatemala, Honduras, Panamá, El Salvador, Argentina, Chile, Ecuador, Peru, Uruguay, Venezuela, Puerto Rico, Dominican Republic.

Dates: Programs start every week or every month. Cost: Depends on location. Prices start at $175 per week and include classes, homestay, travel insurance, most meals, some cultural activities. Contact: AmeriSpan Unlimited, P.O. Box 40007, Philadelphia, PA 19106; (800) 879-6640, fax (215) 751-1100; info@amerispan.com, www.amerispan.com.

Mexico

Copper Canyon. Outstanding cultural and natural history rail trips. The most dramatic train ride in the western hemisphere. Deeper, wider, greener canyons than Arizona's Grand Canyon. Tarahumara Indian culture, nature walks, birding, waterfalls, spectacular vistas. Historic tours, small groups, personal attention. In-depth interpretation of the Copper Canyon and its people.

Dates: Year round. Cost: $1,695 per person for 8-day trips. Contact: S&S Tours, 865 El Camino Real, Sierra Vista, AZ 85635; (800) 499-5685, fax (520) 458-5258; ss@theriver.com.

El Bosque del Caribe, Cancun. Take a professional Spanish course 25 hours per week and enjoy the Caribbean beaches. Relaxed family atmosphere. No more than 6 students per class. Special conversation program. Mexican cooking classes and excursions to the Mayan sites. Housing with Mexican families. College credit available.

Dates: Year round. New classes begin every Monday. Group programs arranged at reduced fees. Cost: Enrollment fee $100, $175 per week. One week with a Mexican family $150. Contact: Eduardo Sotelo, Director, Calle Piña 1, S.M. 25, 77500 Cancún, Mexico; (011) 52-98-84-10-38, fax 84-58-88; bcaribe@mail.cancun-language.com.mx.

Intensive Spanish in Cuernavaca. Cuauhnahuac, founded in 1972, offers a variety of intensive and flexible programs geared to individual needs. Six hours of classes daily with no more than 4 students to a class. Housing with Mexican families who really care about you. Cultural conferences, excursions, and special classes for professionals. College credit available.

Dates: Year round. New classes begin every Monday. Cost: $70 registration; $650 4 weeks tuition, housing with 3 meals per day $18. Lower prices in off season or fewer weeks of attendance. Contact: Marcia Snell, 519 Park Dr., Kenilworth, IL 60043; (800) 245-9335, fax (847) 256-9475; lankysam@aol.com.

Language Institute of Colima. The Language Institute of Colima Mexico offers a system of total immersion with classes held throughout the year Monday-Friday. Students live with local host families and attend 6 hours of instruction daily; no more than 5 students per class. Many extras, including beach excursions.

Dates: Year round, Monday-Friday. Cost: Registration $80; tuition $415 1st week, $345 after 1st week (for shared room), $445 1st week, $375 after 1st week (for private room). 10 percent discount for 6 or more. Contact: Dennis Bourassa, Language Institute of Colima, P.O. Box 827, Miranda, CA 95553; (800) 604-6579, fax (707) 923-4232; colima@northcoast.com, www.northcoast.com/~colima.

Philippines

Little Children of the Philippines, Inc. LCP is a Christian agency helping to develop caring communities for poor children on Negros Island in central Philippines. LCP has service programs in 7 communities covering health, housing, education, livelihood (agriculture, handicrafts), and value formation. Especially needed: volunteers in marketing, computer technology, journalism, music, carpentry, masonry, and environmental concerns.

Dates: Volunteers negotiate their own period of service. Cost: From East Coast: approx. $1,200 roundtrip airfare, $120 per month for food. Dormitory bed free. Contact: Dr. Douglas Elwood, 361 County Rd. 475, Etowah, TN 37331; Tel./fax (423) 263-2303; lcotw@conc.tds.net.

Spain

don Quijote. don Quijote, Europe's largest specialist in in-country Spanish language courses, offers in Salamanca and Granada special starting dates where students of 50 plus in age are specifically invited. The course includes many cultural and social activities.

Dates: May 11, Jun 8, Sep 14, Oct 12, Nov 9 (1997). Cost: Depends on duration, and accommodations. Contact: don Quijote, Central Promotion Office, Ref. USSC97, Ms. Sue-Ann Lard, Student Services, Apdo. de Correos 333, 37080 Salamanca, Spain; (011) 34-23-26-88-60, fax 26-88-15; donquijote@offcampus.es, www.teclata.es/donquijote.

Spanish for Senior Citizens. Frequently called Spain's leading school of Spanish, Malaca Instituto has designed a course for senior citizens. Offered at levels from beginner to advanced, the program combines studying highly practical everyday Spanish (for the market, restaurant, booking hotels, etc.) with a program of cultural and social activities. On-site residential accommodations are recommended.

Dates: Feb 2, 16; Mar 2, 16; Apr 6, 20; May 4, 18; Oct 5, 19; Nov 2, 16, 30, 1998. Cost: Course: from PTS57,750 (2 weeks); accommodations from PTS32,540 (2 weeks). On-site residence (Club Hispanico) recommended. Contact: Bob Burger, Malaca Instituto, c/Cortada 6, Cerrado de Calderon, 29018 Malaga, Spain; (011) 34-5-229-32-42, fax 229-63-16.

Worldwide

American-Int'l Homestays. Stay in English-speaking foreign homes in over 30 countries. Explore foreign cultures responsibly. Learn foreign languages. Perfect for families or seniors. Learn how other people live by living with them in their homes.

Dates: Year round. Cost: From $59 per night. Contact: Joe Kinczel, American-Int'l Homestays, P.O. Box 1754, Nederland, CO 80466; (303) 642-3088 or (800) 876-2048, fax (303) 642-3365; ash@igc.apc.org.

Amizade Volunteer Vacations. Programs offering mix of community service and recreation that provide volunteers with the opportunity to experience firsthand the culture they are working in—Brazilian Amazon, Peruvian Amazon, Bolivian Andes, or Greater Yellowstone region. Volunteers do not need any special skills, just a willingness to serve.

Dates: Year round. Cost: Varies. $1,500-$2,600 for Latin America; $150-$600 for Yellowstone. Contact: Amizade, 1334 Dartmouth Ln., Deerfield, IL 60015; (847) 945-9402, fax (847) 945-5676; amizade@worldnet.att.net, http://amizade.org.

Earthwatch. Unique opportunities to work with leading scientists on 1- to 3-week field research projects worldwide. Earthwatch sponsors 160 expeditions in over 30 U.S. states and in 60 countries. Project disciplines include archaeology, wildlife management, ecology, ornithology and marine mammalogy. No special skills needed—all training is done in the field.

Dates: Year round. Cost: Tax deductible

contributions ranging from $695-$2,800 support the research and cover food and lodging expenses. Airfare not included. Contact: Earthwatch, 680 Mt. Auburn St., P.O. Box 9104MA, Watertown, MA 02272; (800) 776-0188, (617) 926-8200; info@ earthwatch.org, www.earthwatch.org.

Travel-Study Seminars. Learn from people of diverse backgrounds about their economic, political, and social realities. Emphasis on the views of the poor and oppressed. Programming in Mexico, Central America, South Africa, and China/Hong Kong. Call for a free listing of upcoming seminars.

Dates: Ongoing. Cost: $1,000-$4,500 depending on destination and length of trip. Contact: Center for Global Education, Augsburg College, 2211 Riverside Ave., Box TR, Minneapolis, MN 55454; (800) 299-8889, fax (612) 330-1695; globaled@augsburg.edu, www.augsburg.edu/global.

Family Travel Resources

Travel with your kids. Do it now, before they're bogged down in summer jobs and romances, and while they'll still be seen in public with you, their parents. If you've been hestitating because of the cost, the resources below will erase your excuses.

Youth hostels are cheap, and most have family rooms–no reason to fear that you'll be split up into dormitories with strangers snoring in your ears. Small-town tourist offices in Europe can find you a home to rent for as little as $200 per week, less than you'd pay to put the whole family in a hotel for one night.

Beyond rentals, we've included tour groups and newsletters that specialize in family travel, as well as a raft of books on family travel topics. We've also included a smattering of internet sites. Try our recommended sites–or search for new ones with the key words "family travel" or "kids travel" on your favorite search engine.

Don't save travel for your retirement years. Take the family. Now.

Family Adventure Travel

Backroads, 801 Cedar St., Berkeley, CA 94710-1800; (800) 462-2848. Family biking and walking trips in the U.S., Canada, Czech Republic, France, and Switzerland. Children of all ages welcome.

Butterfield & Robinson, 70 Bond St., Toronto, ON M5B 1X5, Canada; (800) 678-1147. Pricey deluxe family walking and biking trips in Italy, Holland, Morocco, Canada, and Belize for families with teenagers.

Hometours International, P.O. Box 11503, Knoxville, TN 37939; (800) 367-4668. Walking tours in England, much cheaper than Backroads or B&R. Also Israeli "Kibbutz Home" program, apartment and villa rentals, plus B and Bs in Britain, France, Italy.

Hostelling International (AYH), 733 15th St. NW, Suite 840, Washington, DC 20005; (202) 783-6161. Affordable hiking and biking trips in U.S., Europe, and Israel, usually for ages 15 and up. Or plan your own hosteling trip: many hostels have family rooms for all ages.

Journeys, 4011 Jackson Rd., Ann Arbor, MI 48103; (800) 255-8735; info@journeys-intl.com, www.journeys-intl.com. Socially responsible family trips include Himalayan trekking and African safaris plus trips to Australia, the Galapagos, Belize, Panama, Vietnam, the Amazon, and Costa Rica.

Overseas Adventure Travel, 625 Mt. Auburn St., Cambridge, MA 02138; (800) 221-0814. Intercultural adventure trips for families and individuals. Families can choose a Galapagos wildlife adventure, a Serengeti safari, or a Costa Rica natural history trip.

Society for the Protection of Nature in Israel, (212) 398-6750. Operates 1-14-day hikes and nature explorations—even a camel tour—in different parts of Israel. Expert environmental guides and low costs. Accommodations are in the group's field study centers or hostels. Children age 10 and up welcome.

Wildland Adventures, 3516 NE 155th St., Seattle, WA 98155; (206) 365-0686, fax (206) 363-6615. Family trips to Costa Rica, Honduras, Belize, Peru, the Galapagos, Turkey, Africa, and Nepal. Some trips include homestays and other intercultural opportunities.

Family Cultural Travel

AmeriSpan Unlimited, P.O. Box 40513, Philadelphia, PA 19106; (800) 879-6640; info@amerispa n .com, www.amerispan.com. Family language programs in 12 countries in Mexico, Central and South America. Families are placed with a host family with a range of childcare options so older kids can study with their parents.

FAMILYHOSTEL, 6 Garrison Ave., Durham, NH 03824; (800) 733-9753; www.learn.unh.edu. Offers 10-day trips to Austria, Wales, France, and the Czech Republic (destinations vary yearly) to adults traveling with school-age kids. Trips mix learning, sightseeing, and recreation—plus a chance to meet local families.

LEX America, 68 Leonard St., Belmont, MA 02178; (617) 489-5800; www.lexlrf.com. Arranges family homestays in Japan, Korea, Mexico, and France with 25,000 member families. Standard 2-, 4- or 6-week summer or autumn program, or they'll design a custom program—for instance, a homestay to mesh with a business trip.

Inexpensive Rentals

U.S. agencies offer properties starting at about $600 per week. You can rent a house for as little as $200 through many local Tourist Offices in Europe. Or try going directly to some of the following European sources:

British Tourist Office, (212) 986-2200. Ask for a free booklet called "City Apartments" for a selection of reasonably-priced family-sized apartments in cities throughout Britain.

Chez Nous, Bridge Mills, Huddersfield Rd., Holmfirth HD7 2TW, England; (011) 44-1484-684-075, fax 685-852. Directory of French rentals owned by Brits. They charge only for ads; prices are reasonable ($175 per week plus) because there's no commission. And there's no language gap in making arrangements.

Destination Stockholm, Skårgård AB, Lillström, S-18497 Ljustero, Sweden; (011) 46-8-542-481-00, fax 414-00; dess.skarg@stockholm.mail.telia.com. Cottages in the Stockholm archipelago, starting at about $200 in the off season and $350 in midsummer. Book seven to eight months ahead for high season.

Fjordhytter, Lille Markevei 13, P.O. Box 103, 5001 Bergen, Norway; (011) 47-5-23-20-80, fax 24-04. Lovely photo catalog in English with very detailed descriptions. Prices start at $180 off season to $350 high season.

FriFerie Danmark, Liselejevej 60, 3360 Liselejevej, Denmark; (011)-45-42-34-63-34; fax 34-64-53. Catalog in German and Danish only. Rentals start at about $240 per week off season and $460 midsummer.

German Tourist Offices. Many regional tourist offices publish excellent color-photo guides. Three good ones: Familienferien, Schwarzwald Fremdenver- kehrsverband, Postfach 1660, 79016 Freiburg im Breisgau, Germany; (011) 49-761-31317; fax 761-36021. Fränkisches Urlaubskatalog, Tourism-usverband Fran- ken, Am Plärrer 14, 90429 Nürnberg, Germany; (011) 49-911-26-42-02, fax 27-05-47. Urlaub auf Bauern-und Winzerhöfen, Rheinland-Pfalz Tourist Office, Schmittp- forte 2, 55437 Ober-Hilbersheim, Germany; (011) 49-6728-1225, fax 6728-626.

Irish Cottage Holiday Homes, Cork Kerry Tourism, Tourist House, Grand Parade, Cork, Ireland; (011) 353-21-273-251, fax 273-504. Good variety of listings from £100 to £500 per week. Also ads for agencies, walking maps of the area, etc.

Italian Farmstays, Agriturist, Corso Vittorio Emanuele 101, 00186 Rome, Italy; (011) 39-6-685-2342; fax 685-2424. An agriturismo source for Italian farmstays. Fax request for the current price for their catalog.

Maison des Gîtes de France, 59 rue St. Lazare, 75009 Paris, France; (011) 33-1-49-70-75-75, fax 75-76. Source for thousands of inexpensive, simple, rural rentals in France. French language may help in arranging terms. Fax for order form for 90 regional guidebooks, which cost about $6 each.

Swiss Farmstays. Some lodgings include a kitchen; others offer meals with the inhabitants: Fédération du Tourisme Rural de Suisse Romande, c/o Office du Tourisme, 1530 Payerne, Switzerland; (011) 41-37-61-61-61. Ferien auf dem Bauernhof, Buchungszentrale Verein, Raiffeisenbank, 5644 Auw AG, Switzerland; (011) 41-57-48-17-09. Ferien auf dem Bauernhof, Schweizer Reisekasse (REKA), Neuengasse 15, 3001 Bern, Switzerland; (011) 41-31-329-66-33. Color photo directory with over 150 listings direct from REKA or from Swiss NTO. Text is in German with English key and booking info.

Internet Resources

A small sample of online family travel resources.

www.bpe.com/travel. Wonderful compendium of first-person travel experiences from all over the world.

www.travelaus.com.au. Scroll down to "categories" and pick "family" for a comprehensive list of family activities and accommodations in Australia—no description, but complete contact info.

www.family.com. This Disney-sponsored site offers a large collection of family travel resources in the U.S. and abroad.

www.kidscom.com. A "communication playground" for kids 4-15 in English, French, Spanish, or German. Fill in your specs for a pen pal—say, French, age 14, girl, likes skiing—and find your e-mail soulmate.

www.ncrsa.com. Lists of language courses with dates and costs. Indexed by language or by country, including family/teen options. National Registration Center for Study Abroad, Box 1393, Milwaukee, WI 53201; (414) 278-0631.

www.worldwide.edu. "Travel Planner" accesses scores of pen pals, travel programs, etc. WorldWide Classroom, Box 1166, Milwaukee, WI 53201-1166; (414) 224-3476.

Making Friends, Meeting People

Hospitality Exchange, 704 Birch, Helena, MT 59601; (406)449-2103. $20 annual membership gets you directory of 250 members in 26 countries. Some can offer overnight accommodations; others will hook you up with local families.

SERVAS 11 John St., Suite 407, New York, NY 10038; (212) 267-0252; http://servas.org. An international cooperative system of hosts and travelers established to help build world peace, goodwill, and understanding. Families and individuals are welcomed as members. $55 annual membership fee for travelers.

World Pen Pals, P.O. Box 337, Saugerties, NY 12477; Tel./fax (914) 246-7828. Send $3 and 9"x4" SASE for each pen pal desired; specify gender and continent plus preferred country.

Zephyr Press, 13 Robinson St., Somerville, MA 02145; (617) 628-9726. Zephyr publishes a series of "People to People" guides for Russia, Poland, Romania, Czech Republic/Slovak Republic, Hungary/Bulgaria, Baltic Republics. $14 each. While not geared specifically to family travelers, the guides are a good source for family contacts.

Other Family Resources

Family Travel Times, $40 per year. Travel with Your Children, 40 5th Ave., New York, NY 10011; (212) 477-5524. Quarterly newsletter of worldwide family travel news. Lots of tips for traveling with younger kids but rarely any budget or alternative travel information.

Have Children Will Travel, P.O. Box 152, Lake Oswego, OR 97034; (503) 699-5869, fax (503) 636-0895. $39 per year. Quarterly family newsletter of travel resources and tips from an experienced mom.

Family Travel Forum, (888) FT-FORUM. Membership organization ($48 per year) publishes newsletter on family travel.

Idyll, Ltd., P.O. Box 405, Media, PA 19063; (610) 565-5242, fax (610) 565-5142; untours@netreach.net. Arranges apartment rentals for families (including one in a German castle) and includes low-key orientation at your destination.

Traveling with Children, Dan and Wendy Hallinan, 2313 Valley St., Berkeley, CA 94702; (510) 848-0929, fax (510) 848-0935. An experienced traveling family arranges home rentals, airfares, and special itineraries for other traveling families, especially in Europe.

Traveling-With-Kids Books

Adventuring with Children: An Inspirational Guide to World Travel and the Outdoors by Nan Jeffrey. Excellent overseas and domestic advice for active families who want to backpack, sail, bicycle, or canoe. $14.95 from Menasha Ridge Press; (800) 247-9437.

Best Places to Go: A Family Destination Guide by Nan Jeffrey. Recommendations and specifics on budget, culturally-aware family visits to Europe and Central and South

America. $14.95 from Menasha Ridge Press (above).

Children's Book of London, Children's Book of Britain (Usborne Guides). Available through BritRail, 551 5th Ave., Suite 702, NY, NY 10176; (800) 677-8585. Usborne guides are not widely available in the U.S.

Guide de la France des Enfants by Marylène Bellenger. Editions Rouge & Or, 11 rue de Javel, 75015 Paris, France. If you can read French, pick this one up in Paris. Exhaustive guide to sites all over France for kids up to 15.

Kidding Around London, Kidding Around Paris, Kidding Around Spain (John Muir). Guide series written for kids instead of parents, suitable for good readers 8 or older. A solid but unexciting mix of history and sightseeing.

Kids Love Israel; Israel Loves Kids by Barbara Sofer. Second edition includes lodging, camps, language, food, plus over 300 sightseeing ideas for the whole country. $17.95 from Kar-Ben Copies, 6800 Tildenwood Ln., Rockville, MD 20852; (301) 984-8733.

Kids' Britain by Betty Jerman. Pan Macmillan Books, Cavaye Place, London SW10 9PG, England. A comprehensive guidebook available in England but probably unobtainable here. Lists every conceivable site in England, with costs. Buy it when you get to London.

The Family Travel Guide by Carole Terwilliger Meyers (Carousel Press). A collection of first-person accounts from families who've traveled all over the world, with specific tips.

The Family Travel Guides Catalog. Carousel Press, P.O. Box 6038, Albany, CA 94706-0038; (510) 527-5849. The books listed here—and dozens of others—are available through Carousel Press. Send $1 or 55¢ and a long SASE for catalog.

The Traveler's Toolkit: How to Travel Absolutely Anywhere (Menasha Ridge Press). Not specifically for families, but a great book to help new travelers feel comfortable taking on the world.

Travel with Children by Maureen Wheeler (Lonely Planet). 3rd ed. The definitive guide to third world travel with kids, covering both logistics and cultural interchange; first-person stories from other travelers.

Découvrir Paris est un Jeu d'Enfant by Isabelle Bourdial and Valeri Guidoux (Editions Parigramme/CPL, 28, rue d'Assas, 75006 Paris, France). Another great guide in French to buy on arrival. Covers museums, parks, zoos, markets—even pick-your-own farms near Paris.

Family Travel (Blue Panda). Parent-tested trips—where to find them, and what they cost. Includes houseswaps, educational trips with universities, nature trips, and dinosaur digs.

How To Fly—For Kids! (Corkscrew Press). Activities to keep children busy during long, boring plane flights.

Take Your Kids to Europe by Cynthia Harriman. Practical, up-to-date, how-to guide. P.O. Box 6547, Portsmouth, NH 03802; (603) 436-1608.

CHAPTER 6

DISABILITY TRAVEL RESOURCES

Persons with disabilities are participating in increasing numbers in all forms of international travel: educational programs, voluntary service, and independent and group travel. The following organizations, web sites, planning guides, agencies, and programs will assist the approximately 49 million travelers with disabilities in the U.S. to find the option that best meets their needs.

Agents

Directions Unlimited, 720 N. Bedford Rd., Bedford Hills, NY 10507; (800) 533-5343 or (914) 241-1700, fax (914) 241-0243. Specializes in arranging vacations and tours for persons with disabilities. Individuals only.

Disability Travel Sites

Access-Able, www.access-able.com/. Good source for web-based information on travel for persons with disabilities. Includes tours, letters from readers, links to other sites, as well as a list of other books, organizations, and newsletters that focus on traveling with disabilities.

Accessible Journeys, www.disabilitytravel. com/. 35 West Sellers Ave., Ridley Park, PA 19078; (800) TINGLES or (610) 521-0339, fax (610) 521-6959. Tour agency that specializes in designing accessible holidays and escorting groups on accessible vacations exclusively for slow walkers, wheelchair travelers, their families and their friends.

Disability Travel Services Online, www.dts.org. Information on travel for persons with special needs, plus e-mail lists and a bulletin board for consumers to exchange information.

Global Access, www.geocities.com/Paris/ 1502/. Network for disabled travelers to share experiences, with many international contributors.

National Patient Air Transport Helpline, www.npath.org. (800) 296-1217. Provides information and referrals for specialized evaluation, diagnosis, treatment, rehabilitation, and/or recovery necessitated by illness or accident. Call or visit their website for referral information on the availability of charitable long-distance air medical transport. Referrals are based on the patient's medical condition, type of transport required, and departure and destination location.

New Mobility, www.newmobility.com. 23815 Stuart Ranch Road, P.O. Box 8987, Malibu, CA 90267; (800) 543-4116 or (310) 317-4522, fax (310) 317-9644. An extension of the print magazine, New Mobility. Includes many links to other sites, as well as some information on travel for persons with disabilities.

Society for the Advancement of Travel for the Handicapped, www.ten-ioo.com/sath. SATH, 347 5th Ave., Suite 610, New York, NY 10016; (212) 447-0027, fax (212) 725-8253. SATH has championed the rights of travelers with disabilities since 1975. Their website includes a calendar of events, information on their Partnership in Awareness program. A good way for on-line travelers with disabilities to learn more about this organization.

The National Clearinghouse on Disability and Exchange, www.miusa.org/clearing.htm. Mobility International USA, P.O. Box 10767, Eugene, OR 97440; (541) 343-1284 voice/TDD, fax (541) 343-6812; clearinghouse@miusa.org. Provides information and support to individuals seeking exchange opportunities and organizations trying to become more inclusive.

Organizations

Barrier Free Travel, Ian J. Cooper, 36 Wheatley St., North Bellingen, NSW 2454, Australia; (011) 61-066-551-733. Provides information on travel for persons with disabilities.

Calvert Trust, Exmoor, Wistlandpound, Kentisbury, Barnstaple, Devon, EX31 4SJ, U.K. Offers holidays for people of all abilities.

Mobility International USA (MIUSA), P.O. Box 10767, Eugene, OR 97440; (541) 343-1284 Voice and TDD, fax (541) 343-6812. MIUSA is a national, nonprofit organization whose purpose is to promote and facilitate opportunities for people with disabilities to participate in international exchange and travel.

Moss Rehab Hospital Information Service, 1200 W. Tabor Rd., Philadelphia, PA 19141; (215) 456-9603. A telephone information and referral center on international travel accessibility.

Society for Advancement of Travel for the Handicapped, 347 5th Ave., Suite 610, New York, NY 10016; (212) 447-7284. Membership $30 for students and seniors, $45 others. Publishes newsletter and information booklets on trip planning for persons with disabilities.

Planning Guides

A World of Options edited by Christa Bucks (Mobility International USA, 3rd ed., 1997). $25 (members), $30 (non-members), $40 (organizations) plus $5 s/h from MIUSA, P.O. Box 10767, Eugene, OR 97440; (541) 343-1284, fax (541) 343-6812. A comprehensive guide to international exchange, study, and volunteer opportunities for people with disabilities with more than 1,000 resources on exchanges, rights, travel, and financial aid. Includes personal experience stories.

Able to Travel: A Rough Guides Special edited by Alison Walsh with Jodi Abbott and

Peg L. Smith (Rough Guides). Over 100 accounts by and for travelers with practical information and resource listings. ISBN 1-85828-110-5, $19.95.

Access to the World: A Travel Guide for the Handicapped by Louise Weiss (Books on Demand). $68.20. To order call (503) 233-3936.

Guide for the Disabled Traveller by The Automobile Association, Norfolk House, Priestly Road, Basingstoke, Hampshire, RG24 9NY, U.K. Lists places to visit selected from AA publication, **Days Out in Britain and Ireland**. Includes information on accessibility and accommodations at sites of interests, restaurants, and lodgings. £3.99.

Holidays in the British Isles 1997: A Guide for Disabled Travellers by Royal Association for Disability and Rehabilitation (RADAR), 12 City Forum, 250 City Rd., London EC1V 8AF, U.K.; (011) 44-71-250-3222. Over 1,000 places to stay in all parts of the U.K. and Republic of Ireland. £13 postpaid.

Loud Proud & Passionate: Including Women with Disabilities in International Development Programs by MIUSA. Contact MIUSA (above) for ordering information. Includes guidelines to ensure inclusion of women with disabilities into the development process, as well as personal experiences, and resources.

TDI National Directory of TTY Numbers by Telecommunications for the Deaf, Inc., 8630 Fenton St., Suite 604, Sliver Spring, MD 20910-3803; (301) 589-3786 or (301) 589-3006 TTY.

Travel Tips for Hearing Impaired People by American Academy of Otolaryngology; (703) 836-4444.

Vacances Pour Personnes Handicapees by Centre d'Information et de Documentation Jeunesse, CIDJ, 101, quai Branly, 75740 Paris, Cedex 15, France. Forty-one pages of addresses for holidays in France, including information on cultural activities, tourism, and sports. To order send 6 International Reply Coupons.

Directory of Travel Agencies for the Disabled by Helen Hecker (Twin Peaks Press). $19.95 plus $3 s/h from Twin Peaks Press, P.O. Box 129, Vancouver, WA 98666-0129; (800) 637-2256 (credit card orders), (360) 694-2462, fax (360) 696-3210; 73743-2634@compuserve. com. Lists more than 370 travel agencies and tour operators in U.S. and worldwide.

Disability Travel Services Online. www.dts.org. Information on travel for persons with special needs plus e-mail lists and a bulletin board for consumers to exchange information.

Travel for the Disabled by Helen Hecker (Twin Peaks Press, address above). $19.95 plus $3 s/h. How and where to find information, travel tips, and access guides to travelers with disabilities.

Wheelchair Through Europe. Graphic Language Press, P.O. Box 270, Cardiff by the Sea, CA 92007; (619) 944-9594. $13. Resources on accessible sites in Europe.

Senior Tour Organizers

Accessible Kiwi Tours New Zealand, Ltd. Adventure or leisure tours for all including disabled or elderly. Group or individual tours New Zealand-wide. Accessible Kiwi Tours New Zealand, Ltd., P.O. Box 550, Opotiki, New Zealand; (011) 64-7-315-7867, fax 315-5056; kiwitours@wave.co.nz.

Tour Agencies

Accessible Journeys, Howard J. McCoy, 35 W. Sellers Ave., Ridley Park, PA 19078; (800)

846-4537, fax (610) 521-6959; sales@ disabilitytravel.com, www.disabilitytravel. com. Slow walkers, wheelchair walkers, friends and family.

Accessible Vans of Hawaii, David McKown, 186 Mehani Circle, Kihei, HI 96753; (808) 879-5521, (800) 303-3750, fax (808) 879-0649; avavans@mauinet, www.accessible-vans.com.

Alaska Snail Trails, James G. Stone, P.O. Box 210894, Anchorage, AK 99521; (800) 348-4532, (907) 337-7517, fax (907) 337-7517.

Alaska Welcomes You, Paul Sandhofer, P.O. Box 91333, Anchorage, AK 99509; (907) 349-6301;awy@customopu.com, http://ourworld.compuserve.com/homepage/alaskaupdate.

Breckenridge Outdoor Education Center, Rich Cook, Breckenridge Outdoor Education Center, P.O. Box 697, Breckenridge, CO 80424; (970) 453-6422, fax (970) 453-4676; boec@colorado.net, www.brecknet.com/boec.

Destination World, I Can Tours, Lynette Wilson, P.O. Box 1077, Santa Barbara, CA 93102; (800) 426-3644, fax (805) 569-3795.

Flying Wheels Travel, Inc., Barbara Jacobson, 143 W. Bridge St., P.O. Box 382, Owatonna, MN 55060; (800) 535-6790.

Gateway Travel, Linda Abrams, 23A Middle Neck Rd., Great Neck, NY 11021; (516) 466-2242.

Hospital Audiences, Inc., Tricia Hennesey, 220 W. 42nd St., 13th Floor, New York, NY 10036; (212) 575-7663 or HAI Hotline: (888) 424-4685.

Mobility International USA, Susan Sygall, P.O. Box 10767, Eugene, OR 97440; (541) 343-1284. Voice and TTY.

Search Beyond Adventures, Connie Magnuson, 400 S. Cedar Lake Rd., Minneapolis, MN 55405; (800) 800-9979.

The Guided Tour, Inc., 7900 Old York Rd., Suite 114B, Elkins Park, PA 19027-2339; (800) 783-5841 or (215) 782-1370, fax (215) 635-2637. Programs for persons with developmental and physical challenges. Free brochure.

Wilderness Inquiry, Jennifer MacLeod, 1313 SE, 5th St., P.O. Box 84, Minneapolis, MN 55414; (800) 728-0719.

Travel Agencies

Able to Travel/Partnership Travel, Inc., 41 Highland Ave., Suite 1, Randolph, MA 02368; (800) 986-0053.

Hinsdale Travel Service, Janice Perkins, 201 E. Ogden Ave., Suite 100, Hinsdale, IL 60521; (708) 469-7349.

Holiday Care Service, Imperial Buildings, 2nd Floor, Victoria Rd., Horley, Surrey, RH6 7PZ, U.K.; (011) 44-1293-774-535, fax 784-647. The U.K.'s central source of holiday information for disabled and disadvantaged persons.

Wheelchair Journeys, Carol Lee Power, 16979 Redmond Way, Redmond, WA 98052; (425) 828-4220.

Wheelchair Travel, Ltd., Trevor Pollitt, 1 Johnston Green, Guildford, Surrey, GU2 6XS, England; (011) 44-1483-233640, fax 1483-23772. A self-drive rental, taxi, and tour service specifically for disabled people, especially the wheelchair-user.

Travel Newsletters

Access to Travel. Will DeRuve, publisher. 29 Bartlett Ln., Delmar, NY 12054; (518) 439-

4146, fax (518) 439-9004. Four-color magazine for travelers with disabilities. Four issues. 416. Outside U.S. add $14. New resource magazine.

*Disability Newsletter, Milliman and Robertson, Inc., 8500 Normdale Lake Blvd., Suite 1850, Minneapolis, MN 55437; (612) 897-5300, fax (612) 897-05301. Published 3 times a year $85.

*Traveling Healthy 108-48 70th Rd., Forest Hills, NY 11375; (718) 268-7290, fax (718) 261-9082; travelhealth@aol.com. Each bimonthly, 8-page issue is devoted to an in-depth report on a specific medical consideration affecting travelers. Editor Karl Neumann is a practicing pediatrician and chairs the publication committee of the Wilderness Travel Society. An annual subscription is $33, 2 years $55.

Access First News, Access First Travel, 45A Pleasant St., Malden, MA 02148; (800) 557-2047, (617) 322-1610, fax (617) 397-8610. Contains destination descriptions, calendar of events, other accessibility information.

Connecting: News for Solo Travelers, P.O. Box 29088, 1996 West Broadway, Vancouver, BC V6J 5C2, Canada; Tel./fax (604) 737-7791; 76420.1200@compuserve.com. Provides travel reports, helpful tips, and information for the solo traveler. Includes publications on accessibiilty and assistance.

Families and Disability Newsletter, Beach Center on Families and Disability, 3111 Haworth Hall, Univ. of Kansas, Lawrence, KS 66045; (913) 864-7600, fax (913) 864-7605. Published three times free to U.S., $5 Mexico, Canada, $10 other. Cindy Higgens, ed.

Insider Travel Secrets, Consumer Club International, P.O. Box 64980, Dept. 267, Dallas, TX 75206. Monthly $29.95.

New Directions, 5276 Hollister Ave., Suite 207, Santa Barbara, CA 93111; (805) 967-2841, (805) 964-7344. Highlights international travel and exchange opportunities.

The Cool Traveler Newsletter, Rome Cappucino Review, P.O. Box 11975, Philaelphia, PA 19145; (215) 440-0592. Publi shed four times a year. Cost is $11.80.

The Diabetic Traveler, P.O. Box 8223, Stamford, CT 06905; (203) 327-5832. $18.95 per year. Articles and information of particular interest to travelers with diabetes.

Travel Companions Exchange, Inc., P.O. Box 833, Amityville, NY 11701; (516) 454-0880, fax (516) 454-0170. $48 per year, sample $6. Travel Companion, bimonthly, lists travelers looking for partners and offers travel tips and bargains.

CHAPTER 7

DISABILITY TRAVEL TOURS AND PROGRAMS

The following list of international travel tours and programs for persons with disabilities was supplied by the organizers.

Programs

Mobility International USA (MIUSA). MIUSA sponsors international educational exchanges to countries around the world, including the U.S. Exchanges include delegates with and without disabilities ages 15 and up. Delegates participate in leadership training, disability rights workshops and recreational activities.

Dates: Vary. Cost: Vary, scholarships available. Contact: Mary Ann Curulla, P.O. Box 10767, Eugene, OR 97440; (541) 343-6812, fax (541) 343-1284; exchange@miusa.org.

Services for Handicapped Travelers. Janice Perkins, a wheelchair traveler and professional travel agent, provides a liaison between disabled clients and travel suppliers.

Dates: Year round. Cost: Varies according to services provided. Contact: Janice Perkins, Hinsdale Travel Service, 201 E. Ogden Ave., Hinsdale, IL 60521; (630) 469-7349 or (630) 325-1335 or (630) 325-1342, fax (630) 469-7390.

Costa Rica

Enjoy Learning Spanish Faster. Techniques developed from our ongoing research enable students at Centro Linguistico Latinoamericano to learn more, faster, in a comfortable environment. Classes are 2-5 students plus group learning activities; conversations with middle-class homestay families (1 student per family). Homestays are within walking distance of school in small town (14,000 population) near the capital, San Jose.

Dates: Year round. Classes begin every

Monday, at all levels. Cost: $295 per week for 25 hours of classes. Includes tuition, all meals (7 days a week), homestay, laundry, all materials, Costa Rican dance and cooking classes, and airport transportation. $25 one-time registration. Contact: Susan Shores, Registrar, Latin American Language Center, 7485 Rush River Dr., Suite 710-123, Sacramento, CA 95831; (916) 447-0938, fax (916) 428-9542; lalc@madre.com.

United Kingdom

Disability Travel. Outdoor activities, holidays and courses for people with disabilities. The Centre is situated 4 miles outside Keswick overlooking Bassenthwaite Lake. A traditional Cumbrian farmstead converted and adapted to give fully accessible accommodations. Activities led by experienced and qualified staff include climbing, canoeing, kayaking, sailing, riding, trap driving, hill walking, orienteering, archery, and camping.

Dates: Year round. Cost: £160-£290. Full week includes full board and activities. Contact: The Calvert Trust, Little Crosthwaite, Keswick, Cumbria CA12 4QD, U.K.; (011) 44-17687-72254, fax 73941.

Worldwide

Access-Able Travel Source. We provide free access information to mature and disabled travelers. Accommodations, attractions, transportation, disability and travel links to travel agents who have accessible tours or who can plan trips. Wheelchair or scooter rental and repairs, and more.

Contact: Access-Able Travel Service, P.O. Box 1796, Wheat Ridge, CO 80034; (303) 232-2979, fax (303) 239-8486; carol@access-able.com, www.access-able.com.

CHAPTER 8

RESPONSIBLE TRAVEL RESOURCES

Throughout the 1980s and 1990s Transitions Abroad *magazine has reported on the growing trends of responsible tourism and ecotravel and how highly consumeristic forms of tourism are unsustainable. Readers tell us there is an urgent need for more realistic information to assist them in making wise travel choices.*

Use the resources below to help you look beyond the "green" labels and promotion materials. Ask yourself, "How can I change the destructive, unsustainable forms of the tourism industry?" And:

Be a sceptic about glossy travel literature that often presents a very skewed version of the destination. Do your homework–understand the real conditions of the places you visit.

Make the connections between environmental and social issues and programs in your own community and those in the communities you visit. These linkages, such as an opportunity to volunteer on an eco-farm in Costa Rica, can provide insightful experiences. One of the growing number of responsible tourism groups described below can help you make those links. In addition, a number of educational and sci-

entific programs, community designed and operated alternative tours, and innovative ecotour operators in the U.S. can be very helpful to you.

Above all, share your experience with others when you return home–this is the most useful kind of information and the most reliable form of travel advertising.

Ecotourism Organizations

Alaska Wilderness Recreation and Tourism Assn. (AWRTA), P.O.Box 22827, Juneau, AK 99802; (907) 463-3038, fax (907) 463-3280; awrta@alaska.net, www.alaska. net/ ~awrta. Membership organization of small, locally-owned ecotour operators, native-owned ecotourism programs. Promotes the protection of Alaska's wild places.

Alternative Tour Thailand, 14/1 Soi Rajatapan, Rajaprarop Rd., Tayathai, Bangkok 10400, Thailand; (011) 66-2-245-2963. Supports environmental efforts of small communities throughout Thailand by organizing low-impact tours and homestays.

Annapurna Conservation Area Project (ACAP), ACAP Headquarters Ghandruk, Ghandruk Panchayat, Kaski District, Nepal. An international project that uses trekkers' fees to protect the environment and culture of the Gurung people in north central Nepal.

Appropriate Technology Tours, 1150 Janes Rd., Medford, OR 97501; (541) 773-2435. Promotes alternative technologies through travel programs.

Baikal Reflections, Inc., P.O. Box 310, Mesa, CO 81643-0310; (970) 268-5885, fax (970) 268-5884; baikal@igc.apc.org. Offers programs to Siberia.

Belize Ecotourism Association, 195A Vista Del Mar, Ladyville 025-2806, Belize. Membership ecotourism groups.

Bina Swadaya Tours, Jl. Gunung Sahari 111/7, Kakarta Pusat, P.O. Box 1456, Jakarta, 10014, Indonesia; (011) 62-21-420-4022. Travelers visit communities and learn about Indonesia's rural and ethnic cultures, lifestyles, and community development efforts.

Conservation International, Ecotourism Dept., 2501 M St., NW, Suite 200, Washington, DC 20037; (202) 429-5660, fax (202) 887-0193. Works with grassroots groups, communities, and environmental NGOs around the world in developing ecotourism programs, such as Eco-escuela in Guatemala.

Eco-Source, P.O. Box 4694, Annapolis, MD 21403-6694; (410) 263-2128, fax (410) 268-0923; Carolyn@podi.com, www.podi. com/ecosource. Connects individuals with environmentally responsible groups worldwide.

Eco-Travel Services, 5699 Miles Ave., Oakland, CA 94618; (510) 655-4054; ecotravel @wonderlink.com. Nationwide individual and corporate travel arrangements; supports local economies and environmentally conscious operations instead of quick profits; publishes newsletter.

Ecotourism Association of Australia, P.O. Box 3839, Alice Springs, Northern Territory 0871, Australia; (011) 61-89-528-308.

Ecotourism Society (TES), P.O. Box 755, North Bennington, VT 05257; (802) 447-2121, fax (802) 447-2122; ecomail@ ecotourism.org, www.ecotourism.org. A membership organization of ecotour operations around the world.

Ecoventure is helping develop a database, BaseCamp, to provide travelers with information on ecotourism. Contact ziegler@ wsu.edu or Ronald Ziegler, Washington State Univ. Libraries, Pullman, WA 99164-5610; fax (509) 335-6721.

Environmental Travel, 119-66 80th Rd., Kew Gardens, NY 11415; (800) 876-0048. Travel agency caters to needs of vegetarians, vegans, and animal rights advocates.

European Center for Eco Agro Tourism, P.O. Box 10899, Amsterdam 1001 EW, The Netherlands. Promotes eco-agro tourism, a sustainable tour option for people with green thumbs.

Euroter, 82, rue Francois Rolland, F 94130 Nogent-sur-Marne, France; (011) 331-4514-6421. Publishes principles for developing green tourism in European villages.

Friends of Malae Kahana, P.O. Box 305, Laie, HI 96762; (808) 293-1736. Native Hawaiian civic group operates ecotourism and low-impact tourism along historic beach.

Hawaii Ecotourism Association, P.O. Box 61435, Honolulu, HI 96839; (808) 956-2866; tabata@hawaii.edu, www.planet-hawaii.com.hea. Promotes responsible tourism, resource network for Hawaii and the Pacific.

Himalayan High Treks, 241 Delores St., San Francisco, CA 94103-2211; (800) 455-8735; effie@well.com. A small trekking company that specializes in trips to Bhutan, India, Nepal, and Tibet; offers specialized programs for women; publishes newsletter.

Indonesian Ecotourism Network (INDECON), Jalan H. Samali No. 51, Pejaten Barat, Pasar Minggu, Kaharta 12510, Indonesia; (011) 62-21-799-3955; indecon@cbn.net.id. Helps link ecotourists with a wide range of opportunities throughout Indonesia.

International Sonoran Desert Alliance, Box 687, Ajo, AZ 85321-0687; (520) 387-6823; alianzason@aol.com. Involved with ecotourism in Mexico.

Journeys International, 4011 Jackson Rd., Ann Arbor, MI 48103; (313) 665-4407 or (800) 255-8735; www.journeys-intl.com. A well-established ecotour operator; guides are either natives or residents of the countries they visit; part of their profits support environmental preservation.

Kodukant Ecotourism Initiative, SAARISOO, EE 3482 Joesuu, Parnumaa, Estonia; (011) 372-446-6405. A network of small tour operators living in or nearby protected areas.

Lisle, Inc., 433 West Sterns Rd., Temperance, MI 48182-9568; (313) 847-7126 or (800) 477-1538, fax (419) 537-7719; mkinney@utnet.utoledo.edu, www.lisle.utoledo.edu. Pioneer people-to-people program.

Oceanic Society Expeditions, Fort Mason Center, Building E, San Francisco, CA 94123; (415) 441-1106. Promotes environmental stewardship, education, and research through ecotourism.

Pax World Tours, 1111 16th St., NW, Suite 120, Washington, DC 20036; (202) 293-7290; info@paxworld.org. Works for peace and justice through innovative programs that encourage peacemaking and community-based development. Promotes people-to-people links and responsible tourism.

Samoan Ecotourism Network (SEN), P.O. Box 4606, Matautu-utu, Western Samoa; (011) 685-26-940, fax 25-993; ecotour@pactok.peg.apc.org. Concerned about deforestation of primary rainforests, offers ecotours as a form of education and vacation.

Sikkim Biodiversity and Ecotourism, Opp. Krishi Bhawan, PO Tadong, 737 102, Sikkim, India; Tel./fax (011) 91-3592-233-35. Developing regional ecotourism program with local communities in the Himalayas.

South American Explorer's Club (SAEC), 126 Indian Creek Rd., Ithaca, NY 14850; (607) 277-0488; explorer@samexplo.org, www.samexplo.org. Hiking club promotes ecologically responsible tourism.

The Travel Specialists, 120 Beacon St., Somerville, MA 02143-4369; (617) 497-8151 or (800) 370-7400, ext. 51. Evaluates travel programs, operators, and the travel industry; arranges alternative trips and programs around the world.

Toledo Ecotourism Association (TEN), San Miguel Village, Toledo District, Belize; (011) 501-72-2119. Network of indigenous farm cooperatives in pristine Mayan lands.

Top Guides, Treks & Tours, 1825 San Lorenzo Ave., Berkeley, CA 94707-1840; top4adven@aol.com. Contact: Kathryn Levenson.

Tour de Cana, P.O. Box 7293, Philadelphia, PA 19101; (215) 222-1253, fax (215) 222-1253, ext. 21; tourdecana@igc.apc.org. An outgrowth of the organization Bikes Not Bombs, this group offers bike trekking with a social, cultural, and political spin.

Travel Quest, 3250 Barham Blvd., Los Angeles, CA 90068; (213) 876-3250; 74732.3153 @compuserve.com. Promotes greater care and understanding of the planet, people, and other beings.

Turismo Ecologico y Cultural del Pueblo Maya, San Cristobal de las Casas, Chiapas, Mexico. An indigenous-owned alternative ecotour group.

Wilderness Travel, 1102 9th St., Berkeley, CA 94710; (510) 548-0420; info@wildernesstravel.com. Promotes cultural preservation and environmental protection; supports conservation, cultural, and development organizations.

Wildland Adventures, Inc., 3516 NE 155th St., Seattle, WA 98155; (800) 345-4453, (206) 365-0686; info@wildland.com, www.wildland.com. Ecotour operator offers group travel, customized trips for independent travelers and families, rainforest workshops, and responsible trips such as trail cleanups and community services. Contributes part of profits to conservation and community development at the local level.

Wildlife Conservation International, P.O. Box 68244, Nairobi, Kenya; (011) 222254-221-699. Information about ecotourism projects in Kenya.

World Wildlife Fund, 1250 24th St., NW, Washington, DC 20037-1175; (202) 293-4800; www.worldwildlife.org. Offers ecotours throughout the world.

Yukon River Tours, 214 2nd Ave., Fairbanks, AK 99701-4811; (907) 452-7162. Alaska native-owned ecotours of the Yukon River educate about local history, environment, wildlife, culture, Athabascan fish-camps.

Publications

Adventuring In... (The Sierra Club). Adventure travel guide series for many countries.

All Asia Guide (Charles E. Tuttle Co., 1994, $23.95). A practical Asia guide.

Asia Through the Backdoor by Rick Steves and Bob Effertz (John Muir Publications, 1995, $17.95). Asia on the cheap and off the beaten path.

Beyond Safaris: A Guide to Building People-to-People Ties With Africa by Kevin Danaher (Africa World Press, 1991, $39.95). Global Exchange, San Francisco, CA; (415) 255-7296. A bit old but still one of the best resources for socially conscious travelers in Africa. Lists organizations.

Directory of Environmental Travel Resources is available for $10 from Dianne Brause, One World Family Travel Network, 81868 Lost Valley Lane, Dexter, OR 97431.

E Magazine. The Earth Action Network, Westport, CT; (203) 854-5559.

Earthtrips by Dwight Holing (Living Planet Press, 1991, $12.95).

Eco-Vacations: Enjoy Yourself and Save the Earth by Evelyn Kaye (Blue Panda, 1991, $22.50).

Ecotourist Guide to the Ecuadorian Amazon by Rolfe Wesche. The Pan-American Center for Geographical Studies and Research, 3er piso, Apartado 17-01-4273, Quito, Ecuador; (011) 593-245-1200.

Green Travel Mailing List. For green travel resources on the Internet. To subscribe contact majordomo@igc.apc.org.

Green Travel Sourcebook by Daniel Grotta and Sally Wiener Grotta (John Wiley & Sons, 1992, $16.95).

Holidays That Don't Cost the Earth by John Elkington and Julia Hailes (Victor Gollancz Ltd., 14 Henrietta St., London, WC2E 8QJ, England, 1992, £5.99). A worldwide guide to environmental vacations.

Indigenous Peoples and Global Tourism. Project Report by Deborah McLaren, The Rethinking Tourism Project, 1761 Willard St., NW, Washington, DC 20009 USA. $6 postpaid.

Lonely Planet Guides (Lonely Planet Publications). Books on every country in Asia plus some regional.

Moon Travel Handbooks (Moon Publications). These guides provide thorough cultural, historical, and political coverage, as well as exhaustive practical information.

Natour: Special edition on ecotourism. Contact editor Arturo Crosby, Viriato, 20, Madrid, Spain; (011) 91-593-0831.

Nature Tourism: Managing for the Environment edited by Tensie Whelan (Island Press, 1991, $19.95). Guidelines and essays on nature tourism.

Rethinking Tourism and Ecotravel: The Paving of Paradise and How You Can Stop It by Deborah McLaren (Kumarian Press, 1997, $22). Useful information about the global tourism industry and creative alternatives. You will never travel the same way again.

Structural Adjustment, World Trade and Third World Tourism: An Introduction to the Issues by K.T. Ramesh, Ecumenical Center on Third World Tourism, P.O. Box 35, Senanikhom, Bangkok 10902, Thailand. Contours, August 1995.

Working With the Environment by Tim Ryder (Vacation Work, 9 Park End St., Oxford OX1 1HJ, ENGLAND, 1996, £9.99). Guide to careers that involve working with the environment. Includes a chapter on environmental tourism.

Responsible Tourism Organizations

Airline Ambassadors, 4636 Fairfax Ave., Dallas, TX 75209; (800) 987-7061. Or contact Nancy Larson Rivard at (415) 685-6263.

Asia Tourism Action Network (ANTENNA), 15 Soi Soonvijai 8, New Petchburi Rd., Bangkok 10310, Thailand. A network in Asia and the Pacific promoting locally controlled tourism; publishes a newsletter.

Badri Dev Pande, Environmental Education and Awareness, P.O. Box 3923, Kathmandu, Nepal. Developing a sustainable tourism master plan of Manaslu region of Nepal.

Broken Bud, 1765-D Le Roy, Berkeley, CA 94709; (510) 843-5506. Formed out of the Center for Responsible Tourism. Advocacy against prostitution tourism and child trafficking.

Center for Global Education, Augsburg College, 2211 Riverside Ave., Minneapolis, MN 55454; (800) 299-8889. On travel seminars or semester programs, learn from people of diverse backgrounds about their economic, political, and social realities; emphasis on those struggling for justice. Programming in Mexico, Central America, Southern Africa, and China/Hong Kong.

Center for Responsible Tourism, P.O. Box 827, San Anselmo, CA 94979; (415) 258-

6594. Publishes a monthly newsletter highlighting innovative tourism projects around the world. They are one of the only responsible travel centers in the U.S. and have helped hundreds of travelers, educators, people in other counties. Subscribe—they need your support!

Center for the Advancement of Responsible Travel (CART), 70 Dry Hill Park Rd., Tonbridge, Kent TN10 3BX, U.K. Center of information on responsible tourism in Europe.

Center for Third World Organizing, 1218 East 21st St., Oakland, CA 94606; (510) 533-7583, fax (510) 533-0923; ctwo@igc. org. An excellent resource for information about progressive politics, actions, and organizations in the U.S. and abroad.

Community Action International Alliance (CAIA), 110 Maryland Ave., NE, Suite 504, Washington, DC 20002; (202) 547-2640, fax (202) 547-3136. Organizes environmental justice tours of Washington, DC for local public high school students. No longer involved with international travel.

COOPRENA (National Eco-Agricultural Cooperative Network of Costa Rica), Aptdo. 6939-1000 San Jose, Costa Rica; (011) 506-225-1942; camese@sol.racsa.co. cr. Consortium of cooperatives developing eco-agro tourism and small farms.

Cousteau Society, Project Ocean Search, 870 Greenbriar Cir., #402, Chesapeake, VA 23320; (757) 523-9335. Good marine guidelines and information about threats to the world's oceans.

Earth Island Institute, 300 Broadway, Suite 28, San Francisco, CA 94133-3312; (415) 788-3666. Publishes "How Green Is Your Tour: Questions to Ask Your Tour Operator." Their sea turtle program offers tours

to Mexico where participants learn about and help monitor endangered turtle species.

Earthstewards Network, P.O. Box 10697, Bainbridge Island, WA 98110; (206) 842-7986, fax (206) 842-8918. For Peacetrees projects contact Jerilyn Brusseau at: jerilyn@earthstewards.org; for Middle East Citizen Diplomacy Projects contact Leah at: office@earthstewards.org.

Earthwatch, 680 Mt. Auburn St., Watertown, MA 02272; (617) 926-8200, www.earthwatch. org. Offers working vacations with scientists around the world.

Earthwise Journeys, earthwyz@teleport. com, is an interlink for "earth-friendly travel to discover our global community."

Ecumenical Coalition on Third World Tourism (ECTWT), P.O. Box 616, Bridgetown, Barbados; contours@caribne t. net; or ECTW Asia office: Box 35, Senanikhom, Bangkok 10902, Thailand; (011) 662-939-7111; contours@ksc.net.th. Oldest responsible tourism organization in the world; numerous publications and resources.

Elderhostel, 75 Federal St., Boston, MA 02110-1941; (617) 426-8056. For travelers over 50. Friendly, educational travel programs around the world for seniors.

EQUATIONS: Equitable Tourism Options, No. 198, II Cross, Church Rd. (behind old KEB office), New Thippasandra, Bangalore 560 075, India; (011) 9180-528-2313; admin@equations.ilban.ernet.in. Responsible tourism advocacy; helps travelers locate environmentally and culturally sensitive projects in India.

Europe Conservation, Via Fusetti, 14-20143 Milano, Italy; (011) 39-2-5810-3135.

Friends of PRONATURA, 240 East Limberlost Dr., Tucson, AZ 85705; (520) 887-1188; closfree@aol.com. Network of ecological groups working in Mexico.

Global Exchange, 2017 Mission St., Suite 303, San Francisco, CA 94110; (415) 255-7296; gx-info@globalexchange.org. Reality tours focus on social, cultural, environmental issues in South Africa, Haiti, Cuba, Mexico, and elsewhere.

Global Family, 210 W. 70th St., #1507, New York, NY 10023. Contact: Margo LaZaro, (212) 877-0992, fax (800) 395-5600 or Patrick MacNamara at: patrickUN@aol.com.

Global Service Corps, 300 Broadway, Suite 28, San Francisco, CA 94133; (415) 788-3666 ext. 128, fax (415) 788-7324; gsc@igc.apc.org, www.earthisland.org/ei/gsc/gschome.html. Cooperates with grassroots groups in Costa Rica to send paid volunteers for 2- and 3-week programs.

Golondrinas Cloudforest Conservation Project, Calle Isabel La Catolica 1559, Quito, Ecuador; (011) 593-2-226-602 fax 2-222-390. A conservation organization conserving 25,000 hectares of cloudforests on the northwest slopes of the Andes. They have volunteer and educational programs, including a 4-day trek through the Cerro Golondrinas area.

Hawaiian Ecumenical Coalition on Tourism (HECOT), 766 North King St., Honolulu, HI 96817; (808) 256-7218, fax (808) 843-0711. Research, activism, advocacy, publications.

Indonesia Resources and Information Program (IRIP), P.O. Box 190, Northcote 3070, Australia; (011) 3-481-1581. Fosters active links with Indonesians working for change.

Institute for Central American Development Studies (ICADS), Dept. 826, P.O. Box 025216, Miami, FL 33102-5216, or ICADS, Apartado 3-2070, Sabanilla, San Jose, Costa Rica; (011) 506-225-0508, fax 234-1337; icads@netbox.com. Field course in resource management and sustainable development and interdisciplinary semester internship programs focusing on development issues from ecological and socio-economic perspectives.

International Bicycle Fund, 4887 Columbia Dr. S, #T-7, Seattle, WA 98108; (206) 767-0848; intlbike@scn.org. Promotes bicycle transport; links with autofree and bicycling organizations around the world; publishes essays on environmentally and culturally friendly traveling.

International Institute for Peace Through Tourism, 3680 rue de La Montange, Monteal, PQ, Canada H3G 2AB; (514) 281-1822. Facilitates tourism initiatives that contribute to international peace and cooperation.

International Institute for Peace Through Tourism, Lou D'Amore, 3641 University, Montreal, H3A 2B3, PQ, Canada. (514) 398-3635, fax (514) 398-1530.

Ladakh (India) Project, P.O. Box 9475, Berkeley, CA 94709; (510) 527-3873. An educational program that supports innovative grassroots development efforts of the Ladakhi people who live on the western edge of the Tibetan Plateau in India. Good resource materials on counterdevelopment, books, videos.

Lost Valley Educational Center, 81868 Lost Valley Ln., Dexter, OR 97431; (541) 937-3351; diannebr@aol.com, www.efn.org/~lvec. Dianne G. Brause is a well-known writer and leader in the field of responsible and sustainable travel. She offers opportunities in Central America for participants to live, learn, and work with local people.

Mobility International USA (MIUSA), P.O. Box 10767, Eugene, OR 97440; (541) 343-1284 (voice/TDD), fax (541) 343-6812; miusa@igc.

apc.org. (Use same address for the National Clearinghouse on Disability and Exchange.)

NANET (North American Network for Ethical Travel), Office of Global Education, Church World Service, 2115 N. Charles St., Baltimore, MD 21218-5755; (410) 727-6106. Responsible travel group has database of responsible tourism organizations.

Office of Study Abroad, The Univ. of Kansas, 108 Lippincott Hall, Lawrence, KS 66045; (913) 864-3742. Offers a semester at the port town of Golfito on the southern Pacific coast of Costa Rica in anthropology, ecology, biology, and Spanish.

One World Family Travel, 81868 Lost Valley Ln., Dexter, OR 96431; (503) 937-3357; dianbr@aol.com. *Transitions Abroad* contributing editor Dianne Brause publishes a directory of alternative travel resources.

Okologischer Tourismus in Europa (OTE), Bernd Rath, Am Michaelshof 8-10, 53177 Bonn, Germany. Responsible tourism organization; resources in German.

Our Developing World, 13004 Paseo Presada, Saratoga, CA 95070-4125; (408) 379-4431; fax 408-376-0755; vic_@vval.com. Educational project bringing Third World realities to North Americans. Community programs, teacher training materials, resources library. Study tour to Southeast Asia in August 1998.

Partners in Responsible Tourism, P.O. Box 419085-322, San Francisco, CA 94141; (415) 273-1430; bapirt@aol.com. Members promote cultural and environmental ethics and practices.

Paul Coleman, c/o Scott Barry, 3020 Bridgeway, Suite 234, Sausalito, CA 94965; (415) 679-1744.

Responsible Tourism Network, PO Box 34, Rundle Mall, Adelaide, SA, Australia 5000; (618) 232-2727, fax (618) 232-2808; bwitty@ozemail.com.au. Responsible tourism in Pacific region; works with travel industry and tourism activists; publishes responsible travel guide.

Rethinking Tourism Project, 1761 Willard St., NW, Washington, DC 20009; (202) 797-1251; DMcla75001@aol.com. An educational and networking project for indigenous people. Offers some volunteer opportunities and internships.

School for Field Studies, 16 Broadway, Beverly, MA 01915-4499; (508) 927-7777. Field studies and hands-on opportunities for high school and college students concerned about the environment.

Sierra Club, 85 2nd St., 2nd Fl., San Francisco, CA 94105; (415) 977-5500. Publishes good travel guides, offers conservation-focused tours.

South American Explorers Club. (SAEC), 126 Indian Creek Rd., Ithaca, NY 14850; (607) 277-0488; explorer@samexplo.org, www.samexplo.org. A network with centers in South America for backpackers, hikers, mountaineers, and other interested travelers. Their magazine is a good resource for responsible travel.

Talamanca Association for Ecotourism and Conservation, Puerto Viejo de Talamanca, Limon, Costa Rica. Local environmental organization that offers ecotourism programs.

TERN: Traveler's Earth Repair Network, Friends of the Trees, P.O. Box 1064, Tonasket, WA 98855; (509) 486-4276. A network for travelers who want to make a positive contribution to the environment.

The Travel Specialists, Co-Op America Travel Links, M.J. Kietzke, 120 Beacon St., Somerville, MA 02144; (617) 497-8151; mj@tvlcoll.com.

Third World Tourism European Ecumenical Network (TEN), Nikolaus-Otto Strasse 13, D-70771 Leinfelden-Echterdingen, Germany; (011) 44-7-11-7989-281, fax 7989-123. Responsible tourism.

Tourism Concern, Stapleton House, 277-281 Holloway Rd., London N7 8HN, U.K.; (011) 44-171-753-3330, fax 753-3331; tour concern@gn.apc.org. Excellent resource on issues related to tourism: land rights, displacement, general responsible tourism information.

Tourism Investigation and Monitoring Team, c/o TERRA, 5th Fl., TVS Bldg., 509 Soi Rohitsook, Pracharat Bampgen Rd., Bangkok 10320, Thailand; (011) 66-2-69104-1820. Newsletter about tourism development in the Mekon subregion.

Tourism With Insight (Arbeitsgemeinschaft Tourismus mit Einsicht), Hadorter Str. 9B, D-8130 Starnberg, Germany. Responsible tourism study group.

Transitions Abroad, P.O. Box 1300, Amherst, MA 01004-1300; (800) 293-0373, fax (413) 256-0373; trabroad@aol.com, www.transabroad.com. Publications with programs, resources, and first-hand reports on responsible travel throughout the world.

Tropical Science Center, Apd 8-3870, San Jose 1000, Costa Rica; (011) 506-22-6241. Offers open-air classrooms and labs for tropical science students and professionals.

University Research Expeditions Program, Univ. of California, Berkeley, CA 94720-7050; (510) 642-6586. Volunteer programs for travelers of all ages. Director Jean Colvin has developed codes of conduct for researchers working with indigenous peoples and codes for travelers going to the same areas.

Washington Semester Program—International Environment and Development offers 12 weeks in Washington, DC and 3 weeks in Costa Rica studying tourism and development. Contact WSWCP, Tenley Campus, American Univ., Washington, DC 20016-8083; (202) 895-4900; washsem@american.edu.

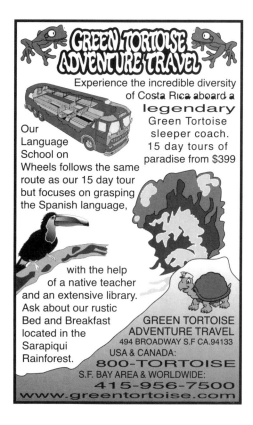

CHAPTER 9

RESPONSIBLE TRAVEL TOURS AND PROGRAMS

The following listing of responsible travel programs was supplied by the organizers. Contact the program directors to confirm costs, dates, and other details. If you do not see the program you want in the country of your choice, look in the "Worldwide" listings at the end of the section for programs located in several different regions.

Africa

Bicycle Africa Tours. Village-based, cross-cultural bicycle tours to all parts of Africa. Cycling difficulty is moderate. Each program is different, but all focus on the diversity of the culture, social institutions, and environment, as well as the complexity of the history, economy, culture, and society. Programs are led by African studies specialists.

   Dates: Jan (Uganda), Feb (Kenya/Tanzania), Apr (Tunisia), Jun-Aug (Zimbabwe), Aug-Sep (Malawi), Sep-Oct (Eritrea/Ethiopia), Oct-Nov (Senegal/Mali), Nov (Burkina Faso/Togo/Benin). Cost: $990-$1,290 plus airfare for 2 weeks. Includes food, lodging, guides, and fees. Contact: David Mozer, Director, International Bi-cycle Fund/Bicycle Africa, 4887 Columbia Dr. S. #T-7, Seattle, WA 98108; Tel./fax (206) 767-0848; intlbike@scn.org; www. halcyon.com/fkroger/bike/bikeafr.htm.

Cultural Tour of Ghana/Kenya. Highlights of places to be visited: Ashanti king's palace, craft and kente weaving villages, tropical rain forest, botanical gardens, slave castles, village meeting with chief and elders, African textiles factory, cocoa processing plant. Opportunity for homestay with Ghanaian family. Also custom designs programs for groups.

   Dates: Feb 9-23; Jul 20-Aug 3, 1998 (Ghana); Kenya, Jun. Cost: $2,950 from NY. One-week optional home stay add-on $200. Contact: Georgina Lorencz, African Travel Seminars, Inc., 3020 Rosewood Ln. North, Minneapolis, MN 55441; (612) 509-

0976, fax (612) 509-0972; georgina_ats_inc@hotmail.com.

Americas

Tours to Exciting Destinations. Gecko Overland Trekking operates small-group tours in Mexico, Central America, and U.S. Our clients are active travelers from all parts of the world. With 9 itineraries and year-long departures, visit the best places these regions offer. Kick back and enjoy the journey. Or be active. Each tour is an adventure.

Dates: Summer and year-long departures, 8 itineraries. Cost: From $690. Includes ground transportation, hotels, admissions to ruin sites and other attractions, and more. Contact: Gecko Overland Trekking, P.O. Box 40-2456, Miami Beach, FL 33140-0456; (800) 628-9161 or (305) 867-2087, fax (510) 974-9716; gecko@geckooverland.com, www.geckooverland.com.

Asia

International Travel Seminar. Themes for trips to Southeast Asia include the impact of tourism, post-Vietnam war society, refugees, and the environment. Call for current trips.

Dates: Trips of 10-20 days to Thailand, Laos, Vietnam, Hong Kong, and China. Cost: Varies. Contact: Travel Seminar Division, Center for Global Education, Augsburg College, 2211 Riverside Ave., Box 307TR, Minneapolis, MN 55454; (612) 330-1159, fax (612) 330-1695.

Orangutan Conservation. In cooperation with the Orangutan Foundation International, Bolder Adventures offers a series of orangutan research study tours. Participants support the work of Dr. Birute Galdikas, who has spent 25 years studying these endangered primates. The 10-day programs take place at Camp Leakey on the island of Borneo in Indonesia.

Dates: Jun 29, Jul 20, Aug 17, Sep 7, Oct 5, Nov 2, 1998. Cost: $2,100 land cost only. Contact: Asia Transpacific Journeys, Southeast Asia Travel Specialists, 3055 Center Green Dr., Boulder, CO 80306; (800) 642-2742, fax (303) 443-7078; travel@southeastasia.com, www.southeastasia.com.

Travel-Study Seminars. Visit with Asians from China, Hong Kong and Indochina as their countries undergo profound economic changes. Pursue critical questions, such as: Do these changes also bring political pluralism? What impact do economic changes have on the education and outlook of youth? On the natural environment? Who benefits from economic restructuring? Call for more information on current trips.

Dates: Varies. Cost: Approx. $3,800-$4,300 depending on length and destinations. Contact: Center for Global Education, Augsburg College, 2211 Riverside Ave., Box 307TR, Minneapolis, MN 55454; (800) 299-8889, fax (612) 330-1695; globaled@augsburg.edu, www.augsburg.edu/global.

Canada

Canada's Canoe Adventures. Canoeing and sea kayaking adventures for all ages and abilities. Canada's Canoe Adventures welcomes those who are seeking an experience of a lifetime that will evoke memories for generations to come. Over 45 trips to all parts of Canada, including: Algonquin Park, Quetico, Temagami, Quebec, Seal, Tweedsmuir, Bowron Lakes, Queen Charlottes, Johnstone Strait, Nahanni, Coppermine, Mountain, and many more. Winter paddling to Belize, Baha, and Bahamas. Proceeds donated to water conservation projects operated by the Canadian Recreational Canoeing Association.

Dates: Year-round. Cost: CAN$250-$5,000. Contact: Canada's Canoe Adventures, P.O. Box 398, 446 Main St. West, Merrickville, ON K0G 1N0, Canada; (613)

269-2910, fax (613) 269-2908; staff@crca.ca, www.crca.ca.

Yoga Study and Retreats. Yasodhara Ashram, a vibrant spiritual community founded 35 years ago by Swami Sivananda Radha, offers yoga courses, workshops, spiritual retreats. Situated on Kootenay Lake in the mountains of southeastern British Columbia, the atmosphere is conducive to reflection, meditation, and renewal. The 10 Days of Yoga, an introduction to ashram courses, is offered every quarter. Programs for young adults are offered at this certified post-secondary institute.

Dates: Year round. Cost: Varies. The 10 Days of Yoga is CAN$825 (CAN$170 deposit). Special youth rates/work programs. Contact: Yasodhara Ashram, Box 9, Kootenay Bay, BC V0B 1X0, Canada; (604) 227-9224 or (800) 661-8711, fax (604) 227-9494; yashram@netidea.com.

Central America

International Travel Seminar. More than 20 trips are offered each year to Nicaragua, El Salvador, Guatemala, and Mexico to meet with the poor and disenfranchised, women's groups, cooperatives, and alternative political parties, as well as decision-makers from the government, businesses, and churches. Programs are designed to bring you face-to-face with Latin American people's struggle for freedom, justice, and human dignity.

Dates: Trips of 7-14 days throughout the year. Cost: From $1,300-$2,500 (includes airfare, food, lodging, and program). Contact: Travel Seminar Division, Center for Global Education, Augsburg College, 2211 Riverside Ave., Box 307TR, Minneapolis, MN 55454; (800) 299-8889, (612) 330-1159, fax (612) 330-1695; globaled@augsburg.edu, www.augsburg.edu/global.

Costa Rica

Costa Rica EcoAdventure. From cloudforests and volcanoes to tropical rivers and beaches, this 8-day ecological adventure lets you discover and experience some of the country's most beautiful and diverse ecosystems. This escorted exploration includes visits to Carrillo National Park, Poás and Arenal volcanoes, Caño Negro, Carara Reserve, Jaco Beach, and Manuel Antonio Park and more.

Dates: Year round. Cost: Varies. Contact: Charlie Strader, Explorations Inc., 27655 Kent Rd., Bonita Springs, FL 34135; (800) 446-9660, fax (941) 992-7666; cesxplor@aol.com.

Costa Rican Language Academy. Costa Rican-owned and operated language school offers first-rate Spanish instruction in a warm and friendly environment. Teachers with university degrees. Small groups or private classes. Included free in the programs are airport transportation, coffee and natural refreshments, excursions, Latin dance, Costa Rican cooking, music, and conversation classes to provide students with complete cultural immersion.

Dates: Year round (start anytime). Cost: $135 per week or $220 per week for program with homestay. All other activities and services included at no additional cost. Contact: Costa Rican Language Academy, P.O. Box 336-2070, San José, Costa Rica; (011) 506-221-1624 or 233-8914 or 233-8938, fax 233-8670. In the U.S.: (800) 854-6057; crlang@sol.racsa.co.cr, www.crlang.co.cr/index.html.

Learn Spanish While Volunteering. Assist with the training of Costa Rican public school teachers in our latest language learning techniques, using classroom computers, K-8 school targeted by Costa Rican government as a model ESL/technology school. Enjoy learning Spanish in the morning, volunteer work in the afternoon/

evening. Spanish classes are 2-5 students plus group learning activities; conversations with middle-class homestay families (1 student per family). Homestays and volunteer project are within walking distance of school in small town (14,000 population) near the capital, San Jose.

Dates: Year round, all levels. Classes begin every Monday, volunteer program is continuous. Cost: $295 per week for 25 hours of Spanish classes. Includes tuition, all meals (7 days a week), homestay, laundry, all materials, Costa Rican dance and cooking classes, and airport transportation. $25 one-time registration for Spanish classes; $100 additional one-time registration fee for volunteer program. Contact: Susan Shores, Registrar, Latin American Language Center, 7485 Rush River Dr., Suite 710-123, Sacramento, CA 95831; (916) 447-0938, fax (916) 428-9542; lalc@ madre.com.

Ecuador

Workshops in the Galapagos Islands. Specializing in comprehensive, educationally-oriented, professionally-led 11-day natural history tours of the Galapagos Islands. Special programs include history-oriented trips that follow Darwin's route as well as National Science Teacher Association (NSTA)-sponsored tours offering 3 graduate credit hours.

Dates: Monthly departures on 16-passenger yachts. Cost: Approx. $3,000. Airfare not included. Contact: Galapagos Travel, P.O. Box 1220, San Juan Bautista, CA 95045; (800) 969-9014, fax (408) 623-2923; galapagos travel@compuserve.com.

El Salvador

El Salvador Encounter (Crispaz). A Third World immersion experience with a faith-based perspective. An intensive week of listening to Salvadorans describe their struggles through the war and hopes for the future, celebrating new life with the Church, visiting historic sites, and reflecting on how our faith is informed and challenged by what we see. El Salvador Encounter will design seminars for your church or community focusing on your interests: theology, education, women, ecology, politics, and economics. Or join nationwide groups throughout the year.

Dates: One- to 2-week "tours" throughout the year. Cost: $65 per day includes room and board, guide, translation, etc. Contact: Stan de Voogd, 1135 Mission Rd., San Antonio, TX 78210; (210) 534-6996; crispaz@igc. apc.org.

France

French and Cookery in a Château. Live and study in 18th-century château. Adult courses in French language and Provençal cookery. Relaxed family atmosphere and good food. Château has 13 acres of park and pool. Single/ en suite and shared rooms. Close to Burgundy, Beaujolais, Auvergne, and cities of Lyons and Roanne. One- to 12-week courses.

Dates: Every Sunday Apr-Nov. Cost: From $999 full board and classes in Château. Contact: Michael Giammarella, P.O. Box 640713, Oakland Gardens, NY 11364-0713; (800) 484-1234 ext 0096 or Ecole des Trois Ponts, Château de Matel, 42300 Roanne; (011) 33-477-70-80-01, fax 477-71-53-00; info@ 3ponts.edu, www.3ponts.edu.

French in France. Among the ways to learn French, total immersion is the most enjoyable and the most effective. We have been doing it for 20 years in a small historical city located in Normandy (west of Paris, close to the seaside). We welcome people at any age and any level in 1- to 10-week programs, intensive or vacation type, from mid-March to mid-November.

Dates: Spring: Mar 23-May 29; summer: Jun 15-Aug 28; fall: Sep 7-Nov 13, 1998. Cost:

From $525 per week (tuition, room and board, and excursions). Contact: Dr. Almeras, Chairman, French American Study Center, 12, 14, Blvd. Carnot, B.P. 176, 14104 Lisieux Cedex, France (011) 33-2-31-31-22-01, fax 31-22-21.

Village Stays. Set in the heart of the old village of Calvisson, this 15th-century house has been restored with patience and talent by its owners and offers you tastefully furnished guestrooms. Calvisson is located 15 km west of Nimes in front of the beaches of Camargue. Painting courses and guided tours of the area.

Dates: Year round. Cost: Double room FF280, single FF230, suite (3 persons); FF350 with breakfasts, meals FF80 with wine. Contact: Corinne Burckel de Tell, Grand Rue 48, 30420 Calvisson, France; (011) 33-466-012391, fax 014219.

Guatemala

Eco-Escuela de Español. The Eco-Escuela de Español offers a unique educational experience by combining intensive Spanish language instruction with volunteer opportunities in conservation and community development projects. Students are immersed in the language, culture, and ecology of Petén, Guatemala—an area renowned for its tropical forests and ancient Maya ruins. Ecological activities integrate classroom with field-based experiences.

Dates: Every Monday year round. Cost: Classes $65 per week (based on 20 hours of individual instruction per week, Monday-Friday). Room and board with local families $60 per week. Registration fee $10. Contact: Eco-Escuela, Conservation International, 2501 M St., NW, Suite 200, Washington, DC 20037; (202) 973-2264, fax (202) 331-9328; ecoescuela@conservation.org.

La Paz Spanish School. Non-profit Spanish language and cultural immersion program. Weekly price includes 25 hours private instruction, family homestay, meals, educational/recreational activities. Volunteer possibilities on projects emphasizing education, natural health, women's empowerment. Qualified, well-trained teachers and friendly, helpful staff. Activities include conferences, videos, hikes, field trips. Peaceful, heart-centered setting.

Dates: Year round. Cost: $100 ($125 Jun-Aug). Room and board, activities, private instruction. Contact: Roy Holman, 5762 26th Ave. NE, Seattle, WA 98105; (206) 729-7664; RoyMundo@aol.com.

Ireland

Irish Language and Culture. Irish language programs at all learning levels for adults are offered by Oideas Gael, which also offers cultural activities, learning programs in hillwalking, dances of Ireland, painting, tapestry weaving, Raku-Celtic pottery, and archaeology.

Dates: Apr-Sep, 1998 (weekly). Cost: $150 plus accommodations (from $90 per week). Contact: Liam O'Cuinneagain, Director, Oideas Gael, Gleann Cholm Cille, County Donegal, Ireland; (011) 353-73-30248; oidsgael@iol.ie.

Italy

Biking and Walking Tours. Specializing in Italy for over 10 years, Ciclismo Classico distills the "Best of Italy," offering more unique Italian destinations than any other active vacation company. Educational, active tours for all abilities in Umbria, Tuscany, Piedmont, the Dolomites, Puglia, Sicily, the Amalfi Coast, Cinque Terre, Sardegna, Abruzzo, Campania, Corsica, and Elba, and Ireland, too. Charming accommodations, expert bilingual guides, cooking demonstrations, wine tastings, support vehicle, detailed route instructions, visits to local festivals, countryside picnics—an unforgettable cultural indulgence.

Dates: Apr-Nov (70 departures). Call for specific dates. Cost: $1,500-$3,000. Contact: Lauren Hefferon, Director, Ciclismo Classico, 13 Marathon St., Arlington, MA 02174; (800) 866-7314 or (781) 646-3377.

Japan

Teaching English in Japan. Two-year program to maximize linguistic and cultural integration of participants who work as teachers' assistants. Placements twice yearly in April and August. Most positions are in junior high schools in urban and rural areas. Bachelor's degree, cultural sensitivity, and some ESL training required.

Dates: Hiring for positions every April and August. Applications accepted year round. Cost: Airfare, salary, housing, health care provided. No application fees. Contact: Earlham College, Institute for Education on Japan, D-202, Richmond, IN 47374; (888) 685-2726; www.earlham.edu/www/departments/AET/home.htm.

Mexico

Cemanahuac Community. Trips are highly educational, with college credit (graduate and undergraduate) available. Focus areas include history, anthropology, archaeology, social issues, cooking and cuisine, and popular and folk art. Previous groups include teachers, social workers, artists, senior citizens, chefs, museum members, alumni groups, and other adult participants. Each trip individually planned.

Dates: Field study trips can be held at any time of the year. Cost: Dependent on require-

ments and length of the field study trips. Contact: Vivian B. Harvey, Educational Programs Coordinator, Cemanahuac Educational Community, Apartado 5-21, Cuernavaca, Morelos, Mexico; (011) 52-73-18-6407, fax 12-5418; 74052.2570@compuserve.com.

Intensive Spanish in Cuernavaca. Cuauhnahuac, founded in 1972, offers a variety of intensive and flexible programs geared to individual needs. Six hours of classes daily with no more than 4 students to a class. Housing with Mexican families who really care about you. Cultural conferences, excursions, and special classes for professionals. College credit available.

Dates: Year round. New classes begin every Monday. Cost: $70 registration fee; $650 4 weeks tuition; housing $18 per night. Contact: Marcia Snell, 519 Park Dr., Kenilworth, IL 60043; (800) 245-9335, fax (847) 256-9475; lankysam@aol.com.

Language and Culture in Guanajuato. We work with innovative teaching techniques, tailoring instruction to each student's needs. Spanish, Mexican History, Politics, Culture-Cuisine, Folk Dancing and Latin American Literature.

Dates: Year round. New classes begin every Monday. Cost: $925. Includes 4 weeks of classes and homestay with 3 meals daily. Contact: Director Jorge Barroso, Instituto Falcon, A.C., Guanajuato, Gto. 36000 Mexico; Tel./fax (011) 52-473-2-36-94, infalcon@redes. int.com.mx, www.infonet. com.mx/falcon.

Mar de Jade Mexico. Tropical ocean-front responsible tourism center in beautiful unspoiled fishing village near Puerto Vallarta offers unique study options: enjoy great swimming, snorkeling, hiking, and boating; study Spanish in small groups taught by native speakers. Or join the longer work/study program that includes working in development projects such as health clinics, teaching, or working in the community of Mar de Jade itself.

Dates: Year round. Cost: For 21 days: room (shared occupancy), board and Spanish classes (12 hours per week of Spanish and 12-15 hours per week of community work) $950. For daily room and board $50. Contact: In Mexico: Mar de Jade, A.P. 81, Las Varas, Nayarit, 63715, Mexico; Tel./fax (011) 52-327-20184; In U.S.: P.O. Box 1280, Santa Clara, CA 95052; (415) 281-0164; mard jade@pvnet.com.mx, www.puerto-vallarta. com/mardejade.

Travel/Study Seminars. Learn from Mexicans of diverse backgrounds about their economic, political, and social realities. Emphasis on the views of the poor and oppressed. Programming in Cuernavaca, Mexico City, and Chiapas. Call for a free list of upcoming programs.

Dates: Ongoing. Cost: $800-$1,900 depending on package, destination, and length of trip. Contact: Center for Global Education, Augsburg College, 2211 Riverside Ave., Box 307TR, Minneapolis, MN 55454; (800) 299-8889, fax (612) 330-1695; globaled@augsburg.edu, www.augsburg. edu/ global.

New Zealand

Dolphin Encounter (Kaikoura). An opportunity to swim with or watch the dusky dolphins in their natural habitat off the Kaikoura coast. At Dolphin Encounter, we let you take part in this experience, so you can witness the beauty, grace and intelligence of these wonderful creatures. Wetsuit, snorkel, and flippers provided.

Dates: Year round but main season is Oct.-May. Cost: NZD$80 to swim; NZD$48 to watch. Contact: Lynette Buurman, Dolphin Encounter, 58 West End, Kaikoura, New Zealand; (011) 64-3-319-6777, fax 319-6534; info@dolphin.co.nz.

New Zealand Wilderness Walking. Small group tours through the South Island, visiting all world heritage areas and six national parks. Daily walking 2-6 hours. Motel/homestay accommodations. Guides expert in New Zealand's natural history, geology, and culture.

Dates: Nov 18-Dec 2; Dec 9-23 (1997); Dec 30-Jan 13; Jan 20-Feb 3; Feb 10-24; Mar 10-24, 1998. Customized tours on demand. Cost: NZ$3,520 includes guide, minibus, all accommodations, meals, boat cruises, goods and services tax. Contact: Anne Braun-Elwert, Alpine Recreation, P.O. Box 75, Lake Tekapo, New Zealand; (011) 64-3-680-6736; fax 680-6765; alprec@voyager.co.nz; www. canterburypages.co.nz/climb/alprec/index.html.

Pacific Region

Hawaii's Kalani Oceanside Retreat. Kalani Educational Retreat, the only coastal lodging facility within Hawaii's largest conservation area, treats you to Hawaii's aloha comfort, traditional culture, healthful cuisine, wellness programs, and extraordinary adventures: thermal springs, a naturist dolphin beach, snorkel pools, kayaking, waterfalls, crater lake, and spectacular Volcanoes National Park. Ongoing offerings in yoga, dance, hula, mythology, language, and massage. Or participate in an annual week-long event: men's/women's/couples conferences, dance/music/hula festivals, yoga/meditation/transformation retreats. Applications are also being accepted for our international Volunteer Scholar program.

Dates: Year round. Cost: Lodging $45-$110 per day. Camping $20-$25. $570-$1,120 per week for most programs, including meals and lodging choice. Contact: Richard Koob, Director, Kalani Retreat, RR2, Box 4500, Pahoa-Beach Rd., HI 96778-9724; (800) 800-6886 or (808) 965-7828 (call for fax info); kh@ilhawaii.net, http://randm.com/kh.html.

Papua New Guinea

Trans Niugini Tours. Nature and culture programs are operated in three areas: the Highlands, the Sepik Area, and a marine environment on the North Coast. Each area has its own distinct culture and environment, with comfortable wilderness lodges located in each.

Dates: Weekly departures. Cost: $889-$3,570 per person (land cost). Contact: Bob Bates, Trans Niugini Tours, P.O. Box 371, Mt. Hagen, Papua New Guinea; (800) 521-7242 or (011) 675-542-1438, fax 542-2470; travel@pngtours.com, www.pngtours.com.

Peru

Peruvian Studies (CIPS). People with an interest in Inca and Pre-Inca cultures travel to remote locations in Peru to study and document ancient cultures and continuing traditions of communities. No experience necessary; however, you must be willing to participate in scientific archaeological research.

Dates: Travel is February-March, June-July-August, and October-November. Choose your preferred time and length of stay. Cost: Approx. $1,400-$2,200 plus airfare to Peru. Cost depends on the length of stay and regions visited. The recommended time is 2 to 3 weeks and 2 regions in Peru. Contact: California Institute for Peruvian Studies, c/o Sandy Asmussen, Executive Director, 45 Quakie Way, Bailey, CO 80421; (303) 838-1215 (leave message). Write a short letter explaining your interest in Peru, or call. Inquiries will be responded to in the order they are received. Inquire at least 6 months prior to your desired time request.

Scotland

Volunteer Care Worker. Living and working in small Camphill community together with young adults with learning disabilities.

Dates: Any dates considered. Full-year stay preferred. Cost: None. £25 pocket money paid per week. Contact: Elisabeth Phethean, Beannacha Camphill Community, Banchory-Deverrick, Aberdeen AB12 5YL, Scotland, U.K.; (011) 44-1224-861200, fax 869250.

South Africa

Reconciliation and Renewal from a Global Perspective. In Johannesburg, Pretoria, Durban, and Cape Town participants will be guests of partner-hosts: religious, political, civic, business, cultural, and grassroots leaders. Opportunities for visits in individual homes and for developing personal contacts. The group will gather each evening for sharing, worship, and issue-based discussion led by experienced staff or hosts.

Dates: Aug 17-Aug 30, 1998. Cost: $3,500 includes tuition, room and board, and travel from New York. Contact: Maralyn R. Lipner, Plowshares Institute, 809 Hopmeadow St., Simsbury, CT 06070; (203) 651-4304, fax (203) 651-4305; evansr@hgc.edu.

Southeast Asia

Intrepid-Small Group Adventures. Intrepid are world leaders in Southeast Asian adventures. See the real Asia, travel on public transport, stay in small, friendly guest houses and let our group leaders do all the hard work. Travelers come from all over the world and we travel in groups of no more than 12 people.

Dates: Many trips depart weekly. Cost: From $420 accommodations, transport, group leader, sightseeing as listed. Contact: Adventure Center, 1311-TR 63rd St., Suite 200, Emeryville, CA 94608; (510) 654-1879, fax (510) 654-4200; res@intrepidtravel.com.au, www.intrepidtravel.com.au.

Vietnam and Laos: A People-Focused Tour. Experience two rich cultures, war's impact, people's effort to rebuild. See Hanoi, Halong Bay, Danang, Hue, and Ho Chi Minh City. Experience beautiful Laos—one of the world's poorest countries where Buddhism is a way of life and virtually no one goes hungry. Visit clinics, schools, co-ops, craftspeople, and villages.

Dates: Aug 3-21, 1998. Cost: $4,495 from San Francisco or Los Angeles. Includes roundtrip airfare, flights within each country, all accommodations, 2 meals per day, guides and land transport. Limited to 10 participants. Contact: Our Developing World, A Nonprofit Educational Project, 13004 Paseo Presada, Saratoga, CA 95070-4125; (408) 379-4431, fax (408) 376-0755; vic_ulmer@ vval.com.

United Kingdom

Eco Research and Education Center. Live on an ecological farm and research center where all the food is produced off the farm in an eco-house, built from products off the farm. Educational courses on criminal welfare and husbandry, horticulture, forestry, etc. Walking and horse riding.

Dates: Year round. Contact: Dr. M. Kiley-Worthington, Little Ash Eco-Farm, Throwleigh, Okehampton, Devon EX20 2HY, U.K.; Tel./fax (011) 44-1647-231394.

United States

River Rafting Expeditions. Adventure is for everyone. All ages are welcome and no experience is necessary. River journeys are 2-6 days through National Parks, wild and scenic Green and Colorado Rivers. Incredible whitewater or moderate and scenic stretches. Choose paddleboats, oarboats, motorized rafts, or inflatable kayaks. Color brochure and video to view. Specialty: Family Goes to Camp, women only.

Dates: May 3-Sep 25 (1997). Cost: $322-$887. Contact: Lee Griffith, Sheri Griffith Expeditions, Inc., P.O. Box 1324, Moab, UT 84532; (800) 332-2439 or (801) 259-8229, fax (801) 259-2226; classriver@aol.com, www. GriffithExp.com.

Worldwide

American-Int'l Homestays. Stay in English-speaking foreign homes in over 30 countries. Explore foreign cultures responsibly. Learn foreign languages. Perfect for families or seniors. Learn how other people live by living with them in their homes.

Dates: Year round. Cost: From $59 per night. Contact: Joe Kinczel, American-Int'l Homestays, P.O. Box 1754, Nederland, CO 80466; (303) 642-3088 or (800) 876-2048, fax (303) 642-3365; ash@igc.apc.org.

Amizade Volunteer Vacations. Programs offering mix of community service and recreation that provide volunteers with the opportunity to experience firsthand the culture they are working in—Brazilian Amazon, Peruvian Amazon, Bolivian Andes, or Greater Yellowstone region. Volunteers do not need any special skills, just a willingness to serve.

Dates: Year round. Cost: Varies. $1,500-$2,600 for Latin America; $150-$600 for Yellowstone. Contact: Amizade, 1334 Dartmouth Ln., Deerfield, IL 60015; (847) 945-9402, fax (847) 945-5676; amizade@ worldnet.att.net, http://amizade.org.

Art and Cultural Learning Journeys. Guided excursions with informative lectures bring to life famous sights and artworks in Italy, Spain, England, and Bali. Free workshops in drawing, painting, photography, etc. Limited scholarships available. Travel with A.R.T.I.S., a nonprofit organization of fine art educators dedicated to providing you with unique and rewarding international cultural experiences. College credit available.

Dates: May-Jul 1998 and Dec 98 for Rome. Ten, 20, or 30 days. Cost: $2,500 to $3,700. Includes airfare, studio space, furnished apartment, workshops, all ground transportation, entry fees, etc. Contact: A.R.T.I.S., 833 E. Holaway Dr., Tucson, AZ 85719; (800) 232-6893, fax (520) 887-5287; dfro@digmo. org, www.artistours. org.

College Semester Abroad, School for International Training. A pioneer in study abroad, The School for International Training (SIT) offers over 57 programs in over 40 countries worldwide. For over 40 years SIT has been a leader in offering field-based study abroad programs to U.S. college and university students.
Dates: Fall and spring semester. Cost: $8,900-$11,900 depending on location. Includes airfare, tuition, room and board, insurance. Contact: School for International Training, P.O. Box 676, Kipling Rd., Brattleboro, VT 05302; (802) 257-7751, fax (802) 258-3500; csa@sit.edu, www.sit.edu.

Coral Cay Conservation Expeditions. Volunteers needed to join major expeditions to help survey and protect coral reefs and tropical forests in the Caribbean, Asia-Pacific, Philippines, Indonesia, Red Sea. No previous experience required. Full accredited training provided (including scuba certification if required). Thousands of CCC volunteers have already helped establish 8 new marine reserves and wildlife sanctuaries worldwide.
Dates: Expeditions depart monthly throughout the year. Cost: From $995 (2 weeks) to $4,415 (12 weeks) excluding flights. Contact: Coral Cay Conservation Ltd., 154 Clapham Park Rd., London SW4 7DE, U.K.; (305) 757-2955 (U.K. office 011-44-171-498-6248, fax 498 8447); ccc@coralcay. demon.co.uk, www.coralcay.org.

Global Volunteers. "An adventure in service." Year-round short-term service programs for people of all ages and backgrounds. Assist mutual international understanding through ongoing development projects in 15 countries throughout Africa, Asia, the Caribbean, Europe, North and South America. Programs are 1, 2, and 3 weeks, ranging from natural resource preservation, light construction and painting to teaching English and assisting with health care. No special skills or foreign languages are required. Ask about our new programs for 1998.
Dates: Over 150 teams year round. Cost: Tax-deductible program fees range from $350 to $1,995. Airfare not included. Contact: Global Volunteers, 375 E. Little Canada Rd., St. Paul, MN 55117; (800) 487-1074, fax (612) 482-0916; email@globalvlntrs.org, www. globalvlntrs.org.

Moon Travel Handbooks. Founded in 1973, Moon Travel Handbooks publishes award-winning, comprehensive travel handbooks to distinct destinations in North America and Hawaii, Mexico, Central America, the Caribbean, Asia, and the Pacific. Environmental and cultural sensitivity set these guides apart from the rest.
Dates: Ongoing publishing schedule includes new editions and titles. Cost: $11.95-$30. Contact: Moon Publications, P.O. Box 3040, Chico, CA 95927-3040; (800) 345-5473, fax (916) 345-6751; travel@moon.com, www.moon.com.

The World for Free. Host/Guest Exchange. Members provide accommodations for other traveling members. Membership includes directory, one annual update, and cheap travel information. Please write for application before sending money.
Dates: Year round. Cost: $25 per year. Contact: c/o Seidboard World Enterprises, The World For Free, P.O. Box 137-TA, Prince St. Station, New York, NY 10012; fax (212) 979-8167; twff@juno.com.

WorldTeach. WorldTeach is a private nonprofit organization based at Harvard Univ. that contributes to educational development and cultural exchange by placing volunteers to teach in developing countries (China, Costa Rica, Ecuador, Honduras, Mexico, Namibia, Thailand, and Vietnam). Volunteers teach English, math, science, and environmental education to students of all ages. All programs last for 1 academic year; except for the summer program in China.

Dates: Year-round departures and deadlines vary depending on the program. Cost: $3,600-$4,400. Includes health insurance, airfare, field support, and training. Contact: Jodi Hullinger, Desk Officer, WorldTeach, Harvard Institute for International Development, 1 Eliot St., Cambridge, MA 02138-5705; (617) 495-5527, fax (617) 495-1599; jhulling@worldteach.org, www.igc.org/worldteach.

STUDY

*Since no two programs or participants are precisely the same, the challenge is
to learn enough about the ways in which programs differ from each other to
develop a short list of programs which best match individual learning styles,
resources, motivations, and interests.*

—WILLIAM HOFFA, PAGE 111

Education Abroad

Criteria for Choosing the Right Program

By William Hoffa, Ph.D.

Study abroad today is largely a buyer's bazaar—at least for students who have the financial and academic support of their parents and college and are thus free to shop widely and wisely and for the program which best corresponds to their individual interests and needs. Ending up in the right program demands informed planning.

As the lists below suggest, study abroad is now something that happens virtually across the curriculum as well as the continents of the world. Students at almost all academic levels can now find a range of suitable programs that span the durational spectrum from a full academic year to a few weeks during the summer or winter term.

While admission to selected programs can sometimes be competitive, in point of fact very few programs operate at anything close to full capacity. Most (including all listed in the following pages) welcome applications from any qualified student. Moreover, competition for enrollments between programs is often intense, a situation which can work to the advantage of interested students.

Since no two programs or participants are precisely the same, the challenge is to learn enough about the ways in which programs differ from each other to develop a short list of programs which best match individual learning styles, resources, motivations, and interests. This is best done with the assistance of campus guidance and the resources listed in this chapter. It should also involve the careful reading of program materials and surfing the Internet for program home pages. The final choice depends on being able to successfully balance the following program variables:

Direct Enrollment. At one extreme are programs offering integrated language and cultural immersion via direct enrollment in a foreign educational institution. Integrated programs allow students to experience a foreign culture at first hand through immersion in its educational and social system.

Participants in integrated programs need to be independent, well-prepared, resourceful, adventurous, and adaptive. They usually have to make their own travel and housing arrangements, and they are responsible for making sure that course work can be successfully transferred back to their home campus for credit. This requires considerable preparation and effort.

U.S. College Sponsored. At the other extreme are U.S. campus or agency initiated programs which transfer the American campus to foreign soil. Such stand-alone or "island" programs offer U.S.-standard course work, support services, excursions and social activities, and often living arrangements. Teaching is done fully or in part by U.S. faculty. This insures that equivalent standards are maintained with regard to work load, class time, grading, attendance, calendar, and the like. Island programs often accommodate large numbers of students and offer cultural enrichment activities, such as tours and excursions.

Students who have never been abroad before, and who need at least initial guidance and direction, are likely to be well-served by these more structured programs. In order to find opportunities for additional intellectual and intercultural experience, however, students must use their own initiative to venture forth outside their program setting.

Hybrid Models. Most programs fall between these poles, borrowing features of each. Most attempt to combine the intercultural advantages of more integrated programming with the more pragmatic advantages and conveniences of what are essentially U.S. branch campuses. Some are able to offer several tracks, so that as students become more involved, venturesome, and linguistically able, they can advance along more challenging paths. Courses offered by foreign institutions are often supplemented by American-style course work, discussion groups, or even tutorials.

At their best, hybrid programs offer a pragmatic and often ingenious blend of cultural enrichment and academic challenges.

When to Venture Overseas. Studying abroad is almost always a remarkably broadening and stimulating experience. It is a productively unsettling component of liberal education, leading participants to ask and answer a number of fundamental questions concerning their real long-range interests, skills, and goals. There is thus plenty to be said for thinking about participation earlier rather than later in the college career, somewhere in the sophomore year, so that after return there is ample time to act on redefined directions and goals.

On the other hand, the curricular strengths of current programs make study abroad ideally suited to juniors and seniors who have chosen an academic concentration and are seeking to deepen and diversify it in ways not possible on campus. While studying abroad toward the end of the undergraduate degree is sometimes seen as a last undergraduate fling, it can also function as an important way to broaden career prospects, especially if it includes a workplace internship or other practical experience.

How Long to Stay. While most observers still believe that the longer the experience, the more long-lasting its intellectual and personal impact will be, something is always better than nothing. The huge variety of program models, courses, and geographical locations make study abroad a real possibility for students who hitherto simply could not have considered it, whatever the program duration. Excellent year, semester, and short-term options abound, each suiting the amount of time students can afford (in an academic and economic sense) to be away from home campus studies. It is important, however, to consider the relative advantages and disadvantages which follow from enrollment in programs of differing lengths.

• The first rule of thumb, affirmed by returned students, is that the longer the program, the greater the intellectual and personal rewards. Academic benefit, crosscultural understanding, career preparation, and maturation all deepen with time. Long-term, fully-integrated programs are thus much more likely to provide students with the crosscultural coping skills favored by global corporations and international service organizations.

• Rule two, however, is that almost any program of any length is likely to offer something of value, and the "right" program can have a tremendous impact, regardless of its length. Short-term programs can be especially valuable if they are part of a continuum which combines pre-departure and post-return studies and professional interests. The key is that program goals are clear from the start and can indeed be accomplished in the allotted time. Students should avoid over-ambition, and also be suspicious of programs which seem to promise too much.

Program Size. Programs vary tremendously in the number of participants they enroll. Small programs enroll as few as five to 10 students, while larger ones regularly enroll 200 or more. Small programs often are ideal at promoting cultural integration with local students and the culture in general. The down side is that the program curriculum may be quite limited and fixed. Larger programs can offer a larger range of curricular offerings, excursions, and support services, which, on an economy of scale, become more affordable. This richness, however, sometimes comes at the expense of cultural integration: the group can become an American ghetto. While no program can predict precise enrollments, its sponsor should be able to estimate normal size.

Group size per se may be less important than where the program is located in relation to other programs in the same area. The proximity of many other programs can affect group dynamics and opportunities for cultural integration in the local environment. Also of concern is whether the program itself does the teaching and provides housing, etc., or whether students directly enroll in a foreign university and have opportunities to mingle with its student population. In short, a large program which integrates its students fully or partially in a foreign university represents a quite different educational and social experience than a small program which keeps them together in the same classroom and accommodations. Each has something to be said in its favor.

Language Instruction and Social Discourse. Language study in U.S. high schools and colleges has been slowly on the rise through the 1990s, but most U.S. students still do not possess enough functional proficiency prior to departure to allow them to study or work abroad exclusively in the language they are learning, at least at the start of their program. Even in programs which place a heavy premium on language acquisition overseas, most courses may still be taught in English. Students without a fluency in a foreign language were until recently limited to English-speaking countries and a handful of other programs. Now, virtually wherever they are, it is temptingly easy to resort to English, the leading world language, with other Americans, with foreign counterparts, and even within host families.

Programs in English, in countries where English is a second language, continue to grow. Some such programs are set up by U.S. institutions hoping to expand study abroad participation to students who otherwise might not consider it. Others were recently established by
countries themselves interested in internationalizing the higher education of their own students by bringing them into contact with students from other countries, using English as the language of instruction because it is the obvious linguistic medium. Students in such programs are almost always given the opportunity to learn the native language but take other course work in English. Many are amazed at how much language they can learn in a short while and the doors opened by their efforts. Most returnees report no relation between their previous efforts to master a foreign language and what they accomplished overseas.

Indeed, studying a foreign language where it is spoken presents unparalleled opportunities for quantum leaps forward in language proficiency, whatever the starting point. The key question is what, if any, level of foreign language proficiency is required by the program in order to function successfully in the unfamiliar linguistic environment of a foreign setting. Home campus instructors are usually the best judges of this. Acquiring a new cultural consciousness via language study, if not proficiency itself, should remain a goal for all program participants.

Where in the World to Go. Study abroad began as an exclusively Eurocentric venture. Indeed, about two-thirds of all current programming still takes place in Western European countries. There of course remain many sound reasons to choose to live and learn in such "traditional" locations, especially if language and other academic preparations for such study are well underway. But other parts of the global village also beckon and should be considered seriously. A variety of new program options now exist in Eastern Europe, for instance, in Russia and countries formerly part of the Soviet Union, and in the Baltic. In addition, excellent programs are now available throughout Latin America, Asia, Africa, Oceania, and the Middle East.

The arguments for considering programs in non-Western regions are compelling, not the least of which is their growing importance to American interests, world geopolitics, and the global economy and job market. Further, study in a developing country, or in a historically rich culture which is dramatically different from U.S. and Europe, can be especially eye-opening and rewarding. Obviously, somewhat different considerations—cost, transportation, communications, ethnicity, language barriers, safety, security, and health—come into play for students and parents considering programs in less-traditional locations. Program sponsors, however, should have responsible and helpful answers to all such questions.

Where one studies can also be very important to potential employers. A semester in Africa, studying its traditional art and culture, is much less likely to impress the average law school admissions committee than a similar period in Brussels studying the European Union. Of course, the opposite could also be true if an employer or graduate school was looking for evidence of adventurousness in applicants. Similarly, an English-language program which visits numerous countries and gives participants a strong sense of, say, comparative ecological systems and government policies, might appeal to a multinational chemical corporation but seem superficial to a company which valued employees with strong linguistic competencies.

Cost. Apart from the first questions concerning how much in the way of family and institutional resources can be realistically afforded to pay the costs, it is most important to determine what is and is not covered in program fees. No two programs, even in the same location, cost the same, nor are there any guarantees that the same features are covered.

Programs which may seem to be more expensive may offer more features or may just be more honest in leveling with students and parents (or, they may in fact offer less but charge more). Programs which list a lower fee may be in fact hiding costs from potential participants. The key for potential participants therefore is to decide what is essential to ensure the quality, integrity, and affordability of the program experience being sought and what is not. This involves carefully comparing not only sticker price but what one's money actually buys.

In sum, shopping widely and wisely involves taking into account program sponsorship, design, size, language, and location, as well as the ideal time to go overseas and how long to stay in order to achieve the maximum personal, educational, and career benefits. In addition, if receiving academic credit and financial aid to support participation in a given program are matters of importance, as they usually are, it is very important to get institutional approval prior to departure.

CHAPTER 10

STUDY ABROAD RESOURCES

Whether you're a student or adviser looking for the right international study program or someone who has the time for a long stay abroad and wants to combine the least expense with the most reward, you will find the information you need in the resources described below.

Much of the material is free for the asking. Books that are too expensive to buy can be found at good public libraries and college and university study abroad offices. We have arranged the listings by country and region and marked those of widest interest with an asterisk.

Ordering information for key study abroad publishers and organizations starts on page 130.

Asia

ABC's of Study in Japan. Association of International Education. Free from the Embassy of Japan, 2520 Massachusetts Ave. NW, Washington, DC 20008. Information on study and research at Japanese universities and graduate schools.

* China Bound (Revised): A Guide to Life in the PRC by Anne Thurston. National Academy of Sciences. 1994. 252 pp. $24.95 plus $4 shipping from National Academy Press, 2101 Constitution Ave. NW, Lockbox 285, Washington, DC 20055; (800) 624-6242. Updated classic on studying or teaching in the People's Republic of China. Invaluable for university students, researchers, and teachers.

Chinese Universities and Colleges. Chinese Education Association for International Exchange. 2nd edition, 1994. 760 pages. $75 plus $4 shipping from IIE. Profiles 1,062 higher education institutes in Peoples' Rep. of China with contact information.

Directory of Japan Specialists and Japanese Studies Institutions in the U.S. and Canada.

Patricia G. Steinhoff, ed. The Japan Foundation. 1995. $50 plus $8 shipping ($12 non-U.S.) from The Association for Asian Studies, 1 Lane Hall, Univ. of Michigan, Ann Arbor, MI 48109; (313) 665-2490, fax (313) 665-3801; postmaster@aasianst.org.

* **Japan: Exploring Your Options—A Guide to Work, Study, and Research in Japan.** Gateway Japan. 1995. 437 pp. $20 ($15 students) plus $5 shipping (checks payable to National Planning Association) from Gateway Japan, NPA, 1424 16th St., NW, Suite 700, Washington, DC 20036-2211; (202) 884-7642, fax (202) 797-5516; www.gw.japan.org. Study, cultural, and homestay programs; fellowships and research; English teaching.

* **Japanese Colleges and Universities, 1995-97** (also Scholarships For International Students). 1995. Available from the Association of International Education, 4-5-29 Komba, Meguro-ku, Tokyo 153, Japan; fax (011) 81-3-5454-5236 for ordering information.

Living in China: A Guide to Studying, Teaching, and Working in the PRC and Taiwan. Rebecca Weiner, Margaret Murphy, and Albert Li. China Books. 1991 (new edition February 1997). $16.95 from China Books and Periodicals, Inc., 2929 24th St., San Francisco, CA 94110. Contains directories of universities in China and Taiwan that offer study abroad or teaching placement.

Studying in India. Published by Indian Council for Cultural Relations. Free from Indian consulates and embassies. Basic information and advice on studies or research in India's numerous educational and scientific institutions.

Survey of Japanese Studies in the United States: The 1990s. $15 plus $4 shipping from Association for Asian Studies, 1 Lane Hall, Univ. Of Michigan, Ann Arbor, MI 48109-1290; (313) 665-2490, fax (313) 665-3801.

Universities Handbook (India). Published biannually. Available from: Association of Indian Universities, AIU House, 16 Kotla Marg, New Delhi 110002. Overview of courses of studies, faculty members, degrees, library and research facilities.

Yale-China Guide to Living, Studying, and Working in the People's Republic of China, Hong Kong, and Taiwan. 1996. The Yale-China Association, Inc., Box 208223, New Haven, CT 06520-8223; ycaffoc@minerva.cis.yale.edu.Asia.

Australia

A Guide to Australian Universities: A Directory of Programs Offered by Australian Universities for International Students. Magabook Pty. Ltd., 1995. P.O. Box 522, Randwick, NSW Australia 2031; (011) 61-2-398-2-5555, fax (011) 62-2-399-9465; info@magabook.com.au, http://www.magabook.com.au. Free. 1995. Highlights of Australian higher education and university profiles.

Studies in Australia: A Guide to Australian Study Abroad Programs. Magabook Pty. Ltd., 1995. Free from Magabook (above). Details on institutions and the courses they offer to North American students (including summer, recreational, and vocational programs) plus practical information on living in Australia.

Studies in Australia: A Guide for North American Students. 1996. Free from Australian Education Office, Australian Embassy, 1601 Massachusetts Ave. NW, Washington, DC 20036; (800) 245-2575. Information on year, semester, and summer programs; undergraduate, graduate, medical, and law degrees; scholarships and financial aid information (for both U.S. and Canadian citizens); internships.

Study Abroad in Australia: A Handbook for North American Students, Guidance Counsellors, Financial Aid Advisors and Study Abroad Staff. Annual. Free 30-page booklet from IDP Education Australia (North American Office), 5722 S. Flamingo Rd., #303, Cooper City, FL 33330; (954) 424-9255, fax (954) 424-9315; austsudy@aol.com. Guide to study abroad published by a consortium of 33 Australian universities.

Study and Travel in Australia: A Directory of Educational Opportunities in Australia for International Students. 1995. Free from Magabook (above). Overview of Australian education system and profiles secondary and vocational schools. Also available on CD-ROM.

Canada

Awards for Study in Canada. Free from Canadian Bureau for International Education (CBIE), 220 Laurier Ave. W., Suite 1100, Ottawa, ON K1P 5Z9; (613) 237-4820. Awards and traineeships open to foreign nationals.

Destination Canada: Information for International Students. Free from CBIE (above). General information on Canadian education system and tuition fees.

Directory of Canadian Universities. Biennial. Free from the Association of Universities and Colleges of Canada (AUCC), Publications Office, 151 Slater St., Ottawa, ON K1P 5N1, Canada. Details on Canadian universities and program offerings.

International Student's Handbook. 6th edition, 1995. 60 pages. CAN$12 postpaid in U.S. funds. Order from CBIE (above). Overview for students new to Canada.

Study Tours '96: The Canadian Guide to Learning Vacations Around the World. CAN$18.95 from Study Tours, Public Affairs, Athabasca Univ., Athabasca, AB T9S 1A1, Canada; (403) 675-6109, fax (403) 675-6467. Over 100 educational travel tours for students, seniors, teachers, professionals, couples, singles.

Europe

Academic Studies in the Federal Republic of Germany. Free from German Academic Exchange Service (DAAD).

Austria: Information for Foreign Students; Summer Language Courses for Foreign Students; Summer Courses in Austria. Annual. Free from the Austrian Cultural Institute, 950 3rd Ave., 20th Fl., New York, NY 10022; (212) 759-5165. Information for foreign students intending to study at an Austrian institution of higher learning.

Compendium: U.S. Assistance to Central and Eastern Europe and the Newly-Independent States. Francis A. Luzzato, ed. 1993. 347 pp. $15 postpaid from Citizen's Democracy Corps, 1735 I St., NW, Suite 720, Washington, DC 20006; (800) 394-1945. Directory to 700 U.S. organizations providing voluntary assistance (everything from volunteer-sending to educational exchanges to scholarships) in Eastern Europe and Russia.

Courses for Foreigners in Spain Sponsored by Spanish Institutions; American Programs in Spain; Study in Spain (entering the Spanish university system). Available from the Education Office of Spain, 150 5th Ave., Suite 918, New York, NY 10011.

Denmark: Guide for Young Visitors. European Youth Information and Counseling Association. 1992. Free. Available from Danish tourist board. Information on living and studying in Denmark for young people.

Directory of Programs in Russian, Eurasian, and East European Studies. AAASS, 8 Story St., Cambridge, MA 02138; (617) 495-0677, fax (617) 495-0680. The most comprehensive source of information available on U.S. university programs in Russian, Eurasian, and East European studies.

Fellowship Guide to Western Europe. Gina Bria Vescovi, ed. 7th edition, 1989. Available for $8 prepaid by check to "Columbia University-CES" from Council for European Studies, 808-809 International Affairs Bldg., Columbia Univ., New York, NY 10027.

The EARLS Guide to Language Schools in Europe 1995. Jeremy J. Garson, ed. 312 pp., $23.95. Order from Cassell, 215 Park Ave. S, 11th Fl., New York, NY 10003; (800) 561-7704, fax (703) 689-0660. Covers the 14 most popular European languages, including Russian. The guide profiles selected schools for each major language and gives details of specialized and general courses for children (ages seven and up), teenagers, adults, and business people.

German Language Courses for Foreign Applicants and Students in Austria. Austrian Foreign Student Service (ÖAD). Annual. Free from Austrian Cultural Institute, 950 3rd Ave., 20th Fl., New York, NY 10022.

Grants for Study and Research in the Federal Republic of Germany. Annual. Free from German Academic Exchange (DAAD).

Higher Education in the European Community. Brigitte Mohr and Ines Liebig, eds. 6th edition, 1990. $32.50 plus $3.25 shipping from Oryx Press. Information on study in 12-member nations of EU. New edition planned.

International Research and Exchanges Board (IREX) Grant. Opportunities for U.S. Scholars. Annual. Free from International Research and Exchanges Board, 1616 H. St., NW, Washington, DC 20006; (202) 628-8188. Descriptions of academic exchange programs and special projects administered by IREX in the Baltic States, Central and Eastern Europe, Mongolia, and the successor states of the former Soviet Union.

Sommerkürse in Bundesrepublik Deutschland. Annual. Free from German Academic Exchange Service (DAAD). In German. List of summer university programs for foreign students, including descriptions, dates, costs, and application information. Also information on courses of Goethe Institute, which offers language courses at 16 locations in Germany as well as at 150 cultural centers worldwide.

Studies in France. Free from the French Cultural Services, 972 5th Ave., New York, NY 10021; (212) 439-1455. Basic document outlining various possibilities for study in France, including direct enrollment at French institutions. Also, distributes French Courses for Foreign Students (annual list of French universities and language centers offering summer and year courses for foreigners) and I Am Going to France (extensive overview of university degree programs).

Study in Finland. Annual. Free from Information and Counseling Office, P.O. Box 3, FIN-00014, Univ. of Helsinki, Finland. English language programs and postgraduate studies in Finnish universities.

Study in Scandinavia 1997-98. Annual. Free from the American-Scandinavian Foundation, 725 Park Ave., New York, NY 10021. Summer and academic year programs offered to high school and college students and anyone interested in Scandinavia.

Studying in Denmark. Annual. Free from Danish consulates and embassies. Guide for foreign students who wish to pursue further and higher education in Denmark.

Summer Courses in Austria - "Campus Austria." Annual. Free from Austrian National

Tourist Office, Travel Information Center, P.O. Box 1142, New York, NY 10108-1142; (212) 944-6880 and Austrian Cultural Institute, 950 3rd Ave., 20th Fl., New York, NY 10022; (212) 759-5165.

Latin America/Caribbean

After Latin American Studies. A Guide to Graduate Study and Employment for Latin Americanists. Revised edition, 1995. Shirley A. Kregar and Annabelle Conroy. $10 from Latin American Studies, 4E04 Forbes Quad, Univ. of Pittsburgh, Pittsburgh, PA 15260; (412) 648-2199, fax (212) 249-3444; clas+@pitt.edu, www.pit.edu/~clas.

Guide to Financial Assistance for Students in Latin American Studies. Revised edition, 1996. Shirley A. Kregar and Silvia Lucrecia Del Cid. Free. Center for Latin American Studies (above). Fellowships, internships, doctoral dissertation research.

An International Students' Guide to Mexican Universities. Alan Adelman, ed. 1995. $19.95 plus $2 shipping from IIE. Profiles higher education institutions in Mexico.

*Travel Programs in Central America. Ann Salzarulo-McGuigan and Carolyn Martino, eds. 1996. 91 pp. $8 postpaid from San Diego Interfaith Task Force on Central America (IFTF), c/o 56 Seaview Ave., North Kingston, RI 02852. Comprehensive guide to over 300 organizations for study, and short- and long-term service in all fields. Essential for finding options located in this region.

Middle East/Africa

Beyond Safaris: A Guide to Building People-to-People Ties with Africa. Kevin Danaher. Africa World Press, Inc. 1991. $14.90 postpaid from Global Exchange, 2017 Mission St., #303, San Francisco, CA 94110; (800) 497-1994.

Handbook on how to help build and strengthen links between U.S. citizens and grassroots development efforts in Africa. Includes volunteering, studying, and socially responsible travel; annotated list of organizations.

Directory of Graduate and Undergraduate Programs and Courses in Middle East Studies in the U.S., Canada, and Abroad. Updated biannually. $20 for nonmembers, $10 for members. Published by Middle East Studies Association of North America, Univ. of Arizona, 1643 E. Helen St., P.O. Box 210410, Tuscon, AZ 85721; (520) 621-5850, fax (520) 626-9095.

A Guide to Israel Programs. Annual. $1.50 from World Zionist Organization, 515 Park Ave., New York, NY 10022. Information on summer study and volunteer work opportunities.

* Guide to Study Abroad in The Middle East, AMIDEAST. Available free through the World Wide Web, summer 1996. For WWW address, contact Kate Archambault at AMIDEAST; (202) 776-9670; karchambault@amideast.org. Study options throughout the Middle East, except Israel.

U.K. and Ireland

Graduate Study and Research in the U.K. The British Council (Education Information Service, 3100 Massachusetts Ave., NW, Washington, DC 20008-3600; fax 202-898-4612; study.uk@bc-washingtondc.sprint.com.) provides information on study opportunities in the U.K. at the graduate and research level, including program information, addresses, and funding.

The Guide to Postgraduate Study in Britain 1997. 1996. £15 plus £2.50 shipping from The Newpoint Publishing Co. Ltd., Windsor Court, East Grinstead House, East Grinstead,

West Sussex RH19 1XA; fax (011) 441 1342 335785. A comprehensive guide including both taught and research degrees.

Study Abroad in Ireland. Annual. Free from Irish Tourist Board offices. Academic programs and travel-study tours.

Study in Britain. Guide to undergraduate study and for visiting students. Free from British Information Services, 845 3rd Ave., New York, NY 10022; (212) 752-5747, fax (212) 758-5395, or from The British Council.

The Underground Guide to University Study in Britain and Ireland. Bill Griesar. 1992. $9.95 postpaid from Intercultural Press. Designed to guide the reader through the entire study abroad experience.

University Courses in Education Open to Students from Overseas 1998/99. £7.50 surface mail from Universities Council for the Education of Teachers, 58 Gordon Square, London WC1H ONT, England. Postgraduate courses in education at British universities open to foreigners.

Young Britain. Annual. Free from British Tourist Authority, 557 W. 57th St., New York, NY 10176-0799. Information on study, work, and accommodations.

Worldwide

* Academic Year Abroad 1997/98. Sara J. Steen, ed. $40.95 postpaid from IIE. Authoritative directory of over 2,400 semester and academic year programs offered by U.S. and foreign universities and private organizations. Indexed for internships, practical training, student teaching, adult courses, volunteer work, as well as fields of study.

The Advising Quarterly. Subscription: $40 ($50 overseas) from AMIDEAST. Quarterly dealing with trends and developments in international educational exchanges.

* Advisory List of International Educational Travel & Exchange Programs. Annual. Council on Standards for International Educational Travel, 3 Loudoun St. SE, Leesburg, VA 22075; (703) 771-2040, fax (703) 771-2046. $8.50. Lists programs for high school students which adhere to CSIET's standards and provides valuable information for prospective exchange students, host families, and schools.

AIFS Advisors' Guides. Various authors and dates. AIFS. Free. Published quarterly by AIFS; (800) 727-AIFS. Study abroad topics include political advocacy, nontraditional programs, promoting ethnic diversity, and reentry.

Archaeological Fieldwork Opportunities Bulletin. Annual in January. Archaeological Institute of America. $13 for AIA members, $15 non-members from Kendall/Hunt Publishing Co., Order Dept., 4050 Westmark Dr., Dubuque, IA 52002; (800) 228-0810. A comprehensive guide to excavations, field schools, and special programs with openings for volunteers, students, and staff worldwide.

Back in the USA: Reflecting on Your Study Abroad Experience and Putting It to Work. Dawn Kepets. NAFSA: Association of International Educators, 1995. $5 plus $2 shipping from NAFSA. A 34-page booklet which helps returning students put their cross-cultural experiences into perspective.

* Basic Facts on Study Abroad. IIE, NAFSA. Single copies free from IIE. Basic information for students interested in an educational experience abroad.

Black Students and Overseas Programs: Broadening the Base of Participation. Holly Carter, ed. 1991. $11.50 postpaid from Council. An 80-page collection of papers by faculty, administrators, and students.

*Commonwealth Universities Yearbook. Compiled by the Association of Commonwealth Universities. 71st edition, 1995. Two-volume set. $235 plus $6 shipping from Stockton Press. (Available in major libraries.) Detailed profiles of universities in all 34 of the Commonwealth countries, with comprehensive guide to degree programs and a register of 230,000 academic and administrative staff.

** Directory of International Internships: A World of Opportunities. Compiled and edited by Charles A. Gliozzo, Vernieka K. Tyson, and Adela Peña. 4th edition, 1997. Available for $25 postpaid from Michigan State Univ., Attn: International Placement, Career Services & Placement, 113 Student Services Bldg., East Lansing, MI 48824. Based on a survey of 4,000 organizations, this directory describes a variety of experiential educational opportunities—for academic credit, for pay, or simply for experience. Useful indexes. This is the only directory to internships entirely located abroad.

Educational Associate. IIE membership newsletter, published five times annually, provides a chronicle of trends and resources in international education.

The Exchange Student Survival Kit. Bettina Hansel. Intercultural Press. 1993. $12.95 plus $2 shipping. Practical guide for U.S. students going abroad or foreign students coming to the U.S.

Film and Video Resources for International Exchange. Lee Zeigler. 1992. NAFSA. Available for $6.50 plus $2 shipping from Intercultural Press. Details on over 300 documentary videos and films of interest to study abroad advisers, foreign student advisers, and ESL instructors on U.S. campuses.

Frontiers: The Interdisciplinary Journal of Study Abroad. Brian Whalen, ed. Annual. $12 per issue from: Frontiers, Boston Univ., International Programs, 232 Bay State Rd., Boston, MA 02215; fax (617) 353-5402; bwhalen@bu.edu. A forum for research-based articles on study abroad.

Guide to Careers and Graduate Education in Peace Studies. 1996. $4.50 from PAWSS, Hampshire College, Amherst, MA 01002. Includes information on internships, fellowships, and relevant organizations.

A Handbook for Creating Your Own Internship in International Development. Overseas Development Network. $7.95 plus $1.50 shipping. How to arrange a position with an international development organization; evaluate your skills, motivations, and learning objectives; practical advice on financing an internship, living overseas, and returning home.

Harvard Guide to International Experience by William Klingelhofer. 1989. 159 pp. $15 postpaid from Office of Career Services, 54 Dunster St., Harvard Univ., Cambridge, MA 02138; (617) 495-2595. Half of this book is devoted to working or volunteering abroad, with numerous reports by students.

The High School Student's Guide to Study, Travel, and Adventure Abroad. Council. 5th edition, 1995., 308 pp. St. Martin's Press. $13.95 from Council. Describes over 200 programs of all types for people aged 13-18.

Home from Home. Central Bureau for Educational Visits and Exchanges. 3rd edition, 1994. $22.95 postpaid from IIE. Compiled from a comprehensive database used by U.K. government agencies, this guide contains details on homestays, home exchanges, hospitality exchanges, and school exchanges worldwide. Includes profiles of organizations by country.

* How to Read Study Abroad Literature. Lily von Klemperer. Reprinted in IIE's Academic Year Abroad and Vacation Study Abroad and in NAFSA's Guide to Education Abroad.

What to look for in ads for a study abroad program.

Including Women with Disabilities in International Development Programs. Cindy Lewis. MIUSA. 1996. Contact MIUSA for price. Describes the efforts and successes of women with disabilities in other countries.

* Increasing Participation of Ethnic Minorities in Study Abroad. 1991. Council. Free. A brochure prepared to assist advisers in increasing enrollments of underrepresented minorities.

International Educator. NAFSA. Quarterly magazine. $24 per year in U.S.; $36 Canada and Mexico; $48 elsewhere. Essays on major issues and trends in international education.

International Exchange Locator. Alliance for International Educational and Cultural Exchange. 1996. $33.95 postpaid from IIE (fax 301-206-9789). Key information on nearly 100 organizations responsible for the exchange of over 100,000 U.S. and foreign nationals annually.

International Handbook of Universities. 14th edition, 1996. $245 plus $6 shipping. International Association of Universities. (Available in major libraries.) Distributed in U.S. and Canada by Stockton Press. Entries for more than 5,700 universities and other institutions of higher education in 170 countries and territories. Complements Commonwealth Universities Yearbook, 1995-96.

NAFSA Newsletter. NAFSA: Association of International Educators; included in annual membership fee. Published 8 times per year, contains current information on international educational exchange and related topics.

* NAFSA's Guide to Education Abroad for Advisers and Administrators, edited by William Hoffa and John Pearson. 1997. 492 pp.

$36 (members) or $45 (non-members) plus $5 shipping from NAFSA Publications; (800) 836-4994. An indispensable reference for education abroad offices, providing an overview of principles and practices, and detailed information for advisers; not a directory of programs. Includes one chapter on advising for work abroad and international careers.

New Manual for Inclusion of Persons with Disabilities in International Exchange Programs. MIUSA. 1996. Contact MIUSA for price. Information on accessibility, resource lists to recruit people with disabilities, and checklists to identify specific needs of participants with disabilities.

Planning for Study Abroad. IIE. 1989. $53.95 (members $26.95) postpaid from IIE. Advising video that presents basic information on study abroad from students acting as peer counselors.

Planning Guides Catalog. Transitions Abroad Publishing, Inc., P.O. Box 1300, Amherst, MA 01004-1300. Free. Descriptive listing of planning guides on international work, study, living, educational and socially responsible travel.

Smart Vacations. The Traveler's Guide to Learning. Council. 1993. 320 pp. $14.95 from Council. Adult traveler's guide to learning abroad includes, in addition to study tours, opportunities for voluntary service, field research and archaeological digs, environmental and professional projects, fine arts, and more.

Student Travels Magazine. Fall and spring. Free from Council. A magazine that covers rail passes, insurance, work and study opportunities abroad, airfares, car rentals, and other services offered by CIEE and Council Travel. Includes articles by students on their experiences abroad.

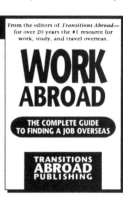

Students Abroad: Strangers at Home—Education for a Global Society. Norman Kauffmann, Judith Martin, and Henry Weaver. 1992. $19.95 plus $3 shipping from Intercultural Press. The study abroad experience examined from the student's viewpoint, followed by a theoretical framework for understanding the effects of study abroad and recommendations for increasing effectiveness of programs.

* Study Abroad 1998: A Guide to Semester, Summer, and Year Abroad Academic Programs. Peterson's Guides. 956 pages. $29.95 plus $6.75 shipping. Over 1,000 pages of detailed information on over 2,000 programs at more than 500 accredited institutions worldwide.

Study Abroad, 1996-1997. UNESCO. Vol. 29, 1995. $29.95 plus $4 shipping from UNIPUB. Describes approximately 4,000 international study programs and sources of financial assistance in more than 100 countries.

Study Abroad: The Astute Student's Guide. David Judkins. Williamson, 1989. $13.95 plus $3 shipping from Intercultural Press. Sound but dated advice on choosing a program abroad.

Survival Kit for Overseas Living by L. Robert Kohls. 3rd ed., 1996. Best-selling guide to adaptation to living abroad. $11.95 plus $3 s/h from Intercultural Press.

Teenager's Vacation Guide to Work, Study, and Adventure Abroad by Victoria Pybus. 1991. £6.95 plus £2.50 shipping or dollar equivalent from Vacation Work. Addressed to a British audience, it covers jobs, study courses, and adventure holidays available in Britain and abroad during school vacations.

Time Out: Taking a Break from School to Travel, Work, and Study in the U.S. and Abroad. Robert Gilpin with Caroline Fitzgibbons. 1992. $12. Simon and Schuster; (800) 223-2348. Describes over 350 programs in U.S. and abroad for high school students who want to travel and learn.

The Travel Journal: An Assessment Tool for Overseas Study. Nancy Taylor. Council. 1991. Occasional Paper on International Educational Exchange No. 27. $5 from Council. Practical guide to writing and evaluating student travel journals.

Update. Monthly. Free. Council's monthly newsletter reports on developments in the field of international educational exchange as well as programs and events organized by the Council.

* Vacation Study Abroad 1998/99. Sara J. Steen, ed. $40.95 postpaid from IIE. Authoritative guide to over 2,000 summer and short-term study programs sponsored by U.S. and foreign organizations and language schools in over 60 countries. Indexed for internships, practical training, student teaching, adult courses, volunteer service, as well as fields of study.

What in the World is Going On? A Guide for Canadians Wishing to Work, Volunteer or Study in Other Countries by Alan Cumyn. 5th edition, 1996. CAN$20 including shipping from Canadian Bureau for International Education, 220 Laurier Ave. W, Suite 1100, Ottawa, ON K1P 5Z9, Canada; (613) 237-4820. Includes a comprehensive listing of work abroad possibilities. Some listings restricted to Canadian citizens. Indexed by country and field.

Whole World Guide to Language Learning by Terry Marshall, 1990. How to learn a language while abroad. $15.95 plus $3 s/h from Intercultural Press (above).

Wilderness U. Opportunities for Outdoor Education in the U.S. and Abroad. Bill

McMillon, 1992. Chicago Review Press. $12.95. A descriptive listing of educational organizations offering programs in and about the great outdoors.

* **Work, Study, Travel Abroad: The Whole World Handbook.** St. Martin's Press. 12th edition, 1994-95. $7.95 plus $1.50 book rate or $3 first class postage from Council. Travel, work, and study opportunities around the world.

* **World Academic Database CD-ROM.** 1996. $435 plus $6 shipping from Stockton Press. Combines the 14th edition of International Handbook of Universities, 20th edition of World List of Universities, with additional information from TRACE. Most complete source of information on education around the world. (This and the two publications following are available in major libraries.)

World List of Universities. 21st edition, 1997. $170 plus $6 shipping from Stockton Press. Addresses of over 9,000 institutions of higher education worldwide.

The World of Learning. 46th edition, 1996. Annual. $415 plus postage from International Publications Service, c/o Taylor & Francis Group, 1900 Frost Rd., Suite 101, Bristol, PA 19007. This authoritative guide lists over 26,000 institutions of higher education by country, gives names of staff and faculty, and includes information on international organizations involved in education throughout the world.

A World of Options: A Guide to International Exchange, Community Service and Travel for Persons with Disabilities. Christa Bucks, Mobility International USA. 3rd edition, 1996. Contact MIUSA for price. A comprehensive guide to international exchange, study, and volunteer opportunities for people with disabilities.

A Year Between. Central Bureau for Educational Visits and Exchanges. 2nd edition, 1994. $23.95 postpaid from IIE. Designed for young British adults who have a year between high school and college, or during college, and want to explore and learn. Volunteer work, internships service, and study options.

Funding for International Activities

Council Scholarships. ISIC Third World Grants cover transportation costs for undergraduates to study, work, or volunteer in developing countries. Available to Council member school students only. Bailey Minority Student Scholarships cover transportation costs for undergraduate students of color to study, work, or volunteer with any Council program. Contact Council at (888) COUNCIL.

Fellowships in International Affairs: A Guide to Opportunities in the U.S. and Abroad. Women International Security. 1994. 195 pp. $17.95 plus $3.50 shipping from Lynne Rienner Publishers, 1800 30th St., Suite #314, Boulder, CO 80301; (303) 444-6684. Well-researched directory to fellowships and grants for students, scholars, and practitioners (most are for graduate and postdoctoral students or professionals). Very useful indexes, including one for non-U.S. applicants.

* **Financial Aid for Research and Creative Activities Abroad 1996-1998** by Gail Ann Schlachter and R. David Weber. 1996. 440 pp. $45 plus $4 shipping from: Reference Service Press, 1100 Industrial Rd., Suite 9, San Carlos, CA 94070; (415) 594-0743, fax (415) 594-0411. Lists over 1,300 funding sources that support research, professional development, teaching assignments, and creative activities. Sources mainly for graduate students, postdoctorates, professionals. Very useful indexes.

* Financial Aid for Study Abroad: A Manual for Advisers and Administrators. Stephen Cooper, William W. Cressey, and Nancy K. Stubbs, eds. 1989. $12 (nonmembers) $8 (members) plus $5 shipping from NAFSA. How to use primarily federal sources of financial aid for study abroad programs for undergraduate students and how to utilize this information to help shape institutional policies.

Financial Aid for Study and Training Abroad 1996-1998 by Gail Ann Schlachter and R. David Weber. 1996. 275 pp. $38.50 plus $4 shipping from Reference Service Press. Lists 1,000 funding sources that support formal educational programs such as study abroad, training, internships, workshops, and seminars. Sources mainly for undergraduate, high school and graduate students, as well as postdoctorates. Very useful indexes.

* Financial Resources for International Study. Sara J. Steen, ed. 1996. IIE. $43.95 postpaid from IIE. Lists funding sources available to support undergraduate, graduate, post-doctorate, and professional learning abroad, from study and research to internships and other work experiences. Very useful indexes, including field of study, internships/work abroad.

Foundation Center Publications Catalog. Free. Call (800) 424-9836. The Foundation Center maintains a comprehensive and up-to-date database on foundations and corporate giving programs.

Fulbright and Other Grants for Graduate Study Abroad. Annual. Free from IIE. Describes grants administered by IIE for study and research abroad.

The Grants Register. 11th edition, 1993-95 (revised biennially in December). St. Martin's Press, Inc. $89.95. Bills itself as "the standard directory of scholarships, fellowships, prizes and other sources of financial aid for professional and academic work beyond the undergraduate level."

The International Scholarship Book. Daniel J. Cassidy. 5th edition, 1996. $24.95 paper, $32.95 cloth plus $4 shipping from Prentice-Hall Publishers, 200 Old Tappan Rd., Old Tappan, NJ 07675; (201) 767-5937. Information on private sector funding sources for study abroad compiled by the National Scholarship Research Service.

Money for International Exchange in the Arts. Jane Gullong and Noreen Tomassi, ed. 1992. 126 pp. $16.95 postpaid from IIE. Lists grant sources, exchange programs, and artists residencies and colonies for individuals and organizations in the creative arts.

Resources for International Arts Exchange. National Endowment for the Arts, 1100 Pennsylvania Ave., Washington, DC 20506; (800) 727-6232 (orders only). Guide for artists and organizations contemplating work abroad.

Internet Resources

INTER-L, SUB request to: listserv@vtvm1.cc.vt.edu. Essential for US university advisers working with foreign students; esoteric for anyone else. Owner: NAFSA.

The following web sites provide links, ordering information for printed material, and a vast variety of other information too recent to be found in books. All web site addresses begin with http://.

www.amideast.org/mideaststudy.html. AMIDEAST's Guide to Study Abroad in the Middle East. Kate Archambault. Up-to-date information on study in Middle East and North Africa.

www.cie.uci.edu/~cie. Univ. of California—Irvine, International Opportunities Program (IOP). Ruth Sylte. One of the most comprehensive sites on the web, with directories of U.S.- and non-U.S.-based study abroad programs and extensive guides for working abroad. Also features a how-to Internet user manual for students and advisers, "The World at Your Fingertips."

www.ciee.org. Council on International Educational Exchange (CIEE)/Council Travel. Information on study, work, and volunteer programs offered through CIEE only, as well as services offered by Council Travel (ISIC student IDs, etc.)

www.finaid.org. Home page of the National Association of Financial Aid Administrators (NASFAA) includes sections on financial aid and scholarships for study abroad.

www.iie.org. Institute of International Education. Provides information about services and publications offered by the IIE, including Fulbright scholarships. Publishes Academic Year Abroad and Vacation Study Abroad, authoritative directories of education abroad programs. Also publishes directories of financial aid for study abroad.

www.istc.umn.edu. Univ. of Minnesota, International Study and Travel Center (ISTC). Richard Warzecha. Excellent searchable database for study abroad, low-cost study abroad, scholarships, and volunteer abroad directory.

www.nafsa.org. NAFSA: Association of International Educators. NAFSA. Essential professional resources for advisers and administrators in international education. Not a directory of overseas programs.

www.petersons.com. Peterson's Education Center, Study Abroad Sector. A commer-cial directory of study abroad programs. Distributes Vacation Work publications.

www.pitt.edu/~cjp/rees.html. REESWeb: Russian and East European Studies, Univ. of Pittsburgh. Karen Rondestvedt. Click on "Academic Programs and Centers" for listings of language and study abroad programs. Links to other REES centers and information.

www.sas.upenn.edu/AfricanStudies/AS.html. African Studies WWW, Univ. of Pennsylvania. Prof. Sandra Barnes. A search using the phrase "study abroad" produces a list of study abroad programs. Outstanding links to African and African-American information.

www.studyabroad.com. Studyabroad.com. Commercial directory of study and work abroad programs.

www.transabroad.com. *Transitions Abroad*'s guide to work, study, and travel abroad. Current educational travel and study resource and program information.

www.wzo.org.il. World Zionist Organization. Information on summer study and volunteer work opportunities, academic year study, internships, and kibbutzim in Israel.

Internships Abroad

* **American-Scandinavian Foundation.** Free brochure on study and scholarships (all fields) and work opportunities. This non-profit organization also offers paid internships in Scandinavia in engineering, teaching English as a foreign language, and agricultural fields. Apply for internships by late Dec. ASF also assists with obtaining work permits for Scandinavia. Contact ASF at 725 Park Ave., New York, NY 10021;

(212) 879-9779, fax (212) 249-3444; asf@amscan.org.

International Health Electives for Medical Students. 1993. American Medical Student Association. $31 ($21 members) for 4-volume set, also available separately, from AMSA Publications, 1902 Association Dr., Reston, VA 20191; (703) 620-6600 ext. 217, fax (703) 620-5873; amsatf@amsa.org, www.amsa.org. Overseas internships for third- or fourth-year medical students. Related titles, **A Student's Guide to International Health** ($7.50/$5.50) and **Cross-Cultural Medicine: What to Know Before You Go** ($7/$5), also available from AMSA.

Key Publishers and Organizations

American-Scandinavian Foundation, Exchange Division, 725 Park Ave., New York, NY 10021. Free publications on study, work, and travel in Scandinavia. Offers scholarships.

AMIDEAST, 1730 M St. NW, Washington, DC 20036-4505; (202) 776-9600.

British Information Services, 845 3rd Ave., New York, NY 10022. Free fact sheets on study in Britain.

French Cultural Services, 972 5th Ave., New York, NY 10021. Free publications on French higher education and opportunities for U.S. students.

German Academic Exchange Service (DAAD), 950 3rd Ave., 19th Fl., New York, NY 10022; (212) 758-3223, fax (212) 755-5780; daad@daad.org, http://www.daad.org. Free materials on German education; offers scholarships.

Global Exchange, 2017 Mission St., #303, San Francisco, CA 94110; (800) 497-1994.

Institute of International Education (IIE), IIE Books, P.O. Box 371, Annapolis Junction, MD 20701-0371; (800) 445-0443, fax (301) 953-2838; iiebooks@iie.org, www.iie.org. Publisher of authoritative directories for study or teaching abroad and financial aid, and distributor of Central Bureau (U.K.) publications on working abroad. Add $2 each shipping for books under $25; $4 each for books over $25, or 10 percent for orders over $100.

Intercultural Press, P.O. Box 700, Yarmouth, ME 04096; (207) 846-5168. Books on intercultural relations, crosscultural communications, and living and working abroad. Free quarterly catalog.

Mobility International USA (MIUSA), P.O. Box 10767, Eugene, OR 97440; (541) 343-1284 (voice and TDD), fax (541) 343-6812. Publications and videos on including persons with disabilities in international exchange and travel programs.

NAFSA Publications, P.O. Box 1020, Sewickley, PA 15143; Fax (412) 741-0609. Free catalog. Publishers of informational materials, geared toward its professional membership, on study, work, and travel abroad opportunities as well as advising and admissions. To rush order publications: (800) 836-4994.

Organizations of American States, General Secretariat, Washington, DC 20006. Materials on Latin America.

Oryx Press, 4041 N. Central Ave., #700, Phoenix, AZ 85012-5397; (800) 279-ORYX. Guides on higher education abroad.

Overseas Development Network, 333 Valencia St., Suite 330, San Francisco, CA 94103; (415) 431-4204, fax (415) 431-5953; odn@igc.org, http://www.igc.apc.org/

odn/. Publishes material on work and internships in international development.

Peterson's Guides, 202 Carnegie Center, P.O. Box 2123, Princeton, NJ 08543-2123; (800) 338-3282. Guides to jobs and careers, study abroad. U.S. distributor for Vacation Work Publications.

Seven Hills Book Distributors, 49 Central Ave., Cincinnati, OH 45202; (800) 545-2005. Carries a wide range of travel books and maps from foreign publishers, including British Tourist Authority publications and Vacation Work publications.

Stockton Press, 345 Park Ave. S., 10th Fl., New York, NY 10010-1707; (800) 221-2123 or (212) 689-9200, fax (212) 689-9711.

Superintendent of Documents, U.S. Government Printing Office, Washington, DC 20402. A wide range of material, including country "Background Notes" series.

The African-American Institute, 833 U.N. Plaza, New York, NY 10017. Publications on Africa.

The Central Bureau, Seymour Mews House, Seymour Mews, London W1H 9PE; (011) 44-71-486-5101. Publishes information for people of all ages on work, study, and travel abroad. Most books available from IIE or Seven Hills.

The Council on International Education Exchange (CIEE), Publication Dept., 205 E. 42nd St., New York, NY 10017-5706; (212) 661-1414, ext. 1108. Publishers of materials on study, job opportunities, and inexpensive travel abroad.

UNIPUB, 4611-F Assembly Dr., Lanham, MD 20706; (800) 274-4888. UNESCO publications on higher education; distributes E.U. publications.

Vacation Work Publications, 9 Park End St., Oxford OX1 1HJ, England; (011) 44-1865-241978, fax 790885. Books on employment and budget travel abroad. Books without U.S. distribution can also be purchased from Seven Hills, 49 Central Avenue, Cincinnati, OH 45202; (800) 545-2005, fax (513) 381-0753.

Williamson Publishing Co., Church Hill Rd., P.O. Box 185, Charlotte, VT 05445; (800) 234-8796. Books on study, careers, and alternative travel abroad.

CHAPTER 11

ADULT STUDY/TRAVEL PROGRAMS

The following list of adult study/travel programs was supplied by the organizers. Contact the program directors to confirm costs, dates, and other details. If you do not see the program you want in the country of your choice, look in the "Worldwide" listings at the end of the section for programs located in several different regions.

Africa

Bicycle Africa Tours. Village-based, cross-cultural bicycle tours to all parts of Africa. Cycling difficulty is moderate. Each program is different, but all focus on the diversity of the culture, social institutions, and environment, as well as the complexity of the history, economy, culture, and society. Programs are led by African studies specialists.

Dates: Jan (Uganda), Feb (Kenya/Tanzania), Apr (Tunisia), Jun-Aug (Zimbabwe), Aug-Sep (Malawi), Sep-Oct (Eritrea/Ethiopia), Oct-Nov (Senegal/Mali), Nov (Burkina Faso/Togo/Benin). Cost: $990-$1,290 plus airfare for 2 weeks. Includes food, lodging, guides, and fees. Contact: David Mozer, Director, International Bicycle Fund/Bicycle Africa, 4887 Columbia Dr. S. #T-7, Seattle, WA 98108; Tel./fax (206) 767-0848; intlbike@scn.org; www. halcyon.com/fkroger/bike/bikeafr.htm.

East Africa with the Experts. Join America's most distinguished museums, zoological societies and wildlife organizations on safaris to East and South Africa. Trips are led by outstanding local naturalists and feature excellent accommodations in the best reserves for animal viewing. Park East Tours has been a leader in travel to East Africa for over 30 years and is the 1996 recipient of the Africa Travel Association Award for Outstanding Achievement in the Promotion of Responsible Tourism to Africa.

Dates: All of 1998. Cost: From $2,995 to $5,995 (depending on program, land and air from New York). Contact: Marcia Gordon, Park East Tours, 1841 Broadway, New York, NY 10023; (800) 223-6078 ext. 316

or (212) 765-4870 ext 316, fax (212) 265-8952.

Travel/Study Seminars. Learn from Southern Africans of diverse backgrounds about their economic, political, and social realities. Emphasis on the views of the poor and oppressed. Programming in South Africa and Namibia. Call for a free listing of upcoming programs.

Dates: Ongoing. Cost: $3,500-$4,400 depending on length of trip. Contact: Center for Global Education, Augsburg College, 2211 Riverside Ave., Box 307TR, Minneapolis, MN 55454; (800) 299-8889, fax (612) 330-1695; globaled@augsburg.edu, www.augsburg.edu/global.

Antarctica

Falklands, South Georgia, and Antarctica. Ecologists Gail and Doug Cheeseman have again chartered an entire ice ship for 25 days. They and their 10 experienced naturalist leaders and 84 passengers will make approximately 25 Zodiac landings at remote penguin and albatross colonies at South Georgia and the Antarctic Peninsula and visit 5 islands in the Falklands. Only eligibility requirement is to agree with nonsmoking policy.

Dates: Oct 12-Nov 5 (1997). Cost: $5,160 plus airfare. The Cheesemans assist with flight bookings. Contact: Gail and Doug Cheeseman, Cheesemans' Ecology Safaris, 20800 Kittredge Rd., Saratoga, CA 95070; (800) 527-5330; cheesemans@aol.com, www.cheesemans.com.

Argentina

Instituto de Lengua Española (ILEE). Located downtown. Dedicated exclusively to teaching Spanish to foreigners. Small groups and private classes year round. All teachers hold a university degree. Method is intensive, conversation-based. Student body is international, mostly European. Highly recommended worldwide. Ask for individual recommendations in U.S.

Dates: Year round. Cost: Four-week intensive program (20 hours a week) including homestay $1,400; 2 weeks $700. Individual classes: $19 per hour. Registration fee (includes books) $100. Contact: ILEE, Daniel Korman, Director, Lavalle 1619, 7º C, (1048) Buenos Aires, Argentina; Tel./fax (011) 54-1-375-0730. In U.S.: David Babbitz, fax (415) 431-5306; ilee@overnet.com.ar, www.studyabroad.com/ilee.

Asia

Travel-Study Seminars. Visit with Asians from China, Hong Kong and Indochina as their countries undergo profound economic changes. Pursue critical questions, such as: Do these changes also bring political pluralism? What impact do economic changes have on the education and outlook of youth? On the natural environment? Who benefits from economic restructuring? Call for more information on current trips.

Dates: Varies. Cost: Approx. $3,800-$4,300 depending on length and destinations. Contact: Center for Global Education, Augsburg College, 2211 Riverside Ave., Box 307TR, Minneapolis, MN 55454; (800) 299-8889, fax (612) 330-1695; globaled@augsburg.edu, www.augsburg.edu/global.

Australia

Special Interest and Study Tours. Personalized programs for individuals and groups of all ages. We combine education, recreation, accommodations (homestay available), and transportation. Based in tropical Cairns with coverage throughout Australia. Subject areas include: aboriginal dreamtime and culture, Great Barrier Reef, rainforest and savannah. Diving, environmental interpretation, flora and fauna, bird watching, tropical islands and wilderness, adventure safaris and farmstay.

Dates: Year round. Start any date. Cost: Prices and customized itineraries on application. Contact: Murray Simpson, Study Venture International, P.O. Box 229A, Stratford Qld., 4870 Australia; (011) 61-70-411622, fax 552044; svi@ozemail.com.au; www.ozemail.au/~svi.

WWOOFING. Work in exchange for keep while learning organic growing with a farmer or enjoy a cultural exchange with Australian small businesses including farms, working for your keep (state your interest).

Dates: Year round. Cost: $25 single, $30 double (includes insurance). Contact: WWOOF Australia, Buchan, Victoria 3885, Australia.

Brazil

Amazon Jungle Safari. An 8-day, natural history adventure offering a valuable rainforest experience. Overnights in serene jungle lodges, located in remote reserves for great bird/wildlife viewing. The small group educational tour is escorted by a qualified U.S. biologist and expert resident guides. Also experience the only Treetop Canopy Walkway in the Americas, over 1,500 feet long and 115 feet high. Also available are Amazon riverboat cruises and extensions to Cuzco and Machu Picchu.

Dates: Monthly. Cost: $1,895 including air from Miami, lodging, all meals, excursions. Contact: Charlie Strader, Explorations Inc., 27655 Kent Rd., Bonita Springs, FL 34135; (800) 446-9660, fax (941) 992-7666; cesxplor @aol.com.

Canada

Canadian Outdoor Leadership Training. Our wilderness-based experiential educa-

tion program will develop your skills to a level required to lead/instruct wilderness and outdoor pursuits at a basic level. It is ideal for those participants anticipating a career in this field and also of great value to those individuals wanting to take time out to develop their own personal direction and potential.

Dates: Mar 23-Jul 6; Apr 18-Jul 31; Aug 14-Nov 26 (1997). Cost: $7,895. Contact: Strathcona Park Lodge C.O.L.T., P.O. Box 2160, Campbell River, BC V9W 5C9, Canada.

Ecole de français, Montréal. For the last 50 years, the Ecole de français has offered courses in French as a second language to students from around the world. The Ecole is continually improving its programs to meet the changing needs of its students. Choose from Oral and Written Communication French (beginner to advanced), Workshop on Teaching French as a Second Language (for teachers), Contemporary Québec Culture (for advanced students), Business French (intermediate to advanced students).

Dates: Summer 1: Jul 6-Jul 24; summer 2: Jul 27-Aug 14; fall 98: Sep 10-Dec 11; winter 99: Jan 8-Apr 13; spring 98: May 19-Jun 11. Cost: Spring, summer: (3 weeks, 60 hours) CAN$495; summer (3 weeks, 45 hours) CAN$390; fall and winter: (12 weeks, 240 hours) CAN$1,495 (subject to change). Contact: Serge Bienvenu, Coordinator, Ecole de français, Faculté de l'education permanente, Université de Montreal, C.P. 6128, succursale Centre-ville, Montréal, PQ, H3C 3J7, Canada; (514) 343-6090, fax (514) 343-2430; infolang@fep.umontreal.ca, http://alize.ere. umontreal.ca/~tousyves/fep.

Language Studies Canada Montréal. Using a multi-skill approach students develop effective communication skills in French. Classes are informative, practical, and enjoyable. Six levels of 4 weeks each, intensive, 6 hours daily or semi-intensive, 4 hours daily. Maximum of 14 students per class. Audio-visual equipment, multi-media Student Resource Center. Optional activity program. Homestay and alternate accommodations available.

Dates: Two-week courses begin any Monday from Jan 13 (1997) year round. Other programs offered: one-on-one instruction, year round; 2-week. Group 5 executive courses, Jun-Oct; Summer Language Adventure (13 to 17-year-olds), 2-9 weeks in Jul and Aug. Cost: Two weeks intensive program $535; homestay accommodations $400. Cost of other services available upon request. Contact: Language Studies Canada Montréal, 1450 City Councillors, Montréal, PQ, H3A 2E6, Canada; (514) 499-9911, fax (514) 499-0332.

Queen's Univ. School of English. The Queen's Univ. School of English offers 5- and 12-week courses year round at one of Canada's oldest and best-known universities in an almost totally English-speaking community. Students have the option of living in a University residence with monitors, in a homestay, or in University cooperative housing. The English Only Rule is strictly enforced.

Dates: 1998: Jan 7-Apr 10, May 6-Aug 7, May 18-Jun 19, July 6-Aug 7, Sep 9-Dec 11. Cost: International students: $2,550 12 weeks; $1,275 5 weeks, plus mandatory health insurance (price varies). Contact: Mrs. Eleanor Rogers, Director, The School of English, Queen's Univ., Kingston, ON K7L 3N6, Canada; (613) 545-2472, fax (613) 545-6809; soe@post.queensu.ca, www.queensu.ca/soe.

Central America

Global Awareness Through Experience (GATE). GATE offers alternative tourism through programs in Mexico, Central America (Guatemala, El Salvador), and Central Europe. Participants connect with Third World people in face-to-face dialogue to explore social, political, economic, religious, and cultural issues. Mutual learning happens between GATE participants and the indigenous people.

Dates: Various open groups. Special groups also welcome. Cost: $650 (Mexico) to $1,500 (Europe) plus airfare. Contact: Beverly Budelier, GATE, 912 Market St., La Crosse, WI 54601; (608) 791-5283, fax (608) 782-6301; gateusa@juno.com, www.fspa.org/Missions/GATE/GATE.html.

International Travel Seminar. More than 20 trips are offered each year to Nicaragua, El Salvador, Guatemala, and Mexico to meet with the poor and disenfranchised, women's groups, cooperatives, and alternative political parties, as well as decision-makers from the government, businesses, and churches. Programs are designed to bring you face-to-face with Latin American people's struggle for freedom, justice, and human dignity.

Dates: Trips of 7-14 days throughout the year. Cost: From $1,300-$2,500 (includes airfare, food, lodging, and program). Contact: Travel Seminar Division, Center for Global Education, Augsburg College, 2211 Riverside Ave., Box 307TR, Minneapolis, MN 55454; (800) 299-8889, (612) 330-1159, fax (612) 330-1695; globaled@augsburg.edu, www.augsburg.edu/global.

Travel/Study Seminars. Learn from Central Americans of diverse backgrounds about their economic, political, and social realities. Emphasis on the views of the poor and oppressed. Programming in El Salvador, Guatemala, and Nicaragua. Call for a free listing of upcoming programs.

Dates: Ongoing. Cost: $1,500-$2,500 depending on length of trip. Contact: Center for Global Education, Augsburg College, 2211 Riverside Ave., Box 307TR, Minneapolis, MN 55454; (800) 299-8889, fax (612) 330-1695; globaled@augsburg.edu, www.augsburg.edu/global.

Costa Rica

COSI (Costa Rica Spanish Institute). COSI offers high quality instruction at reasonable prices. We offer classes in San José and at a beautiful beach. Costa Rican-owned and very efficiently operated.

Dates: Year round. Contact: Marvin Lopez, COSI, P.O. Box 1366-2050, San Pedro, San José, Costa Rica; (011) 506-253-9272, fax 253-2117. From U.S. (800) 771-5184; cosicr@ sol.racsa.co.cr.

Costa Rican Language Academy. Costa Rican-owned and- operated language school offers first-rate Spanish instruction in a warm and friendly environment. Teachers with university degrees. Small groups or private classes. Included free in the programs are airport transportation, coffee and natural refreshments, excursions, and Latin dance, Costa Rican cooking, music, and conversation classes to provide students with complete cultural immersion.

Dates: Year round (start anytime). Cost: $135 per week or $220 per week for program with homestay. All other activities and services included at no additional cost. Contact: Costa Rican Language Academy, P.O. Box 336-2070, San José, Costa Rica; (011) 506-221-1624 or 233-8914 or 233-8938, fax 233-8670. In the U.S.: (800) 854-6057; crlang@ sol.racsa.co.cr., www.crlang.co.cr/index.html.

Enjoy Learning Spanish Faster. Techniques developed from our ongoing research enable students at Centro Linguistico Latinoamericano to learn more, faster, in a comfortable environment. Classes are 2-5 students plus group learning activities; conversations with middle-class homestay families (1 student per family). Homestays are within walking distance of school in small town (14,000 population) near the capital, San Jose.

Dates: Year round. Classes begin every Monday, at all levels. Cost: $295 per week for 25 hours of classes. Includes tuition, all meals (7 days a week), homestay, laundry, all materials, Costa Rican dance and cooking classes, and airport transportation. $25 one-time registration. Contact: Susan Shores, Registrar, Latin American Language Center, 7485 Rush River Dr., Suite 710-123, Sacramento, CA 95831; (916) 447-0938, fax (916) 428-9542; lalc@madre.com.

Learn Spanish While Volunteering. Assist with the training of Costa Rican public school teachers in our latest language learning techniques, using classroom computers, K-8 school targeted by Costa Rican government as a model ESL/technology school. Enjoy learning Spanish in the morning, volunteer work in the afternoon/evening. Spanish classes are 2-5 students plus group learning activities; conversations with middle-class homestay families (1 student per family). Homestays and volunteer project are within walking distance of school in small town (14,000 population) near the capital, San Jose.

Dates: Year round, all levels. Classes begin every Monday, volunteer program is continuous. Cost: $295 per week for 25 hours of Spanish classes. Includes tuition, all meals (7 days a week), homestay, laundry, all materials, Costa Rican dance and cooking classes, and airport transportation. $25 one-time registration for Spanish classes; $100 additional one-time registration fee for volunteer program. Contact: Susan Shores, Registrar, Latin American Language Center, 7485 Rush River Dr., Suite 710-123, Sacramento, CA 95831; (916) 447-0938, fax (916) 428-9542; lalc@madre.com.

Spanish Language. Intercultura Language Institute offers intensive Spanish and homestays with selected Costa Rican families. Academic credit available (with prior notice). Additional free cultural activities: Latin-dance, music, theater, cinema, cooking. Weekend excursions to volcanoes, beaches, rainforest. Volunteer opportunities in social, environmental, and political organizations. Beach campus: optional 1 week per month, study on Pacific coast.

Dates: Year round. Cost: $1,045 per month (shorter stays available). Contact: Laura Ellington, Codirector, Intercultura Costa Rica, Apdo. 1952-3000, Heredia, Costa Rica; (011) 506-260-8480, Tel./fax 260-9243; intercul@sol.racsa.co.cr, www.alphaluz.com/intercultura/.

Total Immersion Spanish. Seven separate year-round language institutes to choose from. Live with a Costa Rican family while taking 3-6 hours of intense language classes a day. Length of program is up to you—from 1 week to 6 months. Locations: cloud forest, beach, country, and San Jose.

Dates: Every Monday except national holidays. Cost: Four-week course with homestay $850 to $2,000. Contact: ISLS, Dana G. Garrison, 1011 E. Washington Blvd., Los Angeles, CA 90021; (800) 765-0025, fax (213) 765-0026; islsspan1@aol.com, www.isls.com.

Denmark

Højskolekurser. Non-formal, adult education in a residential school with many different subjects: liberal arts, creative subjects, sports, civics, literature, history, etc.

Dates: Year round. Cost: Approx. 6,000 krones per month (includes room and board and tuition). Contact: Højskolernes Sekretariat, Nytorv 7, 1450 Kobenhavn K. Copenhagen, Denmark; (011) 45-3313-9822, fax 3313-9870; hs@grundtvig.dk, www.folkehojskoler.dk.

Ecuador

Academia Latinoamericana (Quito). Ecuador's number-one private Spanish language institute in former diplomat's man-sion with swimming pool, hot tub, sauna, sport facilities. Instruction by university-trained teachers, all one-on-one. Customized study programs tailored to the individual. Select host family accommodations. Excursions to haciendas, Indian markets, etc. College credit and internships available.

Dates: Year round. Cost: One-week tuition, lodging, meals $294. Contact: Suzanne Bell, Admissions Director, U.S., 640 East 3990 South, Suite E, Salt Lake City, UT 84107; (801) 268-4608, fax (801) 265-9156; latinoa1@spanish.com.ec, http://ecnct.cc/academia/learnspa.htm.

Europe

Culinary Adventures. Join us in Tuscany or Provence for an exceptional culinary experience. Stay at one of our beautiful villas and enjoy hands-on cooking, fun-filled excursions, and much more. Our chefs will share with you the treasured recipes of France and the warmth of Tuscan cuisine. For a color brochure call (800) 447-1311.

Dates: Spring, summer, and fall. Cost: $1,895 per person (double occupancy, includes food and wine.) Contact: Tim Stone, Rhode School of Cuisine, 216 Miller Ave., Suite 8, Mill Valley, CA 94941; (415) 388-0590, fax (415) 388-4658; www.togastronomy.com.

Issue-Specific Travel Courses. Topics include International Business and Economics, Comparative Educational Systems, Historical Literature, Social Service Systems, and other crosscultural studies. Emphasis on personal interaction between students and European professionals and providing a holistic cultural experience. Two- to 5-week programs. Three to 6 credits hours—undergraduate, graduate, or audit basis—through the Univ. of Missouri-Kansas City.

Dates: Early summer 1998. Cost: Approx. $2,000 (does not include airfare). Contact:

People to People International, Collegiate and Professional Studies Program, 501 E. Armour Blvd., Kansas City, MO 64109-2200; (816) 531-4701, fax (816) 561-7502; collegiateptpi.org, http://cei.haag.umkc.edu/ptp.

France

Discovering Geology in France. Spend 9 stimulating days touring in the western Loire Valley, châteaus and vineyards region. Collect fossils and unique rocks, visit vineyards, churches, museums—enjoy the regional dishes and wines.

Dates: Jul 10-19 (1997). Cost: $1,950 plus airfare. Contact: Roger Steinberg, 327 Katherine Dr., Corpus Christi, TX 78404; Tel./fax (512) 882-4479; piley@falcon.ta.mucc.edu.

French and Cookery in a Château. Live and study in 18th-century château. Adult courses in French language and Provençal cookery. Relaxed family atmosphere and good food. Château has 13 acres of park and pool. Single/en suite and shared rooms. Close to Burgundy, Beaujolais, Auvergne, and cities of Lyons and Roanne. One- to 12-week courses.

Dates: Every Sunday Apr-Nov. Cost: From $999 full board and classes in Château. Contact: Michael Giammarella, P.O. Box 640713, Oakland Gardens, NY 11364-0713; (800) 484-1234 ext 0096 or Ecole des Trois Ponts, Chateau de Matel, 42300 Roanne; (011) 33-477-70-80-01, fax 477-71-53-00; info@3ponts.edu, www.3ponts.edu.

French Language Immersion. International institute on Mediterranean coast. Short- and long-term French courses. Modern air-conditioned premises in large park. Restaurant with terrace. Top-quality homestay, hotels, apartments. Minimum age 17, maximum unlimited. Students, business people, employees, airline staffs, retired people. Charming

medieval town linking Provence to Riviera, lively marina, unspoiled beaches.

Dates: Year round. Cost: From FF1,500 per week (tuition). Contact: Institut ELFCA, 66 ave. du Toulon, 83400 Hyeres, France; (011) 44-4-94-65-03-31, fax 65 81 22; elfaca@compuserve.com, www.worldwide.edu/france/elfca.

Friendly French Immersion/Riviera Vacation. French Riviera specialist: B and B in villa/apartment. Discover the charming provencal heritage through 9 educational and cultural tours: architecture, arts, crafts, gastronomy. Mini-cruises from St. Tropez to Menton. Seasonal programs include Nice/Menton/Mandelieu Carnival (Feb), authentic provencal folkfairs (May-Sep). Two flexible and congenial language programs. Colorful 28-page brochure.

Dates: Year-round and seasonal programs. Cost: (1) Two weeks, homestay, half-board accommodations, 40 hours of visits plus 10 optional hours of informal French discussion, transfer to and from the airport: single $1,710, double $3,350. (2) Seasonal programs: Nice carnival in Feb, Cannes Film Festival in May, Wine Fair in Sep: single $1,990, double $3,780. (3) B and B from U.S. $45-$55 single, $60-$85 double. Accommodations in apartment/villa downtown. Contact: Friendly French Immersion, c/o Michael Grynberg (Marketing and Sales Manager), 4810 Queen Mary, Suite 16, Montreal, PQ H3W 1W3, Canada; (800) 334-0266 or (514) 344-4605, fax (514) 344-6222; ffi@generation.net, www.generation.net/~ffi. In Europe: FFI, c/o Gisele Ninio-Grynberg (President), Val d'Azur, 60 Vallon Barla Bat. C, 06200 Nice, France; Tel./fax (011) 33-93-21-67 26.

Immersion Course in French. Intensive 2- to 4-week course for professional adults in picturesque Villefranche overlooking the French Riviera's most beautiful bay, 8 1/2 hours a day with 2 meals. Audio-visual classes, language lab, practice sessions, discussion-lunch. Evening film showings with discussions, evening outings with teachers, excursions to cultural and scenic landmarks. Accommodations provided in comfortable private apartments.

Dates: Courses start May 5, Jun 2, Jun 30, Aug 4, Sep 1, etc. (year round). Cost: May-Nov (1997): FF16,700 for 4 weeks. Accommodations from FF2,300 to FF5,800 for 4 weeks, depending on type of lodging (individual room, family, studio apartment, etc.) Contact: Elisabeth Martin, Institut de Francais, 23 ave. Général Leclerc, 06230 Villefranche/Mer TR7, France.

Language Study in Loire Valley. Intensive French language (for beginners and/or advanced studies.) Two-, 4-, 8-week courses, 25 hours per week. Small classes (6-8 person maximum). Relaxed family atmosphere. Accommodations in a small castle with pool and numerous sport facilities 170 km southwest of Paris.

Dates: From Feb to Nov. Cost: $1,000 for 2 weeks (25 hours of lessons per week, meals and accommodations). Contact: Mme. Tartière, Chateau Bois Minhy Chemery, 41700 Contres, Loir et Cher, France; (011) 33-2-54795101, fax 54790626.

Learning Vacations in France. Learn French while discovering the Castles of the Loire Valley, the secrets of Provence, or the sandy beaches of the Mediterranean. Programs are designed for independent travelers sharing a passion for the French culture. We offer a choice of locations in Tours, Aix-en-Provence, or Montpellier.

Dates: Year round from 2 weeks to 9 months. Cost: From $1,748 (2 weeks) to $11,589 (9 months) depending on duration and location. Full package includes tuition, fees, roundtrip airfare from New York, Paris visit, housing and meals. Contact: Jim Pondolfino, French-American Exchange, Box 7, 111 Roberts Court, Alexandria, VA 22314; (800) 995-5087, fax (703) 549-2865 or (703) 683-8444; faetours@erols.com.

Germany

German as a Foreign Language. We offer the following educational programs: various levels of German year round; intensive, crash, and long-term courses, individual tuition; special feature: German and Theater; special programs: business German for professionals, German for teachers, German in a teacher's home, German for special purposes. Academic year for high school students, international study year, internship, guest studentship, homestays for groups, courses for firms and other institutions (banking, insurance, doctors, lawyers, etc.), residential language camps for juniors, examination preparation. Various types of accommodations. Full range of activities.

Dates: Year round. Contact: GLS Sprachenzentrum, Barbara Jaeschke, Managing Director, Kolonnenstrasse 26, 10829 Berlin, Germany; (011) 49-30-787-41-52; fax 41-92; gls.berlin@t-online.de.

Study-Travel in Germany, Switzerland. Learn German and travel throughout Germany and Switzerland along Lake Constance—an ideal atmosphere for study, relaxation, and recreation. Included are trips to Neuschweinstein, Munich, Zurich, Lucerne, Strasbourg, Salzburg, as well as Rheintrip and Alpine hike.

Dates: Jul 29-Aug 25, 1998. Cost: $1,495 includes room, food allowance, all excursions. Contact: Dr. Peter Schroeck, German Language School Conference, 1 Hiram Sq., New Brunswick, NJ 08901; (732) 249-9785.

Greece

An Archaeological Tour of Greece. Obtain first-hand knowledge of the art and architecture of ancient Greece through on-site archaeological visits and museum tours. This is the only course of its kind in which students are invited to have one of their lectures inside the Parthenon. Other highlights include visits to Sparta, Corinth, Mycenae, the Olympia Grounds, Delphi, Thermopylae, and Mystra, the world's best-preserved medieval city. The trip ends with 4 days on the island of Mykonos and a visit to the "birthplace" of Apollo.

Dates: Jun 7-Jun 29, 1998. Cost: $2,800 (3 credits) includes roundtrip airfare, double occupancy rooms, breakfast daily, bus, ship, and airport transfers. Contact: Dora Riomayor, Director of International Studies, School of Visual Arts, 209 E. 23rd St., New York, NY 10010-3994; (212) 592-2543, fax (212) 592-2545.

Greek Folk Dances and Culture. Workshops on Greek dance (traditional and ancient) including general courses on Greek culture (music, costume, language, etc.).

Dates: Summer 1998. Cost: $200 a week. Contact: Alkis Raftis, Greek Dances Theatre, 8 Schoiou St., GR-10558, Plaka, Athens, Greece; (011) 30-1-3244395.

Guatemala

Eco-Escuela de Español. The Eco-Escuela de Español offers a unique educational experience by combining intensive Spanish language instruction with volunteer opportunities in conservation and community development projects. Students are immersed in the language, culture, and ecology of Petén, Guatemala—an area renowned for its tropical forests and ancient Maya ruins. Ecological activities integrate classroom with field-based experiences.

Dates: Every Monday year round. Cost: Classes $65 per week (based on 20 hours of individual instruction per week, Monday-Friday). Room and board with local families $60 per week. Registration fee $10. Contact: Eco-Escuela, Conservation International, 2501 M St., NW, Suite 200, Washington, DC 20037; (202) 973-2264, fax (202) 331-9328; ecoescuela@conservation.org.

Escuela de Español "Sakribal". Program provides one-on-one intensive language instruction while giving students the chance to volunteer on student-supported development projects in the surrounding community, working in organic gardens, and in the country's only women's shelter. Family stays, guest lecturers, group discussions, and cultural activities round out the immersion program.

Dates: Classes start every Monday year round. Cost: $120 per week (includes classes, family stay, project work, other school activities). Contact: U.S. Office: 550 Ferncroft Ct., Danville, CA 94526; (510) 820-3632, fax (510) 820-6658; sakribal2@aol.com, http://kcyb.com/sakribal.

India

Sustainable Communities Semester. A Geocommons College Year program in ecological awareness, cooperative community, and mindful living. Participants spend three months at Auroville, an international community of 1,200 people working towards sustainability and "human unity," 2 weeks traveling India, and 1 week at Plum Village, a Buddhist community in France. College credit available.

Dates: Spring semester approx. Jan 3-Apr 25. Cost: Approx. $9,400. Includes tuition, predeparture orientation, international airfare from Boston, lodging, meals, and local transportation. Financial aid accepted. Some scholarships. Contact: Dr. Daniel Greenberg, Program Director, Gaia Education Outreach Institute, Derbyshire Farm, Temple, NH 03084; Tel./fax (603) 654-6705; geo@ic.org, www.ic.org/geo.

Indonesia

Experiencing the Arts in Bali. Providing insight and practice into Bali's arts and crafts, and based in the cultural center, includes island tours, traditional dance performances, and 10 classes in gamelan music, dance, painting, batik, or mask carving, taught by Balinese artists in family compounds. A life-changing experience created by quality guides with 16-year track record. Daily classes in Iyengar Yoga with certified instructor.

Dates: Jul 1-21. Cost: $3,100. Contact: Danu Enterprises, P.O. Box 156, Capitola, CA 95010; Tel./fax (888) 476-0543.

The Healing Arts of Bali. Research Bali's traditional healing practices, observe the work of folk doctors, study herbal medicines, temple offerings, traditional massages, and herbal body revitalization experiences. Participants visit all Bali's top attractions on island tours, attend dance performances and trance rituals, visit artists, and enjoy expert seminars on Balinese culture and religion. Daily classes in Iyengar Yoga with certified instructor.

Dates: Mar 14-27, Jul 28-Aug 12. Cost: $2,900. Contact: Danu Enterprises, P.O. Box 156, Capitola, CA 95010; Tel./fax (888) 476-0543.

Ireland

Irish Language and Culture. Irish language programs at all learning levels, as well as cultural activities. Language learning in hillwalking, dancing, music and archaeology.

Dates: From Easter until Sep (weekly). Cost: $200 including tuition and houseshare. Contact: Liam O'Cuinneagain, Oideas Gael, Gleann Cholm Cille, County Donegal; (011) 353-73-30248, fax 30348; ocdsgael@iol.ie.

Irish Language and Culture. Irish language programs at all learning levels for adults are offered by Oideas Gael, which also offers cultural activities, learning programs in hillwalking, dances of Ireland, painting, tapestry weaving, Raku-Celtic pottery, and archaeology.

Dates: Apr-Sep, 1998 (weekly). Cost: $150 plus accommodations (from $90 per week).

Contact: Liam O'Cuinneagain, Director, Oideas Gael, Gleann Cholm Cille, County Donegal, Ireland; (011) 353-73-30248; oidsgael@iol.ie.

Walking and Trekking Holidays. Countryside Tours, set up in 1990, is the specialist in providing leisurely guided and more challenging self-guided hiking tours. A varied program includes all the major areas of interest such as Kerry, Connemara, Wicklow Mountains, and Ulster. Good food, comfortable accommodations in Irish guesthouses.

Dates: Please ask for brochure. Cost: IR£420 for guided tours, from IR£205 for self-guided tours. Contact: Nick Becker, Countryside Tours Ltd., Glencar House, Glencar, County Kerry, Ireland; (011) 353-66-60211, fax 66- 60217; country@iol.ie.

Israel

Pastor-Parishioner Study Tour. A 2-week program in Israel with daily field trips that concentrate on the geography of Israel and archaeology as they relate to Biblical interpretation. Extensive field trips to Galilee, Dead Sea, Masada, Jerusalem region, including overnights on the Sea of Galilee.

Dates: Oct 28-Nov 10 (1996); Apr 14-Apr 27 and Oct 27-Nov 9 (1997). Cost: $1,325 includes room and board, field trips. Contact: Jerusalem University College, 4249 E. State St., Suite 203, Rockford, IL 61108; (815) 229-5900 or (800) 891-9408, fax (815) 229-5901.

Italy

Biking and Walking Tours. Specializing in Italy for over 10 years, Ciclismo Classico distills the "Best of Italy," offering more unique Italian destinations than any other active vacation company. Educational, active tours for all abilities in Umbria, Tuscany, Piedmont, the Dolomites, Puglia, Sicily, the Amalfi Coast, Cinque Terre, Sardegna, Abruzzo, Campania,

Corsica, and Elba, and Ireland, too. Charming accommodations, expert bilingual guides, cooking demonstrations, wine tastings, support vehicle, detailed route instructions, visits to local festivals, countryside picnics—an unforgettable cultural indulgence.

Dates: Apr-Nov (70 departures). Call for specific dates. Cost: $1,500-$3,000. Contact: Lauren Hefferon, Director, Ciclismo Classico, 13 Marathon St., Arlington, MA 02174; (800) 866-7314 or (781) 646-3377.

Italiaidea. Italiaidea is a center for comprehensive Italian instruction. We offer every level and format of Italian study from intensive short-term "survival Italian courses" to advanced semester-long courses meeting once or twice a week. We offer on-site lectures and visits to historic sites in Italian, conversation, and flexible scheduling. For over 10 years we have been offering college credit courses at numerous U.S. college and university programs in Italy; we now offer both academic assistance and travel/study assistance to our client institutions. Homestays are offered as well as accommodations in shared apartments.

Dates: Year round. Cost: Sixty-hour group course LIT750,000; 25-hour one-on-one program LIT1,170,000; 15 hour-specific purposes or culture LIT1,150,000 (taxes not included). Contact: Carolina Ciampaglia, Co-Director, Piazza della Cancelleria 5, 00186 Roma, Italy; (011) 39-6-68307620, fax 6892997; italiadea@nexus.it, www.italiadea.com.

Italian Language Courses. Institute Galilei specializes in one-to-one courses held in Florence, in the countryside, on the island of Elba with tailored programs to fit the needs of the student. Training in specific vocabularies (economics, law, art history, etc.). All courses are divided into 10 levels. The Institute also organizes small group courses in 3 levels lasting from 2 weeks on.

Dates: One-to-one courses start and end on any days requested; small group courses start every 2 weeks. Cost: Starting from $349 per week. Contact: Institute Galilei, Ms. Alexandra Schmitz, Via degli Alfani 68, 50121 Florence, Italy; (011) 39-55-294680, fax 283481; info.galilei.it.

Late Spring Summer Studies at SACI. Summer studies at Studio Art Centers International (SACI) are open to students enrolled in US institutions who are seeking accredited summer study, independent non-credit students, mature students, and international students interested in studio arts, art history, art conservation and Italian language. The following classes are offered: Drawing, Printing, Printmaking Workshop, Ceramics, Sculpture, Photography, Design Workshop, Batik and Fabric Design, Weaving, Jewelry, Renaissance Art History, Art Conservation, and Italian Language.

Dates: May 14-Jun 22, and Jun 25-Jul 27, 1998. Cost: Tuition: $3,000; housing $950 (5 weeks)/$800 (4 weeks), activity fee $180/$140. Contact: SACI Coordinator, U.S. Student Programs, Institute of International Education, 809 UN Plaza, New York, NY 10017; (800) 344-9186, (212) 984-5548, fax (212) 984-5325; saci@iie.org, www.iie.org/pgms/saci.

Lorenzo de'Medici. Art history, Italian history and culture, cooking programs for adults. All conducted in English. Semester-summer classes-short-term programs. Learn Italian art history, cooking, civilization and culture in the heart of the Renaissance.

Dates: Every month year round. Cost: Package from $1,600, includes hotel, accommodations, meals, lectures, visits, field trips. Tuition: from $150. Contact: Dott. Arch. Gabriella Ganugi, Director, Lorenzo de'Medici, Via Faenza, #43, 50123 Florence, Italy; (011) 39-55-287143, fax 23989 20/287203; ldm@dada.it.

Lorenzo de'Medici Language, Art, Culture. Language courses from 1 week up to 7 months. Art semesters and summer classes in the following subjects: painting, drawing, sculpture, architecture, photography, jewelry, textiles, printmaking, restoration of paintings and frescoes, ceramics, video production, art history, and liberal arts, cooking and wine tasting.

Dates: Year round. Cost: Package from $1,500 includes accommodations, meals, lectures, museum visits. Courses from $100. Contact: Dott. Arch. Gabriella Ganugi, Director, Lorenzo de'Medici, Via Faenza, #43, 50123 Florence, Italy; (011) 39-55-287143, fax (011) 39-55-23989 20/287203; ldm@dada.it.

Painting in the Hilltowns of Italy. The 5 painting workshops are held at La Romita facilities in a 16th-century remodeled monastery in Umbria for all levels of experience; 31 years of experience.

Dates: May 19-Jun 3; Jun 5-Jun 27; Jun 30-Jul 22; Jul 23-Aug 8; Aug 17-Sep 1. Cost: Sessions 2 and 3: $2,300; sessions 1,4, and 5: $1,600. Contact: Paola Quargnali, La Romita School of Art, Inc., 1712 Old Town Rd., NW, Albuquerque, NM 87104; Tel./fax (505) 243-1924; quargnali@apsicc.aps.edu.

Tech Rome. Tech Rome is a 6-week summer travel-study program based in Rome. It features hotel housing, 3 meals per day, tours, and traditional classroom courses combined with field travel for college credit. Up to 13 semester hours may be earned in a choice of over 10 courses in diverse subject areas. Courses are taught by American professors. All disciplines are accredited.

Dates: May 26-Jul 3, 1998. Cost: $4,328 includes tuition, all housing for 6 weeks, 3 meals per day, tours. Group flights and optional tours available. Contact: Tech Rome, P.O. Box 3172, Ruston, LA 71272; (800) 346-8324, http://techrome.latech.edu.

Jamaica

Tropical Marine Biology. Twelve-day course in the biology of Caribbean seashores and coral reefs for persons with a serious interest in snorkeling, shelling and understanding the complex marine biology of the region. Explore sunken shipwreck, fringing and barrier coral reefs, mangrove swamps, rocky shores. Observe animals in our aquaria. Course at Hofstra Univ. Marine Laboratory.

Dates: Jun 26-Jul 7, 1998. Cost: $1,400 (no credit), $2,200 graduate or undergraduate credit (includes airfare, room and board at our own waterfront hotel). Contact: Dr. E. Kaplan, Director, Hofstra Univ. Marine Lab, Gittelson Hall 114, Hempstead, NY 11550; (516) 463-5520, fax (516) 463-6010; bioehk@vaxc. hofstra.edu.

Japan

Lex Homestay Programs. Lex offers homestay programs in which participants, living as members of a Japanese family, absorb the customs and characteristics of their host culture by taking part in daily life activities. Participants may go sightseeing with their families, meet friends and relatives, and attend festivals. Japanese language ability is not a requirement. Host families are fully screened volunteer members of the Lex organization. Adults, students, and entire families are encouraged to apply.

Dates: Jul-Aug: 2, 4- and 6-week programs. Spring: 2-week program. Custom programs year round. Cost: Varies. Four-week summer program $3,030 (includes airfare from West Coast port of departure). Contact: Steffi Samman, Program Manager, Lex America, 68 Leonard St., Belmont, MA 02178; (617) 489-5800, fax (617) 489-5898; exchange@lexlrf. com.

Mexico

Cemanahuac Community. Trips are highly educational, with college credit (graduate and undergraduate) available. Focus areas include history, anthropology, archaeology, social issues, cooking and cuisine, and popular and folk art. Previous groups include teachers, social workers, artists, senior citizens, chefs, museum members, alumni groups, and other adult participants. Each trip individually planned.

Dates: Field study trips can be held at any time of the year. Cost: Dependent on requirements and length of the field study trips. Contact: Vivian B. Harvey, Educational Programs Coordinator, Cemanahuac Educational Community, Apartado 5-21, Cuernavaca, Morelos, Mexico; (011) 52-73-18-6407, fax 12-5418; 74052.2570@compuserve.com.

Copper Canyon. Outstanding cultural and natural history rail trips. The most dramatic train ride in the western hemisphere. Deeper, wider, greener canyons than Arizona's Grand Canyon. Tarahumara Indian culture, nature walks, birding, waterfalls, spectacular vistas. Historic tours, small groups, personal attention. In-depth interpretation of the Copper Canyon and its people.

Dates: Year round. Cost: $1,695 per person for 8-day trips. Contact: S&S Tours, 865 El Camino Real, Sierra Vista, AZ 85635; (800) 499-5685, fax (520) 458-5258; ss@the river.com.

El Bosque del Caribe, Cancun. Take a professional Spanish course 25 hours per week and enjoy the Caribbean beaches. Relaxed family atmosphere. No more than 6 students per class. Special conversation program. Mexican cooking classes and excursions to the Mayan sites. Housing with Mexican families. College credit available.

Dates: Year round. New classes begin every Monday. Group programs arranged at reduced fees. Cost: Enrollment fee $100, $175 per week. One week with a Mexican family $150. Contact: Eduardo Sotelo, Director, Calle Piña 1, S.M. 25, 77500 Cancún, Mexico; (011) 52-98-84-10-38, fax 84-58-88; bcaribe@mail.cancun-language.com.mx.

Instituto Cultural Oaxaca. Spanish Language and Mexican Culture Immersion Program on lovely Oaxacan estate. Grammar and literature and conversation classes offered at 7 levels. Cultural workshops in cooking, pottery, danc-

ing, weaving, music. Local conversation partner. Weekly lectures and cultural activities. Seven contact hours daily. Optional tours to archaeological sites and artisan villages. Homestays available. Special group programs.

Dates: Year-round monthly sessions. Write, call, or fax for specific dates and informative brochure. Cost: $50 registration fee and $400 per 4-week session or $105 per week. Contact: Lic Lucero Topete, Director, Instituto Cultural Oaxaca, Apartado Postal #340, Oaxaca, Oaxaca, C.P. 68000, Mexico; (011)-52-951-53404, fax 53728; inscuoax@antequera.com, http://antequera.com/inscuoax/.

Intensive Spanish in Cuernavaca. Cuauhnahuac, founded in 1972, offers a variety of intensive and flexible programs geared to individual needs. Six hours of classes daily with no more than 4 students to a class. Housing with Mexican families who really care about you. Cultural conferences, excursions, and special classes for professionals. College credit available.

Dates: Year round. New classes begin every Monday. Cost: $70 registration fee; $650 4 weeks tuition; housing $18 per night. Contact: Marcia Snell, 519 Park Dr., Kenilworth, IL 60043; (800) 245-9335, fax (847) 256-9475; lankysam@aol.com.

Intensive Spanish in Yucatan. Centro de Idiomas del Sureste, A.C. (CIS), founded in 1974, offers 3-5 hours per day of intensive conversational Spanish classes with native-speaking, university-trained professors. Maximum 6 students per group, average 3. Program includes beginner courses to very advanced with related field trips and recommended optional homestay. Also special classes in business, legal, medical vocabulary, or Mayan studies.

Dates: Year round. Starts any Monday, except last 2 weeks in Dec. Cost: Tuition (three hours per day program): $330 first 2 weeks, $115 each additional week, tuition (5 hours per day program): $490 first 2 weeks, $195 each additional week. Contact: Chloe C. Pacheco, Director, Centro de Idiomas del Sureste, A.C., Calle 14 #106 x 25, col. Mexico, CP 97128, Mérida, Yucatán, México; (011) 52-99-26-11-55 or (011) 52-99-26-94-94, 20-28-10, fax 26-90-20; cis@sureste.com.

Jewelry in San Miguel de Allende. Explore your creativity and practice your Spanish through silver jewelry classes in San Miguel de Allende, Mexico. Innovative, bilingual 5-day workshop in lost wax casting. All skill levels. No experience required. Individual instruction, small groups. All tools provided. Day trips to historical/archaeological sites available.

Dates: Year round. Contact us for a brochure and latest schedule. Cost: $475 for 5-day courses (includes registration, tuition, supplies, and housing). Contact: Raúl Ybarra, 1900 Fox Dr., Box 84-400T, McAllen, TX 78504; (011) 52-415-27358, fax 26153, Attn: R. Ybarra.

Language and Culture in Guanajuato. We work with innovative teaching techniques, tailoring instruction to each student's needs. Spanish, Mexican History, Politics, Culture-Cuisine, Folk Dancing and Latin American Literature.

Dates: Year round. New classes begin every Monday. Cost: $925. Includes 4 weeks of classes and homestay with 3 meals daily. Contact: Director Jorge Barroso, Instituto Falcon, A.C., Guanajuato, Gto. 36000 Mexico; Tel./fax (011) 52-473-2-36-94, infalcon@ redes. int.com.mx, www.infonet. com.mx/falcon.

Language Institute of Colima. The Language Institute of Colima Mexico offers a system of total immersion with classes held throughout the year Monday-Friday. Students live with local host families and attend 6 hours of instruction daily; no more than 5 students per class. Many extras, including beach excursions.

Dates: Year round, Monday-Friday. Cost:

Registration $80; tuition $415 1st week, $345 after 1st week (for shared room), $445 1st week, $375 after 1st week (for private room). 10 percent discount for 6 or more. Contact: Dennis Bourassa, Language Institute of Colima, P.O. Box 827, Miranda, CA 95553; (800) 604-6579, fax (707) 923-4232; colima@northcoast.com, www. northcoast.com/~colima.

Learn Spanish in Chiapas. Spanish lessons in private sessions or small groups (4 people maximum). Family stays available. School tours to Indian (Mayan) villages, jungle trips available. Extracurricular activities include: Mexican cooking, discussions, and video showings. Teach English in exchange for Spanish lessons. Centro Cultural "El Puente" includes gallery weaver's cooperative, travel agency, cafe, restaurant, phone/fax service.

Dates: Year round. Cost: Highest $220 per week; lowest $75 per week. Contact: Roberto Rivas, Bastidas Centro Bilingüe de Chiapas, C. Real de Guadalupe 55, Centro Cultural "El Puente," San Cristóbal de Las Casas 29230, Chiapas, Mexico; (011) 52-967-8-41-57, fax 967-83723 or Tel./fax (800) 303-4983; cenbili@chisnet.com.mx, www.mexonline.com/centro1.htm.

Mar de Jade. Tropical ocean-front retreat center in a beautiful unspoiled fishing village near Puerto Vallarta offers unique travel options. Enjoy great swimming, kayaking, hiking, massages, and stress-reduction meditation. Study Spanish in small groups. Gain further insight into local culture by studying and working in a farmers' clinic, local construction, cottage industries, or teaching.

Dates: Year round. Cost: $865 for 21-day work/study. Includes room (shared occupancy), board, 12 hours per week of Spanish and 15 hours per week of work. Longer resident program available at lower cost. Vacation/Spanish 1-week minimum $365 room, board, 12 hours of Spanish. Vacation only

$45 per night for any length of time. Contact: In Mexico: Mar de Jade/Casa Clinica, A.P. 81, Las Varas, Nayarit, 63715, Mexico; Tel./fax (011) 52-327-20184; marjade@pvnet.com, www. puerto-vallarta.com/mardejade/. In U.S.: P.O. Box 1280, Santa Clara, CA 95052; (415) 281-0164.

Nepal

Ecosystems and Cultures of Nepal. Join U.S. and Nepali research specialists for an in-depth investigation of the remarkable environmental and cultural elements in the undisturbed ecosystems of Nepal. Engage in a first-hand exploration of Nepal's intertwined natural and human histories. Previous fieldwork experience not required. Projects earn 9 to 14 university credits. Application deadline: May 30, 1998 or until programs are full. Additional programs in Thailand, Russia, New Zealand, and Mexico.

Dates: Jul 1-Aug 18 (summer program); Oct 8-Nov 29 (fall program). Cost: $1,900 academic fee. Contact: Crandall Bay, Director, Wildlands Studies, 3 Mosswood Circle, Cazadero, CA 95421; (707) 632-5665; wildlnds@sonic.net, www.wild-landsstudies.com/ws.

Sojourn Nepal. Sojourn Nepal is a 12-week program comprised of homestay, language study, lectures, village stay, trekking, and opportunities for apprenticeships in a vast variety of areas. Cultural immersion at its finest.

Dates: Fall and spring semesters. Cost: $5,000, airfare not included. Contact: Jennifer Warren, Sojourn Nepal, 2440 N. 56th St., Phoenix, AZ 85008; Tel./fax (602) 840-9197; snepal@aol.com.

North America

Educational Homestays. Foreign students live with host families and learn ESL with teachers, also with optional excursions. Short- or long-term homestays provided for high school or college students in universities, at langauge schools, or just visiting America or Canada.

Dates: Any time of year. Cost: $375-$675 depending on program and area. Includes room, meals, airport transportation, all household amenities and area supervision. Contact: Connections, John Shephard, 17324 185th Ave. NE, Woodinville, WA 98072; (425) 788-9803, fax (425) 788-2785; www.connections.com

Papua New Guinea

Trans Niugini Tours. Nature and culture programs are operated in three areas: the Highlands, the Sepik Area, and a marine environment on the North Coast. Each area has its own distinct culture and environment, with comfortable wilderness lodges located in each.

Dates: Weekly departures. Cost: $889-$3,570 per person (land cost). Contact: Bob Bates, Trans Niugini Tours, P.O. Box 371, Mt. Hagen, Papua New Guinea; (800) 521-7242 or (011) 675-542-1438, fax 542-2470; travel@pngtours.com, www.pngtours.com.

Spain

Escuela Internacional (Madrid, Salamanca, Malaga). Escuela Internacional offers quality programs in Spanish language and culture with U.S. undergraduate credits. Our qualified teachers and small classes (maximum 12 students per class) guarantee you a successful program. Stay with a selected family or in a shared apartment. Enjoy our extensive afternoon activities and weekend excursions. Our professionalism, enthusiasm, and personal touch will make your experience in Spain memorable and fun.

Dates: Year round, 2-48 weeks. Cost: From PTS57,500 for 2 weeks (includes 15 hours per week instruction, room and books) to PTS125,000 (includes 30 hours per week instruction, room and full board, books, activities, and excursion). Contact: Escuela Internacional, Midori Ishizaka,

Director of Admissions, c/Talamanca 10, 28807 Alcalá de Henares, Madrid, Spain; (011) 34-1-8831264, fax 8831301; escuelai@ergos.es, www.ergos.es/escuelai.

Learn Spanish in Spain. Language immersion courses in Spain (Barcelona, Canary Islands, Granada, Madrid, Malaga, San Sebastian, Seville, and Valencia). Private language schools centrally located, convenient to interesting places, cultural events, and sports activities. Programs feature qualified teachers, small classes, attractive surroundings and facilities. Affordable prices for instruction. Accommodations with Spanish families with meals; student residences; apartments; and nearby hotels.
Dates: Year round. Two weeks or more. Cost: Two-week courses with or without accommodations range from $245-$865. Contact: Ms. Lorraine Haber, Study Abroad Coordinator, CES Study Abroad Program, The Center for English Studies, 330 7th Ave., 6th Floor, New York, NY 10001; (212) 629-7300, fax (212) 736-7950.

Painting in Barcelona. A celebrated Spanish faculty made up of Tom Carr and Carme Miquel will conduct a 3-week advanced painting workshop at the spacious studio of Escola d'Arts Plastiques i Disseny "Llotja." Included are 3 museum tours to the Antonio Tapies Foundation, the Miro Foundation, and the Picasso Museum. Three credits.
Dates: Jul 3-Jul 25, 1998. Cost: $2,850. Includes airfare, double occupancy rooms, continental breakfast daily, and 3 tours. Contact: Dora Riomayor, Director of International Studies, School of Visual Arts, 209 E. 23rd St., New York, NY 10010-3994; (212) 592-2543.

Spanish Courses in Malaga. Spanish courses in Malaga, Spain. All grades, small groups, 4 hours daily, courses commencing each month. Living with Spanish families (families or in small apartment in town center).
Contact: F. Marin Fernandez, Director, Centro de Estudios de Castellano, Ave. Juan Sebastian Elcano, 120, 29017 Málaga, Spain; Tel./fax 34-5-2290551; ryoga@arrakis.es, www.arrakis.es/~ryoga.

Spanish in Malaga. Frequently called Spain's leading school of Spanish, Malaca Instituto offers general Spanish courses in small groups year round at all levels. We have many European and Japanese students but very few Americans. Facilities include video rooms, cinema, language lab, self-access study center, bar, restaurant, pool, and on-site residential accommodations. We organize a comprehensive program of cultural and social activities.
Dates: Every 2 weeks. Cost: Course: from PTS72,900 for 4 weeks, Accommodations: residence, host families, student apartments: from PTS62,300 for 4 weeks. Contact: Bob Burger, Marketing Director, Malaca Instituto, c/Cortada 6, Cerrado de Calderon, 29018 Malaga, Spain; (011) 34-5-229-32-42, fax 63-16.

Spanish Language Programs. Intensive Spanish language programs are designed for people wishing to study in small groups (maximum 8 students). Instruction Monday-Friday 9:30-1:15 for 2 weeks. Includes 1 excursion per week. Courses: survival Spanish, Spanish for business/travel/tourism, etc.
Dates: Jun, Jul, Aug, (1997). Cost: PTAS53,000 (tuition, excursions, and study material). Contact: Berlitz Language Centre, Gran Via 80 - 4, 28013 Madrid, Spain; (011) 34-1-541-6215, fax 541-2765.

Summer Study in Salamanca. Spend over 4 weeks in Spain studying Spanish language, literature, and culture at the prestigious Colegio de España in Salamanca. The program is designed for college students, graduates, and teachers, as well as for college-bound high school students. Program Options: A) Intensive Undergraduate Language and Culture; up to 9 credits. B) Literature, Language and Culture, and Business Spanish; 6 graduate or advanced undergraduate credits.

Dates: Jul 1-Jul 30, 1998. Cost: Program A: $1,850. Program B: $2,050. Contact: Prof. Mario F. Trubiano, Director, URI Summer Program in Spain, Dept. of Languages, Univ. of Rhode Island, Kingston, RI 02881-0812; (401) 874-4717 or (401) 874-5911; fax (401) 874-4694.

United Kingdom

Edinburgh Univ. Summer Courses. Scotland past and present: Art, Architecture, History, Literature, Archaeology, Presentation skill, Ethnology, Gaelic, Music, Drama, Creative Writing, Film, Ecology, the Edinburgh Festival. Courses last 1-4 weeks each. Instruction by University professors: highest academic standards. Integral field trips; theatre/concert/cinema tickets provided. Social program. Choice of accommodations.

Dates: Jun-Sep. Contact: Elaine Mowat, Univ. of Edinburgh, Centre for Continuing Education, 11 Buccleuch Pl., Edinburgh EH8 9LW, U.K.; (011) 44-131-650-4400, fax 6097; CCE@ed.ac.uk, www.ed.ac.uk/~cce/summer.

England Afloat. England by canal boat. Historian-skipper, small parties, no fixed itinerary. Also special interest cruises for larger groups: theater, history, painting, etc. Henley for the Regatta? Llangollen for the Eisteddfodd? Two thousand miles of waterways give economic access to all central England. Full board or self-catered.

Dates: Apr-Oct. (by the week). Cost: $695 per week, full board. Camp boats as little as $80. Contact: Jeremy Scanlon, England

Afloat, 66 Old Holyoke Rd., Westfield, MA 01085; Tel./fax (413) 572-9013.

London Academy of Performing Arts. An internationally renowned drama academy, offering classical acting training for students wishing to enter the professional performing arts. Full-time 1- and 2-year courses offered as well as summer schools and 12-week programs. Many graduates work in top theater, film, and T.V. productions.

Dates: Summer schools Jul-Aug. Full-time courses from Sep. Auditions throughout the year. Cost: From £850. Contact: The Administrator, London Academy of Performing Arts, The Church, 2 Effie Rd., Fulham Broadway, London SW6 1TB, U.K.; (011) 44-171-736-0121, fax 371-5624.

Visual Arts and Crafts Courses. Week and weekend courses in painting and drawing, blacksmithing, calligraphy, gardening and garden design, glass engraving, photography, pottery, sculpture, silversmithing, soft furnishing, textiles, and woodcarving and woodworking. Courses for different levels of ability, from complete beginners to master classes, run parallel to 7 full-time Diploma courses.

Dates: Year round. Cost: Short course (residential) weekends £150; 5 days £359; 7 days £483. Contact: Heather Way, Public Relations Coordinator, West Dean College, West Dean, Chichester, West Sussex, PO18 OQZ U.K.; (011) 44-1243-811301, fax 811343; westdean@pavilion.co.uk, www.pavilion.co.uk.

United States

Master of International and Intercultural Management. The School for International Training Master of International and Intercultural Management offers concentrations in sustainable development, international education, and training and human resource development in an academic-year program. This degree is designed for individuals wishing to make a career change or enter the field. A practical training component enables "on-the-job" training and an opportunity to work internationally.

Dates: Through May 29, 1998. Cost: $17,000 (1997-98 tuition). Contact: Kat Eldred, Director of Outreach and Recruitment, Admissions Counselor, School for International Learning, P.O. Box 676, Kipling Rd., Brattleboro, VT 05302; (802) 257-7751, fax (802) 258-3500; admissions@sit.edu, www.sit.edu.

St Giles Language Teaching Center. Earn the Certificate in English Language Teaching to Adults (CELTA) in San Francisco, approved by the Royal Society of Arts/Univ. of Cambridge Examination Syndicate and the California Council for Private Postsecondary and Vocational Education. The course focuses on practical training and teaching methodology. Includes access to international job postings, graduate contacts, and teaching opportunities abroad. EFL school onsite for observation and practice teaching. Part of a group of schools in England, Switzerland, and the U.S. with over 40 years of teaching and training experience, led by highly-qualified instructors with extensive oveseas teaching experience. CELTA courses also offered in Brighton and London, England.

Dates: Feb 2-Feb 27, Apr 20-May 15, Jun 1-Jun 26, Sep 14-Oct 9, Oct 26-Nov 20. Cost: $2,450. Contact: St Giles Language Teaching Center, 1 Hallidie Plaza, Suite 350, San Francisco, CA 94102; (415) 788-3552, fax (415) 788-1923; sfstgile@slip.net, www.stgiles.co.uk.

Worldwide

American-Int'l Homestays. Stay in English-speaking foreign homes in over 30 countries. Explore foreign cultures responsibly. Learn foreign languages. Perfect for families or seniors. Learn how other people live by living with them in their homes.

Dates: Year round. Cost: From $59 per night. Contact: Joe Kinczel, American-Int'l Homestays, P.O. Box 1754, Nederland, CO 80466; (303) 642-3088 or (800) 876-2048, fax (303) 642-3365; ash@igc.apc.org.

Amizade Volunteer Vacations. Programs offering mix of community service and recreation that provide volunteers with the opportunity to experience firsthand the culture they are working in—Brazilian Amazon, Peruvian Amazon, Bolivian Andes, or Greater Yellowstone region. Volunteers do not need any special skills, just a willingness to serve.

Dates: Year round. Cost: Varies. $1,500-$2,600 for Latin America; $150-$600 for Yellowstone. Contact: Amizade, 1334 Dartmouth Ln., Deerfield, IL 60015; (847) 945-9402, fax (847) 945-5676; amizade@worldnet.att.net, http://amizade.org.

CES Study Abroad Program. "Learn The Language Where It Is Spoken": French in France or Monaco; German in Germany or Austria; Italian in Italy; Portuguese in Portugal or Brazil; Spanish in Spain or Mexico. Other languages and locations available. Adult and youth programs. Courses include group instruction at ability level; private instruction; business-language; teacher-refresher; cultural studies; cooking, music, wines, art, history, dance. Housing can be hosted bed and breakfast, homestay half-board or full board, student residences; pensiones, or small hotels. School organized excursions and activities.

Dates: Year round. Two-week minimum and no maximum. Group classes have a maximum of 5-15 students. Cost: With and without accommodations, from $265-$2,700 per 2 weeks. Contact: Ms. Lorraine Haber, CES Study Abroad Program, 330 7th Ave., 6th Fl.,

New York, NY 10001; (212) 629-7300, fax (212) 736-7950.

College Semeter Abroad, School for International Training. A pioneer in study abroad, The School for International Training (SIT) offers over 57 programs in over 40 countries worldwide. For over 40 years SIT has been a leader in offering field-based study abroad programs to U.S. college and university students.

Dates: Fall and spring semester. Cost: $8,900-$11,900 depending on location. Includes airfare, tuition, room and board, insurance. Contact: School for International Training, P.O. Box 676, Kipling Rd., Brattleboro, VT 05302; (802) 257-7751, fax (802) 258-3500; csa@sit.edu, www.sit.edu.

Coral Cay Conservation Expeditions. Volunteers needed to join major expeditions to help survey and protect coral reefs and tropical forests in the Caribbean, Asia-Pacific, Philippines, Indonesia, Red Sea. No previous experience required. Full accredited training provided (including scuba certification if required). Thousands of CCC volunteers have already helped establish 8 new marine reserves and wildlife sanctuaries worldwide.

Dates: Expeditions depart monthly throughout the year. Cost: From $995 (2 weeks) to $4,415 (12 weeks) excluding flights. Contact: Coral Cay Conservation Ltd., 154 Clapham Park Rd., London SW4 7DE, U.K.; (305) 757-2955 (U.K. office 011-44-171-498-6248, fax 498-8447); ccc@coralcay.demon.co.uk, www.coralcay.org.

Earthwatch. Unique opportunities to work with leading scientists on 1- to 3-week field research projects worldwide. Earthwatch sponsors 160 expeditions in over 30 U.S. states and in 60 countries. Project disciplines include archaeology, wildlife management, ecology, ornithology and marine mammalogy. No special skills needed—all training is done in the field.

Dates: Year round. Cost: Tax deductible contributions ranging from $695-$2,800 support the research and cover food and lodging expenses. Airfare not included. Contact: Earthwatch, 680 Mt. Auburn St., P.O. Box 9104MA, Watertown, MA 02272; (800) 776-0188, (617) 926-8200; info@earthwatch.org, www.earthwatch.org.

Eurocentres Language Schools. Immersion course of 20-25 hours per week for beginners to advanced levels. Learn in small classes with students of all ages from around the world. Full organizational social calendar with extended excursions available to students. Homestay living is available, college credit option.

Dates: Begins monthly year round. Cost: Depends on school and length of stay. Contact: Eurocentres, 101 N. Union St., Alexandria, VA 22314; (703) 684-1494 or (800) 648-4809, fax (703) 684-1495; 100632.141@compuserve.com, www.clark.net/pub/eurocent/home.htm.

Global Ecology and Cities in the 21st Century. Two different academic programs to be offered by the International Honors Program in 1998-99. "Global Ecology" is a 2-semester program of around-the-world study and travel to England, Tanzania, India, the Philippines, and Mexico with academic coursework in ecology, anthropology, economics, and environmental issues. The "Cities in the 21st Century" program is a 1-semester program of study and travel to South Africa, India, and Brazil with academic coursework in urban studies, anthropology, sociology, economics, and political science.

Dates: "Global Ecology": Sep 1998-May 1999. "Cities in 21st Century": Jan 1999-May 1999. Cost: "Global Ecology": $21,300 plus airfare, includes tuition, room and board. "Cities in the 21st Century": $11,000 plus airfare, includes tuition, room and board. Contact: Joan Tiffany, Director, International Honors Program, 19 Braddock Pk., Boston,

MA 02116; (617) 267-0026, fax (617) 262-9299; info@ihp.edu, www.ihp.edu.

International Travel Study. Educational faculty-led programs each year range from 1 to 4 weeks in length. Offer university credit. Locations include France, Italy, Greece, Turkey, Mexico, Africa, South America, Great Britain, and more. Travel programs focus on art, language, or geography among a variety of specialties.

Dates: Summer programs May 30-Aug 30; also programs in Jan, spring, and fall. Cost: From $2,300-$5,000. Contact: Mary Pieratt, Director, Travel Programs, San Francisco State Univ., College of Extended Learning, 22 Tapia, San Francisco, CA 94132; (415) 338-1533, fax (415) 585-7345; www.cel.sfu.edu.

Language and Culture Total Immersion. Learn a language and enjoy an exciting variety of cultural and social experiences. Short-term and long-term programs year round for all ages and levels throughout Europe, Asia, Central and South America. Homestays available. Special programs for families, teens, seniors, executives, teachers, professionals. College credit available.

Dates: Year round. Cost: Varies with program. Contact: Nancy Forman, Language Liaison Inc., 20533 Biscayne Blvd., Suite. 4-162, Miami, FL 33180; (800) 284-4448 or (954) 455-3411, fax (954) 455-3413, learn@languageliaison.com, www.languageliaison.com.

Offshore Sailing School. Learn to sail, bareboat cruising preparation, live aboard cruising. Courses meet the needs of varying sailing abilities from beginners to advanced. Offshore has awarded diplomas to over 78,000 successful sailors over 30 years.

Dates: Year round. Cost: Start at $895 including course and accommodations. Contact: Steve and Doris Colgate's Offshore Sailing School, 16731 McGregor Blvd., Ft. Myers, FL 33908; (800) 221-4326, fax (941) 454-1191; offshore@packet.net, www.offshorsailing.com.

Penn Summer Abroad. Academic programs granting Univ. of Pennsylvania credits. Courses focusing on language, culture, economics, theater, anthropology, Jewish studies, cinema, art history, traditional folk medicine, performing arts, and religion. Several programs offer homestays, some offer internships.

Dates: Mid-May-late Aug (2-8 weeks). Cost: Tuition: $1,420 per course. Living costs vary. Contact: Elizabeth Sachs, Penn Summer Abroad, College of General Studies, Univ. of Pennsylvania, 3440 Market St., Suite 100, Philadelphia, PA 19104-3335; (215) 898-5738, fax (215) 573-2053.

Servas International. Servas is an international cooperative system of hosts and travelers established to help build world peace, good will, and understanding by providing opportunities for deeper, more personal contacts among people of diverse cultures and backgrounds. Approved travelers are invited to share life in the home and community of their host for short-term homestays.

Dates: On-going. Cost: $55 per year traveler fee, $25 refundable deposit for the use of host listings (up to 5 countries), $25 suggested host contribution. Contact: U.S. Servas, 11 John St., #407, New York, NY 10038; (212) 267-0252, fax (212) 267-0292; usservas@servas.org, http://servas.org.

Smithsonian Study Tours and Seminars. Smithsonian Study Tours and Seminars offers trips to over 250 destinations worldwide, making it the largest and most diverse program of its kind in the U.S. Tours are designed to meet a variety of budgets and activity levels. All tours provide travelers with rewarding experiences that satisfy their thirst for knowledge and desire to learn. Tours focus on a broad range of interests such as natural history, history, art, architecture, archaeology, gardens, wildlife, and theater.

Dates: Year round. Cost: $895-$12,000. Contact: Smithsonian Study Tours and Seminars, 1100 Jefferson Dr. SW, MRC 702, Washington, DC 20560; (202) 357-4700, fax (202) 633-9250; TSA.Tours@ic.si.edu, www.siedu/tsa/sst, AOL keyword: Smithsonian Travel.

The Lisle Fellowship. Intensive cultural immersion in the social and human development aspects of the host country. Group interaction and process are emphasized. All programs have a unique work component that varies with each such as Habitat for Humanity in Uganda, or repairing an ashram in Bali. The work is unpaid, but limited scholarships are available to defray the program cost. All programs are affiliated with the Univ. of Toledo, and credit is available.

Dates: Summer (1997). Programs are typically 3 to 4 weeks. Cost: $1,000 to $3,500. Includes room and board, and excursion while in host country. In some cases, transportation may be extra. Contact: The Lisle Fellowship, 433 W. Stearns Rd., Temperance, MI 48182; (313) 847-7126 or (800) 477-1538, or Dr. Mark B. Kinney, Executive Director, Univ. of Toledo; fax (419) 530-7719.

WorldTeach. WorldTeach is a private nonprofit organization based at Harvard Univ. which contributes to educational development and cultural exchange by placing volunteers to teach in developing countries (China, Costa Rica, Ecuador, Honduras, Mexico, Namibia, Thailand, and Vietnam). Volunteers teach English, math, science, and environmental education to students of all ages. All programs last for 1 academic year; except for the summer program in China.

Dates: Year-round departures and deadlines vary depending on the program. Cost: $3,600-$4,400. Includes health insurance, airfare, field support, and training. Contact: Jodi Hullinger, Desk Officer, WorldTeach, Harvard Institute for International Development, 1 Eliot St., Cambridge, MA 02138-5705; (617) 495-5527, fax (617) 495-1599; jhulling@worldteach.org, www.igc.org/worldteach.

LANGUAGE SCHOOLS

The following listing of language schools was supplied by the organizers. Contact the program directors to confirm costs, dates, and other details. If you do not see the program you want in the country of your choice, look in the "Worldwide" listings at the end of the section for programs located in several different regions.

Argentina

"Albert Schweitzer" Studio of Education and Culture, International. Spanish for foreigners, English, and German. Expertise is teaching English-speaking expatriates and tourists.

Cost: Average price per classroom—Individual: $20; Group of 2 students $18; 3 students $16; 4 students $14; 5 students $12; 6 students $10. Price is per person. Contact: Albert Schweitzer Studio of Education and Culture, International, Alvear 69, 2nd Fl., Martínez 1640, Buenos Aires, Argentina; (011) 54-1-792-6322/790-6245, fax 793-6888.

Argentine Spanish Language Centre (CEDIC). Offers a completely integrated program in the instruction of the Spanish language with various courses for different levels. Intensive language studies. Immersion experience living in Spanish-speaking community. Private and small group lessons are available with flexible schedules to meet the students' requirements. Accommodations. Social activities with Argentine families and students can also be arranged.

Dates: Year round. Cost: Two weeks intensive program (20 hours a week) $350. Tutor classes $16. Ask for accommodations. Contact: Prof. Susana Bernardi or Prof. Martin Duh, Reconquista 719, 11º E, 1003 Buenos Aires, Argentina; Tel./fax (011) 54-1-315-1156; martinduh@act.net.ar, www.worldwide.edu/argentina/cedic/.

Instituto de Lengua Española (ILEE). Located downtown. Dedicated exclusively to teaching Spanish to foreigners. Small groups and private classes year round. All teachers hold a university degree. Method is intensive, conversation-based. Student body is international, mostly European. Highly recommended worldwide. Ask for individual recommendations in U.S.

Dates: Year round. Cost: Four-week intensive program (20 hours a week) including homestay $1,400; 2 weeks $700. Individual classes: $19 per hour. Registration fee (includes books) $100. Contact: ILEE, Daniel Korman, Director, Lavalle 1619, 7º C, (1048) Buenos Aires, Argentina; Tel./fax (011) 54-1-375-0730. In U.S.: David Babbitz, fax (415) 431-5306; ilee@overnet.com.ar, www.studyabroad.com/ilee.

Instituto de Lengua Española para Extranjeros (ILEE). Located downtown in the most European-like city in Latin America. Dedicated exclusively to teaching Spanish to foreigners. Small groups and private classes year round. All teachers hold Master's degrees. Method is intensive, conversation-based. Student body is international. Highly recommended worldwide. Ask for individual references in U.S.

Dates: Year round. Cost: Four-week intensive program (20 hours per week) including homestay $1,400; 2 weeks $700. Private classes $19 per hour. Registration fee (includes books) $100. Contact: Daniel Korman, ILEE, Director, Lavalle 1619 7 C (1048), Buenos Aires, Argentina; Tel./fax (011) 54-1-375-0730. In U.S.: David Babbitz; (415) 431-8219, fax (415) 431-5306; ilee@overnet.com.ar, www.studyabroad.com/ilee.

Austria

Deutsch in Graz. Learning is experiencing. DiG offers German courses for all ages at all levels. Organized intensive courses, vacation courses, evening and morning classes, and special courses for school classes, German teachers, German for tourist industry. Leisure program, excursions, and accommodations will be arranged.

Dates: Year round. Cost: Example: 3-week intensive course (90 teaching units) ATS7,950. Contact: Deutsch in Graz, Dr. Monika Schneeberger, (manager), Ms. Karin Breyer (administration), A-8010 Graz, Kalchberggasse 10, Austria; (011) 43-316-83 3900, fax 833900-6.

Deutsch-Institut Tirol. German language courses for foreigners above age 16. Any level from beginner to far advanced. Schedule for the typical day: a) mornings: half-day intensive course, in classes of 6 students maximum. Conversation, TV, newspapers, tapes, books, grammar, pronunciation; b) afternoons: three times at least per week diverse recreational programs in company of a teacher: skiing, hiking, swimming, excursions; c) evenings: three times per week 2 lessons, 3 times social programs with teacher.

Dates: Year round. Start at any time. Course length optional. Cost: Course and programs: ATS5,000 per week. Room and breakfast: from ATS200 per day. Evening meal at ATS770 per week possible. Contact: Hans Ebenhöh, Director, Am Sandhügel 2, A-6370 Kitzbühel, Austria; (011) 43-5356-71274, fax 72363; dit@kitz.netwing.at, www.netwing.at/tirol/kitz/ats/dit.

German Courses at the University. German for beginners and advanced students, perfectionist courses, courses for students of the German language and teachers of German in foreign countries (6 levels). Lectures on German and Austrian literature, music, Austria—the country, people, and language. Special courses: translation, commercial German, commercial correspondence, phonetics. Excursions.

Dates: Three sessions: Jul 5-Aug 1, Aug 2-Aug 29, Aug 30-Sep 19, 1998. Cost: Course fee (4 weeks): approx. ATS4,350, accommodations: approx. ATS5,800. Contact: Magister Sigrun Inmann-Trojer, Wiener Internationale Hochschulkurse, Universität, Dr. Karl Lueger-Ring 1, A1010 Wien; (011) 43-1-405-12-54-0, fax 405-12-54-10.

Internationale Hochschulkurse. German courses at the University for beginners and advanced students, perfectionist courses (6 levels). Lectures on German and Austrian literature, music, linguistics, introduction to Austria. Special courses: translation into German, commercial correspondence, business German, medical terminology, communication, phonetics, Vienna waltz, choir singing. Language laboratory. Excursions.

Dates: Jul 6-Aug 2, Aug 3-30, Aug 31-Sep 20. Cost: Course fee (4 weeks): approx. ATS4,300; accommodations: approx. ATS6,000. Contact: Magister Sigrun Anmann-Trojer, Wiener Internationale Hochschulkurse, Universität, Dr. Karl Lueger-Ring 1, A1010 Wien, Austria; (011) 43-1-405-12-54 or 405-47-37, fax 405-12-54-10.

Intl. Summer—Univ. of Vienna. European studies focusing on political, economic, legal, and cultural aspects of the New Europe (taught in English) plus German language instruction. Outstanding academic reputation. Most conducive conditions for intercultural and social exchange. Beautifully located on the shore of Wolfgangsee/Salzburg. Excellent sports facilities. Excursions to Salzburg and Vienna.

Dates: Jul 12-Aug 11 (1997). Application deadline: May 31 (1997). Cost: ATS29,000 shillings (approx. $2,900). Includes registration, full board and tuition for 4-week session, use of all sports facilities (tennis, sailing and wind surfing lessons), a ticket to the Salzburg Festival, all planned excursions, and a trip to Vienna (half-board). Contact: Univ. of Vienna, International Summer Program Office, Dr. Karl Lueger-Ring 1, A1010 Vienna, Austria; Tel./fax (011) 43-1-40-34-988; sommerhochschule@univie.ac.at, www.univie.ac.at/Sommerhochschule.

Vienna Summer School. Annual program in art history, music history, German and Austrian literature, Eastern European literature, modern Austrian history, international communication, German I and II. Vienna: Values in Transit seminar, side trips to Budapest, Bratislava, Prague, Salzburg, Austrian Alps.

Dates: May 21-Jul 4, 1998. Cost: $3,800 includes 6 credit hours, housing, 2 meals per day, transportation, 4 weekend trips. Contact: Dr. Stephen I. Hemenway, English Dept., Hope College, Holland, MI 49422-9000; (616) 395-7616, fax (616) 395-7134.

Brazil

Portuguese Language Courses. Casa Do Brasil is a pioneer school founded in 1988 with the purpose of diffusing the Brazilian culture and the Portuguese language among foreigners. The center's program includes theoretical and practical classes on varied themes of linguistic, social, and cultural interest.

Dates: Mar 3-14, Mar 17-27, Mar 31-Apr 11, etc. New courses every 2 weeks. Cost: Sixty units of 45 minutes: $540 plus book ($35). Contact: Casa Do Brasil, Centro De Língua, Arte E Cultura, Rua Milton De Oliveira 231-Barra, 40140-100 Salvador-BA, Brazil; Fax (011) 55-71-245866.

Canada

Columbia College ESL. Seven- and 14-week programs, 25 hours per week. Small classes. Organized activities. International college also offering Senior, Secondary, and University Transfer programs. Facilities include tutorial center, library, computer center, gymnasium, cafeteria, counseling. Located 20 minutes from downtown Vancouver, near major shopping center and on excellent public transit routes.

Dates: Jan 2-Apr 10, May 5-Aug 14, and Sep 2-Dec 11 (1997). Cost: Tuition CAN$1,850 (7 weeks), CAN$3,500 (14 weeks); application fee CAN$75. Contact: Mr. John Helm, Columbia College, 6037 Marlborough Ave., Barnaby (Greater

Vancouver), BC V5H 3L6 Canada; (604) 430-6422, fax (604) 439-0548; columbia_college @mindlink.bc.ca.

Ecole de français, Montréal. For the last 50 years, the Ecole de français has offered courses in French as a second language to students from around the world. The Ecole is continually improving its programs to meet the changing needs of its students. Choose from Oral and Written Communication French (beginner to advanced), Workshop on Teaching French as a Second Language (for teachers), Contemporary Québec Culture (for advanced students), Business French (intermediate to advanced students).

Dates: May 19-Jun 11; Jul 6-Jul 24; Jul 27-Aug 14 ; Sep 10-Dec 11, 1998; Jan 8-Apr 13, 1999. Cost: Spring, summer: (3 weeks, 60 hours) CAN$495; summer (3 weeks, 45 hours) CAN$390; fall and winter: (12 weeks, 240 hours) CAN$1,495 (subject to change). Contact: Serge Bienvenu, Coordinator, Ecole de français, Faculté de l'education permanente, Université de Montreal, C.P. 6128, succursale Centre-ville, Montréal, PQ, H3C 3J7, Canada; (514) 343-6090, fax (514) 343-2430; infolang@fep.umontreal.ca, http:// alize.ere.umontreal.ca/~tousyves/fep.

English Language Centre, Univ. of Victoria. The English Language Centre at the Univ. of Victoria is known throughout the world for its high standards of English language instruction. Established in 1970, the ELC offers quality language programs aimed at international and Canadian students wishing to improve their English language and cross-cultural skills for personal, professional, and academic purposes. The 12-week Intensive English Language Program is offered 3 times each year, and a series of spring and summer programs are available. UVic is a mid-sized university with 17,000 students and is a friendly and comfortable place to study. It was rated the #1 Comprehensive Univ. in Canada for 2 consecutive years.

Dates: Apr 9-Jul 2; Sep 10-Dec 2, 1998; Jan 7-Mar 31, 1999 (tuition $2,950 per term). Cost: Short-term 1998: Jan 5-Feb 13 ($1,925); Mar 30-May 8, ($1,925); May 25-Jun 26 ($1,585); Jul 6-Jul 31 ($1,295); Jul 6-Aug 14 ($1,925); Aug 3-28 ($1,295). Contact: Bronwyn Jenkins or Maxine Macgillivray, Program Directors, English Language Centre, Univ. of Victoria, P.O. Box 1700, Victoria, BC V8W 2Y2, Canada; (250) 721-8469, fax (250) 721-6276; elc@uvcs.uvic.ca.

Intensive English Second Language. Intensive training in speaking, listening, writing, and reading. Advanced level. Students may combine post-secondary courses and language study. Program open to students at basic, intermediate, and advanced language levels. Students may enhance their language studies through participation in extracurricular activities and homestay with Canadian families.

Dates: Sep-Dec, Jan-Apr. Cost: CAN$3,750 tuition only (for 1 semester). Contact: Ms. Suzanne Woods, International Project Officer/Advisor, Sir Sandford Fleming College, Brealey Dr., Peterborough, ON, Canada; (705) 749-5530 ext. 1262, fax (705) 749-5526; swoods@flemingc.on.ca.

Language Studies Canada Montréal. Using a multi-skill approach students develop effective communication skills in French. Classes are informative, practical, and enjoyable. Six levels of 4 weeks each, intensive, 6 hours daily or semi-intensive, 4 hours daily. Maximum of 14 students per class. Audiovisual equipment, multi-media Student Resource Center. Optional activity program. Homestay and alternate accommodations available.

Dates: Two-week courses begin any Monday from Jan 13 (1997) year round. Other programs offered: one-on-one instruction, year round; 2-week. Group 5 executive courses, Jun-Oct; Summer Language Adventure (13 to 17-year-olds), 2-9 weeks in Jul and Aug. Cost: Two weeks intensive program $535; homestay accommodations $400. Cost

of other services available upon request. Contact: Language Studies Canada Montréal, 1450 City Councillors, Montréal, PQ, H3A 2E6, Canada; (514) 499-9911, fax (514) 499-0332.

Okanagan Univ. College (OUC). OUC offers extensive English as a Second Language programs to upgrade academic English levels and/or enhance conversational skills; offer intensive language training such as summer immersion; focus on specialized areas such as tourism or business; combine language instruction with activities introducing Canadian culture and lifestyles. Some ESL courses can be combined with university courses. OUC provides a range of learning opportunities including degree programs. Main campus is in Kelowna (pop. 90,000) in south central British Columbia.

Dates: Start dates: Jan 6, 1998; summer immersion Jul 7. Application deadlines normally 6-8 weeks prior to semester start. Cost: CAN$3,350 per 4-month semester; $1,750 9 weeks; Summer English Immersion $1,625 per 6 weeks. Contact: International Education, Okanagan Univ. College, 1000 K.L.O. Rd., Kelowna, BC V1Y 4X8, Canada; (250) 862-5443, fax (250) 862-5470; inted@okanagan.bc.ca, www.okanagan.bc.ca.

Queen's Univ. School of English. The Queen's Univ. School of English offers 5- and 12-week courses year round at one of Canada's oldest and best-known universities in an almost totally English-speaking community. Students have the option of living in a University residence with monitors, in a homestay, or in University cooperative housing. The English Only Rule is strictly enforced.

Dates: Jan 7-Apr 10, May 6-Aug 7, May 18-Jun 19, July 6-Aug 7, Sep 9-Dec 11, 1998. Cost: International students: $2,550 12 weeks; $1,275 5 weeks, plus mandatory health insurance (price varies). Contact: Mrs. Eleanor Rogers, Director, The School of English, Queen's Univ., Kingston, ON K7L 3N6, Canada; (613) 545-2472, fax (613) 545-6809; soe@post.queensu.ca, www.queensu.ca/soe.

Special Intensive French Program. McGill Univ. was founded in 1821 and is internationally renowned for its high academic standards. The Special Intensive French courses is offered at 5 levels and run for 9 weeks. Classes are limited to about 15 students per class. There are 4 sessions per year. Instructional methods include the use of a modern language laboratory, audio-visual equipment, and a wide range of activities stressing the communicative approach.

Dates: Winter: Jan 19-Mar 20; spring: Apr 6-Jun 5; summer: Jun 22-Aug 21; fall: Sep 21-Nov 20, 1998.Cost: CAN $1,795 for international students, CAN$1,450 for Canadian citizens and permanent residents. Contact: Ms. M. Brettler, 770 Sherbrooke St. W., Montreal PQ, H3A 1G1 Canada; (514) 398-6160, fax (514) 398-2650; lang@conted.lan.mcgill.ca.

Univ. of New Brunswick ELP. Established in 1954 in eastern Canada, tradition of expertise with international clientele. Language contract base; courses designed for client needs; experienced staff; residential approach. Participants live and learn in English: nonstop, weekday and weekend. Classes extend into the community. Extensive diagnosis, ongoing assessment, constant quality control.

Dates: Three-week format (monthly Sep-Apr) in homestay; 5-week format (May-Jun, Jul-Aug) in university residence. Cost: Three weeks CAN$3,473; 5 weeks CAN$1,800. Includes tuition fees. Contact: Mrs. Mary E. Murray, Director, Univ. of New Brunswick, English Language Programme, P.O. Box 4400, Fredericton, NB E3B 5A3, Canada; (506) 453-3564, fax (506) 453-3578.

Caribbean

Le Français en Guadeloupe. An intensive French immersion course on the Caribbean island of Guadeloupe for adults with intermediate to advanced French skills. This is a total immersion in French language and Caribbean French culture on a beautiful tropical island. Our Guadeloupian friends provide instruction, local cuisine, excursions, and homestays—all in nonstop French.

Dates: Jan 9-26, 1998. Cost: $1,450 includes everything except airfare. Contact: Julia Schulz, President, Penobscot School, 28 Gay St., Rockland, ME 04841; (207) 594-1084, fax (207) 594-1067; penobscot@midcoast.com.

Chile

CWU Semester Program in Chile. Semester abroad program hosted by the Universidad Autral de Chile (Valdivia) that combines intensive language training, core electives in Latin American politics, history and literature, direct enrollment courses, and field research/independent study. Participants enjoy cross-cultural learning experience in the beautiful lake region of southern Chile.

Dates: Spring semester Mar 15-Jul 6 (approx.); fall Aug 15-Dec 15. Cost: Approx. $4,000 (tuition, housing and meals). Contact: Darci Wahl, Study Abroad Advisor, Central Washington Univ., Office of International Studies and Programs, 400 E. 8th Ave., Ellensburg, WA 98926-7408; (509) 963-3623, fax (509) 963-1558; wahld@cwu.edu.

Spanish and Latin American Studies. Santiago offers intensive language studies fulfilling up to 2 years of university Spanish requirements in 1 semester, with additional courses in literature, business, teacher ed., history, political science. Week-long program-oriented field trips to the south and north of Chile, homestays, and many university activities at Chilean university.

Dates: Fall semester Aug 27-Dec 16, 1997; spring semester Jan 7-May 5, 1998. Cost: One semester $3,790; fall and spring $6,340. Contact: University Studies Abroad Consortium (USAC), Univ. of Nevada, Reno #323, Reno, NV 89557-0093; (702) 784-6569, fax (702) 784-6010; usac@admin.unr.edu, www.scs.unr.edu/~usac.

China

Mandarin Language Study. Study intensive Mandarin Chinese at Beijing Language and Culture Univ., the only university in China specializing in teaching Mandarin to foreigners. Classes are intensive with 20 hours of classroom instruction per week. Fees include tuition, textbooks, double-occupancy accommodations, sightseeing in Beijing, cultural activities, orientation, visa processing, and roundtrip airfare from San Francisco.

Dates: Spring, summer, fall programs, and 1-year program. Cost: Six weeks $3,110, 20 weeks $4,720, 12 weeks $3,950, 1 year $6,850. Contact: China Advocates, 1635 Irving St., San Francisco, CA 94122; (800) 333-6474, fax (415) 753-0412; chinaadv@aol.com.

Colombia

CEUCA Intensive Summer Session. Designed for both beginners and more advanced students, this session stresses total immersion. Students live with Colombian host families. Also, classes are small and taught by Colombian faculty. Students can register for Spanish, Latin American Culture, and Handcrafts, but independent studies can be arranged. The session also includes field trips within and outside of Bogota.

Dates: Jun 3-Aug 1. Cost: $3,200. Includes room, board, and all land transportation. Contact: CEUCA, Jennifer Jones, U.S. Program Coordinator, P.O. Box 14942, Gainesville, FL 32604; Tel./fax (352) 376-5515; ceuca@gnv.fdt.net, http://gnvfdt.net/~ceuca/.

Costa Rica

Costa Rican Language Academy. Costa Rican-owned and- operated language school offers first-rate Spanish instruction in a warm and friendly environment. Teachers with university degrees. Small groups or private classes. Included free in the programs are airport transportation, coffee and natural refreshments, excursions, Latin dance, Costa Rican cooking, music, and conversation classes to provide students with complete cultural immersion.

Dates: Year round (start anytime). Cost: $135 per week or $220 per week for program with homestay. All other activities and services included at no additional cost. Contact: Costa Rican Language Academy, P.O. Box 336-2070, San José, Costa Rica; (011) 506-221-1624 or 233-8914 or 233-8938, fax 233-8670. In the U.S.: (800) 854-6057; crlang@sol.racsa.co.cr., www.crlang.co.cr/index.html.

Enjoy Learning Spanish Faster. Techniques developed from our ongoing research enable students at Centro Linguistico Latinoamericano to learn more, faster, in a comfortable environment. Classes are 2-5 students plus group learning activities; conversations with middle-class homestay families (1 student per family). Homestays are within walking distance of school in small town (14,000 population) near the capital, San Jose.

Dates: Year round. Classes begin every Monday, at all levels. Cost: $295 per week for 25 hours of classes. Includes tuition, all meals (7 days a week), homestay, laundry, all materials, Costa Rican dance and cooking classes, and airport transportation. $25 one-time registration. Contact: Susan Shores, Registrar, Latin American Language Center, 7485 Rush River Dr., Suite 710-123, Sacramento, CA 95831; (916) 447-0938, fax (916) 428-9542; lalc@madre.com.

ILISA and Language Link. ILISA offers intensive Spanish language programs with a professional emphasis in the quiet university area of San Pedro, a suburb of San Jose, Costa Rica. Your choice of either 4 hours daily of small classes (never more than 4 students), a combination of 4 hours group and 2 hours private, or completely private. Professional adults, college students, and all Spanish levels. Academic credit through accredited university. Caring homestays and 3 additional weekly activities included. Excursion program. A well-developed program is available for families, with nanny care.

Dates: Year round, 2-12 weeks, start any Monday. Summer months fill very early. Cost: Four hours daily of group classes and homestay: 2 weeks $745. Includes registration, insurance, tuition, materials, airport pickup, private room, and 2 meals daily. Contact: Kay G. Rafool, Language Link Inc., P.O. Box 3006, Peoria, IL 61612; (800) 552-2051, fax (309) 672-2926; info@langlink.com, www.langlink.com.

Instituto de Lenguaje "Pura Vida". Only minutes from the capitol in the fresh mountain air of Heredia. Intense total immersion methods of teaching. Morning classes and daily cultural activities all conducted in Spanish, maximum 5 students per class. Teachers hold university degrees. Latin music and dance lessons, tours, trips, parties. Learn Spanish fast.

Dates: Classes for all levels start every Monday year round. Cost: Language only, 20 hours per week $230; total immersion, 35 hours per week with homestay $370; children's classes with homestay $370 per week, daycare available. Contact: Instituto de Lenguaje "Pura Vida," P.O. Box 730, Garden Grove, CA 92842; (714) 534-0125, fax (714) 534-1201; BS7324@aol.com, www.arweb.com/puravida.

Intensive Spanish-San Jose. In San Jose, at Centro Linguisticó Conversa, Spanish language, Costa Rican homestay, breakfast and 1 other meal daily, 6-8 credits, depending on option chosen. Hotel stay at extra cost. Upper division (junior-senior level) credit.

Dates: Operates in 1-month cycles throughout the year. Cost: $1,860 initial cycle; $1,720 each additional cycle. Contact: Reinaldo Changsut, Study Abroad Adviser, Miami-Dade Community College, 11011 SW 104th St., Miami, FL 33176-3393; (305) 237-2535, fax (305) 237-2949; rchangsu@kendall.mdcc.edu.

Intensive Spanish-Santa Ana. In Santa Ana, about 10 km from San Jose, the campus is a 6-acre "finca" with sports facilities and swimming pool. Operates in 1-month cycles throughout the academic year. Earn 6-7 credits on 1 month, or do a "Language Semester" in 2 months and earn 12-14 credits while mastering Spanish, 110 hours per month, classes of 4 students each. Peace Corps-style techniques. Costa Rican homestay, all meals. Optional lodging on campus at extra cost.

Dates: Operates in 1-month cycles throughout the year. Cost: $2,540 per 1-month cycle. Contact: Reinaldo Changsut, Study Abroad Adviser, Miami-Dade Community College, 11011 SW 104th St., Miami, FL 33176-3393; (305) 237-2535, fax (305) 237-2949; rchangsu@kendall.mdcc.edu.

Spanish and More in Heredia. Heredia offers intensive language studies which fulfills up to 2-year university Spanish requirements in a semester or 1 year in the 8-week summer program. Additional courses offered in political science, history, biology, teacher ed., business, literature, etc. Program organized week-long and weekend field trips, homestays, and many local university activities.

Dates: Spring term: Jan 8-May 10, 1998; summer session: May 22-Jun 27 and Jun 22-Jul 27 (1997); fall term: Aug 27-Dec 19 (1997). Cost: One semester $3,790; year: $6,340; summer $1,770 per session; $3,380 both sessions. Contact: University Studies Abroad Consortium (USAC), Univ. of Nevada, Reno #323, Reno, NV 89557-0093; (702) 784-6569, fax (702) 784-6010; usac@admin.unr.edu, www.scs.unr.edu/~usac.

Spanish at Universal de Idiomas. Our international Spanish programs are designed to provide students with total immersion in the Spanish language. Classes are fun and our homestay program provides a natural setting in which to practice Spanish. Our 15 years of experience in language teaching is a definite plus to learning Spanish and meeting friendly Costa Ricans.

Dates: Year round. Two- to 4-week courses. Cost: Economical Global Package: 4-week tuition room and board $950. Contact: Vilma de Castro, Instituto Universal de Idiomas, Spanish Department, P.O. Box 751-2150, Moravia, Costa Rica; (011) 506-257-0441, fax 223-9917; www.universal-edu.com.

Spanish Immersion Program. The Institute for Central American Development Studies (ICADS) offers 30-day programs of Intensive Spanish Languages—4 1/2 hours daily, 5 days a week. Small classes (4 students or less) geared to individual needs. Extra lectures and activities emphasize environmental issues, women's studies, economic development, and human rights. ICADS offers optional afternoon internship placements in grassroots organizations. Supportive informal learning environment. Homestays and field trips. A great alternative for the socially conscious.

Dates: Programs begin first Monday of each month. Cost: One month $1,225 (includes airport pick-up, classes, books, homestay, meals, laundry, lectures, activities, field trips, and placement). Ten percent discount after first month. Contact: Sandra Kinghorn, PhD, Director, ICADS, Dept. 826, P.O. Box 025216, Miami, FL 33102-5216; (011) 506-225-0508, fax 234-1337; icads@netbox.com.

Spanish Immersion Program. Nestled in colonial Barva, equidistant from Heredia's National Univ. and surrounding mountains, Escuela Latina offers an intensive, experience-based Spanish language and culture program. Students live in nearby homestays. Classes (max. 6 students) are taught entirely in Spanish. Tuition includes 20 hours of Spanish, 1 hour of cooking, 4 hours of Latin dance, and 1 hour of music each week.

Dates: Classes begin every Monday. Cost: $875 for 4 weeks including homestay. Contact: Jill Dewey, Apdo 203-3000, Heredia, Costa Rica; (011) 506-237-5709, or 506-261-5233, fax 506 237-5450. In the U.S.: Roger Dewey, (520) 776-7189, fax (520) 445-2546.

Spanish Language. Intercultura Language Institute offers intensive Spanish and homestays in selected Costa Rican families. Academic credit available (with prior notice). Additional free cultural activities: Latin-dance, music, theater, cinema, cooking. Weekend excursions to volcanoes, beaches, rainforest. Volunteer opportunities in social, environmental, and political organizations. Beach campus: optional 1 week per month, study on Pacific coast.

Dates: Year round. Cost: $1,045 per month (shorter stays available). Contact: Laura Ellington, Codirector, Intercultura Costa Rica, Apdo. 1952-3000, Heredia, Costa Rica; (011) 506-260-8480, Tel./fax (011) 506-260-9243; intercul@sol.racsa.co.cr, www.alphaluz.com/intercultura/.

Summer Study in Costa Rica. The purpose of this program is to study Spanish and gain an appreciation for the people and culture of Costa Rica. Participants live with Costa Rican families and are provided 2 meals per day as well as laundry service. Excursions to Orosi Valley, Arenal Volcano, and Manuel Antonio National Park and Beach.

Dates: Jun 28-Jul 26. Cost: $1,750. Contact: Dr. Bill Hart, Compton Community College, 1111 E. Artesia Blvd., Compton, CA 90221-5393; (310) 637-2660 ext. 2545, fax (310) 608-3721.

Total Immersion Spanish. Seven separate year-round language institutes to choose from. Live with a Costa Rican family while taking 3-6 hours of intense language classes a day. Length of program is up to you—from 1 week to 6 months. Locations: cloud forest, beach, country, and San Jose.

Dates: Every Monday except national holidays. Cost: Four-week course with homestay $850 to $2,000. Contact: ISLS, Dana G. Garrison, 1011 E. Washington Blvd., Los Angeles, CA 90021; (800) 765-0025, fax (213) 765-0026; islsspan1@aol.com, www.isls.com.

Cuba

Cuba Language School. Global Exchange, together with the Univ. of Havana, offers a unique language program combining Spanish study and the opportunity to learn about Cuba's complex political and economic situation and rich culture. Study Spanish throughout the week at the University and then sharpen your conversational skills during weekly meetings to explore the issues confronting Cubans. Additional weekend excursions take you to rural areas, beaches, and salsa dancing. Spanish classes are 5 days a week, 4-5 hours per day. Beginning, intermediate, and advanced students are welcome.

Dates: Year round sessions. Two-week and 1-month summer sessions begin May 31, Jun 28, and Aug 2. Cost: One-month program $1,750 from Cancún, México; 2-week program $1,200. Includes roundtrip airfare from Cancún to Havana, visa fees, double room accommodations at a guest house, airport transfers, transportation for day trips, language instruction, 2 meals per day, cultural program. Program extensions and hotel accommodations available. Contact: Michael O'Heaney, Cuba Language Coordinator, Global Exchange, 2017 Mission St., #303, San Francisco, CA 94110; (415) 255-7296, fax (415) 255-7498; gx-michael@global-exchange.org.

Ecuador

Academia Latinoamericana (Quito). Ecuador's number-one private Spanish language institute in former diplomat's mansion with swimming pool, hot tub, sauna, sport facilities. Instruction by university-trained teachers, all one-on-one. Customized study programs tailored to the individual. Select host family accommodations. Excursions to haciendas, Indian markets, etc. College credit and internships available.

Dates: Year round. Cost: One-week tuition, lodging, meals $294. Contact: Suzanne Bell, Admissions Director, U.S., 640 East 3990 South, Suite E, Salt Lake City, UT 84107; (801) 268-4608, fax (801) 265-9156; latinoa1@spanish.com.ec, http://ecnct.cc/academia/learnspa.htm.

Intensive Spanish Language. Specially designed programs for foreign students. One-on-one instruction, up to 7 hours daily. Courses based on conversation, vocabulary, and grammar at all levels. Cultural and social activities provided weekly. The system is self-paced and it is possible to start at any time. Live with an Ecuadorian family, 1 student per family.

Dates: Year round. Cost: $1,430 for 4 weeks. Includes tuition, meals, housing, fees, airport transfer. Contact: Edgar J. Alvarez, Director, Academia de Español, Quito, P.O. Box 17-15-0039-C, Quito, Ec-

uador; (011) 593-2-553647 or 554811, fax 506474; edalvare@pi.pro.ec.

Egypt

The American Univ. in Cairo. Intensive Arabic language training in Modern Standard, Egyptian Colloquial, and Fusha at the elementary, intermediate, and advanced levels is given by the Arabic Language Institute of The American Univ. in Cairo. Full use is made of the Arabic speaking environment of Cairo and classes are enhanced by field trips.

Dates: Sep-Jan; Feb-Jun; Jun-Aug. Cost: Approx. $5,030 per semester for tuition and academic fees. Contact: Mary Davidson, Office of Student Affairs, American Univ. in Cairo, 420 5th Ave., 3rd Fl., New York, NY 10018; aucegypt@aucnyo.edu.

El Salvador

Melida Anaya Montes Spanish School. The MAM Spanish School offers intensive courses at all levels, utilizing popular education methodology and participatory techniques. An integral part of the program includes participation in afternoon meetings with popular organizations and weekend excursions to developing communities and other places of interest, and housing with Salvadoran families with diverse interests.

Dates: Classes begin the 1st and 3rd Monday of every month, except on national holidays (Easter week, May 10, Jun 22, 1st week of Aug, Sep 15, Nov 2, and Christmas and New Year's week). Cost: Weekly costs: Spanish classes $95, Administrative Fee $12.50, Cultural Program $20, Room and Board $60. Contact: CIS MAM Language School, Boulevard Universitario, Casa #4, San Salvador, El Salvador, Centro America; Tel./fax (011) 503-226-2623; cis@nicarao.org.ni.

Europe

Language and Culture Immersion. By choosing one of our schools in France (17 different locations), Italy (Firenze, Roma, Siena), or Spain (Barcelona, Granada, Malaga, Salamanca), you are choosing the guarantee of quality. We have the support of the European Commission (Program Lingua-Socrates) and offer intensive courses for all levels and all ages: general language and specialty courses and methodology classes for teachers. All types of accommodations are available: family-stay, apartment, hotel. You will speak the language of the country all day long thanks to continuous contact with native people.

Dates: Year round, beginning every Monday. Cost: From $400 per week (including course, accommodations, meals and extracurricular activities). Contact: Promotion-Marketing-International, Pascale Mora, Director, 919 N. Kenmore St., Arlington, VA 22201; (703) 528-5300 or (703) 534-0668, fax (703) 528-5316; pascalem@aol.com, www.studyoverseas.com.

Language Immersion Programs. Learn a language in the country where it's spoken. Intensive foreign language training offered in Spain, France, Italy, Germany, and Ecuador for students aged 16 and older. Classes are taught in up to 8 different proficiency levels and are suitable for beginners as well as people with advanced linguistic skills. All courses include accommodations and meals. Lots of extracurricular activities available. Students can earn college credit through Providence College.

Dates: Courses start every second Monday year round. Year programs commence in Sep., semester programs in Jan. Cost: Varies with program, approx. $950 per 2-week course. Contact: Kari Larsen, Admissions Coordinator, EF International Language Schools, 204 Lake St., Boston, MA 02135; (800) 992-1892 or (617) 746-1700, fax (617) 746-1800; ils@ef.com.

France

French and Cookery in a Château. Live and study in 18th century château. Adult courses in French language and Provençal cookery. Relaxed family atmosphere and good food. Château has 13 acres of park and pool. Single/en suite and shared rooms. Close to Burgundy, Beaujolais, Auvergne, and cities of Lyons and Roanne. One- to 12-week courses.

Dates: Every Sunday Apr-Nov. Cost: From $999 full board and classes in Château. Contact: Michael Giammarella, P.O. Box 640713, Oakland Gardens, NY 11364-0713; (800) 484-1234 ext 0096 or Ecole des Trois Ponts, Chateau de Matel, 42300 Roanne; (011) 33-477-70-80-01, fax 477-71-53-00; info@3ponts.edu, www.3ponts.edu.

French in Brittany. Study French in a 19th century manor house overlooking the Bay of Brest, then go home to a welcoming French host family. Small classes taught by professionally-trained French language teachers are offered year round. Use our toll-free number or e-mail address to get all the information you need to choose the right program for you.

Dates: Courses start every Monday of the year; special start dates for beginners. Cost: $500 per week includes 20 hours instruction, materials, homestay with 2 meals per day. Contact: Patty Hayashi, International Summerstays, 620 SW 50 Ave., Suite 400, Portland, OR 97204; (800) 274-6007, fax (503) 274-9004; homestay@teleport.com.

French Language Courses. La Ferme is a residential school of French operating since 1978 for adults in 2 restored 18th century manor houses near the South Atlantic coast. Courses for individuals or small groups include Intensive French, Business French, and this year a new extension course in Paris. See La Ferme's web site at www.edunet.com/laferme.

Dates: May-Oct. at La Ferme; all year in Paris. Cost: From FF4,850-FF11,200 per week and per person including instruction, lodging, and most food. Contact: Mireille or Farrar Richardson, owners and managers, La Ferme, La Petite Eguille, 17600 Saujon, France; (011) 33-46-22-84-31, fax 22-91-38; fer@filnet.fr.

French Language Immersion. International institute on Mediterranean coast. Short- and long-term French courses. Modern air-conditioned premises in large park. Restaurant with terrace. Top-quality homestay, hotels, apartments. Minimum age 17, maximum unlimited. Students, business people, employees, airline staffs, retired people. Charming medieval town linking Provence to Riviera, lively marina, unspoiled beaches.

Dates: Year round. Cost: From FF1,500 per week (tuition). Contact: Institut ELFCA, 66 ave. du Toulon, 83400 Hyeres, France; (011) 44-4-94-65-03-31, fax 65-81-22; elfaca@compuserve.com, www.worldwide.edu/france/elfca.

French Studies (Pau). Pau offers intensive language studies—up to 4 semesters of university language courses in 1 semester, 1 year in the 8-week summer program, in addition to art, political science, history, literature, second language teaching methods, etc. Program organized week-long field trips to Paris, homestay or student residence, and many activities at the French university.

Dates: Spring semester: Jan 3-May 1, 1998. Summer sessions: May 26-Jun 30 (1997) and Jun 24-Aug 1 (1997); fall semester: Sep 2-Dec 19, (1997). Cost: One semester $3,975; 2 semesters $6,980; summer $1,770 per session $3,380 both sessions. Contact: University Studies Abroad Consortium (USAC), Univ. of Nevada, Reno #323, Reno, NV 89557-0093; (702) 784-6569, fax (702) 784-6010; usac@admin.unr.edu, www.scs.unr.edu/~usac.

French-American Exchange. FAE offers language programs in Montpellier, Tours, and Aix-en-Provence from 2 weeks to a full academic year. Housing is arranged with families, in apartments, student residences, or hotels. All programs begin with a weekend in Paris and include tuition, fees, housing, and meals (transportation may also be arranged at additional charge). Ideal for the independent traveler.

Dates: Summer: Jun, Jul, Aug, Sep; trimester: Oct-Dec, Jan-Mar, Apr-Jun; semester: Sep/Oct-Jan, Jan-May, Feb-Jun; year: Sep-Jun, Oct-May; 2 or more weeks year round. Cost: summer $1,742 (4 weeks); trimester $3,020; semester $5,330-$5,502; year $9,795-$14,050; 2 weeks starting from $775. Contact: Jim Pondolfino, Director, 111 Roberts Ct., Box 7, Alexandria, VA 22314; (800) 995-5087, fax (703) 549-2865; faetours@erols.com.

Immersion Course in French. Intensive 2- to 4-week course for professional adults in picturesque Villefranche overlooking the French Riviera's most beautiful bay, 8 1/2 hours a day with 2 meals. Audio-visual classes, language lab, practice sessions, discussion-lunch. Evening film showings with discussions, evening outings with teachers, excursions to cultural and scenic landmarks. Accommodations provided in comfortable private apartments.

Dates: Courses start May 5, Jun 2, Jun 30, Aug 4, Sep 1, etc. (year round). Cost: May-Nov (1997): FF16,700 for 4 weeks. Accommodations from FF2,300 to FF5,800 for 4 weeks, depending on type of lodging (individual room, family, studio apartment, etc.) Contact: Elisabeth Martin, Institut de Francais, 23 ave. Général Leclerc, 06230 Villefranche/Mer TR7, France.

Learn French in France. Language immersion courses in France (Paris, Nice, Antibes, Bordeaux, Cannes, Monaco, Aix-en-Provence, Tours). Private language schools centrally located, convenient to interesting places, cultural events, sports activities. Programs feature qualified teachers, small classes, attractive surroundings and facilities. Affordable prices for instruction. Accommodations with French families with meals, student residences, apartments, and nearby hotels.

Dates: Year round. Two weeks or more. Cost: Two-week courses with or without accommodations range from $605 to $2,260. Contact: Ms. Lorraine Haber, Study Abroad Coordinator, CES Study Abroad Program, The Center for English Studies, 330 7th Ave., 6th Fl., New York, NY 10001; (212) 629-7300, fax (212) 736-7950.

Live and Learn French. Live with a carefully selected, welcoming French family in the Paris region. Learn from a family member/teacher who has a university degree and will tailor a private course to suit your needs. Share in a cultural and learning experience that will develop both your understanding of the language and the people who speak it. Minimum of 1 week stay. We also offer touristic stays conducted in English or French.

Dates: Year round. Cost: Fifteen hours of study per week $1,150; 20 hours of study per week $1,310. Two people coming together $1,675 per week. Prices include room, 3 meals a day, and instruction. Contact: Sara S. Monick, Live & Learn, 4215 Poplar Dr., Minneapolis, MN 55422; (612) 374-2444, fax (612) 374-3290.

Penn-in-Tours. For students interested in French language, literature, art, and civilization. Penn-in-Tours also offers various cultural opportunities and excursions in the beautiful Loire Valley. Students live with local families.

Dates: May 27-Jul 10. Cost: Tuition $2,840; family lodging $1,350; excursion and activity fee $250. Contact: Penn Summer Abroad, College of General Studies, Univ. of Pennsylvania, 3440 Market St., Suite 100, Philadelphia, PA 19104-3335; (215) 898-5738, fax (215) 573-2053.

Germany

Collegium Palatinum. A German language institute located in downtown Heidelberg, offering German at all levels from beginner to advanced. Two-, 4- and 8-week courses year round. Combination courses, one-on-one, and customized courses for groups. Recreational and cultural program. Accommodations: residential, guest family, private arrangement, or hotel.

Dates: Year round. Cost: Four weeks DM2,370; 8 weeks DM1,730. Activity program extra. Contact: Mrs. Martine Berthet-Richter, PR Director, Adenauerplatz 8, D-69115 Heidelberg, Germany; (011) 49-6221-46289, fax 182023; schillerus@aol.com.

German as a Foreign Language. We offer the following educational programs: various levels of German year round; intensive, crash, and long-term courses, individual tuition; special feature: German and Theater; special programs: business German for professionals, German for teachers, German in a teacher's home, German for special purposes. Academic year for high school students, international study year, internship, guest studentship, homestays for groups, courses for firms and other institutions (banking, insurance, doctors, lawyers, etc.), residential language camps for juniors, examination preparation. Various types of accommodations. Full range of activities.

Dates: Year round. Contact: GLS Sprachenzentrum, Barbara Jaeschke, Managing Director, Kolonnenstrasse 26, 10829 Berlin, Germany; (011) 49-30-787-41-52; fax 41-92; gls.berlin@t-online.de.

German as a Foreign Language. Students from all over the world are taught in small groups or on an individual basis. The school accepts all levels from total beginner to advanced, prepares for official examinations, offers courses for specific purposes, etc. Part of all courses: transmission of German culture, history, and news. The variety of art, culture and leisure activities in and around Munich provides each student endless possibilities. Baviera even has a Travel Service offering flights, tours, etc.

Dates: Year round except Christmas. Courses start every Monday. Cost: Small group: DM506 per week. Accommodations extra. Contact: Baviera, Nymphenburger Str. 154, 80634 Munich, Germany; (011) 49-89-1665599, fax 1665530; baviera@t-online.de.

German in Bavaria. We offer a wide range of courses to suit all needs: short-term, long-term, and intensive courses in Munich and other places of interest in one of the most beautiful regions of Bavaria. Program includes tuition, certificate, accommodations in residential centers or with a host family, excursions, and leisure activities.

Dates: Year round. Cost: From $1,700 for 2 weeks (half-board, tuition, leisure activities and excursions). Contact: Cornelia Kossakowski, BWS Germanlingua, Westliche Zwingergasse 11, D-94469, Deggendorf, Germany; (011) 49-0-991-370210, fax 3702121; BWS@edevau.net.

German Language Courses. 1. Group tuition available at all levels. 2. One-on-one tuition, tailor made. 3. Summer school in Aug for ages 11-16. 4. Cultural program.

Dates: Any Monday, year round. Cost: Two week group tuition, 10 lessons a week DM720; half board, single room DM410. Contact: Inlingua, Senalinger-Tor-Platz 6, D-80336 Munich, Germany; (011) 49-89-2311530, fax 2609920; info@inlingua.de, www.inlingua.de.

German Language in Munich. Group tuition available at all levels. Choose 20, 26, or 30 lessons a week or preparation for officially recognized exams. One-to-one tuition with 10, 20, 30, 40, or 50 lessons a week.

Dates: Every Monday, year round. Cost: Twenty lessons a week (group): DM720 (tuition only, 2 weeks); half board, single room DM367 per week. Contact: Inlingua School, Sendlinger-Tor-P 6, D-80336 Muenchen, Germany; (011) 49-89-2311530, fax 2609920; info@inlingua.de, www.inlingua.de.

German Studies. Intensive language study—up to 2 years of university language requirements in 1 semester. Additional courses in history, political science, culture, literature, etc. Program-organized field trips and housing. Beautiful city only 30 minutes from Hamburg.

Dates: Spring semester: Jan 6-May 19, 1998; Summer: May 23-Jun 27 (1997) and Jun 22-Jul 27 (1997); fall semester: Aug 26-Dec 16 (1997); Cost: One semester: $3,575; fall and spring: $5,575; summer: $1,385 per session, $2,385 both sessions. Contact: University Studies Abroad Consortium (USAC), Univ. of Nevada, Reno #323, Reno, NV 89557-0093; (702) 784-6569, fax (702) 784-6010; usac@admin.unr.edu, www.scs.unr.edu/~usac.

Learn German in Germany or Austria. Language immersion courses in Germany (Berlin, Freiburg, Stuttgart, Munich, Hamburg, Frankfurt) or Austria (Vienna). Private language schools centrally located, convenient to interesting places, cultural events, sports activities. Programs feature qualified teachers, small classes, attractive surroundings and facilities. Affordable prices for instruction. Accommodations with German or Austrian families with meals, student residences, apartments, and nearby hotels.

Dates: Year round. Two weeks or more. Cost: Two-week courses with or without accommodations range from $465-$1,355. Contact: Ms. Lorraine Haber, Study Abroad Coordinator, CES Study Abroad Program, The Center for English Studies, 330 7th Ave., 6th Floor, New York, NY 10001; (212) 629-7300, fax (212) 736-7950.

Penn-in-Freiburg. For students interested in coursework in intensive intermediate German. This program offers German language students an opportunity to gain proficiency skills and cultural insight while studying in the center of Renaissance Germany.

Dates: Jul 15-Aug 21. Cost: Tuition $2,840; housing and activities $600. Contact: Penn Summer Abroad, College of General Studies, Univ. of Pennsylvania, 3440 Market St., Suite 100, Philadelphia, PA 19104-3335; (215) 898-5738, fax (215) 573-2053.

Summer School for German Language. Language instruction on all levels (mornings); seminars and lectures on German literature, society, culture (afternoons); excursions, parties, concerts, theater (evenings).

Cost: DM810 (does not include room and board). Contact: Gisela Plock, Internationaler Ferienkurs, Seminarstr. 2, D-69117 Heidelberg, Germany; (011) 49-6221-54-23-38, fax 54-23-32.

Greece

CYA Summer 1998. Three- and 6-week programs on Ancient Greek Civilization, Modern Greek Language (4 levels).

Dates: Jun 9-Jul 17, 1998. Cost: $3,450 (Jun 9-Jul 17, including study-travel); $1,750 (Jun 29-Jul 17 on island of Paros); $1,550 (Jun 9-Jun 26 in Athens). Covers tuition, housing, and course materials. Contact: College Year in Athens, North American Office, Dept. T, P.O. Box 390890, Cambridge, MA 02139-0010; (617) 494-1008, fax (617) 494-1662; cyathens@aol.com.

Intensive Modern Greek Language. Beginning, intermediate, and advanced levels of modern Greek classes meet for a total of 60 hours of intensive exercises and instruction in speaking, vocabulary, role-playing, grammar, reading, and writing. Held on the island of Paros.

Dates: Jun 29-Jul 17, 1998. Cost: $1,750. Includes tuition, course materials, housing. Contact: College Year in Athens, North American Office, Dept. T, P.O. Box 390890, Cambridge, MA 02139-0010; (617) 494-1008, fax (617) 494-1662; cyathens@aol.com.

Modern Greek Language. The modern Greek language program is a comprehensive, integrated approach to learning modern Greek. Courses are year round, and include beginning through advanced proficiency levels. The syllabus has been created to teach the language to adults of all nationalities, using textbooks developed at the Center. Classes are small, with an average of 8-12 participants in each course. Three-week summer courses offered in July on the island of Spetses.

Dates: Year round, new courses begin every month. Cost: $415 per 60-hour course. Contact: Rosemary Donnelly, Program Director, 48 Archimidous St., Athens 116 36, Greece; (011) 301-701-5242, fax 701-8603.

Modern Greek Language Courses. Modern Greek classes are offered at all levels throughout the year. Students are taught to speak, read, write, and understand Modern Greek through the communicative approach that emphasizes the development of fluency in the real use of the language. Pair and group work is used to maximize active student participation.

Dates: Oct-Sep. Cost: GRD75,000 (registration, fees). Contact: Dimitrios Tolias, Hellenic American Union, 22 Massalias St., 10680 Athens, Greece; (011) 30-1-3607305 or 3633174; hol@hau.gr.

The Aegean School. This course focuses on the ancient Greek idea of the structure of society and its culture as the highest form of art (techne) starting with the art and mythology of the pre-Classical periods through the Classical and Hellenistic periods to Byzantine times. Members explore the ways in which varying philosophies, mythology, literature, drama, and art and architecture contributed to ancient Greek and Byzantine life. Most major archaeological sites and museums throughout Greece are visited and studied; lessons and seminars in modern Greek language and culture are presented. The program is rigorous and each applicant should be in good physical condition.

Dates: Jun 22-Jul 25. Cost: $1,900. Tuition includes all intra-Greece travel, taxes, and transfer fees; room and board averages $40 per day. Airfare fluctuates with prevailing seasonal rates. Contact: Professor Philip Drew, Aegean School of Classical Studies and Philosophy, P.O. Box 3602, Arlington, VA 22203; (703) 528-3375.

Guatemala

Casa de Español Xelajú. A socially responsible program in Quetzaltenango offers Spanish and Quiché language instruction, internships, voluntary work, and educational tours. One-on-one instruction 5 hours a day. Graduate/undergraduate credit in Spanish available, transferable nationwide. Homestay, daily activities, excursions, reforestation/community projects, and lectures on women, development, cultural issues.

Dates: Year round. Classes begin every Monday. Cost: For Spanish program and homestay: from Sep-May $145 per week; Jun-Aug $170 per week. For internships: $55 per week including homestay. $40 registration for both programs. For other programs, please contact us. Contact: CEX, P.O. Box 3275, Austin, TX 78764-3275; (512) 416-6991, fax (512) 416-8965; cexspanish@aol.com, http://members.aol.com/cexspanish. In Guatemala: Apartado Postal 302, Queltzaltenango, Guatemala; (011) 502-761-2628; voces@aol.com.

Centro Linguistico Maya (CLM). One-on-one Spanish instruction at one of Antigua's most respected institutions. Flexible programs from 4 to 7 hours of instruction per day include local excursions twice a week. Airport reception any time and homestay placement upon arrival. Wide range of hotels are available.

Dates: Ongoing. Cost: $135 per week includes 4 hours of instruction per day and room and board with a local family. $25 for airport reception. $50 inscription fee.

Contact: Guatemala Unlimited, P.O. Box 786, Berkeley, CA 94701; (800) 733-3350, fax (415) 661-6149; guatemala1@aol.com.

Centro Maya de Idiomas (CMI). CMI is a cooperative created by indigenous people with an indigenous philosophy, structure, and image. Learn Spanish or a Mayan language: K'iche', Kaqchikel, Mam, Jakalteko, Q'anjob'al, and Q'eqchi'. Learning one of the languages will enable you to live within the spirit of the community.

Dates: Year round. Cost: $120 per week; summer tuition $140 (May 15-Sep 15). Includes classes, family stay and activities. Contact: Max Kintner and Mary Pliska, 710 Webster, New Orleans, LA 70118; (504) 899-4666, fax (504) 899-1869; centromaya@aol.com.

Centro Pop Wuj. This teacher-owned cooperative uses profits from the school to address problems of poverty, health, and environmental degradation in Guatemala. Centro Pop Wuj provides materials for community self-help projects and scholarships for local indigenous students. The program consists of 4 1/2 hours of one-on-one instruction in Spanish 5 days per week plus a variety of extracurricular activities, including community service work projects, conferences, films, and trips. Students have the opportunity to live with a Guatemalan family.

Dates: Year round. Classes begin each Monday. Cost: $125 per week includes homestay (room and meals) with Guatemalan family. $20 registration fee additional. Contact: Current U.S. volunteer info: Centro de Estudios Pop Wuj, P.O. Box 158, Sandstone, WV 25985-0158; (304) 466-2685, fax (304) 466-4399; popwuj@aol.com. In Guatemala: Apdo. Postal 68, Quetzaltenango, Guatemala; Tel./fax (011) 502-761-8286; popwujxel@pronet.net.gt.

Eco-Escuela de Español. The Eco-Escuela de Español offers a unique educational experience by combining intensive Spanish language instruction with volunteer opportunities in conservation and community development projects. Students are immersed in the language, culture, and ecology of Petén, Guatemala—an area renowned for its tropical forests and ancient Mayan ruins. Ecological activities integrate classroom with field-based experiences.

Dates: Every Monday year round. Cost: Classes $65 per week (based on 20 hours of individual instruction per week, Monday-Friday). Room and board with local families $60 per week. Registration fee $10. Contact: Eco-Escuela, Conservation International, 2501 M St., NW, Suite 200, Washington, DC 20037; (202) 973-2264, fax (202) 331-9328; ecoescuela@conservation.org.

Escuela de Español "Sakribal." Program provides one-on-one intensive language instruction while giving students the chance to volunteer on student-supported development projects in the surrounding community, working in organic gardens and in the country's only women's shelter. Family stays, guest lecturers, group discussions, and cultural activities round out the immersion program.

Dates: Classes start every Monday year round. Cost: $120 per week (includes classes, family stay, project work, other school activities). Contact: U.S. Office: 550 Ferncroft Ct., Danville, CA 94526; (510) 820-3632, fax (510) 820-6658; sakribal2 @aol.com, http://kcyb.com.sakribal.

ICA Spanish/Guatemalan Culture. Our complete immersion program consists of one-on-one personalized language instruction 5 hours per day, 5 days per week, living with a Guatemalan family, and daily cultural activities include visits to surrounding villages, markets, cultural conferences, etc. It is also possible to do volunteer work for projects that help benefit the community.

Dates: Year round, 1-week classes. Cost: $120 per week Sep-May, $130 per week

Jun-Aug. Contact: Bonnie and Dale Barth, U.S. Contacts, RR #2, Box 101, Stanton, NE 68779; Tel./fax (402) 439-2943. Or: Enrique Diaz, Director, la Calle 16-93, Zona 1, 09001 Quetzaltenango, Guatemala, C.A.; Tel./fax (011) 502-763-1871; icaxela13@pronet.net.gt.

Juan Sisay Spanish School. Extremely active, unique nonprofit educational collective. Encourages student participation in local community/social projects. Percentage of student's tuition returned to Mayan development programs. Usually only one student per family. Daily planned afternoon activities led by teachers: reforestation projects, hiking to volcanoes/hot springs, visiting Mayan villages, orphanages, and festivals.

Dates: Year round. Cost: $110 per week, ($125 per week from Jun 1-Aug 15). Includes: 25 hours instruction, room and board with family, afternoon activities. Contact: Juan Sisay Spanish School, 15 av. 8-38 Zona 1, Quetzattenango, Guatemala; Fax (011) 502-7-63-1684; bufetej@ pronet. net.gt. In U.S.: (770) 436-6283.

Kie-Balam Spanish Language School. The school features one-on-one instruction with university-degreed teachers. Special group rate program for teachers, social workers and medical personnel. Course work transfers to degree programs. School starts rural lending libraries, helps at a battered women's shelter, and works with a special education school.

Dates: Year round, classes start Mondays. Cost: Application fee $50; tuition $100 per week (includes room and board). Contact: Martha Weese, 1007 Duncan Ave., Elgin, IL 60120; (847) 888-2514 (U.S.), (011) 502-7-611636; fax 610391(Guatemala from U.S.); moebius@super-highway.net.

La Paz Spanish School. Non-profit Spanish language and cultural immersion program. Weekly price includes 25 hours private instruction, family homestay, meals, educational/recreational activities. Volunteer possibilities on projects emphasizing education, natural health, women's empowerment. Qualified, well-trained teachers and friendly, helpful staff. Activities include conferences, videos, hikes, field trips. Peaceful, heart-centered setting.

Dates: Year round. Cost: $100 ($125 Jun-Aug). Room and board, activities, private instruction. Contact: Roy Holman, 5762 26th Ave. NE, Seattle, WA 98105; (206) 729-7664; roymundo@aol.com.

P.L.F.M. of Antigua. Proyecto Linguistico Francisco Marroquin of Antigua offers intensive Spanish language programs in the charming colonial city of Antigua, Guatemala. Includes 7 hours daily of one-on-one instruction. Professional adults, students, retirees, and families at all Spanish levels are accommodated in this nonprofit school, dedicated to the preservation of the Mayan languages, as well as to teaching Spanish. P.L.F.M. is authorized to administer the Foreign Service Institute exam to evaluate Spanish competency. Homestays in private rooms with local families are available. Programs of 1 to 12 weeks. Registration and airport pickups can be easily arranged through our toll-free phone.

Dates: Year round. New classes begin every Monday. (Summer months fill very early.) Cost: Registration fee $35, $135 per week tuition, $65 per week homestay. Includes all meals (except Sundays). Contact: Kay G. Rafool, Language Link Inc. (U.S. Office for P.L.F.M.), P.O. Box 3006, Peoria, IL 61612; (800) 552-2051, fax (309) 692-2926; info@plfm-antigua.org, www.plfm-antigua.org.

Spanish Immersion Program. Probigua is dedicated to two goals: 1) providing the beginning, intermediate, and advanced Spanish student with an intensive, toal immersion experience with one-one-one instruction, trips, daily group activities and homestays; 2) helping the children of Guatemala by donating the school's profits to establish and maintain libraries in many rural villages.

Dates: Year round. Cost: Homestay $50 per week; 4 hours of daily classes $70 per week; 5 hours $80 per week; 6 hours $90 per week; 7 hours $100 per week. Contact: Rigoberto Zamora Charuc, General Manager, Academia de Español Probigua, 6a. Avenida Norte #41-B, La Antiqua 03001, Guatemala; Tel./fax (011) 502-8320-860, fax 8320-082; conex@ibm.net.

Spanish School San José el Viejo. One teacher to 1 student, 32 1/2 hours per week. Spanish language, culture, and conversation, and live in a Guatemalan home. Other languages available. Easy transport from Guatemala International Airport.

Dates: Every Monday year round. Cost: $175 per week. Includes private tutor, homestay, and meals in a Guatemalan home. School only: full day $90 per week, 32 1/2 hours per week; 4 hours a.m. or p.m. $65; 2 hours p.m. $40. Registration fee $10. Contact: Joan Ashton, P.O. Box 1218, Crystal Bay, NV 89402-1218; Tel./fax (702) 832-5678 or (800) JOAN ASH (562-6274). Or (allow 2 months for reply if writing to Guatemala): Spanish School San José el Viejo, 5a Avenida Sur 34, Antigua, Guatemala, Central America; (011) 502-832-3028, fax 832-3029. Allow 3 weeks if writing to Miami mail drop: Spanish School San José el Viejo, Sec. 544, Box 02-5289, Miami, FL 33102; e-mail USA: joanash@aol.com; e-mail to Guatemala: spanish@guate.net.

Honduras

Centro Internacional de Idiomas. Learn Spanish in the Caribbean in historic Trujillo or La Ceiba. Students learn Spanish in a relaxed, tropical atmosphere with a one-to-one student to teacher ratio. Programs emphasize intensive conversation and survival skills, grammar, and vocabulary. Most teachers are university graduates and many are bilingual.

Dates: Year round. Cost: $175 for 4-hour classes, 5 days per week, 7 days homestay. Contact: Belinda Linton, Director, Centro Internacional de Idiomas, TGU 00068, P.O. Box 025387, Miami, FL 33102-5387; Tel./fax (011) 504-44-4777.

Eco Escuela Spanish School. Honduras is beautiful, safe, economical. Our school, located on the beach, has one-to-one student to teacher ratio. Very friendly homestays available. International airport, diving only 20 minutes away. Many activities, volunteer programs, Mayan ruins of Copan.

Cost: $125. Contact: Tom Ellis, Eco Escuela Spanish School, P.O. 797, La Ceiba, Honduras; (011) 504-41-1302, fax 43-0700; escuela@tropicohn.com, http://txinfinet.com/ mader/ecoescuela/eco.html.

Ixbalanque Escuela de Español. Study just 1 km from the ruins or 2 km from the beach. We now have 2 campuses, one next to the Mayan Ruins of Copan and the other in Trujillo, located on the north coast of Honduras. We offer one-to-one student to teacher ratio, a library with games, and study areas. All teachers are Honduran and are trained and certified to teach.

Dates: Closed during the week of Easter, Mar 24-28, 1998. Cost: $185 per week for 4 hours of class, 5 days per week, 7 nights of room and board with local family; $125 for classes only. Contact: Darla Brown de Hernández, Ixbalanque Escuela de Español, Copán Ruinas, Honduras, C.A.; Tel./fax (011) 504-61-4432. In Trujillo: (011) 504-44-4461; ixbalan@gbm.hn.

Spanish Language School. Spend a week or more in a spectacular setting—the magnificent Mayan ruins of Copan, or the tropical beaches of Trujillo while learning Spanish from your own private instructor. Programs include 4 hours of instruction daily (weekdays), and 7 nights room and board with a Honduran family. Hotel based stays also available. All levels of instruction. Small groups and student groups welcome.

Dates: Year round (advance reservations recommended for summer; closed Holy Week). Cost: Single: $235 (7 nights), $410 (14 nights), $615 (21 nights); 2 or more: $205 (7 nights), $410 (14 nights), $615 (21 nights). Contact: Roatan Charter, Inc., P.O. Box 877, San Antonio, FL 33576; (800) 282-8932 or (904) 588-4132, fax (904) 588-4158.

Ireland

EFL/TEFL. DAELS: 1-year full-time postgraduate Diploma in Advanced English Language Studies: English language, linguistics, one other academic subject; Summer school: 15-23 hours per week, 1- to 10-week stay. Levels from elementary to advanced. Options in English for language teachers, business English. Cambridge CTEFLA/DTEFLA teacher training.

Dates: DTEFLA, DAELS Oct-Jun; summer school Jul-Sep. (TEFLA at intervals throughout the year.) Cost: Tuition fees DAELS: IR£1,781 per year, DTEFLA IR£1,600, CTEFLA IR£850; summer school: IR£90 to IR£165 per week. Contact: Steven Dodd/Vivienne Lordan, Language Centre, Univ. College Cork, Republic of Ireland; (011) 353-21-904090 or 904102.

Irish Language and Culture. Irish language programs at all learning levels for adults are offered by Oideas Gael, which also offers cultural activities, learning programs in hillwalking, dances of Ireland, painting, tapestry weaving, Raku-Celtic pottery, and archaeology.

Dates: Apr-Sep, 1998 (weekly). Cost: $150

plus accommodations (from $90 per week). Contact: Liam O'Cuinnea-gain, Director, Oideas Gael, Gleann Cholm Cille, County Donegal, Ireland; (011) 353-73-30248; oidsgael@iol.ie.

Israel

Master of Arts Degree. Ancient History of Syro-Palestine, Middle Eastern Studies, New Testament Backgrounds, Hebrew Language, Hebrew Bible Translation. Two-year MA degrees. Extensive fieldwork and study in the languages, geography, history, culture, social, and religious aspects of Israel and the Middle East.

Dates: Sep-May every year. Cost: Approx. $7,000 per semester. Includes tuition, room and board, fees. Contact: Jerusalem University College, Amelia Nakai, Program Coordinator, 4249 E. State St., Suite 203, Rockford, IL 61108; (815) 229-5900 or (800) 891-9408, fax (815) 229-5901.

Master of Arts in Hebrew Language. A 2-year program studying modern and Biblical Hebrew in Israel. The institute is an evangelical Christian university located on Mt. Zion, Jerusalem with 40 years experience in Hebrew language and Hebrew Bible translation. Other programs also available.

Dates: MA programs begin every fall semester. Cost: Approx. $7,000 per semester. Includes tuition, room and board, fees. Contact: Jerusalem University College, Amelia Nakai, Program Coordinator, 4249 E. State St., Suite 203, Rockford, IL 61108; (800) 891-9408 or (815) 229-5900.

Italy

American Univ. of Rome. Programs for students of international business, international relations, Italian civilization and culture, Italian studies and communications. Credits fully transferable through affilia-tions with U.S. institutions. Housing in studio apartments. All courses (except language classes) in English. All programs are designed to provide students with studies of immediate relevance in a highly competitive job market.

Dates: Fall and Spring semesters plus May/Jun summer sessions. Cost: $4,634 per semester, tuition/housing $2,500. Contact: Mary B. Handley, Dean of Administration, American Univ. of Rome, Via Pietro Roselli 4, Rome 00153, Italy; (011) 39-6-58330919, fax 58330992.

Babilonia-Italian Language School. Study Italian, stroll through historic monuments, climb a volcano, swim aqua-blue waters. Babilonia, the only Italian language school in Sicily, offers: a communicative based approach, 6 levels (4 weeks each), courses from 2 weeks to 6 months length, special courses, extracurricular activities, excursions, accommodations, and much more.

Dates: Year round. Cost: Standard course (4 hours per day) LIT250,000 per week. Contact: Alessandro Adorno, Director, Babilonia, via del Ginnasio 20, 98039 Taormina, Italy; Tel./fax (011) 39-942-23441; babilonia@nti.it, www.nti.it/babilonia.

Business, Economics, Italian Studies. Turin offers a diversified curriculum in English and in business and economics, plus intensive courses in Italian language and culture, literature, etc., at the foot of the majestic Alps. Program-organized housing and field trips and many Italian university activities.

Dates: Spring semester: Jan 4-Apr 30, 1998; summer sessions: Jun 30-Jul 25, 1998; (fall semester: Aug 29-Dec 17, 1997). Cost: $3,975 per semester, $6,980 fall and spring semesters; summer: $1,570 per session $2,900 both sessions. Contact: University Studies Abroad Consortium (USAC), Univ. of Nevada, Reno #323, Reno, NV 89557-0093; (702) 784-6569, fax (702) 784-6010; usac@admin.unr.edu, www.scs.unr.edu/~usac.

Get to Know Italy. Study Italian in a 16th century Renaissance palace in the center of Florence, or in a classic Tuscan town just 30 minutes from the sea. Koiné Center's professional language teachers and small class sizes encourage active participation by each student. Cultural program, guided excursions, choice of accommodations including host families.

Dates: Year round; starting dates each month. Cost: Two-week intensive program $365; 3 weeks $460; homestay accommodations from $115 per week. Contact: In Italy: Dr. Andrea Moradei, Koiné Center, Via Pandolfini 27, 50122 Firenze, Italy; (011) 39-55-213881. In North America: (800) 274-6007; homestay@teleport.com.

Italiaidea. Italiaidea is a center for comprehensive Italian instruction. We offer every level and format of Italian study from intensive short-term "survival Italian courses" to advanced semester-long courses meeting once or twice a week. We offer on-site lectures and visits to historic sites in Italian, conversation, and flexible scheduling. For over 10 years we have been offering college credit courses at numerous U.S. college and university programs in Italy; we now offer both academic assistance and travel/study assistance to our client institutions. Homestays are offered as well as accommodations in shared apartments.

Dates: Year round. Cost: Sixty-hour group course LIT750,000; 25-hour one-on-one program LIT1,170,000; 15 hour-specific purposes or culture LIT1,150,000 (taxes not included). Contact: Carolina Ciampaglia, Co-Director, Piazza della Cancelleria 5, 00186 Roma, Italy; (011) 39-6-68307620, fax 6-6892997; italiadea@nexus.it, www.italiadea.com.

Italian in Rome. Located a few minutes walk from the Colosseum, the school offers intensive and non-intensive, group and individual courses at all levels. A rich extracurricular program includes guided tours, excursions, seminars on art history, architecture, literature, and cinema. Accommodations with family or apartments with cooking facilities.

Dates: Year round, begins every 2 weeks. Cost: Two-week course: LIT470,000, 4-week course: LIT900,000, 12-week course: LIT2,610,000. Contact: Pier Luigi Arri, Director, via Bixio, 74 - 00185, Rome, Italy; (011) 39-6-7008434 or 70474976, fax 70497150; babele@flashnet.it, www.nube.com/babele.

Italian Language (Florence). Intensive courses of Italian language and culture in small groups with maximum of 8 students per class. Four or 6 lessons per day, 5 days per week. Duration: From 2 weeks to 6 months. Full leisure time program. Accommodation facilities: family/half board, rooms with Italians/use of kitchen, holiday apartments.

Dates: New courses start every 2 weeks. Cost: Two weeks, 4 lessons per day LIT500,000; 4 weeks LIT740,000. Contact: CLIC, Centro Lingua Italiana Calvino, Viale Fratelli Roselli 74, 50123 Florence, Italy; (011) 39-55-288081, fax 288125; clic@tzident.nettuno.it.

Italian Language and Culture. Italian language and culture courses (4 to 8 hours per day), small classes, 6 levels of ability, experienced teachers, lots of cultural activities. Locations: Florence, Rome, and Siena, all in the city center.

Dates: Year round, starting every 2 weeks. Cost: From LIT390,000 (2 weeks), language course. Contact: Scuolo Leonardo da Vinci, L'italiano dal vivo a Firenze, Roma, Siena, via Brunelleschi 4, 50123, Firenze, Italy; (011) 39-55-29-03-05, fax 29-03-96; scuola-leonardo@trident.nettuno.it, www.trident.nettuno.it/Mall/leonardo.

Italian Language and Culture. Courses in Italian Language and Culture at all levels. Twenty-five hours tuition per week. Small classes. Special courses in Italian for business and Italian musical culture for opera singers. Housing provided with host families or furnished apartments. Situated in Urbania, small town in central Italy. Where you can live "All Italiana" with Italians.

Dates: Courses non-stop from Mar-Oct. Winter courses for organized groups. Cost: LIT790,000 for a 4-week course includes tuition, guided visits and all teaching material. Housing depends on students' choice. Contact: Centro Studi Italiani, Via Boscarini, 1-60149, Urbania (PS), Italy; (011) 39-722-318950, fax 722-317286; urbania1@internetforce.com, www.pesaro.com/urbania-study.

Italian Language Courses. Group and individual Italian language courses (6 levels). Cultural courses (literature, art history, history of Florence, history of opera, operatic Italian, and libretti), conversation courses, written expression, Italian politics, geography, Italian for business and commerce, Italian for tourism, wine course, cooking course.

Dates: Call or write for details. Cost: Call or write for details. Contact: Dr. Stefano Burbi, Director, Istituto Parola, Corso del Tintori 8, 50122 Florence, Italy; (011) 39-55-24-21-82, fax 24-19-14; lstituto. parola@agora.stm.it, www.alba.fi.it/parola.

Italian Language Lessons. Individual Italian language lessons. Accommodations provided by the school (with a family in hotel or apartment). Course levels: beginners, intermediate, advanced.

Dates: Year round. Cost: From LIT310,000 per week. Contact: Prof. Luigi Foschi, Isttituto Studium, Via Baldini 22, 47042 Cesenatico (FO), Italy; Tel./fax (011) 39-547-84442.

Italian Language, Art Culture. Italian language taught in the heart of Florence. The method is total immersion in the culture. Additional seminars, museum visits, field trips, excursions. Tutor available for extra help at no charge.

Dates: Every Monday (beginners only the first Monday of each month). Cost: From $120. Contact: Dr. Gabriella Ganugi, Lorenzo de'Medici, Via Faenza, #43, 50123 Florence, Italy; (011) 39-55-287360, fax 23989 20; ldm@dada.it.

Italian Studies in Florence. For students interested in intensive beginning and intermediate language courses and cultural studies in literature, cinema, and art history taught in one of the world's most beautiful cities. Numerous cultural opportunities and field trips offer a valuable supplement to class work.

Dates: Jun 3-Jul 12. Cost: Tuition $2,700; housing $1,250-$1,800; travel $800. Contact: Penn Summer Abroad, College of General Studies, Univ. of Pennsylvania, 3440 Market St., Suite 100, Philadelphia, PA 19104-3335; (215) 898-5738, fax (215) 573-2053.

Learn Italian in Italy. Language immersion courses in Italy (Rome, Florence, Siena, Viareggio, Rimini, Bologna, Portico, Milan). Private language schools centrally located, convenient to interesting places, cultural events, sports activities. Programs feature qualified teachers, small classes, attractive surroundings and facilities. Affordable prices for instruction. Accommodations with Italian families with meals, student residences, apartments, and nearby hotels.

Dates: Year round. Two weeks or more. Cost: Two-week courses with or without accommodations range from $295-$905. Contact: Ms. Lorraine Haber, Study Abroad Coordinator, CES Study Abroad Program, The Center for English Studies, 330 7th Ave., 6th Floor, New York, NY 10001; (212) 629-7300, fax (212) 736-7950.

Japan

Lex Homestay Programs. Lex offers homestay programs in which participants, living as members of a Japanese family, absorb the customs and characteristics of their host culture by taking part in daily life activities. Participants may go sightseeing with their families, meet friends and relatives, and attend festivals. Japanese language ability is not a requirement. Host families are fully screened volunteer members of the Lex organization. Adults, students, and entire families are encouraged to apply.

Dates: Jul-Aug: 2, 4- and 6-week programs. Spring: 2-week program. Custom programs year round. Cost: Varies. Four-week summer program $3,030 (includes airfare from West Coast port of departure). Contact: Steffi Samman, Program Manager, Lex America, 68 Leonard St., Belmont, MA 02178; (617) 489-5800, fax (617) 489-5898; exchange@lexlrf.com.

Latin America

Spanish Immersion Programs. Study with small groups or private tutor. Live with local host families or in hotels. One-week to 6 months. All ages and levels. Various settings: beaches, mountains, small towns, large cities, etc. Country options: Costa Rica, Guatemala, Honduras, Panamá, El Salvador, Argentina, Chile, Ecuador, Peru, Uruguay, Venezuela, Puerto Rico, Dominican Republic.

Dates: Rolling admission. Programs start every week or every month. Cost: Depends on location. Prices start at $175 per week and include classes, homestay, travel insurance, most meals, some cultural activities. Contact: AmeriSpan Unlimited, P.O. Box 40007, Philadelphia, PA 19106; (800) 879-6640, fax (215) 751-1100; info@amerispan.com, www.amerispan.com.

Mexico

Centro de Estudios Americanos Language School/Homestay. Wonderful opportunity to study Spanish culture, language, and literature in sunny Saltillo, Coahuila, Mexico.

One-on-one studies throughout year, any dates. Homestay program. Beginning levels to Master's degrees. Great excursions, evening and weekend programs. Tutors provided to beginning and intermediate students. All ages accepted.

Dates: Jul 14-Aug 1 (1997). Cost: $950 (housing, meals, all schooling). Contact: Susie Cook, Centro de Estudios Americanos, 306 Flynn Rd., Branson, MO 65616; (800) 528-7235, fax (417) 334-7735; www.worldwide.edu/mexico/CEA/index.html.

Communicative Spanish Courses. Our team of highly qualified professors has designed a practical, dynamic, and communicative method to learn Spanish in a spontaneous and natural way: 20 hours per week of intensive Spanish in a classroom with a maximum of 10 students. Ten hours per week of seminars, working groups, and guided walking tours.

Dates: Each month begins a 4-week session. Cost: Per person, all sessions: 1-week $100, 2-week $190, 3-week $280, 4-week $360. Minimum enrollment 1 week. Lessons and books included. One-on-one instruction ($10 per hour) and personalized courses (business, teachers, etc.) available upon request. Contact: Angélica Rodriguez de Tonelli, Director, Instituto "Habla Hispana," Calzada de la Luz #25, Apdo 689, C.P. 37700, San Miguel de Allende, GTO, Mexico; Tel./fax (011) 52-415-2-07-13; hhispana@iname.com or 74054.1400@compuserve.com, www.vms.utexas.edu/~kcargill/index.html.

El Bosque del Caribe, Cancun. Take a professional Spanish course 25 hours per week and enjoy the Caribbean beaches. Relaxed family atmosphere. No more than 6 students per class. Special conversation program. Mexican cooking classes and excursions to the Mayan sites. Housing with Mexican families. College credit available.

Dates: Year round. New classes begin every Monday. Group programs arranged at reduced fees. Cost: Enrollment fee $100, $175 per week. One week with a Mexican family $150. Contact: Eduardo Sotelo, Director, Calle Piña 1, S.M. 25, 77500 Cancún, Mexico; (011) 52-98-84-10-38, fax 84-58-88; bcaribe@mail.cancun-language.com.mx

Encuentros. Encuentros is a Spanish immersion program in Cuernavaca, Morelos that focuses on the language needs of adults who need Spanish for professional reasons or other specific purposes—such as travel. Visits included in the schedule relate to students' reasons for acquiring the language. Beginners to advanced students. Groups of 4 students maximum.

Dates: Year round, classes begin each week. Contact: Encuentros, Calle Morelos 36, Colonia Acapantzingo, 62440 Cuernavaca, Morelos, Mexico; (011) 52-73-12-50-88; encuent@infosel.net.mx or encuent@microweb.com.mx, http://cuernavaca.infosel.com.mx/encuentros/spanish/htm.

Guadalajara Summer School. For the 46th year, the Univ. of Arizona Guadalajara Summer School will offer intensive Spanish in the 6-week session, intensive Spanish in the 3-week session, and upper-division Spanish and Mexico-related courses in the 5-week session. Courses may be taken for credit or audit.

Dates: Jul 6-Aug 20. Cost: $1,038-$2,000 includes tuition and host family housing with meals. Contact: Dr. Macario Saldate IV, Director, Guadalajara Summer School, The Univ. of Arizona, P.O. Box 40966, Tucson, AZ 85717; (520) 621-5137; janeg@u.arizona.edu, www.coh.arizona.edu/gss.

Instituto Allende. Arts and crafts, Spanish at all levels, Mexican studies, field trips, lectures. BFA, MFA programs. College transfer credit. Incorporated with the Univ. of Guanajuato since 1953. Noncredit students of all ages also welcome. Campus is the 18th century hacienda of the Counts of Canal.

Dates: Year round. Cost: Tuition, Spanish $150-$420 per 4 weeks, depending on hours. Contact: Rodolto Fernandez, Executive Director, Instituto Allende, San Miguel de Allende, Guanajuato, Mexico 37700; (011) 52-415-2-01-90, fax 2-45-38; allende1@celaya.ugto.mx.

Instituto Cultural Oaxaca. Spanish Language and Mexican Culture Immersion Program on lovely Oaxacan estate. Grammar and literature and conversation classes offered at 7 levels. Cultural workshops in cooking, pottery, dancing, weaving, music. Local conversation partner. Weekly lectures and cultural activities. Seven contact hours daily. Optional tours to archaeological sites and artisan villages. Hometays available. Special group programs.

Dates: Year-round monthly sessions. Write, call, or fax for specific dates and informative brochure. Cost: $50 registration fee and $400 per 4-week session or $105 per week. Contact: Lic Lucero Topete, Director, Instituto Cultural Oaxaca, Apartado Postal #340, Oaxaca, Oaxaca, C.P. 68000, Mexico; (011)-52-951-53404, fax 53728; inscuoax@antequera.com, http://antequera.com/inscuoax.

Intensive Spanish Course. The Academia Hispano Americana, the oldest full-time specialized Spanish language program in Mexico, offers students 35 hours per week of activities in the Spanish language. Courses are held year round and start almost every 4 weeks. San Miguel is a pleasant mountain community with clear air and many cultural opportunities.

Dates: Jan 5, Feb 2, Mar 2, Mar 30, May 4, Jun 1 and 29, Jul 27, Aug 24, Sep 21, Oct 19, Nov 16, 1998. Cost: Tuition $400 per session, discounts after first full session. Room and board from $15 per day. Contact: Gary De Mirjyn, Director, Academia

Hispano Americana, Mesones 4, San Miguel de Allende, Gto., Mexico; (011) 52-415-2-0349 or 2-4349, fax 2-2333; academia@unisono.net.mx.

Intensive Spanish in Cuernavaca. Cuauhnahuac, founded in 1972, offers a variety of intensive and flexible programs geared to individual needs. Six hours of classes daily with no more than 4 students to a class. Housing with Mexican families who really care about you. Cultural conferences, excursions, and special classes for professionals. College credit available.

Dates: Year round. New classes begin every Monday. Cost: $70 registration fee; $650 4 weeks tuition; housing $18 per night. Contact: Marcia Snell, 519 Park Dr., Kenilworth, IL 60043; (800) 245-9335, fax (847) 256-9475; lankysam@aol.com.

Intensive Spanish in Yucatan. Centro de Idiomas del Sureste, A.C. (CIS), founded in 1974, offers 3-5 hours per day of intensive conversational Spanish classes with native-speaking, university-trained professors. Maximum 6 students per group, average 3. Program includes beginner courses to very advanced with related field trips and recommended optional homestay. Also special classes in business, legal, medical vocabulary, or Mayan studies.

Dates: Year round. Starts any Monday, except last 2 weeks in Dec. Cost: Tuition (3 hours per day program: $330 first 2 weeks, $115 each additional week); tuition 5 hours per day programs $490 first 2 weeks, $195 each additional week. Contact: Chloe C. Pacheco, Director, Centro de Idiomas del Sureste, A.C., Calle 14 #106 X25, col. Mexico, CP 97128, Mérida, Yucatán, México; (011) 52-99-26-11-55 or (011) 52-99-26-94-94, 20-28-10, fax (011) 26-90-20.

Language and Culture in Guanajuato. We work with innovative teaching techniques, tailoring instruction to each student's needs. Spanish, Mexican History, Politics, Culture-Cuisine, Folk Dancing and Latin American Literature.

Dates: Year round. New classes begin every Monday. Cost: $925. Includes 4 weeks of classes and homestay with 3 meals daily. Contact: Director Jorge Barroso, Instituto Falcon, A.C., Guanajuato, Gto. 36000 Mexico; Tel./fax (011) 52-473-2-36-94, infalcon@red es.int.com.mx, www.infonet.com.mx/falcon.

Language Institute of Colima. The Language Institute of Colima, Mexico offers a system of total immersion with classes held throughout the year Monday-Friday. Students live with local host families and attend 6 hours of instruction daily; no more than 5 students per class. Many extras, including beach excursions.

Dates: Year round, Monday-Friday. Cost: Registration $80; tuition $415 1st week, $345 after 1st week (for shared room), $445 1st week, $375 after 1st week (for private room). 10 percent discount for 6 or more. Contact: Dennis Bourassa, Language Institute of Colima, P.O. Box 827, Miranda, CA 95553; (800) 604-6579, fax (707) 923-4232; colima@northcoast.com, www. northcoast. com/~colima.

Learn Spanish in Chiapas. Spanish lessons in private sessions or small groups (4 people maximum). Family stays available. School tours to Indian (Mayan) villages, jungle trips available. Extracurricular activities include: Mexican cooking, discussions, and video showings. Teach English in exchange for Spanish lessons. Centro Cultural "El Puente" includes gallery weaver's cooperative, travel agency, cafe, restaurant, phone/fax service.

Dates: Year round. Cost: Highest $220 per week; lowest $75 per week. Contact: Roberto Rivas, Bastidas Centro Bilingüe de Chiapas, C. Real de Guadalupe 55, Centro

Cultural "El Puente," San Cristóbal de Las Casas 29230, Chiapas, Mexico; (011) 52-967-8-41-57, fax 967-83723 or Tel./fax (800) 303-4983; cenbili@chisnet.com.mx, www.mex online.com/centro1.htm.

Loyola Univ. in Mexico City. Loyola offers 17 Spanish courses as well as courses on Latin American studies, communications, economics, history, political science, philosophy, sociology, and visual arts at the Jesuit Universidad Iberoamericana in Mexico City. Financial aid available. Trips to Cuernavaca, Taxco, Teotihuacan, and Tula. Three summer sessions and semester and year abroad program available.

Dates: Jan 9-May 14, 1998. Cost: $2,480 and $2,160 for 6- and 4-week sessions; $6,758 for 17-week semester program. Contact: Maurice P. Brungardt, Director, Mexico Program, Loyola Univ., New Orleans, LA 70118; (504) 865-3539 (day) or (504) 861-3402 (evening), fax (504) 865-2010; brungard@beta.loyno.edu.

Mar de Jade, Mexico. Tropical ocean-front responsible tourism center in a beautiful unspoiled fishing village near Puerto Vallarta offers unique study options. Learn Spanish in small groups and enjoy great swimming, kayaking, hiking, horseback riding, and meditation. Gain insight into rural culture by studying and working in a farmers' clinic, local construction, cottage industries, or teaching.

Dates: Year round. Cost: $865 for 21-day work/study. Includes room (shared occupancy), board, 12 hours per week of Spanish and 15 hours per week of work. Longer resident program available at lower cost. Vacation/Spanish 1-week $365 (includes room, board, and 12 hours of Spanish) 1 week minimum; 21-day Vacation/Spanish $950. Vacation only $45 per night for any length of time. Contact: In Mexico: Mar de Jade/Casa Clinica, A.P. 81, Las Varas, Nayarit, 63715, Mexico; Tel./fax (011) 52-327-20184. In U.S.: P.O. Box 423353, San Francisco, CA 94142; (415) 281-0164.

Spanish. Vancouver Language Centre offers various Spanish language courses in Guadalajara, Mexico. Part-time and full-time courses range from 1 week to 1 year. The curriculum is sophisticated and well-organized, with 8 levels. Teachers are native Spanish speakers with formal training in teaching Spanish as a Foreign Langauge. VLC also offers homestay accommodations and a variety of leisure and sightseeing activities.

Dates: Monthly. Cost: $150 per week (tuition only). Contact: Vancouver Language Centre, Avenida Vallarda 1151, Col. Americana, CP 44100, Guadalajara, Jalisco, Mexico; (011) 52-3-826-0944, fax 825-2051; vic@vec.bc.ca, www.vec.bc.ca.

Spanish in the Land of the Maya. Learn, live and love Spanish in the spring semester: Jan 4-Apr 30, 1998. spring semester: Jan 4-Apr 30, 1998. Land of the Maya. Discover Mayan ruins and visit living Mayan Villages. Enjoy the relaxed atmosphere of colonial San Cristóbal de las Casas, Chiapas and experience the lush vegetation of the Chiapas' Highlands and the only tropical forest in North America.

Dates: Year round starting lessons every Monday and homestays any day of the week. Cost: $170 per week (group lessons, double occupancy). For upper scale lodging, single room and private instruction please inquire. Includes stay with a local family, 3 meals per day, 15 hours of Spanish instruction per week, workbooks, participation in cultural activities, access to dark room and screen printing shop, certificate. Contact: Centro Bilingüe Roberto Rivas-Bastidas or Israel Rivas-Bastidas, rrivas@sancristobal.podernet.com. mx, www.mexonline.com/centro1.htm. Centro Bilingüe Calle Real de Guadalupe 55, Centro Cultural "El Puente," San Cristóbal de las Casas, Chiapas, Mexico, 29230; Fax/voice (011) 52-967-8-3723, Fax/voice mail 8-4157; spanish@sancristobal.podernet.com.mx.

Spanish Language Institute. The Institute offers a complete immersion Spanish program. Maximum 5 students per class. Cultural courses cover politics, economics, art, history, Mexico today. The Institute offers an 8-hour executive program with a private instructor, with a field trip related to her/his area of interest; semi-private with 8-hour program, 3 with private instructor. The programs are complemented with host Mexican families and excursions.

Dates: Year round. Classes begin every Monday. Cost: Registration fee $100. Regular program $150. Housing with 3 meals per day $15/$22. Contact: Francisco Ramos, Spanish Language Institute, Apartado Postal 2-3, Cuernavaca, Morelos 62191, Mexico.

Universal Centro de Lengua. Universal offers Spanish language programs specifically tailored to meet the needs of each student. Spanish courses are offered at all levels, individually or in groups, and are complemented by diverse lectures. Classes range from 2 to 5 students and meet 5 hours daily with hourly breaks of 10 minutes.

Dates: Year round. Cost: Normal $140 per week, advanced $180 per week, professional $200 per week. Contact: Ramiro Cuellar Hernandez, Universal Centro de Lengua, J.H. Preciado #171, Col. San Anton, Cuernavaca, Morelos, Mexico; (011) 52-73-18-29-04 or 12-49-02, fax 18-29-10; students@universal-spanish.com, universa@laneta.apc.org.

Peru

Excel of Cuzco, Peru, and Language Link. Excel, located in the historic former capital of the Inca Empire, high in the Andes Mountains, offers intensive Spanish language programs. Completely private classes for 4 hours daily. Professional adults, college students, and all Spanish levels accommodated. Programs of 2-6 weeks starting on any Monday. Also included is a trip to Machu Picchu or the Inca Trail Trek. Homestays or hotels.

Dates: Year round. New classes begin every Monday. Cost: Two weeks with family stay: $699, with hotel stay: $815; 4 weeks with family stay: $1,299, with hotel stay $1,562. Includes registration, tuition, insurance, homestay with 3 meals or hotel without meals, complete trip to Machu Picchu or trek. Additional excursions including river rafting in 4-week stay. Contact: Kay G. Rafool, Language Link Inc., P.O. Box 3006, Peoria, IL 61612; (800) 552-2051, fax (309) 692-2926; info@langlink.com; www.langlink.com.

Portugal

Portuguese Courses in Lisbon. Intensive Portuguese courses of 60 hours per month. Small groups with an average of 6 students. Portuguese is taught in a fully communicative context. Courses start every 4 weeks. A cultural program of visits included. Accommodation arranged.

Dates: Jan 5, Feb 2, Mar 3, Apr 2, May 5, June 2, Jul 7, Aug 4, Sep 1, Oct 6, Nov 3, Dec 2, Cost: From $600 for 4 weeks intensive (3 hours per day) group course. Contact: Resgate Bertardo da Costa, International House, Rua Marqués Sá Da Bandeira 16, 1050 Lisbon, Portugal; (011) 351-3151496, fax 3530081; imlisbon@mai.telepac.pt.

Puerto Rico

Euskalduna Instituto Internacional. Spanish language and culture program on a beautiful Caribbean island. Travel with 2 weeks notice, no passport or visa needed. We offer: communicative, learner-centered classes with a maximum of 6 students. U.S. university credit; monthly calendar of events; classes at all levels; and an optional homestay program.

Dates: Classes begin second and fourth Monday of every month. Cost: Programs starting at $560. Contact: Director of Study Abroad, NESOL/EII, Edif. Euskalduna, Calle Navarro #56, Hato Rey, PR 00918; (787) 281-8013, fax (787) 767-1494; nesol@coqui.net.

Spanish the Easy Way. Flexible schedules, economy rates, total immersion.

Dates: Year round. Contact: Luis Dueño, Spanish the Easy Way, Ponce de Leon Ave. 661, San Juan, PR 00907; (787) 724-4082, fax (787) 721-3887; Spanish@PRTC.net.

Spain

"El Pueblo" School of Languages. Innovative new language program ideally situated in a small village in the heart of Castile Spain offers true immersion in both language and culture. Courses individually tailored around each new group's particular interests. Emphasis on communicative interaction with the community reinforced with classroom study. All levels. Prescreened host family accommodations.

Dates: Year round. Cost: $459 (1 week), $775 (2 weeks), $1,075 (3 weeks), $1,345 (1 month); includes 25 hours instruction per week, all materials, housing (private rooms), 2 meals per day. Contact: John Cancilla, Director, Plaza Mayor 1, 40430 Bernardos (Segovia), Spain; Tel./fax (011) 3421-56 65 14. In U.S.: Lynda Denman, 954 W. Leadora Ave., Glendora, CA 91741; Tel./fax (626) 914-0494. Portfolio of information available on request.

Commercial Spanish Course. Thirty hours of classes per week in groups of 3-6 students.

Two-week course. Basic and advanced levels. Certificates and examinations in our center. Recognized by Chamber of Commerce and Industry. All course materials. Activities and visits organized by the school are optional. Telefax facilities. Diploma. Exam dates: Mar 15, May 31, Jul 12, Nov 1.

Dates: Mar 3, May 19, Jun 30, Oct 20. Cost: Two weeks PTS85,000; inscription for exam PTS12,000. Contact: Mrs. Renate Urban, Director, Escuela de Idiomas "Nerja," C/ Almirante Ferrándiz, 73, Apdo 46, 29780 Nerja, Málaga, Spain; (011) 34-5-252-16-87, fax 252-21-19; idnerja@gandalf.leader.es.

CP Language Institutes. A Spanish language institute located in the town center of Madrid. Two- to 8-week standard and intensive courses, 4 hours per day. One-on-one instruction, customized courses for groups and combination courses. All levels available. Classes are small and thus offer a great deal of attention to the student. Cultural activities are an integral part of the program. Accommodations in selected guest families.

Dates: Year round (except for the month of Aug). Cost: PTS21,000 per week; PTS23,000 (approx.) full board accommodations. Contact: CP Language Institutes, c/o Schiller International Univ., Mrs. Maria Dolores Romero, Calle San Bernardo 97/99, 28015 Madrid, Spain; schillerus@aol.com.

Escuela Internacional (Madrid, Salamanca, Malaga). Escuela Internacional offers quality programs in Spanish language and culture with U.S. undergraduate credits. Our qualified teachers and small classes (maximum 12 students per class) guarantee you a successful program. Stay with a selected family or in a shared apartment. Enjoy our extensive afternoon activities and weekend excursions. Our professionalism, enthusiasm, and personal touch will make your experience in Spain memorable and fun.

Dates: Year round, 2-48 weeks. Cost: From PTS57,500 for 2 weeks (includes 15 hours per week instruction, room and books) to PTS125,000 (includes 30 hours per week instruction, room and full board, books, activities, and excursion). Contact: Escuela Internacional, Midori Ishizaka, Director of Admissions, c/Talamanca 10, 28807 Alcalá de Henares, Madrid, Spain; (011) 34-1-8831264, fax 8831301; escuelai @ergos.es, www.ergos.es/escuelai.

Group 5 Course on Costa del Sol. Thirty hours of classes per week in groups of 4-6 students. Courses from 2-16 weeks. All course materials. Activities and excursions organized by the school are optional. Telefax facilities. Certificate/diploma. Intermediate and advanced students: any Monday.

Dates: Jan 7, Feb 3, Mar 3 and 31, May 5, Jun 2 and 30, Jul 14, Aug 4 and 18, Sep 1 and 15, Oct 6, Nov 3, Dec 1. Cost: Two weeks PTS80,000; 4 weeks PTS145,000. Contact: Mrs. Renate Urban, Director, Escuela de Idiomas "Nerja," C/ Almirante Ferrándiz, 73, Apdo 46, 29780 Nerja, Málaga, Spain; (011) 34-5-252-16-87, fax 252-21-19; idnerja@ gandalf.leader.es.

Intensive Course on Costa del Sol. Twenty hours of classes per week in groups of 5-10 students. From 2-24 weeks. Registration and all course materials. Activities and visits organized by the school are optional. Continuous progress testing. Certificate of attendance/diploma. Intermediate and advanced students: any Monday.

Dates: Jan 7, Feb 3, Mar 3 and 31, May 5, Jun 2 and 30, Jul 14, Aug 4 and 18, Sep 1 and 15, Oct 6, Nov 3, Dec 1. Cost: Two weeks PTS46,000; 4 weeks PTS68,000. Contact: Mrs. Renate Urban, Director, Escuela de Idiomas "Nerja," C/ Almirante Ferrándiz, 73, Apdo 46, 29780 Nerja, Málaga, Spain; (011) 34-5-252-16-87, fax 252-21-19; idnerja@gandalf.leader.es.

La Coruña Summer Program. Intensive language program providing participants with the opportunity to study Spanish language, civilization, and culture in one of the most beautiful regions in Spain. Cultural immersion is further achieved through homestays with Spanish families. Cultural excursions include Madrid and nearby Santiago de Compostela, site of the famous pilgrimage of Saint James.

Dates: Approx. Jul 1-31. Cost: Approx. $1,700 (tuition and room and board). Contact: Darci Wahl, Study Abroad Advisor, Central Washington Univ., Office of International Studies and Programs, 400 E. 8th Ave., Ellensburg, WA 98926-7408; (509) 963-3623, fax (509) 963-1558; wahld@ cwu.edu.

Learn Spanish in Spain. Language immersion courses in Spain (Barcelona, Canary Islands, Granada, Madrid, Malaga, San Sebastian, Seville, and Valencia). Private language schools centrally located, convenient to interesting places, cultural events, and sports activities. Programs feature qualified teachers, small classes, attractive surroundings and facilities. Affordable prices for instruction. Accommodations with Spanish families with meals; student residences; apartments; and nearby hotels.

Dates: Year round. Two weeks or more. Cost: Two-week courses with or without accommodations range from $245-$865. Contact: Ms. Lorraine Haber, Study Abroad Coordinator, CES Study Abroad Program, The Center for English Studies, 330 7th Ave., 6th Floor, New York, NY 10001; (212) 629-7300, fax (212) 736-7950.

One-to-One, A, B, C Courses. A: 8 hours per day; B: 6 hours per day; C: 4 hours per day. In course A, the student lunches with one of the teachers (meals excluded). Classes Monday-Friday. All course materials. Activities and excursions organized by the school are optional. Telefax facilities.

Met at the airport and transported to your accommodations. Certificate and diploma.

Dates: Any Monday. Cost: Two weeks: A PTS320,000; B: PTS240,000; C: PTS160,000. Contact: Mrs. Renate Urban, Director, Escuela de Idiomas "Nerja," C/ Almirante Ferrándiz, 73, Apdo 46, 29780 Nerja, Málaga, Spain; (011) 34-5-252-16-87, fax 252-21-19; idnerja@gandalf.leader.es.

Penn-in-Alicante. For students interested in the language, literature, and culture of Spain, this program combines classroom instruction with visits to points of cultural and historical interest, including Madrid and Toledo. Students live with local families.

Dates: Jun 25-Jul 26. Cost: Tuition $2,840; room and board $1,500; travel $890. Contact: Penn Summer Abroad, College of General Studies, Univ. of Pennsylvania, 3440 Market St., Suite 100, Philadelphia, PA 19104-3335; (215) 898-5738, fax (215) 573-2053.

Refresher Course for Teachers. Thirty hours of classes, 1 week course. This program seeks to bring teachers up to date on the practical aspects of teaching Spanish as a foreign language and on the reality of Spain today. All learning material included. Telefax facilities. Certificate.

Dates: Apr 7, Jun 9, Jun 16, Jun 30, Jul 28, 1997. Cost: PTS53,000. Contact: Mrs. Renate Urban, Director, Escuela de Idiomas "Nerja," C/ Almirante Ferrándiz, 73, Apdo 46, 29780 Nerja (Málaga) Spain; (011) 34-5-252-16-87, fax 252-21-19; idnerja@gandalf.leader.es.

Semester in Spain. Study Spanish in Seville for a semester, a year, a summer term, or our new January term. Earn 12-16 credits per semester, 4-8 for summer terms or January term. Classes are offered for beginning, intermediate, and advanced Spanish language students. Students live with Spanish families. Outstanding professors, small classes, and lots of fun. Approximately 50 students each semester.

Dates: Fall: Aug 27-Dec 18; spring: Jan 29-May 22; summer: May 28-Jun 19 and/or Jun 30-Jul 23; January 7-25. Cost: Fall or spring: $7,500. Includes room and board, tuition, books. Summer and January: $2,000 (1 term), $4,000 (2 terms). Airfare not included. Contact: Debra Veenstra, U.S. Coordinator, Semester in Spain, 6601 W. College Dr., Dept. TA, Palos Heights, IL 60463; (800) 748-0087 or (708) 396-7440, fax (708) 385-5665; spain@trnty.edu.

Semester in Spain. Semester, year, summer, and January terms for high school graduates, college students, and adult learners. Beginning, intermediate, and advanced Spanish language studies along with Spanish literature, culture, history, and art. All courses taught in Spanish by native Spaniards. Four courses per semester, 4 credits each. Homestays are arranged for all students. January term and summer terms also.

Dates: Fall: Aug 26-Dec 18; spring: Jan 27-May 22; summer: Jun 1-Jun 25 and/or Jul 1-20. Cost: Fall or spring $7,600; year approx. $15,200; summer and Jan term approx. $2,000 each term. Includes tuition, books, room and board. Contact: Debra Veenstra, U.S. Coordinator, Semester in Spain, Dept. TA, 6001 W. College Dr., Palos Heights, IL 60463; (800) 748-0087 or (708) 239-4766, fax (708) 239-3986.

Spanish and Basque Studies. San Sebastian offers intensive language (Spanish or Basque) that fulfill up to 2 years of university language requirements in 1 semester. Plus courses in history, literature, political science, economics, art, teacher education, etc. Program organized field trips to Madrid and elsewhere, housing, and many local university activities in this beautiful seaside resort.

Dates: Sspring semester: Jan 7-May 13, 1998. Summer sessions: May 27-Jul 1, Jun 27-Jul 30, Jul 30-Aug 28 (1997); fall semester: Aug 26-Dec 12 (1997) Cost: Each summer session $1,880; fall or spring semester

$5,990; year $9,370; $4,460 both sessions. Contact: University Studies Abroad Consortium (USAC), Univ. of Nevada, Reno #323, Reno, NV 89557-0093; (702) 784-6569, fax (702) 784-6010; usac@admin.unr.edu, www.scs.unr.edu/~usac.

Spanish and Basque Studies (Bilbao). Bilbao offers intensive language studies (Spanish or Basque) that fulfill up to 2 years of university language requirements in 1 semester, plus courses in history, political science, art, culture, economics, teacher education, literature, etc. Program organized field trips, housing, and many local university activities at this seaside city.

Dates: Spring semester: Jan 7-May 13, 1998; fall semester: Aug 26-Dec 12 (1997); Cost: Fall or spring semester $4,270; year $6,950. Contact: University Studies Abroad Consortium (USAC), Univ. of Nevada, Reno #323, Reno, NV 89557-0093; (702) 784-6569, fax (702) 784-6010; usac@admin.unr.edu, www.scs.unr.edu/~usac.

Spanish Courses in Malaga. Spanish courses in Malaga, Spain. All grades, small groups, 4 hours daily, courses commencing each month. Living with Spanish families (families or in small apartment in town center).

Contact: F. Marin Fernandez, Director, Centro de Estudios de Castellano, Ave. Juan Sebastian Elcano, 120, 29017 Málaga, Spain; 34-5-2290551; ryoga@arrakis.es, www.arrakis.es/~ryoga.

Spanish Language Courses. Raising Language Academy classes are designed for all levels. Lodging provided close to the academy, with easy access to beach, shopping, sports, and nightlife. Excursions to "white villages," Granada, Sevilla, and Cordoba.

Dates: Year-round. For 2 weeks, 1 month, or more. Cost: Varies according to length of stay and kind of accommodations. Contact: Ellen Solomon, Director, Sales and Marketing, USA, 107 W. 82nd St., New York, NY 10024; (212) 362-0709, fax (212) 595-2225; skph48c@prodigy.com.

Spanish Language Programs. Intensive Spanish language programs are designed for people wishing to study in small groups (maximum 8 students). Instruction Monday-Friday 9:30-1:15 for 2 weeks. Includes 1 excursion per week. Courses: survival Spanish, Spanish for business/travel/tourism, etc.

Dates: Jun, Jul, Aug (1997). Cost: PTAS53,000 (tuition, excursions, and study material). Contact: Berlitz Language Centre, Gran Via 80 - 4, 28013 Madrid, Spain; (011) 34-1-541-6215, fax 541-2765.

Study in Your Teacher's Home. A total immersion experience with a friendly family in Barcelona. Don't expect to speak English; expect to improve your Spanish—fast—and have fun. Individualized, private instruction, pool on-site; squash, tennis, horseback, swimming, golf, hiking, beaches, skiing nearby. Also offered in Italy and France. (For other language, arts, or sports programs, see our Europe listing.)

Dates: From 1 week to months, year round. Cost: $830 per week (includes 20 hours per week private instruction, 3 meals per day, private room, airport transfers, laundry service, and 2 organized excursions per week). Contact: Mary Ann Puglisi, eduVacations, 1431 21st St., NW, Suite 302, Washington, DC 20036; (202) 857-8384, fax (202) 835-3756; eduvacate@aol.com.

Summer in Madrid. Students study Spanish language and/or culture: Spanish 2 (Beginning Spanish 2); Spanish 3 (intermediate Spanish 1); Spanish 9 (civilization of Spain); Spanish 4 (intermediate Spanish 2).

Dates: Jun 28-Jul 25, 1998. Contact: Nancy Nieman, Santa Monica College, 1900 Pico Blvd., Santa Monica, CA 90405; (310) 452-9270, fax (310) 581-8618; nnieman@smc.edu.

Univ. of Leon Language and Culture. Our courses include Spanish language and Spanish culture (history, literature, art, etc.). Our students receive a diploma awarded by Spanish Higher Education Institution. Courses at 3 levels: elementary, intermediate, and advanced. Small groups (about 15 students). Students can choose from university residence, living with a family, and flats shared with Spanish students. An attractive cultural-touristic option is also available.

Dates: Summer courses: first session Jul (1997), second session Aug (1997). Permanent courses: second session Feb-Jun 1998. Cost: Summer courses: 1-month PTS 65,000, 2-month PTS85,000. Permanent courses: 1 4-month session PTS95,000; 2 4-month sessions PTS180,000. Contact: Rafael de Paz Ureña, Secretary of International Relations, Avda. de la Facultad, 25, E-24071, Léon, Spain; (011) 34-87-291646 or 291650, fax 291693; germmc@isidoro.unileon.es.

URI Summer Study Program (Salamanca) Spain. Spend over 4 weeks in Spain studying Spanish language, literature, and culture at the prestigious Colegio de España in Salamanca. The program is designed for college students, graduates, and teachers, as well as for college-bound high school students. Program A: Intensive Undergraduate Language and Culture. Up to 9 credits. Program B: Literature, Language and Culture, and Business Spanish. Six graduate or advanced undergraduate credits.

Dates: Jul 1-Jul 30, 1998. Cost: Program A $1,850; Program B $2,050. Contact: Mario F. Trubiano, Director, Summer Program in Spain, Dept. of Languages, Univ. of Rhode Island, Kingston, RI 02881-0812; (401) 874-4717 or (401) 874-5911 or (after 5 p.m.) (401) 789-9501, fax (401) 874-4694.

Sweden

Swedish as a Foreign Language. Intensive summer courses in Swedish (Uppsala) Jul and Aug.

Beginners, intermediate, and higher intermediate levels.

Dates: Jul 6-Jul 24 and Jul 27-Aug 14, 1998. Cost: Approx. $875. Includes tuition, study material, study visits, welcoming lunda. Contact: Marlene Wälivara, Folkuniversitetet, Box 386, 75106 Uppsala, Sweden; (011) 46-18-68000, fax 693484; marlene.walivara@folkuni.se.

Uppsala Univ. International Summer Session. Sweden's oldest academic summer program focuses on learning the Swedish language. All levels from beginners to advanced. Additional courses in Swedish history, social institutions, arts in Sweden, Swedish film. Excursions every Friday. Extensive evening program includes both lectures and entertainment. Single rooms in dormitories or apartments. Open to both students and adults. Credit possible.

Dates: Jun 21-Aug 14; Jun 21-Jul 17; Jul 19-Aug 14, Jul 5-Aug 14, 1998. Cost: SEK21,400 (approx. $2,740) for the 8-week session, SEK11,700 (approx. $1,500) for the 4-week session. Includes room, some meals, all classes, evening and excursion program. Contact: Dr. Nelleke Dorrestÿn, Uppsala Univ. Int. Summer Session, Box 513, 751 20 Uppsala, Sweden; (011) 31-71-541 4955, fax 541 7705; nduiss@worldaccess.nl, www.uuiss.uu.se.

Switzerland

CP Language Institutes. The language school is located in Leysin, a beautiful mountain resort above Lake Geneva in a former Grand Hotel. CP offers 2- to 32-week intensive French and English courses at all levels. International student body, highly experienced teachers and a unique atmosphere. Classes are small and thus offer a great deal of attention to the student. Activity and recreational programs offered. Courses can be taken in conjunction with university courses at the American College of Switzerland.

Dates: Year round. Cost: Per week: Tuition SFR 377, room and board SFR 300. Contact: Mrs. Françoise Bailey, CP Language Institutes, c/o ACS, CH 1854 Leysin, Switzerland; (011) 41-24-494-22-23, fax 494-13-46; schillerus@aol.com.

Intensive French. Founded in 1908, Lemania College is located in the city of Lausanne in a peaceful setting on the shore of Lake Geneva. The professional team of experienced teachers, the individual syllabuses, the computer-assisted language learning method, and the French-speaking area will bring students up to their expected level for official examinations. Leisure activities, sports, and excursions available.

Dates: Year round. Cost: Per week: tuition $450; lodging in boarding house $800, with family: $400; in apartment $170. Contact: Lemania College, Miss E. Perni, International Admissions Office, Chemin de Préville 3, 1001 Lausanne, Switzerland; (011) 41-21-320-15-01, fax 312-67-00; hirtlemania@fasnet.ch.

International Finishing and Language School for Girls. French and English obligatory basic program. Optional courses: cookery, etiquette, dressmaking, design/painting, ceramics, photography, history of art, computer, small business management, German, Italian, Spanish, television studies, tourism, sports.

Dates: Sept, Jan, Apr. Cost: $9,750 for full board, lodging, French and English. Contact: Mr. F. Sidler, Surval Mont-Fleuri, Route de Glion 56, 1820 Montreux, Switzerland; (011) 41-21-9638663, fax 9637013; surval@surval.ch.

Univ. of Geneva Summer Courses. French language and civilization at all levels, beginners to advanced. All instructors have a university diploma. Excursions and visits to Geneva and its surroundings. Class of 15-20 students. Minimum age 17.

Dates: Jul 14-31, Aug 4-22, Aug 25-Sep 12, Sep 15-Oct 3. Cost: SF470 for 3 weeks (tuition). Contact: Mr. Gérard Benz, Univ. of Geneva, Summer Courses, rue de Candolle 3, CH-1211 Geneva 4, Switzerland; (011) 41-22-705-74-34, fax 705-74-39; uni2a.unige.ch.

Thailand

Southeast Asian Studies (Bangkok). Diverse courses in culture, language, economics, business, society, and religions provide a fascinating, well-balanced approach to Southeast Asia. Program-organized field trips, student residence halls, and many university activities at one of Thailand's most modern universities.

Dates: Summer session: Jun 6-Jul 30, 1997; fall semester: Aug 20-Dec 23, 1997; spring semester: Jan 9-May 12, 1998. Cost: One semester: $2,450; year: $4,100; summer session: $1,100. Contact: University Studies Abroad Consortium (USAC), Univ. of Nevada, Reno #323, Reno, NV 89557-0093; (702) 784-6569, fax (702) 784-6010; usac@admin.unr.edu, www.scs.unr.edu/~usac.

United Kingdom

Le Cordon Bleu, L'Art Culinaire. Le Cordon Bleu in London offers the highest diploma in culinary education in just 9 months. Cuisine and pastry classes begin every 10 weeks. Summer abroad program—ICHP—in Paris and London. Catering program for professionals.

Dates: Jun 10-Aug 17 (1996). Trimesters begin every 10 weeks. Cost: From $6,000 to $30,000 for cuisine and pastry 9-month diploma. Contact: In U.S.: (800) 457-CHEF, fax (914) 426-0104. In U.K.: Le Cordon Bleu, 114 Marylebone Ln., WIM 6HH, London, U.K.

Teach English as a Foreign Language. Courses in central London leading to the Cambridge/RSA Certificate (CELTA), regarded internationally as the ideal qualification in TEFL. International House has 40 years experience in training teachers and can offer jobs to those recently qualified in its 110 schools in 27 countries.

Dates: Four-week (110 hours) intensive courses begin Jan 5, Feb 2, Mar 2, Apr 14, May 11, Jun 8, Jul 6, Aug 3, Sep 1, Sep 28, Oct 26, Nov 23, 1998. Cost: £944 includes Cambridge/RSA registration. Contact: Teacher Training Development, International House, 106 Piccadilly, London W1V 9FL, England; (011) 44-171-491-2598, fax 499-0174; teacher@dial.pipex.com.

UCLES RSA CTEFLA. This is the most widely recognized introductory course to the TEFL profession allowing successful participants to work worldwide. The course is extremely practical, develops classroom skills and language awareness as well as dealing comprehensively with methodology, thus providing a sound basis in all aspects of TEFL teaching.

Dates: Oct-Nov, Apr-Jun, Jan-May. Cost: £832. Contact: Guidance Centre, Thames Valley Univ., 18-22 Bond St., Ealing, London W5 5AA, U.K.; (011) 44-181-579-5000, fax 231-2900.

United States

Boston TEFL Course. International TEFL Certificate, limited enrollment, no second language necessary, second career persons welcome, global placement guidance, humanistic orientation to cross-cultural education, teacher training at American English Language Foundation, Harvard Univ. Club or other accommodations, PDP eligible by Massachusetts Department of Education. Also offers the Certificate in Teaching Business-English (Cert. TBE), Executive English, and Accent reduction program.

Dates: Full-time intensive course monthly; part-time courses offered periodically throughout the year. Cert.TBE Course - Intensive 1-week course offered monthly. Cost: $2,300 includes tuition, nonrefundable $95 application fee, internship, international resume, job placement guidance, video lab, all books and materials. Contact: Thomas A. Kane, PhD, Worldwide Teachers Development Institute, 266 Beacon St., Boston, MA 02116; (800) 875-5564, fax (617) 262-0308; bostontefl@aol.com; www.to-get.com/BostonTEFL.

Language Education. Language training in English and all other languages. Flexible schedules by the week or by the month. Individual and group classes. Special programs available in accent reduction and writing skills.

Dates: Year round. Cost: Variable—depends on program length and intensity. Contact: Kelly Keelean, Director, InLingua School of Languages, 200 W. Madison, Suite 1835, Chicago, IL 60606; (312) 641-0488 or (800) 755-8753, fax (312) 641-1724.

St Giles Language Teaching Center. Earn the Certificate in English Language Teaching to Adults (CELTA) in San Francisco, approved by the Royal Society of Arts/Univ. of Cambridge Examination Syndicate and the California Council for Private Postsecondary and Vocational Education. The course focuses on practical training and teaching methodology. Includes access to international job postings, graduate contacts, and teaching opportunities abroad. EFL school onsite for observation and practice teaching. Part of a group of schools in England, Switzerland, and the U.S. with over 40 years of teaching and training experience, led by highly-qualified instructors with extensive oveseas teaching experience. CELTA courses also offered in Brighton and London, England.

Dates: Feb 2-Feb 27, Apr 20-May 15, Jun 1-Jun 26, Sep 14-Oct 9, Oct 26-Nov 20. Cost: $2,450. Contact: St Giles Language Teaching Center, 1 Hallidie Plaza, Suite 350, San Francisco, CA 94102; (415) 788-3552, fax (415) 788-1923; sfstgile@slip.net, www.stgiles.co.uk.

Univ. of Cambridge CELTA. St Giles Colleges (established 1955 in London) offer 4-week intensive teacher training programs approved by the Royal Society of Arts/University of Cambridge Examination Syndicate and, in San Francisco, the California State Department of Postsecondary Education. Program focuses on practical training and teaching methodology. Information on jobs, conditions in specific countries, resume writing, interviewing included. EFL school on site for observation.

Dates: Jan 27-Feb 21, Mar 24-Apr 18, May 5-30, Jun 16-Jul 11, Sep 8-Oct 3, Oct 27-Nov 2. Cost: $2,250. Contact: Teacher Training Coordinator, St Giles Language Teaching Center, 1 Hallidie Plaza, Third Floor, San Francisco, CA 94102; (415) 788-3552; (415) 788-1923.

Venezuela

Spanish as a Second Language. Beginners, intermediate, advanced, and conversation. Grammar-based program encourages the 4 skills: reading, writing, speaking, and listening. Lead students toward communicative competence in Spanish, 20 hours per level.

Dates: Classes begin every Monday. Cost: $147.50 per level. Contact: Carmen Montilla, Instituto Latinoamericano de Idiomas, Avenida las Américas C.C. Mamayeya, 4th Piso, Merida, Venezuela; Tel./fax (011) 58-74-447808.

Worldwide

Academic Credit for Travel. Language immersion programs, work-intern-volunteer experiences worldwide. Independent study courses that provide academic credit for travel undertaken anywhere/anytime in the world. Open to high school, college students, and teachers. Undergraduate and post graduate. Language (Spanish, Italian, French) credit available. Suitable for study abroad, language immersion, short trips, and sabbaticals.

Dates: Year round. Cost: $65 per credit. Contact: Professor Steve Tash, Langue and Travel Study Programs, P.O. Box 16501, Irvine, CA 92623-6501; (800) 484-1081, ext. 7775 (9 a.m.-9 p.m. PST), fax (714) 552-0740; travelstudy@juno.com.

Diploma Program in ESL. The Diploma Program is a noncredit, intensive, 8-week professional training program offered in summers for teachers and prospective teachers of English as a Second or Foreign Language. It covers all essential aspects of English language teaching from a practical classroom perspective. Totals 210 hours of instruction, including practicum.

Dates: Mid-Jun-mid-Aug. Cost: $2,300 tuition (plus room and board and materials). Contact: Daniel W. Evans, PhD, Acting Director, TESL Graduate Programs, School of International Studies, Saint Michael's College, Colchester, VT 05439; (802) 654-2684, fax (802) 654-2595; sis@smcvt.edu.

English Language Intensive Courses for Overseas Students. The Australian College of English (ACE) is one of the oldest and largest independent English language colleges in Australia. Since 1981, students from over 35 different countries have come to ACE to learn practical English for traveling, work and further studies.

Dates: Monthly Intakes. Cost: Tuition: AUS$290 per week, homestay accommodations: AUS$170 per week. Contact: The Registrar, Australian College of English, Level 1, 237 Oxford St., Bondi Junction NSW 2022, Australia or P.O. Box 82, Bondi Junction, NSW 2022, Australia; (011) 61-2-9380-0133,

CHAPTER 12 / LANGUAGE SCHOOLS

fax 9389-6880; info@ace.edu.au, www.ace. edu.au.

English Language Programs. The School of International Studies offers 5 levels of intensive English language instruction. Small classes in oral and written communication. Afternoon electives. Activities program. Twenty-five hours per week. Openings every 4 weeks. We also offer a semester program in University Academic Preparation (UAP).

Dates: Intensive English Program (IEP) openings every 4 weeks year round (closed Dec 21-Jan 9, 1998). UAP semester program: Jan 12-May 11-Aug 8, and Aug 28-Dec 20. Cost: IEP: $1,222 for 4 weeks; UAP Semester Program: $9,324.33 (both include room and board, tuition, infirmary). Contact: Sheena Blodgett, Assistant Director of English Programs, Saint Michael's College, Winooski Park, Colchester, VT 05439; (802) 654-2355, fax (802) 654-2595; sis@smcvt.edu.

Eurocentres Language Schools. Immersion course of 20-25 hours per week for beginners to advanced levels. Learn in small classes with students of all ages from around the world. Full organizational social calendar with extended excursions available to students. Homestay living is available, college credit option.

Dates: Begins monthly year round. Cost: Depends on school and length of stay. Contact: Eurocentres, 101 N. Union St., Alexandria, VA 22314; (703) 684-1494 or (800) 648-4809, fax (703) 684-1495; 100632. 141@compuserve.com, www.clark.net/pub/euroc ent/home.htm.

International Universities. International Universities, established in 1980, is a private educational organization dedicated to providing the highest quality in foreign language and intercultural studies. Travel/study programs are offered in Mexico, Costa Rica, France, Italy, Austria, and Canada (Spanish, French, Italian, and German). Programs,

open to all interested adults, range from 2 weeks to 8 weeks.

Dates: Summer sessions for all countries; some winter intersessions and year-round starting dates in some locations. Cost: $625-$2,395 (includes tuition, housing, meals). Contact: International Universities, 1101 Tijeras Ave., NW, Albuquerque, NM 87102; (800) 547-5678; iu@rt66.com.

Language, Arts, and Sports. Instructional, fun, worldwide. French, Spanish, Italian; sail, windsurf, dive, ski, tennis, golf; photography, painting, French wines, Italian and French cooking; motorcycling, horseback tours and clinics; walking, bicycling tours; cattle ranches, excavations, and more. Combine language study with a sport or art; e.g., French/ski. Join an international mix of people. Let us know your "eduvacational" interests and where you'd like to go.

Dates: Programs run from 1 week to months. Cost: Include room and board, tuition. Contact: Mary Ann Puglisi, eduVacations, 1431 21st St. NW, Suite 302, Washington, DC 20036; (202) 857-8384, fax (202) 835-3756; eduvacate@aol.com.

Master of Arts (MATESL). The MATESL Program is a 36-credit program (39 credits with thesis option) designed for both prospective and experienced teachers. Theoretical and methodological training is integrated with practical coursework to prepare graduates for professional roles in TESL/TEFL or continued graduate study. A variety of practicum experiences are offered both domestically and abroad.

Dates: Begin in Sep, Jan, or Jun. Cost: $260 per credit. Contact: Daniel W. Evans, PhD, Acting Director, TESL Graduate Programs, School of International Studies, Saint Michael's College, Colchester, VT 05439; (802) 654-2684, fax (802) 654-2595; sis@ smcvt.edu.

Peace Corps Opportunities. Since 1961, more than 140,000 Americans have joined the Peace Corps. Assignments are 27 months long. Volunteers must be U.S. citizens, at least 18 years old, and in good health. Peace Corps has volunteer programs in education, business, agriculture, the environment, and health.

Dates: Apply 9 to 12 months prior to availability. Cost: Volunteers receive transportation to and from assignment, a stipend, complete health care, and $5,400 after 27 months of service. Contact: Peace Corps, Room 8506, 1990 K St. NW, Washington, DC 20526; (800) 424-8580 (mention code 824); www.peace corps.gov.

Univ. of Hawaii N.I.C.E. Program. Our program offers 2 courses: E.C.P. (English for Conversational Purposes) focuses on general everyday English; I.S.E. (Intensive Spoken English) focuses on academic and career-oriented English. Students may choose between the two and, in addition, enjoy all the facilities of a university student. Four-week courses offered in the winter and summer.

Dates: Jan 9-Mar 20, Feb 2-Feb 27, Apr 9-Jun 19, Jul 10-Sep 18, Jul 27-Aug 21, Oct 9-Dec 18, 1998. Cost: $1,300 for 10-week terms, $640 for 4-week terms. Includes application and language lab fee. Contact: Ms. Judy Ensing, N.I.C.E. Program, 2500 Dole St., Krauss Hall, Rm. 004, Honolulu, HI 96815; (808) 956-7753, fax (808) 956-3421; nice_info@mail.summer.hawaii.edu, www.nice.hawaii.edu.

CHAPTER 13

STUDY PROGRAMS

The following listing of study programs was supplied by the organizers. Contact the program directors to confirm costs, dates, and other details. If you do not see the program you want in the country of your choice, look in the "Worldwide" listings at the end of the section for programs located in several different regions.

Africa

Development Work. In Zimbabwe you will teach at a school for disadvantaged youth or at a rural health and education project. The Angola project focuses on tree-planting and community work with people of all ages. In Mozambique you will teach street children or at vocational schools. Zimbabwe and Angola are 12-month programs, Mozambique is a 20-month program. Open to students and adults and includes preparation and follow-up periods in the U.S.

Dates: Zimbabwe and Angola: Feb 15 and Aug 15 (1996). Mozambique: Nov 1 (1996). Cost: $4,600. Includes training, room and board, airfare, health insurance, and other direct program costs. Contact: IICD, Institute for International Cooperation and Development, Josefin Jonsson, Administrative Director, P.O. Box 103-T, Williamstown, MA 01267; (413) 458-9828, fax (413) 458-3323.

Kalamazoo in Africa. Programs combine academics and experiential learning. Course work in a host-country setting (with local students in university courses) gives participants a broad overview of the host country. Instruction in the local language as well as internships or independent projects provide opportunities for greater understanding of the host culture.

Dates: Senegal and Kenya: early Sep-early Jun; Zimbabwe: mid-Aug-Jun. Cost: (1996-1997) $19,663. Includes roundtrip international transportation, tuition and fees, room and board, and some excursions. Contact: Center for International Programs, Kalamazoo College, 1200 Academy, Kalamazoo, MI 49006; (616) 337-7133, fax (616) 337-7400; cip@kzoo.edu.

Univ. of Wisconsin in West Africa. Study abroad in Francophone Africa at the Université de Saint Louis in Saint Louis, Senegal. Students experience a blend of Africa, French, and Muslim traditions while they live in dorms with Senegalese roommates. Classes taught in French in a variety of humanities and social sciences. Includes a year-long course in Wolof and an independent fieldwork project. Orientation includes several days in Madison and 2 weeks in Dakar, Senegal. Four semesters of French or equivalent required. Application deadline: first Friday in Feb. Late applications considered on a space-available basis.

Dates: Mid-Sep-mid-Jun. Cost: Call for current information. Contact: Office of International Studies and Programs, 261 Bascom Hall, Univ. of Wisconsin, 500 Lincoln Dr., Madison, WI 53706; (608) 262-2851, fax (608) 262-6998; abroad@macc.wisc.edu.

Argentina

Argentina Universities Program. A loosely structured integrated program based in Buenos Aires. Courses available at 3 universities: Univ. del Salvador, Univ. Torcuato Di Tella, and Univ. de Buenos Aires. Participants can also take program-sponsored courses in Argentine society and Latin American literature. Six-week summer language and culture program is also available.

Dates: Fall semester: Jul-Dec; Spring semester: Mar-Jul; summer program: Jun-mid-Jul. Cost: $4,800 includes tuition, registration fees, excursions, orientation, and partial insurance, site director, support services. Contact: IPA, Univ. of Illinois at Urbana-Champaign, 115 International Studies Bldg., 910 S. 5th St., Champaign, IL 61820; (800) 531-4404, fax (217) 244-0249; ipa@uiuc.edu.

Instituto de Lengua Española (ILEE). Located downtown. Dedicated exclusively to teaching Spanish to foreigners. Small groups and private classes year round. All teachers hold a university degree. Method is intensive, conversation-based. Student body is international, mostly European. Highly recommended worldwide. Ask for individual recommendations in U.S.

Dates: Year round. Cost: Four-week intensive program (20 hours a week) including homestay $1,400; 2 weeks $700. Individual classes: $19 per hour. Registration fee (includes books) $100. Contact: ILEE, Daniel Korman, Director, Lavalle 1619, 7º C, (1048) Buenos Aires, Argentina; Tel./fax (011) 54-1-375-0730. In U.S.: David Babbitz, fax (415) 431-5306; ilee@overnet.com.ar, www.study-abroad.com/ilee.

Instituto de Lengua Española para Extranjeros (ILEE). Located downtown in the most European-like city in Latin America, Buenos Aires. Dedicated exclusively to teaching Spanish to foreigners. Small groups and private classes year round. All teachers hold Master's degrees. Method is intensive, conversation-based. Student body is international. Highly recommended worldwide. Ask for individual references in U.S.

Dates: Year round. Cost: Four-week intensive program (20 hours per week) including homestay $1,400; 2 weeks $700. Private classes $19 per hour. Registration fee (includes books) $100. Contact: Daniel Korman, ILEE, Director, Lavalle 1619 7 C (1048), Buenos Aires, Argentina; Tel./fax (011) 54-1-375-0730. In U.S.: David Babbitz; (415) 431-8219, fax (415) 431-5306; ilee@overnet.com.ar, www.study-abroad.com/ilee.

Australia

Advanced Diploma in Hospitality. This 3-year program prepares students for careers at middle and senior management levels in the hospitality industry. After 2 years students graduate with a Diploma in Hospitality (Management) with the skills to operate as a manager. After 1 year, students graduate with a

Certificate in Hospitality with supervisor skills.

Dates: Feb 10, Jul 14, 1997; Feb 9, Jul 20, 1998. Cost: $3,145 tuition per semester plus living expenses approx. $7,500 per year, ($145 per week). Contact: Mr. Vernon Bruce, Manager, International Education, William Angliss Institute of TAFE, 555 La Trobe St., Melbourne, 3000 Australia; (011) 61-3-96062139, fax 9670-9348; international@angliss.vic.edu.au.

Advanced Diploma in Tourism. This 3-year program prepares students for careers at middle and senior management levels in marketing, sales, and related administrative areas in the travel and tourism industry. After 2 years students can graduate with a Diploma in Tourism. After 1 year, students can graduate with a Certificate in Tourism with supervisor skills, coordinating, or tour planning skills.

Dates: Feb 10, Jul 14, 1997; Feb 9, Jul 20, 1998. Cost: $2,960 tuition per semester plus living expenses approx. $7,500 per year ($145 per week). Contact: Mr. Vernon Bruce, Manager, International Education, William Angliss Institute of TAFE, 555 La Trobe St., Melbourne, 3000 Australia; (011) 61-3-96062139, fax 9670-9348; international@angliss.vic.edu.au.

AustraLearn: Study in Australia. AustraLearn is the most comprehensive Australian study abroad program for U.S. students. You can choose from universities throughout Australia (Queensland, Victoria, Western Australia, New South Wales, Australian capital Territory, South Australia, Tasmania, and the Northern Territory). Semester, year, graduate, short-term experiential, and internship programs are available. Pre-trip orientation.

Dates: Semester/year (Feb or Jul admit), summer or winter abroad short courses. Cost: Semester: $6,500-$9,500, short-term internship: $3,500-$4,200. Contact: Ms. Cynthia Flannery-Banks, Director, AustraLearn, 110 16th St., CSU Denver Center, Denver, CO 80202; (800) 980-0033, fax (303) 446-5955; cflannery@vines.colostate.edu.

Certificate in Asian Cookery. This 15-week program provides students with industry-recognized qualifications in Asian cookery, covering the cuisines of regional China and Southeast Asia such as Cantonese, Sichuan, Chui Chow, Northern Chinese, Thai, Vietnamese, Malaysian, Indonesian, and Nonya.

Dates: Feb 10, Jul 14, 1997; Feb 9, Jul 20, 1998. Cost: $2,775 tuition plus living expenses approx. $7,500 per year ($145 per week). Contact: Mr. Vernon Bruce, Manager, International Education, William Angliss Institute of TAFE, 555 La Trobe St., Melbourne, 3000 Australia; (011) 61-3-96062139, fax 9670-9348; international@angliss.vic.edu.au.

Certificate in Baking. This 6-month course provides basic skills in breadmaking, pastrycooking, and baking. Graduates are eligible to apply for employment in the baking/pastrycooking industry.

Dates: Feb 9, Jul 20, 1998. Cost: $2,960 plus living expenses approx. $7,500 per year ($145 per week). Contact: Mr. Vernon Bruce, Manager, International Education, William Angliss Institute of TAFE, 555 La Trobe St., Melbourne, 3000 Australia; (011) 61-3-9606 2139, fax 9670-9348; international@angliss.vic.edu.au.

Certificate in Professional Cookery. This 6-month course provides students with industry-recognized qualifications in cookery. Graduates are eligible to seek employment as cooks in clubs, restaurants, casinos, motels, reception rooms, hospitals, employee food services, institutions, commercial venues, and private catering businesses.

Dates: Feb 10, Jul 14, 1997; Feb 9, Jul 20, 1998. Cost: $5,000 tuition plus living expenses approx. $7,500 per year ($145 per week). Contact: Mr. Vernon Bruce, Manager, International Education, William Angliss Institute of TAFE, 555 La Trobe St., Melbourne, 3000 Australia; (011) 61-3-96062139, fax 9670-9348; international@angliss.vic.edu.au.

ECU Study Abroad Program. ECU is a multi-campus institution within the metropolitan area of Perth with 21,000 students, including over 1,000 international students from 58 different countries. Two hundred courses are offered at undergraduate and post-graduate level through 6 faculties: Arts, Business, Health and Human Services, Education, Science, Technology and Engineering, and the Academic of Performing Arts.

Dates: Feb-late Jun (Sem I); late Jul-late Nov (Sem II). Cost: AUS$5,500 per semester plus AUS$188 medical insurance. Contact: Joan Wurm, Coordinator, Study Abroad Programme, Edith Cowan Univ., Pearson St., Churchlands, W. Australia 6018; (011) 619-273-8240, fax 273-8732.

Education Australia. Study abroad for a semester or a year at Australian National Univ. (Canberra), Deakin Univ. (Victoria), Univ. of Ballarat (Victoria), Univ. of Tasmania (Tasmania), Univ. of Wollongong (New South Wales), or the Australian Catholic Univ. (several states). In New Zealand courses are offered at the Univ. of Canterbury and Lincoln Univ. (Christchurch). Liberal arts, science, business, biology, psychology, education, Australian studies, etc. Customized internships in all fields are also available.

Dates: Mid-Jul-mid-Nov, mid-Feb-late Jun. Cost: Tuition approx. $4,400, accommodations approx. $2,250. Airfare. Contact: Dr. Maurice A. Howe, Executive Director, Education Australia, P.O. Box 2233, Amherst, MA 01004; (800) 344-6741, fax (413) 549-0741; edaust@javanet.com, www.javanet.com/~edaust.

General Studies in Australia. Victoria offers nearly every discipline in undergraduate/graduate levels at 5 different university campus sites: Australian studies, art, journalism, performing arts, women's studies, biology, chemistry, math, business, computing, etc. Known as the Garden State, Victoria has some of the country's most beautiful mountain and coastal areas.

Dates: First semester: Jul 12-Nov 14 (1997); second semester: Feb 20-Jun 27, 1998. Cost: $4,315 per semester, $7,775 for 1 year. Contact: University Studies Abroad Consortium (USAC), Univ. of Nevada, Reno #323, Reno, NV 89557-0093; (702) 784-6569, fax (702) 784-6010; usac@admin.unr.edu, www.scs.unr.edu/~usac.

Special Interest and Study Tours. Personalized programs for individuals and groups of all ages. We combine education, recreation, accommodations (homestay available), and transportation. Based in tropical Cairns with coverage throughout Australia. Subject areas include: aboriginal dreamtime and culture, Great Barrier Reef, rainforest and savannah. Diving, environmental interpretation, flora and fauna, bird watching, tropical islands and wilderness, adventure safaris and farmstay.

Dates: Year round. Start any date. Cost: Prices and customized itineraries on application. Contact: Murray Simpson, Study Venture International, P.O. Box 229A, Stratford Qld., 4870 Australia; (011) 61-70-411622, fax 552044; svi@ozemail.com.au; www.ozemail.au/~svi.

Study in Australia. Nine programs available in Sydney, Melbourne, Brisbane and Gold Coast, including summer opportunities in cooperation with the National Institute of Dramatic Art and the Univ. of New South Wales. Full range of program services. Need-based scholarships available.

Dates: Fall, Spring, Academic Year, Summer. Cost: Varies. Call for current fees. Contact: Christopher Hennessy, Beaver College CEA, 450 S. Easton Rd., Glenside, PA 19038-3295; (888) BEAVER-9, fax (215) 572-2174; cea@beaver.edu, www.beaver.edu/cea.

Undergraduate and Postgraduate. QUT offers courses in 8 faculties: Arts, Built Environment and Engineering, Business, Education, Health, Information Technology, Law, and Science. The University's reputation for "real-world" education is due to close involvement of employers and professional bodies in course planning, and a balance of theory and practical skills in all courses.

Dates: Semester 1: Feb-Jun; semester 2: Jul-Nov/Dec. Cost: From AUS$5,250 per semester. Contact: QUT International, Victoria Park Rd., Kelvin Grove, Queensland, Australia 4059; (011) 61-7-3864-3142, fax 3864-3529; www.qut.edu.au/.

Univ. of South Australia. The Univ. of South Australia hosts study abroad programs for university students wishing to undertake a semester (or 2) of their studies overseas and have the credits transferred to their home institution. U-SA offers many field-based units, giving the students the opportunity to study in different environments and to learn about something unavailable at home: Aboriginal culture, Australia's environmental settings, South Australian history.

Dates: Semester 1: Feb 23-Jul 4, 1998; Semester 2: Jul 27-Nov 30, 1998. Cost: Call for details. Contact: Study Abroad Adviser, Int'l. Office, Univ. of South Australia, GPO Box 2471, Adelaide, South Australia 5001; (011) 618-302-2169, fax 302-2233; chris.haas@unisa.edu.au. For students in the U.S. and Canada: American Univ. Int'l. Program, 246 Forestry Bldg., Colorado State Univ., Ft. Collins, CO 80523; (970) 491-5511, fax (970) 491-2255; aukerman@crn.colstate.edu or Australearn, 315 Aylesworth Hall, Colorado State Univ., Ft. Collins, CO 80523; (970) 491-0228, fax (970) 491-5501; cflannery@vines.colostate.edu.

Austria

AHA Vienna Program. Subject areas include business, economics, literature, history, politics, cultural, music, art history, and psychology. All courses, other than German language, are conducted in English. No German language experience required for admission. Full academic year or individual semesters.

Dates: Sep-Dec (fall) and Jan-Apr (winter). Cost: Approx. $6,500 per semester. Includes tuition, housing, some meals, international student identity card, texts, local transportation, excursions, and insurance. Financial aid accepted. Contact: Gail Lavin, Assoc. Director for Univ. Programs, American Heritage Association, 741 SW Lincoln St., Portland, OR 97201-3178; (800) 654-2051 or (503) 295-7730, fax (503) 295-5969; 96trab@amheritage.org.

Art Seminar in the Austrian Alps. A 2- or 4-week session exploring the Baroque technique of Fa Presto as well as its contemporary expression. Taught by Michael Fuchs and Philip Jacobson, the seminar will be held at Castle Kuenburg and includes a student exhibition and trips to Vienna, 1 hour away.

Dates: Jun 2-29 (1997). Cost: $1,575-$4,925 depending on length of stay, noncredit or credit option, housing choice. Includes tuition, housing, most meals, and excursions. Contact: School of Continuing Education, The Naropa Institute, 2130 Arapahoe Ave., Boulder, CO 80203; (800) 411-5229.

European Studies in Vienna. Semester program with 3 distinct tracks of study: Central European Studies (fall), European Integration: European Union (spring), and Hungary, Romania, Bulgaria, and Former Yugoslavia Studies (spring). No knowledge of German required, study of German during program. Extensive field study trips.

Dates: Fall, spring, academic year. Presessions in Intensive German Language. Cost: Varies. Call for current fees. Contact: Helene Cohan, Associate Director, Beaver College Center for Education Abroad, 450

S. Easton Rd., Glenside, PA 19038-3295; (888) BEAVER-9, fax (215) 572-2174; cea@beaver.edu, www.beaver.edu/cea.

Internationale Hochschulkurse. German courses at the University for beginners and advanced students, perfectionist courses (6 levels). Lectures on German and Austrian literature, music, linguistics, introduction to Austria. Special courses: translation into German, commercial correspondence, business German, medical terminology, communication, phonetics, Vienna waltz, choir singing. Language laboratory. Excursions.

Dates: Jul 6-Aug 2, Aug 3-30, Aug 31-Sep 20. Cost: Course fee (4 weeks): approx. ATS4,300; accommodations: approx. ATS6,000. Contact: Magister Sigrun Anmann-Trojer, Wiener Internationale Hochschulkurse, Universität, Dr. Karl Lueger-Ring 1, A1010 Wien, Austria; (011) 43-1-405-12-54 or 405-47-37, fax 54-10.

Intl. Summer—Univ. of Vienna. European studies focusing on political, economic, legal, and cultural aspects of the New Europe (taught in English) plus German language instruction. Outstanding academic reputation. Most conducive conditions for intercultural and social exchange. Beautifully located on the shore of Wolfgangsee/Salzburg. Excellent sports facilities. Excursions to Salzburg and Vienna.

Dates: Jul 12-Aug 11 (1997). Application deadline: May 31. Cost: ATS29,000 shillings (approx. $2,900). Includes registration, full board and tuition for 4-week session, use of all sports facilities (tennis, sailing and wind surfing lessons), a ticket to the Salzburg Festival, all planned excursions, and a trip to Vienna (half-board). Contact: Univ. of Vienna, International Summer Program Office, Dr. Karl Lueger-Ring 1, A1010 Vienna, Austria; Tel./fax (011) 43-1-40-34-988; sommerhochschule@univie.ac.at,www.univie.ac.at/Sommerhochschule.

Master Courses in Vienna. Master classes in: singing, opera, piano, violin, cello, guitar, chamber music, conducting, bassoon. Two-week courses, diploma per active participation, final concert, 20 hours per week.

Dates: Jun 30-Aug 15 (1997). Cost: Registration fee AS1,500; active participation: AS5,200; listener: AS2,700. Contact: Elisabeth Keschmann, Monika Wildauer, Reisnerstrasse 3, A-1030 Vienna, Austria; (011) 43-222-714-8822, fax 714-8821.

Slippery Rock Univ. in Vienna. Students can spend a semester or year in Vienna earning 15 credits per semester (9-12 in language and 3 taught in English, an econ. seminar—EU or music).

Dates: Fall 1997: Sep 1-Nov 28 with 2-week holiday Sep 28-Oct 5; winter 1998: Jan 7-Mar 28; spring 1998: Mar-May 29. Cost: $3,390. Includes tuition and room. Contact: Stan Kendziorski, Director of International Studies, Slippery Rock Univ., Slippery Rock, PA 16057; (412) 738-2603, fax (412) 738-2959; stanley.kendziorski@sru.edu.

Webster Univ. in Vienna. Webster Univ. in Vienna has more than 400 students from 59 countries. Students may pursue a degree program leading to a BA, MA, or MBA. In addition, students may enroll for a study abroad semester or year (summer session and other short-term options also available). All courses are taught in English and are fully accredited. Major areas of study include: business, Central and Eastern European studies, computer science, economics, psychology, international relations, management, and marketing plus a complete range of electives.

Dates: Five entry terms: late Aug, mid-Oct, mid-Jan, mid-Mar, late May. Cost: $20,000 (1996-97 academic year), $10,000 (1996-97 semester). Estimate includes tuition, room and board, books, local transportation, social activities. Contact: Study Abroad Office, Webster Univ., 470 E. Lockwood, St. Louis, MO 63119; (314) 968-6988 or (800) 984-6857, fax (314) 968-7119; brunote@websteruniv.edu, http://webster2.websteruniv.edu.

Belgium

MA in Business. The MA program combines several key courses from the MBA program with subjects concerning the theory and implementation of communication and public relations. European Univ. graduates are prepared for careers in public relations, human resources, and training development and organizational consulting. A full-time student can complete the program in 1 academic year.

Dates: Early Oct through Dec, early Jan through mid-Mar, and mid-Mar through mid-Jun. Cost: Tuition BEF355,000 per program (full-time or part-time). Contact: Mr. Luc Van Mele, Dean, Jacob Jordaenstraat 77, 2018 Antwerp, Belgium; (011) 32-3-248-54-31, fax 218-58-68; eutunia@pophost.eunet.be.

MBA. The MBA program covers many aspects of international operations. The emphasis is on international finance and marketing as well as strategic management; it includes a solid foundation in the traditional management disciplines. A full-time student can complete the program in 1 academic year.

Dates: Early Oct to Dec, early Jan to mid-Mar, and mid-Mar to mid-Jun. Cost: Tuition BEF355,000 per program (full-time or part-time). Contact: Mr. Luc Van Mele, Dean, Jacob Jordaenstraat 77, 2018 Antwerp, Belgium; (011) 32-3-248-54-31, fax 218-58-68; eutunia@pophost.eunet.be.

Vesalius College. Vesalius College is the international undergraduate English language college of the Vrije Univ. Brussel-VUB. It offers American-style, liberal arts and sciences programs in coordination with Boston Univ. BA and BS in business economics, international affairs, political studies, literature, communications and computing. About 400 students representing over 60 nationalities have access to excellent research and sports facilities. Over 90 percent of faculty hold PhDs.

Dates: Aug-Dec (fall), Jan-May (spring), Jun-Jul (summer). Cost: $4,200 per semester (tuition and fees) Contact: Admissions Dept. 64/7, Vesalius College-VUB, Pleinlaan 2, B-1050 Brussels, Belgium; (011) 32-2-629-36-26, fax 36-37; vesalius@vub.ac.be, www.vub.ac.be/veco.

Brazil

Economy and Business. Study and observe the business climate and process of economic development in Brazil. Open to students of all majors. Lasts 6 weeks: early Jun to mid-Jul. Seminars taught in English by faculty from the Univ. of Sao Paulo a series of field trips allow students to observe first-hand the process of economic development in an emerging market. All students take intensive language course. No knowledge of Portuguese necessary. Housing with local families.

Dates: Early Jun-mid-Jul. Cost: $3,100 includes tuition, registration fees, room and board, field trips, and partial insurance coverage. Contact: IPA, Univ. of Illinois at Urbana-Champaign, 115 International Studies Bldg., 910 S. 5th St., Champaign, IL 61820; (800) 531-4404, fax (217) 244-0249; ipa@uiuc.edu.

Canada

Ecole de français, Montréal. For the last 50 years, the Ecole de français has offered courses in French as a second language to students from around the world. The Ecole is continually improving its programs to meet the changing needs of its students. Choose from Oral and Written Communication French (beginner to advanced), Workshop on Teaching French as a Second Language (for teachers), Contemporary Québec Culture (for advanced students), Business French (intermediate to advanced students).

Dates: Summer 1: Jul 6-Jul 24; summer 2: Jul 27-Aug 14; fall 98: Sep 10-Dec 11; winter 99: Jan 8-Apr 13; spring 98: May 19-Jun 11. Cost: Spring, summer: (3 weeks, 60 hours) CAN$495; summer (3 weeks, 45 hours) CAN$390; fall and winter: (12 weeks, 240 hours) CAN$1,495 (subject to change). Contact: Serge Bienvenu, Coordinator, Ecole de français, Faculté de l'education permanente, Université de Montréal, C.P. 6128, succursale Centre-ville, Montréal, PQ, H3C 3J7, Canada; (514) 343-6090, fax (514) 343-2430; infolang@fep.umontreal.ca, http://alize.ere.umontreal.ca/~tousyves/fep.

École de langue française de Trois-Pistoles. The oldest university-sponsored French immersion school in Canada, our school offers two 5-week sessions each year. Courses are offered in the areas of French language, culture, theater, and political science. Guided by dynamic monitors, students participate in an afternoon workshop and a varied sociocultural program. Accommodations and meals, as well as an opportunity to practice French in an informal setting, provided by families in Trois-Pistoles.

Dates: May 11-Jun 12; Jul 6-Aug 7, 1998. Cost: Approx. CAN$1,700 plus CAN$200 program deposit ($100 refundable). Contact: Maryanne Giangregorio, Administrative Assistant, The Univ. of Western Ontario, École de langue française de Trois-Pistoles, Univ. College 219, London, ON N6A 3K7, Canada; (519) 661-3637, fax (519) 661-3799; tp@courier.ptce.uwo.ca, www.ptce.uwo.ca/trp.

English Language Centre, Univ. of Victoria. The English Language Centre at the Univ. of Victoria is known throughout the world for its high standards of English language instruction. Established in 1970, the ELC offers quality language programs aimed at international and Canadian students wishing to improve their English language and cross-cultural skills for personal, professional, and academic purposes. The 12-week Intensive English Language Program is offered 3 times each year, and a series of spring and summer programs are available. UVic is a mid-sized university with 17,000 students and is a friendly and comfortable place to study. It was rated the #1 Comprehensive Univ. in Canada for 2 consecutive years.

Dates: Apr 9-Jul 2; Sep 10-Dec 2, 1998; Jan 7-Mar 31, 1999 (tuition $2,950 per term). Cost: Short-term 1998: Jan 5-Feb 13 ($1,925); Mar 30-May 8, ($1,925); May 25-Jun 26 ($1,585); Jul 6-Jul 31 ($1,295); Jul 6-Aug 14 ($1,925); Aug 3-28 ($1,295). Contact: Bronwyn Jenkins or Maxine Macgillivray, Program Directors, English Language Centre, Univ. of Victoria, P.O. Box 1700, Victoria, BC V8W 2Y2, Canada; (250) 721-8469, fax (250) 721-6276; elc@uvcs.uvic.ca.

Language Studies Canada Montréal. Using a multi-skill approach students develop effective communication skills in French. Classes are informative, practical, and enjoyable. Six levels of 4 weeks each, intensive, 6 hours daily or semi-intensive, 4 hours daily. Maximum of 14 students per class. Audio-visual equipment, multi-media Student Resource Center. Optional activity program. Homestay and alternate accommodations available.

Dates: Two-week courses begin any Monday from Jan 13 (1997), year round. Other programs offered: one-on-one instruction, year round; 2-week. Group 5 executive courses, Jun-Oct; Summer Language Adventure (13 to 17-year-olds), 2-9 weeks in Jul and Aug. Cost: Two weeks intensive program $535; homestay accommodations $400. Cost of other services available upon request. Contact: Language Studies Canada Montréal, 1450 City Councillors, Montréal, PQ, H3A 2E6, Canada; (514) 499-9911, fax (514) 499-0332.

Univ. of New Brunswick ELP. Established in 1954 in eastern Canada, tradition of expertise with international clientele. Language contract base; courses designed for client needs; experienced staff; residential approach. Participants live and learn in English nonstop weekday and weekend. Classes extend into the community. Extensive diagnosis, ongoing assessment, constant quality control.

Dates: Three-week format (monthly Sep-Apr) in homestay; 5-week format (May-Jun, Jul-Aug) in university residence. Cost:

Three weeks CAN$3,473; 5 weeks CAN$1,800. Includes tuition fees. Contact: Mrs. Mary E. Murray, Director, Univ. of New Brunswick, English Language Programme, P.O. Box 4400, Fredericton, NB E3B 5A3, Canada; (506) 453-3564, fax (506) 453-35 78.

Univ. of Regina Language Institute. A variety of non-credit programs are offered in 3 streams: English for Academic Purposes (EA), which prepares students for attending university; English for Business (EB) which focuses on increasing students' understanding and use of business vocabulary and concepts; and English for Communication (EC) which focuses on increasing students' oral communication. Evening courses, conversation partners, and short-term customized courses are also available.

Dates: (1997): Jan 10-Apr 4 (12 weeks); Apr 18-Jun 13 (8 weeks); Jun 27-Aug 22 (8 weeks); Sep 12-Dec 5 (12 weeks). Cost: (Winter 1997): $1,825. Spring/summer (1997): $1,625. Fall (1997): $1,945. Conversation partners: $110 per semester. Placement fee for housing: $160. Plus rent, security, and telephone deposits. Contact: Penthes Rubrecht, English as a Second Language Centre, Univ. of Regina, Rm. 211, Language Institute, Regina, SK, Canada S4S 0A2; (306) 585-4585, fax (306) 585-4971; esl@max.cc.uregina.ca, www.uregina.ca/~esl.

Chile

CWU Semester Program in Chile. Semester abroad program hosted by the Universidad Autral de Chile (Valdivia) that combines intensive language training, core electives in Latin American politics, history and literature, direct enrollment courses, and field research/independent study. Participants enjoy cross-cultural learning ex-perience in the beautiful lake region of southern Chile.

Dates: Spring semester Mar 15-Jul 6 (approx.); fall Aug 15-Dec 15. Cost: Approx. $4,000 (tuition, housing and meals). Contact: Darci Wahl, Study Abroad Advisor, Central Washington Univ., Office of International Studies and Programs, 400 E. 8th Ave., Ellensburg, WA 98926-7408; (509) 963-3623, fax (509) 963-1558; wahld@cwu.edu.

Public Policy/Language and Culture. The Public Policy Semester offers students the opportunity to conduct an in-depth research policy on issues facing Chilean government and society. Research preceded by intensive courses on contemporary economcs, history, and politics. Housing with local families. Graduate and undergraduate credit available. A summer language and culture program is also available.

Dates: Spring semester: Mar-Jul; fall semester: Jul-Dec; summer: Jun-mid-Jul. Cost: $5,800 (spring 1997 fee) includes tuition, room and board, registration fees, excursions, orientation, site director, partial insurance coverage. Contact: IPA, Univ. of Illinois at Urbana-Champaign, 115 International Studies Bldg., 910 S. 5th St., Champaign, IL 61820; (800) 531-4404, fax (217) 244-0249; ipa@uiuc.edu.

Spanish and Latin American Studies. Santiago offers intensive language studies fulfilling up to 2 years of university Spanish requirements in 1 semester, with additional courses in literature, business, teacher ed., history, political science. Week-long program-oriented field trips to the south and north of Chile, homestays, and many university activities at Chilean university.

Dates: Spring semester: Jan 7-May 5, 1998; fall semester Aug 27-Dec 16 (1997). Cost: One semester $3,790; fall and spring $6,340. Contact: University Studies Abroad

Consortium (USAC), Univ. of Nevada, Reno #323, Reno, NV 89557-0093; (702) 784-6569, fax (702) 784-6010; usac@admin.unr.edu, www.scs.unr.edu/~usac.

China

AHA Chinese Language Program. This language program available at 70 major universities in China offers tailored programs from 4 weeks to 1 year. Study is in an integrated environment with other foreign students. Courses are taught at 4 different levels, based on the students' previous language skills. Courses meet 20 hours per week.

Dates: Application deadlines vary. Cost: Varies depending on length of course. Tuition lodging, meals, books, and materials approximate $1,100 for 4 weeks. Contact: Cascade Huan, Assoc. Director for Program Development, American Heritage Association, 741 SW Lincoln St., Portland, OR 97201-3178; (800) 654-2051, fax (503) 295-5969; chuan@amheritage.org.

BCA Program in Dalian. Earn 16-20 credits per semester at the Dalian Univ. of Foreign Languages in China, with a 1-week orientation period, field trips, and extended study tours through Beijing and northern or southern China. Year students could study second semester in Sapporo, Japan. Marcel Green is BCA Director in Residence. Students from all U.S. colleges and universities accepted. No foreign language prerequisite. All levels of Chinese language available plus Russian and Japanese, Chinese History and Culture, internships.

Dates: Sep 2-Jan 20 (fall), Feb 10-Jul 10 (spring), Sep 2-Jul 10 (year). Cost: $13,395 (academic year 1997-1998); $7,995 (semester 1997-1998) includes international transportation, tuition, room and board, insurance, group in-country travel. Contact: Beverly S. Eikenberry, 605 E. College Ave.,

North Manchester, IN 46962; (219) 982-5238, fax (219) 982-7755; bca@manchester.edu, www.studyabroad.com/bca.

Friends World Program. A semester or year program at Zhejiang Univ. in Hangzhou, including Chinese language instruction. Classes include Chinese culture, customs, Chinese arts or calligraphy. Students also have their own research projects which may include the study of Chinese medicine, gender issues, religion, or environmental issues. Students may earn 12-18 credits per semester.

Dates: Fall: mid-Oct-end of Jan; spring: beg. of Mar-beg of Jul. Cost: $10,185 per semester in 1996/1997. Includes tuition, travel, room and board, fees, and books. Contact: James Howard, Friends World Program, 239 Montauk Highway, Southampton, NY 11968; (516) 287-8475; jhoward@sand.liunet.edu.

Mandarin Language Study. Study intensive Mandarin Chinese at Beijing Language and Culture Univ., the only university in China specializing in teaching Mandarin to foreigners. Classes are intensive with 20 hours of classroom instruction per week. Fees include tuition, textbooks, double-occupancy accommodations, sightseeing in Beijing, cultural activities, orientation, visa processing, and roundtrip airfare from San Francisco.

Dates: Spring, summer, fall programs, and 1-year program. Cost: Six weeks $3,110, 20 weeks $4,720, 12 weeks $3,950, 1 year $6,850. Contact: China Advocates, 1635 Irving St., San Francisco, CA 94122; (800) 333-6474, fax (415) 753-0412; chinaadv@aol.com.

Colombia

CEUCA Intensive Summer Session. Designed for both beginners and more advanced students, this session stresses total immersion. Students live with Colombian host families. Also, classes are small and taught by Colombian faculty. Students can register for Spanish, Latin American Culture, and Handcrafts, but independent studies can be arranged. The session also includes field trips within and outside of Bogota.

Dates: Jun 3-Aug 1. Cost: $3,200. Includes room, board, and all land transportation. Contact: CEUCA, Jennifer Jones, U.S. Program Coordinator, P.O. Box 14942, Gainesville, FL 32604; Tel./fax (352) 376-5515; ceuca@gnv.fdt.net, http://gnvfdt.net/~ceuca/.

Community Internships in Latin America. Emphasis on community participation for social change. Students work 3 days a week in an internship, meet together for core seminar and internship seminar, and carry out independent study project. Wide range of internship opportunities in community development and related activities. Based in Bogotá. Family homestay. Latin American faculty. Full semester's credit, U.S. transcript provided. All majors, 2 years Spanish language required.

Dates: Early Feb-mid-May. Cost: $9,000 (1998-99). Includes tuition, room and board, field trips. Contact: Rebecca Rassier, Director of Student Services, HECUA, Mail #36, Hamline Univ., 1536 Hewitt Ave., St. Paul, MN 55104-1284; (612) 646-8832 or (800) 554-9421, fax (612) 659-9421; hecua@hamline.edu, www.hamline.edu/~hecua.

South American Urban Semester. Innovative approach combines classroom experience with extensive field work. Courses include introduction to Latin America, urbanization and development in Latin America, Spanish language, and independent study. Based in Bogotá, with field study and travel in Colombia, Guatemala, and Ecuador. Family homestay. Latin American faculty. Full semester's credit, U.S. transcript provided. All majors, 2 years Spanish language required.

Dates: Late Aug-early Dec. Cost: $9,000 (1998-99). Includes tuition, room and board, field trips. Contact: Rebecca Rassier, Director of Student Services, HECUA, Mail #36, Hamline Univ., 1536 Hewitt Ave., St. Paul, MN 55104-1284; (612) 646-8832 or (800) 554-1089, fax (612) 659-9421; hecua@hamline.edu; www.hamline.edu/~hecua.

Costa Rica

Costa Rican Language Academy. Costa Rican-owned and operated language school offers first-rate Spanish instruction in a warm and friendly environment. Teachers with university degrees. Small groups or private classes. Included free in the programs are airport transportation, coffee and natural refreshments, excursions, Latin dance, Costa Rican cooking, music, and conversation classes to provide students with complete cultural immersion.

Dates: Year round (start anytime). Cost: $135 per week or $220 per week for program with homestay. All other activities and services included at no additional cost. Contact: Costa Rican Language Academy, P.O. Box 336-2070, San José, Costa Rica; (011) 506-221-1624 or 233-8914 or 233-8938, fax 233-8670. In the U.S.: (800) 854-6057; crlang@sol.racsa.co.cr., www.crlang.co.cr/index.html.

Intensive Spanish-San José. In San José, at Centro Linguisticó Conversa, Spanish language, Costa Rican homestay, breakfast and 1 other meal daily, 6-8 credits, depending on option chosen. Hotel stay at extra cost. Upper division (junior-senior level) credit.

Dates: Operates in 1-month cycles throughout the year. Cost: $1,860 initial cycle; $1,720 each additional cycle. Contact: Reinaldo Changsut, Study Abroad Adviser, Miami-Dade Community College, 11011 SW 104th St., Miami, FL 33176-3393; (305) 237-2535, fax (305) 237-2949; rchangsu@kendall.mdcc.edu.

Intensive Spanish-Santa Ana. In Santa Ana, about 10 km from San José, the campus is a 6-acre "finca" with sports facilities and swimming pool. Operates in 1-month cycles throughout the academic year. Earn 6-7 credits in 1 month, or do a "Language Semester" in 2 months and earn 12-14 credits while mastering Spanish, 110 hours per month, classes of 4 students each. Peace Corps-style techniques. Costa Rican homestay, all meals. Optional lodging on campus at extra cost.

Dates: Operates in 1-month cycles throughout the year. Cost: $2,540 per 1-month cycle. Contact: Reinaldo Changsut, Study Abroad Adviser, Miami-Dade Community College, 11011 SW 104th St., Miami, FL 33176-3393; (305) 237-2535, fax (305) 237-2949; rchangsu@kendall.mdcc.edu.

Intercultura and Language Link. Intensive Spanish language programs in peaceful Costa Rica. Your choice of either 4 hours daily of small classes, a combination of 4 hours group and 2 hours private, or completely private. Professional adults, college students, and all Spanish levels accommodated. Programs of 1 to 12 weeks starting on any Monday. U.S. graduate and undergraduate credit through accredited university. Free weekly activities, caring homestays, and excursions to rainforests, volcano parks of great natural beauty. Intercultura located in Heredia, a small university town, located 30 minutes outside the busy capital city. Option of a week's stay at our beach campus.

Dates: Year round. New classes begin every Monday. (Summer months fill very early.) Cost: Four hours daily of group classes and homestay: 2 weeks $545, 4 weeks $960. Includes registration, insurance, tuition, airport pickup, private room, and 2 meals daily. Contact: Kay G. Rafool, Language Link Inc., P.O. Box 3006, Peoria, IL 61612; (800) 552-2051, fax (309) 692-2926; info@langlink.com; www.langlink.com.

Learn Spanish While Volunteering. Assist with the training of Costa Rican public school teachers in our latest language learning techniques, using classroom computers, K-8 school targeted by Costa Rican government as a model ESL/technology school. Enjoy learning Spanish in the morning, volunteer work in the afternoon/evening. Spanish classes are 2-5 students plus group learning activities; conversations with middle-class homestay families (1 student per family). Homestays and volunteer project are within walking distance of school in small town (14,000 population) near the capital, San Jose.

Dates: Year round, all levels. Classes begin every Monday, volunteer program is continuous. Cost: $295 per week for 25 hours of Spanish classes. Includes tuition, all meals (7 days a week), homestay, laundry, all materials, Costa Rican dance and cooking classes, and airport transportation. $25 one-time registration for Spanish classes; $100 additional one-time registration fee for volunteer program. Contact: Susan Shores, Registrar, Latin American Language Center, 7485 Rush River Dr., Suite 710-123, Sacramento, CA 95831; (916) 447-0938, fax (916) 428-9542; lalc@madre.com.

Save the Rainforest Adventures. Outward Bound Costa Rica (CRROBS) creates courses that help your rainforest experience endure beyond the canopy of Latin America. We offer year round, multi-element (rafting, kayaking, canopy or rock climbing, hiking, and homestays). Costa Rica courses for any age group or individual. We also offer an 85-day tri-country (Costa Rica, Ecuador, and Peru) semester course (biology, anthropology, Spanish credit). Spanish/biology emphasis are available on all courses. Save the Rainforest Adventures offers excursions catered to the needs and interests of each group or individual.

Dates: Year round 8-, 10-, 12-, 15-, 25-, 30-, and 85-day courses. Cost: $1,000-$2,600 for multi-day; $6,800 for 85-day tri-country semester. Scholarships available. Contact: Outward Bound Costa Rica and Save the

Rainforest Adventures, P.O. Box 243, Quepos, Costa Rica; (800) 676-2018, fax (011) 506-777-1222; crrobs@sol.racsa.co.cr, www.centralamerica.com/cr/crrobs.

Semester in Costa Rica. At Universidad Veritas, San Jose: Spanish language, literature; Costa Rica Colloquim, International Business; Ecology. Courses taught in English. Advanced students may take courses in regular university program. Costa Rican homestay. Upper division credit (junior-senior). A College Consortium for International Studies program.

Dates: Mid-Sep-Dec/Jan-Apr. Cost: Approx. $4,400. Includes tuition, housing, some meals, excursions. Contact: Reinaldo Changsut, Study Abroad Adviser, Miami-Dade Community College, 11011 SW 104th St., Miami, FL 33176-3393; (305) 237-2535, fax (305) 237-2949; rchangsu@kendall.mdc.edu.

Spanish and More in Heredia. Heredia offers intensive language studies which fulfills up to 2-year university Spanish requirements in a semester or 1 year in the 8-week summer program. Additional courses offered in political science, history, biology, teacher ed., business, literature, etc. Program organized week-long and weekend field trips, homestays, and many local university activities.

Dates: Spring term: Jan 8-May 10, 1998; summer sessions: May 22-Jun 27 and Jun 22-Jul 27 (1997); fall term: Aug 27-Dec 19, (1997). Cost: One semester $3,790; year: $6,340; summer $1,770 per session; $3,380 both sessions. Contact: University Studies Abroad Consortium (USAC), Univ. of Nevada, Reno #323, Reno, NV 89557-0093; (702) 784-6569, fax (702) 784-6010; usac@admin.unr.edu, www.scs.unr.edu/~usac.

Spanish Language. Intercultura Language Institute offers intensive Spanish and homestays in selected Costa Rican families. Academic credit available (with prior notice).

Additional free cultural activities: Latin-dance, music, theater, cinema, cooking. Weekend excursions to volcanoes, beaches, rainforest. Volunteer opportunities in social, environmental, and political organizations. Beach campus: optional 1 week per month, study on Pacific coast.

Dates: Year round. Cost: $1,045 per month (shorter stays available). Contact: Laura Ellington, Codirector, Intercultura Costa Rica, Apdo. 1952-3000, Heredia, Costa Rica; (011) 506-260-8480, Tel./fax (011) 506-260-9243; intercul@sol.racsa.co.cr, www.alpha-luz.com/intercultura.

Universidad de Costa Rica. A graduate and undergraduate program at the Universidad de Costa Rica for students interested in studying courses in language, literature, culture and civilization, composition, and history of Costa Rica. All courses are taught by full-time faculty members from the Univ. of Costa Rica, the most prestigious university in Costa Rica. A lot of extra activities and excursions are organized for students. Students stay with Costa Rican families.

Dates: Summer: Jun-Jul; semester: fall and winter. Cost: Total cost from $1,885 including airfare. Contact: Modern Language Studies Abroad, P.O. Box 623, Griffith, IN 46319; Tel./fax (219) 838-9460.

Czech Republic

Penn-in-Prague. For students interested in Jewish studies and Czech culture, this program, located amidst the fairy tale beauty of Prague and affiliated with Charles Univ. and the Jewish Museum of Prague, offers an insight into the rich history and urgent contemporary problems of this important region, as well as an opportunity to learn beginning and intermediate Czech. Some internships can be arranged with the Jewish Museum.

Dates: Jul 8-Aug 16. Cost: Tuition $2,840; housing and excursion $750. Contact: Penn

Summer Abroad, College of General Studies, Univ. of Pennsylvania, 3440 Market St., Suite 100, Philadelphia, PA 19104-3335; (215) 898-5738, fax (215) 573-2053.

Ecuador

Academia de Español Quito. The Academia de Español Quito offers intensive Spanish language programs in the exciting capital of Ecuador. Choose from 4 to 7 hours daily of completely private classes, one-on-one instruction. Professional adults, college students, and all Spanish levels accommodated in a very well-organized school. Programs of 1 to 12 weeks starting on any Monday. U.S. graduate and undergraduate credit. Earn 6 credits in 3 weeks. Caring homestays and many additional weekly activities included. In the Activa program students study 4 hours in the morning in the classroom and in the afternoon explore Quito and surrounding area with their teacher. The Anaconda is a 1-week program located on an island in an Amazon River tributary. Group classes in the morning; explore the jungle and rainforest in the afternoon. Also discounted Galapagos trips.

Dates: Year round. New classes begin every Monday. (Summer months fill very early.) Cost: Four hours daily private classes and homestay: $260 per week; 7 hours daily Activa program (includes all transportation, entry fees, etc.): $385 per week; Anaconda program $470. Includes tuition, insurance, materials, airport pickup, private room, 3 meals daily, and laundry. Contact: Kay G. Rafool, Language Link Inc., P.O. Box 3006, Peoria, IL 61612; (800) 552-2051, fax (309) 692-2926; info@langlink.com; www.langlink.com.

Academia Latinoamericana (Quito). Ecuador's number-one private Spanish language institute in former diplomat's mansion with swimming pool, hot tub, sauna, sport facilities. Instruction by university-trained teachers, all one-on-one. Customized study programs tailored to the individual. Select host family accommodations. Excursions to haciendas, Indian markets, etc. College credit and internships available.

Dates: Year round. Cost: One-week tuition, lodging, meals $294. Contact: Suzanne Bell, Admissions Director, U.S., 640 East 3990 South, Suite E, Salt Lake City, UT 84107; (801) 268-4608, fax (801) 265-9156; latinoa1@spanish.com.ec, http://ecnct.cc/academia/learnspa.htm.

BCA Program in Quito. Earn 13-18 credits per semester at Universidad San Francisco de Quito, with a 4-week intensive language and orientation, homestay with Ecuadoran families, field trips, extended study tour to Amazon headwaters and Galápagos Islands. Students from all U.S. colleges and universities accepted. Intermediate level college Spanish required. Full liberal arts curriculum available. Ecology field studies and internships.

Dates: Aug 1-Dec 15 (fall), Jan 2-May 20 (spring), Aug 1-May 20 (year). Cost: $18,395 (1997-1998 academic year); $10,295 (1997-1998 semester). Includes international transportation, room and board, tuition, insurance, group travel in country. Contact: Beverly S. Eikenberry, 605 E. College Ave., North Manchester, IN 46962; (219) 982-5238, fax (219) 982-7755; bca@manchester.edu, www.studyabroad.com/bca.

Environmental Studies in Ecuador. The program focuses on the growing conflict between the development of Ecuador's economy and the preservation of its ecological resources. Program includes course work in Spanish with Ecuadoran students at the Universidad San Francisco de Quito, field study trips to several regions of the country, and an independent research project. Minimum 2 years college Spanish and strong background in biology required.

Dates: Jan-mid-Jun. Cost: (1996-1997) $12,118 includes roundtrip international transportation, tuition and fees, field study trips, room and board, and some excursions.

Contact: Center for International Programs, Kalamazoo College, 1200 Academy, Kalamazoo, MI 49006; (616) 337-7133, fax (616) 337-7400; cip@kzoo.edu.

Golondrinas Cloudforest Project. We welcome students to assist in or carry out research concerning sustainable agriculture (agroforestry) and forest resource management. Fluency in Spanish is necessary. The reserve spans 3 different ecosystems, lending to great biodiversity, making it a fascinating area for study. If interested, request list of studies to be conducted.

Dates: Year round. Cost: Depending on duration of stay between $210 and $185 per month. Contact: Fundación Golondrinas, Attn: Piet S. Sabbe, c/o Calle Isabel la Católica, 1559, Quito, Ecuador; manteca@uio.satnet.net.

Univ. of San Francisco de Quito. Students take courses with Ecuadorian students at the Univ. of San Francisco de Quito. Courses are available in a variety of subject areas for semester or year. Housing arranged in local homes. Resident director conducts orientation and excursions. Courses taught in Spanish; 4 semesters of college-level Spanish required.

Dates: Fall semester: Aug-Dec; spring semester: Jan-May; year: Aug-May. Cost: $5,850 (spring 1997 fee) includes: tuition, registration, excursions, orientation, room and board, support services, on-site director, partial ins. Contact: IPA, Univ. of Illinois at Urbana-Champaign, 115 International Studies Bldg., 910 S. 5th St., Champaign, IL 61820; (800) 531-4404, fax (217) 244-0249; ipa@uiuc.edu.

Egypt

The American Univ. in Cairo. Study for 1 or 2 semesters with Egyptian students at an American-style liberal arts university in the heart of Cairo. Study abroad students may elect courses from the general course offerings; most popular are those dealing with Middle East, Egyptian, and Arab history, politics, culture, Egyptology, Islamic studies, Arabic language. Language of instruction is English.

Dates: Sep-Jan, Feb-Jun, Jun-Aug. Cost: Approx. $5,030 per semester for tuition and fees. Contact: Matrans Davidson, Office of Student Affairs, American Univ. in Cairo, 420 5th Ave., 3rd Fl., New York, NY 10018; aucegypt@aucnyo.edu.

Europe

Art Under One Roof. Applied Arts Institute-Europe. Study for a semester or academic year with us in Florence or Paris, learn a language and live the arts. Painting, sculpture, restoration, fresco painting, jewelry making, furniture and interior design, boutique design, shoe and handbag design, furniture restoration, tiffany arts, and many more.

Dates: Jan-Apr, May-Jul, Sep-Dec 1998. Cost: $2,500 per semester. Includes tuition only. Contact: Art Under One Roof (Arte Sotto un Tetto), Via Pandolfini, 46-R - 50122 Florence, Italy; Tel./fax (011) 39-55-247-8867; berarducci@iol.it.

AuPair Homestay Abroad. Immerse yourself in the culture of your choice. Develop language skills and earn a monthly stipend while caring for the children of your host family. This is AuPair Homestay Abroad, an innovative program of World Learning, offering participants ages 18-29 the opportunity for experiential learning overseas within the comfort and security of a family setting. Placement in Europe and Argentina also.

Dates: Individual departure with stays from 3 to 12 months and extensions possible. Cost: $775. Includes interviewing, screening, matching with a host family, predeparture materials, program support in U.S. and while overseas. Contact: Imelda R. Farrell, Program Specialist, AuPair Homestay Abroad, 1015 15th St., NW, Washington, DC 20005; (202)

408-5380, fax (202) 408-5397; imelda.farrell
@worldlearning.org.

Business/Liberal Arts Abroad. Undergraduate and graduate business programs located in Brussels, Paris, Madrid, Maastricht, Tartu and Florence. Semester, year long and short-term programs available. Bentley is AACSB accredited. Coursework offered primarily in English; collateral study of native language required. Beginner-advanced instruction offered.
Dates: Year: Sep-May, semester: Sep-Dec, Jan-May. Cost: Varies. Includes tuition, room and board, orientation, ISIC. Contact: Jennifer Scully, Director of Study Abroad, Bentley College, 175 Forest St., Waltham, MA 02154, (617) 891-3474, fax (617) 891-2819; inprinfo@bentley.edu, www.bentley.edu.

Friends World Program. A semester or year program in Europe at Friends World Center in London includes an intensive introduction into European culture and history. The program offers seminars, field study, travel, and independent work. The center serves as a base to explore all regions and cultures in the European continent. Field studies in literature, politics, arts, history, peace studies, theater, education, and community development are all available. Students may earn 12-18 credits per semester.
Dates: Fall: mid-Sep-mid-Dec; spring: mid-Jan-mid-May. Cost: $11,600 per semester (in 1996/1997). Includes tuition, travel, room and board, fees and books. Contact: James Howard, Friends World Program, 239 Montauk Hwy., Southampton, NY 11968; (516) 287-8475; jhoward@sand.liunet.edu.

ICCE Cultural Exchange. Enjoy an affordable all-inclusive top-quality academic learning vacation package—French and Italian on the Riviera, Spanish on the Costa del Sol, or German in Austria or Germany. All levels. Also painting workshop and summer opera festivals in Italy and Eastern Europe. Absorb the culture and atmosphere of your host country.

Dates: Summer and all year. Cost: $2,989 up, all inclusive (air, room, and board). Contact: Dr. Stanley I. Gochman, Program Coordinator, ICCE, 5 Bellport Ln., Bellport, NY 11713; (516) 286-5228.

Language and Culture Immersion. By choosing one of our schools in France (17 different locations), Italy (Firenze, Roma, Siena), or Spain (Barcelona, Granada, Malaga, Salmanca), you are choosing the guarantee of quality. We have the support of the European Commission (Program Lingua-Socrates) and offer intensive courses for all levels and all ages: general language and specialty courses and methodology classes for teachers. All types of accommodations are available: family-stay, apartment, hotel. You will speak the language of the country all day long thanks to continuous contact with native people.
Dates: Year round, beginning every Monday. Cost: From $400 per week (including course, accommodations, meals and extracurricular activities). Contact: Promotion-Marketing-International, Pascale Mora, Director, 919 N. Kenmore St., Arlington, VA 22201; (703) 528-5300 or (703) 534-0668, fax (703) 528-5316; pascalem@aol.com, www.studyoverseas.com.

Language Immersion Programs. Learn a language in the country where it's spoken. Intensive foreign language training offered in Spain, France, Italy, Germany, and Ecuador for students aged 16 and older. Classes are taught in up to 8 different proficiency levels and are suitable for beginners as well as people with advanced linguistic skills. All courses include accommodations and meals. Lots of extracurricular activities available. Students can earn college credit through Providence College.
Dates: Courses start every second Monday year round. Year programs commence in Sep., semester programs in Jan. Cost: Varies with program, approx. $950 per 2-week course. Contact: Kari Larsen, Admissions Coordina-

tor, EF International Language Schools, 204 Lake St., Boston, MA 02135; (800) 992-1892 or (617) 746-1700, fax (617) 746-1800; ils@ef.com.

Study in Paris or Florence. Experience overseas education in Paris or Florence. Accent offers programs for fall/spring semesters and for the summer term hosted by sponsoring institutions with transferable credit. Language classes, art history, art, civilization, ecology, and others. Also includes: accommodations, cultural activity series, excursions, overseas resource centers, and more.

Dates: Summer in Paris with San Francisco Univ.: Jun 30-Aug 1; Summer in Florence with SFSU: Jun 27-Jul 26 (1997). Semester in Paris with City College of San Francisco: fall/spring semester; Semester in Florence with CCSF: fall/spring semester. Cost: Paris semester $5,450, Paris summer $2,550; Florence semester $3,950, Florence summer $2,800. Includes accommodations, cultural activity series, museum visits, excursions, onsite resource center, and more. Contact: Accent, 425 Market St., 2nd Fl., San Francisco, CA 94105; (800) 869-9291, fax (415) 904-7759; sfaccent@aol.com.

France

AHA Avignon Program. Courses are tailored to the needs of American students and are designed to take advantage of the Avignon setting. Language classes are available for nearly every level of French proficiency. Excursions are an important part of the program.

Dates: Sep-Dec (fall); Jan-Mar (winter); Mar-Jun (spring). Cost: $5,300 per term. Includes tuition, housing, meals, international student identity card, texts, local transportation, excursions, and insurance. Financial aid accepted. Contact: Nancy Murray, Assoc. Director for Univ. Programs, American Heritage Association, 741 SW Lincoln St., Portland, OR 97201-3178; (800) 654-2051 or (503) 295-7730, fax (503) 295-5969; taa@amheritage.org.

BCA in Strasbourg or Nancy. Earn 14-16 credits per semester at either the Université de Nancy or the Université de Strasbourg, with a 4-week intensive language training and orientation plus field trips and extended study tour to Paris and/or Provence. Selective Honors Program offered in both universities. Internships available. Students accepted from all U.S. colleges and universities. Intermediate level college French required.

Dates: Sep 5-Jan 20 (fall), Jan 18-Jun 15 (spring), Sep 5-Jun 1 5 (year). Cost: $18,395 (1997-1998 academic year), $10,295 (1997-1998 semester). Includes international transportation, room and board, tuition, insurance, group travel in country. Contact: Beverly S. Eikenberry, 605 E. College Ave., North Manchester, IN 46962; (219) 982-5238, fax (219) 982-7755; bca@manchester.edu, www.studyabroad.com/bca.

CCIS Semester in France. In Aix-en-Provence at the Institute for American Universities. Courses in French language (all levels), literature and civilization. Many courses taught in English: humanities, art history, history, geography, psychology, international relations, international business. Homestay with half-board. A College Consortium for International Studies program. All courses carry upper-division (junior-senior level) credit.

Dates: Mid-Sep-Dec/Jan-end May. Cost: Consult sponsor. Contact: Reinaldo Changsut, Study Abroad Adviser, Miami-Dade Community College, 11011 SW 104th St., Miami, FL 33176-3393; (305) 237-2535, fax (305) 237-2949; rchangsu@kendall.mdcc.edu.

College Cevenol International. College Cevenol, a French Lyceé in the Cevennes mountains (Le Chambon), offers a summer International Work Camp (students 18-25) and an intensive course in French Language and Culture (14-18). Programs culminate in optional travel to Paris/Normandy. Two years French required U.S. students may also attend the academic year (1-3 trimesters) enrolling in special French and courses leading to the Baccalaureate.

Dates: Work camp and summer school: Jul 15-Aug 6, Academic year: Sep-Jun. Cost: Work camp $150; summer school $1,500; academic year $8,100. Contact: Meg Warren, U.S. Representative, College Cevenol, 79 Oriole Ave., Providence, RI 02906; mwarren@ids.net.

Cooking with the Masters. A 1-week series of intensive hands-on culinary education in the kitchens of French master chefs, including professional visits to vineyards, markets, local artisans, etc.

Dates: Jan-Feb; Jun; Sep-Oct. Next series: Sep 20-29, 1996. Cost: Approx. $2,550 per person. Includes dbl. occupancy, airfare. Single supplement applies. Contact: Michel Bouit, President, MBI Inc., P.O. Box 1801, Chicago, IL 60690; (312) 663-5701, fax (312) 663-5702.

Cornell in Paris (EDUCO). Spend a semester or year studying at leading universities of Paris: Paris I (Pantheon-Sorbonne), Paris VII, and Institut d'Etudes Politiques (Sciences Po). Extensive orientation, language preparation, and special coursework at the Cornell-Duke (EDUCO) Center on rue Montparnasse. Housing arranged in private residences or apartments. Four semesters of university-level French required.

Dates: Mid-Sep-late Jan and late Jan-mid-Jun. Cost: $13,300 per semester (1996-1997). Includes tuition and fees, housing, some meals, orientation, language instruction, field trips, and excursions. Contact: Cornell Abroad, 474 Uris Hall, Ithaca, NY 14853-7601; (607) 255-6224, fax (607) 255-8700; cuabroad@cornell.edu.

En Famille Overseas. En Famille Overseas arranges stays for students of all ages with French families to improve their knowledge of the French language. Visits can be arranged for any period from 1 week to 1 year. Stays combined with language courses for all standards available in Paris, Tours, and Valladolid, Spain.

Dates: Year round. Cost: From FF250 per week, full board upwards. Contact: En Famille Overseas, 60b Maltravers St., Arundel, W. Sussex BN18 9BG, U.K.; (011) 44-903-883266, fax 883582.

English as a Second Language. The ESL Program at the American Univ. of Paris is designed for intermediate to advanced level students to prepare them for integration into the University's regular undergraduate program. Students take 1-3 courses, depending on level, stressing writing, reading and literary analysis, and aural/oral skills. Small classes and close contact with teachers insure rapid progress.

Dates: Fall application deadline May 1, spring application deadline Dec 1. Cost: Approx. $12,785 for 1 semester; $25,210 for 1 year. Contact: The American Univ. of Paris, U.S. Office, 80 E. 11th St., Suite 434, New York, NY 10003-6000; (212) 677-4870, fax (212) 475-5205; nyoffice@aup.fr, www.aup.fr.

French as a Second Language. Semester or year intensive program. Four-week intensive program in summer. Short sessions. All levels of French, open to everyone. DEFL, DALF "Credits." Optional day trips to châteaux de la Loire, Anjou, Normandie, Bretagne. Accommodations guaranteed with a French family. Great atmosphere. Attractive surroundings. Angers is located in the Loire Valley (90 minutes from Paris).

Dates: Jul 1-30, Sep 2-28, Oct 2-Feb 1, Feb 6-Jun 7. Cost: Tuition and fees: Jul FF3,650, Sep FF4,250, 1 semester FF7,600. Contact: Renée Cochin, CIDEF, Université Catholique de l'ouest, 3, place André Leroy, BP 808, 49008 Angers Cedex 01, France; (011) 33-41-88-30-15, fax 87-71-67.

French in France. Among the ways to learn French, total immersion is the most enjoyable and the most effective. We have been doing it for 20 years in a small historical city located in Normandy (west of Paris, close to the seaside). We welcome people at any age and any level in from 1- to 10-week programs, intensive or vacation type, from mid-March to mid-November.

Dates: Spring: Mar 23-May 29; summer: Jun 15-Aug 28; fall: Sep 7-Nov 13, 1998. Cost: From $525 per week (tuition, room and board, and excursions). Contact: Dr. Almeras, Chairman, French American Study Center, 12, 14, Blvd. Carnot, B.P. 176, 14104 Lisieux Cedex, France (011) 33-2-31-31-22-01, fax 31-22-21.

French Language and Culture. Intensive French program. Classes at all levels from beginning to advanced. Placement tests determine language ability. A wide choice of cultural courses plus Business French. Progress monitored with graded exercises, assignments, midterm and final examinations. Credits transferred. Cultural activities and excursions, board and lodging (several solutions), sessions for teachers of French.

Dates: Jul 2-27, Sep 2-28; Academic year: Sep-Dec, Feb-Jun. Cost: Tuition and fees: Jul FF3,500, Sep FF4,100, 1 semester FF7,600 Contact: Renée Cochin, Directrice, 3, place André Leroy, BP 808, 49008 Angers Cedex 01, France; (011) 33-41-88-30-15, fax 87-71-67.

French Language Sessions. An intensive immersion program, linking daily French classes in small groups with a large variety of activities, and with the daily life of French residents in a beautiful southern French village; an authentic and personalized (only 12 participants per session) experience of language and culture.

Dates: Feb 13-May 7 and Sep 11-Dec 3, 1998. Cost: $4,880 includes tuition, room and full board, all activities and excursions. Contact: La Sabranenque, Jacqueline C. Simon,

217 High Park Blvd., Buffalo, NY 14226; (716) 836-8698; http://perso.wanadoo.fr/sabranenque.

French Language Studies. Five-week intensive program in Paris, emphasizing language proficiency, culture and civilization, and contemporary French literature. Open to all students with at least 2 semesters of college-level French or equivalent. Field trips. Six credit hours: undergraduate, graduate.

Dates: Late Jun-early Aug. Cost: Approx. $2,800. Airfare not included. Contact: Office of International Education, SUNY New Paltz, HAB 33, New Paltz, NY 12561; (914) 257-3125, fax (914) 257-3129; international @newpaltz.edu, www.newpaltz.edu/oie.

French Studies (Pau). Pau offers intensive language studies—up to 4 semesters of university language courses in 1 semester, 1 year in the 8-week summer program, in addition to art, political science, history, literature, second language teaching methods, etc. Program organized week-long field trips to Paris, homestay or student residence, and many activities at the French university.

Dates: Spring semester: Jan 3-May 1, 1998; summer sessions: May 26-Jun 30 (1997) and Jun 24-Aug 1 (1997), fall semester: Sep 2-Dec 19 (1997). Cost: One semester $3,975; 2 semesters $6,980; summer $1,770 per session $3,380 both sessions. Contact: University Studies Abroad Consortium (USAC), Univ. of Nevada, Reno #323, Reno, NV 89557-0093; (702) 784-6569, fax (702) 784-6010; usac@admin. unr.edu, www.scs.unr.edu/~usac.

French-American Exchange. FAE offers language programs in Montpellier, Tours, and Aix-en-Provence from 2 weeks to a full academic year. Housing is arranged with families, in apartments, student residences, or hotels. All programs begin with a weekend in Paris and include tuition, fees, housing, and meals (transportation may also be arranged at additional charge). Ideal for the independent traveler.

Dates: Summer: Jun, Jul, Aug, Sep; trimester: Oct-Dec, Jan-Mar, Apr-Jun; semester: Sep/Oct-Jan, Jan-May, Feb-Jun; year: Sep-Jun, Oct-May; 2 or more weeks year round. Cost: summer $1,742 (4 weeks); trimester $3,020; semester $5,330-$5,502; year $9,795-$14,050; 2 weeks starting from $775. Contact: Jim Pondolfino, Director, 111 Roberts Ct., Box 7, Alexandria, VA 22314; (800) 995-5087, fax (703) 549-2865; faetours@erols.com.

Homestays with Families. A nonprofit organization founded in 1978 arranging homestays and language course in southwest of France. Accommodations with carefully selected families of similar backgrounds and interests with children of same age where appropriate.

Dates: Year round. Cost: Full board: FF1,490 per week; courses: FF800 for 10 courses. Contact: Aquitaine Service Linguistique (ASL), 15 rue Guénard, 33200 Bordeaux, France; (011) 33-5-56-08-33-23, fax 08-32-74.

Institute for American Universities. The Institute for American Universities, established in 1957 under the auspices of the Université d'Aix-Marseille, offers full-year, semester, and summer programs with centers in Aix-en-Provence and Avignon. IAU's general studies programs include the specialized areas of French language and literature, studio art and art history, political science, international relations, international business, archaeology and ancient history.

Dates: Jun 15-Jul 25; Sep 2-Dec 21, 1998; Jan 13-May 28, 1999. Cost: $3,510. Includes tuition, books, site visits, insurance, room and half-board; 1998-1999: semester $8,740. Includes tuition, books, insurance, room and half-board, activity deposit, damage deposit. Contact: Institute for American Universities, U.S. Office, P.O. Box 592, Evanston, IL 60204; (800) 221-2051, fax (847) 864-6897; iauusa@univ-aix.fr.

Intensive French in the Loire Valley. All levels, all ages: intensive courses to develop students' accuracy in listening, speaking, reading, and writing French language, business French; courses of civilization, literature, history of France, music, arts, philosophy. Jul-Sep (1); Jul-Sep academic year (1 and 2). Credits, accommodations, cultural visits, activities. Univ. in town, 90 minutes from Paris.

Dates and Cost: Oct 2 (1996) Jun 6 (1997) FF14,800; Jul 1-30 (1997). FF3,650; Sep 2-28, (1997) FF4,250. Contact: Madame Renée Cochin, Directrice, CIDEF, 3, place André Leroy, BP 808, 49008 Angers Cedex 01, France; (011) 33-0141-88-30-15, fax 87-71-67.

Internships in Francophone Europe. IFE is an academic internship program—accredited at a number of schools—that places student interns in mid- to high-levels of French public life including government, politics, the press, social institutions, NGOs, etc. IFE is a selective admissions program for highly-motivated students, already proficient in French, who are interested in immersion in the working life of a French institution and in today's France. The program includes intensive preparatory course work in French history, sociology, and politics, high-level language training, and the completion of a research project related to the internship. Open to undergraduates and recent graduates.

Dates: May 1 deadline for fall semester (Aug 21-Dec 22); Nov 1 deadline for spring semester (Jan 22-May 24). Cost: $5,950 (tuition only); tuition plus housing $7,660. Need-based scholarships available, especially for post BA's. Contact: Bernard Riviere Platt, Director, Internships in Francophone Europe, 26, rue Cmdt. Mouchotte J108, 75014 Paris, France; (011) 33-1-43-21-78-07, fax 42-79-94-13; 100662.1351@compuserve.com.

Kalamazoo in Clermont-Ferrand. This university-integrated program begins with an intensive French course and an orientation. Participants enroll in regular courses at the Ecole Supervieve Normale de Commerce. All participants complete a local businss project working with French students in small groups. Minimum of 2 years of college French is required.

Dates: Early Sep-Jun (academic year); early Sep-mid-Feb (fall). Cost: Academic year: 1996-97 $19,663; 1 semester $12,118 includes roundtrip international transportation, tuition and fee, room and board, and some excursions. Contact: Center for International Programs, Kalamazoo College, 1200 Academy, Kalamazoo, MI 49006; (616) 337-7133, fax (616) 337-7400; cip@kzoo.edu.

Penn-in-Bordeaux. For students interested in anthropology, archaeology, and the origins of humankind. This program is located near Lascaux and Cro-Magnon, areas where anthropologists have unearthed much of our knowledge about the beginnings of modern humankind. It will center on the issue of what makes us human and how this quality evolved. Lectures will be augmented with the examination of artifacts and fossils as well as visits to important sites.

Dates: Jun 17-Jul 4. Cost: Tuition $1,420; housing and excursions $450. Contact: Penn Summer Abroad, College of General Studies, Univ. of Pennsylvania, 3440 Market St., Suite 100, Philadelphia, PA 19104-3335; (215) 898-5738, fax (215) 573-2053.

Penn-in-Compiegne. For students with some proficiency in French who are interested in international relations, economics, or business. The program, affiliated with The Universite de Technologie de Compiegne, also offers a 2-week internship in a French enterprise. Students live with local families.

Dates: May 28-Jul 4; with internship: May 28-Jul 20. Cost: Tuition $2,840; room and board, and activities $900 (study only) or $1,200 (full program). Contact: Penn Summer Abroad, College of General Stud-

ies, Univ. of Pennsylvania, 3440 Market St., Suite 100, Philadelphia, PA 19104-3335; (215) 898-5738, fax (215) 573-2053.

Penn-in-Tours. For students interested in French language, literature, art, and civilization. Penn-in-Tours also offers various cultural opportunities and excursions in the beautiful Loire Valley. Students live with local families.

Dates: May 27-Jul 10. Cost: Tuition $2,840; family lodging $1,350; excursion and activity fee $250. Contact: Penn Summer Abroad, College of General Studies, Univ. of Pennsylvania, 3440 Market St., Suite 100, Philadelphia, PA 19104-3335; (215) 898-5738, fax (215) 573-2053.

Sarah Lawrence College in Paris. Combine individually crafted programs of study with total immersion in the academic and social life of Paris. Options include enrollment in the great French institutions of learning, with access to a full range of courses usually open only to French students, small seminars, and the creative arts. Private tutorials with French faculty, focusing on student interests.

Dates: Sep-May (may attend for semester or year). Cost: $10, 725 per semester. Includes all academic expenses, field trips, and cultural activities. Merit scholarships are available. Contact: Celia Regan, Sarah Lawrence College in Paris, Box CR, Bronxville, NY 10708; (800) 873-4752.

Semester in Avignon. French language and literature at the Centre d'Etudes Françaises. Complementary courses in international business, art history, history and international relations. All courses taught in French. Homestay with half-board. Full college credit (upper division). A College Consortium for International Studies program.

Dates: Mid-Sep-Dec/Jan-end May. Cost: Consult sponsor. Contact: Reinaldo

Changsut, Study Abroad Adviser, Miami-Dade Community College, 11011 SW 104th St., Miami, FL 33176-3393; (305) 237-2535, fax (305) 237-2949; rchangsu@kendall.mdcc.edu.

SRU/College International de Cannes. Students can spend a semester or year in Cannes earning 15 credits per semester (9 in language and 6 from selected courses taught in English).

Dates: Mar 1-May 30, 1998; Sep 28-Dec 20 (1997). Cost: $5,595. Includes tuition, meals, and room. Contact: Stan Kendziorski, Director of International Studies, Slippery Rock Univ., Slippery Rock, PA 16057; (412) 738-2603, fax (412) 738-2959; stanley.kendziorski@sru.edu.

Studio Art in Provence. At the Marchutz School of Drawing and Painting of the Institute for American Universities. Full college credit. Courses taught in English. Homestay with half board. Atelier in Le Tholonet, Aix-en-Provence. Courses in French language available. A College Consortium for International Studies program.

Dates: Mid-Sep-Dec/Jan-end May. Cost: Consult sponsor. Contact: Reinaldo Changsut, Study Abroad Adviser, Miami-Dade Community College, 11011 SW 104th St., Miami, FL 33176-3393; (305) 237-2535, fax (305) 237-2949; rchangsu@kendall.mdcc.edu.

Study in Besancon. Fall, spring, or academic year programs in French language, culture, and civilization at the Univ. of Franche-Comte Center for Applied Linguistics, one of the top language schools of Europe. Dormitory housing, native resident director, field trips, on-site orientation, 12-18 undergraduate credits per semester. Requires a minimum of 3 semesters college-level French or the equivalent.

Dates: Fall: early Oct-late Jan; spring: late Jan-late May. Cost: Approx. $5,100 fall, $5,300 spring. Includes tuition, fees, orientation, room and board, and insurance. (Non-New York state residents add $2,100 per semester.) Contact: Office of International Education, SUNY New Paltz, HAB 33, New Paltz, NY 12561; (914) 257-3125, fax (914) 257-3129; international@newpaltz.edu, www.newpaltz.edu/oie.

Study Programs in France. Four majors: fine arts, fashion, interior design, and language.

Dates: Throughout year. Cost: One month $2,700 (includes lodging), academic year $9,500 (tuition only). Contact: Richard Roy, Paris American Academy, 9, rue des Ursulines, 75005 Paris, France; (011) 44-41-99-20, fax 41-99-29.

Summer in France. Five weeks in Aix-en-Provence and 1 week in Paris. French homestay, breakfast and evening meal on class days in Aix, field trips. In Paris, hotel with breakfast, half-day city tour, Louvre and Orsay museum visits, Metropass. 6-9 credits. A College Consortium for International Studies program.

Dates: Mid-Jun-end Jul. Cost: $3,695. Contact: Reinaldo Changsut, Study Abroad Adviser, Miami-Dade Community College, 11011 SW 104th St., Miami, FL 33176-3393; (305) 237-2535, fax (305) 237-2949; rchangsu@kendall.mdcc.edu.

Sweet Briar College Junior Year in France. September pre-session in Tours, academic year in Paris. Enrollment in regular university courses at Sorbonne Nouvelle, Paris-Sorbonne or Universite Denis Diderot, and public and private institutions of higher learning such as Institut Catholique de Paris, art studios. Live with selected families, foyers or pensions de famille. Now in its 50th year.

Dates: Sep-May. Cost: $21,900 (1997-1998). Contact: Prof. Emile A. Langlois, Director, Junior Year in France, Sweet Briar College, Sweet Briar, VA 24595; (804) 381-6109 or (804) 381-6283; jyf@sbc.edu, www.jyf.sbc.edu.

Germany

AHA Cologne Program. Subject areas include business, German language, art, business, economics, history, literature, political science. All courses, other than German language, are conducted in English. Fall term is 12-week business and humanities program, consisting of 2-week intensive German language study, followed by 10 weeks of business, humanities, and German language. No German language experience required for admission. Spring term is 11-week liberal arts curriculum, 2 terms or 1 semester of German language required.

Dates: Sep-Dec (fall); Apr-Jun (spring). Cost: Approx. $5,200 per term. Includes tuition, housing, meals, excursions, texts, international student identity card, local transportation, insurance. Financial aid accepted. Contact: Gail Lavin, Assoc. Director, Univ. Programs, American Heritage Association, 741 SW Lincoln St., Portland, OR 97201-3178; (800) 654-2051, fax (503) 295-5969; 96trab@amheritage.org.

BCA Program in Marburg. Earn 14-16 credits per semester at Phillipps-Universität in Marburg, with a 4-week intensive language training and orientation, field trips, and an extended study tour to Eastern Germany or Prague. Internships available. Students accepted from all U.S. colleges and universities. Intermediate level college German required.

Dates: Sep 5-Feb 15 (fall); Feb 25-Jul 24 (spring); Sep 5-Jul 24 (year). Cost: $18,395 (1997-1998 academic year), $10,295 (1997-1998 semester). Includes international transportation, room and board, tuition, insurance, group travel in country. Contact: Beverly S. Eikenberry, 605 E. College Ave., North Manchester, IN 46962; (219) 982-5238, fax (219) 982-7755; bca@manchester.edu, www.studyabroad.com/bca.

German as a Foreign Language. We offer the following educational programs: various levels of German year round; intensive, crash, and long-term courses, individual tuition; special feature: German and Theater; special programs: business German for professionals, German for teachers, German in a teacher's home, German for special purposes. Academic year for high school students, international study year, internship, guest studentship, homestays for groups, courses for firms and other institutions (banking, insurance, doctors, lawyers, etc.), residential language camps for juniors, examination preparation. Various types of accommodations. Full range of activities.

Dates: Year round. Contact: GLS Sprachenzentrum, Barbara Jaeschke, Managing Director, Kolonnenstrasse 26, 10829 Berlin, Germany; (011) 49-30-787-41-52; fax 41-92; gls.berlin@t-online.de.

German Language in Munich. Group tuition available at all levels. Choose 20, 26, or 30 lessons a week or preparation for officially recognized exams. One-to-one tuition with 10, 20, 30, 40, or 50 lessons a week.

Dates: Every Monday, year round. Cost: Twenty lessons a week (group): DM720 (tuition only, 2 weeks); half board, single room DM367 per week. Contact: Inlingua School, Sendlinger-Tor-P 6, D-80336 Muenchen, Germany; (011) 49-89-2311530, fax 2609920; info@inlingua.de, www.inlingua.de.

German Language Studies. Seven weeks of intensive instruction in intermediate and advanced German and contemporary German civilization. Three weeks of classes in and family stay in Stade, 3 weeks of classes in Hamburg, and a 1-week field trip to Berlin, as well as other excursions. Nine undergraduate credit hours.

Dates: Jun-early Aug. Cost: Approx. $3,300. Airfare not included. Contact: Office of International Education, SUNY New Paltz, HAB 33, New Paltz, NY 12561; (914) 257-3125, fax (914) 257-3129; international@newpaltz.edu, www.newpaltz.edu/oie.

German Studies. Intensive language study—up to 2 years of university language requirements in 1 semester. Additional courses in history, political science, culture, literature, etc. Program-organized field trips and housing. Beautiful city only 30 minutes from Hamburg.

Dates: Spring semester: Jan 6-May 19, 1998 summer: May 23-Jun 27 (1997) and Jun 22-Jul 27 (1997); fall semester: Aug 26-Dec 16 (1997). Cost: One semester: $3,575; fall and spring: $5,575; summer: $1,385 per session, $2,385 both sessions. Contact: University Studies Abroad Consortium (USAC), Univ. of Nevada, Reno #323, Reno, NV 89557-0093; (702) 784-6569, fax (702) 784-6010; usac@admin.unr.edu, www.scs.unr.edu/~usac.

Kalamazoo in Erlangen. This university-integrated program begins with a 5-6-week intensive German course. Participants then enroll in regular courses at the Univ. of Erlangen-Nuernberg. All participants complete an individualized cultural research project or internship of personal interest under the guidance of a local mentor. Minimum of 2 years of college German required.

Dates: Mid-Sep-late Jul (academic year); mid-Sep-late Feb (fall); Apr-late-Jul (spring). Cost: (1996-97) Academic year: $19,663; one semester $12,118 includes roundtrip international transportation, tuition and fees, room and board, and some excursions. Contact: Center for International Programs, Kalamazoo College, 1200 Academy, Kalamazoo, MI 49006; (616) 337-7133, fax (616) 337-7400; cip@kzoo.edu.

Maryland at Schwäbisch Gmünd. UMUC at Schwäbisch Gmünd is a 4-year residential campus located 33 km from Stuttgart in scenic southern Germany. Through classes taught in English, individualized attention, and an international student body, UMUC provides an ideal environment for academic achievement and cultural enrichment. Applications are invited from potential freshman, transfer, and semester or academic year abroad students.

Dates: Semesters run from Aug-Dec and Jan-May. Cost: Approx. $13,000 per year for tuition, approx. $5,500 for double room with full board. For Maryland residents, tuition is $5,700 per year for tuition. Contact: Allison Roach, International Admissions Counselor, UMUC-International Programs, University Blvd. at Adelphi Rd., College Park, MD 20742-1644; (301) 985-7442, fax (301) 985-7959; aroach@nova. umc.edu or Admissions Office, UMUC, Universitätspark, 73525 Schwäbisch Gmünd, Germany; (011) 49-7171-18070, fax 180732; tshea@admin.sg.umuc.edu.

Penn-in-Freiburg. For students interested in coursework in intensive intermediate German. This program offers German language students an opportunity to gain proficiency skills and cultural insight while studying in the center of Renaissance Germany.

Dates: Jul 15-Aug 21. Cost: Tuition $2,840; housing and activities $600. Contact: Penn Summer Abroad, College of General Studies, Univ. of Pennsylvania, 3440 Market St., Suite 100, Philadelphia, PA 19104-3335; (215) 898-5738, fax (215) 573-2053.

Schiller International Univ. at Heidelberg. Schiller Univ. is an American-style university with all courses except language classes taught in English. Schiller's particular strengths are in international business and international relations but it offers courses in the humanities and social sciences as well. Students may take German at Schiller or intensive German at the Collegium Palatinum, a specialized language division. One semester college German or equivalent is required.

Dates: Fall: late Aug-mid-Dec; spring: mid-Jan-mid-May. Cost: Sring 1998 (estimate): $6,355 per semester. Estimates include full-day orientation before departure, application fee, room and food allowance in residence hall, mandatory German insurance, airfare, books and supplies, health and accident insurance, German Residence Permit, administrative fees. SUNY tuition not included. Contact: Dr. John Ogden, Director, Office of International Programs, Box 2000, SUNY Cortland, Cortland, NY 13045; (607) 753-2209, fax (607) 753-5989; studyabroad@snycorva.cortland.edu, www.studyabroad.com/suny/cortland

Semester in Regensburg. This program combines German language courses at the beginning and intermediate levels with a range of courses in humanities, German culture, finance, and international business taught in English. Language courses are taught by Univ. of Regensburg faculty and others by Murray State Univ. faculty. No prior knowledge of German is required.

Dates: Aug 27-Dec 10 (1997). Cost: $2,895 program fee, MSU tuition ($1,030 for KY residents, $2,770 others), airfare. Contact: Dr. Fred Miller, Regensburg Program Director, Murray State Univ., P.O. Box 9, Murray, KY 42071; (502) 762-6206, fax (502) 762-3740; flmiller@msumusikmursuky.edu, or Ms. Linda Bartnik, Center for International Programs, P.O. Box 9, Murray State Univ., Murray, KY 42071; (502) 752-4152, fax (502) 762-3237; lbartnik@msumusik.mursuky.edu, www.mursuky.edu/qacd/cip/sirprog.htm.

Greece

An Archaeological Tour of Greece. Obtain first-hand knowledge of the art and architecture of ancient Greece through on-site archaeological visits and museum tours. This is the only course of its kind in which students are invited to have one of their lectures inside the Parthenon. Other highlights include visits to Sparta, Corinth, Mycenae, the Olympia Grounds, Delphi, Thermopylae, and Mystra, the world's best-preserved medieval city. The trip ends with 4 days on the island of Mykonos and a visit to the "birthplace" of Apollo.

Dates: Jun 7-Jun 29, 1998. Cost: $2,800 (3

credits) includes roundtrip airfare, double occupancy rooms, breakfast daily, bus, ship, and airport transfers. Contact: Dora Riomayor, Director of International Studies, School of Visual Arts, 209 E. 23rd St., New York, NY 10010-3994; (212) 592-2543, fax (212) 592-2545.

BCA Program in Athens. Earn 15-16 credits per semester at the Univ. of La Verne Athens, with a 1-week orientation and survival Greek training. Field trips and an extended study tour to Cairo or Istanbul. All classes taught in English by international faculty. No foreign language prerequisite. Graduate courses in business and education. Students from all U.S. colleges and universities accepted. Full liberal arts curriculum for undergraduates.

Dates: Sep 1-Nov 21 (fall), Mar 8-Jun 15 (spring), Sep 1-Jun 15 (year). Cost: $18,395 (1997-1998 academic year), $10,295 (1997-1998 semester). Includes international transportation, room and board, tuition, insurance, group travel in country, and 1 travel tour. Contact: Beverly S. Eikenberry, 605 E. College Ave., North Manchester, IN 46962; (219) 982-5238, fax (219) 982-7755; bca@manchester.edu, www.studyabroad.com/bca.

Beaver College Study in Greece. An individualized opportunity to learn about Greece, its people and its heritage. Courses available in classical, byzantine, and modern Greek studies, with required study of modern Greek language (no prior knowledge of Greek required). On-site resident director and expert specialist faculty. Field trips. Full range of program services. Need-based scholarships available.

Dates: Fall, spring, Full year and summer. Cost: Summer (1996): $3,300; full year: (1996-97) $15,500; fall or spring semester: $8,000. Contact: Audrianna Jones, Beaver College CEA, 450 S. Easton Rd., Glenside, PA 19038-3295; (888) BEAVER-9, fax (215) 572-2174; cea@beaver.edu, www.beaver.edu/cea.

Classic Theatre Study Abroad. Students, teachers, and professionals spend 3 weeks on an idyllic Greek island with classes mornings and rehearsal evenings. The fourth week they go on tour, presenting an ancient drama in classic and modern amphitheaters and visiting major classic sites.

Dates: Mid-Jun-mid-Jul. Cost: $3,500 participant or $4,500 with 6 hours credit. Contact: Dr. Arthur J. Beer, Univ. of Detroit Mercy, P.O. Box 19900, Detroit, MI 48219-0900.

College Year in Athens. One- or 2-semester programs during the academic year. The 2-track curriculum offers a focus on either Ancient Greek Civilization or Mediterranean Studies and is supplemented by at least 10 days each semester of study and travel within Greece. Instruction is in English. Credit is granted by prearrangement with the home institution.

Dates: Aug 31-Dec 18, 1998; Jan 18-May 21, 1999. Cost: Semester fee of $9,900 includes tuition, housing, partial board, study, travel, most course materials, $100 refundable damage deposit. Contact: College Year in Athens, North American Office, Dept. T, P.O. Box 390890, Cambridge, MA 02139-0010; (617) 494-1008, fax (617) 494-1662; cyathens@aol.com.

CYA Summer 1998. Three- and 6-week programs on Ancient Greek Civilization, Modern Greek Language (4 levels).

Dates: Jun 9-Jul 17, 1998. Cost: $3,450 (Jun 9-Jul 17, including study-travel); $1,750 (Jun 29-Jul 17 on island of Paros); $1,550 (Jun 9-Jun 26 in Athens). Covers tuition, housing, and course materials. Contact: College Year in Athens, North American Office, Dept. T, P.O. Box 390890, Cambridge, MA 02139-0010; (617) 494-1008, fax (617) 494-1662; cyathens@aol.com.

Ithaka Cultural Study in Crete. The Ithaka Semester combines intensive study of ancient and modern Greek culture with cultural immersion on Crete. Good writing, wide reading emphasized. Required local internships, frequent field trips. Warm, dynamic learning community with 5 tutors to 15 students in traditional neighborhood. Challenging program is superb preparation for college; restores vigor, excitement to learning for college students.

Dates: Spring semester: Feb 10-May 15 (1997); fall semester: Sep 10-Dec 15. Cost: $10,500. Includes tuition, room, board, field trips, and overnight excursions. Partial financial assistance available. Contact: Alice Brown, U.S. Director, Ithaka Cultural Study Program in Greece, 1692 Massachusetts Ave., Cambridge, MA 02138; (617) 868-4547, fax (617) 661-1904.

The Aegean School. This course focuses on the ancient Greek idea of the structure of society and its culture as the highest form of art (techne) starting with the art and mythology of the pre-Classical periods through the Classical and Hellenistic periods to Byzantine times. Members explore the ways in which varying philosophies, mythology, literature, drama, and art and architecture contributed to ancient Greek and Byzantine life. Most major archaeological sites and museums throughout Greece are visited and studied; lessons and seminars in modern Greek language and culture are presented. The program is rigorous and each applicant should be in good physical condition.

Dates: Jun 22-Jul 25. Cost: $1,900. Tuition includes all intra-Greece travel, taxes, and transfer fees; room and board averages $40 per day. Airfare fluctuates with prevailing seasonal rates. Contact: Professor Philip Drew, Aegean School of Classical Studies and Philosophy, P.O. Box 3602, Arlington, VA 22203; (703) 528-3375.

Guatemala

Centro Pop Wuj. This teacher-owned cooperative uses profits from the school to address problems of poverty, health, and environmental degradation in Guatemala. Centro Pop Wuj provides materials for community self-help projects and scholarships for local indigenous students. The program consists of 4 1/2 hours of one-on-one instruction in Spanish 5 days per week plus a variety of extracurricular activities, including community service work projects, conferences, films, and trips. Students have the opportunity to live with a Guatemalan family.

Dates: Year round. Classes begin each Monday. Cost: $125 per week includes homestay (room and meals) with Guatemalan family. $20 registration fee additional. Contact: Current U.S. volunteer info: Centro de Estudios Pop Wuj, P.O. Box 158, Sandstone, WV 25985-0158; (304) 466-2685, fax (304) 466-4399; popwuj@aol.com. In Guatemala: Apdo. Postal 68, Quetzaltenango, Guatemala; Tel./fax (011) 502-761-8286; popwujxel@pronet.net.gt.

Eco-Escuela de Español. The Eco-Escuela de Español offers a unique educational experience by combining intensive Spanish language instruction with volunteer opportunities in conservation and community development projects. Students are immersed in the language, culture, and ecology of Petén, Guatemala—an area renowned for its tropical forests and ancient Mayan ruins. Ecological activities integrate classroom with field-based experiences.

Dates: Every Monday year round. Cost: Classes $65 per week (based on 20 hours of individual instruction per week, Monday-Friday). Room and board with local families $60 per week. Registration fee $10. Contact: Eco-Escuela, Conservation International, 2501 M St., NW, Suite 200, Washington, DC 20037; (202) 973-2264, fax (202) 331-9328; ecoescuela@conservation.org.

Kie-Balam Spanish Language School. The school features one-on-one instruction with university-degreed teachers. Special group rate program for teachers, social workers and medical personnel. Course work transfers to degree programs. School starts rural lending libraries, helps at a battered women's shelter, and works with a special education school.

Dates: Year round, classes start Mondays. Cost: Application fee $50; tuition $100 per week (includes room and board). Contact: Martha Weese, 1007 Duncan Ave., Elgin, IL 60120; (847) 888-2514 (U.S.), (011) 502-7-611636; fax 610391(Guatemala from U.S.); moebius@super-highway.net.

La Hermandad Educativa. The nonprofit network of language schools is a sisterhood of 3 nonprofit educational collectives in Quetzaltenango and Todos Santos, Guatemala. All offer 5 hours per day of one-on-one instruction with experienced Spanish teachers and room and board with local families. Daily activities include conferences, field trips, films, and discussions about the culture, history, and political and social reality of Guatemala.

Dates: Classes begin every Monday. Cost: $120 per week Sep-May and $150 per week Jun, Jul, and Aug, $100 per week year round in Todos Santos. Contact: La Hermandad Educativa, 915 Cole St., #363, San Francisco, CA 94117; (800) 963-9889; www.infoserve.net/hermandad/hermandad.htm.

Honduras

Centro Internacional de Idiomas. Learn Spanish in the Caribbean in historic Trujillo or La Ceiba. Students learn Spanish in a relaxed, tropical atmosphere with a one-to-one student to teacher ratio. Programs emphasize intensive conversation and survival skills, grammar, and vocabulary. Most teachers are university graduates and many are bilingual.

Dates: Year round. Cost: $175 for 4-hour classes, 5 days per week, 7 days homestay. Contact: Belinda Linton, Director, Centro Internacional de Idiomas, TGU 00068, P.O. Box 025387, Miami, FL 33102-5387; Tel./fax (011) 504-44-4777.

Hong Kong

Syracuse Univ. in Hong Kong. Focus on international business and economy in Asia. Courses on business, economics, political science, history, Chinese language, sociology. Internships in Hong Kong, field trips to Beijing, Shanghai, elsewhere. Based at City Univ. of Hong Kong. Housing in residence halls, apartments.

Dates: Aug-Dec 1997 and Jan-May 1998. Cost: $8,755 tuition (1997-98); $6,450 includes housing, excursions, roundtrip travel. Contact: James Buschman, Associate Director, Syracuse Univ., 119 Euclid Ave., Syracuse, NY 13244-4170; (800) 235-3472, fax (315) 443-4593; suabroad@syr.edu.

India

BCA Program in Cochin. Earn 16-18 credits per semester at the Cochin Univ. of Science and Technology, with an orientation period, field trips, and extended study tour to Bangalore, Bombay, Madras, Madurai, Mysore, or Trichy. Students from all U.S. colleges and universities accepted. No foreign language prerequisite. Liberal arts curriculum including Hindi, Gandhian Studies, and sustainable development.

Dates: Sep 5-Dec 15 (fall only). Cost: $7,995 (semester 1997-1998). Includes international transportation, room and board, tuition, insurance, group travel in country. Contact: Beverly S. Eikenberry, 605 E. College Ave., North Manchester, IN 46962; (219) 982-5238, fax (219) 982-7755; bca@manchester.edu, www.studyabroad.com/bca.

BCA Program in Cochin. Earn 16-18 credits per semester at Cochin Univ. of Science and Technology with a 2-week orientation in country, field trips, and extended study tour to Madras, Bombay, Madurai, and Mysore. Courses in all academic disciplines taught in English. Students accepted from all U.S. colleges and universities.

Dates: Sep 10-Dec 21 or Jan 24 (fall only). Cost: $7,945 (1997). Includes international transportation, room and board, tuition, insurance, group travel in country. Contact: Beverly S. Eikenberry, 605 E. College Ave., North Manchester, IN 46962; (219) 982-5238, fax (219) 982-7755; bca@manchester.edu, www.studyabroad.com/bca.

Community Development. This study/travel course based in rural India, offers intensive study of 3 connected issues: community development at the village and city street level, the environment, and the roles of women in balancing the demands of the community. Each of the 4 sequential courses begins with an orientation; students then visit development projects where they observe and are taught by development professionals. Appropriate for students from many majors. While the program introduces the religions and cultures of India to students as essential to understanding and learning, the focus of the course is on current issues of development in India.

Dates: Sep-Dec. Contact: Ruth S. Mason, Director of International Education, Gustavus Adolphus College, St. Peter, MN 56082; (507) 933-7545, fax (507) 933-6277.

Friends World Program. A semester or year program in India at the Friends World Center in Bangalore includes orientation, intensive seminars, field studies, travel, and independent work. The core curriculum serves as an introduction to India's complex cultures. Independent study sample topics include: Gandhian studies, sustainable development, Buddhist studies in Nepal, dance, women's studies, philosophy, and traditional medicine. Students may earn 12-18 credits per semester.

Dates: Fall: mid-Sep-mid-Dec; spring: mid-Jan-mid-May. Cost: $10,000 per semester (in 1996/1997). Includes tuition, travel, room and board, fees, and books. Contact: James Howard, Friends World Program, 239 Montauk Hwy., Southampton,

NY 11968; (516) 287-8475; jhoward@sand. liunet.edu.

Peace Studies. Certificate course for 3 months on Indian Culture, Gandhian Thought, and Peace Studies. Send for brochure.
  Dates: Nov-Feb. Cost: $10 form fee plus $1,000 course fee after securing admission. Contact: Coordinator, Peace Research Centre, Gujarat Vidyapith, Ahmedabad 380014, India; (011) 91-79-446148, fax 79-6569547; gujvi@adinet.ernet.in.

Penn-in-India. For students interested in South Asian studies, performing arts, religion, economics, and traditional medicine, PSA's newest program offers students a survey of both India's rich cultural history and its burgeoning industrial life. The program is located in Pune, a cosmopolitan city of 4,000,000 which is a thriving arts center, a hub of scholarship, and a growing economic presence. Students will live with Indian families in the area and be involved in community projects.
  Dates: Jun 28-Aug 9. Cost: Tuition $2,840; program cost $1,860. Contact: Penn Summer Abroad, College of General Studies, Univ. of Pennsylvania, 3440 Market St., Suite 100, Philadelphia, PA 19104-3335; (215) 898-5738, fax (215) 573-2053.

Wisconsin College Year in India. The program provides integrated language training, tutorial instruction, and independent fieldwork projects, beginning with summer school in the U.S. The 4 program sites are at Banaras Hindu Univ. (for Hindu-Urdu students); Hyderabad Univ., Hyderabad, A.P. (for Telugu students); Madurai Kamaraj Univ. (for Tamil students), and Kerala Univ., Thiruvanantha-puram, Kerala (for Malayalam students).
  Dates: Summer in Madison: early Jun-mid-Aug; academic program abroad: late Aug-Apr. Cost: Call for current information. Contact: Office of International Studies and Programs, 261 Bascom Hall, 500 Lincoln Dr., Madison,

WI 53706; (608) 262-2851, fax (608) 262-6998; abroad@macc.wisc.edu.

Indonesia

Study in Bali. Join the Naropa Institute (NCA accredited) program in Bali, Indonesia. Bali, often called the Island of the Gods, is the ideal setting for exploring art in everyday life. The Naropa Institute Program in Bali offers courses in culture, language, gamelan music, dance, painting, maskmaking, batik, and meditation. All classes are taught by master Balinese artists and scholars, as well as Naropa faculty.
  Dates: Mid-Feb-mid-Apr, 1998. Cost: $5,250 (in 1997). Includes tuition (9 semester credits), room and partial board, program expenses. Airfare not included. Contact: Study Abroad Office, The Naropa Institute, 2130 Arapahoe Ave., Boulder, CO 80302; (303) 546-3594, fax (303) 444-0410.

Ireland

Archaeological Field School. Survey and excavation of a post-medieval deserted village: Slievemore, Achill, Co. Mayo. Activities include: surveying, excavation procedure, recording geology and botany of island, field trips, lectures and seminars. No previous knowledge required. Maximum 6 credits.
  Dates: Weekly Jul 15-Aug 30. Cost: Weekly: IR£85 p.p. $200 course fee plus accommodations. Contact: Theresa McDonald, M.A. Director, Achill Archaeological Field School, St. O'Hara's Hill, Tullamore, Co. Offaly, Ireland; (011) 353-1-505-21627, fax 506-21627.

Burren College of Art. The Burren College of Art is located on the west coast of Ireland. It offers studio art courses in a variety of media for year, semester, and 4- and 8-week summer sessions. Students will find the setting and environment of the College conducive to individual growth and self expression, with ample contact between students, teaching staff, and visiting artists. Housing in shared cottages.

Dates: Sep-Dec, Jan-Jun; 4- and 8-week summer programs available as well. Cost: Semester: $8,000; summer: $2,200-$4,000. Includes tuition, housing, some art materials, support services, excursions, partial insurance coverage. Contact: IPA, Univ. of Illinois at Urbana-Champaign, 115 International Studies Bldg., 910 S. 5th St., Champaign, IL 61820; (800) 531-4404, fax (217) 244-0249; ipa@uiuc.edu.

Internships in Dublin. Interns live with families or in apartments. Two programs available: 6-credit internship plus 9-credit classwork in Irish Studies through the Institute of Public Administration or full-time (15-16 credits) internship. IPA placements may be in Parliament, municipal government, health care administration, radio/TV, and at the Irish Times. Full-time placements available in social services, communication, film, advertising and others.

Fields: Public Administration, Parliamentary Internships, Political Science, Technology, Finance, Health and Communications. Fifteen-16 credits per semester, 10 for Summer. Prerequisites: 2.5 GPA for traditional full-time internships, 3.0 for IPA internships. Adaptability and maturity. Strong performance in major. Application materials: SUNY application.

Dates: Fall: early Sep-mid-Dec (application deadline Feb 1); spring: early Jan-late Apr (application deadline Sep 1); summer: early Jun-mid-Aug (application deadline Feb 1). Cost: Fall (1997) and spring 1998 estimates: IPA $4,400 for Dublin internships (full-time) $3,500; summer 1997 $3,415 (Dublin internships only, IPA not available). Estimates include full-day orientation before departure, application fee, room and board, food allowance, health and accident insurance, roundtrip airfare from N.Y., bus pass. SUNY tuition not included. Contact: Dr. John Ogden, Director, Office of International Programs, Box 2000, SUNY Cortland, Cortland, NY 13045; (607) 753-2209, fax (607) 753-5989; studyabroad@snycorva.cortland.edu, www.studyabroad.com/suny/cortland.

Ireland and Northern Ireland. Twelve program opportunities in the Republic and the North. University study and special subject area programs including internships in the Irish parliament. Program provides a full range of services including a full-time resident director and staff in Dublin, orientation, homestay, and guaranteed housing.

Dates: Fall, spring, academic year, and summer. Semesters and terms. Cost: Varies. Call for current fees. Contact: Meghan Mazick, Beaver College Center for Education Abroad, 450 S. Easton Rd., Glenside, PA 19038-3295; (888) BEAVER-9, fax (215) 572-2174; cea@beaver.edu, www.beaver.edu/cea.

Ireland Study Abroad. The Irish College for the Humanities offers a residential program of liberal arts courses with specialized concentrations in Irish Studies, Social Sciences, Literature, and the Arts for full U.S. college credit. Weekly guided study trips to sites of oustanding historic, cultural, and scenic importance complement the course of study.

Dates: Full year: Sep to mid-May; fall: Sep to mid-Dec; Jan (4 weeks); spring: Feb to mid-May; Jun (4 weeks); summer (weekly study tours). Cost: Fall, spring: $9,500 (12-15 credits); Jan: $2,875 (3 credits); Jun: $3,650 (6 credits); summer: $1,500 (noncredit). Includes orientation, tuition, room, board, transcript, and travel on all organized study trips. Contact: U.S. Admissions Office; (800) 610-2858; ichireland@aol.com or Administrator, Irish College for the Humanities, Collis-Sandea House, Oakpark, Tralee, Co. Kerry, Ireland; Tel./fax (011) 353-66-20540; ichkerry@iol.ic; http://ns.ric.tralee/humanities/humanhp.html.

Study Abroad Institute. Semester, academic year, or summer term. Two to 6 courses per semester. Graduate credit available in summer courses. Courses taught in English. Typical class size 25. Less than 25 percent of each class are program participants. Other students are from host institution, host country, other programs. Seminars and tutorials also used for instruction. Unstructured time each week to be used at students' leisure.

Dates: Late Sep-mid-Dec (fall), early Jan-late May (spring). Approx. dates. Apply by Jul 1 for fall or full year, by Oct 1 for spring, and by Apr 1 for summer. Cost: 1996-1997: semester $6,000-$8,500, year $11,500-$16,500, summer $1,000-$2,950. Contact: Elizabeth Strauss, Associate Director, or Amy Armstrong, Operations Manager, North American Institute for Study Abroad, P.O. Box 279, Riverside, PA 17868 ; (717) 275-5099, fax (717) 275-1644.

Univ. College Cork. First opened in 1849, the Univ. College Cork (UCC) is 1 of 3 constituent colleges of the National Univ. of Ireland. Eight faculties comprise the educational offerings of UCC: Arts, Celtic Studies, Commerce, Law, Science, Food Science and Technology, Engineering and Medicine. Enrollment in regular UCC classes with Irish students. Cortland's program specializes in language, history, and culture, but other courses may be available. Housing arranged prior to departure from U.S. in apartments near campus. Fall, spring, summer, academic year.

Dates: Fall: Early Sep-mid-Dec:, spring: mid-Jan-early Jun; summer: early Jul-end of Jul. Cost: Fall (1997) estimate: $6,385; spring 1998: $6,850; summer: $2,950; academic year: $12,750. Estimates include full-day orientation before departure, application fee, apartment rental (including utilities), food allowance, health and accident insurance, roundtrip airfare from NY, books and supplies. SUNY tuition not included. Contact: Dr. John Ogden, Director, Office of International Programs, Box 2000, SUNY Cortland, Cortland, NY 13045; (607) 753-2209, fax (607) 753-5989; studyabroad@snycorva.

cortland.edu, www.studyabroad.com/suny/cortland.

Israel

Ben Gurion Univ. Located in Beer-Sheva, BGU offers the opportunity to live with Israelis, learn Hebrew, and be truly immersed in Israeli culture and society. Students can participate in community internships or conduct individual research in university departments. Courses are taught in English in such areas as anthropology, archaeology, economics, ecology, Judaic studies, political science, and women's studies. Program includes optional kibbutz stay and archaeological dig. Financial aid available.

Dates: Spring: Jan 5-Jun 5 (1997); Aug 4-Dec 26 (1996) fall. Cost: Semester: $5,580; year: $8,770. Includes tuition, room, health insurance, Hebrew ulpan, activity fee (trips). Contact: Caroline Fox, Associate Director, 342 Madison Ave., Suite 1224, New York, NY 10173; (212) 687-7721, fax (212) 370-0805; outside NY (800) 962-2248; bguosp@haven.ios.com, www.bgu.ac.il/osp.

Field Study Internship Program. Designed for students with an interest in policy applications of social science research and/or area studies interest in Israel, this semester program gives students the opportunity to carry out an individual research project on an aspect of Israel's socio-economic development. Also included are instruction in research methods, a background course on Israel's development and instruction in basic conversational Hebrew. Study tours and field trips are important components in this program.

Dates: Jan 14-May 13 (1997); Aug 20-Dec 18 (1996). Cost: Tuition: $4,700 fall, spring. Room $150 per month, board $400 per month (optional). Contact: Dr. Aliza Fleischer, Field Study Program Coordinator, Development Study Center, P.O. Box

2355, Rehovot 76122, Israel; fax (972) 8-9475884; xsvinn@weizmann.weizmann.ac.il.

Geography, History, Archaeology. A 3-week program (4 semester hours of graduate/undergraduate credit) with extensive field trips throughout the region. Introduces the student to the geography, history, and archaeology of Israel and Trans-Jordan as they relate to Biblical studies.

Dates: Call for dates, programs run year round. Cost: $1,695 on campus; $1,865 off campus. Contact: Jerusalem University College, 4249 E. State St., Suite 203, Rockford, IL 61108; (815) 229-5900 or (800) 891-9408, fax (815) 229-5901.

Jesus and His Times. A 2-week (2-semester hour) program of studies related to the geography, history, culture, and archaeology of the Second Temple period (time of Christ). Concentrations in the Jerusalem and Galilee regions.

Dates: Jul each year. Cost: $1,100 on campus; $1,325 off campus. Contact: Jerusalem University College, 4249 E. State St., Suite 203, Rockford, IL 61108; (815) 229-5900 or (800) 891-9408, fax (815) 229-5901.

Long-Term Study Programs. Two-year master of arts degrees in the history of Syro-Palestine; Middle Eastern studies; Hebrew language; Hebrew Bible translation; New Testament backgrounds. Also 1-year graduate studies certificates and semester abroad for undergraduates.

Dates: Year round. Cost: Approx. $7,000 per semester. Includes tuition and room and board. Contact: Jerusalem University College, 4249 E. State St., Suite 203, Rockford, IL 61108; (815) 229-5900 or (800) 891-9408, fax (815) 229-5901.

Master of Arts Degree. Ancient History of Syro-Palestine, Middle Eastern Studies, New Testament Backgrounds, Hebrew Language, Hebrew Bible Translation. Two-year MA degrees. Extensive fieldwork and study in the languages, geography, history, culture, social, and religious aspects of Israel and the Middle East.

Dates: Sep-May every year. Cost: Approx. $7,000 per semester. Includes tuition, room and board, fees. Contact: Jerusalem University College, Amelia Nakai, Program Coordinator, 4249 E. State St., Suite 203, Rockford, IL 61108; (815) 229-5900 or (800) 891-9408, fax (815) 229-5901.

Italy

AHA Siena Program. Subject areas include Italian language, architecture, art history, civilization and culture, classical studies, economics, history, political science. All courses other than Italian language are conducted in English. No Italian language experience required for admissions. Full academic year or individual 10-week terms, fall, winter, spring.

Dates: Sep-Dec (fall), Jan-Mar (winter), Apr-Jun (spring). Cost: Approx. $5,200 per term. Includes tuition, housing, some meals, excursions, texts, international student identity card, local transportation, insurance. Financial aid accepted. Contact: Gail Lavin, Assoc. Director, Univ. Programs, American Heritage Association, 741 SW Lincoln St., Portland, OR 97201-3178; (800) 654-2051, fax (503) 295-5969; 96trab@amheritage.org.

American Univ. of Rome. Programs for students of international business, international relations, Italian civilization and culture, Italian studies and communications. Credits fully transferable through affiliations with U.S. institutions. Housing in studio apartments. All courses (except language classes) in English. All programs are designed to provide students with studies of immediate relevance in a highly competitive job market.

Dates: Fall and Spring semesters plus May/Jun summer sessions. Cost: $4,634 per semester, tuition/housing $2,500. Contact: Mary B. Handley, Dean of Administration, American Univ. of Rome, Via Pietro Roselli 4, Rome 00153, Italy; (011) 39-6-58330919, fax 58330992.

Art Under One Roof. Live the arts in Florence at Art Under One Roof. Study for a month, a semester, or academic year. With over 30 applied art programs we're sure to satisfy you. Enrollments in all courses are limited to 10 to ensure the maximum amount of attention to each student's individual needs.

Dates: Year round. Cost: From $400-$6,000. Contact: Art Under One Roof, Admissions, Borgo dei Greci, 14, 50122 Florence, Italy; Tel./fax (011) 39-55-239-6821; berarducci@iol.it.

Buffalo State Siena Program. Experience a medieval city as your neighborhood through placement with a family and access to university facilities. Enjoy a unique, economical program revolving around art, Italian language, and civilization. Participate in classroom work complemented by excursions, workshops, and frequent informal gatherings. Learn from bilingual instructors in a user-friendly atmosphere (average student-teacher ratio 8:1).

Dates: Early Sep to mid-Dec; late Jan-early May. Cost: (Spring 1997): $6,731 per semester for New York state residents, nonresidents add $2,450. Includes tuition fees, room, board, required field trips, insurance, airfare. Contact: Dr. Lee Ann Grace, Director, Buffalo State College, 1300 Elmwood Ave., Buffalo, NY 14222-1095; (716) 878-4620, fax (716) 878-3054; gracela@snybufaa.cs.snybuf.edu, www.snybuf.edu (under Academic Programs).

Business, Economics, Italian Studies. Turin offers a diversified curriculum in English and in business and economics, plus intensive courses in Italian language and culture, literature, etc., at the foot of the majestic Alps. Program-organized housing and field trips and many Italian university activities.

Dates: Summer sessions: Jun 30-Jul 25, 1998; fall semester: Aug 29-Dec 17 (1997); spring semester: Jan 4-Apr 30, 1998. Cost: $3,975 per semester, $6,980 fall and spring semesters; summer: $1,570 per session $2,900 both sessions. Contact: University Studies Abroad Consortium (USAC), Univ. of Nevada, Reno #323, Reno, NV 89557-0093; (702) 784-6569, fax (702) 784-6010; usac@admin.unr.edu, www.scs.unr.edu/~usac.

Dance in Italy. Located in the Renaissance city of Urbino, this 3-week intensive modern dance workshop will include daily technique class, development of performance skills, and on-site performance. Three undergraduate credits.

Dates: Early Jul-late Jul. Cost: Approx. $1,500. Airfare not included. Contact: Office of International Education, SUNY New Paltz, HAB 33, New Paltz, NY 12561; (914) 257-3125, fax (914) 257-3129; international@newpaltz.edu, www.newpaltz.edu/oie.

Italian Language Courses. Group and individual Italian language courses (6 levels). Cultural courses (literature, art history, history of Florence, history of opera, operatic Italian, and libretti), conversation courses, written expression, Italian politics, geography, Italian for business and commerce, Italian for tourism, wine course, cooking course.

Dates: Call or write for details. Cost: Call or write for details. Contact: Dr. Stefano Burbi, Director, Istituto Parola, Corso del Tintori 8, 50122 Florence, Italy; (011) 39-55-24-21-82, fax 24-19-14; lstituto.parola@agora.stm.it, www.alba.fi.it/parola.

Italian Language Studies. Four-week intensive program in Urbino, emphasizing language proficiency, culture and civilization, and contemporary Italian literature. Open to all students at all levels. Field trips. Six credit hours: undergraduate, graduate.

Dates: Late Jun-early Aug. Cost: Approx. $3,200. Airfare not included. Contact: Office of International Education, SUNY New Paltz, HAB 33, New Paltz, NY 12561; (914) 257-3125, fax (914) 257-3129; international@newpaltz.edu, www.newpaltz.edu/oie.

Italian Studies in Florence. For students interested in intensive beginning and intermediate language courses and cultural studies in literature, cinema, and art history taught in one of the world's most beautiful cities. Numerous cultural opportunities and field trips offer a valuable supplement to class work.

Dates: Jun 3-Jul 12. Cost: Tuition $2,700; housing $1,250-$1,800; travel $800. Contact: Penn Summer Abroad, College of General Studies, Univ. of Pennsylvania, 3440 Market St., Suite 100, Philadelphia, PA 19104-3335; (215) 898-5738, fax (215) 573-2053.

Lorenzo de' Medici. Art history, Italian history and culture, studio art, business and economics. All conducted in English. Semester, summer classes, short-term programs. Learn Italian art history, cooking, civilization, and culture in the heart of the Renaissance. U.S. credits available.

Dates: Sep/Dec-Jan-Apr. Summer: May, Jun, Jul, Aug. Cost: Tuition: Semester $3,500, summer: approx. $1,100. Contact: Dott. Arch. Gabriella Ganugi, Director, Lorenzo de'Medici, Via Faenza, #43, 50123 Florence, Italy; (011) 39-55-287143, fax 23989 20/287203; ldm@dada.it.

Macerata Program. Subject areas include Italian language, architecture, art history, civilization and culture, economics, history, literature, politics. All courses other than Italian language are conducted in English. No Italian language experience required for admission. Full academic year or individual semesters, fall, winter.

Dates: Sep-Dec (fall), Jan-Apr (winter). Cost: Approx. $6,500 per semester. Includes tuition, housing, some meals, excursions, texts, international student identity card, local transportation, insurance. Financial aid accepted. Contact: Gail Lavin, Assoc. Director, Univ. Programs, American Heritage Association, 741 SW Lincoln St., Portland, OR 97201-3178; (800) 654-2051, fax (503) 295-5969; 96trab@amheritage.org.

Sarah Lawrence College in Florence. Individually designed programs with total immersion in the academic and social life of Florence. Options include enrollment in the Univ. of Florence, studio arts, music, and internships. Frequent field trips and excursions are included. Private tutorials and small seminars with distinguished Italian faculty.

Dates: Sept-Jun or Jan-Jun. Cost: $21,450 (full year). Includes all fees, excursions, field trips, and cultural activities. Contact: Celia Regan, Sarah Lawrence College in Florence, Box CR, Bronxville, NY 10708; (800) 873-4752.

Studio Art Centers International. Located in central Florence, SACI is the largest and most comprehensive studio art program in Italy. There are 5 different programs of study to meet the diverse needs of students: year/semester abroad, 2-year diploma, post-baccalaureate certificate, master of fine arts, late spring and summer studies. Field trips take students to Pisa, Siena, San Gimiganano, Lucca, Arezzo, Assisi, Rome, Bologna, etc.

Dates: Sep-Dec; Jan-Apr; May-Jun; Jun-Jul. Cost: Fall/spring 1997/98 tuition $7,500 per term; post-baccalaureate $7,500 per term; tuition late spring/summer 1997 $2,600; 1998 $3,000. Contact: SACI Coordinator, U.S. Student Programs, Institute of International Education, 809 UN Plaza, New York, NY 10017-3580; (800) 344-9186, (212) 984-5548, fax (212) 984-5325; lmoore@iie.org, www.iie.org/pgms/saci/.

Study in Urbino. An academic year program in the Renaissance city of Urbino, offering intensive Italian language and regular university courses at the Univ. of Urbino. Dormitory housing, native resident director, field trips, 12-18 undergraduate credits per semester. Qualifications: junior or above; minimum of 2 years college-level Italian or the equivalent. Qualified applicant may be considered for spring-only program.

Dates: Late Sep-early Jun. Cost: Approx. $10,100. Includes tuition, fees, room and board, and insurance (non-New York state residents add $4,900). Contact: Office of International Education, SUNY New Paltz, HAB 33, New Paltz, NY 12561; (914) 257-3125, fax (914) 257-3129; international@newpaltz.edu, www.newpaltz.edu/oie.

Summer in Rome. The program is open to high school seniors and college students at any accredited university or college in the U.S., and to secondary school teachers. No previous knowledge of Italian is required since the program offers language courses at the elementary, intermediate, and advanced levels, and the art and culture courses are conducted in English. Double occupancy and 3 meals a day are provided at the designated residence in Rome. Participants must register for 6 credits.

Dates: Jun 27-Jul 25 (1997). Cost: $2,100 includes room and board, excursions. Airfare and tuition additional. Contact: Study Abroad Office, Univ. at Stony Brook, Melville Library E5340, Stony Brook, NY 11794-3397; (516) 632-7030, fax (516) 632-6544; bgilkes@ccmail.sunysb.edu.

Tech Rome. Tech Rome is a 6-week summer travel-study program based in Rome. It features hotel housing, 3 meals per day, tours, and traditional classroom courses combined with field travel for college credit. Up to 13 semester hours may be earned in a choice of over 10 courses in diverse subject areas. Courses are taught by American professors. All disciplines are accredited.

Dates: May 26-Jul 3, 1998. Cost: $4,328 includes tuition, all housing for 6 weeks, 3 meals per day, tours. Group flights and optional tours available. Contact: Tech Rome, P.O. Box 3172, Ruston, LA 71272; (800) 346-8324; http://techrome.latech.edu.

UGA Studies Abroad at Cortona. Studio art (ceramics, drawing, book arts, design, interior design, jewelry and metalworking, painting, papermaking, printmaking, photography, sculpture, and watercolor), art history, beginning Italian, Italian culture, landscape architecture, and women studies for undergraduate and graduate university credit. Courses vary each quarter. Deadlines: Jan 10, spring; Apr 10, summer; and Jun, 10 fall.

Dates: (1997): Mar 31-Jun 5 (spring); Jun 16-Aug 20 (summer); Sep 7-Nov 11 (fall). Cost: $6,300. Includes tuition for 2 courses, lodging and 2 meals per day, airfare, and land travel with the program. $125 out-of-state fee. Contact: Larry Millard, Director, UGA Studies Abroad, Visual Arts Building, Univ. of Georgia, Athens, GA 30602-4102; (706) 542-7011, fax (706) 542-2467; cortona@uga.cc.uga.edu.

Wisconsin Summer in Perugia. This intensive Italian language program gives students an opportunity to study at the Universitá Italiana per Stranieri in Perugia, a train-ride away from Florence and Rome. Students take courses in Italian language, at any level, and a 1-credit cultural survey, taught in English. No previous knowledge of Italian required. Application deadline: First Friday in Mar. Late applications considered on a space-available basis.

Dates: Late May through Jul (8 weeks). Cost: Call for current information. Contact: Office of International Studies and Programs, 261 Bascom Hall, Univ. of Wisconsin, 500 Lincoln Dr., Madison, WI 53706; (608) 262-2851, fax (608) 262-6998; abroad@macc.wisc.edu.

Japan

BCA Program in Sapporo. Earn 15-18 credits per semester at Hokusei Gakuen Univ. in Sapporo, with a 1-week orientation, homestay with Japanese families, field trips, and extended study tour through Honshu. Year program could include first semester or 2-month interterm in Dalian, China. Students accepted from all U.S. colleges and universities. No foreign language prerequisite. All levels of Japanese language study available. Practica and internships available.

Dates: Aug 16-Dec 19 (fall), Mar 19-Jul 21 (spring), Aug-Jul or Mar-Dec (year). Cost: $18,395 (academic year 1997-1998); $10,295 (semester 1997-1998). Includes international transportation, room and board, tuition, insurance, group travel in country. Contact: Beverly S. Eikenberry, 605 E. College Ave., North Manchester, IN 46962; (219) 982-5238, fax (219) 982-7755; bca@ manchester. edu, www.study-abroad. com/bca.

Friends World Program. A semester or year program at the Friends World Center in Kyoto includes intensive seminars focused on Japanese culture, language, and the arts. Writing workshops are also offered. Students design internships and independent research projects. Sample topics include: traditional medicine, education, Buddhism, gender studies, peace movements, and environmental policy. Student may earn 12-18 credits per semester.

Dates: Fall: mid-Sep-mid-Dec; spring: mid-Jan-mid-May. Cost: $11,875 per semester in 1996/1997. Includes tuition, travel, room and board, fees, and books. Contact: James Howard, Friends World Program, 239 Montauk Hwy., Southampton, NY 11968; (516) 287-8475; jhoward@ sand.liunet.edu.

Intensive Language and Culture. In this collboration between Washington Univ. and KCP International Language Institute, Tokyo, earn 1 year of college Japanese language credit in 9 weeks (15 quarter credit hours). Japanese language classes offered at all academic levels. No language requirements. Homestay with most meals, or private dormitory room provided. Eductional excursions include trips to many cultural, historical, and political sites around Tokyo, including company visits. Local transportation pass between home and school provided.

Dates: Summer: Jul 2-Sep 12; fall: Oct 2-Dec 12; winter: Jan 7-Mar 17; spring: Apr 13-Jun 16. Cost: $4,500. Includes tuition and fees, airport pick-up, on-site orientation, homestay, breakfast and dinners, local transportation pass between home and school, educational excursions, minor medical insurance, transferable academic credit from Western Washington Univ. Contact: Michael Anderson, Director, KCP International USA, 304 36th St., Suite 223, Bellingham, WA 98225; (888) KCP-7020 (toll free) or (360) 647-0072, fax (360) 647-0736; kcp@kcp-usa.com., http://kcp-usa.com/~kcp.

Japan Exchange and Teaching Program. Contact: JET Program Office, Embassy of Japan, 2520 Massachusetts Ave. NW, Washington, DC 20008; (202) 238-6772, (202) 265-9484; eojjet@erols.com.

Kenya

Friends World Program. A semester or year program in Kenya at Friends World Center in Machakos. Includes intensive seminars, field study, homestays, travel, and independent study. Seminars are offered in historical and contemporary East Africa and Swahili language. Field projects have been done in the areas of sustainable development, education, traditional medicine, agroforestry, marine ecology, wildlife studies, and music. Students may earn 12-18 credits per semester.

Dates: Fall: mid-Sep-mid-Dec.; spring: mid-Jan-mid-May. Cost: $10,600 per semester (in 1996/1997). Includes tuition, travel, room and board, fees, and books. Contact: James Howard, Friends World Program, 239 Montauk Hwy., Southampton, NY 11968; (516) 287-8475; jhoward@sand.liunet.edu.

Korea

Penn-in-Seoul. For students interested in East Asia, Korea, international relations and other business disciplines. This program, offered in conjunction with Kyung Hee Univ., includes courses in the area of international relations as well as internships with multinational corporations, government agencies, and think tanks. Field trips exploring Korean history and culture are integral to the program.

Dates: Jun 14-Aug 17. Cost: Tuition $2,840; housing $850. Contact: Penn Summer Abroad, College of General Studies, Univ. of Pennsylvania, 3440 Market St., Suite 100, Philadelphia, PA 19104-3335; (215) 898-5738, fax (215) 573-2053.

Latin America

Development Work. Programs in Nicaragua and Brazil. In the 11-month Nicaragua program you do construction work in a rural cooperative and travel and study in countries in Central America. In the 6-month program in Brazil you live and work in a rural cooperative and urban settlement and travel throughout the country. Both programs are open to students and non-students and include preparation and follow-up in the U.S.

Dates: Nicaragua: Sep 15 (1996); Brazil: Jan 4 (1997). Cost: Nicaragua: $4,600; Brazil: $3,400. Includes training, room and board, airfare, health insurance, and other direct program costs. Contact: IICD, Institute for International Cooperation and Development, Josefin Jonsson, Administrative Director, P.O. Box 103-T, Williamstown, MA 01267; (413) 458-9828, fax (413) 458-3323.

Friends World Program. A semester or year in Latin America at Friends World Center in San José, Costa Rica, incorporates seminars, field study, travel, and independent projects. Seminars to introduce students into Latin America and its culture include Central America today, intensive Spanish for any level student, ecology and development, women's studies in Latin America. Independent work has included: ecology, community development, peace studies, health and refugee studies. Students may earn 12-18 credits per semester.

Dates: Fall: mid-Sep-mid-Dec; spring: mid-Jan-mid-May. Cost: $10,010 per semester (1996/1997). Includes tuition, travel, room and board, fees and books. Contact: James Howard, Friends World Program, 239 Montauk Hwy., Southampton, NY 11968; (516) 287-8475; jhoward@sand.liunet.edu.

Mexico

AHA in Morelia. Semester weeks. Courses are taught at the Centro Mexicano Internacional (CMI). Intensive Spanish classes, history, politics, art, literature, business, and field study.

Dates: Jan-Dec 12, intensive Spanish in the summer. Cost: Univ. programs approx. $5,200 semester. Intensive Spanish approx. $245 first week, $195 subsequent weeks. Housing and meals $12 per day double occupancy. Contact: Linda Kopfer, Assoc. Director of Univ. Programs, American Heritage Association, 741 SW Lincoln St., Portland, OR 97201-3178; (503) 295-7730 or (800) 654-2051, fax (503) 295-5969; 96trab@amheritage.org.

Autonomous Univ. of Guadalajara/Doing Business in Mexico. Innovative teaching methods combine with cultural immersion and a specialized Beaver-taught class in English, culminating in an extensive field study trip. Semester for beginning and intermediate Spanish speakers with business related major also available. Full range of program services. On-site representative. Need-based scholarships available.

Dates: Fall, spring, full year, summer. Cost: Full year: $10,200; Semester: $6,500, Business semester: $6,500; Summer: $1,350. Contact: Meredith Chamorro, Beaver College Center for Education Abroad, 450 S. Easton Rd., Glenside, PA 19038-3295; (888) BEAVER-9, fax (215) 572-2174; cea@beaver.edu, www.beaver.edu/cea.

BCA Program in Xalapa. Earn 15-18 credits per semester at Univ. Veracruzana with a 4-week intensive language and orientation period, homestay with families, field trips, and extended study tour. Intermediate college level Spanish required for regular university courses. Students with lower level Spanish accepted for language and culture study only.

Dates: Aug 2-Dec 12 or Jan 17 (fall), Feb 15-Jun 12 or Jul 10 (spring), Aug 2-Jun 12 or Jul 10 (year). Cost: $13,395 (academic year 1997-1998); $7,995 (semester 1997-1998). Includes international transportation, room and board, tuition, insurance, group travel in country. Contact: Beverly S. Eikenberry, 605 E. College Ave., North Manchester, IN 46962; (219) 982-5238, fax (219) 982-7755; bca@manchester.edu, www.studyabroad.com/bca.

Centro de Idiomas/Language Link. The Centro de Idiomas offers intensive Spanish language programs in the exciting Pacific coastal city of Mazatlan, Mexico. Combine a beach vacation with your study. Your choice of 2-4 hours daily of group classes with only 6 students or private classes. Professional adults, college students, and all Spanish levels accommodated in a very well organized school. Programs of 1-12 weeks. Academic credit. Caring homestays and

many additional weekly activities include all water sports and excursions with marine biologists.

Dates: Year round. New classes begin every Monday. Cost: $105 registration deposit. Four hours daily group classes and homestay: $270 per week; 4 hours daily private classes: $430 per week. Includes tuition, insurance, shared room (private $20 extra), and 3 meals daily. Contact: Kay G. Rafool, Language Link Inc., P.O. Box 3006, Peoria, IL 61612; (800) 552-2051, fax (309) 692-2926; info@langlink.com; www.langlink.com.

El Bosque del Caribe, Cancun. Take a professional Spanish course 25 hours per week and enjoy the Caribbean beaches. Relaxed family atmosphere. No more than 6 students per class. Special conversation program. Mexican cooking classes and excursions to the Mayan sites. Housing with Mexican families. College credit available.

Dates: Year round. New classes begin every Monday. Group programs arranged at reduced fees. Cost: Enrollment fee $100, $175 per week. One week with a Mexican family $150. Contact: Eduardo Sotelo, Director, Calle Piña 1, S.M. 25, 77500 Cancún, Mexico; (011) 52-98-84-10-38, fax 84-58-88; bcaribe@mail.cancun-language.com.mx

Guadalajara Summer School. For the 46th year, the Univ. of Arizona Guadalajara Summer School will offer intensive Spanish in the 6-week session, intensive Spanish in the 3-week session, and upper-division Spanish and Mexico-related courses in the 5-week session. Courses may be taken for credit or audit.

Dates: Jul 6-Aug 20. Cost: $1,038-$2,000 includes tuition and host family housing with meals. Contact: Dr. Macario Saldate IV, Director, Guadalajara Summer School, The Univ. of Arizona, P.O. Box 40966, Tucson, AZ 85717; (520) 621-5137; janeg@u.arizona.edu, www.coh.arizona.edu/gss.

Intensive Spanish in Cuernavaca. Cuauhnahuac, founded in 1972, offers a variety of intensive and flexible programs geared to individual needs. Six hours of classes daily with no more than 4 students to a class. Housing with Mexican families who really care about you. Cultural conferences, excursions, and special classes for professionals. College credit available.

Dates: Year round. New classes begin every Monday. Cost: $70 registration fee; $650 4 weeks tuition; housing $18 per night. Contact: Marcia Snell, 519 Park Dr., Kenilworth, IL 60043; (800) 245-9335, fax (847) 256-9475; lankysam@aol.com.

Language and Culture in Guanajuato. We work with innovative teaching techniques, tailoring instruction to each student's needs. Spanish, Mexican History, Politics, Culture-Cuisine, Folk Dancing and Latin American Literature.

Dates: Year round. New classes begin every Monday. Cost: $925. Includes 4 weeks of classes and homestay with 3 meals daily. Contact: Director Jorge Barroso, Instituto Falcon, A.C., Guanajuato, Gto. 36000 Mexico; Tel./fax (011) 52-473-2-36-94, infalcon@redes.int.com.mx, www.infonet.com.mx/falcon.

Language Institute of Colima. The Language Institute of Colima, Mexico offers a system of total immersion with classes held throughout the year Monday-Friday. Students live with local host families and attend 6 hours of instruction daily; no more than 5 students per class. Many extras, including beach excursions.

Dates: Year round, Monday-Friday. Cost: Registration $80; tuition $415 1st week, $345 after 1st week (for shared room), $445 1st week, $375 after 1st week (for private room). 10 percent discount for 6 or more. Contact: Dennis Bourassa, Language Institute of Colima, P.O. Box 827, Miranda, CA 95553; (800) 604-6579, fax (707) 923-4232; colima@northcoast.com, www.northcoast.com/~colima.

Learn Spanish in Chiapas. Spanish lessons in private sessions or small groups (4 people

maximum). Family stays available. School tours to Indian (Mayan) villages, jungle trips available. Extracurricular activities include: Mexican cooking, discussions, and video showings. Teach English in exchange for Spanish lessons. Centro Cultural "El Puente" includes gallery weaver's cooperative, travel agency, cafe, restaurant, phone/fax service.

Dates: Year round. Cost: Highest $220 per week; lowest $75 per week. Contact: Roberto Rivas, Bastidas Centro Bilingüe de Chiapas, C. Real de Guadalupe 55, Centro Cultural "El Puente," San Cristóbal de Las Casas 29230, Chiapas, Mexico; (011) 52-967-8-41-57, fax 967-83723 or Tel./fax (800) 303-4983; cenbili@chisnet.com.mx, www.mexonline.com/centro1.htm.

Loyola Univ. in Mexico City. Loyola offers 17 Spanish courses as well as courses on Latin American studies, communications, economics, history, political science, philosophy, sociology, and visual arts at the Jesuit Universidad Iberoamericana in Mexico City. Financial aid available. Trips to Cuernavaca, Taxco, Teotihuacan, and Tula. Three summer sessions and semester and year abroad program available.

Dates: Jan 9-May 14, 1998. Cost: $2,480 and $2,160 for 6- and 4-week sessions; $6,758 for 17-week semester program. Contact: Maurice P. Brungardt, Director, Mexico Program, Loyola Univ., New Orleans, LA 70118; (504) 865-3539 (day) or (504) 861-3402 (evening), fax (504) 865-2010; brungard@beta.loyno.edu.

Semester in Mexico. At the American International College of Mexico, Queretaro, operating under the auspices of the Universidad del Valle de Mexico. Spanish language, Mexico colloquium, government and politics of Mexico, history of Mexico. Courses taught in English. Also, students may select from courses offered in regular program of Americom. Mexican homestay. Upper division credit (junior-senior). A College Consortium for International Studies Program.

Dates: Mid-Sep-Dec/Jan-May. Cost: Approx. $4,300 per semester. Contact: Reinaldo Changsut, Study Abroad Adviser, Miami-Dade Community College, 11011 SW 104th St., Miami, FL 33176-3393; (305) 237-2535, fax (305) 237-2949; rchangsu@ kendall.mdcc.edu.

Spanish in the Land of the Maya. Learn, live and love Spanish in the Land of the Maya. Discover Maya ruins and visit living Maya Villages. Enjoy the relaxed atmosphere of colonial San Cristóbal de las Casas, Chiapas and experience the lush vegetation of the Chiapas' Highlands and the only tropical forest in North America.

Dates: Year round starting lessons every Monday and homestays any day of the week. Cost: $170 per week (group lessons, double occupancy). For upper scale lodging, single room and private instruction please inquire. Includes stay with a local family, 3 meals per day, 15 hours of Spanish instruction per week, workbooks, participation in cultural activities, access to dark room and screen printing shop, certificate. Contact: Centro Bilingüe Roberto Rivas-Bastidas or Israel Rivas-Bastidas, rrivas@sancristobal.podernet.com. mx, www.mexonline.com/centro1.htm. Centro Bilingüe Calle Real de Guadalupe 55, Centro Cultural "El Puente," San Cristóbal de las Casas, Chiapas, Mexico, 29230; Fax/ voice (011) 52-967-8 37 23, Fax/voice mail 8 41 57; spanish@sancristobal.podernet. com.mx.

Spanish Institute of Cuernavaca. Become a participant in Mexican culture by studying Spanish at the Spanish Language Institute in beautiful Cuernavaca on the dates of your choice. Students and professionals from ages 18 to 80 at all language levels study 6 hours daily in classes of 5 students in a small school of excellent reputation dedicated to personal attention and professionalism. U.S. graduate and undergraduate credit (6 credits in 3 weeks) available.

Caring family stays and full excursion program. Longer stays and additional credits also possible.

Dates: Year round, begin any Monday. Cost: $100 registration, $150 per week tuition, $105 (shared), $154 (private) per week for homestay, all meals, school transportation. Form a group of 12 and your trip is complimentary. Contact: Kay G. Rafool, Language Link Inc., P.O. Box 3006, Peoria, IL 61612; (800) 552-2051, fax (309) 692-2926; info@langlink.com, www.langlink. com.

Universal Centro de Lengua. Universal offers Spanish language programs specifically tailored to meet the needs of each student. Spanish courses are offered at all levels, individually or in groups, and are complemented by diverse lectures. Classes range from 2 to 5 students and meet 5 hours daily with hourly breaks of 10 minutes.

Dates: Year round. Cost: Normal $140 per week, advanced $180 per week, professional $200 per week. Contact: Ramiro Cuellar Hernandez, Universal Centro de Lengua, J.H. Preciado #171, Col. San Anton, Cuernavaca, Morelos, Mexico; (011) 52-73-18-29-04 or 12-49-02, fax 18-29-10; students@universal-spanish.com, universa@laneta.apc.org.

Wisconsin Summer in Oaxaca. Students live in a beautiful and historic setting with local families while they study Spanish language and Latin American literature and culture. All classes are taught in Spanish by local instructors under the direction of a Univ. of Wisconsin director. Includes excursions to local Indian villages and pre-Columbian ruins. Intermediate Spanish language ability required. Application deadline: First Friday in Mar. Late applications considered on a space-available basis.

Dates: Approx. late May-mid-Jul. Cost: Call for current information. Contact: Office of International Studies and Programs, 261 Bascom Hall, Univ. of Wisconsin, 500

Lincoln Dr., Madison, WI 53706; (608) 262-2851, fax (608) 262-6998; abroad@ macc.wisc.edu.

WSU Puebla Summer Program. The WSU Summer Program in Puebla provides an outstanding opportunity for students, teachers, and other interested individuals to study the Spanish language, gain the invaluable experience of living in another country, and earn college credit toward a degree or teaching certification. Students in the program spend 6 weeks in Puebla, either in the Hotel Colonial or in a private home with a Mexican family or both.

Dates: Jun 22-Jul 31, 1998. Cost: $1,725. Contact: John H. Koppenhaver, Wichita State Univ., Wichita, KS 67260-0122; (316) 978-3232, fax (316) 978-3777; koppenha@ twsuvm.uc.twsu.edu.

Middle East

Friends World Program. A semester or year program in the Middle East at Friends World Center in Jerusalem consists of intensive seminars that introduce students to the culture of the Middle East. Field work, travel, and independent research are also offered. Sample topics include desert agriculture, archaeology, anthropology, journalism, public health, conflict resolution, religious studies. Fieldwork can be conducted in Israel, Jordan, and other countries and may earn 12-18 credits per semester.

Dates: Fall: mid-Sep-mid-Dec; spring: mid-Jan-mid-May. Cost: $10,770 per semester in 1996/1997. Includes tuition, travel, room and board, fees and books. Contact: James Howard, Friends World Program, 239 Montauk Hwy., Southampton, NY 11968; (516) 287-8475; jhoward@sand.liunet.edu.

Seminar in the Middle East. The Seminar in the Middle East includes 4 weeks of intensive study on the Baldwin Wallace College campus followed by a 6-week tour through Egypt, Jordan, Israel, and Turkey. The focus will be on the religious and cultural heritage of the Middle East and will include visits to historical sites in all 4 countries, with significant exposure to modern cultures as well.

Dates: Apr 1-Apr 24 (on-campus), Apr 27-Jun 8 (overseas). Contact: Dorothy Hunter, Coordinator, The Study Abroad Center, Baldwin-Wallace College, 275 Eastland Rd., Berea, OH 44017; (216) 826-2231, fax (216) 826-3021; dhunter@ rs6000.baldwin.edu.

Morocco

Passage to Morocco. "Passage to Morocco" is a 3-week study visit consisting of: Standard Arabic study, cultural diversity exploration home stays, lectures on Morocco and related North African issues, as well as visits to historical and cultural attractions.

Dates: Tentatively set for Jun 6-Jul 3, 1998. Cost: $2,000. Contact: Andrea Akova, National Council on U.S.-Arab Relations, 1140 Connecticut Ave., NW, Suite 1210, Washington, DC 20036; (202) 293-0801, fax (202) 293-0903; pzm@ncusar.org, www.ncusar.org.

Wisconsin Summer in Morocco. Study at the Mohammed V Univ., the most prestigious institution of higher education in Morocco. Primary courses are taught in English on Moroccan history, culture, and society. Additional Moroccan Arabic course, and 1-week educational excursions. Initial 1-week family homestay, then stay with the family or live in university dormitories. Co-sponsored with Univ. of Wisconsin at Milwaukee. Application deadline: First Friday in Feb. Late applications considered on a space-available basis.

Dates: Late May-mid-Jul. Cost: Call for current information. Contact: Office of International Studies and Programs, 261 Bascom Hall, Univ. of Wisconsin, 500 Lincoln Dr., Madison, WI 53706; (608) 262-2851, fax (608) 262-6998; abroad@macc.wisc.edu.

Nepal

Sojourn Nepal. Sojourn Nepal is a 12-week program comprised of homestay, language study, lectures, village stay, trekking, and opportunities for apprenticeships in a vast variety of areas. Cultural immersion at its finest.

Dates: Fall and spring semesters. Cost: $5,000 all inclusive. Airfare not included. Contact: Jennifer Warren, Sojourn Nepal, 2440 N. 56th St., Phoenix, AZ 85008; Tel./fax (602) 840-9197; snepal@aol.com.

Study Abroad in Nepal. Join the Naropa Institute (NCA accredited) program in Nepal. On this program, our students are immersed in Nepali and Tibetan traditions through coursework in meditation, arts and culture, music and dance, Buddhist traditions, language, and independent study/travel. Classes are taught by Nepali and Tibetan scholars and artists, as well as Naropa faculty.

Dates: Early-Sep-mid-Dec, 1998. Cost: $6,900 (1997). Includes tuition (12 semester credits), room and board, program expenses. Airfare not included. Contact: Study Abroad Office, The Naropa Institute, 2130 Arapahoe Ave., Boulder, CO 80302; (303) 546-3594, fax (303) 444-0410.

Wisconsin Year in Nepal. The program provides integrated language training, tutorial instruction, and independent fieldwork projects. Participants attend summer school in U.S. prior to the term abroad for intensive language study and orientation to South Asian life and cultures. The first semester begins with a homestay period, in a 1-month village-study tour. The entire second semester is devoted to fieldwork projects.

Dates: Summer school in Madison: early Jun-mid-Aug; academic program abroad: late Aug-Apr. Cost: One-way airfare from the U.S. West Coast to Nepal, room, board and pocket money while abroad. Summer school and related expenses additional. Call for current information. Contact: Office of International Studies and Programs, 261 Bascom Hall, Univ. of Wisconsin, 500 Lincoln Dr., Madison, WI 53706; (608) 262-2851, fax (608) 262-6998; abroad@macc.wisc.edu.

Netherlands

School of Child Neuropsychology. Advanced training for graduate students from all countries. Classes (Thursdays and Fridays) are taught in English. Requirement to apply: Master's degree in psychology, medicine, special education, speech pathology, or equivalent qualification. Module A: basics and child neuropsychological syndromes. Module B: child neuropsychological assessment and treatment. Diploma: Satisfactory standards in exams.

Dates: A: Sep-early Nov; B: Jan-early Mar. Cost: A: DFL4,500; B: DFL4,500; A and B: DFL8,200. Contact: Professor Dirk J. Bakker, Ph.D., Director, Paedological Institute, P.O. Box 303, 1115 ZG Duivendrecht, Netherlands; (Tuesday, Thursday, Friday) (011) 31-20-6982131, fax 6952541.

Webster Univ. in Leiden. Webster Univ. in Leiden has more than 250 students. Students may pursue a degree program leading to a BA, MA, or MBA. In addition, students may enroll for a study abroad semester or year (summer session and other short-term options also available). All courses are taught in English and are fully accredited. Major areas of study include: business, international relations, management, marketing and psychology. A complete range of electives is also offered.

Dates: Five entry terms: late Aug-mid-Oct, mid-Jan, mid-Mar, late May. Cost: $19,000 (1996-97 academic year), $9,500 (semester 1996-97). Estimate includes tuition, room and board, books, local transportation, social activities. Contact: Study Abroad Office, Webster Univ., 470 E.

Lockwood Ave., St. Louis, MO 63119-3194; (314) 968-6988 or (800) 984-6857, fax (314) 968-7119; brunote@websteruniv. edu. Visit our website at http://webster2. websteruniv.edu.

New Zealand

General Studies in New Zealand. Located in the City of Hamilton at the Univ. of Waikato, students are able to take a variety of courses in several disicplines. The courses concerning New Zealand/Pacific Society and Culture are especially popular with international students. Students are able to enjoy excellent study facilities and participate in organized university activities.

Dates: Jul 5-Oct 31 (fall); Feb 18, 1998-Jun 26 (winter). Cost: $4,315 fall or winter; $7,775 year. Contact: University Studies Abroad Consortium (USAC), Univ. of Nevada, Reno #323, Reno, NV 89557-0093; (702) 784-6569, fax (702) 784-6010; usac@admin.unr.edu, www.scs.unr.edu/~usac.

Norway

Norwegian Nature and Culture. Fall semester or year program at Telemark College concentrates on the interaction of humans with their environment from a Scandinavian perspective. Students will examine the way environmental protection and management are implemented in public, institutional, and private sectors. Courses include Norwegian Language, Environmental Philosophy, Environmental Management, and in-depth field studies. Instruction in English.

Dates: Aug 20-Dec 15 (fall); Jan 12-Jun 15 (spring). Cost: Approx. $3,800 (fall), $3,800 (spring), $7,600 (full year). These costs do not include airfare, food, books and materials, or personal expenses. Contact: Scandinavian Seminar, 24 Dickinson St., Amherst, MA 01002; (413) 253-9736, fax (413) 253-5282.

Oslo International Summer School. The International Summer School of the Univ. of Oslo in Norway welcomes qualified participants from all parts of the world from late Jun-early Aug. The ISS is a center for learning in an international context, offering courses in the humanities, social sciences, and environmental protection to more than 500 students from over 80 nations every summer.

Dates: Jun 27-Aug 7, 1998. Cost: Approx. $2,425 (basic fees, room and board). Contact: Torild Homstad, Administrator, Univ. of Oslo, International Summer School, North American Admissions-A, St. Olaf College, 1520 St. Olaf Ave., Northfield, MN 55057-1098; (800) 639-0058 or (507) 646-3269, fax (507) 646-3732; iss@stolaf.edu.

Scandinavian Urban Studies Term. Courses include urbanization and development in Scandinavia, Scandinavia in the world, art and literature/perspectives on social change, and Norwegian language. Incorporates many experiential learning activities. Offered in cooperation with Univ. of Oslo, housing in student village with field study-travel to Stockholm, Sweden, and Tallin, Estonia, plus 2 weekend homestays in Norway. Full semester's credit. All majors. No language requirement.

Dates: Sep-Dec. Cost: $9,850 (1998-99). Includes tuition, room and board, field trips. Contact: Rebecca Rassier, Director of Student Services, HECUA, Mail #36, Hamline Univ., 1536 Hewitt Ave., St. Paul, MN 55104-1284; (612) 646-8832 or (800) 554-1089, fax (612) 659-9421; hecua@hamline.edu, www.hamline.edu/~hecua.

Poland

Penn-in-Warsaw. For students interested in Polish history and culture, as well as international relations, economics, and other business disciplines. Taught in English, this program will acquaint students with the political and economic changes occurring in Poland and provide insight into the conditions for doing business in a changing economy. Short-term internships with Polish or joint-venture institutions will complement class instruction.

Dates: Jun 21-Jul 30. Cost: Tuition $3,250; housing $400. Contact: Penn Summer Abroad, College of General Studies, Univ. of Pennsylvania, 3440 Market St., Suite 100, Philadelphia, PA 19104-3335; (215) 898-5738, fax (215) 573-2053.

Polish Language and Culture. Jagiellonian Univ. (founded in 1364) offers intensive and non-intensive Polish language courses; 8 levels; academic methods. Courses on Polish history, literature, art, economy, politics, folklore, etc. Cultural program; trips to places of interest. Up to 8 credits for the language and/ or 6 credits for other programs (transcripts of studies issued).

Dates: Four weeks: Jul 4-Aug 31; 6 weeks: Jul 4-Aug 14; 3 weeks: Jul 4-24, Jul 28-Aug 17. Cost: Four weeks $940 plus $30 registration fee; 6 weeks $1,220 plus $30; 3 weeks $690 plus $30. Room, board and tourist program included. Contact: Ewa Nowakowska, Program Director, Summer School, ul. Garbarska 7a, 31-131, Krakow, Poland; (011) 48-12-213692, fax 227701; uknowako@cyf-kr.edu.pl, www.if.uj.edu.pl/uj/sl.

Polish Language and Culture. The objective of the academic program offered by the Polonia Institute is to teach Polish language and culture to students interested in past and contemporary Poland. The Institute organizes Polish language classes on all levels, computer-assisted teaching and learning, courses in Polish linguistics, history, sociology, economics, culture, literature, and film.

Dates: (Oct 1 1997-Feb 6, 1998); Feb 16-Jun 11, 1998. Cost: $200 registration fee; for students of Polish ancestry: $1,050 plus $200; for students of nonPolish ancestry: $1,500 plus $200. Contact: Agnieszka Pasieka, Instytut Polonijny Uniwersytetu Jagiellonski ego, 30-252 Kraków, ul. Jodlowa 13; (011) 48-12 219855, fax 219877; register@filg.uj.edu.pl.

Portugal

Wisconsin in Portugal. Study at the Univ. of Coimbra, one of the world's oldest universities, founded in 1285. Students enroll in the Portuguese Language and Culture course for international students in the Faculty of Arts. Courses in Portuguese grammar, conversation, composition, history, art, geography. Advanced study includes linguistics and literature. Students with advanced language skills may register for regular university courses. Application deadline: Second Friday in Oct for spring, first Friday in Feb for fall or year.

Dates: Mid-Oct-mid-Jun. Semester or year option. Cost: Call for current information. Contact: Office of International Studies and Programs, 261 Bascom Hall, Univ. of Wisconsin, 500 Lincoln Dr., Madison, WI 53706; (608) 262-2851, fax (608) 262-6998; abroad@macc.wisc.edu.

Russia

ACTR Russian Language Program. ACTR's semester, academic-year, and summer programs maximize linguistic and cultural immersion into Russian society. The academic program emphasizes the development of practical speaking, listening, reading, and writing skills, while providing participants with a structured opportunity to learn about contemporary Russian society and cuture in country.

Dates: Summer, academic-year, fall, and spring. Cost: Vary according to program and length of stay. Contact: Margaret Stephenson, ACTR, 1776 Massachusetts Ave., NW, Suite

700, Washington, DC 20036; (202) 833-7522, fax (202) 833-7523; stephens@actr.org.

St. Petersburg State Univ. Designed to meet the needs of students with as little as 2 semesters of college-level Russian. The curriculum focuses on contemporary Russian language, culture, and politics. All courses taught at St. Petersburg State Univ. Resident director arranges excursions and volunteer/internship assignments for students. Housing in the Chaika, an apartment complex on the beach of the Gulf of Finland. Semester and summer program available.

Dates: Fall semester: Aug-Dec; spring semester: Feb-mid-May; summer program: late May-mid-Jul. Cost: $6,700 (spring 1997 fee) includes tuition, registration fees, housing, excursions, visa, ISIC card, airfare, partial insurance coverage. Contact: IPA, Univ. of Illinois at Urbana-Champaign, 115 International Studies Bldg., 910 S. 5th St., Champaign, IL 61820; (800) 531-4404, fax (217) 244-0249; ipa@uiuc.edu.

Summer Program in Russian. Seven weeks in Russia, based in Pskov at Volny Univ.'s campus in the heart of the ancient city. Includes a 6-week homestay, 12 hours per week of skills-based, practical Russian instruction, small classes with professional native leaders, extensive cultural program plus excursions to Pushkin's Estate, Novgorod, 3 days each Moscow and Petersburg.

Dates: Approx. Jul 1-Aug 20 (1997). Cost: $2,495 for everything except airfare. Contact: Larry Cothren, President, Interweave, 413 17th Ave. SE, Olympia, WA 98501; (360) 956-3229; 75463.3464@compuserve.com.

Spain

BCA Program in Barcelona. Earn 14-16 credits per semester at Universidad de Barcelona, with a 4-week intensive language training and orientation, field trips, and an extended study tour to Madrid and Toledo or Andulcía. Internships and practica available. Students from all U.S. colleges and universities accepted. Intermediate level college Spanish required. Courses in all academic disciplines taught by university professors.

Dates: Sep 8-Dec 19 or Jan 23 (fall), Jan 18-Jun 5 (spring), Sep 8-Jun 5 (year). Cost: $18,395 (academic year 1997-1998); $10,295 (semester 1997-1998). Includes international transportation, room and board, tuition, insurance, group travel in country. Contact: Beverly S. Eikenberry, 605 E. College Ave., North Manchester, IN 46962; (219) 982-5238, fax (219) 982-7755; bca@manchester.edu, www.studyabroad.com/bca.

CLIC of Sevilla and Language Link. Your choice of group classes with only 6-12 students, intensive groups of 3-6 students, or completely private classes. Professional adults, college students, and all Spanish levels accommodated in a very well organized school. Programs of 2-16 weeks starting on any Monday. Graduate and undergraduate credit through accredited U.S. university. Earn 6 units in 4 weeks. Homestays or residence hall. In Jul and Aug beach campus on Isla Cristina on the Costa de la Luz. Combine 2 weeks there with 2 weeks in Seville. Summer program also for high school teens in Jul. Additional weekly activities included.

Dates: Year round. New classes begin every Monday. Cost: Four hours daily of group (6-12) classes and homestay: 2 weeks $576; 4 hours intensive (3-6) classes and homestay: 2 weeks $688; Isla Cristina program combined with Seville: 4 weeks $1,216. Includes registration, tuition, insurance, accommodation arrangements fee, homestay with 2 meals or residence hall. Contact: Kay G. Rafool, Language Link Inc., P.O. Box 3006, Peoria, IL 61612; (800) 552-2051, fax (309) 692-2926; info@langlink.com; www.langlink.com.

Escuela Internacional (Madrid, Salamanca, Malaga). Escuela Internacional offers quality programs in Spanish language and culture with U.S. undergraduate credits. Our qualified teachers and small classes (maximum 12 students per class) guarantee you a successful program. Stay with a selected family or in a shared apartment. Enjoy our extensive afternoon activities and weekend excursions. Our professionalism, enthusiasm, and personal touch will make your experience in Spain memorable and fun.

Dates: Year round, 2-48 weeks. Cost: From PTS57,500 for 2 weeks (includes 15 hours per week instruction, room and books) to PTS125,000 (includes 30 hours per week instruction, room and full board, books, activities, and excursion). Contact: Escuela Internacional, Midori Ishizaka, Director of Admissions, c/Talamanca 10, 28807 Alcalá de Henares, Madrid, Spain; (011) 34-1-8831264, fax 8831301; escuelai@ergos.es, www.ergos.es/escuelai.

Hispalengua Spanish for Foreigners. Small groups with qualified teachers, intensive courses from 2 weeks in selected homestays or hotels. We specialize in Spanish for young American students and provide personal escorts and introductions to local young people.

Dates: Year round. Cost: PTS170,000 for 4 weeks tuition and full board. Contact: Hispalengua, Julio Lalmolda, San Miguel 16, 500 001 Zaragoza, Spain; (011) 34-76-221810 or 211120, fax 212010.

Hispanic Studies Program. Collaboration of the Univ. of Virginia and Valencia, offering summer, fall, spring, and year programs for undergraduates; summer only for teachers of high school Spanish. Located in Valencia, on the Mediterranean coast of Spain, we offer homestays, and classes taught by Spanish professors in language, literature, history, art, and culture.

Cost: Summer: $3,330; fall $5,525; spring $6,035; year $9,725 includes roundtrip from NY, room and board, tuition, insurance, and use of Univ. of Valencia facilities. Contact: F. Operé, Univ.

of Virginia, 115 Wilson Hall, Charlottesville, VA 22903; (804) 924-7155; aam4s@faraday.clas.virginia.edu.

International Program in Toledo. Participants with 2 years of Spanish select courses to suit individual needs from a wide spectrum of the humanities taught in Spanish. Summer term requires only 1 year of Spanish. Monday-Thursday courses are enhanced by excursions. Housing available in an historic residence or with Spanish host families. Univ. of Minnesota accredited.

Dates: 1997-98 fall and/or spring semesters, summer term. Cost: $8,250 (fall or spring), $3,400 (summer). Includes tuition, study abroad and registration fees, room and board, and one-day excursions. Contact: The Global Campus, Univ. of Minnesota, 102T Nicholson Hall, 216 Pillsbury Dr. SE, Minneapolis, MN 55455-0138; (612) 625-3379, fax (612) 626-8009; globalc@tc.umn.edu, www.isp.umn.edu.

La Coruña Summer Program. Intensive language program providing participants with the opportunity to study Spanish language, civilization, and culture in one of the most beautiful regions in Spain. Cultural immersion is further achieved through homestays with Spanish families. Cultural excursions include Madrid and nearby Santiago de Compostela, site of the famous pilgrimage of Saint James.

Dates: Approx. Jul 1-31. Cost: Approx. $1,700 (tuition and room and board). Contact: Darci Wahl, Study Abroad Advisor, Central Washington Univ., Office of International Studies and Programs, 400 E. 8th Ave., Ellensburg, WA 98926-7408; (509) 963-3623, fax (509) 963-1558; wahld@cwu.edu.

Painting in Barcelona. A celebrated Spanish faculty made up of Tom Carr and Carme Miquel will conduct a 3-week advanced painting workshop at the spacious studio of Escola d'Arts Plastiques i Disseny "Llotja." Included are 3 museum tours to the Antonio Tapies

Foundation, the Miro Foundation, and the Picasso Museum. Three credits.

Dates: Jul 3-Jul 25, 1998. Cost: $2,850. Includes airfare, double occupancy rooms, continental breakfast daily, and 3 tours. Contact: Dora Riomayor, Director of International Studies, School of Visual Arts, 209 E. 23rd St., New York, NY 10010-3994; (212) 592-2543.

Penn-in-Alicante. For students interested in the language, literature, and culture of Spain, this program combines classroom instruction with visits to points of cultural and historical interest, including Madrid and Toledo. Students live with local families.

Dates: Jun 25-Jul 26. Cost: Tuition $2,840; room and board $1,500; travel $890. Contact: Penn Summer Abroad, College of General Studies, Univ. of Pennsylvania, 3440 Market St., Suite 100, Philadelphia, PA 19104-3335; (215) 898-5738, fax (215) 573-2053.

Santa Monica College in Madrid. Students attend classes in Spanish language, culture, literature, media, art, communications, international relations, business, and social studies in Spanish and English with Spaniards at College for International Studies. Homestays, excursions.

Dates: Jan-May, Sep-Dec, 1998. Contact: Nancy Nieman, Santa Monica College, 1900 Pico Blvd., Santa Monica, CA 90405; (310) 452-9270, fax (310) 581-8618; nnieman@smc.edu.

Semester in Spain. Semester, year, summer, and January terms for high school graduates, college students, and adult learners. Beginning, intermediate, and advanced Spanish language studies along with Spanish literature, culture, history, and art. All courses taught in Spanish by native Spaniards. Four courses per semester, 4 credits each. Homestays are arranged for all students. January term and summer terms also.

Dates: Fall: Aug 26-Dec 18; spring: Jan 27-May 22; summer: Jun 1-Jun 25 and/or Jul 1-20. Cost: Fall or spring $7,600; year approx.

$15,200; summer and Jan term approx. $2,000 each term. Includes tuition, books, room and board. Contact: Debra Veenstra, U.S. Coordinator, Semester in Spain, Dept. TA, 6001 W. College Dr., Palos Heights, IL 60463; (800) 748-0087 or (708) 239-4766, fax (708) 239-3986.

Simmons College in Córdoba. The Simmons in Córdoba Program, sponsored by Simmons College, offers students the opportunity to live and study—for either a semester or an academic year—in one of Spain's oldest and historically most important cities. Open to undergraduates and MA students. Fields: (Spanish) Foreign Language. Internships available for undergraduates.

Dates: Fall: Sep 3-Dec 18 (1997). Spring: Jan 12-Apr 30, 1998. Application deadline: Mar 30 (Fall); Oct 15 (Spring). Late applications are considered on a space available basis. Cost: $12,174 per semester (1996-1997). Contact: Professor Susan Keane, Foreign Study Advisor, or Racquel María Halty, Program Director, Simmons College, Foreign Languages and Literatures, Boston, MA 02115; fax (617) 521-3199; swilliams2@vmsvaxsimmons.edu.

Spanish and Basque Studies. San Sebastian offers intensive language (Spanish or Basque) that fulfill up to 2 years of university language requirements in 1 semester. Plus courses in history, literature, political science, economics, art, teacher education, etc. Program organized field trips to Madrid and elsewhere, housing, and many local university activities in this beautiful seaside resort.

Dates: Summer sessions: May 27-Jul 1, Jun 27-Jul 30, Jul 30-Aug 28, 1997; fall semester: Aug 26-Dec 12, 1997; spring semester: Jan 7-May 13, 1998. Cost: Each summer session $1,880; fall or spring semester $5,990; year $9,370; $4,460 both sessions. Contact: University Studies Abroad Consortium (USAC), Univ. of Nevada, Reno #323, Reno, NV 89557-0093; (702) 784-6569, fax (702) 784-

6010; usac@admin.unr.edu, www.scs.unr.edu/~usac.

Spanish and Basque Studies (Bilbao). Bilbao offers intensive language studies (Spanish or Basque) that fulfill up to 2 years of university language requirements in 1 semester, plus courses in history, political science, art, culture, economics, teacher education, literature, etc. Program organized field trips, housing, and many local university activities at this seaside city.

Dates: Fall semester: Aug 26-Dec 12, 1997; spring semester: Jan 7-May 13, 1998. Cost: Fall or spring semester $4,270; year $6,950. Contact: University Studies Abroad Consortium (USAC), Univ. of Nevada, Reno #323, Reno, NV 89557-0093; (702) 784-6569, fax (702) 784-6010; usac@admin.unr.edu, www.scs.unr.edu/~usac.

Spanish Language Studies. Four-week intensive language and culture studies program in Asturias and Andalusia, Spain. Open to students at all levels. Field trips. Six credit hours: undergraduate, graduate.

Dates: Late Jun-late Jul. Cost: Approx. $2,700. Airfare not included. Contact: Office of International Education, SUNY New Paltz, HAB 33, New Paltz, NY 12561; (914) 257-3125, fax (914) 257-3129; international@newpaltz.edu, www.newpaltz.edu/oie.

Student Tours in Spain. Bravo Tours is a tour operator specializing in programs to Spain for high school and college students organized and chaperoned by your own school's teachers. Our programs cover Madrid, Barcelona, Mallorca, Toldeo, Avila, Segovia, Tenerife, Santiago, Sevilla, Granada, and more.

Contact: See our website at www.bravotours.com or call us at (800) 272-8674.

Study in Oviedo. Fall or spring programs in Spanish language, culture, and civilization at the Universidad de Oviedo Cursos Para Extranjeros. Students share apartments and prepare their own meals, 12-15 undergraduate credits per semester. Qualifications: Junior or above; 2 or more years college-level Spanish or the equivalent.

Dates: Fall: mid-Sep-late Dec; spring: mid-Jan-late May. Cost: Approx. $4,700 per semester. Includes tuition, fees, room and board, and insurance. (Non-New York state residents add $2,450.) Contact: Office of International Education, SUNY New Paltz, HAB 33, New Paltz, NY 12561; (914) 257-3125, fax (914) 257-3129; international@newpaltz.edu, www.newpaltz.edu/oie.

Study in Seville. Fall, spring, or academic year programs in Spanish language, culture, and civilization at the Universidad de Sevilla Cursos Para Extranjeros. Family owned student housing, native resident director, field trips, on-site orientation, 12-18 undergraduate credits per semester. Qualifications: junior or above; 5 semesters college-level Spanish or equivalent.

Dates: Fall: late Sep-late Dec; spring: mid-Jan-early Jun. Cost: Approx. $5,400 (fall); $6,000 (spring). Includes tuition, fees, orientation, room and board, and insurance. (Non-New York residents add $2,450 per semester.) Contact: Office of International Education, SUNY New Paltz, New Paltz, HAB 33, New Paltz, NY 12561; (914) 257-3125, fax (914) 257-3129; international@newpaltz.edu, www.newpaltz.edu/oie.

Univ. of Cádiz Summer Study. The Summer Study Program is designed for those students 17 years and older who wish to increase their proficiency in Spanish and to be immersed in the Spanish culture and civilization. Host family placement tour: Sevilla, Granada, Cordoba, etc. Six credits available. Ask for free brochure and program booklet.

Dates: Jun 27-Aug 2, 1997 (depending on flight arrangements). Cost: $3,300 incudes tuition, tour of Sevilla, Granada, Cordoba, and other cities as is outlined in brochure, host family stay, 3 meals a day, and transfers. Contact: Carol McCloskey, Euro-Study, Inc., P.O.

Box 1023, Blue Bell, PA 19422; Tel./fax (215) 646-2492; jemcclos@aol.com.

Univ. of Salamanca. Founded in the 13th century, the Univ. of Salamanca is one of the most distinguished centers of learning in Europe. SUNY Cortland is celebrating the 30th consecutive year in this "City of the Golden Stones." The lives of Cervantes, Lope de Vega, Santa Teresa, and Miguel de Unamuno were all linked to the Univ. of Salamanca. Fields of study include Spanish language and literature, humanities, social sciences. Upper division and some qualified sophomores may apply. Requires at least 4 semesters college-level Spanish for fall, 6 semesters for spring. Homestays.

Dates: Fall: early Sep-mid-Dec; spring: early Jan-mid-Jun. Cost: Spring 1998: $4,950. Includes full-day orientation before departure, application fee, room and food allowance, mandatory Spanish insurance, airfare, transportation from Madrid to Salamanca, books and supplies, repatriation, insurance, walking tour of Salamanca, 2 excursions, administrative fees. SUNY tuition not included. Contact: Dr. John Ogden, Director, Office of International Programs, Box 2000, SUNY Cortland, Cortland, NY 13045; (607) 753-2209, fax (607) 753-5989; studyabroad@snycorva. cortland.edu, www.studyabroad.com/suny/cortland.

Universidad Compultense de Madrid. A graduate and undergraduate program at the Universidad Compultense de Madrid for students interested in studying courses in language, literature, culture and civilization, composition, art history, philosophy of Spain. Students are taught by full-time faculty members from the Universidad Compultense de Madrid, the most prestigious university in Spain. A lot of extra activities and excursions are organized for students.

Dates: Summer program: Jul; semester:

fall, winter, spring. Cost: Summer: total cost from $1,985 including airfare; year: $10,250 total cost including airfare. Contact: Modern Language Studies Abroad, P.O. Box 623, Griffith, IN 46319; Tel./fax (219) 838-9460.

Sweden

Uppsala Univ. International Summer Session. Sweden's oldest academic summer program focuses on learning the Swedish language. All levels from beginners to advanced. Additional courses in Swedish history, social institutions, arts in Sweden, Swedish film. Excursions every Friday. Extensive evening program includes both lectures and entertainment. Single rooms in dormitories or apartments. Open to both students and adults. Credit possible.

Dates: Jun 21-Aug 14; Jun 21-Jul 17; Jul 19-Aug 14, Jul 5-Aug 14, 1998. Cost: SEK21,400 (approx. $2,740) for the 8-week session, SEK11,700 (approx. $1,500) for the 4-week session. Includes room, some meals, all classes, evening and excursion program. Contact: Dr. Nelleke Dorrestÿn, Uppsala Univ. Int. Summer Session, Box 513, 751 20 Uppsala, Sweden; (011) 31-71-541 4955, fax 71-5417705; nduiss@worldaccess.nl, www.uuiss.uu.se.

Switzerland

American Studies. Two programs of 5 months of studies each at the undergraduate and pre-MBA levels recognized by American accredited universities as one academic year in terms of transfer credits (up to 36). Learn French and get a European background in a truly multi-cultural environment.

Dates: Feb-Jun or Aug-Dec. Cost: Tuition, insurance, lodging, activities approx. $11,500 total. Contact: Lemania College,

Ms. E. Perni, International Admissions Office, Chemin de Préville 3, 1001 Lausanne, Switzerland; (011) 41-21-320-15-01, fax 312-67-00; info.lemania@lshp1.fastnet.ch.

Bookbinding and Book Restoration. Centro del bel libro is a professional school for artisanal bookbinding and book restoration. Courses are offered year round.

Dates: Call or write for information. Cost: Call or write for information. Contact: Office Centro del bel libro, Ascona, Viale Portone 4, P.O. Box 2600, CH-6501, Bellinzona, Switzerland; (011) 41-91-825-11-62, fax 825-85-86.

Franklin College—Switzerland. Opportunities for study abroad for year, semester, and summer. Transfer opportunities available. Subjects available: Art, Art History, Communications, French Language, German Language, History, International Business, International Relations, Italian Language, Literature, Music, Political Science, Social Sciences. Middle states accredited.

Dates: Summer session I: May 26-Jun 26; Summer session II: Jun 30-Jul 31; fall (1997): Aug 25-Dec 20; spring 1998: Jan 14-May 8. Cost: Tuition: $7,950 per semester; residence: $3,000 per semester; academic travel: $1,600 per semester. Contact: James O'Hara, Associate Director of Admission, Franklin College-Switzerland, 135 E. 65th St., New York, NY 10021; (212) 772-2090, fax (212) 772-2718.

French Courses. All courses are in French in 4 series of 3 weeks each. For beginners courses are at least for 6 weeks. More series may be attended. Classes are constituted according to the students' tested level of competence. Students can also practice sports at the Sports Centre or use our Multimediacentre (videos, tapes, and Macintosh).

Dates: Series I: Jul 6-Jul 24, 1998, SeriesII: Jul 27-Aug 14, 1998, Series III: Aug 17-Sep 4, 1998; Series IV: Sep 7-Sep 25, 1998. Cost:

FF470 for 3 weeks; FF1,050 for beginners (6 weeks). Contact: Université de Lausanne, Cours de Vacances, BFSH2, CH-1015 Lausnne, Switzerland; (011) 41-21-692-30-90, fax 30-85; coursde-vacances@cvac.unil.ch, www.unil.ch/cvac.

Univ. of Geneva Summer Courses. French language and civilization at all levels, beginners to advanced. All instructors have a university diploma. Excursions and visits to Geneva and its surroundings. Class of 15-20 students. Minimum age 17.

Dates: Jul 14-31, Aug 4-22, Aug 25-Sep 12, Sep 15-Oct 3. Cost: SF470 for 3 weeks (tuition). Contact: Mr. Gérard Benz, Univ. of Geneva, Summer Courses, rue de Candolle 3, CH-1211 Geneva 4, Switzerland; (011) 41-22-705-74-34, fax 705-74-39; http://uni2a.unige.ch.

Webster Univ. in Geneva. Webster Univ. in Geneva has more than 400 students from 65 countries. Students may pursue a degree program leading to a BA, MA, or MBA. In addition, students may enroll for a study abroad semester or a year (summer session and some short-term options also available). All courses are taught in English and are fully accredited. Major areas of study include: business, computer science, economics, human resources management, psychology, sociology, international relations, refugee studies, management, marketing. A complete range of electives is also offered.

Dates: Five entry terms: late Aug, mid-Oct, mid-Jan, mid-Mar, late May. Cost: $20,000 (1996-97 academic year), $10,000 (semester 1996-97). Estimate includes tuition, room and board, books, local transportation, social activities. Contact: Study Abroad Office, Webster Univ., 470 E. Lockwood, St. Louis, MO 63119; (314) 968-6988 or (800) 984-6857, fax (314) 968-7119; brunote@websteruniv.edu. Visit our website at http://webster2.websteruniv.edu.

Syria

Summer in Syria. Summer in Syria is a 6-week study visit. The program consists of 4 weeks of courses at the Univ. of Aleppo that include history, culture, and anthropology of Syria. One week of archaeological site visits, and 1 week exploring Syria's numerous historical and cultural attractions.

Dates: Jun-Jul. Cost: $3,000. Contact: Andrea Akova, National Council on U.S.-Arab Relations, 1140 Connecticut Ave., NW, Suite 1210, Washington, DC 20036; (202) 293-0801, fax (202) 293-0903; sis@ncusar. org, www.ncusar.org.

Thailand

College Year in Thailand. The program at Chiang Mai Univ. features Thai language study, subject tutorials, and a fieldwork project. Students attend summer school in Madison before the term abroad for intensive Thai language study as well as cultural and academic orientation. Application deadline: Second Friday in Feb. Late applications are considered on a space-available basis.

Dates: Summer school in Madison Jun-mid-Aug; academic year abroad late Aug-May. Cost: Call for current information. Contact: Office of International Studies and Programs, 261 Bascom Hall, Univ. of Wisconsin, 500 Lincoln Dr., Madison, WI 53706; (608) 262-2851, fax (608) 262-6998; abroad@macc.wisc.edu.

Engaged Buddhism in Siam. Join the Naropa Institute (NCA accredited) program in Siam (Thailand). during this 1-month travel/study program, we will focus on Engaged Buddhism and Buddhist-inspired environmental and development projects. This program will be lead by Sulak Sivaraska, a Thai human rights advocate who was nominated for the Nobel Peace Prize by the Dalai Lama in 1994.

Dates: Mid-Dec to Mid-Jan. Cost: $2,050 (in 1997) for noncredit. The cost is 42,600 for 3 semester credits. Includes room and board, program expenses. Airfare not incuded. Contact: Study Abrod Office, The Naropa Institute, 2130 Arapahoe Ave., Boulder, CO 80302; (303) 546-3594 or (303) 444-0410.

Southeast Asian Studies (Bangkok). Diverse courses in culture, language, economics, business, society, and religions provide a fascinating, well-balanced approach to Southeast Asia. Program-organized field trips, student residence halls, and many university activities at one of Thailand's most modern universities.

Dates: Summer session: Jun 6-Jul 3 (1997); fall semester: Aug 20-Dec 23 (1997); spring semester: Jan 9-May 12, 1998. Cost: One semester: $2,450; year: $4,100; summer session: $1,100. Contact: University Studies Abroad Consortium (USAC), Univ. of Nevada, Reno #323, Reno, NV 89557-0093; (702) 784-6569, fax (702) 784-6010; usac@admin.unr.edu. www.scs.unr.edu/~usac.

Turkey

Live and Study in Istanbul. Here is your chance to live in Istanbul for 7 weeks while studying at Bogaziçi Univ. All courses taught in English by Bogaziçi faculty; a wide variety of courses are available. Resident director arranges orientation program and excursions. Housing in residence hall with full board plan. No knowledge of Turkish necessary.

Dates: Late Jun-mid-Aug. Cost: $2,800 includes tuition, registration, room and board, orientation, excursion, partial insurance coverage, support services. Contact: IPA, Univ. of Illinois at Urbana-Champaign,

115 International Studies Bldg., 910 S. 5th St., Champaign, IL 61820; (800) 531-4404, fax (217) 244-0249; ipa@uiuc.edu.

Uganda

Workcamps and Development. Workcamps aim to: assist needy communities, bind communities together in all apects of life, create common understanding people to people, work for the welfare of African society and the world at large, and link an experience with comparible organizations in the world.

Dates: May, Sep, Dec. Cost: $200 per workcamp, lasts 14 days each. Contact: Mr. G. Stuart Semakula, National Chairman, Uganda Voluntary Workcamps Association, P.O. Box 3367, Kampala, Uganda; Fax (011) 256-41-234168/250668.

United Kingdom

Art and Design in Britain. Studio Art (including painting, sculpture, graphic and industrial design, ceramics, printmaking, film, etc.) programs offered at 5 British universities: Chelsea College of Art, De Montford Univ., Norwich School of Art, Univ. of Northumbria, and Univ. of Wolverhampton. Courses integrated with British students. Housing in university residence halls or shared apartments. Resident director organizes orientation program, monitors students' academic progress.

Dates: Sep-Dec, Jan-Jun. Cost: Varies by programs: semester $5,580-$9,880; year $12,300-$14,300. Contact: IPA, Univ. of Illinois at Urbana-Champaign, 115 International Studies Bldg., 910 S. 5th St., Champaign, IL 61820; (800) 531-4404, fax (217) 244-0249; ipa@uiuc.edu.

BCA Program in Cheltenham. Earn 15-16 credits per semester at the Cheltenham and Gloucester College of Higher Education with a 2-week orientation in country, field trips, and an extended study tour to Wales or Kent. Courses in all academic disciplines including women's studies. Internships and practica available. Students accepted from all U.S. colleges and universities.

Dates: Sep 9-Dec 20 (fall), Feb 8-May 20 (spring), Sep 9-May 20 (year). Cost: $18,395 (academic year 1997-1998); $10,295 (semester 1997-1998). Includes international transportation, room and board, tuition, insurance, group travel in country. Contact: Beverly S. Eikenberry, 605 E. College Ave., North Manchester, IN 46962; (219) 982-5238, fax (219) 982-7755; bca@manchester.edu, www.studyabroad.com/bca.

Bignor Roman Villa. Various 5-day and 2-day training courses will take place as part of the season of excavations. Courses include: Excavation Techniques, Archaeological Surveying, Timber-Framed Buildings, and Planning and Section Drawing. Academic credit option.

Dates: Jul and Aug (1997). Cost: Varies £50-£110 (tuition only). Contact: Mrs. Sheila Maltby, Field Archaeology Unit, Institute of Archaeology, Univ. College in London, 1 West St., Ditchling, Hassocks, W. Sussex BN6 8TS, U.K.; (011) 44-1273-845497, fax 844187; tcrndrr@uc.ac.u.

British Studies at Oxford. British Studies at Oxford is designed to give vital, first-hand exposure to the historical, artistic, political, cultural, and commercial milieu that informed literary and political works, business management, communication, educational theories, and fine arts studied in our courses. The participants live in private rooms tidied daily by the college staff, who also serve 3 bountiful and tasty meals a day in the Great Hall. Wednesdays are travel days—plays in Stratford and London.

Dates: Summer: Jun 29-Jul 19; Jul 20-Aug 9. Cost: $2,800 per session or $5,200 for 2 sessions. Contact: M.B. Pigott, Oakland Univ., Rochester, MI 48309; (810) 370-4131, fax (810) 650-9107; pigott@vela. acs.oakland.edu.

Crafts and Arts Courses. Week and weekend courses. Summer schools in art, ceramics, woodworking, textiles, sculpture, silver-smithing, music, and art appreciation. One-, 2-, and 3-year diploma courses in conservation and restoration of antique furniture, clocks, ceramics, fine metalwork, and rare books and manuscripts; tapestry weaving (also 6-week modules); making early stringed musical instruments. Validation at postgraduate level is by the Univ. of Sussex.

Dates: Diploma courses start each year and end in July. Short courses year round. Cost: Diploma courses £6,498 per annum. Residential accommodations £2,802 per annum. Short courses (residential) 5 days £349, weekends £146, 7 days £469. Contact: Heather Way, Public Relations, West Dean College, West Dean, Chichester, W. Sussex PO18 0QZ, England; (011) 44-1243-811301, fax 811343; westdean@pavilion.co.uk.

Fashion Design/Merchandising. London College of Fashion is the only College in the British university sector to specialize in fashion. Located in the center of London, we offer you: a choice of 2 specialist programs, each covering seven subject areas; 16 credits per program; internship opportunities, plus optional Paris field trip.

Dates: Fall semester: Sep 21-Dec 11, 1998; spring semester: Jan 4-Mar 26, 1999. Cost: 1998/1999 tuition fees £2,425 per 12-week semester. Airfare and accommodations not included. Contact: Alanah Cullen, Business Manager, DALI at London College of Fashion, 20 John Princes St., London W1M 0BJ, England; (011) 44-171-514-7411, fax 514-7490; lcfdali@london-fashion.ac.uk.

General Studies (Brighton). Brighton offers courses in many disciplines: art, business, sports science, engineering, computing, geography, design, education, math, etc. Organized field trips, housing in student residence halls. Summer graduate program in teacher education. Only 45 minutes from London.

Dates: Summer: Jun 29-Aug 2 (1997); fall semester: Aug 31-Dec 14 (1997); spring: Jan 4-May 15, 1998. Cost: Fall or spring: $3,140; year: $5,375; summer: $1,250. Contact: University Studies Abroad Consortium (USAC), Univ. of Nevada, Reno #323, Reno, NV 89557-0093; (702) 784-6569, fax (702) 784-6010; usac@admin.unr.edu, www.scs.unr.edu/~usac.

General Studies (Reading). Reading offers courses in nearly every academic disciplines: art, business, literature, performing arts, engineering, computing, geography, education, agriculture, etc. Housing in student residence halls. Only 25 minutes from London.

Dates: Fall semester: Sep 11-Dec 12, 1997; winter: Jan 6-Mar 20, 1998; Apr 27-Jul 2, 1998. Cost: Fall semester: $3,450; winter or spring quarter: $2,950; year: $7,450. Contact: University Studies Abroad Consortium (USAC), Univ. of Nevada, Reno #323, Reno, NV 89557-0093; (702) 784-6569, fax (702) 784-6010; usac@admin.unr.edu, www.scs.unr.edu/~usac.

Harlaxton College. Harlaxton College is owned and operated by the Univ. of Evansville in Indiana. Therefore, all courses are U.S. accredited and usually transfer easily. Students live and study in a magnificent 19th-century Victorian manor house in the English Midlands. Assistance is available with air arrangements and airport pickup; optional field trips are available throughout England, Ireland, Scotland, Wales, and the Continent. Harlaxton is a full-service study abroad program with help every step of the way.

Dates: Fall 1998: Aug 28-Dec 10; spring 1999: Jan 8-Apr 22. Cost: $9,085 per semester (1996-97). Includes tuition, room and board. Contact: Suzy Lantz, Harlaxton Coordinator, Univ. of Evansville, 1800 Lincoln Ave., Evansville, IN 47722; (800) UKMANOR or (812) 488-1040; sl5@evansville.edu.

Ithaca College London Center. British and international faculty teach undergraduate courses in business, communications, humanities, music, social sciences, and theater. Field trips and excursions to various sites throughout London and the U.K. are an integral part of the curriculum. Internships are available to juniors and seniors majoring in art history, business, communications, economics, English, history, politics, psychology, sociology, and theater arts. A special intensive drama program is offered in the spring semester.

Dates: Aug 20-Dec 13, 1998 and/or Jan 7-May 1, 1999. Cost: Approx. $15,100 per semester. Includes tuition, fees, books, room and board, college-sponsored excursions, and airfare. Costs may vary depending on students' lifestyles and spending habits. Contact: Andrea M. Kiely, Coordinator of Study Abroad, International Programs, Ithaca College, 214 Muller Ctr., Ithaca, NY 14850-7150; (607) 274-3306, fax (607) 274-1515.

Laban Centre London. Program for students outside the U.K. to spend 1 year (2 semesters) in London studying contemporary dance, choreography, and related subjects. Courses are planned for your individual needs and credits are given for subjects taken. Please ask for a booklet.

Dates: Sep-Jul. Contact: Admissions Officer, Laban Centre London, Laurie Grove, London SE14 6NH, U.K.; (011) 44-181-692-4070, fax 694-8749; info@laban.co.uk.

London. Full academic year or one trimester. Courses are tailored for American students and are designed to take advantage of the London setting. Classes meet 3 or 4 times per week and students generally enroll in 3 or 4 courses. Academic focus is theater, literature, history, economics, and art.

Dates: Sep-Dec (1996); Jan-Mar (1997); Mar-Jun, 1997. Cost: Approx. $5,300 per term. Includes tuition, books, housing, meals, international student identity card, excursions, insurance, all-London transportation pass. Financial aid accepted. Contact: Linda Kopfer, Assoc. Director of Univ. Programs, American Heritage Association, 741 SW Lincoln St., Portland, OR 97201-3178; (800) 654-2051, fax (503) 295-5969; 96trab@am-heritage.org.

London Academy of Performing Arts. An internationally-renowned classical theater school. Summer school in Shakespearean acting (all levels). One-year graduate training, and single semester programs (credits available).

Dates: Summer schools: Jul-Aug, full-time courses from Sep. Cost: From £850. Contact: The Administrator, London Academy of Performing Arts, The Church, 2 Effie Rd., London SW6 1TB, U.K.; (011) 44-171-736-0121, fax 371-5624.

OASP Visiting Student Program. OASP's students become Visiting Students of the Univ. of Oxford and associate students Lady Margaret Hall, an undergraduate college. Individual instruction in liberal arts and other subjects plus univ. lectures. Tuition arranged to meet home university requirements in most cases. Orientation, excursions, single rooms, bursaries, e-mail. Ten years experience.

Dates: Term or academic year. Cost: Term: $8,950; year: $22,400 includes tuition, housing, fees, lectures. Contact: E Derow, OASP Visiting Student Program in cooperation with Lady Margaret Hall, Oxford, England, 7B Dunstan Rd., Headington, Oxford OX3 9BY, England; Tel./fax (011) 44-1865-762495; 100645.3460@compuserve.com.

Oxford Advanced Studies Program. The program is an academic and cultural summer course held at Magdalen College, one of Oxford's oldest and most famous colleges. Students select 2 or 3 subjects from a wide choice; teaching is in a combination of small seminar groups and individual tutorials. The social and cultural program is packed with a variety of exciting experiences.

Dates: Jul 6-Jul 31, 1998. Cost: $4,950.

Contact: Mrs. J. Ives, U.S. Registrar, Oxford Advanced Studies Program, P.O. Box 2043, Darien, CT 06820; (203) 966-2886, fax (203) 972-3083.

Penn-in-London. For students interested in theater and literature, this program offers first-hand opportunities to experience the best in traditional and contemporary British theater, from page to footlights.

Dates: Jun 29-Aug 2. Cost: Tuition $2,840; theater tickets $450; housing $750. Contact: Penn Summer Abroad, College of General Studies, Univ. of Pennsylvania, 3440 Market St., Suite 100, Philadelphia, PA 19104-3335; (215) 898-5738, fax (215) 573-2053.

Sarah Lawrence College at Oxford. Work individually with Oxford scholars in private tutorials, the hallmark of an Oxford education. The only American-sponsored program that gives students from other colleges access to the full range of tutors and disciplines of Oxford Univ.'s 37 colleges. Social and academic privileges with Visiting Student status through Wadham College. Frequent field trips and cultural activities.

Dates: Oct-Jun. Cost: $26,650. Includes all academic and housing expenses, field trips, and activities. Contact: Celia Regan, Sarah Lawrence College at Oxford, Box CR, Bronxville, NY 10708; (800) 873-4752.

Schumacher College. International center for ecological studies running residential courses on: ecological economics and development issues; links between philosophy, psychology and ecology; new understandings emerging from recent scientific discoveries. Courses led by world-renowned thinkers, including Fritjof Capra, James Hillman, Vandana Shiva, Stanislav Grof. Students come from all ages; countries and backgrounds.

Dates: Short courses throughout the year. Cost: £350 (approx.) per course week. Includes tuition, residential accommodations, food, and field trips. Some scholarships available for U.S. citizens. Contact: Hilary Nicholson, Schumacher College, The Old Postern, Dartington, Totnes, Devon TQ9 6EA; (011) 44-1803-865934, fax 866899; schumcoll@gn.apc.org.

Study Abroad in Northern Ireland. The Queen's Univ. of Belfast offers study abroad opportunities in all subject areas except medicine. Attendance can be for 1 or 2 semesters; students usually take 3 modules per semester.

Dates: First semester: Sep 28, 1998-Jan 29, 1999; second semester: Feb 8-Jun 18, 1999 (3 weeks vacation at Christmas and Easter). Cost: Tuition fee for 1997-98 was £2,350 for 1 semester, £4,700 for 2 semesters (rate for 1998-99 not available at press time). Accommodations range from £40-£55 per week. Contact: Mrs. C. McEachern, Administrative Officer, International Liaison Office, The Queen's Univ. of Belfast, Belfast BT7 1NN, Northern Ireland, U.K; (011) 44-1232-335415, fax (011) 44-1232-687297; ilo@ qub.ac.uk.

Study Abroad—Strathclyde. Participants will integrate fully into student life at the Univ. of Strathclyde, Scotland's largest university. Choose from a vast range of courses in engineering, business, science, education, and arts including Scottish history, literature, and politics. Full credit is normally awarded and transferred upon the completion of the course.

Dates: Oct-Jun; Oct-Dec. Cost: $5,500 includes tuition and accommodations for 1 semester; $11,000 includes tuition and accommodations for 2 semesters. Contact: Michelle Stewart, International Office, Univ. of Strathclyde, 50 George St., Glasgow G1 1QE, Scotland, U.K.; m.stewart@mis.strath.ac.uk, www.strath.ac.uk.

Study in Great Britain. Thirty-three program opportunities in England, Scotland, and Wales. University study and special subject area programs, including internships, for fall, spring, academic year and summer. Program provides a full range of services including predeparture advising, orientation, homestay, and guaranteed housing. Need-based scholarships available.

Dates: Fall, spring, academic year. Summer semester and terms. Cost: Varies. Call for current fees. Contact: Beaver College Center for Education Abroad, 450 S. Easton Rd., Glenside, PA 19038-3295; (888) BEAVER-9, fax (215) 572-2174; cea@beaver.edu, www.beaver.edu/cea.

Study in London. Four-week program offering a wide selection of regular university courses at Middlesex Univ. University housing, field trips and cultural activities. Six credit hours, undergraduate

Dates: Mid-Jul-mid-aug. Cost: Approx. $3,100. Airfare not included. Contact: Office of International Education, SUNY New Paltz, HAB 33, New Paltz, NY 12561; (914) 257-3125, fax (914) 257-3129; international@newpaltzedu, www.newpaltz.edu/oie.

Study in Wales. Opportunities for either year-long or semester study abroad at the Univ. of Wales Swansea (10,500 students, located by the sea) in fully integrated programs. Host family and summer internship programs are available. University housing, orientation, and cultural events are integral to all programs. Swansea is a lively maritime city with great social life and numerous outdoor activities.

Dates: Sep-Dec/Jan-May/May-Jul. Cost: From $4,500. Contact: Emma Frearson, Study Abroad Swansea, American Studies Centre, Univ. of Wales Swansea, Singleton Park, Swansea SA2 8PP, Wales, U.K.; (011) 44-1-792-295135, fax 295719; e.frearson@swansea.ac.uk, www.swan.ac.uk/sao/saohp.html.

Summer Academy. Summer Academy offers study holidays at 15 British and Irish universities. The course fee includes full board accommodations for 6 to 7 nights. Tuition fees and course related excursions. Study topics inlcude: heritage, the arts, countryside and creative writing. Accommodations are in single rooms in university halls of residence. Locations include: Aberystwyth, Canterbury, Cork (Ireland), Durham, Exeter, Glasgow, Lancaster, Maynooth (Ireland), Norwich, Oxford, Sheffield, Southampton, Stirling, Swansea, and York.

Dates: Jun 20-Sep 5, 1998. Cost: £370-£460 (see above for what fee includes). Contact: Andrea McDonnell, Marketing and Reservations Coordinator, Summer Academy, Keynes College, The Univ., Canterbury, Kent CT2 7NP; (011) 44-1227-470402/823473, fax 784338; summeracademy@ukc.ac.uk.

Teach English as a Foreign Language. Courses in central London leading to the Cambridge/RSA Certificate (CELTA), regarded internationally as the ideal qualification in TEFL. International House has 40 years experience in training teachers and can offer jobs to those recently qualified in its 110 schools in 27 countries.

Dates: Four-week (110 hours) intensive courses begin Jan 5, Feb 2, Mar 2, Apr 14, May 11, Jun 8, Jul 6, Aug 3, Sep 1, Sep 28, Oct 26, Nov 23, 1998. Cost: £944 includes Cambridge/RSA registration. Contact: Teacher Training Development, International House, 106 Piccadilly, London W1V 9FL, England; (011) 44-171-491-2598, fax 499-0174; teacher@dial.pipex.com.

The European Fashion Industry. London College of Fashion is the only college in the British university sector to specialize in fashion. Unique 4-credit summer program; specialist courses in design, marketing and merchandising, cosmetics and beauty; historical and cultural studies; plus optional 4-week internship.

Dates: Jun 22-Jul 17, 1998. Cost: £1,450 for 4 weeks. London accommodations not included. Contact: Alanah Cullen, Business Manager, DALI at London College of Fashion, 20 John Princes St., London W1M 0BJ, England; (011) 44-171-514-7411, fax 514-7490; lcfdali@londonfashion.ac.uk.

The London Theater Program. Study with some of Britain's most distinguished actors and directors. Undergraduate program co-sponsored by Sarah Lawrence College and the British American Drama Academy exposes you to the rigor and excitement of professional British training in acting. Frequent trips to West End and fringe productions. Apartment living is available.

Dates: Sep-Apr (may attend semester or year). Cost: $10,275. Includes all academic expenses, field trips, and cultural activities. Contact: Celia Regan, Sarah Lawrence College, Box CR, Bronxville, NY 10708; (800) 873-4752.

Travel and Study with Rockland. Enrolling in one of Rockland's summer or January study abroad program enables you to travel with an objective...to enrich your course of study and to broaden your perspectives on the world. Short-term study abroad through Rockland Community College is open to college students and adult members of the community.

Dates: Summer, Jan term. Cost: Varies. Contact: Jody A. Dudderar, Rockland Community College, 145 College Rd., Suffern, NY 10901; (914) 574-4205, fax (914) 574-4423; jdudderar@sunyrockland.edu.

UCLES RSA CTEFLA. This is the most widely recognized introductory course to the TEFL profession allowing successful participants to work worldwide. The course is extremely practical, develops classroom skills and language awareness as well as dealing comprehensively with methodology, thus providing a sound basis in all aspects of TEFL teaching.

Dates: Oct-Nov, Apr-Jun, Jan-May. Cost: £832. Contact: Guidance Centre, Thames Valley Univ., 18-22 Bond St., Ealing, London W5 5AA, U.K.; (011) 44-181-579-5000, fax 231-2900.

Univ. of Cambridge International Summer Schools. Largest and longest-established program of summer schools in the U.K. Intensive study in Cambridge as part of an international community. Term I (6 weeks) and Term II (2 weeks) of the International Summer School offer over 60 different courses. Three-week specialist programs: Art history, Medieval Studies, History, English Literature, and Shakespeare. Wide range of classes on all programs. U.S. and other overseas institutions grant credit for study at the Univ. of Cambridge Summer School. Guidelines available.

Dates: Jul 5-Aug 15, 1998. Cost: Tuition from £460-£625 (2 to 4 weeks), accommodations from £240-£925 (2 to 4 weeks). Six-week period of study also possible by combining 2 summer schools. Contact: Sarah Ormrod, Director, International Division, Univ. of Cambridge Board of Continuing Education, Madingley Hall, Madingley, Cambridge CB3 8AQ, England; (011) 44-1954-210636, fax 210677; rdi1000@cam.ac.uk, www.cam.ac.uk.

Univ. of Essex. Undergraduates (sophomores, juniors, or seniors) can normally select 4 courses from all regular undergraduate courses in the Univ. (subject to prerequisites, schedules, and space). Guaranteed single occupancy, fully integrated with British students. On-campus accommodations are less than 1 hour from London. Full support services including transcripts of credit and grades. Students can come for full year or autumn term or spring and summer terms.

Dates: Academic year: Oct 3 (1996); Jun 28 (1997); autumn term: Oct 3-Dec 14 (1996); spring and summer terms: Jan 13-Jun 28 (1997). Cost: (1995-96): full year £5,945; spring and summer terms £3,585; autumn term £2,390 (costs for tuition only). Contact: Mrs. Gloria Vicary, Coordinator of International Programmes, Univ. of Essex, Wivenhoe Park, Colchester CO4 3SQ, England.

Univ. of North London. SUNY Cortland celebrates its 25th consecutive year at UNL, the prestigious public university formerly known as London Polytechnic. Over 400 courses are offered. Fields of study include education, natural sciences, humanities, communications, social sciences, business, health, theater arts. Credits per semester: 12-16. Prearranged housing in flats in the Bayswater district. Internships available.

Dates: Fall: mid-Sep-mid-Dec:, spring: end-Jan-mid-May. Cost: Fall 1997 estimate: $5,000, spring 1998: $5,385; academic year: $9,980. Estimates include full-day orientation in the U.S., application fee, apartment rental, meals, commuter ticket on underground for semester, London tour and Thames cruise, insurance, roundtrip airfare from N.Y., transportation from airport to downtown London upon arrival, books and supplies, various cultural activities, administrative fees. SUNY tuition not included. Contact: Dr. John Ogden, Director, Office of International Programs, Box 2000, SUNY Cortland, Cortland, NY 13045; (607) 753-2209, fax (607) 753-5989; studyabroad@snycorva.cortland.edu, www.studyabroad.com/suny/cortland.

Visual Arts and Crafts Courses. Week and weekend courses. Summer schools in art, ceramics, woodworking, textiles, sculpture, silversmithing, music, and art appreciation. One-, 2-, and 3-year diploma courses in conservation and restoration of antique furniture, clocks, ceramics, fine metalwork, and rare books and manuscripts; tapestry weaving (also 6-week modules); making early stringed instruments. Vaidation at postgraduate level is by the Univ. of Sussex.

Dates: Diploma courses start each year and end in July. Short courses are year round. Cost: Diploma courses £6,921 per annum; residential accommodations £2,979 per annum; short courses (residential) £359, weekends £150, 7 days £483. Contact: Heather Way, Press and Public Relations Coordinator, West Dean College, West Dean, Chichester, West Sussex, PO18 0QZ U.K.; (011) 44-1243-811301, fax 811343; westdean@pavilion.co.uk, www.pavilion.co.uk.

Webster Univ. in London. Webster Univ. in London, located on the campus of Regent's College, has students from more than 50 countries. Students may pursue a degree program leading to a BA, MA, or MBA. In addition, students may enroll for a study abroad semester or year (summer session and other short-term options also available). Each semester more than 70 courses are available in 15 different disciplines. Major areas of study include: business, computer science, economics, psychology, international relations, management, marketing.

Dates: Five entry terms: late Aug, mid-Oct, mid-Jan, mid-Mar, late May. Cost: $20,000 (1996-97 academic year); $10,000 (semester 1996-97). Estimate includes tuition, room and board, books, local transportation, social activities. Contact: Teresa Bruno, Study Abroad Office, Webster Univ., 470 E. Lockwood Ave., St. Louis, MO 63119-3194; (314) 968-6988 or (800) 984-6857, fax (314) 963-6051. Visit our website at http://webster2.websteruniv.edu.

United States

Master of International and Intercultural Management. The School for International Training Master of International and Intercultural Management offers concentrations in sustainable development, international education, and training and human resource development in a 1 academic-year program. This degree is designed for individuals wishing to make a career change or enter the field. A practical training component enables "on-the-job" training and an opportunity to work internationally.

Dates: Sep 1, 1997-May 29, 1998. Cost: $17,000 (1997-98 tuition). Contact: Kat Eldred, Director of Outreach and Recruitment, Admissions Counselor, School for International Learning, P.O. Box 676, Kipling Rd., Brattleboro, VT 05302; (802) 257-7751, fax (802) 258-3500; admissions@sit.edu, www.sit.edu.

Vietnam

Vietnam Program (Ho Chi Minh City). Includes Vietnamese language, business economics, political science, history, geography, and Vietnamese literature course. All courses taught in English except literature, which has a language proficiency pre-requisite. Spring and fall terms are 11-week programs including a 3-day excursion to Hanoi. Accreditation from Western Washington Univ.

Dates: Spring: Apr 8-Jun 10; fall: Sep 17-Dec 2. Cost: $5,500 per term includes tuition, housing, meals. Contact: Cheryl Brown, Program Coordinator or Roger Edginton, Senior Director, American Heritage Association, 741 SW Lincoln St., Portland, OR 97201-3178; (800) 654-2051, fax (503) 295-5969; vn@amheritage.org.

Worldwide

AIYSEP. AIYSEP is a nonprofit high school foreign exchange program based in the U.S. which establishes exchange programs for students in Europe, America, and many other foreign countries. Area counselors are located in Europe, U.S., Australia, New Zealand, South America, Peru, Canada, and Japan. AIYSEP believes a greater international understanding is accomplished among people and countries through cultural homestay programs.

Dates: Year, semester, and summer homestay programs. Cost: Year $3,995-$6,000; semester $3,495-$4,000; summer $1,900-$3,000. Contact: American International Youth Student Exchange, 200 Round Hill Rd., Tiburon, CA 94920; (800) 347-7575 or (415) 435-4049, (415) 499-7669, fax (415) 499-5651; aiysep@compuserve.com.

Art and Cultural Learning Journeys. Guided excursions with informative lectures bring to life famous sights and artworks in Italy, Spain, England, and Bali. Free workshops in drawing, painting, photography, etc. Limited scholarships available. Travel with A.R.T.I.S., a nonprofit organization of fine art educators dedicated to providing you with unique and rewarding international cultural experiences. College credit available.

Dates: May-Jul 1998 and Dec 98 for Rome. Ten, 20, or 30 days. Cost: $2,500 to $3,700. Includes airfare, studio space, furnished apartment, workshops, all ground transportation, entry fees, etc. Contact: A.R.T.I.S., 833 E. Holaway Dr., Tucson, AZ 85719; (800) 232-6893, fax (520) 887-5287; dfro@digmo.org, www.artis-tours.org.

Boston Univ. International Programs. Offering internship and language/liberal arts programs in 15 cities on 6 continents and in 9 different languages. Course offerings range from intermediate-level language and liberal arts study through advanced-level, direct enrollment in local universities. Internship programs combine coursework with an academic internship. Application materials: 2 references, transcript, essays, and academic approval.

Dates: Fall, spring, and summer (length varies). Application deadline: Mar 15 (summer and fall); Oct 15 (spring). Cost: $4,500-$14,770; application fee: $35. Contact: Boston Univ., International Programs, 232 Bay State Rd., 5th Fl., Boston, MA 02215; (617) 353-9888, fax (617) 353-5402; abroad@bu.edu, http://web.bu.edu/abroad.

Center for Global Education-Undergraduate Semester Programs. The center facilitates cross-cultural learning experiences that prepare students to think more critically about global issues and to work toward a more just and sustainable world. Programs include homestays, community learning, and regional travel. Students explore women's issues and issues of social change, sustainable development, and human rights. Programs in Mexico, Central America, and Namibia/South Africa.

Dates: Semesters (Sep-Dec or Feb-May). Cost: Contact the Center for current costs. Contact: Academic Programs Abroad, Center for Global Education, Augsburg College, 2211 Riverside Ave., Box 307TR, Minneapolis, MN 55454; (800) 299-8889, fax (612) 330-1695; globaled@augsburg.edu, www.augsburg.edu/global.

Center for Global Education. The center facilitates cross-cultural learning experiences that prepare students to think more critically about global issues and to work toward a more just and sustainable world. Programs include homestays, community learning, and regional travel. Students explore women's issues and issues of social change, sustainable development, and human rights. Programs in Mexico, Central America, Namibia and South Africa.

Dates: Semesters (Sep-Dec or Feb-May), Jan term. Cost: Contact the Center for current costs. Contact: Academic Programs Abroad, Center for Global Education, Augsburg College, 2211 Riverside Ave., Box 307TR, Minneapolis, MN 55454; (800) 299-8889, fax (612) 330-1695; globaled@augsburg.edu, www.augsburg.edu/global.

College Semester Abroad. Through College Semester Abroad (CSA) you have the opportunity to learn firsthand about our interdependent world and its diversity through interdisciplinary study in more than 40 countries worldwide. The structure of each program provides you with the best possible opportunity to immerse yourself into the culture of the host country.

Dates: Fall and spring semesters (vary). Cost: Average $9,700 (room and board, tuition, international travel, insurance, excur-

sions). Contact: Admissions College Semester Abroad, SIT, P.O. Box 676, Kipling Rd., Brattleboro, VT 05302; (802) 257-7751, fax (802) 258-3500; csa@sit@worldlearning.org, www.worldlearning.org/csa.html.

College Semeter Abroad, School for International Training. A pioneer in study abroad, The School for International Training (SIT) offers over 57 programs in over 40 countries worldwide. For over 40 years SIT has been a leader in offering field-based study abroad programs to U.S. college and university students.

Dates: Fall and spring semester. Cost: $8,900-$11,900 depending on location. Includes airfare, tuition, room and board, insurance. Contact: School for International Training, P.O. Box 676, Kipling Rd., Brattleboro, VT 05302; (802) 257-7751, fax (802) 258-3500; csa@sit.edu, www.sit.edu.

Cooperative Education Program. Paid employment and internships for college and university students for a period of 8-12 weeks in 8 European and one Asian country. Employment depends on foreign language knowledge, major, and previous work experience. Work permits and housing are provided.

Dates: From Jun-Sep. Cost: Students must pay for air transportation and have a reserve of at least $800 for initial expenses. Contact: Günter Seefeldt, PhD, Director, International Cooperative Education Program, 15 Spiros Way, Menlo Park, CA 94025; (415) 323-4944, fax (415) 323-1104.

Coral Cay Conservation Expeditions. Volunteers needed to join major expeditions to help survey and protect coral reefs and tropical forests in the Caribbean, Asia-Pacific, Philippines, Indonesia, Red Sea. No previous experience required. Full accredited training provided (including scuba certification if required). Thousands of CCC volunteers have already helped establish 8 new marine reserves and wildlife sanctuaries worldwide.

Dates: Expeditions depart monthly throughout the year. Cost: From $995 (2 weeks) to $4,415 (12 weeks) excluding flights. Contact: Coral Cay Conservation Ltd., 154 Clapham Park Rd., London SW4 7DE, U.K.; (305) 757-2955 (U.K. office 011-44-171-498-6248, fax 498 8447); ccc@coralcay.demon.co.uk, www.coralcay.org.

European University. European University offers undergraduate and graduate programs in Business Administration, International Hospitality and Tourism Management, Business Communications and Public Relations, Information Systems, and European Languages.

Dates: Courses begin Oct, Jan, Mar. Cost: SF3,0850. Contact: Prof. D. Craen, European Univ. Les Bosquets, 1817 Montreaux, Switzerland; (011) 41-21-964-84-64, fax 964-84-68, eurmon@iprolink.ch.

Friends World Program. A full year program in comparative religion and culture. Students will study for three 10-week terms in Japan, India, and Israel. The field course will be based on experiential approaches, emphasizing participation, observation, and involvement in local religious life. Culture's relation to religion will be emphasized.

Dates: Mid-Sep-mid-May. Cost: $23,500 for year (1996/1997). Includes tuition, travel, room and board, fees and books. Contact: James Howard, Friends World Program, 239 Montauk Hwy., Southampton, NY 11968; (516) 287-8475; jhoward@sand.liunet.edu.

Global Ecology and Cities in the 21st Century. Two different academic programs to be offered by the International Honors Program in 1998-99. "Global Ecology" is a 2-semester program of around-the-world study and travel to England, Tanzania, India, the Philippines, and Mexico with academic coursework in ecology, anthropology, economics, and environmental issues. The "Cit-

ies in the 21st Century" program is a 1-semester program of study and travel to South Africa, India, and Brazil with academic coursework in urban studies, anthropology, sociology, economics, and political science.

Dates: "Global Ecology": Sep 1998-May 1999. "Cities in 21st Century": Jan 1999-May 1999. Cost: "Global Ecology": $21,300 plus airfare, includes tuition, room and board. "Cities in the 21st Century": $11,000 plus airfare, includes tuition, room and board. Contact: Joan Tiffany, Director, International Honors Program, 19 Braddock Pk., Boston, MA 02116; (617) 267-0026, fax (617) 262-9299; info@ihp.edu, www.ihp.edu.

Global Routes: Internship Program. Global Routes interns are assigned in pairs to remote villages where they teach in local schools and complete at least 1 community service project. Each intern lives separately with a local family in a simple, traditional home. Training, support, and adventure travel are an integral part of the programs. Programs offered in Costa Rica, Ecuador, Kenya, Thailand, Navajo Nation.

Dates: Year round in 3-month sessions. Cost: $3,550 summer, $3,950 during year. Includes all expenses (room, board, adventure travel) except airfare to and from country. Scholarships and fundraising information available. Contact: Global Routes, 1814 7th St., Suite A, Berkeley, CA 94710; (510) 848-4800, fax (510) 848-4801; mail@global-routes.org, www.lanka.net.globalrts.

Partnerships International. A short-term, school-to-school pairing program designed to foster long-term academic and cultural partnerships between secondary schools in the U.S. and other countries. Once schools are linked, a group of 6-15 students, accompanied by a faculty member, visits their partner school for approximately 3 weeks. During this time, students live in the homes of host students, attend classes, participate in another way of life, and discover local points of interest.

Dates: Vary with academic year. Cost: Range $800-$1,900 depending on country of destination. Contact: Partnership International/NASSP, 1904 Association Dr., Reston, VA 22091; (800) 253-7746, fax (703) 476-6319.

Peace and Conflict Studies at EPU. A unique opportunity to study with the world's foremost experts in the areas of peace, conflict, and development at the European Peace Institute. Campuses in Spain and Austria. Full range of program services. Need-based scholarships available.

Dates: Fall, winter, and spring semesters. Full academic year. Cost: Semesters $7,400 (1997-98). Contact: Helene Cohan, Beaver College Center for Education Abroad, 450 S. Easton Rd., Glenside, PA 19038-3295; (888) BEAVER-9, fax (215) 572-2174; cea@beaver.edu, www.beaver.edu/cea.

Phenix International Campuses, Inc. Spring and summer language programs to Germany, France, Spain, Mexico, Costa Rica. Combination of homestay and travel. Small groups with teacher chaperones. Individualized programs possible with your itinerary. Recommendations from former students and teachers. All inclusive prices. Twenty-eight years experience.

Dates: Spring and summer vacation times. Cost: Each program individually priced. Contact: Nellie Jackson, Director, Phenix International Campuses, 7651 N. Carolyn Dr., Castle Rock, CO 80104; (303) 688-9397, fax (303) 688-6543.

Program Coordinator. World Experience in Agriculture offers FFA members and agriculture students a chance to work and live with agricultural host families for 3, 6, or 12 months to gain practical training and learn the culture of another country.

Dates: Year-round departures. Cost: Ranges from $2,000-$6,000 depending on destination. Contact: Bruce White, Student Services Specialist, National FFA Organization, P.O. Box 15160, Alexandria, VA 22309.

Programs in European Studies. The Center for European Studies, Maastricht Univ., offers semester, year, and summer programs. Students compose their own "package" of courses—all taught in English, fully integrated with European students in international dormitories. Maastricht, on the border of Belgium, Germany, and the Netherlands is the oldest city of the Netherlands.

Dates: Spring: Jan 5-Apr 30; summer: Jul 3-Aug 18; fall: Aug 20-Dec 20. Cost: $300 per credit (1 semester per 16 credits $800). Other: $600 per month (housing food, miscellaneous). Contact: Karin Quanten, Coordinator Undergraduate Programs, Center for European Studies, Witmakersstraat 10, 6211 JB Maastricht, the Netherlands; (011) 31-43-26-27, fax 325-73-24; k.quantn@ces.unimaas.nl, www.unimaas.nl.

Study Abroad in Australia. Study 1 semester in a wide range of courses including humanities, arts, social sciences, economics, education, science, Australian studies.

Dates: Feb-Jun or Jul-Nov. Cost: Approx. $5,500 Contact: International Office, Univ. of New England, Armidale, NSW Australia 2351.

Summer Study Abroad. Summer opportunities in Australia, Austria, England, Ireland, Mexico, and Scotland, including internships, fine arts, drama, history, literature, environmental studies, psychology and languages. Full range of program services. Guaranteed housing.

Dates: Vary. Call for tentative dates. Cost: Varies. Call for fees. Contact: Beaver College Center for Education Abroad, 450 S. Easton Rd., Glenside, PA 19038-3295; (888) BEAVER-9, fax (215) 572-2174; cea@beaver.edu, www.beaver.edu/cea.

The Global Campus. Choose from 30 programs featuring language, theme, area studies, integrated classroom and field study. Program courses include language, culture, humanities, internships, and international relations. Destinations range from Austria to Venezuela with Third World internship programs in Ecuador, India, Kenya, and Senegal. Open to all students and professionals.

Dates: Quarter, semester, summer, and academic year options. Cost: From $2,600-$14,000 (most $3,800). Contact: The Global Campus, Univ. of Minnesota, 102T Nicholson Hall, 216 Pillsbury Dr. SE, Minneapolis, MN 55455-0138; (612) 625-3379, fax (612) 626-8009; globalc@tc.umn.edu, www.isp.umn.edu.

Trent International. Trent's International study and exchange programs provide students with an opportunity to spend an academic study year abroad. Students from all academic disciplines may pursue one of a number of formalized exchange or study abroad or language programs. Some programs involve an international work placement component. Students take regular courses and examinations at a host university, and credits earned abroad are counted toward their undergraduate degree.

Dates: Full academic year (often Oct-Jun). Cost: Differs according to program but generally pay Trent's tuition and (often) residence fees. Contact: Cynthia Bennett Awe, Int'l. Programs and Services Manager, Trent Univ., Peterborough, ON K9J 7B8, Canada; (705) 748-1300, fax (705) 748-1626; cawe@trentu.ca.

Vienna Master Courses for Music. Master classes (2 weeks) in: singing, opera, lied, piano, violin, cello, guitar, chamber music, conducting, flute. Diploma for active participation, certificate for listeners, final concerts. Twenty lessons per week. Instructors are leading artists or renowned teachers.

Dates: Jul 6-Aug 15, 1988. Cost: Registration fee: AS1,500; course fee active: AS5,200; listen AS2,700. Contact: Vienna Master Courses, A-1030 Vienna, Reisnerstr. 3, Austria; (011) 43-1-714-88-22, fax 714-88-21.

(Elisabeth Keschmann or Monika Wiladauer).

World Experience Student Exchange Program. World Experience offers an opportunity to have an experience of a lifetime. Learn another language while living with a host family from 1 of 30 countries for a semester or school year. Attend school locally. Add a new dimension to your life. Eligibility: 15-18 years. 3.0 GPA.

Dates: Aug or Jan departure for 1 to 2 semesters. Cost: $2,640 plus individual country fees for 1 year; $2,265 plus individual country fees for 1 semester. Contact: World Experience, 2440 Hacienda Blvd #116, Hacienda Heights, CA 91745; (800) 633-6653, fax (626) 333-4914; weworld@aol.com.

WorldTeach. WorldTeach is a private nonprofit organization based at Harvard Univ. which contributes to educational development and cultural exchange by placing volunteers to teach in developing countries (China, Costa Rica, Ecuador, Honduras, Mexico, Namibia, Thailand, and Vietnam). Volunteers teach English, math, science, and environmental education to students of all ages. All programs last for 1 academic year; except for the summer program in China.

Dates: Year-round departures and deadlines vary depending on the program. Cost: $3,600-$4,400. Includes health insurance, airfare, field support, and training. Contact: Jodi Hullinger, Desk Officer, WorldTeach, Harvard Institute for International Development, 1 Eliot St., Cambridge, MA 02138-5705; (617) 495-5527, fax (617) 495-1599; jhulling@worldteach.org, www.igc.org/worldteach.

CHAPTER 14

HIGH SCHOOL EXCHANGE RESOURCES

Never before has the high shool student been so fortunate in the choice of overseas educational travel options. Gone are the days when a student eager to travel overseas had only a few creative alternatives to a whirlwind bus and train tour of Europe.

Options now include academic enrichment, cultural immersion, and environmental studies as well as travel.

For summer programs alone, *Peterson's Guide to Summer Opportunities for Kids and Teenagers 1997* ($26.95 plus shipping, 800-338-3282) lists over 600 different overseas options to suit students' varied interests, including community service in Costa Rica or the Fiji Islands, language study and homestays in France or Italy, conservation biology in Belize, and learning outdoor skills in Chile.

Start your search for the program that is best for you with the college counselor at your high school or at the study abroad office at your local college or university. The following organizations provide information on travel and study abroad for high school-age students.

Organizations

Alliance for International Educational and Cultural Exchange, 1090 Vermont Ave. NW, Washington, DC 20005; (202) 371-2070. Publishes the International Exchange Locator: A Guide to U.S. Organizations, Federal Agencies, and Congressional Committees Active in International Exchange. Annual. $29.95 plus $4 s/h. Lists high school and college exchange organizations and others involved in international exchange at all levels.

American Association of School Administrators (AASA), 1801 N. Moore St., Arlington, VA 22209; (703) 528-0700. Publications include: **Development Education: Building a Better World,** a guidebook for integrating Third World issues and ideas into school curricula.

Council on International Educational Exchange (Council), Council-Pubs Dept., 205 E. 42nd St., New York, NY 10017-5706; (888)-COUNCIL, fax (212) 822-2699; info@ciee.org, http://www.ciee.org. Publishers of materials on work, study, and travel abroad, especially for students; also administers the Council Work Abroad Program and Council Workcamps.

Council on Standards for International Education Travel (CSIET), 212 S Henry St., Alexandria, VA 22314; (703) 771-2040, fax (703) 771-2046. CSIET is a nonprofit organization committed to quality international educational travel and exchange. It established standards for organizations operating international educational travel and exchange programs at the high school level and monitors compliance with those standards by annually reviewing those programs that submit themselves for evaluation. It also disseminates information on international educational travel organizations. Advisory List of International Educational Travel & Exchange Programs, published annually, ($10 postpaid, $15 overseas) lists programs for high school students which adhere to CSIET's standards and provides valuable information for prospective exchange students, host families, and schools.

EF Foundation for Foreign Study (known internationally as EF High School Year), 1 Memorial Drive, Cambridge, MA 02142; (617) 252-6000, fax (617) 621-1930; http://ef.com/hsy/. Non-profit organization dedicated to encouraging cultural awareness and mutual respect between nations through cultural exchange. Over 40,000 students from 25 countries since 1979.

Intercultural Press, P.O. Box 700, Yarmouth, ME 04096; (207) 846-5168, fax (207) 846-5181; interculturalpress@mcimail.com, http://www.bookmasters.com/interclt.htm. Intercultural Press publishes numerous books on international living, travel, study, and cross-cultural experiences. Titles include:

Host Family Survival Kit: A Guide for American Host Families, Survival Kit for Overseas Living, Exchange Student Survival Kit.

Institute of International Education (IIE), IIE Books, P.O. Box 371, Annapolis Junction, MD 20701-0371; (800) 445-0443, fax (301) 953-2838; iiebooks@iie.org, www.iie.org. Publisher of authoritative directories for study or teaching abroad and financial aid, and distributor of Central Bureau (U.K.) publications on working abroad. Add $2 each shipping for books under $25; $4 each for books over $25, or 10 percent for orders over $100.

International Youth Exchange Staff (USIA), 301 4th St., Room 314, SW, Washington, DC 20547; (202) 619-6299. The International Youth Exchange Staff of USIA oversees activities initiated under the President's International Youth Exchange Initiative and works closely with other organizations involved in international educational exchange activities.

NAFSA: Association of International Educators, P.O. Box 1020, Sewickley, PA 15143; (800) 836-4994, fax (412) 741-0609. Essential publications for advisers and administrators in international educational exchange. For membership information, contact NAFSA: Association of International Educators, 1875 Connecticut Ave. NW, Suite 1000, Washington, DC 20009-5728, (202) 939-3103 or (202) 462-4811, fax (202) 667-3419; inbox@nafsa.org, http://www.nafsa.org.

National Association of Secondary School Principals, 1904 Association Dr., Dept. CS, Reston, VA 20191-1537; (703) 860-7200, fax (703) 476-9319; sherardm@nassp.org. A professional association of more than 43,000 school administrators. Administers School Partnerships, International, a short-term, school-to-school pairing program designed to foster long-term academic and cultural partnerships between secondary schools in the U.S. and other countries. A U.S. secondary school is "linked" with a similar secondary school abroad. The partner schools exchange information, educational and cultural materials, and, ultimately, groups averaging six to 15 students, accompanied by a faculty member, for three to four weeks. Students live with a host family, attend classes, and participate in school activities. Cultural orientation is provided upon arrival in the host country before transferring to the partner school location. Cost to participants is $650 to $1,995, including transportation and insurance.

U.S. Information Agency (USIA), Exchange Visitor Program Services, 301 4th St., (FEMA Room 200), SW, Washington, DC 20547; (202) 475-2389. The USIA evaluates not-for-profit organizations to determine whether they meet Criteria for Teenage Visitor Programs. It grants authorization to issue Forms IAP-66 for securing J-1 visas to enter the U.S.

Youth For Understanding 3501 Newark Street. N.W., Washington, DC 20016; (800) TEENAGE or (202) 966-6800; fax (202) 895-1104; USA@mail.yfu.org, www.yfu.org/. Nonprofit educational organization provides opportunities for teenagers between the ages of 15 and 18 to spend a summer, semester or year with a host family in another culture. More than 180,000 participants from 40 nations since 1951.

HIGH SCHOOL EXCHANGE PROGRAMS

The following listing of high school exhange programs was supplied by the organizers. Contact the program directors to confirm costs, dates, and other details. If you do not see the program you want in the country of your choice, look in the "Worldwide" listings at the end of the section for programs located in several different regions.

Australia

Custom Designed Professional Development Internships. Upon application, participants are asked to describe their internship needs, after which the placement service in Australia locates suitable programs. Responsibilities vary by placement. Excellent professional development and career building opportunities. Opportunities to travel in Australia before and after the placement. Flexible duration and start dates. Interns are not usually placed as a group. On-call support service, airport transfers, academic or professional supervisor provided in Australia. Pre-trip support for air travel, visas and orientation.

Fields: Management, Marketing, Finance and Accounting, Communications (radio, television, newspaper, public relations), Law, Politics, The Arts, Social Work, Biology, Wild-life Management, Natural Resources, and Marine Science. Academic credit can be arranged through home university. One-hundred-200 internships per year. Prerequisites: Pursuing or have obtained a university/college degree. Application materials: application and transcript(s).

Dates: Six, 8, 10, 12, 16 weeks or more (52 weeks maximum) placements. Year-round start dates. Sign up at least 4 months prior to intended departure. Cost: $3,240 (6 weeks) to $4,480 (16 weeks). Includes room, 2 meals per day in homestay (or no meals in an apartment), internship placement, liaison service in Australia, airport transfers. Compensation: placements are typically unpaid due to immigration rules. Application fee: $500 deposit with application. Eighty percent refundable for cancellation after placement is found. Contact: AustraLearn, U.S. Center for Australian Universities, 110 16th St., CSU Denver Center, Denver, CO 80202; (800) 980-0033, fax (303) 446-5955; cflannery@ vines.colostate.edu.

Special Interest and Study Tours. Personalized programs for individuals and groups of all ages. We combine education, recreation, accommodations (homestay available), and transportation. Based in tropical Cairns with coverage throughout Australia. Subject areas include: aboriginal dreamtime and culture, Great Barrier Reef, rainforest and savannah. Diving, environmental interpretation, flora and fauna, bird watching, tropical islands and wilderness, adventure safaris and farmstay.

Dates: Year round. Start any date. Cost: Prices and customized itineraries on application. Contact: Murray Simpson, Study Venture International, P.O. Box 229A, Stratford Qld., 4870 Australia; (011) 61-70-411622, fax 552044; svi@ozemail.com. au; www.ozemail.au/~svi.

Costa Rica

Enjoy Learning Spanish Faster. Techniques developed from our ongoing research enable students at Centro Linguistico Latinoamericano to learn more, faster, in a comfortable environment. Classes are 2-5 students plus group learning activities; conversations with middle-class homestay families (1 student per family). Homestays are within walking distance of school in small town (14,000 population) near the capital, San Jose.

Dates: Year round. Classes begin every Monday, at all levels. Cost: $295 per week for 25 hours of classes. Includes tuition, all meals (7 days a week), homestay, laundry, all materials, Costa Rican dance and cooking classes, and airport transportation. $25 one-time registration. Contact: Susan Shores, Registrar, Latin American Language Center, 7485 Rush River Dr., Suite 710-

123, Sacramento, CA 95831; (916) 447-0938, fax (916) 428-9542; lalc@madre. com.

Spanish Language Training. Nonprofit organization. Program includes intensive Spanish language training, optional excursions, lodging with a Costa Rican host family or hotel, introductory orientation, WEF certificates.

Dates: Four-week programs start any Monday of the year. Cost: $825 includes room and food. Contact: José O. Arauz, Executive Director, World Education Forum, P.O. Box 383-4005, San Antonio de Belén, Heredia, Costa Rica; Fax (506) 239-2254.

Germany

German as a Foreign Language. We offer the following educational programs: various levels of German year round; intensive, crash, and long-term courses, individual tuition; special feature: German and Theater; special programs: business German for professionals, German for teachers, German in a teacher's home, German for special purposes. Academic year for high school students, international study year, internship, guest studentship, homestays for groups, courses for firms and other institutions (banking, insurance, doctors, lawyers, etc.), residential language camps for juniors, examination preparation. Various types of accommodations. Full range of activities.

Dates: Year round. Contact: GLS Sprachenzentrum, Barbara Jaeschke, Managing Director, Kolonnenstrasse 26, 10829 Berlin, Germany; (011) 49-30-787-41-52; fax 41-92; gls.berlin@t-online.de.

India

Studies Abroad for Global Education (SAGE). Year-abroad program in India for high school students in grades 9-12 at accredited international schools offering college preparatory courses and many extracurricular activities. Includes a winter tour of India and volunteer opportunities between semesters.

Cost: Fee $10,500. Does not include travel to and from India. Contact: Jane Cummings, KWI, 159 Ralph McGill Blvd., #408, NE, Atlanta, GA 30308; (404) 524-0988, fax (404) 523-5420.

Japan

Lex Homestay Programs. Lex offers homestay programs in which participants, living as members of a Japanese family, absorb the customs and characteristics of their host culture by taking part in daily life activities. Participants may go sightseeing with their families, meet friends and relatives, and attend festivals. Japanese language ability is not a requirement. Host families are fully screened volunteer members of the Lex organization. Adults, students, and entire families are encouraged to apply.

Dates: Jul-Aug: 2, 4- and 6-week programs. Spring: 2-week program. Custom programs year round. Cost: Varies. Four-week summer program $3,030 (includes airfare from West Coast port of departure). Contact: Steffi Samman, Program Manager, Lex America, 68 Leonard St., Belmont, MA 02178; (617) 489-5800, fax (617) 489-5898; exchange@lexlrf.com.

Latin America

Iberoamerican Cultural Exchange Program. U.S. Spanish students live as a member of a foreign host family for periods of 6 weeks, 3 months, 1 semester, or 1 school year. The program includes pre-experience orientation, local supervision, and—depending on time of year—school attendance. Participants must be 15 to 18 years of age and have studied a minimum of 2 years of Spanish. Appli-

cations due 3 months prior to start of program.

Dates: Programs begin Aug, Jan, and Jun. Cost: Six weeks $850, 3 months $950; semester $1,300; school year $2,600. Does not include airfare and insurance. Contact: Bonnie P. Mortell, 13920 93rd Ave., NE, Kirkland, WA 98034; (206) 821-1463, fax (206) 821-1849; icepbpm@aol.com.

Mexico

Intensive Spanish in Cuernavaca. Cuauhnahuac, founded in 1972, offers a variety of intensive and flexible programs geared to individual needs. Six hours of classes daily with no more than 4 students to a class. Housing with Mexican families who really care about you. Cultural conferences, excursions, and special classes for professionals. College credit available.

Dates: Year round. New classes begin every Monday. Cost: $70 registration fee; $650 4 weeks tuition; housing $18 per night. Contact: Marcia Snell, 519 Park Dr., Kenilworth, IL 60043; (800) 245-9335, fax (847) 256-9475; lankysam@aol.com.

Intensive Spanish Language (Cuernavaca). The Cemanahuac Educational Community offers intensive Spanish language study taught by native speakers. Special classes on history, literature, art, and anthropology of Mexico and Latin America, with field study excursions led by Cemanahuac anthropologists. Group programs with special fees. College credit available for juniors and seniors. Family homestay highly recommended.

Dates: Classes begin each Monday, year round program. Cost: Registration, tuition, room and board with Mexican family for 4 weeks: $1,296. Contact: Vivian B. Harvey, Educational Programs Coordinator, Cemanahuac Educational Community, Apartado 5-21, Cuernavaca, Morelos, Mexico; (011) 52-73-18-6407, fax 12-5418; 74052.2570@compuserve.com.

Language and Culture in Guanajuato. We work with innovative teaching techniques, tailoring instruction to each student's needs. Spanish, Mexican History, Politics, Culture-Cuisine, Folk Dancing and Latin American Literature.

Dates: Year round. New classes begin every Monday. Cost: $925. Includes 4 weeks of classes and homestay with 3 meals daily. Contact: Director Jorge Barroso, Instituto Falcon, A.C., Guanajuato, Gto. 36000 Mexico; Tel./fax (011) 52-473-2-36-94, infalcon@redes.int.com.mx, www.infonet.com.mx/falcon.

Spain

High School Exchange Programs. Locations of the programs include Alicante, Castellon, Barcelona, Tarragona, Lerida, Tervel, Zaragoza, Bilbao, San Sebastian, Vitoria. Students can participate in short-term programs during the summer (2, 4, or 6 weeks) or in semester/academic year programs. Students my live with families only, or they may take academic courses. Boarding school option is also available.

Dates: Year round. Cost: Varies by program. Contact: Ann Marie Coyle, FEYDA, 1670 Sheffield Ct., Aurora, IL 60504; (630) 978-4223; amcoyle@aol.com.

Student Tours in Spain. Bravo Tours is a tour operator specializing in programs to Spain for high school and college students organized and chaperoned by your own school's teachers. Our programs cover Madrid, Barcelona, Mallorca, Toldeo, Avila, Segovia, Tenerife, Santiago, Sevilla, Granada, and more.

Contact: See our website at www.bravotours.com or call us at (800) 272-8674.

Summer Spanish Courses for Older Teenagers. Frequently called Spain's leading school of Spanish, Malaca Instituto offers a special program designed specifically for young people (16-22 years). It combines serious study of Spanish with sports and cultural ac-

tivities. Accommodations in our on-site residence or host families. Facilities include: video rooms, cinema, language lab, self-access study center, bar, restaurant, and pool.

Dates: Jun 23, Jul 7, 21, Aug 4, 18 (1997). Cost: Course: from PTS42,000 for 2 weeks, Accommodations: residence, host families, student apartments: from PtS32,540 for 2 weeks. Contact: Bob Burger, Marketing Director, Malaca Instituto, c/Cortada 6, Cerrado de Calderon, 29018 Malaga, Spain; (011) 34-5-229-32-42, fax 63-16.

Switzerland

Bookbinding and Book Restoration. Centro del bel libro is a professional school for artisanal bookbinding and book restoration. Courses are offered year round.

Dates: Call or write for information. Cost: Call or write for information. Contact: Office Centro del bel libro, Ascona, Viale Portone 4, P.O. Box 2600, CH-6501, Bellinzona, Switzerland; (011) 41-91-825-11-62, fax 85-86.

Worldwide

American International Youth Student Exchange. American International Youth Student Exchange Program (AIYSEP) was established in 1981 as a nonprofit, high school exchange program. Based in the U.S., it establishes exchange programs for students in Europe, America, and many other foreign countries. Area counselors are located in Europe, U.S., Australia, New Zealand, South America, Peru, Russia, Croatia, Yugoslavia, Canada, and Japan. AIYSEP believes a greater international understanding is accomplished among people and countries through cultural homestay programs.

Dates: Year (Aug-Jun); semester (Jan-Jun), (Aug-Jan); summer 4, 6, 8 weeks (Jun, Jul, Aug). Cost: Year $3,995-$6,000; semester $3,495-$4,000; summer $1,900-$3,000. Contact: American International Youth Student

Exchange, 200 Round Hill Rd., Tiburon, CA 94920; (800) 347-7575 or (415) 435-4049, (415) 499-7669, fax (415) 499-5651; aiysep @compuserve.com.

English Course. This course consists of general class, conversation, TOEFL, G-MAT, SAT, and private tutoring. We recruit English teachers with BA degrees and TESL/TEFL/RSA certification, preferably those who have teaching experience in Asian countries.

Dates: Year round. Contact: Triad English Centre, JL. Purnawarman, No. 76, Bandung 40116, Indonesia; (011) 6222 431309, fax 431149; triad09@ibm.net.

World Experience Student Exchange Program. World Experience offers an opportunity to have an experience of a lifetime. Learn another language while living with a host family from 1 of 30 countries for a semester or school year. Attend school locally. Add a new dimension to your life. Eligibility: 15-18 years. 3.0 GPA.

Dates: Aug or Jan departure for 1 to 2 semesters. Cost: $2,640 plus individual country fees for 1 year; $2,265 plus individual country fees for 1 semester. Contact: World Experience, 2440 Hacienda Blvd #116, Hacienda Heights, CA 91745; (800) 633-6653, fax (626) 333-4914; weworld@aol.com.

WORK

*Any individual with guts and gusto,
from students to grandmothers,
has the potential for funding themselves
as they travel to the corners of the globe.*
—SUSAN GRIFFITH, PAGE 269

Working Abroad

Experiencing a Foreign Culture from the Inside

By Susan Griffith

We look for alternatives to the conventional two-week vacation for a multitude of reasons: traveling in out-of-the-ordinary ways or to out-of-the-ordinary places is, by definition, one of the best ways to shake off the boredom which comes with routine. Other reasons are more positive: to experience a foreign culture from the inside rather than as an onlooker, to fill a gap of time in our life (perhaps between graduation and the working world or one job and another) in a productive way, to improve our knowledge of foreign languages and cultures, to gain practical skills.

Underlying all these worthy motives for shunning mass market tourism is a belief that the experience of doing it our way and traveling outside the safe parameters will be more rewarding and even more fun. Experiences which require some personal input are potentially more valuable than those purchased off the peg.

Working abroad for an extended period gives us the chance to absorb a foreign culture, to meet foreign people on their own terms. The kind of job we find obviously determines the stratum of society in which we will mix and therefore the content of the experience. The traveler who spends a few weeks picking olives for a Cretan farmer will get very different insights and have more culturally worthwhile experiences than the traveler who settles for working at a beach cafe frequented only by partying foreigners.

Generalizations about the valuable cultural insights afforded by working in a foreign land should be tempered with a careful consideration of the reality of doing a job abroad. True "working holidays" are rare, though they do exist. Traveling Americans have exchanged their labor for a free trip with an outback Australian camping tour operator or on a cruise to the midnight sun. But jobs tend to be jobs wherever you do them. There is little scope for visiting historic sights or even making friends if you are stranded in an obscure industrial town teaching English six days a week or cooped up in a damp caravan which serves as an office for a camping holiday operator.

Yet those who have shed their unrealistic expectations are normally exhilarated by the novelty and challenge of working abroad. Any individual with guts and gusto, from students to grandmothers, has the potential for funding themselves as they travel to the corners of the globe. In hopes of soothing the minds of the irresolute, here are some general guidelines to preface the specific information and contact addresses included in this *Alternative Travel Directory.*

Motives. Some travelers have future career prospects in view when they go abroad; a few go in search of highly paid jobs. Success is easier for people with acknowledged qualifications such as nurses and pipe-fitters, though cherry pickers and pot washers have been known to earn and save substantial sums. Those on open-ended trips may decide to postpone cashing their last traveler's check by looking around for ways of boosting their travel fund. They may find paid work, or they may decide to volunteer their labor in exchange for a bed and board.

Advance Planning. The aspiring working traveler either arranges a definite job before leaving home or gambles on finding something on the spot. There is a lot to recommend prior planning, especially for people who have never traveled abroad and who feel some trepidation at the prospect. Jobs can be pre-arranged either through private contacts or with the help of a mediating organization.

A range of organizations, both public and private, can offer advice and practical assistance to those who wish to arrange a job before leaving home. Some accept a tiny handful of individuals who satisfy stringent requirements; others accept almost anyone who can pay the required fee. Many work schemes and official exchanges require a lot of advance planning since it is not unusual for an application deadline to fall six or nine months before departure.

While it's easy to arrange a job to teach English in the former Soviet Union or work on an Israeli kibbutz, the price you pay for this security is that you commit yourself to a new life, however temporary, sight unseen. Furthermore, a participation fee in some cases can be as expensive as booking a conventional holiday.

The alternative to these packaged arrangements is to wait until after arrival at your destination to explore local job possibilities. In the course of research for my book *Work Your Way Around the World*, I have come across many examples of fearless travelers who are prepared to arrive in a foreign city with very little money, confident that a means by which they can earn money will present itself. In most cases it does, but not without a few moments of panic and desperation.

Like job-hunting in any context, it will be much easier to contend with the inevitable competition if prospective employers can meet you in the flesh and be assured that you are available to start work the minute a vacancy crops up. For casual work on farms or arranging a passage on a transatlantic yacht, a visit to a village pub frequented by farmers or yachties is worth dozens of speculative applications from home.

The more unusual and interesting the job the more competition it will attract. Only a small percentage of applicants for advertised jobs actually get the chance to work as underwater models in the Caribbean. Other, less glamorous, options can absorb an almost unlimited number of people. International workcamps, for example, mobilize thousands of volunteers from many countries every year to build footpaths, work with disabled persons, etc.

Red Tape. Work permits and residence visas are not readily available in many countries and for many kinds of jobs. In most cases, job-seekers from overseas must find an employer willing to apply to the immigration authorities on their behalf well in advance of the job's starting date, while they are still in their home country. This is easier for nuclear physicists and foreign correspondents than for mere mortals, though in certain countries English teachers are welcomed by the authorities. In an organized exchange program like the ones administered by Council on International Educational Exchange and InterExchange the red tape is taken care of by the sponsoring organization.

Temporary jobs like apple picking and burger flipping seldom qualify for a work permit, and unofficial employment can quite often lead to exploitative working conditions.

Improving Your Chances. Preparation will improve your chances either of being accepted on an organized work scheme or convincing a potential employer of your superiority to the competition. For example, before leaving home you might take a short course in teaching English as a foreign language, cooking, word processing, or sailing—all skills which have been put to good use by working travelers. If you are serious, you might learn or improve your knowledge of a foreign language.

Even if you are not lucky enough to have friends and family scattered strategically throughout the world, it is always worth broadcasting your intentions to third cousins, pen friends, and visiting Oriental professors. The more widely publicized your travel plans, the better your chance of a lead.

Even if you set off without an address book full of contacts, your fellow travelers are undoubtedly the best source of information on job prospects; most are surprisingly generous with their information and assistance. Youth hostels can be a gold mine for the job seeker. Jobs may even be advertised on the notice board. Any locals or expatriates you meet are a potential source of help. Any skill or hobby, from jazz music to motor car racing, can become the basis for pursuing contacts.

Local English language newspapers like Mexico City's *The News*, the *Bangkok Post*, or *FUSAC* in Paris may carry job advertisements appropriate to your situation, or may be a good place for you to advertise your services. The most effective method of finding a job overseas is to walk in and ask. As in any job hunt, it helps to have a neat appearance and show keenness and persistence. If you want a job for which there appear to be no openings, volunteer. If you prove yourself competent, you will have an excellent chance of filling a paid vacancy if one does occur.

Seasonal jobs are the ones most likely to go to itinerant foreigners. In times of recession the number of temporary jobs available may even increase since employers are not eager to expand their permanent staff but will need extra help at busy times.

Farmers and hotel/restaurant managers are the best potential sources of employment. English teaching normally requires some experience and a nine-month commitment, though many travelers from Bangkok to Buenos Aires have used the Yellow Pages to direct them to local language schools willing to employ native speakers of English as conversational assistants. In most cases, one setback leads to a success once you are on the track.

Young women and (increasingly) young men who want the security of a family placement and who may also wish to learn a European language, may choose to live with a family helping to look after the children in exchange for pocket money. Such positions can be found on the spot by means of advertisement or in advance through agencies, like AuPair Homestay.

Volunteering. Paid work in developing nations is rarely available, yet many travelers arrange to live for next to nothing doing something positive. Charities and aid organizations offer a range of volunteer opportunities around the world. Many volunteer agencies require more than curiosity about a country; they require a strong wish to become involved in a specific project and in many cases an ideological commitment to a cause. Almost without exception, volunteers must be self-funding.

For anyone with a green conscience, conservation organizations throughout the world welcome volunteers for short or long periods in projects ranging from tree planting to gibbon counting. Unfortunately, the more glamorous projects, such as accompanying scientific research expeditions into wild and woolly places, charge volunteers a great deal of money for the privilege of helping. However, most provide detailed assistance with fund-raising.

Whether you set off to work abroad with the help of a mediating organization or with the intention of living by your wits, you are bound to encounter interesting characters and lifestyles, collect a wealth of anecdotes, increase your self-reliance, and feel that you have achieved something. Inevitably there will be some surprises along the way.

In the words of Oscar Wilde, "It is better to regret something you have done than to regret something you haven't done."

CHAPTER 16

WORK
ABROAD
RESOURCES

Looking for international work, whether abroad or in the U.S. with an international organization, can be daunting–and downright frustrating without good resources. Fortunately, there are now useful guides for almost any field in almost any country.

But you won't find many in your bookstore. Some of the best guides, published by small organizations, lack retail distribution. Even books by major publishers may not be stocked. To help you in your search, we provide complete contact information (if no address is given, see the last section, Key Publishers and Organizations).

Worldwide Overviews and *Overviews by Geographic Area* (pages 276 and 278) include information about work, study, and travel options, either worldwide or for a specific region.

Short-Term Paid Work Abroad Resources (page 280) are for casual work abroad, often—though not always—for students or recent graduates, and generally not career-related. The positions last from a summer to six months. Typical location: Western Eu-

rope. Look into these a few months before going.

International Internships (page 282), like the international careers they can help open up, may be either located in the U.S. with international organizations, or overseas. They are often unpaid. Start your search early, as applications can be due three to nine months in advance.

Teaching English (page 285) may not require any special credentials other than having English as your native language and a year's commitment (and usually a college degree). Typical locations: Eastern Europe and Asia. Apply as early as December prior to the fall you want to start.

Teaching K-12/University Level (page 287) includes resources for teachers with credentials. Typical locations: worldwide. Major K-

12 job fairs are in February (apply in November).

Volunteer Options (page 289) are the best choice for working in developing countries or for social causes anywhere. Many do "pay," at least room and board, and it may be possible to defer educational loans during the volunteer assignment. Typical locations: Africa, Eastern and Western Europe, Latin America, and North America (with international volunteer organizations). For summer workcamps apply March-May. For long-term options like the Peace Corps, apply six to nine months in advance.

International Careers (page 292) resources offer help in planning for a "global" lifetime, which more often than not develops in several stages. Typical home-base location for American citizens: U.S.

International Job Listings (page 296) include newsletters specializing in international job openings in all sectors, but advertised jobs tend to be only a fraction of those actually available.

Internet Resources (page 297) lists some of the most useful e-mail discussion groups and websites for work abroad and international careers.

* *Resources of broadest interest*–and thus essential for libraries–are marked with an asterisk.

** *Best resources to start with*, or for a small library, are marked with two asterisks.

We have made every possible attempt to ascertain the latest edition of each resource. You are welcome to send updates to us at the address indicated at the end of this section.

Worldwide Overviews

** **Academic Year Abroad / Vacation Study Abroad,** edited by Sara Steen. 1997 (revised annually). 650/432 pp. $42.95/$36.95 plus $5 shipping per book from Institute of International Education; (800) 445-0443. Authoritative and comprehensive directories of over 4,150 study and work abroad programs offered by U.S. and foreign universities and pri-

vate organizations (semester/summer). Indexes for internships, practical training, student teaching, volunteer/service, professional and adult courses, as well as fields of study and location. Can be found in most college libraries and study abroad offices.

* **Council Scholarships. (1) ISIC Travel Grants for Educational Programs in Developing Countries,** cover transportation costs for undergraduates to study, work or volunteer in developing countries. (2) **Bailey Minority Student Scholarships** cover transportation costs for undergraduate students of color to study, work, or volunteer with any Council program. Contact Council toll-free at (888) COUNCIL for applications.

Fellowships in International Affairs: A Guide to Opportunities in the United States and Abroad, edited by Gale Mattox. 1994. 195 pp. Women in International Security. $17.95 plus $3 shipping from Lynne Rienner Publishers, 1800 30th St., Suite 314, Boulder CO 80301; (303) 444-6684. Well-researched directory of fellowships and grants for students, scholars and practitioners (most are for graduate and postdoctoral students or professionals). Indexes for level of study and geographic specialization.

* **Financial Aid for Research and Creative Activities Abroad 1996-1998,** edited by Gail Ann Schlachter and R. David Weber. 1996. 440 pp. $45 plus $4 shipping from Reference Service Press, 5000 Windplay Dr., Suite 4, El Dorado Hills, CA 95762; (916) 939-9629, fax (916) 939-9626; findaid@aol.com. Lists over 1,300 funding sources available to support research, professional development, teaching assignments, or creative activities. Sources mainly for graduate students, postdoctorates, and professionals. Indexes for level of study, location, and subject.

* **Financial Aid for Study and Training Abroad 1996-1998,** edited by Gail Ann Schlachter and R. David Weber. 1996. 275

pp. $38.50 plus $4 shipping from Reference Service Press, 1100 Industrial Rd., Suite 9, San Carlos, CA 94070; (415) 594-0743, fax (415) 594-0411. Lists 1,000 funding sources available to support formal educational programs such as study abroad, training, internships, workshops, or seminars. Sources for high school, undergraduate and graduate students, postdoctorates; some for professionals. Indexes for level of study, location, and subject.

** Financial Resources for International Study: A Guide for US Nationals, edited by Sara Steen. 1996. $39.95 plus $5 shipping from IIE. Authoritative and comprehensive directory (600 entries) based on a survey of over 5,000 organizations and universities in the U.S. and abroad. Lists funding sources available to support undergraduate, graduate, postdoctorate, and professional learning abroad, from study and research to internships and other work experiences. Indexes for level of study, subject, and organization.

* The High-School Student's Guide to Study, Travel, and Adventure Abroad, edited by Richard Christiano. 1995. 308 pp. St. Martins. $6.95 from Council. Describes over 200 programs for high-school students, including language programs, summer camps, homestays, study tours, and work and volunteer opportunities. Indexes for program type and location (out of print but worth a library search).

** Intercultural Press Catalog. Updated quarterly. Free from Intercultural Press, Inc., or see www.bookmasters.com/interlt.htm. Catalog of practical books on international cross-cultural issues in settings ranging from academic to business.

** International Job, Career, and Travel Resources for the 1990s. Free from Impact Publications, or see www.impactpublications.com. Catalog of hard-to-find books on international jobs and careers which can be ordered from Impact.

* Money for International Exchange in the Arts, edited by Jane Gullong and Noreen Tomassi. 1992. 126 pp. $14.95 from IIE. Lists grant sources, exchange programs, artists' residencies and colonies for individuals and organizations in the creative arts.

* NAFSA's Guide to Education Abroad for Advisers and Administrators, edited by William Hoffa and John Pearson. 1997. 492 pp. $36 (members) or $45 (non-members) plus $5 shipping from NAFSA Publications; (800) 836-4994. An indispensable reference for education abroad offices, providing an overview of principles and practices, and detailed information for advisers; not a directory of programs. Includes one chapter on advising for work abroad and international careers.

* Peterson's Study Abroad: A Guide to Semester, Summer and Year Abroad Academic Programs. 1997 (revised annually). 1,008 pp. $26.95 plus $6.75 shipping from Peterson's Guides. Detailed information on over 2,000 study abroad programs worldwide. Includes essays on credit, financial aid, nontraditional destinations, internships and volunteering, and travelling (also for those with disabilities). Indexes for field of study, location, host institutions, and internships.

Smart Vacations: The Traveler's Guide to Learning Abroad. 1993. 320 pp. St. Martin's Press. $14.95 from Council. Guide to programs for adults lists study tours, opportunities for voluntary service, field research and archaeological digs, environmental and professional projects, fine arts, and more.

* Taking Time Off: Inspiring Stories of Students Who Enjoyed Successful Breaks

from College and How You Can Plan Your Own. By Colin Hall and Ron Lieber. 1996. 288 pp. The Noonday Press. $12 from Farrar, Strauss and Giroux, 19 Union Square W., New York, NY 10003. Thoughtful book that gives reports of individuals who studied abroad or interned, worked, volunteered, or traveled both abroad and in the U.S. Useful directories to other resources.

Teenager's Vacation Guide to Work, Study, and Adventure Abroad by Victoria Pybus. 1992. Vacation Work. $16.95 from Seven Hills. Addressed to a British audience, this guide covers jobs, study courses, and adventure holidays available for teenagers in Britain and abroad during school vacations.

** Transitions Abroad. Available from Transitions Abroad, Dept. TRA, Box 3000, Denville, NJ 07834, (800) 293-0373; trabroad@aol.com, www.transabroad.com. $24.95/6 issues. Also available in bulk for educators. Published six times a year, this is the only U.S. periodical which gives extensive coverage to work abroad options, in addition to all other varieties of education abroad.

What in the World is Going On? A Guide for Canadians Wishing to Work, Volunteer or Study in Other Countries by Alan Cumyn. 1995. CAN$21 postpaid from Canadian Bureau for International Education, 220 Laurier Ave. W, Suite 1100, Ottawa, Ontario K1P 5Z9, Canada; (613) 237-4820. Includes a comprehensive listing of work abroad possibilities, organized according to skills required and location. Invaluable for Canadians.

Work, Study, Travel Abroad: The Whole World Handbook 1994-1995, edited by Lazar Hernandez and Max Terry. 1994. 605 pp. St. Martin's Press. $13.95 from Council. Overview of opportunities around the world for college students. Lists only programs of Council members. Indexes for country and field.

* Working with the Environment by Tim Ryder. 1996. 271 pp. Vacation Work. Available for $17.95 from Seven Hills. This new book provides the first survey of international environmental work possibilities, from volunteer to career. Addressed to a British audience, it provides in-depth coverage of Great Britain and Ireland, but also includes organizations (including U.S.-based ones) offering placements worldwide.

* A World of Options, edited by Christa Bucks (Mobility International USA, 3rd ed., 1997). $30 (members), $40 (non-members), $45 (organizations) from MIUSA, P.O. Box 10767, Eugene, OR 97440; (541) 343-1284, fax (541) 343-6812. A comprehensive guide to international exchange, study, and volunteer opportunities for people with disabilities.

Overviews By Geographic Area

** After Latin American Studies: A Guide to Graduate Study and Fellowships, Internships, and Employment by Shirley A. Kregar and Annabel Conroy. 1995. $10 (check payable to Univ. of Pittsburgh) postpaid from: Center for Latin American Studies, 4E04 Forbes Quad, Univ. of Pittsburgh, Pittsburgh, PA 15260; (412) 648-7392, fax (412) 648-2199; clas+@pitt.edu, www.pitt.edu/~clas. The essential resource for anyone with career or scholarly interests in this region—an information-packed bargain. Most listings not overseas. Extensive bibliography. Also available, free: **A Guide to Financial Assistance for Graduate Study, Dissertation Research and Internships for Students in Latin American Studies. 1996.

Beyond Safaris: A Guide to Building People-to-People Ties with Africa by Kevin Danaher. Africa World Press, Inc. 1991. 193 pp. $12.95 from Global Exchange. Tells how to build links between U.S. citizens and grassroots development efforts in Africa;

one brief chapter on volunteering and studying abroad.

Bridging the Global Gap: A Handbook to Linking Citizens of the First and Third Worlds by Medea Benjamin and Andrea Freedman. 1989. 338 pp. Seven Locks Press. $12.95 from Global Exchange. Information on ending hunger and poverty and building peaceful international ties through direct action. For overseas options see **The Peace Corps and More** (below).

** ** China Bound (Revised): A Guide to Life in the PRC** by Anne Thurston. 1994. 272 pp. National Academy of Sciences. $24.95 plus $4 shipping from National Academy Press, 2101 Constitution Ave. NW, Lockbox 285, Washington, DC 20055; (800) 624-6242. Updated classic on studying or teaching in the People's Republic of China. Invaluable for university students, researchers, and teachers.

* **Complete Guide to the Israel Experience.** Annual. Available from the World Zionist Organization, 110 E. 59th St., 3rd Fl., New York, NY 10022; (800) 274-7723, fax (212) 755-4781; usd@net-com.com,www.wzo. org.il.

* **The Directory of Work and Study In Developing Countries** by Toby Milner. 1997. 256 pp. Vacation Work. $16.95 from Seven Hills. Comprehensive guide to employment, voluntary work, and academic opportunities in developing countries.

** ** Japan: Exploring Your Options—A Guide to Work, Study and Research in Japan,** edited by Gretchen Shinoda and Nicholas Namba. 1995. 437 pp. $20 ($15 students) plus $5 shipping; (888) GNJAPAN or (703) 883-0504. A comprehensive directory of study, cultural, and homestay programs; fellowships and research; and teaching opportunities. A must for anyone interested in Japan. You can read the book online at www.gwjapan.com/html/xjeo.html.

Korea Calling by Allegra Specht and Jay Freeborne. 1997. $18 postpaid from Woodpecker Press, P.O. Box 2081, Pt. Townsend, WA 98368 (WA residents add $1.20). A comprehensive guide to living and working in Korea.

* **Living in China: A Guide to Teaching and Studying in China Including Taiwan** by R. Weiner, M. Murphy, and A. Li. 1997. 312 pp. $19.95 from China Books and Periodicals, Inc., 2929 24th St., San Francisco, CA 94110; (415) 282-2994, fax (415) 282-0994; info@chinabooks.com, www.china-books.com. Practical advice with extensive directories of schools and colleges as well as organizations which offer study abroad or teacher placement.

* **The Peace Corps and More: 120 Ways to Work, Study, and Travel in the Third World** by Medea Benjamin. 1996. 107 pp. Seven Locks Press. $6.95 from Global Exchange. Describes 120 programs that allow anyone to gain Third World experience while promoting the ideals of social justice and sustainable development. Lacks indexes.

* **The Post-Soviet Handbook: A Guide to Grassroots Organizations and Internet Resources in the Newly Independent States** by M. Holt Ruffin, Joan McCarter, and Richard Upjohn. 1996. 416 pp. Univ. of Washington Press. $19.95 plus $4 shipping from Center for Civil Society International, 2929 N.E. Blakely St., Seattle, WA 98105; (206)-523-4755, fax (206) 523-1974; ccsi@u.washington.edu, http://solar.rtd.utk.edu/~ccsi/ccsihome.html. Up-to-date source for organizations that may welcome volunteers.

* **Studying and Working in France: A Student Guide** by Russell Cousins, Ron Hallmark, and Ian Pickup. 1994. 314 pp. $17.95

from Manchester Univ. Press (U.S. distributor St. Martin's Press). Very useful information for directly enrolling in French universities or language courses; one brief chapter on working.

** **Travel Programs in Central America, 1995-96,** edited by Kim Harley and Ann Salzarulo-McGuigan. 1995 (revised annually). 91 pp. $8 postpaid from San Diego Interfaith Task Force on Central America (IFTF), c/o Ann Salzarulo-McGuigan, 56 Seaview Ave., North Kingston, RI 02852 (written orders only). Comprehensive guide to 250 organizations for study, conferences, environmental projects, human rights, and short- and long-term service in all fields. Essential for finding options in this region.

Short-Term Paid Work Abroad

The Au Pair & Nanny's Guide to Working Abroad by Susan Griffith and Sharon Legg. 1997. 304 pp. Vacation Work. $16.95 from Seven Hills. Practical, insightful advice on how to prepare for and find a child care job in another country. Lists agencies worldwide. **Work Your Way Around the World** (below) has some of this information.

** **Council Work Abroad.** Free brochure from Council Work Abroad, 205 E. 42nd St., New York, NY 10017-5706; (888) COUNCIL; wabrochure@ciee.org. Application for paying work exchange programs through Council, a large non-profit organization, for college students and recent grads in Britain, Canada, Costa Rica, France, Germany, Ireland, Jamaica, and New Zealand. Approx. 6,000 U.S. participants annually.

** **Council Work Abroad Participant's Handbooks** can be requested from Council at (888) COUNCIL by college study abroad or

career planning offices; otherwise for program participants only (not for sale).

* **The Directory of Overseas Summer Jobs,** edited by David Woodworth. Updated each Jan. 256 pp. Vacation Work. $15.95 from Peterson's Guides. More than 30,000 temporary jobs, paid and volunteer, in over 50 countries: who to contact, pay rates, how and when to apply. Valuable information on work permits required. Council, 205 E. 42nd St., New York, NY 10017-5706; (888) COUNCIL; wabrochure@ciee.org and AIPT, 10400 Little Patuxent Parkway, Suite 250, Columbia, MD 21044-3510; (410) 997-2200, fax (410) 992-3924; aipt@aipt.org; www.softaid .net/aipt/aipt.html can assist Americans in obtaining work permits.

* **The Directory of Summer Jobs in Britain (1996),** edited by David Woodworth. Updated each Jan. 255 pp. Vacation Work. $15.95 from Peterson's Guides. More than 30,000 jobs listed, ranging from internships, farming, and hotel work to volunteering. Listings include wages, qualifications, and contacts. Americans need a work permit—contact Council or AIPT.

Emplois d'Été en France (1996). Vac-Job, Paris. Updated annually. $14.95. Available from Ulysses Books. Lists temporary summer jobs in France, including names and addresses of employers. In French.

Employment in France for Students. 1991. Free from French Cultural Services, 972 5th Ave., New York NY 10021; (212) 439-1400, fax (212) 439-1455. Work regulations and work possibilities. Also free: **Au Pair Work in France.**

Le guide du Job-Trotter en France by Emmanuelle Rozenzweig. 1994. 204 pp. Dakota Editions (France). $18.95 from Ulysses Books. In French. Guide to temporary jobs in France.

Guide to Cruise Ship Jobs by George Reilly. 1994. 40 pp. $6.95 from Pilot Books. Step-by-step guidance.

How to Get a Job with a Cruise Line by Mary Fallon Miller. 1997. 208 pp. $17.95 ($24 foreign) from Ticket to Adventure, Inc., P.O. Box 41005, St. Petersburg, FL 33743; (800) 929-7447 or (813) 822-1515; ticket2@gte.net, www.artquarter.com/cruisejobs. Detailed information on how to apply plus tips from cruise line employees. Bibliography.

** **Work Your Way Around The World** by Susan Griffith. 1997. 512 pp. Vacation Work. $17.95 from Peterson's Guides. The authoritative (and only) guide to looking for short-term jobs while abroad. Extensive country-by-country narratives include first-hand reports.

* **Working Abroad (InterExchange).** Free brochure from InterExchange, Inc., 161 6th Ave., New York, NY 10013; (212) 924-0446, fax (212) 924-0575; interex@earthlink.net, www.interexchange.org. Non-profit program offers placements for paid work abroad, internships, English teaching, and au pair in Europe.

** **Working in Asia** by Nicki Grihault. In Print Publishing Ltd. (U.K.). 1996. 444 pp. $16.95 from Weatherhill, 568 Broadway, Suite 705, New York, NY 10012; Tel./fax (800) 557-5601. This is the first book to give an overview of all work options, from volunteer to teaching to career opportunities, throughout Asia—from the Indian subcontinent to Southeast Asia to Northern Asia. Includes specifics on U.S. and other organizations.

* **Working Holidays 1997.** Updated annually. 382 pp. Central Bureau (U.K.). $18.95 from IIE. Thoroughly researched information on 101,000 paid and voluntary work opportunities in over 70 countries. Written for a British audience, it sometimes omits relevant U.S. organizations.

Working in Ski Resorts—Europe and North America by Victoria Pybus. 1997. 304 pp. Vacation Work. $16.95 from Seven Hills. Available jobs plus reports from resorts.

* **Worldwide Internships and Service Education (WISE).** Free brochure from WISE, 303 S. Craig St., Suite 202, Pittsburgh, PA 15213; fax (412) 681-8187; wise@unix.cls.pitt.edu. Non-profit program offers experiential learning placements for au pair (Europe), service and internships (U.K.), farm work (Norway), and low-cost language immersion programs.

International Internships

** **Academic Year Abroad / Vacation Study Abroad** edited by Sara Steen. 1997 (revised annually). 650/432 pp. $42.95/$36.95 plus $5 shipping per book from Institute of International Education; (800) 445-0443. Indexes for internships, practical training, volunteering, and student teaching list over 1,100 programs, most of which charge tuition and give academic credit.

** **The ACCESS Guide to International Affairs Internships in the Washington, DC Area,** edited by Matthew T. Higham and Hilary Berkey. 1997. 146 pp. $19.95 plus $5 shipping from ACCESS, 1701 K St. NW, 11th Fl., Washington, DC 20006; (202) 223-7949, fax (202) 223-7947. Listings for 226 organizations and agencies (U.S. government, foreign embassies, international organizations, and nongovernmental agencies) in and around Washington, DC that offer internships in the field of international affairs. The most up-to-date directory for the city with the most internships in international affairs.

* **American-Scandinavian Foundation.** Free brochure on study and scholarships (all fields) and work opportunities. This non-profit organization also offers paid internships in Scandinavia in engineering,

teaching English as a foreign language, and agricultural fields. Apply for internships by late Dec. ASF also assists with obtaining work permits for Scandinavia. Contact ASF at 725 Park Ave., New York, NY 10021; (212) 879-9779, fax (212) 249-3444; asf@amscan.org.

** **Association for International Practical Training (AIPT) / International Association for the Exchange of Students for Technical Experience (IAESTE).** Free brochures. Non-profit organization provides paid internships in over 60 countries in engineering and science (apply by Dec 10), and in tourism and hotel and restaurant management. They can also assist in obtaining work permits for career-related practical training in other fields. Contact them at 10400 Little Patuxent Parkway, Suite 250, Columbia, MD 21044-3510; (410) 997-2200, fax (410) 992-3924; aipt@aipt.org; www.softaid.net/aipt/aipt.html.

* **CDS International, Inc.** Non-profit organization offers several paying internship programs (deadlines as early as Dec) in Germany in fields ranging from business to engineering. Knowledge of German necessary. CDS also assists with obtaining work permits for Germany. Contact them at 330 Seventh Ave., New York, NY 10001; (212) 760-1400, fax (212) 268-1288; www.cdsintl.org.

* **Center for Interim Programs.** Free information from CIP, P.O. Box 2347, Cambridge, MA 02238; (617) 547-0980, fax (617) 661-2864; interimcip@aol.com. Organization provides placements in approx. 3,000 "non-academic but structured" opportunities, from internships to teaching, worldwide for people aged 16-70. Some provide room and board.

* **Development Opportunities Catalog: A Guide to Internships, Research, and Employment with Development Organizations,** edited by Sri Indah Prihadi. 1993 (1996 insert,

$5). 127 pp. $7 (students), $10 (individuals), $15 (institutions) plus $1.50 shipping from Overseas Development Network, 333 Valencia St., Suite 330, San Francisco, CA 94103; (415) 431-4204; odn@igc.org. Descriptions of 79 development organizations offering internships or staff positions in the U.S. (and a few abroad). Indexed by subject and location. Also available from ODN, a nationwide student organization for development issues: **Career Opportunities in International Development in Washington, D.C.,** edited by Brian Dunn. 1994. 98 pp. $6 (students), $9 (individuals), $12 (institutions). **Opportunities in Grassroots Development in California,** edited by Wesley Batten. 1994. 89 pp. $7 (students), $10 (individuals), $15 (institutions). **Opportunities in International Development in New England,** edited by Michelle Burts. 1993. $7 (students), $10 (individuals), $15 (institutions). Add $1.50 shipping for each book. In addition ODN offers directories, information packs, and research services related to volunteer and internship opportunities.

Directory of International Internships: A World of Opportunities by Charles Gliozzo, Vernicka Tyson, Adela Pena, and Bob Dye. 1994. 168 pp. Michigan State University. $25 postpaid from Career Development and Placement Services, Attn: International Placement, MSU, 113 Student Services Bldg., East Lansing, MI 48824; (517) 355-9510 ext. 371. Describes experiential educational opportunities offered through educational institutions, government, and private organizations—for academic credit, for pay, or simply for experience. Indexed by subject and country, this is the only directory listing academic and non-academic internships located abroad.

* **The Directory of Summer Jobs in Britain** edited by David Woodworth. Updated each Jan. 255 pp. Vacation Work. $15.95 from Peterson's Guides. Includes listings of intern-

ships in Britain ("traineeships"). The **CIEE/ BUNAC Work in Britain Participant's Handbook** is an even better source.

The Guide to International Affairs Internships: Europe and the Former Soviet Union, edited by Matthew T. Higham. 1997 (forthcoming). 150 pp. $25 plus $5 shipping from ACCESS, 1701 K St. NW, 11th Fl., Washington, DC 20006; (202) 223-7949, fax (202) 223-7947. Contains listings for organizations in Europe and the successor states of the former Soviet Union that provide internships in the field of international affairs. Includes information on visa requirements and language skills needed. Produced in cooperation with women in International Security, Univ. of Maryland at College Park.

* **A Handbook for Creating Your Own Internship in International Development** by Natalie Folster and Nicole Howell. 1994. 98 pp. $7.95 plus $1.50 shipping from Overseas Development Network, 333 Valencia St., Suite 330, San Francisco, CA 94103; (415) 431-4204; odn@igc.org. How to arrange a position; evaluate your skills, motivations and learning objectives. Not a directory of opportunities.

* **International Cooperative Education Program.** Free information from ICE, 15 Spiros Way, Menlo Park CA 94025; (650) 323-4944, fax (650) 323-1104; ICEmenlo@aol.com. Organization offers 450 paid summer internships for students with knowledge of foreign languages in Europe, Asia. U.S. or Canadian citizens only. Apply in fall or winter.

International Directory of Youth Internships by Michael Culligan and Cynthia T. Morehouse. 1993. 52 pp. $7.50 plus $3.50 shipping from Apex Press, Publications Office, P.O. Box 337, Croton-on-Hudson, NY 10520; Tel./fax (914) 271-6500. Comprehensive guide to U.N. agencies and U.N.-affiliated organizations that regularly use interns and volunteers. Most internships are in the U.S. and unpaid.

International Health Electives for Medical Students. 1993. American Medical Student Association. $31 ($21 members) for 4-volume set, also available separately, from AMSA Publications, 1902 Association Dr., Reston, VA 20191; (703) 620-6600 ext. 217, fax (703) 620-5873; amsatf@amsa.org, www.amsa.org. Overseas internships for third- or fourth-year medical students. Related titles, **A Student's Guide to International Health** ($7.50/$5.50) and **Cross-Cultural Medicine: What to Know Before You Go** ($7/$5), also available from AMSA.

* **The Internship Bible** by Mark Oldman and Samer Hamadeh. 1995. 614 pp. $25 by Princeton Review—Random House, available through Velarde Publicity; (212) 572-2870, fax (212) 572-6026; interninfo@aol.com. New directory describes in detail paid and unpaid internships offered by more than 900 mostly non-academic organizations. Around 120 of these may offer overseas internships, listed in an index for location. Other indexes for field, benefits, level of study, minority programs, and deadlines.

* **Internships International.** Free information from Judy Tilson, Director, 1116 Cowper Dr., Raleigh, NC 27608; Tel./fax (919) 832-1575; intintl@aol.com, http://rtpnet.org/ ~intlintl. Organization offers unpaid, not-for-credit internship placements for college graduates in London, Paris, Stuttgart, Florence, Dublin, Madrid, Melbourne, Budapest, and Santiago.

Mexico: Oportunidades de Empleo. 1997 (revised annually). Available from American Chamber of Commerce of Mexico, Lucerna 78, Col. Juárez, 06600 México, D.F.; (011) 52 724-3800, fax 703-3908 or 703-2911. Lists internships in Mexico for Mexican and U.S. students.

* U.S. Department of State Student Intern Program. Free brochure and application from U.S. Department of State, Student Intern Program, Recruitment Division, Box 9317, Arlington, VA 22219; (703) 875-4884; www.state.gov. Nearly 1,000 unpaid and paid internships annually in Washington and abroad. Only for currently-enrolled undergraduate and graduate students who will continue studies after the internship. Competitive. Deadlines: Nov 1 (summer), Mar 1 (fall), Jul 1 (spring).

* A Year Between: The Complete International Guide to Work, Training, and Travel in a Year Out. Central Bureau (U.K.). 1994 (new edition, 1997). 288 pp. $18.95 from IIE. Addressed to a British audience, this book describes over 100 internships, teaching, and volunteer possibilities of up to 1 year, primarily in Britain and Europe.

Teaching English Abroad

Asia Employment Program. (See **Now Hiring!: Jobs in Asia** below.)

The ELT Guide. 1996. 216 pp. $19.95. Comprehensive reference for English language teaching worldwide. Country-by-country guide with recruitment information, school listings, and training courses. Order from TESOL, 1600 Cameron St., Suite 300, Alexandria, VA 22314; (703) 836-0774, fax (703) 836-6447; publ@tesol.edu, www.tesol.edu. Also publishes the The ESL/EFL Job Search Handbook (edited by Adelaide Parsons, 1995. 92 pp. $19.95 + $3.50 s/h) and The Directory of Professional Programs in TESOL in the U.S. and Canada (1995, 300 pp., $34.95 + $3.50 s/h).

English in Asia: Teaching Tactics for the Classrooms of Japan, Korea, Taiwan by John Wharton. 1992. 214 pp. $12.95 plus $2 shipping ($4 first-class) from Global Press, 697

College Pkwy., Rockville, MD 20850; (202) 466-1663. Overview of teaching methodologies and practical details of living in Japan, Korea, and Taiwan. Extensive lists of schools.

* Fulbright English Teaching Assistantships. Applications free from USIA Fulbright, U.S. Student Program, 809 United Nations Plaza, New York, NY 10017-3580; (212) 984-5330. Enrolled students should apply through own college. English teaching options for graduates in Belgium/Luxembourg, France, Germany, Hungary, Korea, and Taiwan. Application deadline is Oct 23, 1996 (1 month earlier through campuses) for teaching in 1997-98.

** Japan Exchange Teaching Program (JET). FREE brochures. Office of the JET Program, Embassy of Japan, 2520 Massachusetts Ave. NW, Washington, DC 20008; (202) 939-6772 or (202) 939-6773 or (800) INFO-JET, or contact any Japanese embassy or consulate. The largest program for teaching English abroad, with more than 4,000 placements annually. Offers 2 types of positions in Japan: English-teaching assistantships in secondary schools or Coordinator for International Relations (latter requires Japanese proficiency). Application deadline early Dec.

** Japan: Exploring Your Options—A Guide to Work, Study and Research in Japan. edited by Gretchen Shinoda and Nicholas Namba. 1995. 437 pp. $20 ($15 students) plus $5 shipping; (888) GNJAPAN or (703) 883-0504. Detailed descriptions of English teaching possibilities, through both U.S.- and Japan-based organizations.

Jobs in Japan: The Complete Guide to Living and Working in the Land of Rising Opportunity by John Wharton. 1993. 270 pp. $14.95 plus $2 shipping ($4 first-class) from Global Press, 697 College Pkwy., Rockville,

MD 20850; (202) 466-1663. More about the details of living in Japan than on teaching. Recent users say it makes the on-site job search sound easier than it now is.

The Korea Super Job Catalog by James F. Haddon. 1993. 215 pp. Bonus Books. $13 postpaid from Korea Services Group, 2950 S.E. Stark, Suite 200, Portland, OR 97214; (503) 230-6932, fax (503) 233-9966; tricia@e-z.net. Practical guide to jobs in Korea for non-Koreans; lists hundreds of employers in most fields. KSG also offers placements, primarily for English teachers.

* **Living in China: A Guide to Teaching and Studying in China Including Taiwan** by R. Weiner, M. Murphy, and A. Li. 1997. 312 pp. $19.95 from China Books and Periodicals, Inc., 2929 24th St., San Francisco, CA 94110; (415) 282-2994, fax (415) 282-0994; info@chinabooks.com, www.chinabooks.com. Useful tips and hundreds of addresses for anyone who wants to teach English in China or Taiwan; wait for new edition.

Make a Mil-¥en: Teaching English in Japan by Don Best. 1994. 176 pp. $14.95 plus $2 (book rate) or $3.50 (first-class) shipping from Stone Bridge Press, P.O. Box 8208, Berkeley, CA 94707; (800) 947-7271, fax (510) 524-8711; sbp@stonebridge.com, www.stonebridge.com. Guide has up-to-date information on everything from the job search to settling in.

* **More Than a Native Speaker: An Introduction for Volunteers Teaching Abroad** by Don Snow. 1996. 320 pp. $29.95 plus $3.50 shipping from TESOL (see below). Comprehensive source of ideas and techniques for ESL/EFC teaching.

Native Speaker: Teach English and See the World by Elizabeth Reid. 1996. 93 pp. $7.95 plus $3 shipping from In One Ear Publications, P.O. Box 637, Campo, CA 91906; (800) 356-9315. Guide by an American who taught

English in Latin America; main focus on teaching tips.

* **Now Hiring! Jobs in Asia** by Jennifer Dubois, Steve Gutman, and Clarke Canfield. 1994. 289 pp. $17.95 from Perpetual Press, P.O. Box 45628, Seattle, WA 98145-0628. Guide to finding an English teaching job in Japan, South Korea, or Taiwan. Lists U.S. placement organizations and overseas schools. Some information on living and teaching abroad. Similar **Asia Employment Program**, (several authors are the same) is direct-marketed for $50, supposedly with a guarantee of employment, by Progressive Media Inc., P.O. Box 45220, Seattle, WA 98145-0220. Perpetual Press also publishes *Now Hiring! Jobs in Eastern Europe** by Clarke Canfield. 1996. 330 pp. $14.95.

* **O-Hayo Sensei: The Newsletter of Teaching Jobs in Japan.** edited by Lynn Cullivan. Bi-weekly listings by e-mail, $1 per issue or free on the Web. Contact: Editor, O-Hayo Sensei, 1032 Irving St., Suite 508, San Francisco, CA 94122; fax (415) 731-1113; editor@ohayosensei, www.ohayosensei.com.

Opportunities in Teaching English to Speakers of Other Languages by Blyth Camenson. 1995. 143 pp. $11.95 from VGM Career Horizons. Overview of the professional field of Teaching English as a Foreign/Second Language.

Teach Central Europe by Stephanie Hinton and Judy Moore. 1995. 184 pp. $19.95 plus $4.75 shipping from Teach Central Europe, 536 Mosswood Shoals, Stone Mountain, GA 30087; outside U.S.: Teach Central Europe, Belgicka 36, 120 00 Praha 2, Czech Republic; (011) 422 2423-1730, fax 2423-1731. Over 400 addresses of schools and universities which supposedly offer English teaching positions; little information about living or teaching there.

Teach English in Japan by Charles Wordell and Greta Gorsuch. 1992. 212 pp. Japan Times. $18.25 plus $5 shipping from

Kinokuniya Book Store, 10 W. 49th St., New York, NY 10020; (212) 765-1461. Valuable for its realistic reports by experienced American teachers; no job search information.

The Teach English in Mexico Employment Guide by Mark S. Farley. 1997. 33 pp. $14.95 + $4 s/h from Inter/Networks, Order Dept., 3023 N. Clark St., #791, Chicago, IL 60657; www.employnow.com/Mexico.htm. Most of this overpriced booklet is devoted to basic travel tips; only a few pages cover teaching.

** **Teaching English Abroad: Talk Your Way Around the World** by Susan Griffith. Vacation Work. 1994 (new edition Jan 1997). 368 pp. $16.95 from Peterson's Guides. The only guide with extensive worldwide coverage (including Western and Eastern Europe, the Middle East, and other regions ignored in other guides), this outstanding volume gives in-depth information on everything from preparation to the job search. Extensive directories of schools.

* **Teaching English in Asia: Finding a Job and Doing it Well** by Galen Harris Valle. 1995. 178 pp. $19.95 from Pacific View Press, P.O. Box 2657, Berkeley, CA 94702. Detailed yet lively overview of teaching English in East and S.E. Asia, with comprehensive teaching tips, by a professional teacher. Few contact addresses provided.

Teaching English Guides (Passport Books/In Print Publishing series). Books in this British series offer extensive advice by professional teachers on teaching and living abroad, tailored to the specific regions covered. All would be valuable for teachers headed abroad, but provide few job search addresses. Available in the U.S. from Passport Books, 4255 W. Touhy Ave., Lincolnwood, IL 60646; (800) 323-4900; elsewhere from In Print Publishing Ltd., 9 Beufort Terrace, Brighton BN2 2SU, U.K.; (011) 44 1273 682836, fax 620958.

* **Teaching English in Asia** by Jerry and Nuala O'Sullivan. 1996. $14.95. Covers PR China, Hong Kong, India, Indonesia, Japan, South Korea, Malaysia, Philippines, Singapore, Taiwan, Thailand, and Vietnam.

Teaching English in Italy by Martin Penner. 1996. $14.95. Note that the job search in Italy will be extremely difficult for citizens of non-European-Union countries.

** **Teaching English** in Eastern & Central Europe by Robert Lynes. 1996. $14.95. The only book to date with extensive coverage of this region, including Bulgaria, the Czech and Slovak Republics, Hungary, Poland, and Romania.

* **Teaching English in Japan** by Jerry O'Sullivan. 1996. $14.95.

TESOL Placement Bulletin. TESOL members: $21/year hard copy, $26/year electronic copy; nonmembers: $27/year hard copy, $32/year electronic copy. Monthly bulletin lists position openings for qualified ESL/EFL teachers and administrators. Also includes resume bank. TESOL, 1600 Cameron St., Suite 300, Alexandria, VA 22314; (703) 836-0774, fax (703) 836-6447; place@tesol.edu, www.tesol. edu.

** **Work Abroad: the Complete Guide to Finding Work Overseas** 1997. 221 pp. $15.95 plus $4 s/h from Transitions Abroad. Comprehensive book with informative articles and hundreds of contacts essential for success in the international workplace.

** **Working in Asia.** (See description in Short-Term Paid Work, above.)

Teaching Abroad: K-12 And University-Level

** **China Bound (Revised): A Guide to Life in the PRC** by Anne Thurston. 1994. 272 pp. National Academy of Sciences. $24.95 plus

$4 shipping from National Academy Press, 2101 Constitution Ave. NW, Lockbox 285, Washington, DC 20055; (800) 624-6242. Invaluable for university students, researchers and teachers.

* College Teaching Abroad: A Handbook of Strategies for Successful Cross-Cultural Exchanges by Pamela Gale George. 256 pp. Longwood (hardcover). $35.95 plus $649 shipping from Allyn and Bacon, 160 Gould St., Needham Heights, MA 02194; (800) 278-3525. Thought-provoking yet practical guide to the cross-cultural dimensions of teaching abroad, based on the reports of 700 Fulbright exchange participants. Essential reading for any teacher headed overseas.

* Fulbright Teacher Exchange: Opportunities Abroad for Educators. Free information from the U.S. Information Agency, Fulbright Teacher Exchange Program, 600 Maryland Ave. S.W., Room 235, Washington, DC 20024-2520; (800) 726-0479, fax (202) 401-1433; advise@usia.gov. Program descriptions and application for direct exchanges in over 30 countries for currently employed K-12 and community college faculty and administrators.

* Fulbright Scholar Program: Grants for U.S. Faculty and Professionals. Free information from Council for International Exchange of Scholars, 3007 Tilden St. NW, Suite 5M, Washington, DC 20008-3009; (202) 686-7877; info@ciesnet.cies.org. Information and application for university-level opportunities for lecturing and research abroad; most positions require doctoral degrees and/or equivalent professional experience. Deadlines for 1998-99: Aug 1 (lecturing and research awards); Nov 1 (international education administrators); Jan 1, 1998 (NATO scholars).

The International Educator. Fifty-page newspaper published quarterly. Annual subscription $25. TIE, P.O. Box 513, Cummaquid, MA 02637; (508) 362-1414, fax (508) 362-1411; tie@capecod.net. Each issue features an "Educators Wanted" section where American and international schools advertise their teaching and administrative vacancies. These schools are generally K-12 schools, all taught in English.

* The ISS Directory of Overseas Schools, edited by Gina Parziale. 1996. 531 pp. International Schools Services. $34.95 from Peterson's Guides, or ISS Inc., P.O. Box 5910, Princeton, NJ 08543; (609) 452-0990, fax (609) 452-2690; edustaffing@iss.edu, www.iss.edu. The most comprehensive and up-to-date directory to overseas K-12 schools that hire qualified American teachers. Available FREE from ISS: NewsLinks, a bimonthly news magazine for the international school community; and Teaching and Administrative Opportunities Abroad, application to ISS job fairs (apply in Nov) for teaching overseas.

Overseas Academic Opportunities. Monthly bulletin. $38/year from Overseas Academic Opportunities, 72 Franklin Ave., Ocean Grove, NJ 07756; Tel./fax (908) 774-1040. Openings primarily for new teachers in all K-12 subject areas for jobs where the only language needed is English and state certification is not required.

Overseas American-Sponsored Elementary Schools Assisted by the U.S. Department of State. Free 30-page pamphlet available from the Office of Overseas Schools, Room 245, SA-29, U.S. Department of State, Washington, DC 20522-2902; (703) 875-7800. Information on private overseas K-12 schools. Fact Sheets, also free, provide more detailed information.

Overseas Employment Opportunities for Educators. Annual. Free from Department of Defense Dependents Schools, Teacher Recruitment Section, 4040 N Fairfax Dr., Alexandria, VA 22203; (703) 696-3255. Application for K-12 employment opportunities in over 200 schools worldwide serving U.S. military bases. Minimum academic requirement is a baccalaureate degree with at least 18 hours of education courses.

* Overseas Placement Service for Educators. Registration materials for one of the two largest U.S. placement fairs (the other is ISS, above) for certified K-12 teachers. $5 from Overseas Placement Service for Educators, Univ. of Northern Iowa, Cedar Falls, IA 50614-0390; (319) 273-2083, fax (319) 273-6998; overseas.placemnt@uni.edu, www.uni.edu/placement/student/internat.html. The Fair, held each Feb, attracts over 100 American international schools. Fact book and newsletters are included with registration.

Overseas Teaching Opportunities. Friends of World Teaching. $20 for first three country lists, $4 for each additional country from Friends of World Teaching, P.O. Box 1049, San Diego, CA 92112-1049; (800) 503-7436; fowt@worldnet.att.net. List of over 1,000 English-speaking schools in over 100 countries where educators may apply.

1998-99 Schools Abroad of Interest to Americans. ISBN 0-87558-138-2, 9th ed. 1998. $45 plus $4.50 shipping from Porter Sargent Publishers, 11 Beacon St., Suite 1400, Boston, MA 02108. Descriptive listings of 800 elementary and secondary schools enrolling American and English-speaking students in 130 countries.

Teach Abroad. Central Bureau (U.K.). 1993. 192 pp. $18.95 from IIE. Addressed to a British audience, this Central Bureau publication is a guide to work and volunteer teaching opportunities, including teacher exchanges.

Teaching Opportunities in the Middle East and North Africa. 1987. 222 pp. $18 from AMIDEAST, 1730 M St. N.W., Suite 1100, Washington, DC 20036-4045; (202) 776-9600, fax (202) 776-7000. Still-useful survey of 140 K-12 and postsecondary institutions.

Teaching Overseas: The Caribbean and Latin American Area, edited by Carlton H. Bowyer and Burton Fox. 1989. 106 pp. $4 from Inter-Regional Center for Curriculum and Materials Development, P.O. Box 013449, Tuscaloosa, AL 35403. Comprehensive handbook on teaching in 30 U.S.-sponsored schools in Latin America and the Caribbean.

Workplace. Central Bureau (U.K.). 1997. 224 pp. $18.95 from IIE. Addressed to a British audience, this new publication is a guide to work experience, internships, and practical training.

Volunteer Abroad

** Working in Asia. (See description in Short-Term Paid Work, above.)

** Alternatives to the Peace Corps: A Directory of Third World and U.S. Volunteer Opportunities by Phil Lowenthal, Stephanie Tarnoff, and Lisa David. 1996. 88 pp. $9.95 plus $4 shipping from Food First Books, 398 60th St., Oakland, CA 94618; (510) 654-4400 (book orders 800-274-7826); fax (541) 847-6018; foodfirst@igc.apc.org. Thoroughly researched guide to voluntary service, study, and alternative travel overseas and in the U.S. with organizations which "address the political and economic causes of poverty." Excellent bibliography.

Archaeological Fieldwork Opportunities Bulletin, compiled by Susanna Burns. 144 pp. Updated each Jan. Archaeological Institute of America. $9 for AIA members ($11 non-members) from Kendall/Hunt Publishing Co., Order Dept., 4050 Westmark Dr., P.O. Box 1840, Dubuque, IA 52004-1840; (800) 228-0810. Comprehensive guide to excavations, field schools, and programs worldwide with openings for volunteers, students, and staff. AIA also publishes **Archaeology** magazine, which lists volunteer opportunities in the Old World (Mar/Apr) and the New World (May/Jun). For membership in AIA or subscriptions, call (617) 353-9361 or fax (617) 353-6550.

Archaeology Abroad, 31-34 Gordon Square, London WC1H 0PY, U.K. Three annual bulletins (Mar, May, and Oct). Lists worldwide projects and provides details on staffing needs.

Directory of Volunteer Opportunities, edited by Kerry L. Mahoney. 1992. 90 pp. CAN$10 (Canadian residents $10.70) in advance from Volunteer Directory, Career Resource Centre, Univ. of Waterloo, Waterloo, ON N2L 3G1, Canada; (519) 885-1211 ext. 3001. Over 100 listings of part- and full-time volunteer opportunities in North America and overseas. Especially useful for Canadians.

From the Center of the Earth: Stories out of the Peace Corps, edited by Geraldine Kennedy. 1991. 223 pp. $12.95 from Clover Park Press, P.O. Box 5067, Santa Monica, CA 90409-5067. Interesting accounts by Peace Corps volunteers.

Going Places: A Catalog of Domestic and International Internship, Volunteer, Travel and Career Opportunities in the Fields of Hunger, Housing, Homelessness and Grassroots Development by Joanne Woods. 1991 (new edition, 1997). 63 pp. $6.25 postpaid from National Student Campaign Against Hunger and Homelessness, 11965 Venice Blvd., #408, Los Angeles, CA 90066; (800) NOHUNGE or (310) 397-5270 ext. 324; fax (310) 391-0053. Well-researched descriptions of more than 90 organizations and selected graduate programs.

* **How to Serve and Learn Effectively: Students Tell Students** by Howard Berry and Linda Chisholm. 1992. 77 pp. $7.00 from Partnership for Service Learning, 815 2nd Ave., Suite 315, New York, NY 10017, (212) 986-0989, fax (212) 986-5039; pslny@aol.com. Reality-testing and exploration of motivations for students considering volunteering overseas. Not a directory of opportunities.

* **InterAction Member Profiles 1995-1996.** 1995. 350 pp. $40 ($20 members) from Interaction Publications, 1717 Massachusetts Ave. NW, Suite 801, Washington, DC 20036; (202) 667-8227, fax (202) 667-8236; iac@interaction. org. Up-to-date information on 150 U.S. private voluntary organizations in relief and development work. Details which agencies are doing what in which countries. Also by Interaction: **Monday Developments.** $65 per year (individuals); $275 per year (institutions). Biweekly job listing in this field. **The Essential Internet.** 47 pp. $12. Also see Internet Resources section below.

* **The International Directory of Voluntary Work** by David Woodworth. 1997. 272 pp. Vacation Work. $15.95 from Peterson's Guides. Directory of over 500 agencies offering volunteer jobs and how to apply. Most comprehensive listing of volunteer opportunities in Britain and Europe of any directory.

* **International Voluntary Service Guide: Peace Through Deeds, Not Words.** Updated each Apr. $5 postpaid from SCI-IVS, 5474 Walnut Level Rd., Crozet, VA 22932; (804) 823-1826, fax (804) 823-5027; sciivsusa@igc.apc.org. Describes short-term volunteer options in Europe, Africa, Asia, and North America available through SCI-IVS.

* **International Workcamper (VFP).** Free brochure available from Volunteers for Peace (VFP), International Workcamps, 43 Tiffany Rd., Belmont, VT 05730; (802) 259-2759, fax (802) 259-2922; vfp@vfp.org, www.vfp.org. The **VFP International Workcamp Directory** (136 pp.), available each Apr for $15 from VFP, describes over 900 short-term service placements in over 65 countries available through VFP for the summer and fall of the year of publication.

* International Volunteer Projects (Council). Free brochure available from Council, 205 E. 42nd St., New York, NY 10017-5706; (888) COUNCIL or (212) 822-2695; IVPBr ochure@ciee.org, www.ciee.org. Describes over 600 short-term summer voluntary service options available through Council in 23 countries of Europe, Africa, and North America. The **Council International Volunteer Projects Directory** (82 pp.), available each Apr for $12 postpaid, describes the workcamps in depth.

* **Kibbutz Volunteer** by Victoria Pybus. 1997. 192 pp. Vacation Work. $15.95 from Seven Hills. Now the most up-to-date resource on volunteering in Israel. New edition lists over 200 kibbutzim at different sites in Israel; also includes information on work on a moshav and other employment opportunities in Israel.

** **Peace Corps Information Packet.** Free from Peace Corps, 1990 K St. NW, Room 8508, Washington, DC 20526; (800) 424-8580 code 824; www.peacecorps.gov. The largest U.S. volunteer-sending organization, with approx. 3,000 placements annually. Two-year assignment. One of the best job opportunities (paid, too) in the developing world and Eastern Europe for Americans. Apply 9 to 12 months prior to availability. Volunteers receive transportation to and from assignment, a stipend, health care, and $5,400 after 27 months of service.

* **The Post-Soviet Handbook: A Guide to Grassroots Organizations and Internet Resources in the Newly Independent States** by M. Holt Ruffin, Joan McCarter, and Richard Upjohn. 1996. 416 pp. Univ. of Washington Press. $19.95 plus $4 shipping from Center for Civil Society International, 2929 N.E. Blakely St., Seattle, WA 98105; (206) 523-4755, fax (206) 523-1974; ccsi@u. washington.edu, http://solar.rtd.utk.edu/~ccsi/ccsihome.html. Most up-to-date source for organizations which may welcome volunteers.

* **Response: Volunteer Opportunities Directory of the Catholic Network of Volunteer Service.** 1997. 90 pp. Free (donations accepted) from CNVS, 4121 Harewood Rd. NE, Washington, DC 20017; (800) 543-5046 or (202) 529-1100, fax (202) 526-1094; cnvs@ari.net. Directory also on-line at www2.ari.net/home3/cnvs/. Directory of lay mission opportunities in the U.S. and abroad. Indexes by type of placement, location, length of time, couples, parents, etc.

** **Travel Programs in Central America,** edited by Kim Harley and Ann Salzarulo-McGuigan. 1995 (revised annually). 91 pp. $8 postpaid from San Diego Interfaith Task Force on Central America (IFTF), c/o Ann Salzarulo-McGuigan, 56 Seaview Ave., North Kingston, RI 02852 (written orders only). The most comprehensive listing of volunteer opportunities in this region.

** **Volunteer: The Comprehensive Guide to Voluntary Service in the U.S. and Abroad,** edited by Richard Christiano. 1995. 188 pp. $12.95 from Council. Detailed descriptions of nearly 200 voluntary service organizations recruiting volunteers for work in the U.S. and abroad. Organized by short- and long-term opportunities, with indexes by country and type of work. Absolutely the best place to start exploring volunteer options.

* **Volunteer & Internship Possibilities in Israel,** by Leon Dow. 1994. $10 postpaid from Univ. Student Department, American Zionist Youth Foundation, 110 E. 59th St., 3rd Floor, New York, NY 10022; (800) 274-7723.

* **Volunteer Vacations: Short-Term Adventures That Will Benefit You and Others** by Bill McMillon. 1997. 480 pp. $16.95 from Chicago Review Press, 814 N. Franklin St., Chicago, IL 60610; (312) 337-0747. Describes more than 250 organizations sponsoring projects in the U.S. and abroad. Indexed by cost, length of time, location, type of project, and season. Opportunities from 1 weekend to 6 weeks.

* **Volunteer Work: The Complete International Guide to Medium & Long-Term Voluntary Service.** Central Bureau (U.K.). 1995. 240 pp. Available for $18.95 from IIE. A thoroughly researched British survey of volunteer possibilities worldwide, with many listings not found elsewhere. Indexed by country and type of work.

International Careers

The Adventure of Working Abroad: Hero Tales From the Global Frontier by Joyce Sautters Osland. 1995. 269 pp. $25 from Jossey-Bass Inc., 350 Sansome St., 5th Fl., San Francisco, CA 94104; (800) 956-7739. Thirty-five American expatriates assigned abroad tell about the perils and opportunities of working in a new culture. Suggestions for employers and employees for preparation, support, and reentry.

** **The Almanac of International Jobs and Careers: A Guide to Over 1001 Employers** by Ronald Krannich and Caryl Krannich. 1994. 334 pp. $19.95 from Impact Publications. Companion volume to **The Complete Guide to International Jobs and Careers**, this is a comprehensive source of hard-to-find information, tips on other resources, and trends in international employment for Americans.

* **American Jobs Abroad** by Victoria Harlow and Edward Knappman. 1994. 882 pp. $65 from Visible Ink Press, a division of Gale Research Inc., 835 Penobscot Bldg., Detroit, MI 48226-4094; (800) 776-6265, fax (313) 961-6083. The only directory listing the number of Americans working abroad for specific organizations; most employees worked in the U.S. before being assigned abroad. Gives con-

tact information. Useful indexes by country and job category. Out-of-print but copies available from Gale or Impact Publications.

Building an Import/Export Business by Kenneth D. Weiss. 1997. $19.95 from John Wiley & Sons. Detailed guide to entering the import/export business.

* **The Canadian Guide to Working and Living Overseas** by Jean-Marc Hachey. 1995 (new edition, Jan 1998). 1,000 pp. $37 postpaid from Intercultural Systems, P.O. Box 588, Station B, Ottawa, ON K1P 5P7, Canada; (800) 267-0105 or (613) 238-6169, fax (613) 238-5274; www.international-careers.com. The most comprehensive single volume on working and living abroad; listings emphasize Canadian organizations. Americans can benefit from the thorough overseas job-search advice, and from the most extensive bibliography anywhere—describing 550 publications.

Career Opportunities for Bilinguals and Multilinguals: A Directory of Resources in Education, Employment, and Business by Vladmir Wertsman. 1994. 308 pp. $35 plus $3 shipping from Scarecrow Press, 4720 Boston Way, Lanham, MD 20706; (800) 462-6420. Lists thousands of local organizations across the U.S. that may need people with foreign language skills. Cross-indexed by location and language.

Careers for Foreign Language Aficionados and Other Multilingual Types by Ned Seelye and Laurence Day. 1992. 114 pp. $12.95 from VGM Career Horizons. Mainstream and offbeat jobs for those who want to use a foreign language. Includes profiles.

** **Careers in International Affairs,** edited by Maria Pinto Carland and Michael Trucano. 1996. 320 pp. $17.95 plus $4.75 shipping from Georgetown Univ. Press, P.O. Box 4866, Hampden Station, Baltimore, MD 21211-0866; (800) 246-9606, fax (410) 516-6998.

New edition is the most up-to-date U.S. overview of international career fields; provides survey-based specifics on major organizations in all international sectors. Highly recommended.

Careers In International Business by Edward J. Halloran. 1995. 97 pp. $12.95 from VGM. Overview of education for international business and types of opportunities, from employment to entreprenuers.

Careers in International Law, edited by Mark W. Janis. 1993. 229 pp. $19.95 plus $3.95 shipping from American Bar Association, ABA Orders and billing Services, P.O. Box 10892, Chicago, IL 60611; (312) 988-5522. Essays on how to plan for a career in international law by lawyers in the field. Also lists ABA-approved study abroad programs.

** The Complete Guide to International Jobs and Careers by Ronald L. Krannich and Caryl R. Krannich. 1992. 306 pp. $13.95 from Impact Publications. The best introduction to strategies and skills for landing an international job in the 1990s, along with listings of resources for researching international employers.

Directory of American Firms Operating in Foreign Countries. 1996. $220 plus $9.50 s/h from Uniworld, 257 Central Park West, Suite 10A, New York, NY 10024-4110; Tel./fax (212) 496-2448, fax (212) 769-0413. Lists 3,000 American companies with subsidiaries and affiliates in 138 foreign countries. Check your local library for this and dozens of other expensive specialized international directories that are beyond the scope of this bibliography. Impact Publications also carries many of these. Individual and regional directories are also available ($29) that contain information for employment overseas.

* The Directory of Jobs and Careers Abroad, edited by André DeVries. 1997. 352 pp. Vacation Work Publications. $16.95 from

Peterson's Guides. The only career guide with country-by-country coverage of everything from professional fields to short-term and volunteer possibilities. British publication, but usually includes relevant U.S. organizations.

Directory of Opportunities in International Law, edited by Paul Brinkman. 1992. 204 pp. $20 ($10 for students) from John Bassett Moore Society of International Law, Univ. of Virginia School of Law, Charlottesville, VA 22901; (804) 924-3087. Law firms, agencies, and organizations with international practices, and a partial list of U.S. law schools that provide international training.

* Directory of U.S. Based Agencies Involved in International Health Assistance. 1996. 254 pp. $65 ($35 members) postpaid from National Council for International Health, 1701 K St. NW, Suite 600, Washington, DC 20006; (202) 833-5900, fax (202) 833-0075; ncih@ncih.org. Lists organizations in international health fields by specialty and location. **Career Network** ($120 non-members, $60 members per year) is the NCIH job bulletin.

Employment Abroad: Facts and Fallacies, edited by Rachel Theus. 1993. $7.50 plus $3 shipping from the International Division of the U.S. Chamber of Commerce, 1615 H St. NW, Washington, DC 20062; (202) 463-5460, fax (202) 463-3114; www. uschamber. org. Booklet stresses the realities of international employment.

Evaluating an Overseas Job Opportunity by John Williams. 1992. 39 pp. $5.95 from Pilot Books. Booklet with good advice (career gamble, family, financial factors) for anyone considering an overseas assignment.

Getting Your Job in the Middle East by David Lay. 1992. 184 pp. DCL International. $19.95 from DCL Publishing. An overview of career possibilities in the Middle East, along with information about Middle East history, culture, and recent events.

Great Jobs Abroad by Arthur H. Bell. 1997. 378 pp. McGraw-Hill. $14.95 from Impact Publications. Describes strategies for getting hired with corporations based in the U.S., in hopes of being assigned abroad. Tips on research, resumes, interviewing, and using the internet. Most of this book consists of information available in directories, such as U.S. corporations with international operations, U.S. embassies and consulates abroad, etc.

Great Jobs for Foreign Language Majors by Julie DeGalan and Stephen Lambert. 1994. 242 pp. VGM Career Horizons. $11.95. Covers careers in all sectors which involve foreign languages, either directly or as an auxiliary skill, as well as career strategies. Advice often innacurate.

Guide to Careers, Internships & Graduate Education in Peace Studies. 1996. 71 pp. $4.50 from PAWSS Publications, Hampshire College, Amherst, MA 01002. Includes information on internships, fellowships, and relevant organizations.

Health Professionals Abroad by Tim Ryder. 1997. 256 pp. Vacation Work. Available for $17.95 from Seven Hills. New guide provides the first overview (from a British perspective) of working abroad in all areas of health care, from volunteer to career. Professions include doctors, nurses, pharmacists, physiotherapists, and others.

How to Be an Importer and Pay for Your World Travel (Revised) by Mary Green and Stanley Gilmar. 1993. 215 pp. $9.95 plus $3.50 shipping from Ten Speed Press, P.O. Box 7123, Berkeley, CA 94707; (800) 841-BOOK.

* How to Get a Job in Europe: The Insider's Guide by Robert Sanborn. 1995. 546 pp. $17.95 plus $3 shipping from Surrey Books, Inc., 230 E. Ohio St., Suite 120, Chicago, IL 60611; (800) 326-4430. Good source for country-by-country employer addresses (otherwise found in expensive directories) and general suggestions for finding a job.

How to Get the Job You Want Overseas by Arthur Liebers. 1990. 39 pp. $4.95 from Pilot Books. Sketchy advice on private industry and government opportunities.

* International Careers: An Insider's Guide by David Win. 1987. 222 pp. Williamson Publishing Co. Analyzes why international careers are different from domestic ones and suggests strategies for developing one. Out-of-print.

* International Job Finder by Daniel Lauber. Nov 1997. 200 pp. $16.95 + $5 s/h from Planning/Communications, 7215 Oak Ave., River Forest, IL 60305; (800) 829-5220; lauber@jobfindersonline.com, www.jobfindersonline.com. Book by a leading career expert promises to provide useful information on the best sources for an international job search, including: specialty and trade periodicals, job hotlines, internet job and resume databases, job placement services, directories, and salary surveys. Author provides updates to purchasers of this book.

* International Jobs: Where They Are and How to Get Them by Eric Kocher. 1993. 394 pp. $16 from Addison-Wesley; (800) 822-6339, fax (617) 944-4968. An overview of international career fields and how to prepare for them.

International Opportunities: A Career Guide for Students. 1993. 128 pp. David M. Kennedy International Center. $10.95 postpaid from Brigham Young Univ., Kennedy Center for International Studies, Publication Services, P.O. Box 24538, Provo, UT 84602; (800) 528-6279, fax (801) 378-5882; www.byu.edu/. Useful guide for the student interested in international career opportunities.

Jobs Worldwide by David Lay and Benedict A. Leerburger. 1996. 374 pp. Impact. $17.95. An overview of career possibilities in the Caribbean, Europe, Africa, Middle East, Asia, and South Pacific. Information about each country including history, culture, recent events, and demographics.

The Job Hunter's Guide to Japan by Terra Brockman. 1990. 232 pp. Kodansha International. $12.95. Insightful first-hand interviews with Americans working in Japan in various professions.

* **Jobs For People Who Love Travel** by Ronald and Caryl Krannich. 1995. 304 pp. $15.95 from Impact Publications. Information for those who want to work the world before settling down, including but going far beyond the travel industry. Explores motivations; 50 myths about jobs involving travel.

* **Jobs in Russia and the Newly Independent States** by Moira Forbes. 1994. 228 pp. $15.95 from Impact Publications. Provides much-needed help in finding work opportunities, in this rapidly changing region.

* **Jobs Worldwide** by David Lay and Benedict Leerburger. 1996. 377 pp. $17.95 from Impact Publications. Country-by-country examination of employment opportunities; identifies key employers.

Journal of Career Planning and Employment. Periodical published by National Association of Colleges and Employers (formerly College Placement Council), 62 Highland Ave., Bethlehem, PA 18017, (800) 544-5272. Articles by career planning professionals. See especially "Student Dreams and the Real International Job Market," by Jeffrey B. Wood, and other articles on international jobs, in the Nov 1992 issue; see also the May 1994 issue.

The Korea Super Job Catalog, by James F. Haddon. 1993. 215 pp. Bonus Books. $13

postpaid from Korea Services Group, 2950 S.E. Stark, Suite 200, Portland, OR 97214; (503) 230-6932, fax (503) 233-9966; tricia@e-z.net. Includes professional listings.

Live and Work in ... (series): Australia & New Zealand (1996); Belgium, The Netherlands, and Luxembourg (1993); France (1994); Germany (1992); Italy (1992); Scandinavia (1995); Spain & Portugal (1991). Vacation Work. 336 pp. $16.95 each from Seven Hills. Excellent British series for long-term stays. Information on employment, residence, home buying, daily life, retirement, and starting a business. More useful for those on overseas assignment than for those looking for a job.

Living and Working in ... (series): Britain (1995), France (1996), Spain (1995) Switzerland (1996), USA (1995) by David Hampshire. Survival Books. $21.95 plus $3.50 shipping each from Seven Hills, 49 Central Ave., Cincinnati, OH 45202; (800) 545-2005, fax (513) 381-0753. Detailed information for long-term stays on everything from working to buying a house. More useful for those on overseas assignment than for those looking for a job.

* **Making It Abroad: The International Job Hunting Guide** by Howard Schuman. 1988. 168 pp. John Wiley & Sons. Positive insight into career patterns in various international career fields and employment sectors. Out-of-print, but available in libraries.

Opportunities in Foreign Languages Careers by Wilga Rivers. 1993. 151 pp. $11.95 from VGM Career Books. Harvard professor emerita discusses the use of languages as an auxiliary skill; also covers teaching languages and working as a translator or interpreter. Short on practical advice.

Opportunities in International Business Careers by Jeffry Arpan. 1995. 150 pp. $11.95 from VGM Career Books. General overview of careers in international business, with discussion of types of international business degrees and specific business schools.

OPTIONS. Job opening newsletter available for $25 per year (6 issues) from Project Concern's OPTIONS/Service, 3550 Afton Rd., San Diego, CA 92123; (619) 279-9690. Places doctors, nurses, and other healthcare professionals in Third World countries and underserved areas of the U.S.

Special Career Opportunities for Linguists/ Translators/Interpreters. Free pamphlet from U.S. Department of State, Language Services Division, Room 2212, Washington, DC 20520; (202) 647-1528, fax (202) 647-0749.

Tax Guide for U.S. Citizens Abroad (Publication 54). Free from Forms Distribution Center, P.O. Box 25866, Richmond, VA 23260.

Trade & Culture (magazine). $32.95 for 12 issues from Trade & Culture Inc., P.O. Box 10988, Baltimore, MD 21234-9871; (410) 342-4444, fax (410) 342-8560. Focus on the cross-cultural aspects of doing business abroad.

* U.S. Department of State Foreign Service Officer Careers. Free pamphlet available from Recruitment Division, Department of State, Box 12226, Arlington, VA 22219; (703) 875-7490; www.state.gov. Application for the Foreign Service Officer Program. Available from above address (written requests only). Applications for 1998 exam must be postmarked by Jan 16 (overseas locations) or Jan 30 (U.S.). **Study Guide to the Foreign Service Officer Written Examination and Assessment Procedure.** $11.95 postpaid from FSO Study Guide, Educational Testing Service, P.O. Box 6736, Princeton, NJ 08618-6736; (609) 771-7243.

** Working in Asia. (See description in Short-Term Paid Work, above.)

* Working in France: The Ultimate Guide to Job Hunting and Career Success à la Française by Carol Pineau and Maureen Kelly. 1991. 194 pp. Frank Books. Exceptionally useful guide to working in France, focusing on cross-cultural differences in the workplace, written by 2 Americans who live there. Out-of-print but well worth a search.

Working in the Persian Gulf by Blythe Camenson. 1993. 149 pp. $16.95 plus $3 shipping from Desert Diamond Books, P.O. Box 4065, Deerfield Beach, FL 33442. Subtitled "Survival Secrets," this useful book combines details on finding jobs with tips on what to expect when you do.

International Job Listings

International Career Employment Opportunities. Biweekly listings of 600-800 international job openings (about 70 percent located overseas) organized by career fields: international education, foreign policy, international commerce, environment, development, program administration, health care. Main listings are for professionals, typically asking for two to five years or more experience. One section in each issue covers internships; these are nearly all in U.S. Subscriptions available from two months ($29 individuals, $35 institutions) to two years ($229/$350) from International Employment Opportunities, 1088 Middle River Rd., Stanardsville, VA 22973; (804) 985-6444, fax (804) 985-6828; intlcareers@internetmci.com.

International Employment Gazette. Each biweekly issue includes more than 400 overseas job openings by region and field. Good for private-sector business and technical jobs, although many of these require extensive experience, as well as teaching and volunteer positions. $35 for 3 months (6 issues); $55 for 6 months (13 issues); $95 for 1 year (26 issues) from International Employment Gazette, 220 N. Main St., Suite 100, Greenville,

SC 29601; (800) 882-9188, fax (864) 235-3369. Also publishes **The International Directory of Employment Agencies and Recruiters**, which contains information on nearly 200 international recruiters, including complete contact information as well as the occupations and geographic regions for which they recruit. Available for $29.95, including shipping and handling.

** **International Employment Hotline,** edited by Will Cantrell. $39 for 12 issues from Worldwise Books, P.O. Box 3030, Oakton, VA 22124; (703) 620-1972, fax (703) 620-1973. Monthly reports by an international careers expert on who's hiring now in private companies, government, and nonprofit organizations. Lists overseas job openings, both entry-level and mid-career. Each issue has information-packed articles of lasting value on topics such as internships, organizations recruiting for teaching English abroad, and more. An outstanding bargain.

Job Registry, NAFSA: Association of International Educators. 10 issues a year for $30 ($20 members) from NAFSA Job Registry, 1875 Connecticut Ave. NW, Suite 1000, Washington, DC 20009-5728; (202) 462-4811. The best job listing for those interested in the field of international educational exchange.

Internet Resources

E-mail discussion groups and World Wide Web sites on work abroad are free (for the most part), but none of them displace print resources in terms of quality and quantity of useful information. You need access to the internet or other online service to use these.

E-MAIL DISCUSSION GROUPS ("lists").
To sign on to any e-mail list, send a message to the LISTSERV address where the group is based, along with a SUBSCRIBE command in the body of the message. For example: 1) Send e-mail message to: LISTSERV@ cmuvm. csv.cmich.edu. 2) Leave subject blank, and in message section, type only: SUB PCORPS-L yourfirstname yourlastname. 3) Post the message, and you will shortly receive a confirmation message with information about the group. Save it for instructions!

* **PCORPS-L,** SUB request to: listserv@ cmuvm.csv.cmich.edu. Great discussions by former and prospective Peace Corps volunteers, of interest to anyone interested in studying or working in developing countries.

* **JET-L,** SUB request to: listserv@listserv. arizona.edu. Very interesting discussions by former and prospective participants in the JET program (ESL) of the Japanese goverment.

SECUSS-L, SUB request to: listserv@ listsrv.assu.buffalo.edu. Discussion group maintained by NAFSA volunteers Art Neisberg, Ruth Sylte, and Katherine Yngve. The best way to plug into the vast wealth of knowledge of fellow education abroad advisors/administrators. Dozen or more messages daily.

TANEWS-L *Transitions Abroad*'s bimonthly newsletter highlights new educational and travel abroad programs and resources including study, short-term work, internships, and volunteer placements. To subscribe, address an e-mail message to listserv@peach. ease.lsoft.com; in the body of the message, write: SUBSCRIBE TANEWS-L.

WORLD WIDE WEB SITES You'll have the best luck using standard search tools such as Infoseek or Yahoo and experimenting with key words such as Work Abroad, TESL, TESOL, ESL or other fields and countries. Here are a few sites which are excellent places to start:

www.careermosaic.com. CareerMosaic's site offers a searchable, comprehensive database of job listings for over 50 countries. Their "International Gateway" page is a good place to start.

www.cdsintl.org. Internship exchanges with Germany.

** **www.ciee.org/work/index.htm.** Council Work Abroad, the largest work abroad exchange (6,000 US students annually), and Council International Volunteer Projects.

www.cies.org. Fulbright University Teaching exchanges.

http://clover.slavic.pitt.edu/~aatseel/jobs/intern/intern-index.html. Guide to internships in Central and Eastern Europe by the American Association of Teachers of Slavic and East European Languages (AATSEEL). Not available in hardcopy.

www.dbm.com/jobguide. Resources for International Opportunities, from the Riley Guide. Country-by-country lists of web and Gopher sites listing job opportunities. Best overview of online job services, but most postings are for experienced specialists in computers, engineering, and business.

www.gwjapan.org. Gateway Japan's guide to study and work opportunities in Japan.

www.interaction.org/ia. Interaction is a Washington, DC clearinghouse for international volunteer organizations.

* **www.istc.emn.edu.** Ann Halpin's directory of organizations offering overseas volunteer placements. Searchable.

www.istc.umn.edu. Univ. of Minnesota, International Study and Travel Center (ISTC). Richard Warzecha. Excellent searchable database for study abroad, low-cost study

abroad, scholarships, and volunteer abroad directory.

www.monster.com. "The Monster Board" lists over 50,000 jobs. It's "Monster Search" will let you search by job category or region.

www.oneworld.org/vso. Voluntary Service Overseas's site offers application information for volunteer positions throughout the world.

* **www.overseasjobs.com.** Comprehensive site that offers job search capabilities as well as links to other relevant sites.

www.pitt.edu/~ian/index.html. International Affairs Network Web provides information on graduate programs and careers in international relations.

* **www.softaid.net/aipt/aipt.html.** AIPT/IAESTE, non-profit with exchanges in 65+ countries, can also assist with work permits for internship exchanges.

http://solar.rtd.utk.edu/~ccsi/ccsihome.html. Center for Civil Society, Univ. of Washington, information on voluntary assistance and NGOs for Russia and the NIS.

www.state.gov. U.S. State Dept offers 1,000 internships annually; complete information and application on home page.

** **www.transabroad.com.** *Transitions Abroad*'s web site contains an online database that serves as a complete guide to working, living and learning overseas. This searchable database is a compilation of a selection of the articles and resource directories published in Transitions' bimonthly magazine. You can order any of their publications online.

www.umich.edu/~icenter. Bill Nolting's guides to work abroad, developed for the Univ. of Michigan.

http://units.ox.ac.uk/departments/ slavonic. Univ. of Oxford's (U.K.) guide to internships in Central and Eastern Europe. Not available in hardcopy.

* www.usia.gov. Information on all Fulbright scholarships (study, research, teaching abroad).

Key Publishers And Organizations

Council (Council on International Educational Exchange), Council-Pubs Dept., 205 E. 42nd St., New York, NY 10017-5706; (888) COUNCIL, fax (212) 822-2699; info@ ciee.org, www.ciee.org. Publishers of materials on work, study, and travel abroad, especially for students; also administers the Council Work Abroad Program and Council Workcamps. Add $1.50 (book rate) or $3 (first-class) shipping for each book.

Global Exchange, 2017 Mission St., Room 303, San Francisco, CA 94110; (415) 255-7296, fax (415) 255-7498; globalexch@ igc.org. Distributes books on solidarity with developing countries; also organizes "reality tours." Add $1.75 ($3 first class) shipping for each book ordered.

Impact Publications, 9104-N Manassas Dr., Manassas Park, VA 22111; (703) 361-7300, fax (703) 335-9486; www.impactpublications. com. The best one-stop source for international career books published by Impact and many other publishers. Add $4 shipping for the first book ordered plus $1 for each additional one.

Institute of International Education (IIE), IIE Books, P.O. Box 371, Annapolis Junction, MD 20701-0371; (800) 445-0443, fax (301) 206-9789; iiebooks@pmds.com; www.iie.org. Publisher of authoritative directories for study or teaching abroad and financial aid, and distributor of Central Bureau (U.K.) publications on working abroad. Add $2 each shipping for books under $25; $5 each for books over $25, or 10 percent for orders over $100.

Intercultural Press, P.O. Box 700, Yarmouth, ME 04096; (207) 846-5168, fax (207) 846-5181; interculturalpress@internetmci.com, www.bookmasters.com/interclt.htm. Numerous publications dealing with cross-cultural issues in settings ranging from academic to business.

John Wiley & Sons, 1 Wiley Dr., Summerset, NJ 08875; (908) 469-4400. Publications on careers.

NAFSA Publications, P.O. Box 1020, Sewickley, PA 15143; (800) 836-4994, fax (412) 741-0609. Essential publications for advisers and administrators in international educational exchange. For membership information, contact NAFSA: Association of International Educators, 1875 Connecticut Ave. NW, Suite 1000, Washington, DC 20009-5728, (202) 939-3103 or (202) 462-4811, fax (202) 667-3419; inbox@nafsa. org, www.nafsa.org.

Peterson's Guides, 202 Carnegie Center, P.O. Box 2123, Princeton, NJ 08543; (800) 338-3282; www.petersons.com. Guides to jobs and careers, study abroad. U.S. distributor for many of the **Vacation Work Publications** (U.K.). Add $4.75 shipping for each book or avoid this charge by ordering through a bookstore.

Pilot Books, 127 Sterling Ave., P.O. Box 2102, Greenport, NY 11944; (800) 79-PILOT, fax (516) 477-0978. Booklet-sized guides to international jobs and budget travel. Add $2 shipping for each book ordered.

Seven Hills Book Distributors; 49 Central Ave., Cincinnati, OH 45202; (800) 545-2005, www.sevenhillsbooks.com. Carries a wide range of travel books and maps from foreign publishers. U.S. distributor for many Vacation Work Publications.

Seven Locks Press, P.O. Box 68, Arlington, VA 22210; (800) 354-5348, fax (310) 834-2835. Books on social change. Add $3 for first book, $.75 for each additional title.

Vacation Work Publications, 9 Park End St., Oxford, OX1 1HJ, U.K.; (011) 44-1865-241978, fax 1865-790885. Publisher of numerous books on work abroad and international careers. Many are distributed in the U.S. by Peterson's Guides. Those which lack U.S. distribution have recently been picked up by Seven Hills, 49 Central Ave., Cincinnati, OH 45202; (800) 545-2005, fax (513) 381-0753.

VGM Career Horizons, a division of NTC Publishing Group, 4255 West Touhy Ave., Lincolnwood, IL 60646-1975. Books on careers. Available through bookstores.

Worldwise Books, P.O. Box 3030, Oakton, VA 22124; (703) 620-1972, fax (703) 620-1973. Publisher of books on international jobs and careers as well as the newsletter *International Employment Hotline.*

CHAPTER 17

SHORT-TERM WORK ABROAD: THE KEY EMPLOYERS

The major fields of temporary employment abroad are tourism and agriculture (both seasonal), au pairing (almost exclusively for women), English teaching (difficult for periods of less than nine months), and volunteer work.

Everyone will tell you that the more research you do before you go abroad the better. But the limited information available is often discouraging, misleading, or useless. Remain determined in the face of discouragement and use these and the Work Abroad Resources to clarify what you want to do and determine what is possible.

As a first step in finding a short-term job, contact the embassy or consulate and the tourist office of the countries in which you want to work. Consult their telephone directories and yellow pages for addresses of companies in your field. If you don't have a field, look up English-language teaching institutes. Diplomatic missions should also have newspapers from which you can study the "situations vacant" columns.

Exchanging labor for room and board is an excellent way of gaining worthwhile experience while seeing another country. Be aware that most organizations that take on short-term volunteers look for people willing to finance themselves completely or perhaps even make a financial contribution. (Again, consult the Work Abroad Key Resources.)

If you are searching for a specific kind of job or are qualified in a certain field, you might get leads by consulting the specialist press. For example, you can find out about crewing or yacht delivery possibilities from yachting magazines like **Cruising World.** Professionals should consult their own associations and journals.

Finally, when contacting agencies and potential employers, increase your chances of receiving a reply by enclosing several international reply coupons (IRCs), available from post offices.

International Organizations

AIESEC (International Association for Students in Economics and Business Management), 135 W. 50th St., 20th Fl., New York, NY 10020; (212) 757-3774. Business-related jobs available in over 75 countries. Highly qualified interns must apply through an AIESEC chapter in the U.S.

Alliances Abroad, 2830 Alameda, San Francisco, CA 94103; fax (415) 621-1609; alliancea@aol.com. Range of programs including au pair placement in Europe and volunteer work in Ecuador, Mexico, and Ghana.

* American-Scandinavian Foundation. Free brochure on study and scholarships (all fields) and work opportunities. This nonprofit organization also offers paid internships in Scandinavia in engineering, teaching English as a foreign language, and agricultural fields. Apply for internships by late Dec. ASF also assists with obtaining work permits for Scandinavia. Contact ASF at 725 Park Ave., New York, NY 10021; (212) 879-9779, fax (212) 249-3444; asf@amscan.org.

Association for International Practical Training, 10400 Little Patuxent Parkway, Suite 250, Columbia, MD 21044-3510; (410) 997-3068 or 997-2886. Summer placements in over 60 countries through the International Association for the Exchange of Students for Technical Experience (IAESTE) available to students in science, engineering, math, agriculture, or architecture. Also runs hotel and culinary exchanges to Austria, Finland, France, Germany, Ireland, Netherlands, Switzerland, U.K., Australia, and Japan and Career Development Exchanges for candidates who can find their own employer overseas.

Au Pair in Europe, P.O. Box 68056, Blakely Postal Outlet, Hamilton, ON L8M 3M7, Canada; (905) 545-6305; aupair@prince.ent.com. Au pairs placed in 18 countries including Australia.

AuPair Homestay, World Learning, Inc., 1015 15th St., Suite 750, NW, Washington, DC 20005; (202) 408-5380; imelda.farrell@worldlearning.com. Arranges for young Americans to spend 3-12 months as au pairs in France, Germany, Iceland, the Netherlands, Norway, Finland, Switzerland, U.K., and Argentina. Program fee is $775.

Berlitz, 400 Alexander Park Dr., Princeton, NJ 08540; (609) 514-9650. Teacher vacancies often occur in Latin America, Korea, and Europe. Berlitz teachers must be university graduates and willing to be trained in the Berlitz method.

BUNAC, the British Universities North America Club, operates the "Work in Britian" program enabling U.S. students and recent graduates to take virtually any job in Britain for up to 6 months. P.O. Box 49, South Britain, CT 06487; (800) GO-BUNAC; www.bunac.org. In the U.K.: 16, Bowling Green Ln., London EC1R OBD; (011) 44-171-251-3472.

Council, 205 E. 42nd St., New York, NY 10017-5706; (888) COUNCIL; info@ciee.org coordinates a working holiday program for U.S. college students to Britain, Ireland, France, Germany, Spain, Canada, New Zealand, Australia, and Costa Rica. The participation fee for all programs is $225. Participants receive work documentation and access to job-finding assistance in the destination country. The Canadian equivalent is the Student Work Abroad Program (SWAP) administered by the Canadian Federation of Students, 243 College St., Suite 500, Toronto, ON M5T 2T1, Canada; (416) 977-3703.

ELS International Inc., 5761 Buckingham Parkway, Culver City, CA 90230-6583; (310) 642-0988;international@els.com. International chain of language schools. U.S. office handles the bulk of recruitment for ELS's overseas franchises. Also now runs its own TEFL training courses.

Global Outreach, P.O. Box 3291, Merrifield, VA 22116-3291. Sends students of agriculture to Australia, Costa Rica, Germany, Hungary, Japan, Mexico, Romania, Russia, U.K., etc.

IAEA (International Agricultural Exchange Association), 1000 1st Ave. S, Great Falls, MT 59401; (406) 727-1999. Farm placements of agricultural trainees in many European countries plus Japan, Australia, and New Zealand. A separate agricultural and horticultural work exchange exists between the U.S. and most European countries (including Eastern Europe) and elsewhere; details from Communicating for Agriculture, 112 East Lincoln, Fergus Falls, MN 56538; (218) 739-3241.

Institute of International Education (IIE), IIE Books, P.O. Box 371, Annapolis Junction, MD 20701-0371; (800) 445-0443, fax (301) 953-2838; iiebooks@iie.org, www.iie.org. Publisher of authoritative directories for study or teaching abroad and financial aid, and distributor of Central Bureau (U.K.) publications on working abroad. Add $2 each shipping for books under $25; $4 each for books over $25, or 10 percent for orders over $100.

InterExchange Program, 161 6th Ave., New York, NY 10013; (212) 924-0446; interex@earthlink.net. Work placements for students in Germany and anyone 18-30 in France, Scandinavia, Switzerland, and Eastern Europe. Also au pair placements in Austria, Finland, Netherlands, Italy, Norway, and Spain.

Interlocken International, RR 2, Box 165, Hillsboro, NH 03244; (603) 478-3166. Group leaders needed to escort high school students on tours worldwide.

International Cooperative Education, 15 Spiros Way, Menlo Park, CA 94025; (650) 323-4944. Arranges paid summer work for 2-3 months in Germany, Switzerland, Belgium, Austria, and Japan. Jobs include retail sales, hotels and restaurants, agriculture, offices, etc.; most require knowledge of relevant language.

International House, 106 Piccadilly, London W1V 9FL, U.K.; (011) 44-171-491 2598. With 100 schools in 26 countries, IH is one of the largest English teaching organizations in the world. The Central Department (address above) does much of the hiring of teachers—who must have at least a Cambridge/RSA Certificate (Pass B).

Internships International, 1116 Cowper Dr., Raleigh, NC 27608; Tel./fax (919) 832-1575; intintl@aol.com. Internships (i.e., unpaid work placements) arranged in London, Dublin, Paris, Stuttgart, Florence, Madrid, Africa.

ISS, P.O. Box 5910, Princeton, NJ 08543; (609) 452-0990; edustaffing@iss.mcimail.com. Places state-certified U.S. teachers in international schools worldwide. Recruitment meetings in February, March, and June.

National Future Farmers of America (FFA), P.O. Box 15160, Alexandria, VA 22309. Arranges international farm exchanges in 35 countries.

Taking Off, P.O. Box 104, Newton Highlands, MA 02161; (617) 630-1606, and Center for Interim Programs, P.O. Box 2347, Cambridge, MA 02238. Consulting services aimed primarily at pre-university and university students looking to arrange a worthwhile experience abroad, including paid and voluntary work. Flat fee of $895 and $1,500 respectively.

Wall Street Institute International, Torre Mapfre, Marina 16-18, 08005 Barcelona, Spain; (011) 34 3 225 45 55, fax 225 48 88. Chain of 164 commercial language institutes for adults that employ approximately 350 full-time EFL teachers in Europe and Latin America. In some countries the "Master Center" acts as a clearinghouse for teacher vacancies; addresses from HQ.

WISE (Worldwide Internships & Service Education), 303 S. Craig St., Suite 202, Pittsburg, PA 15213; (412) 681-8120; wiset@pitt.edu. American liaison for European work placement programs—au pairing, farm work in Norway, internships in London, etc. Program fees from $725.

Africa

Travelers sometimes negotiate teaching contracts in East Africa and casual tutoring in Cairo on the spot. It may also be possible to join conservation or scientific research trips for a fee. Additional contacts include:

African-American Institute, Chanin Building, 380 Lexington Ave., New York, NY 10168-4298. Resource center for opportunities for teaching, technical, and voluntary posts in Africa.

CADS (Centre for Alternative Development Strategies), 5 Frazier-Davies Dr., P.M.B. 1290, Freetown, Sierra Leone; (011) 232-22 230964. International volunteer exchange program. Participation fee for up to 4 weeks is $5,000.

Eclaireuses et Eclaireurs du Senegal, 5 Rue Pierre Millon, BP 744, Dakar, Senegal; (011) 221-217367. Volunteers offer practical training to Senegalese young people in various fields.

Foreign Placements cc, P.O. Box 912, Somerset West 7129, South Africa; (011) 27-4457 7677. Casual work arranged for short periods and also contracts for medical staff and tradesmen with skills.

Frontier Conservation Expeditions, 77 Leonard St., London EC2A 4QS, England; (011) 44-171-613-2422, carries out environmental surveys in Tanzania, Uganda, and Mozambique that use paying volunteers for 10-12 weeks.

Global Citizens Network/Harambee, 1931 Iglehart Ave., St. Paul, MN 55104; (612) 644-0960 or (800) 644-9292. Sends paying volunteers to rural Kenya (among other countries worldwide).

Greenforce, 11-15 Betterton St., Covent Garden, London WC2H 9BP, U.K.; (011) 44-171 470 8888. Recruit researchers to join conservation aid projects for 10-12 weeks in Africa. Participation fee approx. £2,700 ($4,500).

Institute for International Cooperation and Development, P.O. Box 103, Williamstown, MA 01267; (413) 458-9828. Teaching and tree-planting project in Angola.

International Language Institute, P.O. Box 13, Embaba, Cairo, Egypt; (011) 20-2-346 3087. English teaching positions are available for people with some TEFL training. Also 10 American Language Centers throughout Morocco, including ALC, 4 Zankat Tanja, Rabat, 10000 Morocco.

Operation Crossroads Africa, 475 Riverside Dr., Suite 242, New York, NY 10115-0050; (212) 870-2106. Runs 7-week projects in rural Africa staffed by self-financing volunteers. Canadian Crossroads International is at 31 Madison Ave., Toronto, ON M5R 2S2, Canada.

Overland Adventure Tours. A number of overland adventure tour operators require expedition leaders for at least 1 year. These include Guerba Expeditions, 40 Station Rd., Westbury, Wiltshire BA13 3JN, U.K.; and Kumuka Africa, 40 Earls Court Rd., London W8 6EJ, England.

Pa Santigie Conteh Farmer's Association (Pasacofaas), 5A City Rd., Wellington, P.M.B. 686, Freetown, Sierra Leone. Sends volunteers to 26 villages in Northern Province to build, teach, plant, harvest, etc. Application fee is $50.

SCORE, South Africa Sports Coaching Program, c/o Netherlands Government representative Steffan Howells; howells@aztec.co.za. Summer program for self-funding volunteers.

Visions in Action. 2710 Ontario Rd., NW, Washington, DC 20009; (202) 625-7403.

Range of volunteer projects in Kenya, Uganda, Zimbabwe, Burkina Faso, South Africa and Tanzania. Volunteers must raise $5,000-$6,000 and commit themselves to stay for 1 year.

Workcamps in Africa. The following organizations arrange workcamps in Africa, though applications should normally be sent to the partner organization in the U.S. (See Voluntary Service below.) For Morocco and Tunisia, a knowledge of French is very useful. **Mouvement Twiza**, A.M.T., 23 rue Echiguer Hammand; **Hay Salam**, B.P. 77, 15000 Khemisset, Morocco. **Pensées et Chantiers**, B.P. 1423, Rabat, 10001 Morocco, (011) 212-7-698338; **Tunisian Assoc. of Voluntary Work**, Maison du RCD, Blvd. 9 Avril, 1938, 1002 Tunis, Tunisia; **Africa Voluntary Service of Sierra Leone**, Private Mail Bag 717, Freetown, Sierra Leone; **Voluntary Workcamps Association of Nigeria**, P.O. Box 2189, Lagos, Nigeria; **Voluntary Development Association**, P.O. Box 48902, Nairobi, Kenya; **Lesotho Workcamps Assn.**, P.O. Box 6, Linare Rd., Maseru 100, Lesotho; **Zimbabwe Workcamps Assoc.**, P.O. Box CY 2039, Causeway, Harare, Zimbabwe; **Joy Relief Association**, P.O. Box 673, Kaneshie-Accra, Ghana (organizes workcamps to help with community projects); and **WWOOF-Ghana**, c/o Ebenezer Nortey-Mensah, P.O. Box 154, Trade Fair Site, La-Accra, Ghana (places volunteers on traditional farms and bicycle workshops in Ghana). Also **WWOOF organization in Togo**: c/o Prosper Agbeko, B.P. 25, Abou gare, Togo; (011) 228-47-1036. Registration fee is $25. **Uganda Voluntary Workcamps Association**, GPO Box 3367, Kampala, Uganda.

WorldTeach (see Voluntary Service section). Recruits college graduates to teach science, English, etc., in Namibia.

Asia

AEON Intercultural USA, 9301 Wilshire Blvd., Suite 202, Beverly Hills, CA 90210; (310) 550-0940. Recruits university graduates to teach in their 190 language schools in Japan.

Bangladesh Workcamps Association, 289/2 Work Camps Rd., North Shahjahanpur, Dhaka 1217, Bangladesh; fax (011) 88-2-956-5506/5483. Attn: BWCA. Development workcamps of 7-10 days, and medium-term projects also. Participation fee $150 plus application fee $25.

China Teaching Program, Western Washington Univ., Old Main 530A, Bellingham, WA 98225-9047; (360) 650-3753; ctp@cc.wwu.edu. Places teachers and teaching assistants in China.

Colorado China Council, 4556 Apple Way, Boulder, CO 80301; (303) 443-1108. Twenty-five ESL teachers placed at institutes throughout China, including Tibet and Mongolia for next year.

Council's Teach in China Program, 205 E. 42nd St., New York, NY 10017; (888) COUNCIL. People with BAs can teach ESL to Chinese college students for a summer or an academic year.

Dakshinayan, F-1169 Chittaranjan Park, New Delhi 110019, India; Tel./fax (011) 91-11-648 4468. Volunteers to help with educational medical projects in tribal lands in remote areas. Contribution of $5 a day is expected.

ELS International, 12 Kuling St., Taipei, Taiwan; (011) 886-2-321-9005. Nine schools needing 200 teachers in Taiwan.

English and Computer College (ECC), 430/17-24 Chula Soi 64, Siam Square, Bangkok 10330, Thailand; (011) 66-2-255-1856. English school with 60 branches in Thailand (half in Bangkok) that employs native-speaker teachers.

English Language Recruitment Center, Inc. (ELRC), 4344 South Archer Ave., Suite 131,

Chicago, IL 60632-2827; (312) 843-9792 or 843-9723. Recruits instructors for language academies throughout South Korea. Minimum requirements: BA and clear speaking voice.

EPIK (English Program in Korea), c/o of any of the 12 Korean Consulates in the U.S. Korean government scheme to recruit up to 1,000 native speaker teachers for Korean schools.

Friendship Club Nepal, P.O. Box 11276, Dillibazar, Kathmandu, Nepal; (011) 977-1-410856. Can assist native speakers with a BA to teach in schools. Volunteers contribute $125 per month for their expenses.

GEOS Corporation, Simpson Tower 2424, 401 Bay St., Toronto, ON M5H 2Y4, Canada; (416) 777-0109. One of Japan's largest recruiters of English teachers.

Grahung Kalika, (Walling Village Development Committee), Bartung, Ward 2, Syngja, Western Nepal. Community needs volunteers from 2 weeks to much longer to teach English. Details from former volunteer Mark Scotton (125 Trowell Rd., Nottingham NG8 2EN, U.K.).

Hess Language Schools, 83 Po Ai Rd. 2F, Taipei, Taiwan. Recruits 200 teachers for 40 schools in Taiwan. Details from 4 Horicon Ave., Glens Falls, NY 12801; Tel./fax (518) 793-6183.

Insight Nepal, P.O. Box 6760, Kathmandu, Nepal; (011) 977-1-418964. Volunteer placements for 3-4 months in Nepali schools for $600 fee.

Interact Nova Group, 2 Oliver St., Suite 7, Boston, MA 02110; (617) 542-5027. Also 1881 Yonge St., Suite 700, Toronto, ON M4S 3C4, Canada. Hires native speaker teachers for its 230 institutes throughout Japan.

International Language Programs (ILP), ILP Centre, Jl. Raya Pasar Minggu, No. 39A, Jakarta, 12780, Indonesia; (011) 62-21-798-5210. Employs qualified instructors for various schools in Indonesia. Also try Triad English Centres, Jalan Letjen S. Parman 6J; Tel./fax (011) 62-21-530 8001.

Jaffe International Education Service, Kunnuparambil Buildings, Kurichy, Kottayam 686549, India; Tel./fax (011) 91-481 430470. Places young foreign volunteer teachers in English high schools, vocational institutes, etc. in Kerala State, including 4-week summer schools (in April and May).

Japan Exchange and Teaching Programs (JET), c/o Japanese Embassy, 2520 Massachusetts Ave. NW, Washington, DC 20008; (202) 939-6772 or (800) INFOJET. Places English language teaching assistants in 1-year contracts throughout Japan.

Missionaries of Charity, 54A A.J.C. Bose Rd., Calcutta 16, India. Runs children's homes for destitute people in Calcutta. Unskilled volunteers can work for short periods.

Narayana Gurukula Botanical Sanctuary, Alattil, P.O., North Wynad, Kerala, India 670644. Rainforest research center welcomes self-funded volunteers; minimum donation $5-$10 per day.

Shin Sizen Juku, Tsuri-Mura, Akan-Gun, Hokkaido 085-12 Japan; (011) 81-154 642821. Free food and accommodations provided in return for teaching English in local community.

State Bureau of Foreign Experts, Friendship Hotel, 3 Bai Shi Qiao Rd., 100873 Beijing; (011) 86-10-849 888 ext. 83500. Coordinates selection of foreign teachers and foreign experts.

The Japan Times and Korea Times. English-language newspapers that carry teaching advertisements.

YBM/ELSI and ECC Language Institutes and ECC Language Institutes. Recruits 400 teachers for language schools throughout Korea. Contact Sisa America, 17420

Carmenita Rd., Cerritos, CA 90703; (800) 501-SISA.

YMCA Overseas Service Corps., 101 North Wacker Dr., Chicago, IL 60606; (800) 872-9622 ext. 167. Twenty-five ESL teachers placed in 9 localities in Taiwan for 1 year.

Australasia

Antarctic Support Associates (ASA), 61 Inverness Dr. E., Suite 300, Englewood, CO 80112; (303) 790-8606. Hires some general assistants as well as skilled staff for research stations like McMurdo in Antarctica for 5 or 12 months.

Au Pair Australia, 6 Wilford St, Corrimal, NSW 2518, Australia; (011) 61-42 846412. Places young women with work visas in live-in childcare positions for a minimum of 3 months.

Australian Trust for Conservation Volunteers, P.O. Box 423, Ballarat, Victoria 3350, Australia; (011) 61-53-331483; atcv@netconnect.com.au. Organizes short- and long-term voluntary conservation projects throughout Australia. Overseas volunteers participate in a 6-week package costing from AUS$840.

Farm Helpers in New Zealand, Kumeroa Lodge, RD1, Woodville 5473; Tel./fax (011) 64-6-376-4582. NZ$20 membership to be put in touch with farmers looking for helpers in exchange for room and board.

New Zealand Wilderness Trust, Box 19200, Hamilton, New Zealand; (011) 64-7-839 6767. Volunteers sent to various conservation projects around the North Island of New Zealand. Volunteers pay NZ$155 per week.

Northern Victoria Fruitgrowers' Association, P.O. Box 394, Shepparton, Victoria

3630, Australia. Actively recruits fruit pickers in February and March. Also Victorian Peach and Apricot Growers' Association, 30A Bank St., Cobram, VIC 3644, Australia.

Stablemate, 156 Pitt Town Rd., Kenthurst, NSW 2156, Australia; (011) 61-2-9654 9643. Supply staff to the horse industry. Operates exchange program with the U.S.

Student Travel Bureau, New Zealand Univ. Students Assoc., NZUSA, P.O. Box 6368, Te Aro, Wellington, New Zealand. Assists American students on the Council Work in New Zealand program find catering and agricultural jobs from May to October.

Wilderness Society, 1st Fl., 263 Broadway, Glebe, Sydney, NSW 2037, Australia; (011) 612-9552-2355. Casual work available as collectors dressed in koala suits.

WWOOF, Mt. Murrindal Cooperative, Buchan, Victoria 3885, Australia; (011) 61-51-550235. Issues a list of 700 member farms in Australia for $25. Also publishes worldwide list of farms and volunteer work opportunities for $15.

WWOOF, P.O. Box 1172, Nelson, New Zealand; (011) 64-25-345711; wwoof-nz@xtra.co.nz. Provides a list of about 450 organic growers for $12.

Eastern and Central Europe

Many new opportunities, especially in English language teaching, have become available in the Baltic, Russia, and the Newly Independent States.

Albanian Youth Council, P.O. Box 1741, Tirana, Albania. Requesting volunteer teachers to tutor children and adults at English classes in Tirana, preferably in summer.

American Language Institute, City University Slovakia, 335 116th Ave. SE, Bellevue, WA

98004; (800) 426-5596, fax (206) 637-6989. Bratislava site: Drienova 34, P.O. Box 78, 820 09 Bratislava; Tel./fax 7-293 114. Trencin site: Bezrucova 64, 911 01 Trencin; Tel./fax 831-529337. Recruit 30-35 teachers (must have teaching experience) for Slovakia.

American Slavic Student Internship Service and Training Corporation (ASSIST), 1535 SE Upper Hall St., Portland, OR 97201; Tel./fax (503) 220-2535; AssistUSA@aol.com. Organizes fee-paying internships in Russia and Latvia for students and graduates in relevant fields.

Avalon '92 Agency, Karoly Krt. 21, Budapest 1075, Hungary; Tel./fax (011) 36-1- 351 3010. Nanny positions available in Hungary year round. Also a few posts for English teachers and secretaries.

Belarusian Association of International Youth Workcamps (ATM), 10a Oktyabrskaya St., P.O. Box 64, 220119 Minsk, Belarus. International youth workcamps lasting 3 weeks, organized as part of Anti-Chernobyl Project. Participants must know some Russian (Russian course can be arranged).

Brontosaurus Movement, Senovázná 2, 11000 Prague 1, Czech Republic; (011) 42-2-2422 3166. Volunteers needed for environmental projects throughout the Czech Republic.

Caledonian School, Vlatavska 24, 150 00 Prague 5, Czech Republic; (011) 42-2 57 31 36 50. Employs 80 teachers with TEFL background to teach English in a large Prague language institute.

Central European Teaching Program, Beloit College, 700 College St., Beloit, WI 53511; (608) 363-2619. Supplies English teachers to Hungary and Romania. Placement fee of $750.

Czech Academic Information Agency, Dum Zahranicnich Sluzeb, Senovázné Námesti 26, 11121 Prague, Czech Repub-

lic; (011) 42-2-24-22-9698. Slovak AIA is at Na vrsku 8, P.O. Box 108, 81000 Bratislava, Slovakia; (011) 42-7-5333 010. Helps prospective English teachers find posts mainly in state schools but also in private institutes.

English for Everybody, Spanielova 1292, 163 00 Prague 6, Czech Republic; Tel./fax (011) 42-2-301-9784. U.S. voice mail (415) 789-7641. EFL teacher training and placement agency with job vacanies throughout Central Europe.

English School of Communication Skills (ESCS), ul. sw. Agnieszki 2/Ip, 31-068 Kraków, Poland; Tel./fax (011) 48-12 22 85 83. Also at ul. Bernrdynska 15, 33-100 Tarnów. Fifteen EFL teachers for summer and winter language camps in Poland.

Foundation for a Civil Society, 1270 Avenue of the Americas, Suite 609, New York, NY 10020; (212) 332-2890. Two-month summer and year-round teaching placements in Czech and Slovak republics for ESL teachers.

Galindo Skola (Sava Centar), Milentija Popovica 9, 11070 Novi Beograd, Yugoslavia; (011) 381-11 311 4568. English teachers to work with children and adolescents for at least 3 months.

International Exchange Center, 2 Republic Sq., LV-1010 Riga, Latvia; (011) 371-2-702 7476. Recruits English-speaking volunteers for summer projects in Latvia and Russia that may involve camp counseling, au pairing, etc.

International House maintains a large contingent of language schools in Poland employing many Certificate-qualified EFL teachers. IH Katowice (U1. Gliwicka 10, 40-079 Katowice), IH Kraków (ul. Pilsudskiego 6, Ip, 31-110 Kraków), IH Opole (U1. Kosciuszki 17, 45-062 Opole), IH Wroclaw, (U1. Ruska 46a, 50-079 Wroclaw) and IH Bielsko-Biala (U1. Karsinskiego 24, 43-300 Bielsko Biala).

International Placement Group, Jezkova 9, 130 00 Prague 3, Czech Republic; (011) 42-2 279568; ipgcz@mbox.vol.cz. Teacher recruitment agency for Central and Eastern Europe.

Language Link Schools, Novoslobodskaya ul. 5 bld. 2, 101030 Moscow; Tel./fax (011) 95-973 2154. Forty native-English teachers for various schools.

Mir-V-Mig, P.O. Box 1085, 310168 Kharkov, Ukraine; (011) 7-0572 653141. Places native speaker teachers at secondary schools and universities in Kiev and Kharkov, Ukraine.

Project Harmony, 6 Irasville Common, Waitsfield, VT 05673; (802) 496-4545 pharmony@igc.apc.org. Teaching Intern Program places teachers in Russia, the Baltics, central Asian republics, etc. Recent college graduates accepted.

Services for Open Learning, North Devon Professional Centre, Vicarage St., Barnstable, Devon EX32 7HB, U.K.; (011) 44-1271-327319. Recruits graduates to teach in schools in Belarus, Croatia, Czech Republic, Hungary, Romania, and Slovakia. Interviews in Eastern Central Europe or U.K.

Soros Professional English Language Teaching Program (SPELT), 888 7th Ave., 31st Fl., New York, NY 10106; (212) 757-2323. Teaching positions in most East European countries for trained, experienced English teachers.

Sunny School, P.O. Box 23, 125057 Moscow, Russia; (011) 7-95-151-2500. Hires university-educated Americans with some teaching experience.

Teachers for Central and Eastern Europe, 21 V 5 Rakovski Blvd., Dimitrovgrad 6400, Bulgaria; (011) 359-391-24787, fax 26218. Appoints native speakers to teach in English language secondary schools on behalf of the Ministry of Education in Bul-

garia, and also in Czech Republic, Hungary, Poland, and Slovakia. Details available from Mr. Bill Morrow; (512) 494-0392; jbmorrow@mail.utexas.edu.

Teaching Abroad, Gerrard House, Rustington, W. Sussex BN16 1AW, U.K.; (011) 44-1903 859911. Short- and long-term voluntary teaching positions in Ukraine, Moscow, and Siberia (also Ghana, Mexico, and India). Fees from about £665 (not including travel).

Travel Teach USA, P.O. Box 357, Rigby, ID 83442; Tel./fax (208) 745-7222. Working holiday opportunities teaching English in Russia, Ukraine, Moldova, Romania, and Lithuania. Placement fee from $500.

UNIO Youth Workcamps Association, Nepszinhaz u. 24, 1081 Budapest, Hungary. Volunteers placed on range of summer workcamps in Hungary.

WWOOF Hungary, Hungarian Association for Organic Farming and the Protection of the Environment and Health, Kitaibel P.U. 4, 1024 Budapest, Hungary; (011) 36-1- 316 2138; figi@biok.datanet.hu. Volunteer workers for organic farms throughout Hungary.

Youth Voluntary Service, 11/60 Lystopadna, Lviv 290034, Ukraine; Tel./fax (011) 380-322 423658. Short-term voluntary projects in the summer.

France

Acorn Venture Ltd., 137 Worcester Rd., Hagley, Stourbridge, West Midlands DY9 0NW, England. Activity holiday centers in France that need instructors and catering staff.

APARE, 41 cours Jean Jaurès, 84000 Avignon, France; (011) 33-490-85-51-15. Runs volunteer workcamps at historic sites in southern France (and in many other countries).

Butterfly et Papillon, 5 Av de Genève, F-74000 Annecy, France; (011) 33-4-50-67-03 51; aupair.France@wanadoo.fr. All nationalities placed as au pairs in French families for 3-18 months.

Centres d'Information et de Documentation Jeunesse (CIDJ). Act as general advisory centers for young people. For leaflets about temporary work possibilities, send 4 IRCs to 101 Quai Branly, 75740, Cedex 15, Paris; Fax (011) 33-1-40-65-02-61. This main Paris branch has a useful notice board for job seekers.

Continental Waterways, 1 Promenade du Rhin, 21000 Dijon, France; (011) 33-380-41-67-73. Employs deck hands on holiday barges on the inland waterways of France.

Fédération Unie des Auberges de Jeunesse, 27 rue Pajol, 75018 Paris, France. Short-term work (catering, reception, sports, instruction, etc.) at youth hostels throughout France. Applications must be sent to individual hostels. FUAJ also organizes voluntary workcamps to renovate hostels; volunteers pay FF350 per week.

Jeunesse et Réconstruction, 10 rue de Trévise, 75009 Paris, France; (011) 33-1-47-70-15-88. Arranges workcamps throughout France and recruits grapepickers.

La Sabranenque, Centre International, rue de la Tour de l'Oume, 30290 Saint Victor la Coste, France; (011) 33-466-50-05-05. Volunteers needed to help preserve and restore monuments in France and Italy. Inquiries to Jacqueline Simon, 217 High Park Blvd., Buffalo, NY 14226; (716) 836-8698.

Ministry of Culture, Sous-Direction de l'Archéologie Documentation, 4 rue d'Aboukir, 75002 Paris, France; (011) 33-1-40-15-77-17. Every year in May publishes a list of excavations throughout France that accept volunteers.

Nature et Progrès, 1 Avenue Géneral de Gaulle, 84130 Le Pontet, France; (011) 33-4-90-31-00-42. Sells "Les Bonnes Adresses de la Bio," a list of organic farmers who need temporary assistants. Current price not confirmed.

PGL Adventure (see United Kingdom section). Needs outdoor activity center staff for holiday centers in France.

REMPART, 1 rue des Guillemites, 75004 Paris, France; (011) 33-1-42-71-96-55. Needs volunteers to care for endangered monuments. Most projects charge FF40-FF50 a day, plus membership of FF220.

The French Embassy publishes the leaflets Employment in France for Students and Au Pair Positions in France which include agency addresses and information on red tape. Contact: Studies Office, Cultural Services, French Embassy, 972 5th Ave., New York, NY 10021. In Paris, look for the publication France-USA Contacts which carry job ads. Also, consult notice boards at American Church, 65 quai d'Orsay, Paris 7, France.

Germany, Switzerland, Austria

Au Pair in Germany/GIJK, Oststr. 8-14, 53173 Bonn, Germany; (011) 49-228-95-73-00; gijk @gijk.de. Au pair placements for all nationalities under the age of 24.

CDS International, 330 7th Ave., 19th Fl. New York, NY 10001-5010; (212) 497-3500 info@cdsintl.org. Arranges 6-month paid internships in Germany for students or recent graduates in business, engineering, and other technical fields. Longer placements of 12-18 months also available.

English for Kids, A. Baumgartnerstr. 44, A/ 7042, 1230 Vienna, Austria; (011) 43-1-667-45-79. TEFL trained teachers needed for residential summer school.

FJM/Freundinnen Junger Mädchen, Zähringerstrasse 36, 8001 Zürich, Switzerland; (011) 41-1-252-38-40. Au pair placements throughout Switzerland.

German Academic Exchange Service/DAAD, 950 3rd Ave., 19th Fl., New York, NY 10022. May be able to advise on teaching opportunities in Germany.

Gruppo Volontari dalla Svizzera Italiana, C.P. 12, CH-6517 Arbedo, Switzerland; (011) 41-92-29-13-37. Reconstruction workcamps manned by volunteers in mountain villages who can speak German, French, or Italian.

IBG, Schlosserstrasse 28, D-70180 Stuttgart, Germany; (011) 49-711-649-11-28. Organizes voluntary workcamps throughout Germany.

Institut du Haut-Lac, 1831 Les Sciernes d'Albeuve, Switzerland; (011) 41-29-84201. Teacher and monitors needed for summer and winter language programs.

International School Kaprun, Alpine Sports and Ski Racing Academy, Postfach 47, 5710 Kaprun, Austria; Tel./fax (011) 43-6547-7106. Young graduates needed to live in on low pay for a year; some teaching and pastoral duties.

Internationale Umweltschutz Korps, P.O. Box 9101, Herisau, Switzerland; (011) 41-71- 515103. Volunteers needed for conservation camps at Zermatt, Saas Fee, etc. Knowledge of German required.

Involvement Volunteers—Deutschland Naturbadstr. 49, 91056 Erlangen, Germany; Tel./fax (011) 49-9135-8075. Conservation organization allied to Involvement Volunteers

in Australia (see Voluntary Service listings below).

Okista, Türkenstrasse 8/11, 1090 Vienna, Austria; (011) 43-1-401-48-8827; rosi.weinmann@oekista.co.at. Live-in childcare positions throughout Austria.

Österreichischer Bauorden, P.O. Box 149, Hornesgasse 3, 1031 Vienna, Austria. Organizes projects staffed by volunteers to help disadvantaged communities.

Pro Filia, 51 rue de Carouge, 1205 Geneva, Switzerland; (011) 41-22-329-84-62. Places live-in babysitters with French-speaking families for a minimum of 1 year; the office at Beckenhofstrasse 16, 8036 Zurich deals with German-speaking Switzerland.

Swiss Travel Service, Bridge House, 55-59 High Rd., Broxbourne, Hertfordshire EN10 7DT, England. Winter and summer resort representatives needed. Interviews held in U.K.

Travelbound/Skibound, Olivier House, 18 Marine Parade, Brighton, East Sussex BN2 1TL, U.K.; (011) 44-1273-677777. Domestic and kitchen staff needed to work summer or winter season for tour operator which runs hotels in Alpine resorts in Austria (and also France).

U.S. military bases throughout Germany have Civilian Personnel Offices (CPOs) that are responsible for recruiting auxiliary staff to work in bars, shops, etc. on base. However, with the scaling down of the U.S. military presence in Europe, fewer vacancies exist. The best bet is at Armed Forces Recreational Centers at Garmisch Partenkirchen, Berchtesgaden, and Chiemsee.

Village Camps S.A., CH-1296 Coppet, Switzerland; (011) 41-22-776 4010; village-camps@compuserve.com. Recruits monitors and counselors to work for the summer or winter season at children's sports camps in several Swiss resorts and Zell-am-See, Austria.

WWOOF (Germany), Thalhauser Fussweg 30, D-85354 Freising, Germany. Volunteer openings on organic farms. Membership costs DM30.

WWOOF (Switzerland), Postfach 615, 9001 St. Gallen, Switzerland; fairtours@gn.apc.org. For details of working for your keep on an organic farm, send 2 IRCs.

Zentralstelle für Arbeitsvermittlung, Feuerbachstrasse 42-46, D-60325 Frankfurt-am L-Main, Germany; (011) 49-69-71-11-0. This federal employment bureau handles student applications from abroad.

Latin America

American Friends Service Committee, 1501 Cherry St., Philadelphia, PA 19102; (215) 241-7000. Sends paying volunteers who speak Spanish to community projects in Mexico and Cuba during the summer. Program fee $750 for Mexico plus travel expenses.

Amigos de las Americas, 5618 Star Ln., Houston, TX 77057. Sends about 500 volunteers with knowledge of Spanish or Portuguese to Brazil, Costa Rica, Dominican Republic, Ecuador, Honduras, Mexico, and Paraguay. Participants pay $2,500-$3,000.

Amizade Volunteer Vacations, 1334 Dartmouth Ln., Deerfield, IL 60015; (847) 945-9402; amizade@worldnet.att.net. Short-term voluntary projects in Brazil, Peru, and Bolivia. Participation fee of $1,500-$3,000 includes travel.

Bermuda Biological Station for Research, Inc., 17 Biological Ln., St. George's, GE01 Bermuda; (809) 297-1880. Volunteer interns help scientists conduct research for 4 months.

Casa de los Amigos, Casa de los Amigos Ignacio Mariscal 132, 06030 Mexico, D.F. Mexico; Tel./fax (011) 52-5-705 0521. Quaker-run community center in Mexico City which assigns volunteers for at least 6 months to worthwhile social projects.

Casa Guatemala, 14th Calle 10-63, Zona 1 Guatemala City; (011) 502-2-1-25517. Run orphanage in the Petén region that need volunteer medical staff, teachers, and nannies.

Centro Cultural Colombo Americano Carrera 43, 51-95 Barranquilla, Colombia. Recruits English teachers. Similar centers in Cali, Bogota, Medellin, etc.

Conservation International, Eco-Escuela d Espanol, 2501 M St., NW, Suite 200, Washington, DC 20037; (202) 973-2264 ecoescuela@conservation.org. Students liv in Guatemalan village and help with devel opment work while studying Spanish.

Fomento Educacional, Educational and Cul tural Exchange Center, Hamburgo 115, Co Juarez, C.P. 06600 Mexico D.F.; (011) 52-5 525-1693; fomec@mpsnet.com.mx. Can ad vise on internships and volunteer work i Mexico.

Foundation for Sustainable Development P.O. Box 37, Carrboro, NC 27510; (919) 932 5975. Summer and year-long internships ar ranged in Guatemala, Mexico, and Nicara gua.

ICADS (Institute for Central American De velopment Studies) Apartado 3, 207 Sabanilla, San Jose, Costa Rica; (011) 506 225-0508. Also P.O. Box 025216, Miami, F 33102-5216. One month Spanish cours combined with voluntary sevice in Costa Ric Nicaragua or Belize. Cost from $1,100.

Latin Link, 325 Kennington Park Rd., Lor don SE11 4QE, England; (011) 44-171-207

WORK AND STUDY ABROAD

 WORK taking care of children (maximum 30 hours a week) living with a European family

 STUDY a foreign language or culture in Paris, London or Madrid

 TRAVEL inexpensively in Europe

SEMESTER		YEAR	
PARIS & LONDON	$3,495	PARIS & LONDON	$5,190
MADRID	$2,995	MADRID	$4,390

...includes one way flight, tuition, private room and meals, $75 weekly pocket money, orientation, cultural activities and on-site support

(800) 727-AIFS • http://www.aifs.com

a program of the **American Institute For Foreign Study**®

☐ **YES,** send me your brochure

I am interested in a ☐ semester ☐ year

Au Pair in

EUROPE

Name _____

Address _____

College/university _____

Phone ( ) _____ E-mail _____

Send to AIFS Au Pair in Europe, Dept. TR, 102 Greenwich Avenue, Greenwich, CT 06830

5880. Runs Short-Term Experience Projects (STEPs) in Argentina, Brazil, Bolivia, Peru, Ecuador, and Nicaragua for committed Christians.

One World Work Force, Rt. 4, Box 963A, Flagstaff, AZ 86001-9320; Tel./fax (520) 779-3639; 1world@infomagic.com. Sends volunteers to assist scientists at wildlife projects along the Pacific coast of Mexico.

Overseas Development Network, 333 Valencia St., Suite 330, San Francisco, CA 94103; (415) 431-4204. Summer internships in Mexico for Spanish speakers.

Programa de Voluntariado Internacional, Servicio de Parques Nacionales, Apdo. 11384-1000, San Jose, Costa Rica; (011) 506-222-50-85. Spanish-speaking volunteers work in national parks for at least 2 months. Cost is $400 per month.

World Education Forum, P.O. Box 383-4005, San Antonio de Belen, Heredia, Costa Rica; (800) 689-1170. Sponsors exchange programs between U.S. and Costa Rica and Mexico. Volunteers teach English while learning Spanish.

Mediterranean

Abruzzo National Park, Viale Tito Livio 12, I-00136 Rome, Italy; (011) 36-6-35403331. Conservation project in the central Italy mountains.

Acorn Venture Ltd. (see under France). Activity instructors and support staff for holiday center on the Costa Brava of Spain.

American Farm School, 1133 Broadway, New York, NY 10010 (212) 463-8434; or Summer Work Activities Program, P.O. Box 23, 55 102 Kalamaria, Thessaloniki, Greece. Young people needed in the summer for ag-

ricultural and maintenance programs on farms near Thessaloniki in northern Greece.

Au Pair International, Via S. Stefano 32, 40125 Bologna, Italy; (011) 39-51-267575. Au pair placements in Italy. Weekly pocket money or about LIT100,000.

Centros Europeos, Calle Principe 12-6°A, 28012 Madrid, Spain; (011) 34-1-532-7230. Au pair placements in Spain. Also vacancies for English teachers October-June.

Club Paradisus, Poste Restante, Koroni 240 04, Messinia, Greece. Conservation volunteers needed for 1-month stints mid-June to end of September to clean up beach and surrounding habitats of the loggerhead turtle near Koroni on the Peloponnese.

Consolas Travel, 100 Eolou St., 10559 Athens, Greece; (011) 30-1-325-4931. This travel agency hires office staff for its branches plus hostel staff for pensions in Athens and the islands.

Coordinatora d'Agricultura Ecològica, Apt de Correus 2580, 08080 Barcelona, Spain. Send 1 IRC for a list of organic farms.

Employment Agencies. Several employment agencies in Athens run a placement service for au pairs and may offer positions in the tourist industry, including: Au Pair Activities P.O. Box 76080, 17110 Nea Smyrni, Athens, Greece; Tel./fax (011) 30-1-932-6016.

European Conservation Volunteers in Greece, 15 Omirou St., 14564 Kifissia, Greece. Voluntary projects to restore old buildings and maintain areas of natural beauty. Apply through a U.S. counterpart (e.g. CIEE, VFP).

Galentina's Childcare Consultancy, P.O. Box 51181, Kifissia, Athens 145 10, Greece; Tel./fax (011) 30-1-808-1005. Places nannies and experienced nurses in private families in Greece (and worldwide).

GIC, Pintor Sorolla Apartado 1080, 46901 Monte Vedat, Spain; Tel./fax (011) 34-6-156-7216. Au pair agency and youth exchange organization.

Greece, Italy, Spain, and Portugal. English-language newspapers such as the Athens-News, Greek News or the Anglo-Portuguese News are helpful sources of tutoring or au pair positions. Many people find work in language schools by applying in person to schools in Madrid, Barcelona, Oporto, Thessaloniki, Milan, etc. Lists of English language schools in Italy may be found in the Italian Yellow Pages under "Scuole di Lingua."

Gruppi Archeologici d'Italia, Via Degli Scipioni 30/A, 00192 Rome, Italy; (011) 39-6-39733786. Volunteers for short archaeological digs throughout Italy.

Instituto da Juventude, Av. da Liberdade 194, 1250 Lisbon, Portugal; (011) 351-3151-955. Arranges workcamps including archaeological digs, throughout Portugal.

Kursolan, S.A., Calle Sándalo 5, 28042, Madrid, Spain; (011) 34-91-320-7500. Runs 2 summer camps outside Madrid employing 40 teacher-counselors.

Malta Youth Hostels Association, 17 Triq Tal-Borg, Pawla PLA 06, Malta; (011) 356-693957; myha@keyworld.net. Volunteers who spend 21 hours a week doing hostel maintenance and administration receive free bed and breakfast for 2 weeks to 3 months.

Mr. Panayotis Passalis, Stavros Kallas, Theologos 85106, Rhodes, Greece; (011) 30-241-41173. Volunteers with knowledge of farming can stay and work on his prop-

erty which he wants to turn into an in national community.

O'Neill School of English, Servicio Au Pair, Ibarluce 20, 48960 Galdakao, Spain; (011) 34-4-456-49-17. Demand for native speakers to live with families and help the children with conversational English.

Proyecto Ambiental Tenerife, c/o 55 Monmouth St., Covent Garden, London WC2H 9DG, England; (011) 44-171-240-6604. Volunteers needed to work 3-4 months in depopulated rural areas of Tenerife, Spain. Must contribute $115 per week to expenses.

Skyros, 92 Prince of Wales Rd., London NW5 3NE, U.K; (011) 44-171-284-3065. Work scholars recruited to assist at Atsitsa alternative holiday center on Greek island of Skyros. Volunteers can participate in courses offered at center such as yoga, holistic medicine, windsurfing, etc.

Summer Camps, Via Roma 54, 18038 San Remo, Italy; Tel./fax (011) 39-184-506070; edu@rosenet.it. Need counselors for multi-activity and English-language camps in northern Italy.

Sunsail, The Port House, Port Solent, Portsmouth, Hampshire P06 4TH, England; (011) 44-1705-222325, hires sailors, hostesses, clubhouse staff, cooks, and nannies for Greece, and Turkey.

Sunseed Trust, Eastside, Huntingdon, PE18 7BY, England; Tel./fax (011) 44-1480-411 784. Invites volunteers to help at a remote research project near Almeria on the south coast of Spain, to help subsidize their stay (costing from about $120 per week).

Sunworld Sailing Ltd., 120 St. Georges Rd., Brighton, E. Sussex BN2 1EA, U.K. Employs instructors, maintenance staff, crew and

ALTERNATIVE TRAVEL DIRECTORY

other staff for sailing and windsurfing holidays in Turkey, Spain, Greece, and Turkey.

Middle East

American Language Center Damascus, c/o USIS, P.O. Box 29, Damascus, Syria; (011) 963-11-332 7236, or c/o USIS, Department of State, Washington, DC 20521-6110. Forty native speaker teachers employed after interview and orientation/training session.

Anglo Nannies, 20 Beverley Ave., London SW20 0RL, England; (011) 44-181-944-6677. Places mother's helpers and nannies in wealthy Istanbul households.

Dogan International Organization (Au Pair and Employment Agency), Sehitmuhtar Caddesi 37/7, Taskim 80090, Istanbul, Turkey; (011) 90 216-235-1599. Places English-speaking au pairs, preferably after interview.

Eilat. This prospering and expanding Red Sea resort employs many passers-through in hotels, bars, marinas, etc. Inquire at the youth hostel or the Peace Cafe about work.

English Fast, Burhaniye Mah-Resmi Efendi Sok. No. 4, Beylerbeyi, Istanbul, Turkey; (011) 90-216-318-7018 or 7019. Openings for teachers in Istanbul, Ankara, and Izmir.

Gençtur, Istiklal Cad. Zambak Sok. 15/5, Taksim, 80080 Istanbul, Turkey; (011) 90-212-249-2515; workcamps@genctir.com.tr. A student travel organization that arranges international workcamps and English language summer camps for which ESL teachers and monitors are needed.

GSM Youth Activities Services, Bayindir Sokak No. 45/9, 06450 Kizilay, Ankara, Turkey; (011) 90-312-417-29-91. Arranges 2-week work camps in Anatolia. Registration fee is DM100.

Hilma's Au Pair Intermediary, Mrs. Hilma Shmoshkovitz, P.O. Box 91, 75100 Rishon-le-Zion, Israel; (011) 972-3-965-99-37; hilma@netvision.net.il. Well-established au pair and nanny agency for Israel. Also has an office in Jerusalem.

Israel Antiquities Authority, P.O. Box 586, Jerusalem 91004, Israel; (011) 972-2-560-2607; harriet@israntique.org.il. Coordinates archaeological excavations throughout Israel. Publishes an annual listing of digs looking for paying volunteers.

Israel Youth Hostels Assoc., 1 Shezer St., P.O. Box 6001, Jerusalem 91060, Israel; (011) 972-2-6558400. Volunteers needed for hostel work throughout Israel. Applications should be sent to individual hostels.

Kibbutz Program Center, 18 Frishman St., Cr. Ben Yehuda, 3rd Fl., Apt. 6, Tel Aviv 61030, Israel; (011) 972-3-527-8874. This office can place you on a kibbutz, although it is better to arrive with a letter of introduction from Kibbutz Program Center, 110 E. 59th St., 4th fl., New York, NY 10022; (800) 247-7852; ProjOren@aol.com. A clearinghouse for American volunteers. Minimum stay 2 months. Registration fee $110. Summer is the busiest time.

Meira's Volunteers, 73 Ben Yehuda St., 1st Fl., Tel Aviv 63435, Israel; (011) 972-3-523-7369. Agent for kibbutzim and moshavim for volunteers already in Israel.

Noah's Ark International, 12 Broadlands Brixworth, Northamptonshire NN6 9BH U.K.; (011) 44-1604-881639. Places qualified TEFL teachers at range of public and private schools in Turkey.

Saday Educational Consultancy, Necatibe Caddesi 92/3, Karakoy, Istanbul, Turkey (011) 90-212-2S43-2078. Supply English tutors to live in with Turkish families.

Transonic Travel, 10 Sedley Pl., London W1R 1HG, U.K.; (011) 44-171-409-3535. Agency which places volunteers on kibbutzim and moshavim for at least 2 months.

UNIPAL (Universities Trust for Educational Exchange with Palestinians), c/o Centre for Middle Eastern and Islamic Studies, South Rd., Durham, DH1 3TG, U.K.; Tel./fax (011) 44-191-386 7124. Sends volunteers to teach English to Palestinians and help with handicapped children in the West Bank, Gaza, and Lebanon.

Netherlands, Belgium, Luxembourg

Activity International, P.O. Box 7097, 9701 JB Groningen, Netherlands; (011) 31-50-3130666; aupair@noord.bart.nl. Au pair placements via Au Pair Homestay Program (see International Organizations section).

Archeolo-j, Avenue Paul Terlinden 23, 1330 Rixensart, Belgium; (011) 2-653-82-68. Residential archaeological digs require paying volunteers.

BLS (Brussels Language Studies), 8 rue du Marteau, 1210 Brussels, Belgium; (011) 32-2-217-23-73. Freelance English teachers needed to teach children and adults during summer holidays and throughout the year.

ICVD, MvB Bastiaan sestraat 56, 1054 SP Amsterdam, Netherlands. Volunteers needed for building restoration and other voluntary camps.

L'Administration de l'Emploi, 38a rue Philippe II, 3rd fl., L-2340 Luxembourg; (011) 352-47-68-55. Operates a Service Vacances for students seeking summer jobs in warehouses, restaurants, etc. Non-European students must visit the office in person.

Luxembourg Accueil Information, 10 Bisserwee, L-1238 Luxembourg-Grund; (011) 352-24-17-17. Welcome center for new arrivals that tries to match au pairs with families looking for help with childcare.

Natuur 2000, Bervoetstraat 33, 2000 Antwerp, Belgium; (011) 32-3-231-26-04. Organizes summer conservation workcamps and study projects throughout Belgium, which cost from BF1,000.

Phone Languages, 65 rue des Echevins, 1050 Brussels, Belgium; (011) 32-2-647-40-20. Telephone teachers recruited for clients throughout Belgium and Luxembourg.

Stufam V.Z.W., Vierwindenlaan 7, 1780 Wemmel, Belgium; (011) 32-2-460-3395. Places au pairs in Belgium for a fee of BF1,000.

The Bulletin. A weekly English-language magazine in Brussels which carries job ads.

Windrose Au Pair Agency, Av. Paul Dejaer 21a, 1060 Brussels, Belgium; (011) 32-2-534 7191. Places all nationalties as au pairs in Belgium.

Scandinavia

American-Scandinavian Foundation (Exchange Division), 725 Park Ave., New York, NY 10021; (212) 879-9779. Places summer trainees in engineering, agriculture, chemistry, etc. throughout Scandinavia.

APØG, Norsk Økologisk Landbrukslag, Langeveien 18, N-5003 Bergen, Norway; (011) 47-55-32-04-80. Service for volunteers who want to work on organic farms in Norway; send $8 or 10 IRCs for list of 50 plus farm addresses.

Atlantis (Norwegian Foundation for Youth Exchange), Rolf Hofmosgate 18, 0655 Oslo, Norway; (011) 47-2-67-00-43. Arranges summer working guest positions on farms for 1-3 months. Also recruits au pairs for a minimum of 6 months. Applications should be sent to InterExchange in New York (see International Organizations).

Center for International Mobility (CIMO), P.B. 343, 00531 Helsinki, Finland; (011) 358-9-7747-7033. Arranges family stays with participant teaching host family English. Also arranges internships for 2-18 months.

Exis, Rebslagergade 3, Postbox 291, 6400 Sonderborg, Denmark; (011) 45-74-42-97-49; exis@po.ia.dk. Au pair placements in Denmark, Norway, and Iceland.

IAL/Internationella Arbetslag, Barnängsgatan 23, 116 41 Stockholm, Sweden; (011) 46-8-643 08 89. Peace and conservation camps organized through the Swedish branch of Service Civil International (see U.S. address at end of Directory).

Icelandic Nature ConservationVolunteers, SJA, P.O. Box 8468, 128 Reykjavik. Recruits volunteers for local short-term summer projects throughout Iceland.

MS/Mellemfolkeligt Samvirke, Studsgade 20, 8000 Aarhus C, Denmark. Two 4-week summer workcamps in Denmark and Greenland. Danish camp fee 885 kroner.

Use It, Youth Information Copenhagen, Radhusstraede 13, 1466 Copenhagen K, Denmark; (011) 45-1-33-15-65-18. Publishes English Language Guide to Copenhagen, Short Cuts, with section on working, for 40 Danish kroner.

VHH, c/o Inga Nielsen, Asenvej 35, 9881 Bindslev, Denmark. For $10 publishes a list of English-speaking farmers looking for volunteers.

WOOF Finland, Luomu-Liiton talkoovälitys, Koiddalamylly, 51880 Koikkala, Finland; (011) 358-9-55-450- 251. New Finnish organic farm organization. Send 2 IRCs to get list of 40 farmers looking for volunteers over the summer.

United Kingdom and Ireland

Aillwee Cave Co., Ltd., Ballyvaughan, Co. Clare, Ireland; (011) 353-65-77036. Cave tour guides and catering/sales staff taken on for summer season at this busy tourist attraction open March to November.

An Oige, 61 Mountjoy St., Dublin 1, Ireland. The Irish Youth Hostels Association makes use of voluntary assistant wardens in the summer months.

British Trust for Conservation Volunteers, 36 Saint Mary's St., Wallingford, Oxfordshire OX10 0EU, England; (011) 44-1491-839766. Organizes 1- or 2-week working breaks for environmentally concerned volunteers.

Community Service Volunteers, Overseas Programme, 237 Pentonville Rd., London N1 9NJ, England; (011) 44-1-71-278-6601. Places volunteers in socially worthwhile projects from 4 months to a year, throughout Britain. U.S. applicants should apply through WISE (see International Organizations).

Conservation Volunteers Ireland, P.O. Box 3836, Ballsbridge, Dublin 4, Ireland; Tel./fax (011) 353-1-668-1844. Coordinates unpaid environmental working holidays throughout Ireland. Membership is £15.

Council for British Archaeology, Bowes Morrell House, 111 Walmgate, York Y01 2UA, England. Publishes CBA Briefing 5 times a year with details of upcoming excavations in Britain. Membership costs £20 (plus postage).

Council, 205 E. 42nd St., New York, NY 10017-5706; (888) COUNCIL. Used to run the Work in Britain Program in conjunction with BUNAC (16 Bowling Green Ln., London EC1R 0BD, England) whereby students can obtain a 6-month work permit to do any job in the British Isles or a 4-month permit for Ireland. Check for current programs.

Dublin Internships, 8 Orlagh Lawn, Scholarstown Rd., Dublin 16, Ireland; Tel./fax (011) 353-1-494-5277. Places American students in salaried internships of varying durations in Dublin. A placement fee is charged.

National Trust, Residential Holidays, P.O. Box 84, Cirencester, Glos. GL7 1ZP, England; (011) 44-1285-644727. One-week outdoor conservation camps throughout the U.K. year round. Volunteers pay £42-50 per week.

Nord-Anglia International Ltd., 10 Eden Pl., Cheadle, Stockport, Cheshire SK8 1AT, England; (011) 44-161-491-4191. Places over 500 young people in English-language summer schools in Britain and Ireland as language and sports instructors. Many positions are nonresidential.

People to People International, 501 E. Armour Blvd., Kansas City, MO 64109-2200; (816) 531-4701. Two-month unpaid internships in London and Dublin.

PGL Adventure, Alton Court, Penyard Ln., Ross-on-Wye, Herefordshire HR9 5NR, England; (011) 44-1989-767833. Hires over 500 people as sports instructors, counselors, and general staff for activity centers throughout Britain. Other children's holiday companies include: Prime Leisure Activity Holidays, Ltd., The Manor Farm House, Dunstan Rd., Old Headington, Oxford OX3 9BY, England; Camp Beaumont, Worth- ington House, 203-205 Marylebone Rd., London NW1 5QP, England; EF Language Travel, 1-3 Farman St., Hove, Sussex BN3 1AL, England; and Action Holidays, Robinwood, Jumps Rd., Todmorden, Lancashire 0L14 8HJ, England. All recruit large numbers of summer staff.

Programme of International Agricultural Workcamps in the U.K. Listing available from Concordia Youth Service Volunteers, Heversham House, 20/22 Boundary Rd., Hove, Sussex BN3 4ET, England; (011) 44-1273-422293 in exchange for 2 IRCs. Recruits foreign students aged 19-25 to pick fruit and hops at over 160 U.K. farms. Applications should be sent between September and December.

TASIS England American School, Cold-Harbour Ln., Thorpe, Surrey KT20 8TE, England; (011) 44-1932-565252. EFL teaching vacancies for qualified Americans and jobs for sports monitors to work at children's summer camp.

Thistle Camps, National Trust for Scotland, 5 Charlotte Sq., Edinburgh EH2 4DU, Scotland; (011) 44-131-243-9470. Similar to National Trust but in Scotland. Includes archaeological digs. Week-long projects cost from £40.

Trident Transnational, Saffron Court, 14B Saint Cross St., London EC1N 8XA, England; (011) 44-171-242-1515 ttn.demon. co.uk. Offers unpaid work placements lasting 3 weeks to 6 months in U.K. businesses. Participants aged 18-26. Fees start at £200 for 2-month attachment.

USIT (Union of Students in Ireland Travel Service), 19 Aston Quay, Dublin 2, Ireland; (011) 353-1-677-8117. Advice on job opportunities for Council work abroad participants.

Winant & Clayton Volunteers, 109 E. 50th St., New York, NY 10022; (212) 751-1616 ext. 271, arranges for U.S. citizens to work 6-10 weeks during the summer in youth clubs, with the homeless, AIDS sufferers, etc. in Britain.

WWOOF (Working for Organic Growers), 19 Bradford Rd., Lewes, Sussex BN7 1RB, England. Connects members with organic farmers throughout Britain (annual membership £10). The Irish equivalent is WWOOF Ireland, Harpoonstown, Drinagh, Co. Wexford, Ireland (membership IR£5).

YHA Recruitment, 8 St. Stephen's Hill, St. albans, Herts AL1 2DY, U.K. Seasonal assistant youth hostel wardens for 240 U.K. hostels. Interviews required.

Voluntary Service

Archaeological Institute of America, in Boston; fax (617) 353-6550 or (800) 228-0810. Publishes each January the Archaeological Fieldwork Opportunities Bulletin listing digs and projects open to volunteers. The Bulletin costs $12.50 from Kendall Hunt Publishing, 4050 Westmark Dr., P.O. Box 1840, Dubuque, IA 52004-1840.

British Trust for Conservation Volunteers, 36 St. Mary's St., Wallingford, Oxfordshire OX10 0EU, U.K.; (011) 44-1491-839766. Conservation projects around the world.

Canadian Crossroads International, 31 Madison Ave., Toronto, ON M5R 2S2, Canada; (416) 967-0801. Various short-term development projects worldwide (for Canadian citizens only).

Concern Worldwide, 104 E. 40th St., New York, NY 10016; (212) 557-8000. Irish agency that sends professional aid workers to developing countries.

Conservation International, Accepts volunteers to work with local people to help save rainforests in Brazil, Colombia, Costa Rica, Indonesia, Botswana, etc.

Europe Conservation Italia, Via Bertini 34, 20154 Milan, Italy; (011) 39-2-33103344; ecomil@imiucca.csi.unimi.it. Fee-paying volunteers for environmental projects in Italy, Thailand, Brazil, and Switzerland.

Global Routes, 1814 7th St., Suite A, Berkeley, CA 94710; (510) 848-4800; mail@global routes.org. Sends interns in pairs to remote villages in Costa Rica, Ecuador, Thailand, Kenya, and Navajo Nation to teach in local schools and do community service.

Global Service Corps, 300 Broadway, Suite 28, San Francisco, CA 94133-3312. Cooperates with grassroots organizations in Kenya, Costa Rica, Guatemala, and Thailand. Sends volunteers for 2-3 weeks (fee $1,500-$1,700).

Global Volunteers, Global Volunteers, 375 E. Little Canada Rd., Little Canada, MN 55117. Sends volunteers to short-term community projects in selected countries.

Partnership for Service Learning, 815 2nd Ave., Suite 315, New York, NY 10017; (212) 986-0989. Sends students to India, Philippines, Ecuador, Mexico, Jamaica, and Europe to teach, help care for disadvantaged people, etc.

Peace Corps, 1990 K St. NW, Washington, DC 20526. The main government agency that recruits volunteers to work in developing countries on 2-year contracts.

Raleigh International, Raleigh House, 27 Parsons Green Lane, London SW6 4HS, England; (011) 44-171-371-8585. Selects young people aged 17 to 25 for 10-week expeditions to carry out scientific research and community aid in remote areas.

Scientific and Conservation Expeditions. A number of organizations recruit paying volunteers to help staff scientific and conservation expeditions throughout the world. Examples are: Earthwatch, 680 Mt. Auburn St., P.O. Box 403, Watertown, MA 02272; and Univ. of California Research Expeditions (UREP), Univ. of California, Berkeley, CA 94720-7050.

Traveler's Earth Repair Network (TERN), c/o Michael Pilarski, P.O. Box 4469, Bellingham, WA 98227; Fax (360) 671-9668. Supplies list of potential hosts worldwide involved in organic farming, tree planting, etc. A subscription costs $50.

Volunteers Exchange International, 134 W. 26th St., New York, NY 10001; (212) 206-7307. U.S. branch of International Christian Youth Exchange. Exchanges with over 33 countries that involve voluntary service in the community.

Volunteers, P.O. Box 218, Port Melbourne, VIC 3207, Australia; Fax (011) 61-3-9646 5504; ivimel@iaccess.com.au. Arranges short-term individual, group, and team voluntary placements in Australia, New Zealand, Fiji, Papua New Guinea, Thailand, India, Germany, Finland, Greece, Ghana, Kenya, Lebanon, and South Africa. Most projects involve conservation. Program fee is AUS$400.

Workcamp Organizations. The major workcamp organizations for American volunteers are: Council, 205 E. 42nd St., New York, NY 10017-5706; (888) COUNCIL.

Service Civil International, 5474 Walnut Level Rd., Crozet, VA 22932; (804) 823-1826, and Volunteers for Peace, 43 Tiffany Rd., Belmont, VT 05730; (802) 259-2759.

World Challenge Expeditions Ltd., Black Arrow House, 2 Chandos Rd., London NW10 6NF, U.K.; (011) 44-181-961-1122; welcome@ world-challenge.co.uk. Expedition leaders for school groups to developing countries.

World Exchange, 121 George St., Edinburgh, Scotland EH2 4YN; (011) 44-131-225-8115. Volunteer program arranged by combined Scottish Churches. Basic training followed by church-affiliated placements worldwide lasting 10-12 months.

WorldTeach, Harvard Institute for International Development, 1 Eliot St., Cambridge, MA 02138; (617) 495-5527. Sends volunteers to teach English, and other subjects for one year in Ecuador, Costa Rica, Poland, Lithuania, Namibia, Vietnam, and Thailand. Also has summer program in China.

CHAPTER 18

VOLUNTEER PROGRAMS

The following listing of volunteer abroad programs was supplied by the organizers. Contact the program directors to confirm costs, dates, and other details. If you do not see the program you want in the country of your choice, look in the "Worldwide" listings at the end of the section for programs located in several different regions.

Africa

African Am. Studies Program. To educate the American public concerning social, cultural, political developments in Africa with educational trips to 25 African countries.

Dates: Feb, Jun, Jul, Aug. Cost: From $1,000 to $5,000. Contact: AASP, 19 S. La Salle, #301, Chicago, IL 60615; (312) 443-0929, fax (312) 773-6967.

Australia

Australian Trust for Conservation Volunteers. ATCV is a national, nonprofit, nonpolitical organization undertaking practical conservation projects, including tree planting, seed col-

lection, flora/fauna surveys, habitat restoration, track construction, and weed eradication. Projects take place year round in all states and territories.

Cost: Six-week Echidna Package: AUS$840. Contact: ATCV, P.O. Box 423, Ballarat, Victoria 3353, Australia (please include IRC); (011) 61-3-5333-1483, fax 5333-2290; atcv@netconnect.com.au.

WWOOFING. Learn about organic growing and/or about life in Australia by working in exchange for keep. Australian list has 720 hosts.

Dates: Year round. Cost: $30 single, $35 couple (includes accident insurance). Contact: WWOOF Australia, Buchan, Victoria 3885, Australia; (011) 61-3-5155-0218.

Canada

Willing Workers on Organic Farms. WWOOF-Canada is an exchange venture. In exchange for your help on one of over 250 farms or homesteads (animal care, weeding, harvesting, construction projects) volunteers receive accommodations, 3 meals daily, and a wonderful learning experience.

Dates: Year round. Most opportunities spring-fall. Cost: $25 (single), $35 (couple) plus 2 IRCs. Contact: WWOOF-Canada, RR 2, S. 18, C. 9 Nelson, BC V1L 5P5, Canada; (250) 354-4417, fax (250) 352-3927.

Central America

Plenty Volunteer Program. Plenty places a limited number of volunteers to work on community-based development projects in food production, communications, crafts marketing, and other appropriate technologies related to increasing local self-sufficiency. Length of service varies per position, but is typically 1-6 months.

Dates: Ongoing. Cost: Volunteer pays travel and living expenses. Contact: Send SASE to: Lisa Wartinger, Plenty, West Coast Office, Dept. T, 22 Harper Canyon Rd., Salinas, CA 93908; (408) 484-5845; www.public.usit.net/plenty1/.

Costa Rica

Casa Rio Blanco Rainforest Reserve. Slow down and enjoy this biodiverse world. Get a better understanding of yourself, blended with a new perspective of a fascinating culture and environment. A unique experience that will last a lifetime, while participating in rainforest conservation and environmental education. Visit us on the web.

Dates: Four-week sessions throughout the year. Contact: Dee Bocock (new owner), Casa Rio Blanco, Apdo 241-7210, Guapiles, Pococi, Costa Rica.

Genesis II Cloudforest Preserve. The main activity during the dry season (Jan to Jun) is trail maintenance and construction. In the rainy season (Jul to Dec) work is done on reforestation in a deforested area.

Dates: Jan 3-31, Feb 7-Mar 6, Mar 13-Apr 10, Apr 17-May 15, May 22-Jun 19, Jun 26-Jul 24, Jul 31-Aug 28, Sep 11-Oct 9, Oct 16-Nov 13. Cost: $600 per unit of 28 days. Inquiries should include 3 IRCs. Contact: Steve or Paula Friedman, Apdo. 655, 7.050 Cartago, Costa Rica.

Learn Spanish While Volunteering. Assist with the training of Costa Rican public school teachers in our latest language learning techniques, using classroom computers, K-8 school targeted by Costa Rican government as a model ESL/technology school. Enjoy learning Spanish in the morning, volunteer work in the afternoon/evening. Spanish classes are 2-5 students plus group learning activities; conversations with middle-class homestay families (1 student per family). Homestays and volunteer project are within walking distance of school in small town (14,000 population) near the capital, San Jose.

Dates: Year round, all levels. Classes begin every Monday, volunteer program is continuous. Cost: $295 per week for 25 hours of Spanish classes. Includes tuition, all meals (7 days a week), homestay, laundry, all materials, Costa Rican dance and cooking classes, and airport transportation. $25 one-time registration for Spanish classes; $100 additional one-time registration fee for volunteer program. Contact: Susan Shores, Registrar, Latin American Language Center, 7485 Rush River Dr., Suite 710-123, Sacramento, CA 95831; (916) 447-0938, fax (916) 428-9542; lalc@madre.com.

Denmark

Internship Program. The World Assembly of Youth (WAY) is an international coordinating body of national youth councils and organizations. WAY recognizes the Universal Declaration of Human Rights as the basis of its actions, and works for the promotion of youth in areas such as population, development, etc. Working knowledge of English essential, knowledge of French and/or Spanish preferred. Interns are 20-30 years old.

Dates: Year round. 6-18 months minimum stay. Cost: Return trip paid by WAY. Scholarship of DKK3,000 month provided. Contact: Mr. Heikki Pakarinen, Secretary General, World Assembly of Youth, Ved Bellahøj 4, DK-2700 Brønshøj, Copenhagen, Denmark; (011) 45-38607770, fax 38605797; wayouth @centrum.dk.

El Salvador

Melida Anaya Montes Language School. Teach small-size English classes, all levels offered. Training provided. Students are adults working in the Salvadoran opposition who need to increase their capacity for their work and/or complete their studies. CIS also seeks volunteers for their human rights work. Volunteers can receive half-price Spanish classes.

Dates: Three-month sessions beginning mid-Jan, Apr, and Aug. Mini-sessions offered Jul and Nov. Cost: No fee. Must pay living costs ($250-$400 per month). Contact: CIS MAM Language School, Boulevard Universitario, Casa #4, San Salvador, El Salvador, Centro America; Tel./fax (011) 503-226-2623; cis@nicarao.org.ni.

Europe

Camphill Village. Live and work with mentally handicapped adults and give them help when needed.

Dates: Minimum 6 months, better one year. Start all year. Cost: No costs. We pay board and living and pocket money. Contact: Per Iverson Staffarsgarden, Box 66, S-82060 Delsbo, Sweden; (011) 466 531 6850, fax 0968.

France

Archaeological Digs. These workcamps undertake restoration and maintenance of medieval buildings and sites. The project concerns 2 fortified chateaux at Ottrott, Alsace, destined as cultural and recreational centers. We provide participants with cultural enrichment and physical exercise.

Dates: Jul 16-30; Aug 1-15, Aug 16-30. Cost: Approx. FF500. Contact: Chantiers d'Études Médiévales, 4, rue du Tonnelet Rouge, 67000 Strasbourg, France; (011) 03-88-37-17-20.

Chantiers d'Etudes Medievales. These workcamps lasting 15 days undertake to restore and maintain medieval buildings and sites. The project includes 2 fortified castles at Oltroh, near Strasbourg.

Dates: Jul 1 - Aug 31. Cost: 450FF Contact: Chantiers d'Etudes Medievales, 4 rue du Tonnelet Rouge, 67000 Strasbourg, France; (011) 33-88-37-17-20.

Germany

Work with Children. Help look after mentally handicapped young people in a residential school where "house parents," trainees, teachers, and other staff live and work together. The work includes caring for a small group of children outside of school hours, organizing recreational time, and helping with housework. Knowledge of German is necessary.

Dates: Year round. Cost: Program provides free board and accommodations, social security, and pocket money of DM350 per month. Contact: Mr. Bruno Wegmüller, Heimsonderschule Brachen- reuthe, 88662 Überlingen, Germany; (011) 49-07551/8007-0, fax 8007-50.

Guatemala

Eco-Escuela de Español. The Eco-Escuela de Español offers a unique educational experience by combining intensive Spanish language instruction with volunteer opportunities in conservation and community development projects. Students are immersed in the language, culture, and ecology of Petén, Guatemala—an area renowned for its tropical forests and ancient Mayan ruins. Ecological activities integrate classroom with field-based experiences.

Dates: Every Monday year round. Cost: Classes $65 per week (based on 20 hours of individual instruction per week, Monday-Friday). Room and board with local families $60 per week. Registration fee $10. Contact: Eco-Escuela, Conservation International, 2501 M St., NW, Suite 200, Washington, DC 20037; (202) 973-2264, fax (202) 331-9328; ecoescuela@conservation.org.

India

Cultural Exchange/Workcamps. CECOWOR is a service organization that conducts cultural exchange workcamps for small groups. Specific skills not necessary.

Dates: Year round. Cost: $130 (food and accommodations for one month). Contact: M. Susai Raj, CECOWOR, No. 9, Rajadesingh Nagar, Desurpattai Rd., Gingee V.R.P. Dt., 604 202, Tamil Nadu, India; (011) 91-4145-22747, fax 413 30057.

Project India. A unique 3-week service program open to people of all ages and backgrounds run by a highly qualified staff of educators, social workers, and cultural advisors. Positions include health care, education, social development, arts/recreation, and more. No skills or experience is required. Volunteers pay a fee which covers all expenses.

Dates: Three-week programs run year round. Longer term placements can be arranged. Cost: $1,650 covers all India based expenses. International airfare, insurance, and visa not included. Program fee is tax deductible. Contact: Steven C. Rosenthal, Cross-Cultural Solutions, P.O. Box 625, Ophir, CO 81426; (970) 728-5551 or (800) 380-4777, fax (970) 728-4577; ccsmailbox@aol.com, http://emol.org/emol/projectindia.

Ireland

Conservation Volunteers Ireland. A program of weekend and week-long conservation-working holidays. Volunteers will have the opportunity to mix with Irish volunteers and experience Irish culture.

Dates: Year round. Cost: Varies from IR£16-IR£50. Contact: Conservation Volunteers Ireland, P.O. Box 3836, Ballsbridge, Dublin 4, Ireland; Tel./fax (011) 353-1-66818-44.

Willing Workers on Organic Farms. Voluntary work in return for food and board on farms and small holdings throughout Ireland. Learn about organic farming methods, rural Ireland and its life. Work is varied and you can volunteer from a few days to a few months.

Dates: Year round. Cost: IR £6. Contact: WWOOF, Harpoonstown, Drinagh, Co. Wexford, Ireland.

Israel

Interns for Peace. An independent, community-sponsored program dedicated to building trust and respect among the Jewish and Arab citizens of Israel. Develop action-oriented projects in education, sports, health, the arts, community and workplace relations, and adult interest groups. Requirements include: a commitment to furthering Jewish-Arab relations; BA, BS, or equivalent degree; proficiency in Hebrew or Arabic; a previous stay in Israel of at least 6 months; background in sports, business, teaching, health care, youth work, art, music, or community organizing (professional work experience is a plus).

Dates: Vary. Cost: Must pay own fare to Israel. Contact: Interns for Peace, 475 Riverside Dr., 16th Fl., New York, NY 10115; (212) 870-2226, fax (212) 870-2119.

Japan

Teaching English in Japan. Two-year program to maximize linguistic and cultural integration of participants who work as teachers' assistants. Placements twice yearly in April and August. Most positions are in junior high schools in urban and rural areas. Bachelor's degree, cultural sensitivity, and some ESL training required.

Dates: Hiring for positions every April and August. Applications accepted year round. Cost: Airfare, salary, housing, health care provided. No application fees. Contact: Earlham College, Institute for Education on Japan, D-202, Richmond, IN 47374; (888) 685-2726; www.earlham.edu/www/departments/AET/home.htm.

Latin America

Volunteer, Internship Positions. In Costa Rica, Mexico, Guatemala, Ecuador, Argentina, Peru, Dominican Republic. Various positions in the fields of health care, education, tourism, ESL, business, law, marketing, administrative, environmental, and social work. Additional customized options available. Two weeks to 6 months. Inexpensive lodging in homestays or dorms. Some positions provide free room and board.

Dates: Year round. Flexible start dates. Cost: $200 placement and application fee. Travel insurance and pre-departure preparation included. Lodging costs depend on location. Some positions provide free room and board. Contact: AmeriSpan Unlimited, P.O. Box 40007, Philadelphia, PA 19106; (800) 879-6640, fax (215) 751-1100; info@amerispan.com, www.amerispan.com.

Malta

MYHA Workcamp. Workcamp open to 16- to- 30-year-olds who want to volunteer for the MYHA and other organizations. Periods: 2 weeks to 3 months. For details send 3 IRCs or $2.

Dates: Year round. Apply 3 months in advance. Cost: A good faith deposit of $45 every 2 weeks, returnable on completion. Contact: The Workcamp Organizer, Malta Youth Hostels Association, 17, Triq Tal-Borg, Pawla PLA 06, Malta; Tel./fax (011) 356-693957; myha@keyworld.net.

Mexico

Learn Spanish in Chiapas. Spanish lessons in private sessions or small groups (4 people maximum). Family stays available. School tours to Indian (Mayan) villages, jungle trips available. Extracurricular activities include: Mexican cooking, discussions, and video showings. Teach English in exchange for Spanish lessons. Centro Cultural "El Puente" includes gallery weaver's cooperative, travel agency, cafe, restaurant, phone/fax service.

Dates: Year round. Cost: Highest $220 per week; lowest $75 per week. Contact: Roberto Rivas, Bastidas Centro Bilingüe de Chiapas, C. Real de Guadalupe 55, Centro Cultural "El Puente," San Cristóbal de Las Casas 29230, Chiapas, Mexico; (011) 52-967-8-41-57, fax 967-83723 or Tel./fax (800) 303-4983; cenbili@chisnet.com.mx, www.mexonline.com/centro1.htm.

Mar de Jade. Tropical ocean-front retreat center in a beautiful unspoiled fishing village near Puerto Vallarta offers unique volunteer opportunities in a 21-day work/study program. Work in community health program, local construction, cottage industries, and teaching. Study Spanish in small groups with native teachers. Relax and enjoy great swimming, kayaking, hiking, boating, horseback riding, and meditation.

Dates: Year round. Cost: (1997 rates) $865 for 21-day work/study. Includes room (shared occupancy), board, 12 hours per week of Spanish and 15 hours per week of community work. Longer resident program available at lower cost. Vacation/Spanish 1 week minimum: $365 room, board, 12 hours of Spanish. Vacation only: $45 per night for any length of time. Contact: Mexico: Mar de Jade/Casa Clinica, A.P. 81, Las Varas, Nayarit, 63715, Mexico; Tel./fax (011) 52-327-20184; U.S.: P.O. Box 1280, Santa Clara, CA 95052; (415) 281-0164; mardjade@pvnet.com.mx, www.puerto-vallarta.com/mardejade.

Third World Opportunities (Tecate). Third World Opportunities is a 2-pronged program utilizing the border with Mexico as a gigantic classroom. Learn about the realities of poverty and hunger and participate in short-term development projects including 1-week straw-bale house building programs with Sustainability International in Tecate and Las Palmas, Mexico. Applicants must be at least 15 years old. Registration fee is due 6 weeks prior to event.

Dates: Call for information. Cost: $200 plus transportation (6-day events). Contact: M. Laurel Gray, Coordinator, 1363 Somermont Dr., El Cajon, CA 92021; (619) 449-9381.

Micronesia

Ponape Agriculture and Trade School. Volunteers with trade skills, agricultural experience, and mechanical or technical skills are needed to teach and supervise Micronesian high school students. The school is privately run and supported by the Catholic church in Micronesia.

Dates: School year: Aug 15-May 15. Only 2-year contracts are considered for volunteer acceptance. Contact: Joseph E. Billotti, S.J., Director, PATS, Box 39, Pohnpei, FM 96941, Federated States of Micronesia.

Nepal

Placement for Volunteer Service. Provides opportunities to those interested in contributing their time and skills to worthwhile community groups throughout Nepal. We arrange a limited number of volunteer placements involving either teaching or working in various organizations.

Dates: Feb, Apr, and Aug. Cost: $600 program fee and visa fee depending on length of stay. Contact: Naresh M. Shrestha, Director, Insight Nepal, P.O. Box 6760, Kathmandu, Nepal; (011) 977-1-418-964, fax 416-144.

Pacific Region

Hawaii's Kalani Oceanside Retreat. Kalani Educational Retreat, the only coastal lodging facility within Hawaii's largest conservation area, treats you to Hawaii's aloha comfort, traditional culture, healthful cuisine, wellness programs, and extraordinary adventures: thermal springs, a naturist dolphin beach, snorkel pools, kayaking, waterfalls, crater lake, and spectacular Volcanoes National Park. Ongoing offerings in yoga, dance, hula, mythology, language, and massage. Or participate in an annual week-long event: men's/women's/couples conferences, dance/music/hula festivals, yoga/meditation/transformation retreats. Applications are also being accepted for our international Volunteer Scholar program.

Dates: Year round. Cost: Lodging $45-$110 per day. Camping $20-$25. $570-$1,120 per week for most programs, including meals and lodging choice. Contact: Richard Koob, Director, Kalani Retreat, RR2, Box 4500, Pahoa-Beach Rd., HI 96778-9724; (800) 800-6886 or (808) 965-7828 (call for fax info); kh@ilhawaii.net, http://randm.com/kh.html.

Philippines

Little Children of the Philippines, Inc. LCP is a Christian agency helping to develop caring communities for poor children on Negros Island in central Philippines. LCP has service programs in 7 communities covering health, housing, education, livelihood (agriculture, handicrafts), and value formation. Especially needed: volunteers in marketing, computer technology, journalism, music, carpentry, masonry, and environmental concerns.

Dates: Volunteers negotiate their own period of service. Cost: From East Coast: approx. $1,200 roundtrip airfare, $120 per month for food. Dormitory bed free. Contact: Dr. Douglas Elwood, 361 County Rd. 475, Etowah, TN 37331; Tel./fax (423) 263-2303; lcotw@conc.tds.net.

Scotland

Edinburgh Cyrenians. Residential volunteers needed. Edinburgh Cyrenians provide long-term accommodations for young homeless men. Volunteers live alongside residents in one of our 2 communities (city project or farm project). We offer 6-month placements for volunteers aged 18-30 as well as access to our time-off flat.

Contact: Project Manager, Edinburgh Cyrenians, 107A Ferry Rd., Edinburgh EH6 4ET, Scotland; Tel./fax (011) 44-1-31-5553707.

Loch Arthur Community. Community in which volunteer workers live and work with adults with mental handicaps. The community is on a 500-acre estate in the southwest of Scotland. There are 6 houses, farms, garden, bakery, creamery, weavery.

Dates: Year round. Cost: No cost but volunteers must pay for transportation to and from community. Contact: Lana Chanarin, Loch Arthur, Beeswing, Dumfries DG2 8JQ, Scotland; (011) 44-1387-760687, fax 1387-760618.

Sierra Leone

JMRRDO Volunteer Exchange. The camp program of the organization is to assist the rural villagers where access to services is not available. The program also helps volunteers to learn our culture and assist to improve the lifestyle of the people. The program will also establish training centers to train villagers and set-up income generating activities in each village.

Dates: Three-month, 6-month, and 1-year programs. Cost: $600, $1,200, $2,400. Contact: Mr. John Musa-Bangalie, Camp Director, JMRRDO, 42 Soldier St., Freetown, Sierra Leone, West Africa; Tel. 227822.

South America

Youth Challenge International (YCI). YCI combines community development, health work and environmental research in adventurous projects conducted by international teams of volunteers aged 18-25, and coordinated by volunteer field staff aged 26 plus. Since 1989 YCI has promoted international cooperation and understanding through dynamic living and working exchanges between the people and cultures of different nations.

Dates: Projects depart in May, Jun, and Feb, and Dec. Cost: Participants must fundraise

$3,750 prior to departure. Contact: Mike Buda, Recruitment and Selection Director, YCI, 11 Soho St., Toronto, ON M5T 1Z6, Canada; (416) 971-9846, fax (416) 971-6863; info@yci.org.

Sweden

Project Assistant. TRN is a network of NGO's, indigenous peoples and nations working for the presentation and sustainable use of the world's boreal forest. Our ongoing program consists of: coordinating consumer campaigns; serving as an information clearinghouse; organizing international meetings and conferences; researching and publishing reports, factsheets, and a bimonthly newsletter. The project assistant position is open to self motivated environmental activists interested in assisting the above activities.

Dates: Year round. Living expenses (room and board). Anne Janssen, Taiga Rescue Network (TRN), Box 116, S-96223, Jokkmokk, Sweden; (011) 46 971 17039, fax 12057; taiga@jokkmokk.se.

Switzerland

Gruppo Volontari. Work on reconstruction projects in the Italian region of Switzerland that has suffered natural disasters. Lodging in a house in the village provided by the municipality. Participate in service projects aimed at helping the populace; e.g., help the aged, cut wood, domestic work, work in the stable and orchard. Volunteers share kitchen, cleaning, shop, and vehicle maintenance duties. Minimum age: 18.

Dates: Jun 1-Sep 30, 7-day minimum, 15-day maximum. Cost: Varies. Contact: Mari Federico, Director, Gruppo Volontari della Svizzera Italiana, CP 12, 6517 Arbedo, Switzerland; (011) 41-071-829-13-37, 079-354-01-61.

Taiwan

Overseas Service Corps YMCA (OSCY). Place BAs to PhDs in ESL teaching positions in community-based YMCAs in Taiwan. Degree in teaching, ESL or general teaching experience preferred. No Chinese language necessary. This conversational English program provides an opportunity for cultural exchange. Must reside in North America and be a citizen of an English-speaking country. Twenty to 30 openings.

Dates: Call anytime for a brochure, apply between Jan 1 and Apr 15 for Sep placement. Cost: $35 application fee. Benefits for successful applicants include: Housing, health insurance, return airfare, paid vacation, bonus, orientation, sponsorship for visa, and monthly stipend. Contact: Janis Sterling, OSCY Manager, International Group, YMCA of the USA, 101 N. Wacker Dr., Chicago, IL 60606; (800) 872-9622 ext. 167, fax (312) 977-0884.

Turkey

Workcamps and Study Tours. Gençtur organizes workcamps in small Anatolian villages with manual projects for people over 18. Lasting 2 weeks, camp language English. Enables close contact with locals. Study tour maintains close contact with students, teachers, lawyers, peasants, workers, journalists, etc.

Dates: Workcamps: Jul-Aug-Sep; Study Tours: Year round. Cost: Workcamps £45; Study Tours: depends on duration and program. Contact: Gençtur, Mr. Zafer Yilmaz, Istiklal Cad. Zambak Sok. 15/5, 80080 Istanbul-TR, Turkey; (011) 90-212-249-25-15, fax 249-25-54; workcamps@genctur.com.tr, www.geocities.com/madisonavenue/1244.

United Kingdom

Archaeological Excavation-Wales. Volunteer accepted on archaeological excavation of late-

Roman and early medieval settlement in rural environment. Training given in varied tasks. No experience required, camp site, food and transportation provided.

Dates: Jul 25-Aug 15, 1998. Cost: £40 per week, includes campsite and food. Contact: Dr. C.J. Arnold, Dept. of Continuing Education, Univ. of Wales, 10-11 Laura Pl., Aberystwyth, Ceredigion, SY23 2AU, U.K.

Independent Living Alternatives. Provides support to disabled people in London to enable them to live in their own homes.

Dates: Year round (6 months). Cost: Travel to United Kingdom. Living expenses and accommodations provided. Contact: Tracey Jannaway, Independent Living Alternatives, Trafalgar House, Grenville Pl., Mill Hill, London NW7 3SA, U.K.; (011) 44-181906-9265.

Lulworth Court. Holiday/respite center for adults with physical disabilities. Relaxed seaside setting. Helpers needed to aid permanent care and nursing staff with physical. Personal care of guests. Plus outings and activities. No experience necessary and lots of friendly support. All board and lodging provided.

Dates: Late Jan and late Dec. for 1-2 weeks annually. Cost: Travel Contact: Mrs. Pat McCallion, Lulworth Court, 25 Chalkwell Esplanade, Westcliff on Sea, Essex, SS0 8JQ, U.K.; (011) 44-171-1702-431725, fax 433165.

The Calvert Trust. The Calvert Trust offers holidays for people of all abilities. In particular we focus on disabled people, and their families and friends and are open to individuals, family groups, and larger organizations.

Contact: Calvert Trust Exmoor, Wistlandpound, Kentisbury, Barnstaple, Devon EX31 4SJ, U.K.; (011) 44-1598-763221, fax 763400.

Welshpool and Llanfair Railway. A chance to participate in the maintenance and operation of this preserved historic steam railway. Opportunities exist in all departments from trackwork through to restoration work on locomotives and rolling stock. Accommodations available in self-catering hostel.

Dates: Year round, particularly winter months. Cost: Small overnight charge for hostel accommodations. Contact: David Moseley, Welshpool and Llanfair Railway, The Station, Llanfair Caereinion, Welshpool, Powys, Wales SY21 0SF, Wales.

Winant-Clayton Volunteers, Inc. Since 1948, WCV has sponsored a summer international visitor exchange program designed for 20 U.S. and 20 U.K. citizens to work in social service settings. Winants depart in early Jun and return mid-Aug, must travel with group from New York and pay group-rate airfare. Application fee: $30, deadline Jan 31.

Dates: Jun-Aug. Cost: Free room and board; anticipate approx. $2,000 for airfare and personal expenses. Contact: Volunteer Coordinator, Winant-Clayton Volunteers, 109 E. 50th St., New York, NY 10019; (212) 378-0271.

United States

Camphill Special School. Volunteers for 6-12 months live in an international community based on Anthroposophy, devoted to providing a wholesome life and education to the mentally retarded child. Days are long, children demanding, 1 day off per week. Orientation course required. Challenging but rewarding. Volunteers for July summer program also only accepted. Minimum age 19; 21 and older preferred.

Dates: End of August to end of July or July only. Cost: Medical and dental exams required before arrival; no other costs. Contact: Andrea Janisch (610-469-9160) or Ursel Pietzner (610-469-9236), c/o 1784 Fairview Rd., Glenmoore, PA 19343.

Institute for Unpopular Culture Internship. The Institute for Unpopular Culture is a nonprofit organization dedicated to assisting and promoting unconventional and/or controversial artists. We're seeking interns to assist with a number of tasks, including writing, research, graphic design, and administrative duties.

Dates: Flexible. Cost: None. Contact: David Ferguson, Institute for Unpopular Culture, 1850 Union St., #1523, San Francisco, CA 94109; (415) 986-4382, fax (415) 986-4354.

Master of International and Intercultural Management. The School for International Training Master of International and Intercultural Management offers concentrations in sustainable development, international education, and training and human resource development in a 1 academic-year program. This degree is designed for individuals wishing to make a career change or enter the field. A practical training component enables "on-the-job" training and an opportunity to work internationally.

Dates: Sep 1, 1997-May 29, 1998. Cost: $17,000 (1997-98 tuition). Contact: Kat Eldred, Director of Outreach and Recruitment, Admissions Counselor, School for International Learning, P.O. Box 676, Kipling Rd., Brattleboro, VT 05302; (802) 257-7751, fax (802) 258-3500; admissions @sit.edu, www.sit.edu.

The Univ. of Arizona. The Dept. of English MA in ESL emphasizes leadership development and is designed for experienced teachers with a strong academic record and leadership experience. Specialized courses are offered in language program administration, comparative discourse, teaching language through literature, sociolinguistics, language testing, and technology. PhD in SLAT.

Dates: Applications due by Feb 1 for the following fall semester. Two years are normally required to complete the program. Cost: $1,005 registration for 7 or more units, plus approx. $244 per unit for nonresident tuition. Contact: Director, English Language/Linguistics Program, English Dept., P.O. Box 210067, The Univ. of Arizona, Tucson, AZ 85721-0067; (520) 621-7216, fax (520) 621-7397; maes1@ccit.arizona.edu.

Worldwide

Amizade Volunteer Vacations. Programs offering mix of community service and recreation that provide volunteers with the opportunity to experience firsthand the culture they are working in—Brazilian Amazon, Peruvian Amazon, Bolivian Andes, or Greater Yellowstone region. Volunteers do not need any special skills, just a willingness to serve.

Dates: Year round. Cost: Varies. $1,500-$2,600 for Latin America; $150-$600 for Yellowstone. Contact: Amizade, 1334 Dartmouth Ln., Deerfield, IL 60015; (847) 945-9402, fax (847) 945-5676; amizade@ worldnet.att.net, http://amizade.org.

Catholic Network of Volunteer Service. We are a coordinating center for full-time, faith-based volunteer programs with placements around the world. We publish the Response directory of volunteer opportunities. Call (800) 543-5046 to receive a free copy.

Contact: Jim Lindsay, Executive Director, CNVS, 4121 Harewood Rd. NE, Washington, DC 20017; (800) 543-5046, fax (202) 526-1094; cnvs@ari.net.

Coral Cay Conservation Expeditions. Volunteers needed to join major expeditions to help survey and protect coral reefs and tropical forests in the Caribbean, Asia-Pacific, Philippines, Indonesia, Red Sea. No previous experience required. Full accredited training provided (including scuba certification if required). Thousands of CCC volunteers have already helped establish 8 new marine reserves and wildlife sanctuaries worldwide.

Dates: Expeditions depart monthly

throughout the year. Cost: From $995 (2 weeks) to $4,415 (12 weeks) excluding flights. Contact: Coral Cay Conservation Ltd., 154 Clapham Park Rd., London SW4 7DE, U.K.; (305) 757-2955 (U.K. office 011-44-171-498-6248, fax 498 8447); ccc@coralcay.demon.co.uk, www.coralcay. org.

Earthwatch. Unique opportunities to work with leading scientists on 1- to 3-week field research projects worldwide. Earthwatch sponsors 160 expeditions in over 30 U.S. states and in 60 countries. Project disciplines include archaeology, wildlife management, ecology, ornithology and marine mammalogy. No special skills needed—all training is done in the field.

Dates: Year round. Cost: Tax deductible contributions ranging from $695-$2,800 support the research and cover food and lodging expenses. Airfare not included. Contact: Earthwatch, 680 Mt. Auburn St., P.O. Box 9104MA, Watertown, MA 02272; (800) 776-0188, (617) 926-8200; info@earthwatch.org, www.earthwatch.org.

Global Citizens Network. Global Citizens Network provides cross-cultural volunteer expeditions to rural communities around the world. Current sites include Belize, Guatemala, Kenya, St. Vincent, the Yucatan, and New Mexico (U.S.). While immersed in the daily life of the community volunteers work on projects initiated by the local people. Projects could include setting up a library, building a health clinic, or planting trees to reforest a village. Trips last 1, 2, or 3 weeks. Specific skills are not required.

Dates: Year round. Cost: $400-$1,300 not including airfare. All trip-related expenses are tax-deductible. Limited partial scholarships available. Contact: Kim Regnier or Carol North, Global Citizens Network, 1931 Iglehart Ave., St. Paul, MN 55104; (800) 644-9292 or (612) 644-0960, fax (612) 644-0960 (by appointment).

Global Service Corps. Service-learning opportunities in Costa Rica, Kenya, or Thailand. Live with a village family while assisting grassroots community organizations on development projects. Assist with: rainforest conservation, sustainable agriculture, AIDS/HIV awareness, women's group projects, teaching English. Experience the challenges of developing countries from the inside out. Short- and long-term placements and internship available.

Dates: Year round. Cost: $1,595-$1,695 for 2-3 week project trips. Long-term projects start at $1,445 for 2 months. Includes in-country expenses (room and board, project fees, transportation, orientation, excursions). Airfare not included, discounts available. Contact: Global Service Corps., 300 Broadway, Suite 28, San Francisco, CA 94133-3312; (415) 788-3666 ext. 128, fax (415) 788-7324; gsc@igc.apc.org, www.earthisland.org/ei/gsc/gschome.html.

Global Volunteers. "An adventure in service." Year round short-term service programs for people of all ages and backgrounds. Assist mutual international understanding through ongoing development projects in 15 countries throughout Africa, Asia, the Caribbean, Europe, North and South America. Programs are 1, 2, and 3 weeks, ranging from natural resource preservation, light construction and painting to teaching English and assisting with health care. No special skills or foreign languages are required. Ask about our new programs for 1998.

Dates: Over 150 teams year round. Cost: Tax-deductible program fees range from $350 to $1,995. Airfare not included. Contact: Global Volunteers, 375 E. Little Canada Rd., St. Paul, MN 55117; (800) 487-1074, fax (612) 482-0916; email@globalvlntrs.org, www.global-vlntrs.org.

Green Volunteers. The World Guide to Voluntary Work in Nature Conservation now lists more than 100 projects and organizations worldwide where you can volunteer from 1 week to 1 year. Projects on marine mammals, primates, sea turtles, African wildlife, birds, and on conservation work in general are listed. Some of the projects do not require a financial contribution from the volunteers.

Dates: Year round. Cost: $16 plus $5 postage. Contact: Green Volunteers: in the U.S.: 1 Greenleaf Woods Dr., #302A, Portsmouth, NH 03810; (800) 525-9379. In Europe: P.O. Box 23, Sandy, Bedfordshire SG19 2XE, U.K.; Tel./fax (011) 44-767-262481; info@greenvol.com, www.greenvol.com.

Health Volunteers Overseas. HVO solicits health volunteers in Africa, Asia, the Caribbean, and Latin America trained in the following specialties: anesthesia, dentistry, general surgery, internal medicine, oral and maxillofacial surgery, orthopaedics, pediatrics, and physical therapy. In most cases, volunteers teach rather than just provide service.

Dates: Year round, 2-week to 1-month assignments. Cost: Volunteers responsible for expenses. Room and board provided in most cases. Contact: Kate Skillman, Program Coordinator, Health Volunteers Overseas, c/o Washington Station, P.O. Box 65157, Washington, DC 20035-5157; (202) 296-0928, fax (202) 296-8018; hvo@aol.com.

Internships International. Quality, professional, full-time internships in all fields for college graduates. Internships are found based on the intern's needs and experiences. Internship locations are: London, Paris, Florence, Madrid, Stuttgart, Dublin, Santiago, Budapest, Melbourne, and Shanghai. Internships are non-paying but it is often possible to "moonlight" while doing an internship. This is a program for individuals who are ready to assume professional responsibility.

Fields: All fields. Prerequisites: college graduate, language ability if appropriate to location or willingness to attend language school. Application materials: 2 references, photo, specific statement of purpose, resume, transcript, interview.

Dates: Flexible, depending on wishes of the intern. Application deadline: none. Cost: Intern pays all expenses (approx. $200 per week). Compensation: none. Application fee: $700 (refundable if intern not placed). Contact: Judy Tilson, Director, Internships International, 1116 Cowper Dr., Raleigh, NC 27608; (919) 832-1575, fax (919) 837-7170; http://rtpnet.org/~int/intl.

Learning Through Service. Learning Through Service provides 45 sites where students or recent graduates of any college may do voluntary service for a summer, semester, or longer. Eleven sites combine service with formal study for academic credit.

Dates: Two months to 2 years; beginning and ending rates vary. Cost: Some volunteer programs offer a stipend; Service-Learning programs (i.e., those that combine service with study) involve tuition fees. Contact: Program Coordinator, Association of Episcopal Colleges, 815 2nd Ave., Suite 315, New York, NY 10017-4594; (212) 986-0989, fax (212) 986-5039; anglican.colleges@ecunet.org.

Medical Ministry International. MMI International conducts over 65 annual 1- or 2-week clinics for people who have no other access to medical and surgical care. Volunteers pay fee plus airfare. MMI is a Christian organization from many traditions. Non-Christians welcome. Needed are dentists, physicians, surgeons, anesthesiologists, nurses (all areas), OR techs, health care professionals, optometrists, opticians, helpers.

Dates: Write for calendar projects. Sign up several months in advance. Cost: $640 for any project. Participants also pay airfare. Expenses are tax deductible. Contact: In U.S.: Medical Ministry International, P.O. Box 940207, Plano, TX 75094; (972) 437-1995, fax (972) 437-1114. In Canada: Medical Group Missions Inc., 15 John St. N, Suite 301, Hamilton, ON L8R 1H1; (905) 524-3544, fax (905) 524-5400.

Mission Service Opportunities. Opportunities are diverse with some positions requiring more experience than others. We need:

educators, office workers, RN's, development and community workers, and youth and social service workers. Both national and international.

Dates: Flexible (summer, full year, 2 or more years). Cost: Varies. Depends on service project (assistance for longer-term projects possible). Contact: Mission Service Recruitment Office, Presbytarian Church (U.S.A.), 100 Witherspoon St., Louisville, KY 40202-1396; (800) 779-6779; www.pcusa.org/msr.

Networked International Volunteering. Involvement Volunteers Association, Inc. (IVI) aims to identify volunteer placements to suit the requirements, abilities, and experiences of individual volunteers. Volunteers are able to share their resources and to gain from their experiences. Countries covered: Australia, England, Fiji, Finland, Germany, Ghana, Greece, India, Kenya, Lebanon, Malaysia, New Zealand, Spain, South Africa, and Thailand. Placements run for a minimum of 2 weeks and relate to sustainable environmental conservation or community-based social service. Projects may be suitable for individual volunteers with or without expertise. Individual placements may be on farms, in historic gardens or national parks; at schools teaching spoken English or special schools for disadvantaged children; at bird observatories, zoological parks or research centers. Individual volunteers from different countries participate in groups assisting community based project. Volunteers can participate in any number of placements in any number of countries over a year. Placements can be planned to coincide with activities such as open water scuba diving courses on the Great Barrier Reef or native animal encounters or camping trips in the Red Center to suite an itinerary in Australia Other countries have other things to do.

Dates: Volunteers are always needed somewhere. Cost: Approx. $350 for program, plus $40 per placement. The volunteer meets all travel costs (including insurance). Most "hosts" provide accommodations and food for free, but some placements (of volunteers choice, in projects or countries with limited resources) may cost up to $70 per week for food. Contact: Mr. Tim B. Cox, Involvement Volunteers Assoc., Inc., P.O. Box 218, Port Melbourne, Victoria 3207, Australia; Tel./fax (011) 61-3-9646 9392, fax 9646 5504; ivimel@iaccess.com.au, www.iaccess.com.au/ivimel/index.html.

Peace Brigades International. PBI provides international human rights observers in areas of extreme conflict. Volunteer teams currently operate in Guatemala, Chiapas, Haiti, Sri Lanka, Colombia, the Balkans, and North American Native communities. PBI is dedicated to the nonviolent resolution of conflicts and works by consensus. Volunteer provide protective accompaniment, peace education, and information.

Dates: Year round (minimum 7 months commitment). Cost: Includes airfare, health insurance, and training costs. Contact: Peace Brigades International, 2642 College Ave., Berkeley, CA 94704; (510) 540-0749, fax (510) 849-1247; pbiusa@igc.apc.org, www.igc.apc.org/pbi.

Peace Corps Opportunities. Since 1961, more than 140,000 Americans have joined the Peace Corps. Assignments are 27 months long. Volunteers must be U.S. citizens, at least 18 years old, and in good health. Peace Corps has volunteer programs in education, business, agriculture, the environment, and health.

Dates: Apply 9 to 12 months prior to availability. Cost: Volunteers receive transportation to and from assignment, a stipend, complete health care, and $5,400 after 27 months of service. Contact: Peace Corps, Room 8506, 1990 K St. NW, Washington, DC 20526; (800) 424-8580 (mention code 824); www.peacecorps.gov.

Peacework. Peacework sponsors international volunteer programs in countries such as

Mexico, Cuba, Honduras, Costa Rica, Haiti, Nicaragua, Russia, and Vietnam. Programs involve work in housing, childcare, agriculture, and/or healthcare with indigenous development organizations and opportunities for travel, community interaction, and examination of regional political and economic issues.

Dates: Usually winter, spring, and summer breaks. Cost: Usually $400-$600 plus airfare, all inclusive. Contact: Stephen Darr, Peacework, 305 Washington St., SW, Blacksburg, VA 24060; (540) 953-1376, fax (540) 552-0119; 75352.261@compuserve.com.

Visions in Action. Visions in Action sends volunteers to Africa and to Latin America to work for nonprofit development organizations. Volunteers are placed in diverse fields such as business management, law, health care, journalism, women's issues, democratization, human rights, children's programs, and environmental concerns.

Dates: Jul: Tanzania, South Africa, Mexico. Sep: Uganda. Oct: Burkina Faso. Jan: Zimbabwe, South Africa, Mexico. Cost: $4,000-$6,000. Contact: Shaun Skelton, Visions in Action, 2710 Ontario Rd. NW, Washington, DC 20009; (202) 625-7403, fax (202) 625-2353; vision@igc.apc.org.

Voluntary Workcamps. Cotravaux coordinates 12 French workcamps. Its role is to promote voluntary work and community projects concerning environmental protection, monument restoration, and social projects. Many of the organizations members of Cotravaux work with Volunteers for Peace and International Voluntary Service.

Dates: Year round; most projects take place between Jun and Oct. Cost: Volunteers must pay for their own transportation to the camps. Room and board is provided (some camps require a small contribution). Contact: Françoise Dore, Cotravaux, 11, rue de Clichy, 75009 Paris, France; (011) 33-1-48-74-79-20.

Volunteers for Peace. Join volunteers from at least 3 other countries in over 1,000 social, environmental, conservation, restoration, archaeological, or agricultural work in over 70 countries. The length of service is 2-3 weeks; multiple placements in the same or different countries is common. Call or write VFP for a free newsletter.

Dates: Most programs are May-Sep, some Oct-Apr. Cost: $200 registration fee per workcamp covers meals and accommodations. Volunteers pay transportation costs. Contact: Peter Coldwell, Executive Director, Volunteers for Peace, Inc. (VFP), 43 Tiffany Rd., Belmont, VT 05730; (802) 259-2759, fax (802) 259-2922; vfp@vfp.org, www.vfp.org.

WorldTeach. WorldTeach is a private nonprofit organization based at Harvard Univ. which contributes to educational development and cultural exchange by placing volunteers to teach in developing countries (China, Costa Rica, Ecuador, Honduras, Mexico, Namibia, Thailand, and Vietnam). Volunteers teach English, math, science, and environmental education to students of all ages. All programs last for 1 academic year; except for the summer program in China.

Dates: Year-round departures and deadlines vary depending on the program. Cost: $3,600-$4,400. Includes health insurance, airfare, field support, and training. Contact: Jodi Hullinger, Desk Officer, WorldTeach, Harvard Institute for International Development, 1 Eliot St., Cambridge, MA 02138-5705; (617) 495-5527, fax (617) 495-1599; jhulling@worldteach.org, www.igc.org/worldteach.

WWOOFING. Learn about organic or traditional growing methods and life in your host country by working in exchange for keep at over 600 places in countries without a WWOOF group.

Dates: Year round. Cost: $20 for a list of 600 places in 50 countries. Contact: WWOOF Australia, Buchan, Victoria 3885, Australia; (011) 61-3-5155-0218.

Youth International. An international travel, community service, and experiential education program for people ages 18-25. Members travel with a team of 12 to Asia, Africa, and the Middle East. Service work includes such projects as teaching and helping to renovate schools in the Philippines; working with Tibetan refugees in northern India; assisting the "Poorest of the Poor" in Mother Theresa's clinics in Calcutta, India; and building water tanks for a remote village in East Africa.

Dates: Jan 24-Oct 24, 1998; Jan 24, 1998-Jun 8, 1999. We are now filling spots for the '98 season. Cost: Nine months: $10,800; 4 1/2 months: $6,000. All expenses covered. Contact: Brad Gillings, Youth International, 1121 Downing St., #2, Denver, CO 80218; (303) 839-5877.

CHAPTER 19

INTERNSHIP PROGRAMS

The following listing of internship programs was supplied by the organizers. Contact the program directors to confirm costs, dates, and other details. If you do not see the program you want in the country of your choice, look in the "Worldwide" listings at the end of the section for programs located in several different regions.

Argentina

Instituto de Lengua Española para Extranjeros (ILEE). Located downtown in the most European-like city in Latin America. Dedicated exclusively to teaching Spanish to foreigners. Small groups and private classes year round. All teachers hold Master's degrees. Method is intensive, conversation-based. Student body is international. Highly recommended worldwide. Ask for individual references in U.S.

Dates: Year round. Cost: Four-week intensive program (20 hours per week) including homestay $1,400; 2 weeks $700. Private classes $19 per hour. Registration fee (includes books) $100. Contact: Daniel Korman, ILEE, Director, Lavalle 1619 7 C (1048), Buenos Aires, Argentina; Tel./fax (011) 54-1-375-0730. In U.S.: David Babbitz; (415) 431-8219, fax (415) 431-5306; ilee@over net.com.ar, www.studyabroad.com/ilee.

Asia

Penn-in-India. Internships found on demand for interested students.

Fields: South Asian Studies, Performing Arts, Religion, Economics, Traditional Medicine. Academic credit offered. Fifteen internships per year. No prerequisites. Application materials: application, transcript, resume, letter of recommendation.

Dates: Summer: 6 weeks. Application deadline: Mar 1. Cost: $4,700 (includes room, food, international airfare, and tuition). Compensation: none. Application fee: $35. Contact: Penn Summer Abroad, Univ. of Pennsylvania, 3440 Market St., Suite 100, Philadelphia, PA 19104-3335; (215) 898-5738, fax (215) 573-2053.

Penn-in-Seoul (Korea). Internships with multinational corporations, government agencies, and think tanks.

Fields: Economics, Social Sciences. Academic credit offered. Fifteen internships per year. No prerequisites. Application materials: Application, transcript, resume, letter of recommendation.

Dates: Summer: 10 weeks. Application deadline: Mar 1. Cost: $3,700 (includes room and tuition). Compensation: Varies. Application fee: $35. Contact: Penn Summer Abroad, Univ. of Pennsylvania, 3440 Market St., Suite 100, Philadelphia, PA 19104-3335; (215) 898-5738, fax (215) 573-2053.

Australia

Australian Internships. Interns are placed with research teams, Australian employers, political administrations, etc. for periods ranging from 6 weeks to a year. The positions are unpaid. Homestay (or other) accommodations are included. Placement is arranged to suit the individual provided 4 months notice is given. Most placements are in Queensland or New South Wales.

Fields: Marine and Wildlife Biology, Business, etc. No academic credit offered. Unlimited internships. Prerequisites: a) High School Graduates, b) Professional Development for Graduates and Junior/Senior college students.

Dates: Year round. Application deadline: Four months before start date. Cost: $2,455 (includes room and food) for 6-week program. Application fee: $500. Contact: Dr. Maurice A. Howe, Education Australia, P.O. Box 2233, Amherst, MA 01004; (800) 344-6741, fax (413) 549-0741; edaust@javanet.com.

Custom Designed Professional Development Internships. Upon application, participants are asked to describe their internship needs, after which the placement service in Australia locates suitable programs. Responsibilities vary by placement. Excellent professional development and career building opportunities. Opportunities to travel in Australia before and after the placement. Flexible duration and start dates. Interns are not usually placed as a group. On-call support service, airport transfers, academic or professional supervisor provided in Australia. Pre-trip support for air travel, visas and orientation.

Fields: Management, Marketing, Finance and Accounting, Communications (radio, television, newspaper, public relations), Law, Politics, The Arts, Social Work, Biology, Wildlife Management, Natural Resources, and Marine Science. Academic credit can be arranged through home university. One hundred-200 internships per year. Prerequisites: Pursuing or have obtained a university/college degree. Application materials: application and transcript(s).

Dates: Six, 8, 10, 12, 16 weeks or more (52 weeks maximum) placements. Year-round start dates. Sign up at least 4 months prior to intended departure. Cost: $3,240 (6 weeks) to $4,480 (16 weeks). Includes room, 2 meals per day in homestay (or no meals in an apartment), internship placement, liaison service in Australia, airport transfers. Compensation: placements are typically unpaid due to immigration rules. Application fee: $500 deposit with application. Eighty percent refundable for cancellation after placement is found. Contact: AustraLearn, U.S. Center for Australian Universities, 110 16th St., CSU Denver Center, Denver, CO 80202; (800) 980-0033, fax (303) 446-5955; cflannery@vines.colostate.edu.

Colombia

Community Internships in Latin America. Emphasis on community participation for social change. Students work 3 days a week in an internship, meet together for core seminar and internship seminar, and carry out independent study project. Wide range of internship opportunities in community development and related activities. Based in Bogotá. Family homestay. Latin American faculty. Full semester's credit, U.S. transcript provided. All majors, 2 years Spanish language required.

Dates: Early Feb-mid-May. Cost: $9,000 (1998-99). Includes tuition, room and board, field trips. Contact: Rebecca Rassier, Director of Student Services, HECUA, Mail #36, Hamline Univ., 1536 Hewitt Ave., St. Paul, MN 55104-1284; (612) 646-8832 or (800) 554-9421, fax (612) 659-9421; hecua@hamline.edu, www.hamline.edu/~hecua.

Costa Rica

Learn Spanish While Volunteering. Assist with the training of Costa Rican public school teachers in our latest language learning techniques, using classroom computers, K-8 school targeted by Costa Rican government as a model ESL/technology school. Enjoy learning Spanish in the morning, volunteer work in the afternoon/evening. Spanish classes are 2-5 students plus group learning activities; conversations with middle-class homestay families (1 student per family). Homestays and volunteer project are within walking distance of school in small town (14,000 population) near the capital, San Jose.

Dates: Year round, all levels. Classes begin every Monday, volunteer program is continuous. Cost: $295 per week for 25 hours of Spanish classes. Includes tuition, all meals (7 days a week), homestay, laundry, all materials, Costa Rican dance and cooking classes, and airport transportation. $25 one-time registration for Spanish classes; $100 additional one-time registration fee for volunteer program. Contact: Susan Shores, Registrar, Latin American Language Center, 7485 Rush River Dr., Suite 710-123, Sacramento, CA 95831;

(916) 447-0938, fax (916) 428-9542; lalc@madre.com.

Czech Republic

Penn-in-Prague. Internships found for interested students in the Jewish Museum in Prague and other organizations.

Fields: Language, Civilization, Political Science, Jewish Studies. Academic credit offered. Fifteen internships per year. Application materials: application, transcript, letter of recommendation, resume.

Dates: Summer: 6 weeks. Application deadline: Mar 15. Cost: $3,600 (includes room and tuition). Compensation: none. Application fee: $35. Contact: Penn Summer Abroad, Univ. of Pennsylvania, 3440 Market St., Suite 100, Philadelphia, PA 19104-3335; (215) 898-5738, fax (215) 573-2053.

Dominican Republic

Dominican Republic Program. Exposes students to career opportunities in business, human service organizations, and government agencies in conjunction with academic program featuring study of Spanish language, Dominican culture, Latin American and Caribbean Studies, and African-American Studies. Direct enrollment at Universidad Nacional PH Ureña also available for fluent Spanish speakers. Housing with host families. Field trips.

Fields: Latin American and African-American Studies. Fifteen credits per semester (fall and spring), of which 3-6 are for the internship. Six to 9 credits for the summer (no internships).

Dates: Fall (Aug-Dec): 16 weeks. Spring (Jan-May): 16 weeks. Summer (May-Jun): 6 weeks. Cost: $5,589 per semester, $2,578 summer (includes room, food, health insurance, local transport, international airfare, books, in-state tuition, and fees, 1997 rates). Some internships may carry a stipend. Contact: Alex M. Shane, Director, Office of International Programs, LI-84, Univ. of Albany, Albany, NY 12222; (518) 442-3525, fax (518) 442-3338; oipua@albany.edu.

Ecuador

Academia Latinoamericana (Quito). Ecuador's number-one private Spanish language institute in former diplomat's mansion with swimming pool, hot tub, sauna, sport facilities. Instruction by university-trained teachers, all one-on-one. Customized study programs tailored to the individual. Select host family accommodations. Excursions to haciendas, Indian markets, etc. College credit and internships available.

Dates: Year round. Cost: One-week tuition, lodging, meals $294. Contact: Suzanne Bell, Admissions Director, U.S., 640 East 3990 South, Suite E, Salt Lake City, UT 84107; (801) 268-4608, fax (801) 265-9156; latinoa1@spanish.com.ec, http://ecnct.cc/academia/learnspa.htm.

France

Internships in Francophone Europe. IFE is an academic internship program—accredited at a number of schools—that places student interns in mid- to high-levels of French public life including government, politics, the press, social institutions, NGOs, etc. IFE is a selective admissions program for highly-motivated students, already proficient in French, who are interested in immersion in the working life of a French institution and in today's France. The program includes intensive preparatory course work in French history, sociology, and politics, high-level language training, and the completion of a research project related to the internship. Open to undergraduates and recent graduates.

Dates: May 1 deadline for fall semester (Aug 21-Dec 22); Nov 1 deadline for spring semester (Jan 22-May 24). Cost: $5,950 (tuition only); tuition plus housing $7,660. Need-based scholarships available, especially for post BA's. Contact: Bernard Riviere Platt, Director, Internships in Francophone Europe, 26, rue Cmdt. Mouchotte J108, 75014 Paris, France; (011) 33-1-43-21-78-07, fax 42-79-94-13; 100662.1351@compuserve.com.

Penn-in-Compiegne. Short-term (2 weeks) internships with banks, mayor's office, advertising agency, hospital, etc.

Fields: Economics, Business French. Academic credit offered. Twelve internships per year. Prerequisites: Intermediate French. Application materials: application, transcript, letter of reference.

Dates: Summer: 5 weeks of study and 2 weeks of internship. Application deadline: Mar 1. Cost: $4,100 (includes room, food, and tuition). Compensation: none. Application fee: $35. Contact: Penn Summer Abroad, Univ. of Pennsylvania, 3440 Market St., Suite 100, Philadelphia, PA 19104-3335; (215) 898-5738, fax (215) 573-2053.

Germany

Schiller International Univ. at Heidelberg. Schiller Univ. is an American-style university with all courses except language classes taught in English. Schiller's particular strengths are in international business and international relations but it offers courses in the humanities and social sciences as well. Students may take German at Schiller or intensive German at the Collegium Palatinum, a specialized language division. One semester college German or equivalent is required.

Dates: Fall: late Aug-mid-Dec; spring: mid-Jan-mid-May. Cost: Spring 1998 estimate: $6,355 per semester. Estimates include full-day orientation before departure, application fee, room and food allowance in residence hall, mandatory German insurance, airfare, books and supplies, health and accident insurance, German Residence Permit, administrative fees. SUNY tuition not included. Contact: Dr. John Ogden, Director, Office of International Programs, Box 2000, SUNY Cortland, Cortland, NY 13045; (607) 753-2209, fax (607) 753-5989; studyabroad@sny corva.cortland.edu, www.studyabroad.com/ suny/cortland

Hong Kong

Syracuse Univ. in Hong Kong. Focus on international business and economy in Asia. Courses on business, economics, political science, history, Chinese language, sociology. Internships in Hong Kong, field trips to Beijing, Shanghai, elsewhere. Based at City Univ. of Hong Kong. Housing in residence halls, apartments.

Dates: Aug-Dec (1997) and Jan-May 1998. Cost: $8,755 tuition (1997-98); $6,450 includes housing, excursions, roundtrip travel. Contact: James Buschman, Associate Director, Syracuse Univ., 119 Euclid Ave., Syracuse, NY 13244-4170; (800) 235-3472, fax (315) 443-4593; suabroad@syr.edu.

Ireland

Dublin Internships. Dublin Internships provides quality international internships across the spectrum of majors, minors, and career options in Dublin, Ireland. The internships are full-time and non-salaried. Credit is awarded by the student's university/college.

Dates: The Internship program schedule includes Spring and Fall semesters, Summer and Jan interim. A minimum of 3 months notice from the student is recommended. Contact: Director, Dublin Internships, 8 Orlagh Lawn, Scholarstown Rd., Dublin 16, Ireland; Tel./fax (011) 3531-1-494-5277.

Internships in Dublin. Interns live with families or in apartments. Two programs available: 6-credit internship plus 9-credit classwork in Irish Studies through the Institute of Public Administration or full-time

(15-16 credits) internship. IPA placements may be in Parliament, municipal government, health care administration, radio/TV, and at the Irish Times. Full-time placements available in social services, communication, film, advertising and others.

Fields: Public Administration, Parliamentary Internships, Political Science, Technology, Finance, Health and Communications. Fifteen-16 credits per semester, 10 for Summer. Prerequisites: 2.5 GPA for traditional full-time internships, 3.0 for IPA internships. Adaptability and maturity. Strong performance in major. Application materials: SUNY application.

Dates: Fall: early Sep-mid-Dec (application deadline Feb 1); spring: early Jan-late Apr (application deadline Sep 1); summer: early Jun-mid-Aug (application deadline Feb 1). Cost: Fall (1997) and spring 1998 estimates: IPA$4,400 for Dublin internships (full-time) $3,500; summer (1997) $3,415 (Dublin internships only, IPA not available). Estimates include full-day orientation before departure, application fee, room and board, food allowance, health and accident insurance, roundtrip airfare from N.Y., bus pass. SUNY tuition not included. Contact: Dr. John Ogden, Director, Office of International Programs, Box 2000, SUNY Cortland, Cortland, NY 13045; (607) 753-2209, fax (607) 753-5989; studyabroad@snycorva.cortland.edu, www.studyabroad.com/suny/cortland.

Ireland and Northern Ireland. Twelve program opportunities in the Republic and the North. University study and special subject area programs including internships in the Irish parliament. Program provides a full range of services including a full-time resident director and staff in Dublin, orientation, homestay, and guaranteed housing.

Dates: Fall, spring, academic year, and summer. Semesters and terms. Cost: Varies. Call for current fees. Contact: Meghan Mazick, Beaver College Center for Education Abroad, 450 S. Easton Rd., Glenside, PA 19038-3295; (888) BEAVER-9, fax (215)

572-2174; cea@ beaver.edu, www.beaver.edu/cea.

Univ. College Cork. First opened in 1849, the Univ. College Cork (UCC) is 1 of 3 constituent colleges of the National Univ. of Ireland. Eight faculties comprise the educational offerings of UCC: Arts, Celtic Studies, Commerce, Law, Science, Food Science and Technology, Engineering and Medicine. Enrollment in regular UCC classes with Irish students. Cortland's program specializes in language, history, and culture, but other courses may be available. Housing arranged prior to departure from U.S. in apartments near campus. Fall, spring, summer, academic year.

Dates: Fall: Early Sep-mid-Dec:, spring: mid-Jan-early Jun; summer: early Jul-end of Jul. Cost: Fall 1997 estimate: $6,385; spring 1998: $6,850; summer: $2,950; academic year: $12,750. Estimates include full-day orientation before departure, application fee, apartment rental (including utilities), food allowance, health and accident insurance, roundtrip airfare from NY, books and supplies. SUNY tuition not included. Contact: Dr. John Ogden, Director, Office of International Programs, Box 2000, SUNY Cortland, Cortland, NY 13045; (607) 753-2209, fax (607) 753-5989; studyabroad@snycorva.cortland.edu, www.studyabroad.com/suny/cortland.

Japan

Japan Exchange and Teaching Program. Contact: JET Program Office, Embassy of Japan, 2520 Massachusetts Ave. NW, Washington, DC 20008; (202) 238-6772, (202) 265-9484; eojjet@erols.com.

Teaching English in Japan. Two-year program to maximize linguistic and cultural integration of participants who work as teachers' assistants. Placements twice yearly in April and August. Most positions are in junior high schools in urban and rural areas. Bachelor's degree, cultural sensitivity, and some ESL training required.

Dates: Hiring for positions every April and August. Applications accepted year round. Cost: Airfare, salary, housing, health care provided. No application fees. Contact: Earlham College, Institute for Education on Japan, D-202, Richmond, IN 47374; (888) 685-2726; www.earlham.edu/www/departments/AET/home.htm.

Latin America

Community Internships. Semester program for academic credit in Bogotá, Colombia, combines 20-hour-per-week internship with core seminar entitled "Community Participation for Social Change," taught by Latin American faculty. Internships available in wide variety of agencies. Program director assists with finding placement appropriate to individual students' interests/goals, provides orientation and on-going supervision. Also includes independent study project, family homestays, field projects, friendships with other interns from across the U.S. and with Colombians.

Fields: Social Sciences, Communications, Health Sciences, Education, Social Work, Peace Studies; open to all majors. Sixteen hours offered, equivalent to 4 semester courses or 24 quarter credits. Fifteen internships per year. Ten-20 applicants. Prerequisites: equivalent of 2 years college-level Spanish language coursework; ability to communicate verbally in Spanish. Application materials: application form, 2 essays, transcript, 2 references (forms provided).

Dates: Feb-May (15 weeks). Application deadline: Nov 1. Cost: $7,300 (1997), includes room and food. Compensation: none. Application fee: $50. Contact: Elizabeth M. Andress, Admissions Director, Higher Education Consortium for Urban

Affairs (HECUA), Mail #36, Hamline Univ., 1536 Hewitt Ave., St. Paul, MN 55104-1284; (612) 646-8832 or (800) 554-1089, fax (612) 659-9421; eabejari@piper. hamline.edu.

Mexico

El Bosque del Caribe, Cancun. Take a professional Spanish course 25 hours per week and enjoy the Caribbean beaches. Relaxed family atmosphere. No more than 6 students per class. Special conversation program. Mexican cooking classes and excursions to the Mayan sites. Housing with Mexican families. College credit available.

Dates: Year round. New classes begin every Monday. Group programs arranged at reduced fees. Cost: Enrollment fee $100, $175 per week. One week with a Mexican family $150. Contact: Eduardo Sotelo, Director, Calle Piña 1, S.M. 25, 77500 Cancún, Mexico; (011) 52-98-84-10-38, fax 84-58-88; bcaribe@mail.cancun-language.com.mx

Learn Spanish in Chiapas. Spanish lessons in private sessions or small groups (4 people maximum). Family stays available. School tours to Indian (Mayan) villages, jungle trips available. Extracurricular activities include: Mexican cooking, discussions, and video showings. Teach English in exchange for Spanish lessons. Centro Cultural "El Puente" includes gallery weaver's cooperative, travel agency, cafe, restaurant, phone/fax service.

Dates: Year round. Cost: Highest $220 per week; lowest $75 per week. Contact: Roberto Rivas, Bastidas Centro Bilingüe de Chiapas, C. Real de Guadalupe 55, Centro Cultural "El Puente," San Cristóbal de Las Casas 29230, Chiapas, Mexico; (011) 52-967-8-41-57, fax 967-83723 or Tel./fax (800) 303-4983; cenbili@chisnet.com.mx, www.mexonline.com/centro1.htm.

Poland

Penn-in-Warsaw (Pepsi, Coopers & Lydbrand, Hewlett Packard, Citibank, etc.). Internships with American Businesses in Warsaw.

Fields: Economics, political science. Academic credit offered. Fifteen internships per year. No prerequisites. Application materials: application, transcript, resume, letter of recommendation.

Dates: Summer: 5 weeks. Application deadline: Mar 1. Cost: $3,250 (includes room and tuition). Compensation: none. Contact: Penn Summer Abroad, Univ. of Pennsylvania, 3440 Market St., Suite 100, Philadelphia, PA 19104-3335; (215) 898-5738, fax (215) 573-2053.

Spain

Univ. of Salamanca. Founded in the 13th century, the Univ. of Salamanca is one of the most distinguished centers of learning in Europe. SUNY Cortland is celebrating the 30th consecutive year in this "City of the Golden Stones." The lives of Cervantes, Lope de Vega, Santa Teresa, and Miguel de Unamuno were all linked to the Univ. of Salamanca. Fields of study include Spanish language and literature, humanities, social sciences. Upper division and some qualified sophomores may apply. Requires at least 4 semesters college-level Spanish for fall, 6 semesters for spring. Homestays.

Dates: Fall: early Sep-mid-Dec; spring: early Jan-mid-Jun. Cost: Fall 1997 estimate: $4,200, spring 1998: $4,950. Estimates include full-day orientation before departure, application fee, room and food allowance, mandatory Spanish insurance, airfare, transportation from Madrid to Salamanca, books and supplies, repatriation, insurance, walking tour of Salamanca, 2 excursions, administrative fees. SUNY tuition not included. Contact: Dr. John Ogden, Director, Office of International Programs, Box 2000, SUNY Cortland, Cortland, NY 13045; (607) 753-2209, fax (607) 753-5989; studyabroad@snycorva.cortland.edu, www.studyabroad.com/suny/cortland.

Switzerland

Bookbinding and Book Restoration. Centro del bel libro is a professional school for artisanal bookbinding and book restoration. Courses are offered year round.

Dates: Call or write for information. Cost: Call or write for information. Contact: Office Centro del bel libro, Ascona, Viale Portone 4, P.O. Box 2600, CH-6501, Bellinzona, Switzerland; (011) 41-91-825-11-62, fax 825-85-86.

Geneva Study Abroad. An opportunity for a part-time voluntary work assignment in which the student can earn academic credit. Many times our students find themselves in responsible non-routine assignments. All students are enrolled in a full course load of at least 12 semester hours.

Dates: Fall and spring semesters each academic year. Cost: $8,670. Includes program fee, transportation package, medical insurance, tuition, and security deposit. Contact: Phyllis L. Dreyer, CICP-Kent State Univ., P.O. Box 5190, Kent, OH 44242-0001; (330) 672-7980, fax (330) 672-4025; pdreyer@kentvm.kent.edu, www.kent.edu/cicp.

United Kingdom

Fashion Design and Merchandising. London College of Fashion is the only college in the British Univ. sector to specialize in fashion. Located in the center of London, students enroll in a selection of semester and summer programs with internship options. While studying in regular classes during part of the week, you can earn credits 2 days a week in professionally oriented internships in public relations, design, marketing, retailing, trend forecasting, and design companies.

Six credits offered. Twenty-four internships per year. Prerequisites: prior work experience is helpful, although it is not mandatory. Application materials: completed application form and resume.

Dates: Fall or Spring: 12 weeks. Summer: 4 weeks. Application deadline: Rolling admission. Cost: £2,425 12-week program, £1,450 4-week program. Contact: Jan Miller, London College of Fashion, 20 John Princes St., London W1M 0BJ, U.K.; (011) 44-171-514-7411, fax 514-7490; lcfdali@london-fashion.ac.uk.

Hansard Scholars Programme. An opportunity for students to become involved in the workings of the British government and British politics, accompanied by a comprehensive study of British politics and British public policy. Students are mainly assigned internships with Members of Parliament, but also to political parties, think tanks, and pressure groups.

Prerequisites: 2 or more years of college. Application materials: transcript, 2 letters of recommendation, and an essay.

Dates: Spring 1998: Jan 5-Mar 27. Summer 1998: May 11-Jul 17. Fall 1998: Sep 28-Dec 18. Cost: 1998: £4,250 per semester (includes housing and London travel costs). Contact: Penny O'Hara, Programme Manager, The Hansard Society, St. Philips, Building North, Sheffield St., London WC2A 2EX, U.K.; (011) 44-171-955-7478, fax 955-7492; hansard@lse.ac.uk.

Study in Great Britain. Thirty-three program opportunities in England, Scotland, and Wales. University study and special subject area programs, including internships, for fall, spring, academic year and summer. Program provides a full range of services including predeparture advising, orientation, homestay, and guaranteed housing. Need-based scholarships available.

Dates: Fall, spring, academic year. Summer semester and terms. Cost: Varies. Call for current fees. Contact: Beaver College Center for Education Abroad, 450 S. Easton Rd., Glenside, PA 19038-3295; (888) BEAVER-9, fax (215) 572-2174; cea@beaver.edu, www.beaver.edu/cea.

Study in Wales. Opportunities for either year-long or semester study abroad at the Univ. of Wales Swansea (10,500 students, located by the sea) in fully integrated programs. Host family and summer internship programs are available. University housing, orientation, and cultural events are integral to all programs. Swansea is a lively maritime city with great social life and numerous outdoor activities.

Dates: Sep-Dec/Jan-May/May-Jul. Cost: From $4,500. Contact: Emma Frearson, Study Abroad Swansea, American Studies Centre, Univ. of Wales Swansea, Singleton Park, Swansea SA2 8PP, Wales, U.K.; (011) 44-1-792-295135, fax 295719; e.frearson@swansea.ac.uk, www.swan.ac.uk/sao/saohp.html.

Univ. of North London. SUNY Cortland celebrates its 25th consecutive year at UNL, the prestigious public university formerly known as London Polytechnic. Over 400 courses are offered. Fields of study include education, natural sciences, humanities, communications, social sciences, business, health, theater arts. Credits per semester: 12-16. Prearranged housing in flats in the Bayswater district. Internships available.

Dates: Fall: mid-Sep-mid-Dec:, spring: end-Jan-mid-May. Cost: Fall 1997 estimate: $5,000, spring 1998: $5,385; academic year: $9,980. Estimates include full-day orientation in the U.S., application fee, apartment rental, meals, commuter ticket on underground for semester, London tour and Thames cruise, insurance, roundtrip airfare from N.Y., transportation from airport to downtown London upon arrival, books and supplies, various cultural activities, administrative fees. SUNY tuition not included. Contact: Dr. John Ogden, Director, Office of International Programs, Box 2000, SUNY Cortland, Cortland, NY 13045; (607) 753-2209, fax (607) 753-5989; studyabroad@snycorva.cortland.edu, www.studyabroad.com/suny/cortland.

United States

Bachelor's Program in World Issues. The School for International Training's Bachelor's Program in World Issues offers a unique opportunity for undergraduates to pursue their passion to make a difference in their world. The 2-year upper-division program is divided into the first year on campus and the second year is spent on an international or domestic internship with evaluation before graduation.

Dates: Aug 28, 1996-Jun 2, 1997. Cost: $12,200 (1996-97 tuition). Contact: Ed Parker, Admissions Counselor, School for International Learning, P.O. Box 676, Kipling Rd., Brattleboro, VT 05302; (802) 257-7751, fax (802) 258-3500; admissions.sit@worldlearning.org, www.worldlearning.org/sit.html.

Institute for Unpopular Culture Internship. The Institute for Unpopular Culture is a nonprofit organization dedicated to assisting and promoting unconventional and/or controversial artists. Seeking interns to assist with a number of tasks, including writing, research, graphic design, and administrative duties.

Dates: Flexible. Cost: None. Contact: David Ferguson, Institute for Unpopular Culture, 1850 Union St., #1523, San Francisco, CA 94109; (415) 986-4382, fax (415) 986-4354.

Master of International and Intercultural Management. The School for International Training Master of International and Intercultural Management offers concentrations in sustainable development, international education, and training and human resource development in a 1 academic-year program. This degree is designed for individuals wishing to make a career change or enter the field. A practical training component enables "on-the-job" training and an opportunity to work internationally.

Dates: Sep 1-May 29 (1997-1998). Cost: $17,000 (1997-98 tuition). Contact: Kat Eldred, Director of Outreach and Recruitment, Admissions Counselor, School for International Learning, P.O. Box 676, Kipling Rd., Brattleboro, VT 05302; (802) 257-7751, fax (802) 258-3500; admissions@sit.edu, www.sit.edu.

Worldwide

Agricultural Internship Program. Gain practical experience with an internship in production agriculture or agribusiness. Most participants live with host families, but some may live in apartments or dormitories. Foreign language knowledge is helpful but not required. Program fee includes U.S. orientation, international airfare, medical insurance, and supervision by Global Outreach. Room and board are provided by the host.

Dates: Orientations available year round. Program length 2-12 months. Cost: $2,600-$4,900, depending on country and length. Contact: Global Outreach, Inc., 203A Liberty St. SW, Leesburg, VA 20175; (703) 443-0548, fax (703) 443-0549.

Agricultural Internship Program. Full-time internships in production agriculture and agribusiness. Placements made according to intern's experience and career goals. Most participants live with host families, but some may live in apartments or dormitories. Foreign language knowledge is helpful but not required.

Fields: Agriculture, Agribusiness, Horticulture. Prerequisites: Knowledge and experience in agriculture. Application materials: Application form.

Dates: Orientations year round; 2-12 months. Application deadline: Four months before program. Cost: $2,600-$4,900 (includes room, food, health insurance, international airfare, orientation). Compensation: None to $120 per week (includes room and food). Intern must arrange. Application fee: $15. Contact: Diane Crow, Global Outreach, Inc., P.O. Box 3291, Merrifield, VA 22116-3291; (703) 385-2995, fax (703) 385-2996; globaloutreach@compuserve.com.

Boston Univ. International Programs. Students enroll in 3 academic courses in conjunction with a professional internship experience. Students choose from internships in: Advertising and Public Relations; The Arts; Business and Economics; Health and Human Services; Hospitality Administration; The Media: Journalism, Film, and Television; Politics; and Prelaw. The internship experience allows students to explore organizations from multi-national corporations to local businesses, from hospitals to community service centers, from major magazine publishers or film production studios to local radio or advertising agencies.

Academic credit offered. Prerequisites: good academic standing, 3.0 GPA; language depending on site. Application materials: 2 references, transcript, essays, academic approval, interview for upper-level language programs.

Dates: Fall, Spring, and Summer (length varies). Application deadline: Mar 15 (Summer and Fall); Oct 15 (Spring). Cost: $4,400-$8,900. Application fee: $35. Contact: Boston Univ., International Programs, 232 Bay State Rd., 5th Fl., Boston, MA 02215; (617) 353-9888, fax (617) 353-5402; abroad@bu.edu, www.bu.edu/abroad.

Brethren Colleges Abroad. Opportunities vary by location. Examples include: business at Siemens Corp. in Germany; social work at a shelter in England; political science at the Council of Europe and The Human Rights

Institute in France; business in import-export companies and an international hotel chain in China and Japan; village development with The Resource Foundation in Ecuador; women's advocacy in India.

Fields: Business, teaching, political science, social work. Academic credit offered. Prerequisites: participation in BCA's academic program overseas for at least 1 semester.

Dates: Before, after, or during academic semesters. Cost: Living expenses. Application fee: $150. Contact: Tamula Drumm, Brethren Colleges Abroad, 605 College Ave., N. Manchester, IN 46962; (219) 982-5045, fax (219) 982-7755; bca@manchester.edu; www.studyabroad.com/bca.

Cooperative Education Program. Paid employment and internships for college and university students for a period of 8-12 weeks in 8 European and one Asian country. Employment depends on foreign language knowledge, major, and previous work experience. Work permits and housing are provided.

Dates: From Jun-Sep. Cost: Students must pay for air transportation and have a reserve of at least $800 for initial expenses. Contact: Günter Seefeldt, PhD, Director, International Cooperative Education Program, 15 Spiros Way, Menlo Park, CA 94025; (415) 323-4944, fax (415) 323-1104.

IAESTE-U.S. IAESTE-U.S. arranges reciprocal exchanges among 63 member countries for students of engineering, architecture, and the sciences to obtain on-the-job practical training with host employers in other countries. The IAESTE program is administered in the U.S. by the Association for International Practical Training (AIPT) in Columbia, MD.

Fields: Technical Fields. Seventy-five-100 internships per year. Three hundred-400 applicants. Prerequisites: Junior level standing, enrolled full-time at time of application. Application materials: application, reference, transcript, language certification.

Dates: Summer placements (other periods available). Application deadline: Dec 10. Cost: $150 placement. Compensation: cost of living. Application fee: $50. Contact: Jeff Lange, Program Assistant/Eric Haines, Program Director, IAESTE-U.S., 10400 Little Patuxent Pkwy., Suite 250 L, Columbia, MD 21044-3510; (410) 997-3068, fax (410) 997-5186; iaeste@aipt.org, www.softaid.net/aipt/aipt.hml.

International Internship Program. People to People International coordinates 2 month, unpaid internships for students and professionals for 6 units of graduate or undergraduate credit. We can place interns in the following cities: London, Dublin, Brisbane, Rockhampton, Seville, Nairobi, Munich, Moscow, Prague, Buenos Aires and Copenhagen. We employ interns in positions that correspond to their academic backgrounds, work experience and career goals. These are full-time, on-the-job learning positions that will give students experience in real working settings in addition to cultural exposure.

Dates: Flexible throughout the year. Cost: $1,675. Includes tuition and placement fee. Housing and airfare not included. Contact: Ms. Dorel Drinkwine, People to People International, 501 E. Armour Blvd., Kansas City, MO 64109-2200; (816) 531-4701, fax (816) 561-7502; ptpi@cctr.umkc.edu, http://cei.haag.umkc.edu/ptp.

Internships International. Quality, professional, full-time internships in all fields for college graduates. Internships are found based on the intern's needs and experiences. Internship locations are: London, Paris, Florence, Madrid, Stuttgart, Dublin, Santiago, Budapest, Melbourne, and Shanghai. Internships are non-paying but it is often possible to "moonlight" while doing an internship. This is a program for individuals who are ready to assume professional responsibility.

Fields: All fields. Prerequisites: college graduate, language ability if appropriate to location or willingness to attend language school. Application materials: 2 references, photo, specific statement of purpose, resume, transcript, interview.

Dates: Flexible, depending on wishes of the intern. Application deadline: none. Cost: Intern pays all expenses (approx. $200 per week). Compensation: none. Application fee: $700 (refundable if intern not placed). Contact: Judy Tilson, Director, Internships International, 1116 Cowper Dr., Raleigh, NC 27608; (919) 832-1575, fax (919) 837-7170; http://rtpnet.org/~int/intl.

Syracuse Internships Abroad. All internships are supervised by Syracuse faculty or approved adjuncts who teach in Syracuse programs abroad. Actual work experience is assigned by an agency supervisor. Interviews and final placements take place overseas. Most internships are part of a varied semester experience including coursework, field trips, and social activities.

Fields: Business, Advertising, Political Science, Social Agencies, Drama, Human Development, Social Work, Education, Photography, Communications. Academic credit offered. Three-6 internship credits, up to 18 total credits. One hundred internships per year. Ninety applicants. Prerequisites: Sophomore status, essays, recommendations, good academic standing. Application materials: application and recommendation forms.

Dates: Fall, Spring, Summer (6 weeks or longer). Application deadline: Mar 15 (summer), Apr 1 (fall), Oct 15 (spring). Cost: $3,500-$15,000 (includes room, food, international airfare, tuition). Compensation: none. Application fee: $50. Contact: Syracuse Univ., 119 Euclid Ave., Syracuse, NY 13244-4170; (800) 235-3472, fax (315) 443-4593; suabroad@syr.edu, http://sumweb.syr.edu/dipa.

WorldTeach. WorldTeach is a private nonprofit organization based at Harvard Univ. which contributes to educational development and cultural exchange by placing volunteers to teach in developing countries (China, Costa Rica, Ecuador, Honduras, Mexico, Namibia, Thailand, and Vietnam). Volunteers teach English, math, science, and environmental education to students of all ages. All programs last for 1 academic year; except for the summer program in China.

Dates: Year-round departures and deadlines vary depending on the program. Cost: $3,600-$4,400. Includes health insurance, airfare, field support, and training. Contact: Jodi Hullinger, Desk Officer, WorldTeach, Harvard Institute for International Development, 1 Eliot St., Cambridge, MA 02138-5705; (617) 495-5527, fax (617) 495-1599; jhulling@worldteach.org, www.igc.org/worldteach.

TEACHING ENGLISH: TRAINING AND PLACEMENT PROGAMS

The following listings of training and placement programs for English teaching was supplied by the organizers. Contact the program directors to confirm costs, dates, and other details.

Asia

Volunteers in Asia. Founded in 1963, Volunteers in Asia (VIA) is a small, non-profit organization that provides Asian communities with volunteer English teachers. VIA's goal is to stimulate long-term interest in Asia and further communication between Americans and Asians. Volunteers generally teach at colleges in Vietnam, Indonesia, China, and Laos.

Dates: Applications due Feb 5, 1998; volunteers depart for Asia June 1998. Cost: $950 for 2 years includes roundtrip airfare. Contact: Amy Tanner, Volunteers in Asia, P.O. Box 4543, Stanford, CA 94309; (650) 723-3228, fax (650) 725-1805; volasia @volasia.org, www.volasia.org.

Canada

ELC, Univ. of Victoria. English Language Centre (ELC), Univ. of Victoria provides intensive (12-week) English language programs 3 times annually for intermediate and advanced international students. Students may choose an Academic Program to improve academic and study skills for future studies or a Communicative Program to improve conversational English language skills for professional or personal development. Short-term programs are available throughout the spring and summer.

Dates: Spring and summer (1997): Mar 31-May 9 ($1,925); May 26-Jun 27 ($1,585), Jul 7-Aug 15 ($1,925), Aug 4-29 ($1,295). 1998: Apr 10-Jul 2, Sep 11-

Dec 3, Jan 8-Apr 1 (tuition $2,700 per term). Contact: Maxine Macgillivray, Program Coordinator, English Language Centre, Univ. of Victoria, P.O. Box 1700 MS8452, Victoria, BC V8W 2Y2, Canada; (604) 721-8469, fax (604) 721-6276; mmacgillivry@uvcs.uvic.ca.

Queen's Univ. School of English. The Queen's Univ. School of English offers 5- and 12-week courses year round at one of Canada's oldest and best-known universities in an almost totally English-speaking community. Students have the option of living in a University residence with monitors, in a homestay, or in University cooperative housing. The English Only Rule is strictly enforced.

Dates: Jan 7-Apr 10, May 6-Aug 7, May 18-Jun 19, July 6-Aug 7, Sep 9-Dec 11. Cost: International students: $2,550 12 weeks; $1,275 5 weeks, plus mandatory health insurance (price varies). Contact: Mrs. Eleanor Rogers, Director, The School of English, Queen's Univ., Kingston, ON K7L 3N6, Canada; (613) 545-2472, fax (613) 545-6809; soe@post.queensu.ca, www.queensu.ca/soe/.

Special Intensive English Program. McGill Univ. was founded in 1821 and is internationally renowned for its high academic standards. The Special Intensive English courses are offered at 6 levels and run for 9 weeks. Classes are limited to about 15 students per class. There are 4 sessions a year. Instructional methods include the use of a modern language laboratory, audio-visual equipment, and a wide-range of activities stressing the communicative approach.

Dates: Spring (1998): Apr 6-Jun 5. Summer (1998): Jun 22-Aug 21. (Fall) 1998: Sep 21-Nov 20. (Winter) 1999: Jan 19-Mar 20. Cost: CAN$1,795 for international students, CAN$1,450 for Canadian citizens and permanent residents. Contact: Ms. M. Brettler, 770 Sherbrooke St. W., Montreal, PQ, H3A 1G1 Canada; (514) 398-6160, fax (514) 398-2650; lang@conted.lan.mcgill.ca.

TESL Certification Program. Located in Vancouver, the ESL Teacher Training Centre features TESL certificate programs. We offer full-time, part-time and correspondence courses of 1-4 months. We are a member organization of the National Association of Career Colleges and the Private Career Training Association of British Columbia.

Dates: Programs are offered year round. Cost: CAN$850. Includes course materials. Contact: ESL Teacher Training Centre, #105-2412 Laurel St., Vancouver, BC V5Z 3T2, Canada; (604) 872-1236, fax (604) 872-1275; teachabroad@ibm.net, www.arnb.com/eslttc.

Univ. of Regina Language Institute. A variety of non-credit programs are offered in 3 streams: English for Academic Purposes (EA), which prepares students for attending university; English for Business (EB) which focuses on increasing students' understanding and use of business vocabulary and concepts; and English for Communication (EC) which focuses on increasing students' oral communication. Evening courses, conversation partners, and short-term customized courses are also available.

Dates: (1997) Jan 10-Apr 4 (12 weeks); Apr 18-Jun 13 (8 weeks); Jun 27-Aug 22 (8 weeks); Sep 12-Dec 5 (12 weeks). Cost: (Winter 1997): $1,825. Spring/summer (1997): $1,625. Fall (1997): $1,945. Conversation partners: $110 per semester. Placement fee for housing: $160. Plus rent, security, and telephone deposits. Contact: Penthes Rubrecht, English as a Second Language Centre, Univ. of Regina, Rm. 211, Language Institute, Regina, SK, Canada S4S 0A2; (306) 585-4585, fax (306) 585-4971; esl@max.cc.uregina.ca, www.uregina.ca/~esl.

Central Europe

Central European Teaching Program. Places teachers in Hungary, Romania, Poland, and Latvia, with expansion to Moscow and China for 1998-99. Orientation, housing, stipend, and basic health insurance are provided.

Dates: Sep 98-Jun 99. Cost: Placement fee: $1,000. Contact: Michael Mullen, CETP Director, Beloit College, 700 College St., Beloit, WI 53511; (608) 363-2619, fax (608) 363-2449; mullenm@beloit.edu, www.beloit.edu/~cetp.

Costa Rica

Learn Spanish While Volunteering. Assist with the training of Costa Rican public school teachers in our latest language learning techniques. Learn Spanish in the morning, volunteer work in the afternoon/evening. Spanish classes are 2-5 students plus group learning activities; conversations with middle-class homestay families (1 student per family). Homestays and volunteer project are within walking distance of school in small town (14,000 population) near the capital, San Jose.

Dates: Year round, all levels. Classes begin every Monday, volunteer program is continuous. Cost: $295 per week for 25 hours of Spanish classes. Includes tuition, all meals, homestay, laundry, all materials, Costa Rican dance and cooking classes, and airport transportation. $25 one-time registration for Spanish classes; $100 additional one-time registration fee for volunteer program. Contact: Susan Shores, Registrar, Latin American Language Center, 7485 Rush River Dr., Suite 710-123, Sacramento, CA 95831; (916) 447-0938, fax (916) 428-9542; lalc@madre.com.

France

French in France. Among the ways to learn French, total immersion is the most enjoyable and the most effective. We have been doing it for 20 years in a small historical city located in Normandy (west of Paris, close to the seaside). We welcome people at any age and any level in from 1- to 10-week programs, intensive or vacation type, from mid-March to mid-November. Homestay of Chélea (deville).

Dates: Spring: Mar 23-May 29; summer: Jun 15-Aug 28; fall: Sep 7-Nov 13, 1998. Cost: From $525 per week (tuition, room and board, and excursions). Contact: Dr. Almeras, Chairman, French American Study Center, 12, 14, Blvd. Carnot, B.P. 176, 14104 Lisieux Cedex, France (011) 33-2-31-31-22-01, fax 31-22-21.

French Language Studies—Sorbonne. Intensive French language at the Univ. of Paris, Sorbonne. All levels are available, 12-15 hours of instruction weekly. All courses are taught in French. Over 100,000 students from around the world have participated in this program.

Dates: Spring semester: Feb 6-May 31; summer: Jul and Aug.; fall: Sep 11-Dec 15. Cost: Semester: $1,895 for 16 weeks. Contact: Philip Virtue, Program Director, Center for Study Abroad, 2802 E. Madison St., #160, Seattle, WA 98112; (206) 726-1498, fax (206) 285-9197; virtuecsa@aol.com.

Ireland

EFL/TEFL. DAELS: 1-year full-time postgraduate Diploma in Advanced English Language Studies: English language, linguistics, one other academic subject; Summer school: 15-23 hours per week, 1- to 10-week stay. Levels from elementary to advanced. Options in English for language teachers, business English. Cambridge CTEFLA/DTEFLA teacher training.

Dates: DTEFLA, DAELS Oct-Jun; summer school Jul-Sep. (TEFLA at intervals throughout the year.) Cost: Tuition fees DAELS:

IR£1,781 per year, DTEFLA IR£1,600, CTEFLA IR£850; summer school: IR£90 to IR£165 per week. Contact: Steven Dodd/ Vivienne Lordan, Language Centre, Univ. College Cork, Republic of Ireland; (011) 353-21-904090 or 904102.

Teaching EFL. Part-time 3-month course; full-time 1-month course both leading to the Univ. of Cambridge Certificate in Teaching English as a Foreign Language to Adults (or as renamed after 1996).

Dates: Three-month course Jan-Mar (1997); 1-month course Jul-Aug (1997). Cost: Tuition fees: IR£850. Contact: Steven Dodd/Vivienne Lordan, Language Centre, Univ. College Cork, Republic of Ireland; (011) 353-21-904090 or 904102, fax 904090 or 904102.

Japan

ESL Placement in Japan. Recruits teachers for their 240 schools in Japan. Requires a bachelor's degree, overseas experience desired. Interview required. Work week is 33-35 hours, maximum 3-4 students per class. Guaranteed monthly salary, furnished housing, insurance, teaching material, paid training provided. Japanese language not required.

Dates: Ongoing, 1-year renewable contracts. Cost: No application fee. Contact: Trevor Phillips, Interact Nova Group, 2 Oliver St., 7th Fl., Boston, MA 02109; (800) 551-6682; 74507.3070@compuserve.com, www. novaja pan.com or Eric Smith, Interact Nova Group, 601 California St., Suite 702, San Francisco, CA 94108; (415) 788-3717.

Japan Employment Pak. Our Japan Employment Pak contains addresses and phones of 100 English conversation schools in Japan, passport and visa information, apartment rental advice, and teaching tips.

Dates: Year round. Cost: $25 (in U.S.), $28 via an interantional poster order (if outside U.S.) Contact: Rob Tschudi, Art of Words,

481 W. Prentice Ave., Suite 303, Littleton, CO 80120-1554; (303) 899-4962; artofwords@ earthlink.net, http://home.earthlink.net/ ~artofwords.

Japan Exchange and Teaching (JET) Program. Sponsored by the Japanese Government, the JET Program invites over 1,000 American college graduates and young professionals to share their language and culture with Japanese youth. One-year positions are available in schools and government offices throughout Japan. Apply by early December for positions beginning in July of the following year.

Dates: One-year contracts renewable by mutual consent. May be renewed twice for a maximum of 3 years on the program. Cost: Participants receive approx. ¥3,600,000 per year in monthly payments. Contact: JET Program Office, Embassy of Japan, 2520 Massachusetts Ave. NW, Washington, DC 20008; (202) 238-6772, fax (202) 265-9484; eojjet@pop.erols.com, www.jet.org.

Nova Intercultural Institute. The largest conversational English school in Japan, employing over 2,100 teachers in 220 schools. Nova offers a fixed, 5-day work schedule, guaranteed monthly salary, visa, paid training, assistance with housing, flight arrangements, health insurance and an extensive support network. Maximum 3-4 students per class. Beginning to advanced levels. Forty to 45 minute classes.

Dates: Jan-Nov (1997). Cost: No application or processing fees. Contact: Trevor Phillips, Interact Nova Group, 2 Oliver St., 7th Fl., Boston, MA 02109; (617) 542-5027, fax (617) 542-3115; www.novajapan.com.

Teach English in Japan at Interac. Interac seeks language consultants to teach corporate clients for a minimum of 1 year. A challenging, cross-cultural working environment with competitive remuneration. Perfect for an outgoing, self-motivated, flexible professional. Send resume, with cover letter and 1-

page essay on reasons for seeking employment in Japan.

Contact: Recruiting Dept., Interac Co., Ltd., Fujibo Bldg., Chiyoda-ku, Tokyo 102, Japan; (011) 81-3-3234-7857, fax 3234-6055; www.alpha-web.or.jp/~interac/.

Teaching English in Japan. Two-year program to maximize linguistic and cultural integration of participants who work as teachers' assistants. Placements twice yearly in April and August. Most positions are in junior high schools in urban and rural areas. Bachelor's degree, cultural sensitivity, and some ESL training required.

Dates: Hiring for positions every April and August. Applications accepted year round. Cost: Airfare, salary, housing, health care provided. No application fees. Contact: Earlham College, Institute for Education on Japan, D-202, Richmond, IN 47374; (888) 685-2726; www.earlham.edu/www/departments/AET/home.htm.

Your Personal Gateway to Japan. Safe Jobs is your unique, personal, and highly affordable gateway to an international teaching job. Not a big corporation or a shady recruiter, we match your unique qualifications with a safe school. Know in detail about your school before you accept a position. Don't go it alone, we can help.

Dates: Ongoing. Cost: Free application. Upon placement, a $95 fee is due 30 days after you arrive in Japan and start your new job. Contact: Safe Jobs in Japan, Aza Nakayaii 20-7, Otsuki-machi, Koriyama-shi, Fukushima-ken, 963-0201 Japan; (908) 231-0994 (phone inquiries only); info@safejobsinjapan.com, www.safejobsinjapan.com.

Korea

Korea Services Group (KSG). KSG provides native-speaking English conversation instructors to Korean foreign language institutes and educational institutions including public or private universities, junior colleges, high schools, middle schools, etc. Pay range is normally $19,000-$25,000 per year for foreign language institutes. Minimum requirement is usually any 4 year BA/BS, but AA/AS acceptable if major is in English or Education. Experience usually not required for language institutes. Send resume, cover letter, photocopy of passport, photocopy of transcripts, diploma, 2 passport sized photos and 2 letters of reference.

Dates: Starts monthly for foreign language institutes. Educational institutions usually start Mar 1 and Sep 1. Cost: $300 (includes most process expenses and cultural and teaching training as required). Contact: Korea Services Group U.S. Headquarters for more information; (503) 230-6932. Korea Services Group, #807-3, Mang Mi-Dong, Suyoung-Gu, Pusan 613-131, Korea.

Mexico

El Bosque del Caribe, Cancun. Take a professional Spanish course 25 hours per week and enjoy the Caribbean beaches. Relaxed family atmosphere. No more than 6 students per class. Special conversation program. Mexican cooking classes and excursions to the Mayan sites. Housing with Mexican families. College credit available.

Dates: Year round. New classes begin every Monday. Group programs arranged at reduced fees. Cost: Enrollment fee $100, $175 per week. One week with a Mexican family $150. Contact: Eduardo Sotelo, Director, Calle Piña 1, S.M. 25, 77500 Cancún, Mexico; (011) 52-98-84-10-38, fax 84-58-88; bcaribe@mail.cancun-language.com.mx.

Language and Culture in Guanajuato. We work with innovative teaching techniques, tailoring instruction to each student's needs. Spanish, Mexican History, Politics, Culture-Cuisine, Folk Dancing, and Latin American Literature.

Dates: Year round. New classes begin every

Monday. Cost: $925. Includes 4 weeks of classes and homestay with 3 meals daily. Contact: Director Jorge Barroso, Instituto Falcon, A.C., Guanajuato, Gto. 36000 Mexico; Tel./fax (011) 52-473-2-36-94, infalcon@redes.int. com.mx, www.infonet.com.mx/falcon.

Learn Spanish in Chiapas. Spanish lessons in private sessions or small groups (4 people maximum). Family stays available. School tours to Indian (Mayan) villages, jungle trips available. Extracurricular activities include: Mexican cooking, discussions, and video showings. Teach English in exchange for Spanish lessons. Centro Cultural "El Puente" includes gallery weaver's cooperative, travel agency, cafe, restaurant, phone/fax service.

Dates: Year round. Cost: Highest $220 per week; lowest $75 per week. Contact: Roberto Rivas, Bastidas Centro Bilingüe de Chiapas, C. Real de Guadalupe 55, Centro Cultural "El Puente," San Cristóbal de Las Casas 29230, Chiapas, Mexico; (011) 52-967-8-41-57, fax 967-83723 or Tel./fax (800) 303-4983; cenbili@chisnet.com.mx, www.mexonline. com/centro1.htm.

New World Teachers. Accelerated 4-week TEFL/TESL Certificate Course available in Puerto Vallarta. Integrates established European Direct Method aimed at trainees with an American education; requires no second language. Includes supervised practice teaching to foreign students, permanent access to job placement guidance and information. Extensive Internet resources. Two-day seminar in Teaching English to Young Learners also available with every course.

Dates: Four-week intensive courses begin in Puerto Vallarta: Feb 16, Mar 16, Apr 20, Jun 8, Jul 20, Aug 31, Sep 28, Oct 26, Dec 14. Cost: $2,900. Includes deposit, registration, books, course materials, and lifetime job placement assistance. Accommodations: single room with private bath, 5 minutes walk from the beach, $300. *Transitions Abroad* readers receive free accommodations package. Contact: New World Teachers, 605 Mar-

ket St., Suite 800, San Francisco, CA 94105; (800) 644-5424; teachersSF@aol.com, www. goteach.com.

Short-Term TEFL Program. Vancouver Language Centre is a large language school in Mexico that offers Spanish and English language instruction to international and local students. VLC also offers 2-week and 4-week TEFL courses to local and foreign teachers. VLC often hires qualified teachers from Canada and the U.S.

Dates: Monthly. Cost: $150 per week (tuition only). Contact: Vancouver Language Centre, Avenida Vallarda 1151, Col. Americana, CP 44100, Guadalajara, Jalisco, Mexico; (011) 52-3-826-0944, fax 825-2051; vic@vec. bc.ca, www.vec.bc.ca.

Portugal

Teacher Training in Lisbon. International House Lisbon offers the following range of intensive teacher training courses. RSA/Cambridge certificate in the teaching of English to adults, RSA/Cambridge certificate in the teaching of English to young learners, RSA/Cambridge diploma in the teaching of English to adults, IHTT introductory course to TEFL.

Dates: May 6-May 31, Jul 1-26, Jul 29-Aug 23, Aug 26-Sep 20, Nov 4-29. Cost: Courses from $400 to $1,400. Contact: Paula de Nagy, International House, Rua Marqués Sá Da Bandeira 16, 1050 Lisbon, Portugal; (011) 351-3151496, fax 3530081; ihlisbon@mail. telepac.pt.

Saudia Arabia

Hail Community College. Opening Fall 1998. Pre-college IEP for academic purposes in an English-medium institution. Beautiful agricultural area. Minimum BA and ESL certificate and 1-year overseas ESL experience. Free housing, in-Kingdom health care, roundtrip air tickets to home-of-record annually, e-mail, gratuity, single/married status. Dates: From Fall 1998: Sep and Feb each year. Cost: Competitive salary and benefits. Contact: Dean, Educational Services, KFUPM, Box 5026, Dhahran 31261, Saudi Arabia; (011) 966-3-860-2395, fax 860-2341; d-dusv@dpc.kfupm.edu.sa.

King Fahd Univ. of Petroleum and Minerals-Dhahran. A pre-university IEP emphasizing English for academic purposes. MA in ESL closely-allied field and 2 years overseas ESL experience required. All-male student body. Free housing, in-Kingdom health care, e-mail, roundtrip air tickets to home-of-record annually, end-of-contract gratuity, single/married status.
Dates: Hiring for Sep and Feb each year. Cost: Competitive salary and benefits package. Dean, Educational Services, KFUPM, Box 5026, Dhahran 31261, Saudi Arabia; (011) 966-3-860-2395, fax 860-2341; ddusv@dpc.kfupm.edu.sa.

Spain

RSA/UCLES Certificate in ELT to Adults. CELTA is the most widely recognized course in teaching English to adults. The course provides initial training for those without previous experience or training in this field. The course is based on daily teaching practice and evaluation of lessons. Highly regarded by employers.
Dates: Twelve 4-week courses per year. Cost: PTS160,000. Contact: Jenny Johnson, Courses Administrator, International House, c/o Trafalgar 14 entlo, 08010 Barcelona, Spain; (011) 34-3-268-4511, fax 268-0239; training@bcn.ihes.com.

Teacher Training Program. Full-time courses in Barcelona leading to the Univ. of Cambridge Certificate in Teaching English as a Foreign Language to Adults (CELTA).
Dates: Jul 6-Jul 31, Sep 1-Sep 29, 1998. Cost:

Entry fee and course fee: 160,000 Ptas. Contact: Ms. Montserrat Solé, York House, Muntaner 479, 08021 Barcelona, Spain; (011) 34-3-2113200, fax 4185866.

Taiwan

Overseas Service Corps YMCA (OSCY). Place BAs to PhDs in ESL teaching positions in community-based YMCAs in Taiwan. Degree in teaching, ESL, or general teaching experience preferred. No Chinese language necessary. This conversational English program provides an opportunity for cultural exchange. Must reside in North America and be a citizen of an English-speaking country. Twenty to 30 openings.
Dates: Call any time for a brochure, apply between Jan 1 and Apr 15 for Sep placement. Cost: $35 application fee. Benefits for successful applicants include: Housing, health insurance, return airfare, paid vacation, bonus, orientation, sponsorship for visa, and monthly stipend. Contact: Janis Sterling, OSCY Manager, International Group, YMCA of the USA, 101 N. Wacker Dr., Chicago, IL 60606; (800) 872-9622 ext. 167, fax (312) 977-0884.

Taiwan, U.S.

Hess Language School. Largest private children's English school in Taiwan. Over 75 branches throughout the island. The curriculum has been tried, tested, and constantly updated to provide the most successful program in teaching English to children. For details and an application visit our web site: www.hess.com.tw. You need a bachelor's degree, a passport from an English-speaking country, a 1-year commitment, and be a native English speaker.
Dates: Application deadlines fall 5 months before quarterly intakes in Jun, Sep, Dec, and Mar. Cost: No fee. We recruit only for our own schools. Contact: North Americans:

contact HLS, 4 Horicon Ave., Glens Falls, NY 12801; Tel./fax (518) 793-6183; dhess@ capitalnet. Main officer serves all other countries: HLS, PoAi Rd., No. 83, 2nd Fl., Taipei 100, Taiwan; (011) 886-2-2382-5439, fax 2382-0799; personne@hess.com.tw.

Thailand

Full- and Part-Time Teaching Jobs. Language schools of over 50 western teachers teaching all academic subjects and languages in one-on-one setting in Bangkok. Wage from $10 per hour. Programs for full-time ESL jobs in Bangkok and in-house staff training for companies. All kinds of test preparation.

Dates: Year round. Contact: John F. Moriarty, TCD Co., Ltd., 399/7 Soi 55-21, Sukhumvit Rd., Bangkok 10110, Thailand; (011) 66-2-391-5670, fax 391-5670;johnstcd@hotmail. com.

Teaching English at Yonok College. Suitable candidates must have a Bachelor's degree and be prepared to sign a 2-year contract. Those chosen will teach Thai university students the fundamental aspects of the English language. Teaching experience is preferred. The salary package includes a monthly stipend, housing, paid vacation time, visas, and health insurance.

Dates: May 1997-May 1999. Cost: Teachers must pay own airfare. Contact: Paul J. McKenney, Assistant to the President, Yonok College, 444 Lampany, Denchai Rd., Lamang, Thailand 52000; (011) 66-54-226-952, x 124, fax 226-957.

United Kingdom

Teach English as a Foreign Language. Courses in central London leading to the Cambridge/RSA Certificate (CELTA), regarded internationally as the ideal qualification in TEFL. International House has 40 years experience in training teachers and can offer jobs to those recently qualified in its 110 schools in 27 countries.

Dates: Four-week (110 hours) intensive courses begin Jan 5, Feb 2, Mar 2, Apr 14, May 11, Jun 8, Jul 6, Aug 3, Sep 1, Sep 28, Oct 26, Nov 23, 1998. Cost: £944 includes Cambridge/RSA registration. Contact: Teacher Training Development, International House, 106 Piccadilly, London W1V 9FL, England; (011) 44-171-491-2598, fax 499-0174; teacher@dial.pipex.com.

United States

American English Programs. American English Programs of New England offers intensive international TEFL certificate training programs. Four week courses include practice teaching sessions, job assistance, a videotape of yourself to use in job applications. No foreign language or teaching experience required. We are the most affordable TEFL Certificate program in North America.

Dates: Year round. Cost: $1,800 fee includes tuition, textbooks (housing extra). Ask about our "early bird scholarships." Contact: Lesley Woodward, Director, 17 South St., Northampton, MA 01060; Tel./fax (413) 582-1812; eflworld@crocker.com, www.crocker.com/~eflworld.

Boston TEFL Course. International TEFL Certificate, limited enrollment, no second language necessary, second career persons welcome, global placement guidance, humanistic orientation to cross-cultural education, teacher training at American English Language Foundation, Harvard Univ. Club or other accommodations, PDP eligible by Massachusetts Department of Education. Also offers the Certificate in Teaching Business-English (Cert. TBE), Executive English, and Accent reduction program.

Dates: Full-time intensive course monthly; part-time courses offered periodically throughout the year. Cert.TBE Course - Intensive 1-week course offered monthly. Cost:

$2,300 includes tuition, nonrefundable $95 application fee, internship, international resume, job placement guidance, video lab, all books and materials. Contact: Thomas A. Kane, PhD, Worldwide Teachers Development Institute, 266 Beacon St., Boston, MA 02116; (800) 875-5564, fax (617) 262-0308; bostontefl@aol.com; www.to-get.com/BostonTEFL.

Cambridge/RSA CELTA. The most prestigious and selective 4-week TEFLA course. Qualified Univ. of Cambridge approved faculty. Intensive teaching practice combined with theoretical work in methodology, materials, and structure of English. Pre-course study materials and job placement assistance are included. Low-cost housing available. Six graduate credits toward MA in TESOL.

Dates: Courses begin every 4 weeks from Jan 12-Oct 19, 1998. Cost: Tuition for courses in 1998: $2,225. Contact: Bruce Sharpe, The Center for English Studies, 330 7th Ave., New York, NY 10001; (212) 629-7300, fax (212) 736-7950; cesnewyork@cescorp.com.

China Teaching Program. A training and placement program for those wanting to teach at institutions of higher education or at secondary schools throughout the P.R.C. Most opportunities are in TEFL, some in business or law. Five-week summer training sessions held on WWU campus. Participants study Chinese language and culture, TEFL methodology, etc. Minimum requirements: BA, native speaker of English. (Placement-only option may be possible.)

Dates: Application deadline for summer session 1998 is Jan 31. Cost: Approx. $1,100 (includes tuition and placement). Contact: China Teaching, Western Washington Univ., OM 530A, Bellingham, WA 98225-9047; (360) 650-3753; ctp@cc.wwu.edu.

Eastern Michigan University. The MATESOL program has a strong practical emphasis based on sound pedagogical and linguistic theory. Students take 20 hours in TESOL (theoretical foundations, pedagogical grammar and pronunciation, observation and analysis methods and materials, language testing, research seminar, practicum) and 12 more hours (at least 6 in English linguistics). There is no comprehensive exam; a thesis is optional. A typical cohort includes about 1/3 international and 2/3 U.S. students from a wide range of ages and experiences. Limited number of assistantships.

Dates: Mar 1 deadline for fall admission; Jul 1 for winter admission. Cost: In-state, $141 per credit hour; out-of-state, $327 per credit hour. Furnished campus apartments $515 per month. Contact: Jo Ann Aebersold, TESOL Adviser, 219 Alexander, Eastern Michigan Univ., Ypsilanti, MI 48197; (313) 487-0130, fax (313) 487-0338.

EFL Teacher Training. Lado Enterprises Inc. offers an intensive Teacher Training Certificate Program in teaching English as a Foreign Language. The program is designed for inexperienced teachers, or those with no teaching experience, seeking employment overseas. This 135-hour course provides practical hands-on classroom experience using fundamental teaching principles and methodologies.

Dates: Monthly sessions held year-round. Ten-week evening program also offered. Cost: $1,950 for tuition and fees. Contact: Will Pickering, Lado Enterprises, Inc., 2233 Wisconsin Ave., NW, Washington, DC 20007; (202) 223-0023, fax (202) 337-1118.

ELS TEFL Certificate Program. Provides intensive practical training for teaching English as a foreign language to the following groups: 1) those who wish to develop skills and learn methods for teaching EFL, 2) current English (language) teachers who wish to update teaching methodologies, 3) program coordinators and administrators who are involved in curriculum design, and 4) native and non-native English speakers and international teachers who wish to teach English in their native countries or in other non-English-speaking countries.

Dates: 1997: Feb 24-Mar 21; Apr 21-May 16; Jun 16-Jul 11; Jul 14-Aug 8; Aug 11-Sep 5, Oct 6-31; Dec 29-Jan 23, 1998. Cost: $1,995 includes registration fee, course fee, books and materials, and job placement services. Contact: Victoria Cabal, Coordinator, ELS Language Centers, 5761 Buckingham Pkwy., Culver City, CA 90230; (310) 642-0982, fax (310) 649-5231; vcabal@els.com.

English For Everybody. Prague and other cities in Central/Eastern Europe. Also, Greece and Vienna. Guaranteed jobs, pre-arranged housing, airport greeting. TEFL Certificate or experience required. College degree preferred.

Cost: $450 assistance fee. Contact: English For Everybody, Spanielova 1292, 163 00 Prague 6, Czech Republic; Tel./fax (011) 42-2-301-9784. U.S. voice mail (415) 789-7641; www.vol.C2/EFE.

ESL Intensive Institute. Learn English pronunciation, listening comprehension, conversation, reading and writing. Includes an orientation to American culture and weekly field trips. By Univ. of New Hampshire in Durham (hour north of Boston and 15 minutes from ocean). For students wanting to learn English before college or who want to improve TOEFL scores (3-10 credits, 4 hours per day).

Dates: Take 1 session or combine them for 3-, 4-, 6-, 7-, or 10-week study. Jun 2-27 (4-week session), Jul 7-25 (3-week session), Jul 28-Aug 15 (3-week session). Cost: $225 per week plus one-time fee of $130. Room and board available at a moderate additional cost. Contact: L. Conti, UNH Continuing Education, ESL Institute, 24 Rosemary Ln., Durham, NH 03824; (603) 862-2069, learn.dce@unh, www.learn.unh.edu.

Eurocentres. Intensive language training 20-25 hours per week for beginners to advanced levels. Immersion philosophy in small classes with students from around the world and homestay living available. A calendar of social and cultural programs with extended excursions available with each course. Business English and college test preparation courses are offered. CELTA teacher-training course offered 4 times a year.

Dates: Two- 4-, and 12-week courses to academic year offered year round. Cost: Ranges by location and length. Contact: Eurocentres, 101 N. Union St., Alexandria, VA 22314; (703) 684-1494 or (800) 648-4809, fax (703) 684-1495; 100632.141@compuserve.com.

Hamline TEFL Certificate Course. Hamline University offers an internationally recognized TEFL Certificate Course for individuals with little or no teaching experience who wish to teach English to adults overseas. An interactive, hands-on approach enables participants to discover the principles and practices of English language teaching. Courses include lectures, workshops, and practice teaching.

Dates: Three 1-month intensives: Apr, Jul, and Aug; 10-week: Jan-Mar. Semi-intensive: Sep-Mar. Evening extensive; On-campus room and board available for Jul. Limited space available for Jan-Apr. Cost: One-month intensive courses: $1960 (10 graduate quarter credits); Semi-intensive and evening: $2,280 (15 graduate quarter credits). Materials: approx. $80. Contact: Betsy Parrish, Associate Professor/Coordinator, TEFL Certificate Program, Graduate Continuing Studies, Hamline Univ., 1536 Hewitt Ave., St. Paul, MN 55104; (800) 888-2182, fax (612) 523-2489; bparrish@gw.hamline.edu.

Master of Arts in Teaching Program. The School for International Training's Master of Arts in Teaching Program offers concentrations in ESOL, French, and Spanish in academic year or 2-summer format. The program emphasizes practical teaching skills, classroom-based research, and innovative methodologies.

Dates: Sep 1, 1997-May 29, 1998; Jun 22-Aug 14, 1998; Jun 21-Aug 13, 1999. Cost: 997-98 tuition for both formats is 17,500. Contact: Kat Eldred, Director of Outreach and Recruitment, School for International Training, Box 676, Kipling Rd., Brattleboro, VT 05302; (802) 257-7751, fax (802) 258-3500; admissions@sit.edu.

Master of International and Intercultural Management. The School for International Training Master of International and Intercultural Management offers concentrations in sustainable development, international education, and training and human resource development in a 1 academic-year program. This degree is designed for individuals wishing to make a career change or enter the field. A practical training component enables "on-the-job" training and an opportunity to work internationally.

Dates: Sep 1, 1997-May 29, 1998. Cost: 17,000 (1997-98 tuition). Contact: Kat Eldred, Director of Outreach and Recruitment, Admissions Counselor, School for International Learning, P.O. Box 676, Kipling Rd., Brattleboro, VT 05302; (802) 257-7751, fax (802) 258-3500; admissions@sit.edu, www.sit.edu.

Master's in TESOL. One of the most sought-after professionals in the world today is the teacher of English as a second or foreign language. Bringing together knowledge and skill from linguistics, education, humanities, and the social sciences, the Seattle Pacific Univ. Division of Humanities MA-TESOL program will prepare you for leadership and service in this growing field.

Contact: MA-TESOL Dept., Seattle Pacific Univ., 3307 3rd Ave. W, Seattle, WA 98119; (206) 281-2670, fax (206) 281-2771; daphynes@spu.edu.

Monterey Institute of International Studies. MA program in Teaching English to Speakers of Other Languages (MATESOL) combines strong academic preparation with practical training language pedagogy, including a core of courses in applied linguistics and pedagogical theories, curriculum development, language testing, and practicum courses organized around the type of tasks encountered in the classroom. Applications must have a minimum 3.0 grade point average on a 4.0 scale, and a minimum 600 TOEFL score.

Dates: The MA program typically takes 3 semesters (fall, spring, fall; or spring, fall, spring). 37 semester units. Cost: $17,200 (fall 1997 and spring 1998). Contact: Admissions Office, Monterey Institute of International Studies, 425 Van Buren St., Monterey, CA 93940; (408) 647-4123, fax (408) 647-6405; admit@miis.edu.

RSA/Cambridge CELTA. Intensive 4-week TEFL training leading to the most widely recognized certification worldwide: The RSA/Cambridge CELTA. Our program offers: 35-hour pre-course assignment, unique post-course development pack, highly professional training, expert job guidance during and after training.

Dates: Every month (except December). Cost: $2,750. Includes tuition, materials and job guidance. Contact: Jeff Mohamed, English International, 655 Sutter St., Suite 200, San Francisco, CA 94102; (415) 749-5633; teflusa@compuserve.com, www.english-international.com.

RSA/UCLES CTEFLA. A course for those without previous TESOL experience. Input includes language awareness, phonology, methodology, classroom management, use of technology, syllabus. Trainees are observed teaching students at elementary and intermediate levels. They observe qualified teachers for 8 hours. Practical emphasis.

Dates: Jan 7-Apr 5; Apr 8-Jun 28; Jul 1-Sep 20; Sep 23-Dec 13, 1997. Cost: AUS$2,190 payable in 1 installment. Contact: Dierdre Conway, St. Mark's International College, 375 Stirling St., Highgate,

Western Australia; (011) 61-9-227-9888, fax 227-9880; smic@iinet.net.au.

RSA/Univ. of Cambridge CELTA. The most widely recognized initial qualification for teaching English as a foreign language to adults, the CELTA is offered at both our Santa Monica and Portland centers year round. You need to be at least 20 years old, have a good standard of education and a recent foreign language learning experience to be qualified.

Dates: Jan-Nov year round. Cost: $2,150. Contact: John Myers, Coast Language Academy, International House, 200 SW Market St., Suite #111, Portland, OR 97201; (503) 224-1960, fax (503) 224-2041; jmyers@coastpdx.com.

School of Teaching ESL. Intensive 4-week courses earn 12 Seattle Univ. education credits (post-baccalaureate or graduate-status) and the Certificate in Teaching English as a Second or Foreign Language. Graduates are teaching throughout the world. Instructors have higher degrees, overseas and U.S. teaching experience, and emphasize the practical. Laboratory ESL school on site. Also available: evening program, advanced certification, Master's in TESOL through Seattle Univ.

Dates: Eleven starting dates per year for the 4-week day intensive course. Evening courses are on the Seattle Univ. quarterly system. Cost: $170 per credit ($2,040 for the 12-credit course). Includes the Seattle Univ. credit fees but not books and materials (approx. $15 per credit). Accommodations: Studio apartments on site. When those are filled, a list of alternative rentals is provided. Contact: The School of Teaching ESL, 2601 N.W. 56th St., Seattle, WA 98107; (206) 781-8607, fax (206) 781-8922; tulare@seattleu.edu.

School of Teaching ESL. Prepare both to teach overseas and to return to work or graduate study afterwards. Earn 12 post-baccalaureate or graduate-status credits from Seattle Univ. and the Certificate in Teaching English as a Second or Foreign Language. Graduates teaching in more than 40 countries, includ-

ing the U.S. International candidates welcome. Reflection, practice, counseling, and much more.

Dates: Eleven starting dates per year for the 4-week day intensive course. Evening program is on the Seattle Univ. quarterly schedule. Cost: $175 per credit ($2,100 for the 12-credit course). Includes the Seattle Univ. credit fees but not books and materials. Reasonably priced accommodations on site. Contact: School of Teaching ESL, 2601 N.W. 56th St., Seattle, WA 98107; (206) 781-8607, fax (206) 781-8922; tulare@seattleu.edu, www.seattleu.edu/soe/stesl.

St Giles Language Teaching Center. Earn the Certificate in English Language Teaching to Adults (CELTA) in San Francisco, approved by the Royal Society of Arts/Univ. of Cambridge Examination Syndicate and the California Council for Private Postsecondary and Vocational Education. The course on practical training and teaching methodology, includes access to international job postings, graduate contacts, and teaching opportunities abroad. EFL school onsite for observation and practice teaching. Part of a group of schools in England, Switzerland, and the U.S. with over 40 years of teaching and training experience, led by highly-qualified instructors with extensive oveseas teaching experience. CELTA courses also offered in Brighton and London, England.

Dates: Feb 2-Feb 27, Apr 20-May 15, Jun 1-Jun 26, Sep 14-Oct 9, Oct 26-Nov 20. Cost: $2,450. Contact: St Giles Language Teaching Center, 1 Hallidie Plaza, Suite 350, San Francisco, CA 94102; (415) 788-3552, fax (415) 788-1923; sfstgile@slip.net, www.stgiles.co.uk

Summer Intensive Language Program Monterey Institute of International Studies offers elementary and intermediate language courses in a 9-week Summer Intensive Language Program for Chinese, Japanese, and Russian, Jun 16-Aug 18, 1998. Eight-week programs in Arabic, French, German, Italian, and Spanish are offered Jun 23-Aug 18

1998. English as a Second Language is offered year round in 8-week programs. Instruction is supplemented with tutors and cultural activities on campus for practice outside of the classroom. Customized programs are available any time during the year, call for information. Monterey is a beautiful venue for language study in a supportive small-class environment. Come join our "global village."

Cost: Nine-week program tuition $2,800, 8-week program tuition $2,600. Contact: Summer Session Office, Monterey Institute of International Studies, 425 Van Buren St., Monterey, CA 93940; (408) 647-4115, fax (408) 647-3534; jwatts@miis.edu, www.miis.edu.

Teaching English Abroad Program. This intensive program consists of 5 courses: Methods of TESOL, Language Structure and Use, Cultural Adjustment Abroad, Teaching English Internationally, and Finding an EFL Job Abroad. The program is intended for native speakers of English wishing to specialize in EFL in order to secure a teaching job overseas.

Dates: Oct-Dec and Apr-Jun. Cost: $1,210 includes all tuition (textbooks extra). Contact: Student Affairs Officer, TESL Dept., Univ. of California Irvine Extension, P.O. Box 6050, Irvine, CA 92616-6050; (714) 824-7845, fax (714) 824-3651; gfrydenb@uci.edu, www.unex.uci.edu/~unex.

The Univ. of Arizona. The Dept. of English MA in ESL emphasizes leadership development and is designed for experienced teachers with a strong academic record and leadership experience. Specialized courses are offered in language program administration, comparative discourse, teaching language through literature, sociolinguistics, language testing, and technology. PhD in SLAT.

Dates: Applications due by Feb 1 for the following fall semester. Two years are normally required to complete the program. Cost: $1,029 registration for 7 or more units, plus approx. $255 per unit for nonresident tuition. Contact: Director, English Language/ Linguistics Program, English Dept., P.O. Box 210067, The Univ. of Arizona, Tucson, AZ 85721-0067; (520) 621-7216, fax (520) 621-7397; maes1@ccit.arizona.edu, www.coh.arizona. edu/ell.

Univ. of Cambridge CELTA. St Giles Colleges (established 1955 in London) offer 4-week intensive teacher training programs approved by the Royal Society of Arts/University of Cambridge Examination Syndicate and, in San Francisco, the California State Department of Postsecondary Education. Program focuses on practical training and teaching methodology. Information on jobs, conditions in specific countries, resume writing, interviewing included. EFL school on site for observation.

Dates: Jan 27-Feb 21, Mar 24-Apr 18, May 5-30, Jun 16-Jul 11, Sep 8-Oct 3, Oct 27-Nov 2. Cost: $2,250. Contact: Teacher Training Coordinator, St Giles Language Teaching Center, 1 Hallidie Plaza, 3rd Floor, San Francisco, CA 94102; (415) 788-3552; (415) 788-1923.

Worldwide

American Language Institute. Study English for academic, personal, or professional reasons. Emphasis on speaking, listening, reading, and writing skills to enhance the students use of English, with special attention to skills needed for success in college.

Dates: Fifteen-week sessions beginning in Jan and Sep; summer sessions also. Cost: $2,300. Includes tuition, books, cultural activities. Contact: Constance Sabo-Risley, Office of International Programs, Univ. of Texas at San Antonio, San Antonio, TX 78249; csabo@utsa.edu.

Diploma Program in ESL. The Diploma Program is a noncredit, intensive, 8-week professional training program offered in summers for teachers and prospective teachers of English as a Second or Foreign Language. It covers all essential aspects of English language teaching from a practical classroom perspective. Totals 210 hours of instruction, including practicum.

Dates: Mid-Jun-mid-Aug. Cost: $2,300 tuition (plus room and board and materials). Contact: Daniel W. Evans, PhD, Acting Director, TESL Graduate Programs, School of International Studies, Saint Michael's College, Colchester, VT 05439; (802) 654-2684, fax (802) 654-2595; sis@smcvt.edu.

ESL Summer Institute. An intensive 5-week program specifically designed for international students planning to study science and engineering in the U.S. Classroom instruction integrates the basic skills and pays attention to English in a technology environment. In addition to CALL, program includes web instruction, oral presentation, and technical writing tutorials and workshops.

Dates: Jul 11-Aug 15, 1998 Cost: $3,060 includes program and activities fees, room and board. Contact: ESL Summer Institute, WPI, 100 Institute Rd., Worcester, MA 01609; www.wpi.edu/devel/iss/esl.

ELS TEFL Certificate Program. Provides intensive 1-month training program (150 hours) for teaching EFL for: 1) those with no prior experience, 2) current teachers who wish to update methodologies. Includes 30-hour student practica, direct placement in our 50 overseas schools for graduates, cultural issues workshops. Success rate of 90 percent for placement within 3 months of graduation.

Dates: Offered 7 times a year. Cost: $1,995 includes books, practica supervision, all fees, and placement. Contact: Susan Matson, Director of Field Operations, International Division, ELS Language Centers, 5761 Buckingham Pkwy., Culver City, CA 90230; (310) 342-4190, fax (310) 342-4104; smatson@els.com.

ESL Teaching. Give the gift of English. Two-year opportunities to teach ESL at locations around the world to students or to teach teachers. Stipend, travel, health insurance provided. Must be Christian to qualify.

Dates: Apply by Jan 15 for spring interviews and Aug 15 for fall. Cost: Some sites require fundraising of stipend only. Contact: Mission Service Recruitment Office, Presbytarian Church (U.S.A.), 100 Witherspoon St., Louisville, KY 40202-1396; (800) 779-6779; www.pcusa.org/msr.

International Schools Services. Last year International Schools Services recruited for nearly 60 ESL positions in K-12 American/international schools worldwide. Applicants must possess teaching certification and have at least 2 years of full-time K-12 teaching experience. Placement services include yearly recruitment centers and ongoing computer searches. Opportunities are as diverse as regions represented globally: salary and benefits vary congruously.

Dates: International Recruitment Centers in Feb, Mar, and Jun. Cost: Application: $100; Recruitment Center registration: $125. There are no placement fees charged to candidates who are placed through the work of ISS. Contact: Erika Pedersen, ISS, P.O. Box 5910, Princeton, NJ 08543; (609) 452-0990, fax (609) 452-2690; edustaffing@iss.edu.

International Schools Services. Teaching opportunities exist in private American and international schools around the world. Learn about these schools and discover how you can carry your education career overseas. Applicants must have a bachelor's degree and 2 years of current relevant experience. Most candidates obtain their overseas teaching positions by attending our U.S.-based International Recruitment Centers (IRCs).

Dates: International Recruitment Centers in Feb and Jun. Cost: Application: $100; International Recruitment Center registration: $150. There are no placement fees charged to candidates who are placed through the work of ISS. Contact: Erika Pedersen, ISS, P.O. Box 5910, Princeton, NJ 08543; (609)

452-0990 or (609) 452-2690; edustaffing@ iss.edu, www.iss.edu.

M.A. TESOL. This 30-unit degree emphasizes research findings in socio- and psycho linguistics as they apply to second language acquisition and ESL/EFL pedagogy at all levels. Additionally, the program offers a special emphasis in English for Specific Purposes that prepares students to design and deliver courses in ESL/EFL workplace settings.

Dates: Fall semester: late Aug-mid-Dec; spring semester late Jan-mid-May. Cost: Non-California residents: State Univ. fee $459 plus $246 tuition per unit. Residents $669 for up to 6 units, $1,002 over 6. Contact: TESOL Coordinator, Dept. of Linguistics and Language Dev., San Jose State Univ., 1 Washington Sq., San Jose, CA 95192-0093; linguist@email. sjsu.edu.

Master of Arts (MATESL). The MATESL Program is a 36-credit program (39 credits with thesis option) designed for both prospective and experienced teachers. Theoretical and methodological training is integrated with practical coursework to prepare graduates for professional roles in TESL/TEFL or continued graduate study. A variety of practicum experiences are offered both domestically and abroad.

Dates: Begin in Sep, Jan, or Jun. Cost: $260 per credit. Contact: Daniel W. Evans, PhD, Acting Director, TESL Graduate Programs, School of International Studies, Saint Michael's College, Colchester, VT 05439; (802) 654-2684, fax (802) 654-2595; sis@smcvt.edu.

Mission Volunteer International. The Presbyterian Church (USA) has over 100 year's experience sending educators to work with partner institutions around the world. English as a Second Language teachers are needed primarily in Africa, Eastern Europe, and Asia. Training and experience preferred. Some positions require volunteer to raise cost of monthly stipend.

Dates: Year round: requires 2-year commit-

ment. Cost: Volunteers receive stipend, housing, and insurance. Contact: Susan Heffner Rhema, Presbyterian Church (USA), 100 Witherspoon St., Louisville, KY 40202-1396; (800) 779-6779.

New World Teachers. Accelerated 4-week TEFL/TESL Certificate Course available in San Francisco, Boston, and Puerto Vallarta, Mexico. Integrates established European Direct Method aimed at trainees with an American education. Includes supervised practice teaching to foreign students, permanent access to job placement guidance and information. Extensive Internet resources, 2-day seminar in Teaching English to Young Learners also available with every course.

Dates: Four-week intensive courses begin in San Francisco: Jan 12, Feb 9, Mar 16, Apr 13, May 18, Jun 22, Jul 20, Aug 17, Sep 14, Oct 12, and Nov 9, 1998. In Boston: Apr 27 and Nov. 9, 1998. In Puerto Vallarta: Feb 16, Mar 16, Apr 20, Jun 8, Jul 20, Aug 31, Sep 28, Oct 26, Dec 14. Ten-week Tuesday evening and Saturday courses begin Jan 27, May 19, Jul 28 and Oct 6, 1998. Cost: San Francisco and Boston: $2,350; Puerto Vallarta: $2,900. Includes deposit, registration, books, course materials, and lifetime job placement assistance. Accommodations: San Francisco $575 per month, Boston $625, Puerto Vallarta $300. *Transitions Abroad* readers receive free accommodations package in Puerto Vallarta. Contact: New World Teachers, 605 Market St., Suite 800, San Francisco, CA 94105; (800) 644-5424; teacherssf@aol.com, www.goteach.com.

Peace Corps Opportunities. Since 1961, more than 140,000 Americans have joined the Peace Corps. Assignments are 27 months long. Volunteers must be U.S. citizens, at least 18 years old, and in good health. Peace Corps has volunteer programs in education, business, agriculture, the environment, and health.

Dates: Apply 9 to 12 months prior to availability. Cost: Volunteers receive transportation to and from assignment, a stipend, complete health care, and $5,400 after 27 months of service. Contact: Peace Corps, Room 8506, 1990 K St. NW, Washington, DC 20526; (800) 424-8580 (mention code 824); www.peacecorps.gov.

Rocky Mountain TESL Summer Institute. Participants will combine theoretical insight and practical application through graduate level courses that are co-taught by university faculty and ESL instructors. Classes will include observation and practicum work with international students. Sponsored by: Language, Literacy and Culture Division, Univ. of Colorado at Denver and Spring International Language Center.

Dates: Two 3-week sessions Jun 15-Jul 2, Jul 6-Jul 24; one 6-week session Jun 15-Jul 24, 1998. Cost: Tuition approx. $570 for a 3-credit course, student I.D., access to all campus facilities. Contact: Janice Oldroyd, Co-ordinator, Spring International Language Center, 900 Auraria Pky., Tivoli Bldg., Suite 454, Denver, CO 80204; (303) 534-1616, fax (303) 534-2424; silcaur@aol.com.

Study Abroad in Australia. Study 1 semester in a wide range of courses including humanities, arts, social sciences, economics, education, science, Australian studies.

Dates: Feb-Jun or Jul-Nov. Cost: Approx. $5,500 Contact: International Office, Univ. of New England, Armidale, NSW Australia 2351.

TESOL Certificate. The College of Sante Fe, in beautiful and historic Sante Fe, New Mexico, offers an alternative, 18-credit-hour, 2-semester TESOL certificate program. Participants must also have 6 credit hours of foreign language and possess a bachelor's degree. The TESOL certificate is for participants who wish to teach outside of the K-12 public school setting, but may qualify as an ESL endorsement for licensed teachers.

Dates: Year round. Cost: $204 per credit. Contact: Wallace K. Pond, PhD, 1600 St. Michael's Dr., Sante Fe, NM 87505; (800)

456-2673, fax (505) 473-6510; edudtp@ fogelson.csf.edu.

TESOL Minor and Certificate. An undergraduate program of courses that outlines major issues about language and trains students to teach ESL. Students may earn a public school ESL teaching endorsement or a 1-year certificate or may simply take the 3-week intensive TESOL Methods course. Field experiences may be arranged.

Dates: May 1-23 (TESOL Methods); Sep 4-Apr 26, other courses. Cost: $1,070 tuition for TESOL Methods; $5,450 tuition per semester. Contact: Carl Barnett, Goshen College, 1700 S. Main St., Goshen, IN 46526; (800) 348-7422, fax (219) 535-7609; admissions@ goshen.edu; www.goshen.edu.

Training for EFL/ESL Teachers. The Australian TESOL Training Centre offers full-time, intensive 4-week courses and part-time 12-week courses leading to the internationally recognized Cambridge/RSA Certificate in English Language Teaching to Adults (CELTA). The Cambridge/RSA CELTA courses are held every month.

Dates: The Introduction to TEFL Methodolgy courses begin on Feb 2, Apr 18, Jul 27, Nov 9. Cost: $1,500 plus $110 examination fee. Introduction course: $290. Contact: Gloria Smith, Australian TESOL Training Centre, P.O. Box 82, Bondi Junction, NSW 2022, Australia; (011) 61-2-9389-0133, fax 9389-6880; info@ace. edu.au, www.ace.edu.au/attc.

TESOL Placement Services is the place to find an ESOL teaching position worldwide: Asia, Central and South America, the Middle East, North America, and Europe. The service includes 10 issues of the TESOL Placement Bulletin per year and a Resume Search Service. TESOL Placement Services also features TESOL's annual Employment Clearinghouse, where over 100 schools recruit onsite every year for their position openings.

Dates: Employment Clearinghouse:

March of year. Placement Bulletin and Re-sume Service Search is ongoing. Cost: Start-ing at $27. Contact TESOL for more infor-mation. Contact: TESOL Placement Services, 1600 Cameron St., Suite 300, Alexandria, VA 22314-2751; (703) 836-0774, fax (703) 836-7864; place@tesol.edu, www.tesol.edu.

WorldTeach. WorldTeach is a private non-profit organization based at Harvard Univ. which contributes to educational develop-ment and cultural exchange by placing vol-unteers to teach in developing countries (China, Costa Rica, Ecuador, Honduras, Mexico, Namibia, Thailand, and Vietnam). Volunteers teach English, math, science, and environmental education to students of all ages. All programs last for 1 academic year; except for the summer program in China.

Dates: Year-round departures and deadlines vary depending on the program. Cost: $3,600-$4,400. Includes health insurance, airfare, field support, and training. Contact: Jodi Hullinger, Desk Officer, WorldTeach, Harvard Institute for International Develop-ment, 1 Eliot St., Cambridge, MA 02138-5705; (617) 495-5527, fax (617) 495-1599; www.tesol.edu.jhulling@worldteach.org, www.igc.org/worldteach.

Geographical
Index

TRANSITIONS ABROAD

For over 20 years, *Transitions Abroad* magazine has helped independent travelers have the overseas experiences they desire. Each issue is packed with the alternatives to mass tourism. "It's the best resource around for practical, clearly-stated information on travel outside the US."–**Rick Steves**

SHORT-TERM JOBS (JAN/FEB)

• Pick up short-term jobs as you go along or volunteer your services for room and board
• The most mobile skill is teaching English. This issue provides a country-by-country directory of schools and programs where you can get training and placement programs.

SPECIAL INTEREST (MAR/APR)

• Whether it's hiking, sailing, or cooking, following your *own* interest is much more satisfying than fighting the crowds.
• You can also choose from our worldwide directory of credit-bearing summer as well as semester and year courses worldwide.

LANGUAGE SCHOOLS (MAY/JUN)

• In Central America, $125 a week buys full room and board plus four hours a day of private tutoring. Our May/June directory features overseas language programs.

WORKING ABROAD (SEP/OCT)

• Whether you're looking for short-term paid work, volunteer vacations, teaching jobs, or an international career, this issue brings together all the sources of information you need to make it happen. Includes a directory of worldwide volunteer opportunities.

RESPONSIBLE TRAVEL (NOV/DEC)

• One of *Transitions Abroad*'s principal objectives is to promote travel that respects the culture and environment of the host country. Our special directory describes responsible adventure travel programs by region and country, with the emphasis on locally organized tourism.